THEORY AND PRACTICE
OF
COST AND MANAGEMENT ACCOUNTING

THEORY AND PRACTICE OF COST AND MANAGEMENT ACCOUNTING

[For BCom (General) and (Honours), MCom, ICWA (Inter), CA (Inter), MBA, CS, and other Professional Courses]

Dr Subir Kumar Dutta

BA (Econ.), MCom, LLB, MPhil, PhD, AICWA

Principal, Khudiram Bose Central College, Kolkata

Sk. Sahajahan Ali

MCom, MPhil

Principal, Dwijendralal College, Krishnanagar, Nadia

Chittaranjan Karmakar

BA (Econ.), MCOM, AICWA

Lecturer, Dum Dum Motijhil Rabindra Mahavidyalaya, Kolkata

New Central Book Agency (P) Ltd

8/1 Chintamoni Das Lane, Kolkata 700 009

INDIA

Theory and Practice
of
Cost and Management Accounting

First Published : October 1998
First Central Edition (Revised and Enlarged) : January 2008

ISBN : 81-7381-566-6

Publisher : New Central Book Agency (P) Ltd
8/1 Chintamoni Das Lane, Kolkata 700 009

Typesetter : Allied Print Systems
197B Muktaram Babu Street, Kolkata 700 007

Printer : New Central Book Agency (P) Ltd
Web-Offset Division, Dhulagarh, Sankrail, Howrah

Cover Designer : Prasenjit Halder

Cover Printer : Biswanath Studio
3 Garanhatta Street, Kolkata 700 006

Proof Checking : Subas Maitra, Sutapa Kar, and Authors

Project Team : Prabhat Jas, Somenath Ganguly

Price : **Rs 265.00** [Rupees Two Hundred and Sixty-five only]

This book is dedicated

to

Our Parents and Teachers

with whose blessings this book is published

CONTENTS

3. Materials 87-137

FOREWORD

A. K. Basu, Professor, Department of Commerce, University of Calcutta

I am delighted to have the opportunity to contribute to this introductory cost accounting textbook "Theory and Practice of Cost and Management Accounting" by writing the *Foreword.* Let me thank Dr Subir Kumar Dutta, Sk. Sahajahan Ali and Chittaranjan Karmakar, the authors of the book, for inviting me to perform such a pleasant task.

Cost Accounting is a branch of accounting that is concerned with the recognition, measurement, interpretation, and presentation of information about the costs associated with the products, services or activities of an organisation. Cost Accounting information is meant for internal use in business. Its main purpose is to facilitate internal managerial decision-making. The information generated by the cost accounting system of an organisation is used by its managers in formulating business strategy, pricing products and services, and in controlling operations.

Although cost accounting techniques have long been used by owners and managers in making business-decisions, the birth of modern sophisticated cost accounting is dated at the end of the nineteenth century. The aim and scope of the subject has, however, changed with the passage of time. As the environment of business has changed, new concepts and ideas have been developed to cope with the new reality. In the past, cost accounting was occupied with manufacturing. Its main emphasis was on product costing for valuing inventory. But, today, service costing has also become one of the focussed areas in cost accounting. Modern cost accounting texts attached a great deal of importance in discussing costing practices in a service setting.

This introductory cost accounting textbook is intended primarily for students of BCom, MBA, CA, ICWA, and other professional accounting and finance courses. It should also be of value to those working in businesses and who find themselves in the position of having to deal with cost accounting information.

The book's main focus is to enable students to acquire a broad perspective of Cost Accounting based upon a sound conceptual foundation. It explores the fundamental concepts and principles that underlie cost accounting information and explains, in a straightforward language, how cost data are accumulated, organised, and presented. The textbook is divided into thirteen chapters, which are arranged in a logical order.

One important feature of the book is that it contains a wealth of carefully worked-out examples, many of which have been drawn from previous university and professional-body examinations. Another noteworthy feature of the book is the extensive end-of-chapter material. At the end of most of the chapters there is a wide array of questions, exercises and problems, which are designed to assist the students in preparing for examinations.

I hope the text will not only bring the students examination success but also a deeper understanding of the basic principles, practices and varied applications of the invaluable subject—Cost Accounting—and that will be invaluable to them—all their life.

PREFACE TO THE FIRST CENTRAL EDITION

It is a great privilege and satisfaction on our part to place before the esteemed readers the Third Revised and Enlarged Edition of the book "Theory and Practice of Cost and Management Accounting". We are grateful to the appreciative readers for giving a warm and hearty response to the previous editions of the book.

The principal concern of this book is to show how Cost and Management Accounting theory can be applied to work-out problems in practice. An attempt has been made to relate theory to practice. Encouraged by the overwhelming response to the earlier editions of this book, we have tried to strengthen the book in the following manner :

- Each topic has been developed gradually and special care has been taken to ensure conceptual clarity.
- Many new topics—Cost Booking and Cost Ledger Control Accounts, Reconciliation of Cost Accounts with Financial Accounts, Budgetary Control, Marginal Costing and Standard Costing—have been added in this edition.
- All old chapters have been thoroughly updated and much expanded.
- All the latest changes in cost accounting terminology have been incorporated in this book.
- Each chapter starts with Authors' comments and suggestions, which the students should air to achieve well.
- In all, the book has 310 solved problems and 450 unsolved problems, with guide to answers, in addition to sufficient number of illustrations.
  Many of the problems presented in the book have been taken from different university and professional examinations.

We take this opportunity to place on record our heartiest thanks to New Central Book Agency (P) Ltd for ably and cooperatively bringing out this book in record time.

We are confident that with all the changes, additions and adaptations, the book will meet all the more extensively the combined requirements of the students for BCom, MCom, MBA, CA, ICSI, ICFAI, ICWAI, and other professional examinations.

While we have taken all possible care to see that the book has no errors, we would be grateful if mistakes or lacunae are pointed out. Suggestions for further improvement would be more than welcome from erudite fellow-teachers and interested students.

25 December 2007
Kolkata

AUTHORS

PREFACE TO THE FIRST EDITION

The world of Cost Accounting is vast and varied. That is why we bring out this manual of Cost Accounting with a new approach and in an inimitable style. This manual opens up the gateway to the world of Cost Accounting to those who go in for the study of Commerce—academically as well as non-academically. The students studying BCom—Pass and Honours, and MCom at different universities of India must, we do hope, make an easy leap into the varied and numerous problems of Cost Accounting with the help of this book and find solutions and the methods of solutions, step-by-step guidelines, and innumerable illustrations easily made. This is not all—special care has been taken for those who opt for professional courses like ICWA (Inter), CA (Inter), CS and other courses of studies in the Commerce stream.

This book goes into details of the principles and techniques of Cost Accounting. It presents a sound theoretical exposition and numerous illustrative problems besides a lot of explanatory notes for facile understanding of the important as well as critical problems of the subject. Numerous problems have been worked-out; charts are given to enrich the knowledge of those who intend to sit for university and professional examinations—both as private and collegiate students.

Chapters are logically set and graded; some of them have been even sectionalised to facilitate the learner-readers' power of grasping the subject and thereby grow self-confidence in the mastery of it.

Besides useful hints, answers to practical exercises are given at the end of each chapter. A lot of Model Questions and Answers, to be rarely found elsewhere, are also to be found here for the all-round understanding for acquiring a wholesome knowledge of Cost Accounting as well.

Suggestions for the improvement of the book are most welcome.

October 1998
Kolkata

AUTHORS

1 Introduction

Concept of Cost—Costing—Cost Accountancy—Financial and Cost Accounting relationship—Objectives—Needs—System—Difficulties—Method and Techniques of Cost Accounting—Limitations—Worked out problems—Exercises.

World is now facing the problem of scarcity of resources. Optimum utilisation of resources is the urgent need of the day. The role of Cost Accountants in this regard play a vital role all over the world. Starting as a branch of Financial Accounting, Cost Accountancy has made a remarkable progress during the last few decades. Until the late 1880s, cost accounting was in the domain of the engineers. Perhaps the first book, entitled 'Cost of Manufacturers' written by Henry Metcalfe, was published in 1885 in New York. It is only after the World War-I that Cost Accounting has increasingly been looked upon as a managerial tool for planning and control of cost.

Cost, Costing, Cost Accounting and Cost Accountancy

Cost Concept

The concept of cost is so critical that truly speaking it covers every aspect of human life and business and it is difficult to give a suitable definition for that; which would cover all its aspects. The Terminology of Cost Accountancy published by the Chartered Institute of Management Accountants (U.K.) defines cost as : (*a*) the amount of expenditure (actual or notional) incurred on, or attributable to a given thing, or (*b*) to ascertain the cost of a given thing. Actually 'cost' represents a sacrifice, a forgoing or a release of something of value. Having defined the thing, for example, cost of each element *i.e.*, material, labour, overhead etc. means the amount of money that had to be paid to procure the item.

Costing

Costing refers to the procedure for measuring cost. It is the technique of measurement and accumulation of cost of different activities, products, processes or services. The term 'Costing' has been defined by the CIMA as "The technique and process of ascertaining cost". In short, costing is the technique consists of a set of rules and principles for ascertaining cost.

Cost Accounting

Cost accounting is a quantitative method which deals with the classification, recording, allocation, summarisation and reporting of current of probable cost of a product. It is a specialised branch of accounting and recording transactions which assists management to control costs. The CIMA has also defined Cost Accounting as : "The process of accounting for cost from the point at which expenditure is incurred or committed to the establishment of its ultimate relatiohship with cost centre and cost units."

Cost Accountancy

Cost Accountancy is the application of costing and cost accounting principles, methods and techniques to the science, art and practice of cost control and the ascertainment of profitability.

It includes the presentation of information derived therefrom for the purpose of managerial decision-making.

Financial Accounting and Cost Accounting—Relationship

The main objective of accounting is to provide information relating to finance to different interested parties. Although both the financial accounting and cost accounting serves the needs of management and outsiders and maintain records separately in order to fulfil different objectives, but it is very difficult to make a clear-cut demarcation between the two. The main reasons behind this are : (*i*) Cost accounting is based on same principles regarding debit and credit like financial accounting. (*ii*) Again, the data used for cost accounting are collected from the records of financial accounting. Nevertheless, both of the two accounts are different in relation to its objectives and uses.

The main difference between the two are :

(*i*) The main objective of financial accounting is to serve external people but objective of cost accounting mainly relates to internal management.

(*ii*) Thus cost accounting serves only to a limited area than financial accounting.

(*iii*) Financial accounting is mostly dependent on historical cost that arises after happening the event, but cost accounting does not restrict itself only to the expost calculations. The cost accounting includes both retrospective and anticipatory calculations.

(*iv*) Financial accounting provides information about the enterprise in a general way to all the interested people through its common financial statements. But under cost accounting separate reports are prepared for different levels and different decision-making areas of management.

(*v*) The financial accounts are to be kept according to the provisions of Companies Act and Income Tax Act. But cost accounts are kept voluntarily as per requirements of management and there is no such provisions under any Act.

(*vi*) The financial accounts reveals the profit and position of the business as a whole while cost accounts measures the performance, skill and profitability of each operation.

(*vii*) In financial accounts, reports are usually published at the end of each accounting period whereas the report under cost accounts are placed as and when required.

(*viii*) The main object of financial accounts is to record the daily transactions without attaching any importance to control. But cost accounts—through its detailed study—assures control of materials, labour and overhead costs.

(*ix*) Cost accounts locate the cause of any increase or decrease in the profit or loss disclosed by the financial accounts.

(*x*) Finally, cost accounts lays main importance on planning, operation, control and decision making. But financial accounting is merely accounts for money entrusted to the business.

Objectives of Costing or Cost Accounting (Purposes)

The main purposes/objectives of costing are :

(*i*) to determine cost with a view to fixing selling prices.

(*ii*) to ascertain the cost of each product, process or operation as well as total cost.

(*iii*) to determine the profitable and unprofitable products with a view to improving the profitability.

(*iv*) to provide a reliable basis upon which quotations or tenders may be submitted.

(*v*) to provide invaluable imformation for the purpose of comparison.

(*vi*) to facilitate in ***detecting*** and ***preventing*** of wastes, leakages and inefficiencies.

(*vii*) to enable the business to ascertain cost of each specific unit of output and the extent to which each element of expenditure contributes to such cost.

(*viii*) to assist management in various policy-making, such as, make or buy, introduction of a new product, utilisation of idle capacity, expansion of existing capacity, replacement of plant etc.

Need for Cost Accounting (Advantages/Importance)

The cost accounting, as a separate branch of accounting, has some added advantages than financial accounting. The importance/necessity of cost accounting can be realised from the following advantages :

(*i*) The cost accounting is very much useful in preparing estimates of new work under various working conditions.
(*ii*) A well-established costing system reveals unprofitable situations with their causes.
(*iii*) Thus, it helps to control waste of material, labour and overhead cost, thereby reducing the cost of production.
(*iv*) All the expenses are classified according to functions, elements and variability. These types of classifications will reveal the controllable and non-controllable portion of overheads.
(*v*) It not only assists to estimate the cost of a product but also helps to determine the reasonable cost of that product through standard costing.
(*vi*) Cost data help to reconcile the periodical results with those shown by financial records.
(*vii*) It helps to reveal operating efficiency or inefficiency in order to take right action at the right time.
(*viii*) Profit planning and price fixing become easier.
(*ix*) It helps the management for taking important decisions such as product mix, capacity utilisation etc.
(*x*) It helps to prepare financial statements in more details.
(*xi*) Market research and value analysis together with cost reduction programme leads to economy.
(*xii*) It provides data to government for price fixation, price control, wage level fixation, payment of dividends, tariff protection and settlement of disputes.
(*xiii*) Cost and responsibility centres may be fixed in order to locate the responsible persons or the centres.
(*xiv*) Installation of uniform costing enables management to make inter-firm comparisons.
(*xv*) It helps in the preparation of financial statements, as cost of inventories can be easily obtained from cost records.

Installation of a Costing System

When the requirement of two firms are alike, the system must be designed to meet the specific needs of a particular organisation. So, for introducing a sound costing system one should ensure that :

(*i*) The technical side of the business is carefully studied to design a suitable costing system.
(*ii*) The system to be adopted must satisfy the needs of the business and unduly elaborate system is avoided.
(*iii*) It is helpful in planning the future and controlling the present.
(*iv*) The system is simple and easy to operate.
(*v*) Standard printed forms, having numbers, are used for control purposes.
(*vi*) The necessary data can be collected regularly and promptly.
(*vii*) The results shown under two sets (*viz.*, cost and financial accounting) are so correlated that reconciliation between the two can be done easily.
(*viii*) The cost accountant must receive full cooperation from the technical staffs and have such a power to access easily to all factory records as and when required.

Difficulties in Introducing a Costing System

To introduce a sound costing system the cost accountant may have to face certain practical difficulties which are as follows :

(*a*) Due to lack of proper education and cooperation the top-management may treat it as duplication of work.

(*b*) Due to ignorance and suspicion, the existing accounting staff may feel that they would lose their importance. Hence they may resist the introduction of the new system.

(*c*) The selected system of costing may not be suitable for the business.

(*d*) The cost of installation and operating a costing system may, sometimes, be so high that only a large organisation can afford them.

(*e*) Due to shortage of trained staff, cost classification, cost analysis, cost control, and cost reduction may not be handled efficiently.

To overcome the above mentioned difficulties, the following measures should be adopted :

(*a*) The related existing staff should be trained properly.

(*b*) The proposed costing system should be simple and practical.

(*c*) The employees and the top management should be convinced of the benefits derived from the costing system.

(*d*) The existing staff as well as management should realise the utility and importance of a sound costing system.

(*e*) Finally, the installation and operating cost of the systems should not supersede its value to the management.

Methods and Techniques of Cost Accounting

Various methods and techniques of cost accounting are used to ascertain cost. They are designed to suit the needs of individual business conditions. The most significant *techniques* of costing are : (*i*) Historical or Absorption Costing (*ii*) Standard Costing (*iii*) Marginal Costing (*iv*) Uniform Costing (*v*) Direct Costing (*vi*) Budgetary Control. The various major methods generally used are : (*i*) Job Costing (*ii*) Process Costing and (*iii*) Farm Costing. In general, at least one of the above methods with one technique are used to find out the cost of a cost unit.

The diagrammatical representation of the above methods and techniques is :

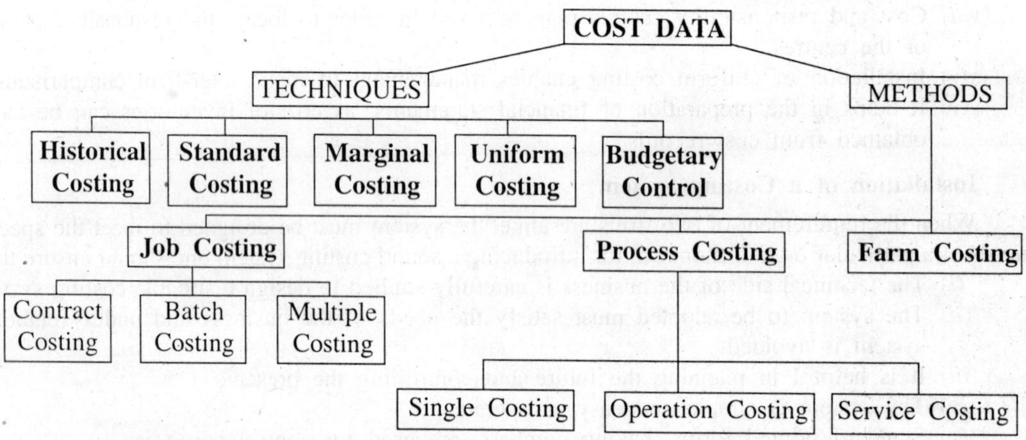

Limitations of Cost Accounting

The limitations of cost accounting are :

(*i*) Like any other accouting system, it is not an exact science but an art which has developed through theories and practices.

(*ii*) Cost accounting is based on some preestimations.

(*iii*) No one cost is suitable for all purposes.

(*iv*) Because of different assumptions, the cost presented by any two cost accountants will generally vary.

(*v*) A cost accountant does not necessarily provide the true cost of a product, as they incorporate a large number of conventions, assumptions etc.

(*vi*) Cost accounting provides information for taking decisions, but it does not give the exact solution to the problem.

EXERCISES

1. Explain what you mean by 'Cost Accounting', 'Cost Accountancy', and 'Costing'.
2. Why is Cost Accounting necessary ? In what respect does Cost Accounting differ from Financial Accounting ?
3. "Costing is an aid to management"—Enumerate the main points in support of this statement.
4. What are the essential requirements of a sound system of costing ? Describe the steps to be taken in installing a costing system in a manufacturing concern.
5. What are the advantages you would expect from the keeping of Cost Accounts ? What are the limitations of Cost Accounting System ?
6. Please describe (*i*) the various points that would be looked into, and (*ii*) Prerequisites which would satisfy before installing the costing system. ***[I.C.W.A. (Int.) Dec. 1994]***
7. "There is no need to instal a costing system when proper financial accounts are to be compulsorily maintained"—Justify the statement. ***[C.U. B.Com. (H) 2003]***
8. What are the general principles which you, as a cost controller, should keep in mind while you set up a costing system. ***[I.C.W.A. Final]***
9. Enumerate the factors which are to be considered before installing a system of cost accounting in a manufacturing organisation. ***[C.A. Inter]***

2 Concept, Analysis and Classification of Cost

Authors' Comments and Suggestions :

1. ***This chapter is very important for B.Com. Examinations of different Universities.***
2. ***At least one problem is expected from this chapter.***
3. ***Students should be very careful in valuation of closing stock of raw materials, WIP and finished goods.***
4. ***Detailed information relating to total as well as per unit of cost is relevant for this purpose.***
5. ***The students should note that, as per revised terminology of the C.I.M.A., the term Prime Cost is the summation of Direct Material and Direct Labour Cost only.***

Different Concepts—Classification—Cost Sheet—Workedout Problems—Exercises.

Different Concepts

Cost and Expense

Cost is the measure of expenditure. It means the total of all expenses—actual, or notional. Cost represents a sacrifice, a forgoing or a release of something for obtaining something. The American Institute of Certified Public Accountants (AICPA) defines the term 'expenses' as 'all expired cost which are deductible from revenues'. Expenditure means payment in cash or otherwise. The term 'expenses' refers to such items as operating, administrative, selling and distribution, interest and taxes.

Cost Centre and Cost Unit

Cost centre may be defined as the smallest part of operation or area of responsibility for which costs are collected. It is a location, person or item of equipment (or group of these) for which cost may be ascertained and used for cost control. Thus cost centres may be of two types *viz.* (*i*) personal; and (*ii*) impersonal cost centres. The personal cost centre consists of a person or group of persons upon whom responsibilities are assigned. The impersonal cost centres consist of a location or item of equipment or a group of these.

Cost unit refers to the unit or quantity of product, service or time units (or combination of these) in relation to which cost may be expressed or ascertained. It is a device used for the purpose of breaking up or separating cost into smaller subdivisons attributable to products or services. For instance we may determine cost per tonne of coal, per kilo-watt hour of power, rate per machine hour, or per tonne-kilometer of a transport service etc.

Elements of Cost

The heading under which various kinds of expenditure is analysed are called elements of cost. Elements of cost are : (*i*) Direct Material (*ii*) Direct Labour (*iii*) Direct expenses (*iv*) Overheads.

Overheads are *classified* according to functions :

(*a*) Factory or Production (*b*) Administration (*c*) Selling (*d*) Distribution.

Now we can discuss the exact meanings of elements of costs :

Direct Materials. Direct materials are those materials that can be treated as a part of the product. It includes :

(*i*) Materials specially purchased for a particular job.

(*ii*) Materials passing from one process to the other.

(*iii*) Primary packing materials such as cardboard, cartons etc.

Direct Labour or Wages. It is all labour expended in the construction, conformation, composition or condition of the product.

It has a linear relationship with the volume of output *i.e.* it directly changes with the change of production unit.

Direct Expenses. Direct expenses are those expenses which are neither direct material nor direct wages but are directly identifiable with a particualr job, product or process.

Examples : (*i*) Cost of drawing and design, (*ii*) Cost of special designs or moulds etc.

Overhead. It may be defined as the cost which is incurred over and above prime cost *i.e.*, it is the aggregate of indirect materials, indirect wages and indirect expenses.

Overhead expenses may be subdivided on the basis of function and behaviour and elementwise.

Functional Classification. The main functions of a manufacturing-cum-selling concern are production, administration, selling and distribution.

The costs which are generally related with these functions are called :

(*a*) Production Cost (*b*) Administration Cost (*c*) Selling and Distribution Cost.

Production Cost or Production Overhead. This type of cost covers all indirect expenditure incurred in the factory.

Administrative Overhead. This includes all expenses incurred in connection with planning, policy making, coordinating, controlling and other general administration.

Selling Overhead. It is the expenses which are incurred in giving service to the existing customers and in prospecting new customers.

Distribution Overhead. This comprises all expenditure incurred in packing, making the packet product ready to despatch, despatching and bringing back the empty cases, upkeep and running of delivery vehicles, salary of despatch clerk etc.

Behavioural Classification

With the change of production units some cost will change directly, some costs will remain unchanged while others will change not in proportion with the change of production. Therefore, behaviour cost can be classified and analysed in following way :

Variable Cost. The cost which tends to vary directly with volume of production units is known as variable cost.

Examples : Direct labour, Direct material, Direct expenses, Consumable cost, Power fuel etc.

Semivariable Cost. Semivariable costs are those costs which are partly variable and partly fixed *i.e.*, this type of costs change with the change of production but not proportionately.

Examples : Repair and maintenance, Telephone charges, Depreciation, service department wages etc.

Fixed Cost. The cost which tends to remain unaffected by the changes in production units.

Examples : Insurance, Managers' Salary, Rent, Rates and Taxes, etc.

Elementwise Classification

Indirect Materials. It may be defined as 'materials which cannot be allocated but which can be apportioned to or absorbed by cost centre or cost units'.

Examples : Stores used in maintenance of machinery, cotton waste etc.

Indirect Labour. The wages of that labour which cannot be allocated but which can be apportioned to or absorbed by cost centre or cost units, is called as indirect labour.

Examples : Supervisors' wages, wages to apprentices, trainees and instructors etc.

Indirect Expenses. These are the expenses which cannot be allocated but can be apportioned to or absorbed by cost centres or cost units.

Examples : Rent, insurance, municipal taxes, general manager's salary, telephone expenses etc.

Chargeable Expenses and Overhead Expenses

The term 'expenses' denote all costs being deducted from revenue in a given period. Expenses may be defined as the cost of services provided to an undertaking and the notional cost of the use of own assets. Expenses are generally divided into two categories—chargeable or direct and indirect expenses.

Chargeable expenses are those expenses which can be directly charged to the product or job. It is a part of the prime cost.

The examples of direct expenses are :

(*i*) Cost of patents and royalty payments.

(*ii*) Cost of experiments in connection with model and pilot schemes.

(*iii*) Architect's charges.

(*iv*) Surveyor's and other consultants' fees.

Overhead may be defined as the aggregate of indirect material in direct wages and indirect expenses.

The overhead expenses can be divided in a number of ways such as according to their nature, behaviour functions, variabilities and normalities.

Cost Sheet. The statement of cost elementwise, is known as cost sheet. In a cost sheet, besides total expenditure, cost per unit of output, and the various stages of cost (from prime cost to total cost) are shown systematically.

Advantages of a cost sheet. The advantages of a cost sheet are :

(a) It shows the total cost and cost per unit of the product produced during the given period.

(*b*) It helps the producers to control over the cost of production.

(*c*) It acts as a guide to the manufacturers and helps them in formulating a definite and profitable production policy.

(*d*) It helps the management in fixing up the selling price of their products.

(*e*) It helps management in comparative study of the various elements of cost with the past result and standard cost.

The specimen of a cost sheet showing the elements of costs is given :

COST SHEET
for the period ended ....

Particulars	*Amount*	*Amount*	*Cost per unit*
DIRECT MATERIALS			
Opening stock of raw materials	—		
Add : Purchases	—		
Add : Carriage inwards/import duty			

Particulars			
Less : Closing stock of raw material	—		
Less : Materials return	—		
Less : Materials lost by fire	—	—	
Direct Material consumed		—	
Direct Labour/Productive wages		—	
Direct Expenses :			
Hire charges for special	—		
Plant & Machinery	—		
Cost of Blue-print for production	—		
Royalty related with production	—		
Research and Development expenses	—		
Other chargeable expenses	—	—	
PRIME COST			
Add : Factory or Works Overhead :	—		
Indirect Wages	—		
Indirect Materials	—		
Factory Rent & Rates		—	
Factory lighting	—		
Factory insurance	—		
Depreciation, repairs and maintenance	—		
Power, lubricating oil etc.	—		
Cost of Idle time	—		
Less : Sale of scrap	—	—	
FACTORY COST			
Add : Office administrative overhead :		—	
Office Rent & Rates			
Office salaries	—		
Remuneration of Management	—		
Office lighting & Insurance	—		
Establishment charges		—	
Depreciation of Office Assets	—		
Audit Fees	—		
Legal Charges	—		
Bank Charges	—		
General office expenses	—		
COST OF PRODUCTION		—	—
Add : Opening finished stock			
Less : Closing finished stock			
COST OF GOODS SOLD			
Add : Selling and distribution overhead	—		
Showroom Rent and Rates	—		
Lighting	—		
Salesmen's salaries	—		
Packing	—		
Commissions	—		
Advertisement	—		
Market Research & Development Cost	—		
Bad Debt	—	—	—

COST OF SALES/TOTAL COST		—	—
Add : Profit		—	—
SALES VALUES		—	—

If a cost sheet is prepared and costs are analysed according to behaviour, then the specimen of cost sheet will be as follows :

	Details	*Total Cost*	*Cost per unit*
Variable Direct Cost :			
Raw materials consumed		—	—
Direct wages			
Direct expenses			
PRIME COST		—	—
Add : Variable factory overhead :		—	—
Variable factory expenses		—	—
Total Variable factory cost			
Add : Variable administration overhead		—	—
Total Variable cost of production		—	—
Add : Variable cost of opening finished stock		—	—
Less : Variable cost of closing finished stock		—	—
Variable cost of Goods sold		—	—
Add : Variable selling & distribution overhead		—	—
Variable or Marginal cost of sales		—	—

Note : (*i*) When the opening and closing working progress is valued at works cost, then these should be adjusted with factory cost. But if the W.I.P. are valued at prime cost, it should be adjusted with prime cost.

The Adjustment for W.I.P. are :

(*a*) *If W.I.P. is valued at work cost*

	Rs.
PRIME COST	—
Add : Factory Overhead	—
Add : Opening W.I.P.	—
	—
Less : Closing W.I.P.	—
FACTORY COST	—

(*b*) *If W.I.P. is valued at prime cost*

Raw materials consumed	—
Direct Wages	—
Direct Expenses	—
	—
Add : Opening W.I.P. at prime cost	—
	—
Less : Closing W.I.P. at prime cost	—
PRIME COST	—

	Details	*Total Cost*	*Cost per unit*
Add : Fixed Factory overhead cost	—		
Fixed Administrative overhead cost	—		
Fixed Selling & Distribution overhead cost	—	—	—
Total Cost		—	—
Add : Profit/Loss		—	
Sales Value		—	—

Specimen of Estimated Price to be Quoted Per Unit for the Period

Particulars	*Amount* *Rs.*	*Amount* *Rs.*
Raw material (new price)	—	
Direct Labour (current rate)	—	
Direct Expenese (current price)	—	
PRIME COST		—
Add : Works Overhead (on the basis of % of Direct wages)		—
WORKS COST		—
Add : *Offices Administrative overhead* (On the basis of % of work cost)		—
COST OF PRODUCTION		—
Add : Selling & Distribution overhead (On the basis of % of work cost or cost per unit)		—
COST OF SALES OR TOTAL COST		—
Add : Estimated Profit (% of Profit on cost)		—
PRICE TO BE QUOTED		—

WORKEDOUT PROBLEMS

Problem 1

The accounts of Basudev Manufactures Ltd. for the year ended 31st December 1988 show the following :

	Rs.
Stock of Material on 1.1.88	6,720
Materials Purchased	1,50,000
Materials returned to suppliers	2,000
Direct Labour	50,000
Direct Expenses	20,000
Factory Expenses	15,300
Office & Administrative Expenses	8,000
Selling & Distribution Expenses	7,900
Stock of Materials on 31.12.88	7,720
Profit	10,000

Find out :
(*a*) Material Consumed (*b*) Prime Cost (*c*) Works Cost
(*d*) Cost of Production (*e*) Total Cost (*f*) Sales.

Solution

Statement of Cost for the year ended 31.12.88

Particulars	Rs.	*Amount* Rs.	*Amount* Rs.
Opening Stock of Materials		6,720	
Add : Purchases of Material	1,50,000		
Less : Materials returned of Suppliers	2,000	1,48,000	
		1,54,720	
Less : Closing Stock of Materials		7,720	
RAW MATERIALS CONSUMED		1,47,000	
Direct Labour		50,000	
Direct Expenses		20,000	
PRIME COST			2,17,000
Factory Overhead			
Factory Expenses			15,300
WORKS COST			2,32,300
Office & Administration Overhead			
Office & Administration Expenses			8,000
COST OF PRODUCTION			2,40,300
Selling & Distribution Overhead			
Selling & Distribution Expenses			7,900
TOTAL COST/COST OF SALES			2,48,200
PROFIT			10,000
SALES			2,58,200

Problem 2

Prepare a Cost Sheet for the year ended 31.3.86 from the following figures extracted from the books of Best Engineering Co.

Opening Stock :

(*i*) Raw Material 40,350, (*ii*) Work-in-Progress 15,000 (*iii*) Finished Stock 35,590.

Cost incurred during the period :

Materials purchased 2,50,000, Wages paid 2,00,000, Carriage inward 2,000, Consumable Stores 10,000, Wages of Storekeeper 7,000, Depreciation of Plant & Machinery 10,000, Materials destoryed by Fire 5,000, Repairs & Renewals 5,010, Office Manager's Salary 10,000, Salary to Office Staff 20,500, Printing & Stationary 10,000, Power 10,500, Lighting for Office Building 2,000, Carriage outward 3,000, Freight 5,000, Entertainment 2,500, Warehousing charges 1,500, Legal charges 2,000, Expenses for participating in Industrial exhibition-6,000.

Closing Stock :

(*i*) Raw material 35,000, (*ii*) Work-in-Progress 14,500, (*iii*) Finished Stock 40,030.

Profit 25% on cost.

Solution

BEST ENGINEERING CO.
COST SHEET
for the year ended 31.3.86

Particulars	*Amount* *Rs.*	*Amount* *Rs.*
Opening Stock of Raw Materials	40,350	
Add : Purchases	2,50,000	
Add : Carriage inward	2,000	
Add : Freight	5,000	
	2,97,350	
Less : Materials destroyed by fire	5,000	
	2,92,350	
Less : Closing Stock of Raw Materials	35,000	
RAW MATERIALS CONSUMED	2,57,350	
Wages	2,00,000	
PRIME COST		4,57,350
Factory Overhead		
Consumable Stores	10,000	
Wages of Storekeeper	7,000	
Depreciation of Plant & Machinery	10,000	
Repairs & Renewals	5,010	
Power	10,500	
		42,510
		4,99,860
Add : Opening work-in-progress		15,000
		5,14,860
Less : Closing Work-in-Progress		14,500
WORKS COST		5,00,360
Office & Administrative Overhead		
Office Manager's Salary		10,000
Salary to Office Staff	20,500	
Printing & Stationery	10,000	
Light for Office Building	2,000	
Legal Charges	2,000	
		44,500
COST OF PRODUCTION		5,44,860
Add : Opening Finished Stock		35,590
		5,80,450
Less : Closing Finished Stock		40,030
COST OF GOODS SOLD		5,40,420

Selling & Distribution Overhead		
Carriage outward	3,000	
Entertainment	2,500	
Warehousing charge	1,500	
Expenses in Industrial Exhibition	6,000	
		13,000
COST OF SALES		5,53,420
PROFIT [25% ON 5,53,420]		1,38,355
SELLING PRICE		6,91,775

Problem 3

From the following figures relating to the manufacture of a Electronic Product during the month of July 1990, prepare a statement showing Cost and Profit per unit :

		Rs.
Raw materials used		50,000
Direct wages		30,000
Labour hours worked		10,500 units
Labour hour rate	Rs. 2·00	
Office overhead		20,000
Selling overhead	Rs. 1·00	
Units produced	20,000 units	
Units sold	18,000 @ Rs. 10	

Solution

Statement Showing Cost

Elements	*Unit*	*Amount* Rs.	*Amount* Rs.	*Per unit* Rs.
Raw Materials used		50,000		
Direct wages		30,000		
PRIME COST			80,000	
Factory Overhead				
Labour hours worked [10,500 units × Rs. 2.00]			21,000	
WORKS COST			1,01,000	
Office overhead			20,000	
COST OF PRODUCTION	20,000		1,21,000	6·05
Less : Closing Stock of Finished Goods [balancing figure]	2,000		12,000	
COST OF GOODS SOLD	18,000		1,08,900	
Selling overhead [18,000 units × Re. 1]			18,000	1·00
COST OF SALES	18,000		1,26,900	7·05

Statement Showing Profit

Particulars	*Units*	*Amount Rs.*	*Amount Rs.*	*Per unit Rs.*
Sales [18,000 units @ Rs. 10 P.U.]			1,80,000	10·00
Less : Cost of Sales			1,26,900	7·05
PROFIT	18,000		53,100	2·95

Working Notes :

Calculation of Closing Finished Stock :

Closing Finished Stock= Opening Finished Stock + Production – Sales

= Nil + 20,000 – 18,000 = 2,000.

Problem 4

The following data are available for 2006 :

Production	50,000 units	*Rs.*
Materials Consumed		75,000
Direct Wages		50,000
Variable Production overhead		1,00,000
Variable Selling overhead		2,00,000
Fixed Expenses		75,000
Selling Price per unit		12

It is expected that in 2007 :

(*a*) Production will be 1,00,000 units

(*b*) Prices of materials will go up by $33\frac{1}{3}$%.

(*c*) Variable selling overhead and fixed expenses will rise by 25% and Rs. 25,000, respectively.

What would be the cost per unit and selling price in 2007, if it is desired to maintain the same rate of profit on sales as in 2006 ?

[*C.U. B.Com. Pass*]

Solution

COST SHEET
for the year ended 2006

Particulars	*Amount Rs.*	*Amount Rs.*	*Per unit Rs.*
		Production :	50,000 units
Materials Consumed	75,000		1·5
Direct Wages	50,000		1·0
PRIME COST		1,25,000	2·5
Add : **Factory Overhead :**			
Variable Production overhead		1,00,000	2·0
WORKS COST		2,25,000	4·5
Add : **Office and Administrative Overhead :**			
Fixed expenses		75,000	1·5
COST OF PRODUCTION		3,00,000	6·0

Add : **Selling & Distribution Overhead :**		
Variable selling overhead	2,00,000	4·0
COST OF SALES	5,00,000	10·0
Add : PROFIT (Balancing figure)	1,00,000	2·0
SALES VALUE	6,00,000	12·0

Working :

(*i*) Calculation for Material Cost per unit in 2007

	Rs.
Material costs per unit in 2006	1·50
Add : Increased $33\frac{1}{3}\%$ in 2007	0·50
	2·00

(*ii*) Calculation for cost per variable selling overhead in 2007

Selling overhead increased by 25% *i.e.* Selling overhead per unit in 2007

= Rs. 4·00 + 25% of Rs. 4 = 4·00 + 1·00 = Rs. 5·00

(*iii*) Fixed expenses in 2007 = 75,000 + 25,000 = 1,00,000

(*iv*) Rate of profit on sales = $\frac{2}{12} \times 100 = 16\frac{2}{3}\%$

COST SHEET
for the year 2007.

Particulars	*Units*	*Amount* Rs.	*Per unit* Rs.
	Production 1,00,000 unit		
Materials Consumed	1,00,000	2,00,000	2·00
Direct wages		1,00,000	1·00
PRIME COST		3,00,000	3·00
Add : **Factory Overhead :**			
Variable Production overhead		2,00,000	2·00
WORKS COST		5,00,000	5·00
Add : **Office & Administrative Overhead**			
Fixed Expenses		1,00,000	1·00
COST OF PRODUCTION		6,00,000	6·00
Add : **Selling & Distribution Overhead :**			
Variable Selling overhead		5,00,000	5·00
COST OF SALES		11,00,000	11·00
Add : PROFIT [$16\frac{2}{3}\%$ on Sales, *i.e.*, $\frac{1}{5}$ of cost]		2,20,000	2·20
SALES VALUE		13,20,000	13·20

Working Notes :

(*i*) Variable overhead changed with production unit.

(*ii*) Fixed expenses assumed related with office and administration.

Problem 5

From the following particulars prepare a Cost Sheet for the month of January 2006 :

	Rs.
Stock of Raw Materials on 1.1.06	3,000
Purchase of Raw Materials	28,000
Stock of Raw Materials on 31.1.06	4,500
Productive Wages	6,300
Depreciation	2,000
Factory Rent	1,800
Material Destroyed by Fire	200
Office Rent	4,800
General expenses	600
Selling overhead	1,500
Number of units produced during the month = 4,000	
Stock of finished goods on 1.1.06 – 2,000 units valued at	3,000
Stock of finished goods on 31.1.06	500 units

Apply FIFO Method.

[*C.U. B.Com. (Pass) Adopted*]

Solution

COST SHEET
for the month of January 1986

Elements of Cost	*Unit*	*Cost* Rs.	*Total Cost* Rs.
Stock of Raw Materials on 1.1.06		3,000	
Add : Purchase of Raw Materials		28,000	
		31,000	
Less : Materials destroyed by Fire		200	
		30,800	
Less : Stock of Raw Materials on 31.1.06		4,500	
RAW MATERIALS CONSUMED		26,300	
Productive Wages		6,300	
PRIME COST			32,600
Factory Overhead :			
Depreciation			2,000
Factory rent			1,800
WORKS COST			36,400
Office & Administrative Overhead :			
Office rent			4,800
General expenses			600
COST OF PRODUCTION	4,000		41,800
Add : Stock of Finished goods on 1.1.06	2,000		3,000
	6,000		44,800
Less : Stock of Finished goods on 31.1.06	500		5,225
COST OF GOODS SOLD	5,500		39,575
Selling & Distribution Overhead			
Selling overhead			1,500
TOTAL COST	5,500		41,075

Working Notes :

(*i*) Calculation for value of closing stock of finished goods :

$$\frac{\text{Total cost of production} \times \text{Closing stock units}}{\text{Total production units}}$$

$$i.e.\ \frac{\text{Rs. } 41{,}800 \times 500}{4{,}000} = \text{Rs. } 5{,}225$$

(*ii*) Abnormal Loss of Materials should be deducted from costs.

Problem 6

Your company manufactures two products *A* and *B*. During a month 300 units of product *A* and 400 units of product *B* have been manufactured.

The total expenses incurred in the said month had been as follows :

	Rs.
Materials	2,97,000
Wages (Direct)	18,000
Stores Overhead	29,700
Machinery maintenance	8,700
Depreciation	4,350
Work amenities	2,250
General works expenses (to be charged as a % of direct wages)	15,000
Administration and Selling Expenses (to be charged as a % of works cost.)	18,750

Other data available are :

	A		B
Material Cost ratio per unit	1	:	2
Direct Labour ratio	2	:	3
Machine utilisation ratio	3	:	5

Calculate cost per unit of each product.

[*C.U. B.Com. (Pass)*]

Solution

Statement of Cost of Products *A* & *B*

For the month of ......

Particulars	*Calculation*	*Total*	*Product*	
			A	*B*
		Rs.	*Rs.*	*Rs.*
Materials	300×1:400×2	2,97,000	81,000	2,16,000
Wages (Direct)	300×2:400×3	18,000	6,000	12,000
PRIME COST		3,15,000	87,000	2,28,000
Factory Overhead				
Stores Overheads [Basis of Material used]	300×1:400×2	29,700	8,100	21,600
Depreciation [Basis of Machine Utilisation]	300×3:400×5	4,350	1,350	3,000

Machinery Maintenance [Basis of Machine Utilisation]	300×3:400×5	8,700	2,700	6,000
Workmen's Amenities [Basis of Direct Labour]	300×2:400×3	2,250	750	1,500
General Work Expenses [Basis of Direct Labour]	300×2:400×3	15,000	5,000	10,000
WORKS COST		3,75,000	1,04,900	2,70,100
Administration & Selling Expenses [Basis of works cost]	1049:2701	18,750	5,245	13,505
TOTAL COST		3,93,750	1,10,145	2,83,605
COST PER UNIT		562·50	367·15	709·01

Problem 7

A factory produced and sold 1,000 units of a product in July 2006, for which following particulars are available :

	Rs.
Stock of Direct Materials on 1.7.06	6,000
Purchases and Receipt of Direct Materials in July 2006	1,44,000
Direct Wages paid in cash in July 2006 (Which includes Rs. 3,000 on account of June 2006 and an advance of Rs. 2,000)	55,000
Works overhead charges for the month	60,000
Stock of Direct Materials on 31-7-06	10,000
Administration and selling overheads	Rs. 25 per unit
Sales price	Rs. 300 per unit

From the above you are required to (*a*) prepare a cost statement for July, and (*b*) estimate the sale price of a unit of the same product in August 2006 assuming :

(*i*) 20% increase in Direct Materials Cost

(*ii*) 10% increase in Direct Wages

(*iii*) 5% increase in Works Overhead Charges.

(*iv*) 20% reduction in Administration and Selling Overhead charges.

(*v*) Same percentage of profit on sales price.

[*C.U. B.Com. (Hons.)*]

Solution (a)

COST SHEET
for the month of July 2006

Particulars	*Amount Rs.*	*Amount Rs.*
Opening Stock of Raw materials	6,000	
Add : Purchases	1,44,000	
	1,50,000	
Less : Closing stock of Raw materials	10,000	
RAW MATERIALS CONSUMED		1,40,000
Direct wages for the month of July 2006	55,000	
Less : Arrear Direct Wages for the month of June 2006	3,000	

	52,000	
Less : Paid in Advance	2,000	50,000
PRIME COST		1,90,000
Add : Works Overhead charges		60,000
WORKS COST		2,50,000
Add : Administration and selling overheads		25,000
COST OF SALES/TOTAL COST		2,75,000
Profit (balancing figure)		25,000
SELLING PRICE [1,000 units × Rs. 300]		3,00,000

(b)

ESTIMATED COST SHEET
for the month of August 2006

Particulars	*Amount* Rs.	*Amount* Rs.
Opening Stock of Raw Materials	10,000	
Estimated Purchases of R.M. $\left[\text{Rs.}\,(1{,}40{,}000 - 10{,}000) \times \frac{120}{100}\right]$	1,56,000	
RAW MATERIALS CONSUMED		1,66,000
Add : Direct wages $\left[\text{Rs.}\,50{,}000 \times \frac{110}{100}\right]$		55,000
PRIME COST		2,21,000
Add : Works overhead $\left[\text{Rs.}\,60{,}000 \times \frac{105}{100}\right]$		63,000
WORKS COST		2,84,000
Add : Administration & Selling overheads $\left[\text{Rs.}\,25{,}000 \times \frac{80}{100}\right]$		20,000
COST OF SALES		3,04,000
Profit [$8\frac{1}{3}\%$ of sale *i.e.* $9\frac{1}{11}\%$ on cost]		27,634
SELLING PRICE		3,31,634

* Per unit Selling Price = $\frac{3{,}31{,}634}{1{,}000}$ = Rs. 331·63

Working Notes :

(*i*) % of Profit of Sales = $\frac{25 \times 100}{300} = 8\frac{1}{3}\%$

Problem 8

The following figures are available from the books of Best Manufacturing Co. for the year ended 31.12.06.

	Rs.
Materials :	
Stock on 1.12.06	1,000
Stock on 31.12.06	2,000
Purchased during 2006	10,000
Wages	7,500
Profit for the year	6,090

Selling overhead	5,250
Factory overhead	4,500
Administrative overhead	4,200

(*a*) Prepare a Cost Sheet showing Prime Cost, Works Cost, Cost of Production, Cost of Sales and Sales.

(*b*) In 2007 the factory receives an order for a job which will require materials of Rs. 1,200 and wages of Rs. 750. Ascertain the sale price of the job if the factory intends to earn a profit of 10% higher than that in 2006. Assume that factory overhead has gone up by $16\frac{2}{3}\%$ and selling overhead has gone down by 20% in 2007. Further assume that factory overhead is recovered as a percentage of the Wages and Adminstration and Selling overhead as a percentage of works cost.

[*C.U. B.Com. (Hons.)*]

Solution

COST SHEET
for the year ended 31.12.06

Particulars	*Amount* Rs.	*Amount* Rs.
Opening Stock of Raw Materials	1,000	
Add : Purchases	10,000	
	11,000	
Less : Closing Stock of Raw Materials	2,000	
RAW MATERIAL CONSUMED	9,000	
Add : Direct Wages	7,500	
PRIME COST		16,500
Add : Factory overhead		4,500
WORKS COST		21,000
Add : Administrative overhead		4,200
COST OF PRODUCTION		25,200
Add : Selling overhead		5,250
COST OF SALES		30,450
Add : Profit		6,090
SALES VALUE		36,540

Working Notes :

(*i*) Calculation for % of Works Overhead on Direct Wages in 2006

$$\frac{4{,}500}{7{,}500} \times 100 = 60\%$$

(*ii*) % of Administrative Overhead on Works Cost in 2006

$$\frac{4{,}200}{21{,}000} \times 100 = 20\%$$

(*iii*) % of Selling overhead on Works Cost $= \dfrac{5{,}250}{21{,}000} \times 100 = 25\%$

(*iv*) % of Profit on Total Cost $= \dfrac{6{,}090 \times 100}{30{,}450} = 20\%$

Percentage of Overheads in 2007

(*i*) Factory overhead on wages :

Factory overhead has gone up by $16\frac{2}{3}\%$

$\therefore$ $60\% + 16\frac{2}{3}\%$ of $60 = 60\% + 10\% = 70\%$

(*ii*) Office and Administrative overhead on works cost :

Office and Administration overhead has not been changed in 2007. Hence it is assumed that the recovery rate is same as 2006, *i.e.* 20% on works cost.

(*iii*) Selling overhead on works cost :

Decreased by 20% in 2007, *i.e.* the % of selling overhead = 25% – 20% of 25%
= 25% – 5% = 20%.

(*iv*) % of Profit on Cost :

Rate of profit in 2007 will be 10% higher than in 2006.

It implies that the rate of profit in 1982 will be 20% + 10% of 20 = 20% + 2% = 22.

ESTIMATED COST SHEET
for the year ended 2007

Elements	*Amount* Rs.	*Amount* Rs.
Material	1,200	
Wages	750	
PRIME COST		1,950
Add : Factory overhead [70% of Rs. 750]		525
WORKS COST		2,475
Add : Office & Administration overhead [20% of Rs. 2,475]		495
COST OF PRODUCTION		2,970
Add : Selling overhead [20% of Rs. 2,475]		495
COST OF SALES		3,465
Add : Profit [22% of Rs. 3,465]		762
SALES		4,227

Problem 9

From the following particulars relating to production and sales for the year ended 31st December 2006, prepare a statement of cost showing, inter alia, the Prime Cost, Factory Cost, Cost of Production, Cost of goods sold and total as well as per unit cost of Sales and Profit :

	As on 1.1.06 Rs.	*As on 31.12.06* Rs.
Materials :	16,000	19,600
Wok-in-progress	12,600	4,600
Finished Goods (at cost) (3,000 units)	16,400	(2,500 units)
Other information for the year :		
Purchase of Raw Materials	1,11,600	
Sales of Finished Goods (40,500 units)	2,83,500	
Productive Wages	67,200	

Office & Administrative Expenses	20,800
Selling & Distribution Expenses	50 paise per unit sold
Machine Hours worked	8,000 hours
Machine hour rate	Rs. 2·50

Assume that sales are made on the basis of 'first in, first out' principle.

[C.U. B.Com. (Hons.)]

Solution

COST SHEET
for the year ended 31.12.06

Particulars	*Amount* Rs.	*Amount* Rs.
Opening Stock of Raw Materials	16,000	
Add : Purchases	1,11,600	
	1,27,600	
Less : Closing Stock of Raw Materials	19,600	
Raw material consumed	1,08,000	
Add : Productive Wages	67,200	
PRIME COST		1,75,200
Add : **Factory Overhead :**		
Machine hours worked [8,000 units × Rs. 2·50]		20,000
		1,95,200
Add : Opening Stock of Work-in-progress		12,600
		2,07,800
Less : Closing Stock of Work-in-progress		4,600
WORKS COST		2,03,200
Add : **Office and Administrative Overhead**		
Office & Administration Expenses		20,800
COST OF PRODUCTION		2,24,000
Add : Opening Stock of Finished Goods		16,400
		2,40,400
Less : Closing Stock of Finished Goods		14,000
COST OF GOODS SOLD		2,26,400
Selling and Distribution Overhead		
Selling & Distribution Expenses [40,500 units × Re. 0·50]		20,250
TOTAL COST		2,46,650
Profit (Balancing Figure)		36,850
SELLING PRICE		2,83,500

$$\text{* Per unit Cost of Sales} = \frac{2,46,650}{40,500} = \text{Rs. } 6{\cdot}09$$

$$\text{** Per unit Profit} = \frac{36,850}{40,500} = \text{Re. } 0{\cdot}91$$

Working Notes :

(*i*) Calculation of goods manufactured during the year :

Sold goods in units	40,500
Add : Closing stock of goods in units	2,500
	43,000
Less : Opening stock of goods in units	3,000
Units produced	40,000

(*ii*) Valuation of Closing Stock of Finished Goods

Cost Price of 40,000 units = Rs. 2,24,000

$\therefore$ Cost Price of 2,500 units $= \dfrac{\text{Rs. } 2{,}24{,}000 \times 2{,}500}{40{,}000}$

= Rs. 14,000

Problem 10

From the following particulars relating to the production and sales for the year ended 30th June 2006, prepare a cost statement showing therein : (*i*) Prime cost, (*ii*) Works Cost, (*iii*) Cost of Production, (*iv*) Cost of Sales and (*v*) Profit per unit :

		Rs.	
Raw Materials as on 1.7.06		12,500	
Work-in-progress as on 1.7.06			
At Prime Cost	Rs. 15,000		
+ Manufacturing Expenses	Rs. 3,000		
		18,000	
Finished goods at cost as on 1.7.06 (8,000 units)			60,000
Raw Materials Purchased		1,10,000	
Freight on Raw Materials Purchased		5,000	
Loss of materials by fire		5,000	
Factory Expenses		70,000	
Chargeable Expenses		25,000	
Direct Labour		1,35,000	
Administrative Expenses Rs. 2 per unit			
Selling Expenses Re. 1 per unit			
Distribution Expenses		15,000	
Sale of Finished Goods (28,000 units)			4,00,000
Raw Materials as on 30.6.07		20,000	
Work-in-progress as on 30.6.07			
At Prime Cost	Rs. 10,000		
+ Manufacturing Expenses	Rs. 8,000		
		18,000	
Stock of Finished Goods on 30.6.07 (10,000 units)			

Assume sales are made on FIFO basis.

[*C.U. B.Com. (Hons.) Adopted*]

Solution

COST SHEET
for the year ended 30.6.07

Particulars	*Amount Rs.*	*Amount Rs.*
Raw Material Consumed :		
Opening stock of materials	12,500	
Add : Purchase of raw material	1,10,000	
Freight of raw material	5,000	
	1,27,500	
Less : Closing stock of raw material	20,000	
	1,07,500	
Less : Material loss by fire	5,000	
	1,02,500	
Add : Direct Wages	1,35,000	
Chargeable Expenses	25,000	
	2,62,500	
Add : Opening W.I.P. at Prime Cost	15,000	
	2,77,500	
Less : Closing W.I.P. at Prime Cost	10,000	
PRIME COST		2,67,500
Factory Overhead :		
Factory Expenses	70,000	
Add : Opening W.I.P. (Manufacturing expenses)	3,000	
	73,000	
Less : Closing W.I.P. (Manufacturing expenses)	8,000	
		65,000
WORKS COST		3,32,500
Office & Adminstrative Overhead :		
Administrative Expenses [30,000 units × Rs. 2]		60,000
Cost of production		3,92,500
Add : Opening stock of finished goods		60,000
		4,52,500
Less : Closing stock of finished goods $\left[3,92,500 \times \frac{10,000}{30,000}\right]$		1,30,833
Cost of goods sold		3,21,667
Selling & Distribution Overhead :		
Selling Expenses [28,000 × Re. 1]		28,000
Distribution overhead		15,000
Cost of sales		3,64,667
*Profit (balancing figure)		35,333
Sales		4,00,000

$$*\text{Per unit profit} = \frac{35{,}333}{30{,}000} = \text{Rs. } 1{\cdot}18$$

Working Notes :

(*i*) Unit manufactured during the year

Unit sold	28,000 units
Add : Closing Stock of Finished Goods	10,000 units
	38,000 units
Less : Opening Stock of Finished Goods	8,000 units
Units manufactured	30,000 units

Problem 11

From the following particulars relating to the production and sales for the year ended 31st March 2007, prepare a statement of cost showing therein (*i*) Prime Cost, (*ii*) Works Cost, (*iii*) Cost of Production, (*iv*) Cost of Sales and (*v*) Profit per unit :

Opening Inventory (1.4.06)		
Raw Materials	Rs. 6,000	
Work-in-progress	Rs. 9,620	
Finished Goods 1,000 units	Rs. 13,680	
Closing Inventory (31.3.07)		
Raw Materials		Rs. 7,000
Work-in-progress	Rs. 8,020	
Finished Goods		?
Raw Materials Purchased	Rs. 72,000	
Productive Wages	Rs. 18,000	
Machine Hours Worked	Hrs. 21,600	
Machine Hour Rate	Rs. 1·50	
Chargeable Expenses	Rs. 16,400	
Office and Administrative overhead	Re. 1·00/unit	
Selling overhead	Re. 0·90/unit	
Units Sold	8,000 units	
Units Produced	8,200 units	
Profit on Sale	10%	

Assume the sales are made on FIFO basis. **[*C.U. B.Com. (Hons.), Adopted*]**

Solution

COST SHEET
for the Production and Sales for the year ended 31.3.07

Particulars	*units*	*Amount Rs.*	*Amount Rs.*	*Per unit Rs.*
Opening Stock of Raw Materials		6,000		
Add : Purchases		72,000		
		78,000		
Less : Closing Stock of Raw Materials		7,000		
RAW MATERIALS CONSUMED		71,000		
Production Wages		18,000		
Chargeable Expenses		16,400		

Particulars	Units	Rs.	Rs.	Per unit
PRIME COST	8,200		1,05,400	12·85
Works Overhead :				
Machine Hours Worked [21,600 Machine hours × 1·50]		32,400		
Add : Opening W.I.P.		9,620		
		42,020		
Less : Closing W.I,P.		8,020		
			34,000	4·15
WORKS COST	8,200		1,39,400	17·00
Office & Administration Overhead [8,200 units × Re. 1]			8,200	1·00
COST OF PRODUCTION	8,200		1,47,600	18·00
Add : Opening Finished Goods	1,000		13,680	
	9,200		1,61,280	
Less : Closing Finished Goods (balancing figure)	1,200		21,600	
COST OF GOODS SOLD	8,000		1,39,680	17·46
Add : Selling overhead [8,000 units × Re 0·90]			7,200	0·90
COST OF SALES			1,46,880	18·36
Profit [10% of sale *i.e.* $\frac{1}{9}$th of cost of sale *i.e.* $\frac{1}{9}$ × 1,46,880]			16,320	2·04
SALES	8,000		1,63,200	20·40

Problem 12

Following figures are extracted from the records of a Co. for the year 1989-90 :

	Rs.
Direct Materials	60,000
Direct Wages	50,000
Works overhead	30,000
Administrative overhead	33,600
Selling overhead	22,400
Distribution overhead	14,000
Profit	52,500

One material had been manufactured and supplied to Mr. *X*, in 1990-91 for which following expenses were incurred :

	Rs.
Direct Material	4,000
Direct Wages	2,000

In 1990-91 works overhead was increased by 20%, Distribution overhead has been decreased by 10% and Selling Administrative overhead each were increased by 12·5%.

At what price the above supply is to be billed to Mr. *X* so as to earn the same rate of profit on selling price as earned in 1989-90.

[*C.U. B.Com. (Hons.)*]

Solution

COST SHEET
for the period 1989-90

Particulars	Rs.	Rs.	Calculation
Direct material	60,000		(*i*) % of works overhead on direct wages
Direct Wages	50,000		$= \frac{30,000}{50,000} \times 100 = 60\%$
PRIME COST		1,10,000	
Add : Works overhead		30,000	
WORKS COST		1,40,000	(*ii*) % of Administrative overhead on works cost $= \frac{33,600}{1,40,000} \times 100 = 24\%$
Add : Administrative overhead		33,600	
COST OF PRODUCTION		1,73,600	
Add : **Selling & Distribution Overhead**			
Selling overhead	22,400		(*iii*) % of selling overhead on works cost $= \frac{22,400}{1,40,000} \times 100 = 16\%$
Distribution overhead	14,000		
		36,400	
Total Cost/Cost of Sales		2,10,000	(*iv*) % of distribution overhead on works cost $\frac{14,000}{1,40,000} \times 100 = 10\%$
Profit		52,500	(*v*) % of Profit on cost $= \frac{52,500}{2,10,000} \times 100 = 25\%$
Sales Value		2,62,500	

For the period 1990-91 :

(*i*) % of Works overhead in 1990-91 = 60% + 20% of 60 = 60% + 12% = 72%
(*ii*) % of Administrative overhead = 24% + 12·5% of 24 = 24% + 3% = 27%
(*iii*) % of Selling overhead = 16% + 12·5% of 16 = 16% + 2% = 18%
(*iv*) % of Distribution overhead = 10% – 10% of 10 = 10% – 1% = 9%

ESTIMATED SELLING PRICE
for the period 1990-91

Particulars	Amount Rs.	Amount Rs.
Direct Material	4,000	
Direct Wages	2,000	
PRIME COST		6,000
Add : Works overhead [72% of Direct wages *i.e.* 72% of Rs. 2,000]		1,440
WORKS COST		7,440
Add : Administrative overhead [27% of works cost *i.e.* 27% of 7,440]		2,009
COST OF PRODUCTION		9,449
Add : **Selling and Distribution Overhead**		
Selling overhead (18% of Works Cost *i.e.* 18% of 7,440)		1,339
Distribution overhead (9% of Works Cost *i.e.* 9% of 7,440)		670

COST OF SALES		11,458
Add : Profit [25% of Total cost of sales, *i.e.* 25% of 11,458]		2,865
SELLING PRICE		14,323

Problem 13

From the following particulars relating to the production and sales for the year ended 31st December 1992, prepare a cost statement showing therein (*i*) the Prime Cost, (*ii*) the Works Cost, (*iii*) the Cost of Production, (*iv*) the Cost of Sales and (*v*) the Profit or Loss.

		Rs.
Stock as on 1.1.92 :		
(*a*) Raw Materials		25,000
(*b*) Work-in-progress		
At Prime Cost	Rs. 30,000	
Add : Manufacturing Exp.	Rs. 6,000	36,000
(*c*) Finished goods [at cost 8,000 units]		1,44,000
Raw Material Purchased		2,00,000
Freight on raw materials		10,000
Machine hour rate		3
Machine hours worked : 48,000 hours		
Chargeable Expenses		50,000
Factory wages for direct labour		2,70,000
Administration Expenses		1,00,000
Selling Expenses		54,000
Distribution Expenses		36,000
Sale proceeds of finished goods (30,000 units)		9,00,000
Stock as on 31st December 1992 :		
(*a*) Raw Materials		45,000
(*b*) Work-in-progress		
At Prime Cost	Rs. 45,000	
Add : Mfg. Expenses	Rs. 9,000	54,000
(*c*) Finished goods at cost (10,000 units)		?

Finished goods produced 32,000 units.

Apply LIFO principle in finished goods valuation. **[*C.U. B.Com. (Hons.)*]**

Solution

STATEMENT SHOWING COST SHEET
for the year ended 31.12.92

Particulars	Amount *Rs.*	Amount *Rs.*
Opening Stock of Raw Materials	25,000	
Add : Purchases	2,00,000	
	2,25,000	
Less : Closing Stock	45,000	
	1,80,000	
Freight on Raw Material	10,000	
	1,90,000	
Add : Direct Wages	2,70,000	
Add : Chargeable Expenses	50,000	

		5,10,000
Add : Opening work-in-progress at cost		30,000
		5,40,000
Less : Closing W.I.P. at cost		45,000
PRIME COST		4,95,000
Add : Factory overhead [48,000 hours × Rs. 3]		1,44,000
		6,39,000
Adjusting for W.I.P. :		
Opening W.I.P. (Manufacturing Exp.)	6,000	
Closing W.I.P. (Manufacturing Exp.)	9,000	
		– 3,000
WORKS COST		6,36,000
Add : Administrative overhead		1,00,000
COST OF PRODUCTION		7,36,000
Add : Opening Finished Stock	1,44,000	
Less : Closing Finished Stock	1,90,000	– 46,000
COST OF GOODS SOLD		6,90,000
Add : **Selling & Distribution Overhead**		
Selling Exp.	54,000	
Distribution Exp.	36,000	90,000
COST OF SALES		7,80,000
Add : PROFIT [Balancing figure]		1,20,000
SALES		9,00,000

Working Notes :

(*i*) *Valuation of Closing Stock (10,000 units) under LIFO Method :*

Value of 8,000 units (at cost)	Rs. 1,44,000
Add : Value of 2,000 units = $\frac{7,36,000 \times 2,000}{32,000}$	Rs. 46,000
	Rs. 1,90,000

Problem 14

Following extracts of costing information relate to commodity *A* for the year ending 31.3.89

		Rs.
Purchase of Raw Materials		48,000
Direct Wages		40,000
Stock on 1.4.88		
of Raw material		8,000
of Finished Goods	1,600 quintals	6,400
Stock on 31.3.89		
of Raw Materials		8,800
of Finished Goods	3,200 quintals	?
Works on Cost		16,800

Work-in-progress :

1st April 1988	1,920
31st March 1989	6,400
Office & Administrative overheads	3,200
Sales (Finished Products)	1,20,000

Advertising, discount allowed and selling cost is Re. 0·40 per quintal. During the year 25,600 quintals of commodity were produced.

Calculate Cost of Production and extend the Cost Sheet to include profit so that it may also be called Production Statement. **[*B.Com. Delhi*]**

Solution

COST SHEET
for the year ended 31.3.89

Particulars	*Unit quintal*	*Total Amount* Rs.	*Total Amount* Rs.	*Per unit* Rs.
Raw Materials Consumed :				
Opening Stock		8,000		
Add : Purchases		48,000		
		56,000		
Less : Closing Stock		8,800		
		47,200		
Direct Wages		40,000		
PRIME COST		87,200		
Factory Overhead :				
Works on Cost		16,800		
Add : Opening Work-in-progress		1,920		
		18,720		
Less : Closing Work-in-progress		6,400		
			12,320	
FACTORY COST			99,520	
Office and Administrative Overhead :				
Office & Administration overhead			3,200	
COST OF PRODUCTION	25,600		1,02,720	
Add : Opening Stock of Finished Goods	1,600		6,400	
	27,200		1,09,120	
Less : Closing Stock of Finished Goods[1]	3,200		12,840	
COST OF GOODS SOLD	24,000		96,280	4·01
Selling and Distribution Overhead				
Advertisement, Discount Allowed & Selling Cost @ Re. 0·40 per unit sold			9,600	0·40
COST OF SALES			1,05,880	4·41
PROFIT (Balancing Figure)			14,120	0·59
SALES	24,000		1,20,000	5·00

Working Notes :

Calculation for value of closing stock of finished goods :

$$\frac{\text{Total Cost of production} \times \text{cl. st. units}}{\text{Total production units}}$$

$$i.e., \frac{\text{Rs. } 1,02,720}{25,600} \times 3,200 = \text{Rs. } 12,840$$

Problem 15

The following figures are available from the books of Best Manufacturing Co. for the year ended 31.12.2001 :

	Rs.
Materials	
Stock on 1.1.2001	1,000·00
Stock on 31.12. 2001	2,000·00
Purchase during 2001	10,000·00
Wages	7,500·00
Profit for the year	6,090·00
Selling overhead	5,250·00
Factory overhead	4,500·00
Administration overhead	4,200·00

(*a*) Prepare a cost sheet showing prime cost, work cost, cost of production, cost of sales and sales.

(*b*) In 2002 the factory receives an order for a job which will require materials Rs. 1,200 and wages Rs. 750. Ascertain the sale price of the job if the factory intends to earn a profit 10% higher than the percentage of profit earned in 2001.

Assume that the factory overhead has gone up by $16\frac{2}{3}\%$ and selling overhead has gone down by 20% in 2002. Further assume that factory overhead is recovered as a percentage of the wages and administration and selling overhead as a percentage of works cost. **[*C.U. B.Com. (Hons.)*]**

Solution

STATEMENT SHOWING COST SHEET

for the year ended 31.12.2001

Particulars	*Amount* *Rs.*	*Amount* *Rs.*
Materials consumed		
Stock on 1.1.2001	1,000·00	
Purchase during 2001	10,000·00	
	11,000·00	
Less : Stock on 31.12.2001	2,000·00	
		9,000·00
Wages		7,500·00
Prime cost		16,500·00
Factory overhead		4,500·00
Works cost		21,000·00
Administration Overhead		4,200·00
Cost of Production		25,000·00
Selling Overhead		5,250·00
Cost of Sales		30,450·00
Profit for the year		6,090·00
Sales		36,540·00

ESTIMATED COST SHEET
and price of Job No. in 2002

Elements	*Amounts* Rs.
Materials	1,200·00
Wages	750·00
PRIME COST	1,950·00
Add : Factory Overhead : 70% of wages (see note-2)	525·00
WORKS COST	2,475·00
Administration Overhead : 19·31% of works cost (see Note 3)	478·00
COST OF PRODUCTION	2,953·00
Add : Selling Overhead : 19·31% of works cost (See Note 4)	478·00
COST OF SALES	3,431·00
Add : Profit : $26\frac{2}{3}$ of Sales. (See Note 5)	1,248·00
SALES PRICE	4,679·00

Working Notes :

(*i*) Cost sheet for the year 2001 taking into consideration the increase or decrease in rates of O/H in 2002.

Elements	*Amounts* Rs.
Materials	9,000·00
Wages	7,500·00
PRIME COST	16,500·00
Add : Factory Overhead : 4,500 + $16\frac{2}{3}$% thereof	5,250·00
WORKS COST	21,750·00
Add : Administration overhead	4,200·00
COST OF PRODUCTION	25,950·00
Add : Selling Overhead : 5,250 – 20% thereof	4,200·00
COST OF SALES	30,150·00

(*ii*) Precentage of factory overhead on wages in 2002 = Rs. 5,250 / Rs. 7,500 × 100 = 70%

(*iii*) Percentage of administration overhead on works cost in 2002 = Rs. 4,200 / Rs. 21,750 × 100 = 19·31%

(*iv*) Percentage of selling overhead on works cost in 2002 = Rs. 4,200 / Rs. 21,750 × 100 = 19·31%

(*v*) Percentage of profit on sale in 2001 = Rs. 6090 / Rs. 36,540 × 100 = $16\frac{2}{3}$%

∴ Percentage of profit on sale in 2002 = $16\frac{2}{3}$% + 10% = $26\frac{2}{3}$%.

(Normally profit is expressed as per percentage of sales. In the problem nothing has been mentioned whether the percentage is on cost or sales. The result will be different if the percentage is applied on cost.)

Problem 16

The following particulars relating to the year 2002 have been taken from the books of a chemical works, manufacturing and selling a chemical mixture :

	Kg	Rs.		Kg.	Rs.
Stock on 1.1.02			Salaries		
Raw materials	2,000	2,000	Factory		72,220
Finished mixture	500	1,750	Office		37,220
Factory stores		7,250	Selling		41,500
Purchase			Expenses		
Raw materials	1,60,000	1,80,000	Direct		18,500
Factory stores		24,250	Office		18,200
Sales			Selling		18,000
Finished mixture	1,53,050	9,18,000	Stock on 31.12.02		
Factory		8,170	Raw materials	1,200	
Factory wages		1,78,650	Finished mixture	450	
Power		30,000	Factory stores		5,550
Depreciation of machinery		18,000			

The Stock of finished mixture at the end of 2002 is to be valued at the factory cost of the mixture for that year. The purchase price of raw materials remained unchanged throughout 2002.

Prepare a statement giving the maximum possible information about cost and its break-up for the year 2002. ***[Delhi, B. Com. (Hons.)]***

Solution

STATEMENT OF COST
for the year ended 31.12.02

Particulars		*Amount Rs.*	*Amount Rs.*
Raw Material Consumed :			
Opening Stock		2,000·00	
Purchase		1,80,000·00	
		1,82,000·00	
Less : Closing Stock		1,350·00	1,80,650·00
(1,200/1,60,000 × Rs. 1,80,000)			
Factory wages			1,78,650·00
Direct expenses			18,500·00
PRIME COST			3,77,800·00
Factory overhead :			
Power		30,400·00	
Depreciation of machinery		18,000·00	
Salary (factory)		72,220·00	
Factory Stores :			
Opening Stock :	7,250·00		
Purchase	24,250·00		
	31,500·00		
Less : Closing Stock	5,550·00	25,950·00	
		1,46,570·00	
Less : Sale of factory scrap		8,170·00	1,38,400·00

COST OF GOODS MANUFACTURED		5,16,200·00
Add : Opening stock of finished mixture		1,750·00
		5,17,950·00
Less : Closing stock of finished mixture (See note)		1,518·00
COST OF GOODS SOLD		5,16,432·00
OFFICE AND ADMINISTRATION OVERHEAD :		
Salary (Office)	37,220·00	
Office expenses	18,200·00	55,420·00
SELLING AND DISTRIBUTION OVERHEAD :		
Salary	41,500·00	
Selling expenses	18,000·00	59,500·00
Cost of sales		6,31,352·00
Profit (balancing figure)		2,86,648·00
SALES		9,18,648·00

Note : Closing stock of finished mixture valued at factory cost.
450/1,53,050 + 450 − 500 × Rs. 5,16,200 = Rs. 1,518·00

Problem 17

Cooling Limited manufactured and sold 1,000 refrigerators in the year ending 31st December 2006. The summarised Trading and Profit & Loss A/c is set out below :

	Dr. Rs.		*Cr. Rs.*
To Cost of Material	80,000	By Sales	4,00,000
To Dirct Wages	1,20,000		
To Other Manufacturing Cost	50,000		
To Gross Profit c/d	1,50,000		
	4,00,000		4,00,000
		By Gross Profit b/d	1,50,000
To Management and Staff Salary	60,000		
To Rent, Rates and Insurance	10,000		
To Selling Expenses	30,000		
To General Expenses	20,000		
To Net Profit	30,000		
	1,50,000		1,50,000

For the year ended 31st December 2007, it is estimated that :

(*a*) Output and Sales will be 1,200 refrigerators. Prices of materials will go up by 20% on the level of previous year.

(*b*) Wages will rise by 5%.

(*c*) Manufacturing cost will rise in proportion to the combined cost of material and wages.

(*d*) Selling cost per unit will remain unaffected.

(*e*) Other expenses will remain constant.

You are required to submit a statement to the Board of Directors showing the price at which the refrigerator should be marked as to show profit at 10% on selling price.

[*B.Com. Bombay*]

Solution

COST SHEET
for the year ended 31st December 2006

Particulars	Total Cost Rs.	Per Unit Cost Rs.
Cost of Materials	80,000	80·00
Direct Wages	1,20,000	120·00
PRIME COST	2,00,000	200·00
Factory Overhead :		
Manufacturing Cost	50,000	50·00
WORKS COST	2,50,000	250·00
Office and Administrative Overhead :		
Management & Staff Salaries	60,000	60·00
Rent, Rates and Insurance	10,000	10·00
General Expenses	20,000	20·00
COST OF PRODUCTION	3,40,000	340·00
Selling & Distribution Overhead :		
Selling Expenses	30,000	30·00
TOTAL COST	3,70,000	370·00
NET PROFIT	30,000	30·00
SALES	4,00,000	400·00

ESTIMATED COST SHEET
for 1,200 Refrigerators

	Total Cost Rs.	Per Unit Rs.
Materials (20% increase)	1,15,200	96·00
Direct Wages (5% increase)	1,51,200	126·00
PRIME COST	2,66,400	222·00
Factory Overhead :		
Manufacturing Cost (25% of Prime Cost)	66,600	55·50
WORKS COST	3,33,000	277·50
Office and Administrative Overhead :		
Management and Staff Salaries	60,000	50·00
Rent, Rates & Insurance	10,000	8·33
Other Expenses	20,000	16·67
COST OF PRODUCTION	4,23,000	352·50
Selling and Distribution Overhead :		
Selling Expenses	36,000	30·00
TOTAL COST	4,59,000	382·50
PROFIT [10% on selling price *i.e.* $\frac{1}{9}$th of Cost Price]	51,000	42·50
SALES	5,10,000	425·00

Working Notes

(*i*) Cost of Material

	Rs.
Old Price per unit	80
Add : 20% increase $\left[\frac{80 \times 20}{100}\right]$	16
	96

(*ii*) Direct Wages

Old rate per unit	120
Add : 5% increase $\left[\frac{120 \times 5}{100}\right]$	6
	126

(*iii*) % of manufacturing expenses calculated is given below

When prime cost is 2,00,000, manufacturing exp. 50,000

When prime cost is 100, manufacturing exp. = $\frac{50{,}000 \times 100}{2{,}00{,}000}$ = 25%

Problem 18

From the following particulars relating to production and sales for the year ended 31st December 1991, prepare statements of Production Cost and Cost of Goods Sold showing, inter alia, the prime cost and the cost per unit. Also prepare the Costing Profit & Loss Account.

	Rs.
Raw Materials as on 1.1.91	25,000
Work-in-progress as on 1.1.91	36,000
Finished goods as on 1.1.91 (8,000 units)	1,44,000 (at cost)
Raw Materials Purchased	2,00,000
Factory Wages	2,70,000
Factory Expenses	1,44,000
Administration Expenses	90,000
Selling Expenses	54,000
Distribution Expenses	36,000
Sale proceeds of finished goods (30,000 units)	9,00,000
Raw materials as on 31.12.91	45,000
Work-in-progress as on 31.12.91	54,000
Finished goods as on 31.12.91 (10,000 units) at cost	

[*C.U. B.Com. (Hons.)*]

Solution

Statement of Cost of Goods Sold for the year ended 31.12.91

Particulars	*Units*	*Total Cost Rs.*	*Cost per unit Rs.*
Raw Materials Consumed :			
Stock on 1.1.91		25,000	
Add : Purchases		2,00,000	
		2,25,000	
Less : Stock on 31.12.91		45,000	
RAW MATERIALS CONSUMED		1,80,000	
Factory Wages		2,70,000	
PRIME COST		4,50,000	
Factory Overhead :			
Factory Expenses		1,44,000	
		5,94,000	
Add : Work-in-progress on 1.1.91		36,000	
		6,30,000	
Less : Work-in-progress on 31.12.91		54,000	
WORKS COST		5,76,000	
Office and Administration Overhead :			
Administrative Expenses		90,000	
COST OF PRODUCTION	32,000	6,66,000	20·812
Add : Finished goods on 1.1.91	8,000	1,44,000	
	40,000	8,10,000	
Less : Finished goods on 31.12.91	10,000	2,08,125	
COST OF GOODS SOLD	30,000	6,01,875	20·625

Statement of Costing Profit & Loss A/c

Particulars	*Rs.*	*Amount Rs.*	*Cost per unit Rs.*
Sales (A)		9,00,000	30·00
Less : Cost of Goods Sold	6,01,875		
Selling Expenses	54,000		
Distribution Expenses	36,000		
TOTAL COST OR COST OF SALES (B)		6,91,875	23·06
∴ PROFIT (A[–]B)		2,08,125	6·94

Working Notes

(*i*) Calculation for units produced during the year

	Units
Units Sold	30,000
Add : Closing Stock of finished goods	10,000
	40,000
Less : Opening Stock of finished goods	8,000
Units produced during the year	32,000

(*ii*) Calculation for value of closing-finished stock at cost :
Closing Finished stock = 10,000 units.
Cost of Production per unit = Rs. 20·8125
∴ Cost of 1,000 units = Rs. 20·8125 × 10,000 = 2,08,125.

Problem 19

From the following information prepare a Cost Sheet showing (*a*) the value of materials consumed, (*b*) the cost of production, (*c*) the cost of sales, (*d*) the Total Net profit; and (*e*) Net profit per ton :

	Rs.
Purchases of Raw Materials	2,64,000
Direct Wages	2,20,000
Carriage inward	3,168
Works on Cost	88,000
Stock on 1.1.06 :	
Raw Materials	44,000
Work-in-progress	10,500
Finished Goods (1,600 tons)	35,200
Stock on 31.12.06 :	
Raw materials	48,928
Work-in-progress	35,200
Finished Goods (3,200 tons)	70,400
Sales	6,60,000
Office on Cost	17,600

Selling expenses amount to 0·75 paise per ton, 25,600 tons were produced during the year.

[*Audit & Accounts Service Exam.*]

Solution

COST SHEET
for the year ended 31.12.06

Particulars	*Amount* *Rs.*	*Amount* *Rs.*
Opening Stock	44,000	
Add : Purchases	2,64,000	
	3,08,000	
Less : Closing Stock	48,928	
	2,59,072	
Add : Carriage inward	3,168	
Raw Materials consumed	2,62,240	
Add : Direct Wages	2,20,000	
PRIME COST		4,82,240
Factory Overhead :		
WORKS COST	88,000	
Add : Opening Work-in-progress	10,500	
	98,500	
Less : Closing Work-in-progress	35,200	
		63,300

WORKS COST		5,45,540
Office & Administrative Overhead :		
Office on Cost		17,600
COST OF PRODUCTION		5,63,140
Add : Opening Finished Goods		35,200
		5,98,340
Less : Closing Finished Goods		70,400
COST OF GOODS SOLD		5,27,940
Selling & Distribution Overhead :		
Selling Expenses [*24,000 tons × Re. 0·75]		18,000
		5,45,940
Add : Profit (balancing figure)		1,14,060
TOTAL SALES		6,60,000

Working Notes :

***Calculation of Sales unit :**

	Tons
Opening Finished Stock	1,600
Add : Produced during the year	25,600
	27,200
Less : Closing Finished Stock	3,200
	24,000

Net Profit per ton : $\dfrac{\text{Net Profit}}{\text{Sales unit}} = \dfrac{1,14,060}{24,000}$ = Rs. 4·75 (approx.)

Problem 20

Sreelekha Mfg. Co. manufactures two types of pens—*P* and *Q*. The cost data for the year ended 30th June 2002 is as follows :

	Rs.
Direct materials	4,00,000
Direct wages	2,24,000
Production overhead	96,000
	7,20,000

It is further ascertained that :

(*a*) Direct materials in type *P* cost twice as much direct materials as in type *Q*.
(*b*) Direct wages for type *Q* were 60% of those of type *P*.
(*c*) Production overhead was of the same rate for both types.
(*d*) Administration overhead for each was 200% fo direct labour.
(*e*) Selling costs were 50 paise per pen for both types.
(*f*) Production during the year :

Type *P*	40,000
Type *Q*	1,20,000

(*g*) Sales during the year :

Type *P*	36,000
Type *Q*	1,00,000

(*h*) Selling prices were Rs. 14 per pen for type *P* and Rs. 10 per pen for type *Q*.

Prepare a statement showing per unit cost of production, total cost, profit and also total sales value and profit separately for the two types of pens *P* and *Q*. **[*ICWA, Inter. Dec. 1990*]**

Solution

STATEMENT OF COST
for the year ended 30.6.02

	Total	P 40,000 units		Q 1,20,000 units	
		Total	Per unit	Total	Per unit
	Rs.	Rs.	Rs.	Rs.	Rs.
Direct Materials					
40,000 × 2 : 1,20,000 × 1	4,00,000	1,60,000	4·00	2,40,000	2·00
Direct Wages					
40,000 × 100 : 1,20,000 × 60	2,24,000	80,000	2·00	1,44,000	1·20
Prime Cost	6,24,000	2,40,000	6·00	3,84,000	3·20
Production Overhead					
40,000 : 1,20,000	96,000	24,000	0·60	72,000	0·60
Works Cost	7,20,000	2,64,000	6·60	4,56,000	3·80
Administration Overhead	4,48,000	1,60,000	4·00	2,88,000	2·40
Cost of Production	11,68,000	4,24,000	10·60	7,44,000	6·20
Less : Closing Stock of Finished Goods : (*P* — 4,000 × Rs. 10·60, *Q* — 20,000 × Rs. 6·20)	1,66,400	42,400	10·60	1,24,000	6·20
Cost of Goods Sold (*P* —36,000, *Q*—1,00,000)	10,01,600	3,81,600	10·60	6,20,000	6·20
Selling Costs @ 50 p. per pen	68,000	18,000	0·50	50,000	0·50
Total Cost	10,69,600	3,99,600	11·10	6,70,000	6·70
Profit (*balancing figure*)	4,34,400	1,04,400	2·90	3,30,000	3·30
Total Sales	15,04,000	5,04,000	14·00	10,00,000	10·00

Working Notes :

(*i*) Let cost of Material for type $Q = A$.

$\therefore$ cost of Materials for Type $P = 2A$.

or, $80{,}000\ A + 1{,}20{,}000\ A = 4{,}00{,}000$

or, $2{,}00{,}000\ A = 4{,}00{,}000 \quad \therefore \quad A = \frac{4{,}00{,}000}{2{,}00{,}000} = 2$

$\therefore$ For type Q = Rs. 2 per unit

Type P = Rs. 2 × 2 = Rs. 4 per unit.

(*ii*) Let Wages for $P = A$

$\therefore$ Q will be $\frac{60}{100}$ A

or, $40{,}000A + 1{,}20{,}000 \times \frac{60}{100} A = 2{,}24{,}000$

or, $40{,}000A + 72{,}000A = 2{,}24{,}000$

or $1{,}12{,}000A = 2{,}24{,}000 \quad \therefore \quad A = \frac{2{,}24{,}000}{1{,}12{,}000} = 2$

$\therefore$ Cost of Wages for quality P = Rs. 2 per unit

Q = $\frac{60}{100}$ × Rs. 2 = Rs. 1·20 per unit

(*iii*) Closing Stock of units

	Type P	*Type Q*
Production during the year	40,000	1,20,000
Sales during the year	36,000	1,00,000
Closing stock during the year	4,000	20,000

Problem 21

P. Ltd. a manufacturer of fans, manufactured and sold 2,000 fans during the year ended 31.3.01. Following is the Profit and Loss Account of the company during the year :

Profit & Loss A/c for the year ended 31.3.01

	Rs.		Rs.
To Opening stock of raw materials	20,000	By Sales	6,00,000
" Purchases of raw materials	1,30,000	" Closing stock of raw materials	30,000
" Wages	1,80,000		
" Manufacturing expenses	75,000		
" Gross profit c/d	2,25,000		
	6,30,000		6,30,000
To Rent, rates and taxes	20,000	By Gross profit b/d	2,25,000
" Administration expenses	1,00,000	" Dividend received	3,000
" Selling and distribution expenses	45,000		
" Preliminary expenses written off	8,000		
" Donation	5,000		
" Net profit c/d	50,000		
	2,28,000		2,28,000

The estimates made by the company for the year ending 31.3.2002 are as under :

(*a*) The production and sales of fans will increase by 50%.
(*b*) The price of material per fan would increase by 20%.
(*c*) The labour cost per fan would go up by 10%.
(*d*) Of the manufacturing expenses Rs. 15,000 are fixed and the balance are variable. The variable portion will be in the same proportion of materials consumed and wages as in the previous year.
(*e*) Administration expenses are to be charged at the same respective percentage as in the previous year.
(*f*) Selling and distribution expenses per fan would remain unchanged.
(*g*) Selling price per fan will decrease by 10%.

You are required to prepare two separate cost sheets for the years 2000-2001 and 2001-2002 showing cost, profit and selling price per fan and the total cost, total profit and total sales.

[C.U. B.Com. (Hons.) 2000]

Solution

COST SHEET
for the year ended 31.03.2001

Output : 2,000 Fans

	Total		Per unit
	Rs.	Rs.	Rs.
Raw Materials Consumed :			
Opening Stock	20,000		
Purchase during the year	1,30,000		
	1,50,000		
Less : Closing Stock	30,000	1,20,000	60·00
Wages		1,80,000	90·00
Prime Cost		3,00,000	150·00

Manufacturing Expenses :			
Fixed	15,000		
Variable	60,000	75,000	37·50
Works Cost		3,75,000	187·50
Office and Administration Expenses :			
Rent, Rates and Taxes	20,000		
Administration Expenses	1,00,000	1,20,000	60·00
Cost of Production		4,95,000	247·50
Selling and Distribution Expenses		45,000	22·50
Cost of Sales		5,40,000	270·00
Profit (*balancing figure*)		60,000	30·00
Sales		6,00,000	300·00

ESTIMATED COST SHEET
for the year ended 31.03.2002

Budgeted Output and Sales : 3,000 Fans

	Total		Per unit
	Rs.	Rs.	Rs.
Raw Materials		2,16,000	72·00
Wages		2,97,000	99·00
Prime Cost		5,13,000	171·00
Manufacturing Expenses :			
Fixed	15,000		
Variable : 20% of Rs. 5,13,000	1,02,600	1,17,600	39·20
Works Cost		6,30,600	210·20
Office and Administration Expenses :			
Rent, Rates and Taxes	20,000		
Administration Expenses : $20\frac{2}{3}$% of *Works Cost*	1,68,160	1,88,160	62·72
Cost of Production		8,18,760	272·92
Selling and Distribution Expenses		67,500	22·50
Cost of Sales		8,86,260	295·42
Loss		76,260	25·42
Sales		8,10,000	270·00

Working Notes :

(*i*) Percentage of variable manufacturing expenses to prime cost : $\frac{60,000}{3,00,000} \times 100 = 20\%$

(*ii*) Percentage of Administration expenses to works cost : $\frac{1,00,000}{3,75,000} \times 100 = 26\frac{2}{3}\%$

(*iii*) Raw material cost per fan in 2001-2002 : 60 + 20% thereof = 72

(*iv*) Labour cost per fan in 2001-02 : 90 + 10% thereof = 99

(*v*) Selling price per fan in 2001-02 : Rs. 300–10% thereof = 270

(*vi*) Div. received, Preliminary expenses, Donations are non-cost items and have been excluded from Cost Sheet.

Problem 22

From the following particulars regarding the single output of Anirban & Co. for the quarter ended on 31st December 2001, prepare (a) a statement of Cost of Production; and (b) a statement of Profit or Loss, assuming Weighted Average Method is followed by the company for valuation of closing stock of finished goods :

Stock	1.10.2001	31.12.2001
	Rs.	Rs.
Raw Materials	40,000	50,000
Work-in-progress	50,000	70,000
Finished Goods	72,000 (4,000 units)	? (5,000 units)
Purchase of Raw Materials		Rs. 1,60,000
Direct Labour		Rs. 1,10,000
Chargeable Expenses		Rs. 40,000
Machine Hour Rate		Rs. 16 per hour
Machine Hours worked		5,000 hours
Office and Administration overhead		@ Rs. 4·80 per unit
Selling and Distribution overhead		@ Rs. 3·00 per unit
Sale of 24,000 units		@ Rs. 26 per unit

What would be the difference in stock value if the company follows FIFO method for valuation of closing stock of finished goods ?

[C.U. B.Com. (H) 2002]

Solution

In the Books of Anirban & Co. Ltd.
Historical Cost Sheet
for the year ended 31.12.2000

Sale = 24,000 units Output = 25,000

	Total Rs.	Per unit Rs.
Opening Raw Materials	40,000	
Add : Purchase of Raw Materials	1,60,000	
	2,00,000	
Less : Closing Raw Materials	50,000	
Raw Materials Consumed	1,50,000	6·00
Add : Direct Labour Cost	1,10,000	4·40
Chargeable Expenses	40,000	1·60
Prime Cost	3,00,000	12·00
Add : Adjustment for work--in-progress	– 20,000	– ·80
Add : Works overhead (Rs. 16 × 5,000)	80,000	3·20
Works Cost	3,60,000	14·40
Add : Office and Administration OHD (Rs. 4·80 × 25,000)	1,20,000	4·80

Cost of Production	4,80,000	19·20
Add : Opening Finished goods	72,000	
	5,52,000	19·03448
Less : Closing Finished goods under WEIGHTED AVERAGE METHOD (5,000 × 19·03448276)	95,172	—
Cost of Goods Sold	4,56,828	19·03448
Add : Selling & Distribution overhead (Rs. 3 × 24,000)	72,000	3·000
Cost of Sales	5,28,828	22·03448
Add : Profit (balancing figure)	95,172	3·96552
Sales	6,24,000	26·00

Part C

Closing Stock under FIFO METHOD = Rs. $\frac{4,80,000}{25,000}$ × 5,000 = Rs. 96,000

Profit would be Rs. 96,000

Rs. 6,24,000 – [4,80,000 + 72,000 – 96,000 + 72,000]

= Rs. 6,24,000 – 5,28,000

= Rs. 96,000

Problem 23

A factory produced 50,000 units P.A. Electric fans at a capacity level of 100%, Estimated cost of production is as under :

Material per unit Rs. 4

Labour per unit Rs. 2

Overhead :

Fixed—50,000 P.A.

Variable—Rs. 5 per unit

Semivariable—Rs. 40,000 P.A. up to 50% capacity, Rs. 5,000 for every 10% increase in capacity.

If the production programmed is as good and the factory wants to make a profit of Rs. 1,00,000. Determine the average sales price—

1st three months 50% capacity

Next nine months 80% capacity

[Adopted—Audit & Accounts Service]

Solution

Statement Showing Average Sales Price

Particulars	*1st 3 months*	*Next 9 months*	*Total*
Production Capacity Level :	50%	80%	
Production Units	6,250	30,000	36,250
Material consumed (@ Rs. 4 P.U)	25,000	1,20,000	1,45,000
Labour (@ Rs. 2 P.U.)	12,500	60,000	72,500
PRIME COST	37,500	1,80,000	2,17,500

Add : **Overhead :**			
Fixed : 50,000 P.A. [Allocated 3:9 ratio]	12,500	37,500	50,000
Variable : [@ Rs. 5 P.U.]	31,250	1,50,000	1,81,250
Semivariable	10,000	45,000	55,000
TOTAL COST	91,250	4,12,500	5,03,750
Add : Profit			1,00,000
TOTAL SALES VALUE			6,03,750

$\therefore$ Average Selling Price $= \dfrac{6{,}03{,}750}{36{,}250} = 16{\cdot}66$ (approx.)

Working : (*i*) Calculation for production unit of 1st 3 months at 50% capacity

$$= 50{,}000 \times \frac{50}{100} \times \frac{3}{12} = 6{,}250$$

(*ii*) Calculation for Production unit of next 9 months at 80% capacity

$$= 50{,}000 \times \frac{80}{100} \times \frac{9}{12} = 30{,}000$$

$\therefore$ Total Production = (6,250 + 30,000) units = 36,250 units.

(*iii*) Semivariable overhead for 1st 3 months $= 40{,}000 \times \dfrac{3}{12} = 10{,}000$

(*iv*) Semivariable overhead at 80% capacity level for 9 months :

Semivariable overhead increased Rs. 5,000 for every 10% increasing capacity over 50%.

Now, capacity level increases in next 9 month = (80 – 50)% = 30%

$\therefore$ Semivariable overhead increased by Rs. $5{,}000 \times \dfrac{30}{10} =$ Rs. 15,000

$\therefore$ Semivariable overhead at 80% level for next 9 months $= \left(40{,}000 \times \dfrac{9}{12}\right) + 15{,}000$

$$= 30{,}000 + 15{,}000 = \text{Rs. } 45{,}000$$

Problem 24

(*a*) The following figures are available from the books of XYZ Ltd. for the year ended 31.12.06 :

Material consumed	Rs. 10,000
Wages	Rs. 8,000
Factory overhead	Rs. 6,000
Office & Administrative overhead	Rs. 4,500
Selling overhead	Rs. 2 per unit

Profit for the year = 20% on cost of sales.

Units produced and sold 3,000

Prepare a Cost Sheet.

(*b*) In the next year the factory received an order of 750 units.

In this year, due to inflation, the cost structure has been changed by the following way.

Price of material increased by 10% Rate of wages increased by 20%, Factory overhead decreased by 20%, Selling overhead reduced to Rs. 1·50.

If the company wants to earn a profit higher than 10% of profit earned in last year, what will be the sales price of the job ?

Solution

COST SHEET
for the year ended 31.12.06

Particulars	*Amount* Rs.	*Amount* Rs.
Material consumed	10,000	
Wages	8,000	
PRIME COST		18,000
Add : Factory overhead		6,000
WORKS COST		24,000
Add : Office & Administrative overhead		4,500
COST OF PRODUCTION		28,500
Add : Selling & Distribution overhead [3,000 units × Rs. 2]		6,000
COST OF SALES		34,500
Add : Profit		6,900
SALES VALUE		41,400

ESTIMATED COST SHEET
for 750 units for the year 2007.

Particulars	*Amount* Rs.	*Amount* Rs.
Material	2,750	
Wages	2,400	
PRIME COST		5,150
Add : Factory overhead [60% of Rs. 2,400]		1,440
WORKS COST		6,590
Add : Office & Administrative Overhead [18·75% of Rs. 6,590]		1,236
COST OF PRODUCTION		7,826
Add : Selling & Distribution overhead [750 units × Rs. 1·50]		1,125
COST OF SALES		8,951
Add : Profit [22% of Rs. 8·951]		1,969
SALES VALUE		10,920

Working Notes :

(*i*) Material consumed as per last year price = $\frac{10,000 \times 750}{3,000}$ = 2,500

Now price of material increased by 10%.

∴ Material for 1985 = 2,500 + 10% of 2,500 = 2,750

(*ii*) Wages for 1985 :

Wages as per last year price = $\frac{8,000 \times 750}{3,000}$ = 2,000

Add : Increased (20% on 2,000) 400

2,400

(*iii*) Calculation for % of Factory overhead on Direct wages in 2006

$$= \frac{6,000 \times 100}{8,000} = 75\%$$

∴ Factory overhead in 2007 = 75% – 20% of 75 = 60%

(*iv*) Per unit selling overhead in 2007 = Rs. 1·50

(*v*) Calculation for % of Office & Administrative overhead on works cost

$$= \frac{4,500 \times 100}{24,000} = 18{\cdot}75\%$$

(*vi*) Calculation for profit on cost in 2006 = $\frac{6,900 \times 100}{34,500} = 20\%$

% of Profit increased in 2007 = 10%

∴ Profit on Cost in 2007 = 20% + 10% of 20 = 22%

Problem 25

The Bengal Pottery Ltd. prepares four types of articles, namely *P, Q. R & S.* The same raw materials are used for manufacture of all these articles. The articles which are found defective on inspection, are sold to the employees at a concessional rate. The ratio of defective articles is 10% of the finished articles, *i.e.,* for every 100 finished stock, 10 are defective.

The following data are collected from the manufacturing A/c for the month of December 2004 :

Type	*Finished Articles*	*Labour P.U.*	*Amount realised from Sale of defective articles Rs.*
P	2,000	1·00	1,200
Q	4,000	1·50	2,100
R	6,000	0·50	1,650
S	8,000	0·75	1,000

One type of article requires one kg of raw material @ Rs. 5 per kg Factory overhead variable 100%, fixed 150% of prime cost.

Find out the factory cost of each article.

Solution

COST SHEET
for the month of December 2004

Particulars	*P*	*Q*	*R*	*S*
Production in units (Finished)	2,000	4,000	6,000	8,000
Add : Defective (10% on finished units)	200	400	600	800
TOTAL PRODUCTION UNITS	2,200	4,400	6,600	8,800
Material consumed @ Rs. 5 per kg per unit	11,000	22,000	33,000	44,000
Labour [Per unit cost × Production unit]	2,200	6,600	3,300	6,600
PRIME COST	13,200	28,600	36,300	50,600
Add : Factory overhead :				
Variable [100% of Prime Cost]	13,200	28,600	36,300	50,600
Fixed [150% of Prime Cost]	19,800	42,900	54,450	75,900
	46,200	1,00,100	1,27,050	1,77,100
Less : Scrap value	1,200	2,100	1,650	1,000

COST OF PRODUCTION		2,80,000
Add : Opening Finished Stock		50,000
		3,30,000
Less : Closing Finished Stock (Missing)		1,70,000
TOTAL COST/COST OF GOODS SOLD		1,60,000

Problem 31

The following is the Manufacturing and Profit & Loss A/c of the Saraswati Trading Co. for the year ended 31st March 2006 :

	Dr. *Rs.*		*Cr.* *Rs.*
To Opening Stock :	-	By Sales	3,40,000
Raw Material	20,000	By Closing Stock :	
W.I.P.	10,000	Raw Materials	30,000
Finished Stock	30,000	W.I.P.	15,000
To Purchase of Raw Materials	1,50,000	Finished Stock	25,000
To Direct Wages	80,000		
To Power	20,000		
To Carriage Inward	4,000		
To Royalty	2,000		
To Cost of Spl. Design	4,000		
To Freight	2,000		
To Gross profit	88,000		
	4,10,000		4,10,000
To Rent, Rates & Taxes	5,000	By Gross Profit B/D	88,000
Carriage Outward	3,000	By Interest on Fixed Deposit	10,000
Provision for Bad Debt	2,500	By Discount Received	12,000
Bad Debt	1,500		
Electricity —Office	500		
—Factory	1,000		
Donation	2,000		
Subscription to Trade Association	2,500		
Income Tax	10,000		
Depreciation on P & M	5,000		
Warehouses Rents	6,000		
Advertisement	2,000		
Fees & Fines	1,000		
Packing Charges	4,000		
Establishment Expenses	20,000		
Net Profit	44,000		
	1,10,000		1,10,000

Prepare a Cost Sheet after considering the following facts : (*i*) 60% of Rent, Rates and Taxes are related to Office & Administration and 40% to Sales Department.

(*ii*) 50% of establishment expenses relate to Office & Administrative Department, 30% to Production Department.

Solution

COST SHEET OF SARASWATI TRADING CO.
for the year ended 31.3.2006

Particulars		Amount Rs.	Amount Rs.
Opening Stock of Raw Materials		20,000	
Add : Purchases		1,50,000	
Add : Carriage Inward		4,000	
Add : Freight		2,000	
		1,76,000	
Less : Closing Stock of Raw Materials		30,000	
RAW MATERIALS CONSUMED		1,46,000	
Add : Direct Wages		80,000	
Direct Expenses :			
Royalty	2,000		
Cost of Spl. Design	4,000	6,000	
PRIME COST			2,32,000
Factory Overhead :			
Power		20,000	
Electricity		1,000	
Depreciation on Plant & Machinery		5,000	
Establishment Expenses (30% of Rs. 20,000)		6,000	
			32,000
			2,64,000
Add : Opening W.I.P.			10,000
			2,74,000
Less : Closing W.I.P.			15,000
FACTORY COST			2,59,000
Office & Administrative Overhead :			
Rent, Rates & Taxes [60% of Rs. 5,000]		3,000	
Office Electricity		500	
Subscription to Trade Association		2,500	
Establishment Expenses [50% of Rs. 20,000]		10,000	
			16,000
COST OF PRODUCTION			2,75,000
Add : Opening Finished Stock			30,000
			3,05,000
Less : Closing Finished Stock			25,000
COST OF GOODS SOLD			2,80,000
Selling & Distribution Overhead :			
Rent, Rates & Taxes (40%)		2,000	
Warehouse rent		6,000	

Advertisement	2,000	
Packing Charge	4,000	
Establishment Expenses (20% of Rs. 20,000)	4,000	
Carriage Outward	3,000	
Bad Debt	1,500	
		22,500
COST OF SALES		3,02,500
Profit (balancing figure)		37,500
Sales		3,40,000

Working Notes :

(*i*) The following items should be excluded from cost sheet, as they are purely financial in nature.

Provision for Bad Debt, Donation, Income Tax, Fees & Fines, Interest on Fixed Deposit, Discount Received.

(*ii*) As bad debts related with sales, hence it should be considered as Selling and Distribution overhead.

Problem 32

The following figures are extracted from the Trial Balance of Gogetter Company on 30th September 2006 :

	Rs.	*Rs.*
Inventories :		
Finished Stock	80,000	
Raw Materials	1,40,000	
Work-in-progress	2,00,000	
Office Appliances	17,400	
Plant & Machinery	4,60,500	
Buildings	2,00,000	
Sales		7,68,000
Sales Return & Rebates	14,000	
Materials Purchased	3,20,000	
Freight incurred as materials	16,000	
Purchase Returns		4,800
Direct Labour	1,60,000	
Indirect Labour	18,000	
Factory Supervision	10,000	
Repairs & Maintenance—Factory	14,000	
Heat, Light & Power	65,000	
Rates & Taxes	6,300	
Miscellaneous Factory Expenses	18,700	
Sales Commission	33,600	
Sales Travelling	11,000	
Sales Promotion	22,500	

Distribution Dept.—Salaries & Expenses	18,000
Office Salaries & Expenses	8,600
Interest on Borrowed Funds	2,000

Further details are available as follows :

(*i*) Closing inventories :

Finished Goods	1,15,000
Raw Materials	1,80,000
Work-in-Progress	1,92,000

(*ii*) Accrued expenses on :

Direct Labour	8,000
Indirect Labour	1,200
Interest on Borrowed Funds	2,000

(*iii*) Depreciation to be provided on :

Office Appliances	5%
Plant & Machinery	10%
Buildings	4%

(*iv*) Distribution of the following costs :

Heat, Light and Power to Factory, Office & Distribution in the ratio 8 : 1 : 1.

Rates & Taxes two-thirds to Factory and one-Third to office.

Depreciation on Building to Factory, Office and Selling in the ratio 8 : 1 : 1.

With the help of the above information, you are required to prepare a condensed Profit & Loss statement of Gogetter Co. for the year ended 30th September 2006, along with supporting schedules of :

(*i*) Cost of Sales.

(*ii*) Selling and Distribution Expenses.

(*iii*) Administration Expenses. **[*C.A. Inter Nov. Adopted*]**

Solution

COST SHEET

Particulars		*Amount* *Rs.*	*Amount* *Rs.*
Opening Stock of Raw Materials		1,40,000	
Add : Purchases	3,20,000		
Less : Returns	4,800		
		3,15,200	
Add : Freight		16,000	
		4,71,200	
Less : Closing Stock of Raw Materials		1,80,000	
RAW MATERIALS CONSUMED		2,91,200	
Direct Labour	1,60,000		
Add : Accrued expenses	8,000		
		1,68,000	
PRIME COST			4,59,200

	Rs.	Rs.	Rs.
Factory Overhead :			
Indirect Labour	18,000		
Add : Accrued expenses	1,200		
		19,200	
Factory Supervision		10,000	
Repairs and Maintenance		14,000	
Heat, Light and Power		52,000	
Rates and Taxes		4,200	
Misc. Factory Expenses		18,700	
Depreciation : Plant	46,050		
Building	6,400		
		52,450	
			1,70,550
WORKS COST (GROSS)			6,29,750
Add : Opening W.I.P.		2,00,000	
Less : Closing W.I.P.		1,92,000	
			8,000
WORKS COST (NET)			6,37,750
Office and Administration Overhead :			
Heat, Light and Power		6,500	
Rates and Taxes		2,100	
Depreciation & Building		800	
Office Appliances		870	
Office Salaries and Expenses		8,600	
			18,870
COST OF PRODUCTION			6,56,620
Add : Opening Stock of Finished Goods		80,000	
Less : Closing Stock of Finished Goods		1,15,000	
			–35,000
COST OF GOODS SOLD			6,21,620
Selling and Distribution Overhead :			
Heat and Light		6,500	
Depreciation Building		800	
Sales Commission		33,600	
Sales Travelling		11,000	
Sales Promotion		22,500	
Distribution Dept. Expenses		18,000	
			92,400
COST OF SALES			7,14,020

GOGETTER COMPANY LTD.

Condensed Profit & Loss Statement for the year ended 30th September 2006

To Cost of Sales	7,14,020	By Sales	7,68,000	
To Interest on Borrowed Funds	4,000	*Less* : Sales Return	14,000	
				7,54,000
To Net Profit	35,980			
	7,54,000			7,54,000

Problem 33

Mr. Rohit has a small furniture factory. He specialises in the manufacture of small drawing tables of standard size of which he can make 15,000 a year. The cost per table worked out as under for the year 2006-07, when he made and sold 10,000 tables :

	Rs.
Materials	30
Labour	10
Overhead (fixed) received @ 50% of Material Cost	15
	55

Price is fixed by adding a standard margin of 10% to the total cost arrived at as above.

In 2006-07, due to fall in the cost of materials, total cost worked out as under :

	Rs.
Materials	20
Labour	10
Overhead (fixed) recovered @ 50% of Material Cost	10
	40

Mr. Rohit maintained his standard margin of 10% on the cost of sales. Sales were at the same level as in 2006-07.

You are asked to :

(*a*) Determine profit or loss for the year 2006-07.

(*b*) Compute the price which should have been charged in 2006-07 to yield the same profit or loss as in 2006-07. **[*I.C.W.A.I. Inter*]**

Solution

Statement Showing the Profit
for the year 2006-07

(a) **Production : 10,000 Tables**

Particulars	*Total* Rs.	*Per Unit* Rs.
Materials (30 × 10,000)	3,00,000	30·00
Labour (10 × 10,000)	1,00,000	10·00
PRIME COST	4,00,000	40·00
Overhead (50% on materials)	1,50,000	15·00
TOTAL COST	5,50,000	55·00
Profit (10% on Total Cost)	55,000	5·50
SELLING PRICE	6,05,000	60·50

Statement Showing the Profit or Loss
for the year 2006-07

Production : 10,000 Tables

Particulars	*Total* Rs.	*Per Unit* Rs.
Total Cost :		
Material (20 × 10,000 units)	2,00,000	20·00

Labour (10 × 10,000 units)		1,00,000	10·00
Overhead (10 × 10,000 units)		1,00,000	10·00
		4,00,000	40·00
Profit @10%		40,000	4·00
SELLING PRICE		4,40,000	44·00
Revised TOTAL COST treating overhead as fixed charge :			
Materials	2,00,000		
Labour	1,00,000		
Overhead	1,50,000		
		4,50,000	45·00
LOSS		10,000	1·00

(b) Computation of price to be charged in 1981-82 to yield the same profit as in 2006-07

	Total Cost *Rs.*	*Per Unit* *Rs.*
Cost	4,50,000	45·00
Profit as 2006-07	55,000	5·50
SELLING PRICE	5,05,000	50·50

Problem 34

The following data are available from the Cost Ledger of Acme Industries for the year 2006 :

	Rs.
Plant Maintenance	25,000
Lighting	6,300
Depreciation on plant	8,100
Rates and Taxes for the Works	3,900
Staff Salaries	32,000
Management Salaries	22,000
Power (for this plant)	10,600
Rental for Leasehold Equipments	9,600
Indirect Wages	37,100
Rectification Cost of Defectives (Normal)	8,400
Consumable Stores	17,600
Selling Expenses	30,000
General Charges	15,600
Sale proceeds from scrap	4,200

During the year total production was 1,20,000 units. The break-up of Prime Cost per unit was Materials Rs. 2·20 and Wages Rs. 1·80. The average selling price was Rs. 6·75 per unit and the entire quantity produced during the year was sold out.

With effect from January 1, 2007, the selling price was reduced to Rs. 6·40 per unit. It was envisaged that production could be enhanced during 2007 by $33\frac{1}{3}\%$ without incurring any overtime or extra-shift work or additional selling expenses.

You are required to prepare statements showing :

(*i*) Actual cost and profit for the year 2006.

(*ii*) Estimated cost and profit for 2007, assuming that the entire production will be sold during the year. Assumptions, if any, required to be made in the above exercise should be clearly noted.

[*I.C.W.A. Inter, Adopted*]

Solution

(*i*) **ACME Limited**

Cost Statement for the year 2006

Output : 1,20,000 Unit

Particulars	*Amount* *Rs.*	*Amount* *Rs.*	*Per Unit* *Rs.*
Materials	2,64,000		2·20
Wages	2,16,000		1·80
PRIME COST		4,80,000	4·00
Add : **Factory Overhead :**			
Variable :			
Power	10,600		
Rectification Cost of Defectives	8,400		
Consumable Stores	17,600		
	36,600		
Less : Sale Proceeds from Scrap	4,200		
		32,400	0·27
Fixed :			
Maintenance of Plant & Machinery	25,000		
Lighting	6,300		
Depreciation for Plant	8,100		
Rates and Taxes for work	3,900		
Rental for Leasehold Equipment	9,600		
Indirect Wages	37,100		
		90,000	0·75
WORKS COST		6,02,400	5·02
Office & Administrative Overhead :			
Staff Salaries	32,000		
Management Salaries	22,000		
General Expenses	15,600		
		69,600	0·58
COST OF PRODUCTION		6,72,000	5·60
Selling & Distribution Overhead :			
Selling Expenses		30,000	0·25
		7,02,000	5·85
Profit		1,08,000	0·90
		8,10,000	6·75

(*ii*)

ESTIMATED COST SHEET FOR 2007

Output : 1,60,000 units

Particulars		*Amount*	*Per unit*
	Rs.	*Rs.*	*Rs.*
Prime Cost		6,40,000	4·00
Variable Charges without Scrap $\left[32{,}400 \times \frac{1{,}60{,}000}{1{,}20{,}000}\right]$		43,200	0·27
		6,83,200	4·27
Fixed Charges :			
Factory	90,000		
Office & Administration	69,600		
Selling & Distribution	30,000		
		1,89,600	1·185
COST OF SALES		8,72,800	5·455
Profit		1,51,200	0·945
SALES		10,24,000	6,400

Problem 35

The following datas are available from the books and records of Q Ltd. for the month of November 1995. You are require to prepare a statement showing the cost of goods manufactured and sold and the profit earned :

Direct Labour cost Rs. 16,000 (160% of the factory overheads)
Cost of goods sold Rs. 56,000

Inventory accounts show the following figures :

	Nov. 1, 1995	*Nov. 30, 1995*
	Rs.	*Rs.*
Raw Materials	8,000	8,600
Work-in-progress	8,000	12,000
Finished goods	14,000	18,000
Selling Expenses		3,400
General and Administration Expenses		2,600
Sales (for the month)		75,000

You are required to prepare a statement showing the cost of goods manufactured and sold and the profit earned. **[*I.C.W.A. (Int.), Dec. '95*]**

Solution

Computation of Raw Material consumed

	Rs.
Cost of goods sold	56,000
Less : Selling Expenses	3,400
Cost of Production	52,600
Less : General and Administration Expenses	2,600
	50,000

Add : Closing Stock of Finished Goods		18,000
		68,000
Less : Opening Stock of Finished Goods		14,000
Work Cost		54,000
Add : Closing Stock of Work-in-progress		12,000
		66,000
Less : Opening Stock of Work-in-progress		8,000
		58,000
Less : Factory Overhead	$\left[16,000 \times \frac{100}{160}\right]$	10,000
Prime Cost		48,000
Less : Direct Labour		16,000
Raw Material consumed		32,000

Statement of Cost and Profit

	Rs.	*Rs.*
Opening Stock of Raw Materials	8,000	
Add : Purchase of Raw Materials (balancing figure)	32,600	
	40,600	
Less : Closing Stock of Raw Materials	8,600	
Raw Materials Consumed		32,000
Add : Direct Labour Cost		16,000
Prime Cost		48,000
Add : Factory Overheads		10,000
		58,000
Add : Opening W.I.P.		8,000
		66,000
Less : Closing W.I.P		12,000
Work Cost		54,000
Add : General and Aministration expenses		2,600
		56,600
Add : Opening Stock of Finished Goods		14,000
		70,600
Less : Closing Stock of Finished Goods		18,000
Cost of Production		52,600
Add : Selling Expenses		3,400
		56,000
Sales		75,000
Profit		19,000

EXERCISES

OVERVIEW OF ACCOUNTING

1. *State which of the following statements are correct or incorrect* :

(*i*) The method of costing used in a refinery is "process costing".
(*ii*) In cost accounting, like financial accounting, absolute accuracy is aimed at.
(*iii*) To design a costing department is not difficult, study another similar organisation and study a book on costing and you know what to do.
(*iv*) Conversion costs and overheads are interchangeable terms.
(*v*) Notional Costs are not included while ascertaining cost.
(*vi*) Cost Accounting is not needed by a non-profit organisation such as a hospital.
(*vii*) If the management is not interested in costing information, there should be no costing department.
(*viii*) Notional Costs and Imputed Costs mean the same thing.
(*ix*) Standard costing tells us what the cost should be.
(*x*) Historical costs are useful solely for estimating cost that lie ahead.
(*xi*) Cost is a fact, price is a policy.
(*xii*) Basically there are two methods of costing *viz.* (1) Specific Order Costing; and (2) Operation Costing.
(*xiii*) Cost Accounting is nothing more than a detailed analysis of expenditure.
(*xiv*) Cost Accounting is nothing but a postmortem of post costs.
(*xv*) Cost Accounting provides cost information to all those who are external to the business.
(*xvi*) Both financial and cost accounts are written up with the same basic documents.
(*xvii*) Cost Accounting is not needed if price is beyond the control of the firm.
(*xviii*) Cost Accounting assists financial accounting with regard to the valuation of inventory.
(*xix*) The scope of cost accounting includes cost ascertainment, cost presentation and cost control.
(*xx*) Cost Accounting helps in the ascertainment of cost beforehand.
(*xxi*) Cost Accounting provides information for ascertaining the financial position as on a particular date.
(*xxii*) Cost Accounting helps in controlling cost.
(*xxiii*) Since pricing is a matter of managerial policy, cost information is useless for price fixation.
(*xxiv*) A cost unit is the same as a cost centre.
(*xxv*) The cost converting raw materials to finished products is known as conversion cost.

Ans. True :- (*i*), (*iii*), (*viii*), (*ix*), (*x*), (*xi*), (*xii*), (*xvi*), (*xviii*), (*xix*), (*xx*), (*xxii*).
False :- (*ii*), (*iii*), (*iv*), (*v*), (*vii*), (*xiii*), (*xiv*), (*xv*), (*xvii*), (*xxi*), (*xxiii*), (*xxiv*), (*xxv*).

2. *Specify the method of costing applicable to the following industries* :

(*i*)	Ship-building	(*ii*)	Dairy
(*iii*)	Printing	(*iv*)	Bicycles
(*v*)	Medicines	(*vi*)	Hospital
(*vii*)	Radio	(*viii*)	Cement
(*ix*)	Textiles	(*x*)	Brewery
(*xi*)	Aerated water	(*xii*)	Canteen
(*xiii*)	Motor car	(*xiv*)	Chemicals
(*xv*)	Oil	(*xvi*)	Road transport
(*xvii*)	Sugar	(*xviii*)	Toy Making

Ans.

(*i*)	**Contract**	(*ii*)	**Process**
(*iii*)	**Job**	(*iv*)	**Multiple**
(*v*)	**Batch**	(*vi*)	**Operating**
(*vii*)	**Multiple**	(*viii*)	**Unit**
(*ix*)	**Process**	(*x*)	**Unit/Process**
(*xi*)	**Unit**	(*xii*)	**Operating**

(*xiii*)	**Multiple**	**(*xiv*)**	**Process**
(*xv*)	**Process**	**(*xvi*)**	**Operating**
(*xvii*)	**Process**	**(*xviii*)**	**Batch**

3. *Match the following* :

(*i*)	The Practice of charging all costs to Product	(*i*)	Facilitates greater degree of control over cost.
(*ii*)	Standard costing	(*ii*)	Absorption costing
(*iii*)	A cost unit which consists of a group of similar products	(*iii*)	Historical costing, estimating costing and standard costing.
(*iv*)	Cost classification	(*iv*)	Batch
(*v*)	Cost accounting involves	(*v*)	Facilities computation of cost variances.
(*vi*)	A group of identical items maintaining identity through one or more stages of production.	(*vi*)	Analysis and synthesis of costs.
(*vii*)	What the costs are, what they are likely to be, and how they should be distinguished, respectively.	(*vii*)	Product Group

[Ans. (*i*), (*ii*); (*ii*), (*v*); (*iii*), (*vii*); (*iv*), (*i*); (*v*), (*vi*); (*vi*), (*iv*); (*vii*), (*iii*).]

4. *Point out the statements which are false—(F)/Correct (C)* :

(*i*) Abnormal cost is controllable.
(*ii*) Cost of production is equal to prime cost plus work cost.
(*iii*) Variable cost increases as the fixed cost.
(*iv*) Financial accounting provides information for cost control.
(*v*) Direct cost is one which can be conveniently identified with and charged to a particular unit of cost.
(*vi*) Total variable cost does not increase in total proportion to output.
(*vii*) Variable cost per unit remains constant.
(*viii*) Sunk costs are relevant for decision-making.
(*ix*) Costing and cost accounting are the same.
(*x*) Fixed cost does not change in the same proportion in which output change.
(*xi*) Administration expenses are mostly fixed.
(*xii*) Decremental cost means the cost of an added unit.
(*xiii*) Standard costs tell as what the cost is.
(*xiv*) Period costs are not assigned to product.
(*xv*) Marginal cost is not at all helpful to management for decision making.
(*xvi*) Fixed cost per unit decreases with rise in output and increases with fall in output.
(*xvii*) Cost centre and cost unit are the same.

[Ans. (*i*) C	**(*ii*) F**	**(*iii*) F**	**(*iv*) F**
(*v*) C	**(*vi*) F**	**(*vii*) C**	**(*viii*) F**
(*ix*) F	**(*x*) F**	**(*xi*) C**	**(*xii*) F**
(*xiii*) F	**(*xiv*) C**	**(*xv*) F**	**(*xvi*) C**
(*xvii*) F			**(*xviii*) F]**

5. *Which of the following is correct* ?

A. Which cost system description applies to the manufacture of 20 engraved doors for the new clubhouse at a golf course ?

(*i*) Contract (*ii*) Process (*iii*) Batch (*iv*) Service

B. An important feature of a cost centre is that :

(*i*) It uses only monetary information.
(*ii*) It has clearly defined boundaries.
(*iii*) It must be one specific location only.
(*iv*) It must be an area of the business through which products pass.

C. Prime cost may be correctly defined as :

(*i*) The sum of direct materials and direct labour cost with all other costs excluded.

(*ii*) The total of all cost items which can be directly charged to product units.

(*iii*) The total cost incurred in producing a finished unit.

(*iv*) The sum of the large cost items in a product cost.

D. Which of the following is a cost behavior-oriented approach to production costing ?

(*i*) Absorption costing (*ii*) Marginal costing

(*ii*) Process costing (*ii*) Job order costing

E. In a process cost system the unit cost is computed for a

(*i*) Job (*ii*) Department

(*iii*) Batch of goods (*iii*) Category of goods.

F. The cost of goods sold under a periodic cost accumulation system is equal to the

(*i*) Cost of goods available for sale less ending finished goods inventory.

(*ii*) Cost of goods available for sale plus beginning finished goods inventory.

(*iii*) Cost of goods manufactured plus beginning finished goods inventory.

(*iv*) Cost of goods sold manufactured less beginning finished goods inventory.

G. The cost of goods manufactured, under a periodic cost accumulation system, is equal to the

(*i*) Beginning finished goods inventory plus purchase.

(*ii*) Beginning work-in-process plus cost of goods in process during the year.

(*iii*) Cost of goods put into production plus beginning work-in-process less ending work-in-process.

(*iv*) Cost of goods sold less beginning work-in-process.

H. For external financial statement purpose, inventories must be reported at

(*i*) Standard costs (*ii*) Actual costs

(*ii*) Period costs (*ii*) Direct costs.

I. The term "conversion costs" refers to

(*i*) Manufacturing costs incurred to produce units of output.

(*ii*) All costs associated with manufacturing other than direct labour costs and raw material costs.

(*iii*) Costs which are associated with marketing, shipping, warehousing and billing activities.

(*iv*) The sum of direct labour cost and all factory overhead costs.

(*v*) The sum of raw material costs and direct labour costs.

J. The term "prime costs" refers to

(*i*) Manufacturing costs incurred to produce unit of output.

(*ii*) All costs associated with manufacturing other than direct labour costs and raw material costs.

(*iii*) Costs which are predetermined and should be attained.

(*iv*) The sum of direct labour costs and all factory overhead costs.

(*v*) The sum of direct material cost and direct labour costs.

K. The term "variable costs" refers to

(*i*) All costs which are likely to respond to the amount of attention devoted to them by a specified manager.

(*ii*) All costs which are associated with marketing, shipping, warehousing and billing activities.

(*iii*) All costs which do not change in total for a given period of time and relevant range but become progressively smaller on a per unit basis as volume increases.

(*iv*) All manufacturing costs incurred to produce units of output.

(*v*) All costs which fluctuate in total in response to small change in the rate of utilization of capacity.

L. The term "cost" refers to

(*i*) An asset that has given benefit and is now expired.

(*ii*) The price of products sold or services rendered.

(*iii*) The value of the sacrifice made to acquire goods or services.

(*iv*) An asset that has not given benefit and is now expired.

(*v*) The present value of future benefits.

M. The term "sunk costs" refers to

(*i*) Past costs that are now irrevocable.

(*ii*) Costs that are directly influenced by unit manager.

(*iii*) Costs that should be incurred in a particular production process.

(*iv*) Costs that may be eliminated if some economic activity is changed or deleted.

(*v*) Benefits lost from rejecting the next best alternative.

N. The process of charging factory overhead to work-in-process based on a predetermined application rate multiplied by actual input is known as :

(*i*) Normal costing (*ii*) Standard costing

(*iii*) Actual costing (*iv*) Product costing

Ans. A (*iii*), B (*ii*), C (*i*), D (*ii*), E (*ii*), F (*i*), G (*iii*), H (*ii*), I (*iv*), J (*v*), K (*iv*), L (*iii*), M (*i*), N (*ii*).

THEORETICAL QUESTIONS

1. Define

(*a*) Direct Material (*b*) Direct wages.

(*c*) Direct expenses. Give few examples. (*d*) Indirect Material

(*e*) Indirect wages. (*f*) Overhead costs.

2. (*a*) What are Elements of Cost ?

(*b*) Classify costs according to element function and variability and give two examples of each. **[*C.U. B.Com. (Hons.) 1992*]**

3. You are required to state why it is important to distinguish between 'fixed' and 'variable' expenses in Cost Accounting and give two examples of each type of expenses. **[*C.U. B.Com. (Hons.)*]**

4. What do you mean by overhead expenditure ? Give the functional classification of overhead expenditure with two examples of each class. **[*C.U. B.Com. (Hons.)*]**

5. (*a*) Explain the 'Elements of cost' with examples.

(*b*) With imaginary figures analyse the total cost of an article into prime cost, factory cost, office cost and cost of sales. If profit is 20% on sales, determine also the sales price. **[*C.U. B.Com. (Hons.)*]**

6. Distinguish between

(*a*) Cost Centre and Cost Unit **[*C.A. (Inter)*]**

(*b*) Variable Cost and Direct Cost **[*C.A. (Inter)*]**

(*c*) Direct Materials and Indirect Materials

(*d*) Fixed Overhead and Variable Overhead.

(*e*) Cost of Sales and Cost of Goods Sold.

7. Write short notes on :

(*a*) Prime cost (*b*) Cost Centre (*c*) Selling and Distribution Overhead (*d*) Semi variable overhead (*e*) Cost unit. **[*I.C.W.A. (Inter) Dec. '89*]**

8. Distinguish between :

(*a*) Cost and Expenses (*b*) Direct Cost and Indirect Cost. (*c*) Cost Unit and Cost Center. (*d*) Cost Estimation and Cost Ascertainment.

9. Write short notes on :

(*i*) Pre-production cost (*ii*) Conversion cost (*iii*) Apportunity cost (*iv*) Sunk cost (*v*) Relevant cost (*vi*) Replacement cost (*vii*) Marginal cost.

10. What do you understand by 'Cost Classification' ? Discuss the various bases of classification of costs and various types of costs.

11. (*a*) What is Cost Sheet ? How does it help in cost centre ?

(*b*) "The classification of costs as controllable and non-controllable depends upon a point of reference"—Discuss.

(*c*) State the important items which are not included in the cost of production.

(*d*) "Direct Costs and Controllable Costs are not necessarily the same"—Comment.

(*e*) What are chargeable expenses ? Give three examples.

(*f*) What is the purpose of the classification of expenditure in cost accounting ?

(*g*) Define Overhead. Point out the different methods of classification of overheads.

(*h*) What are the various elements of cost ? Give the examples of expenses included under each element.

PROBLEMS

1. A radio manufacturer produces three brands of radios. The following figures were collected from the books of accounts for the year ended 31st December 1990 :

Stock and finished inventory on 1.1.90	
Core model	100 Nos.
Super Model	80 Nos.
Deluxe Model	60 Nos.
	Rs.
Work-in-progress on 1.1.90	21,000
Cost of Materials Consumed	1,61,000
Cost of other Stores	48,000
Production Wages	70,000
Works overhead	2,40,000
Work-in-progress on 31-12-90	30,000

The production and sales during the period were :

	Production	*Sales*
Core Model	800 Nos.	760 Nos.
Super Model	600 Nos.	560 Nos.
Deluxe Model	400 Nos.	420 Nos.

The selling rates averaged Rs. 600, Rs. 800 and Rs. 1,000 for the respective models. The cost of production is to be apportioned (at 75% of these ratios) on the basis of sales value of production.

Find out the gross trading profit in a tabular form. **[*C.U. B.Com., Adopted*]**

2. On the basis of the following information of Maa Tara Chemical Works Ltd., prepare a Cost Sheet showing therein total cost and cost per unit for the year ended 30th June 1992 (assuming that the total output for the period is 1,000 units) :

Opening Stock of Raw Materials	50,000
Purchase of Raw Materials	2,80,000
Carriage of Raw Materials	20,000
Closing Stock of Raw Materials	40,000
Direct Wages	1,95,000
Chargeable Expenses	90,000
Factory Rent and Taxes	19,000
Indirect Wages (Factory)	5,000
Factory Lighting	2,500
Factory Heating	500
Motive Power & Fuel	1,300
Sundry Office Expenses	1,800
Estimation (Factory)	1,000
Office Stationery	2,800
Factory Stationery	500
Legal Expenses	4,200
Haulage (Factory)	800
Directors' Fees : Works	2,000
Office	4,000

Factory Cleaning		1,000
Loose Tools Written-off		8,500
Rent & Taxes (Office)		6,000
Water (Factory)		8,800
Insurance :	Office	2,000
	Factory	4,000
Bank Charges		2,800
Rent of Warehouse		2,800
Commission on Sale		1,000
Depreciation :		
Plant & Machinery		6,000
Office Building		8,000
Delivery Vans		1,500
Maintenance of Delivery Vans		1,200
Salaries to Sales Department		3,400
Advertisement		1,200
Bad Debts		1,600

			Per Unit (Rs.)
[Ans.	**Prime Cost**	**Rs. 5,85,000**	**585·00**
	Works Cost	**Rs. 6,45,900**	**645·90**
	Cost of Production	**Rs. 6,77,500**	**677·50**
	Cost of Sales or Total Cost	**Rs. 6,90,200**	**690·20]**

3. From the following particulars of a company, prepare a statement showing (*a*) Raw Materials Consumed, (*b*) Prime Cost, (*c*) Factory Cost, (*d*) Cost of Production, (*e*) Cost of Goods Sold, (*f*) Cost of Sales :

	Rs.
Stock of Raw Materials on 1.4.91	10,000
Work-in-progress on 1.4.91	5,000
Finished Goods on 1.4.91	20,000
Chargeable Expenses	5,000
Carriage Inward	2,000
Purchase of Raw Materials	2,10,000
Raw Materials returned to suppliers	10,000
Direct Wages	1,05,000
Direct Expenses	55,000
Motive Power	3,000
Depreciation of Machinery	6,000
Legal Expenses	3,500
Warehouse Rent	2,000
Godown Rent	3,000
Works Manager's Salary	5,000
Administration Expenses	7,000
Other Office Expenses	2,500
Travelling Expenses of Salesman	500
Free Samples	2,000
Stock of Raw Materials on 31.3.92	15,000
Work-in-progress on 31.3.92	7,000
Finished Goods on 31.3.92	15,000

[Ans. (*a*) Raw Material `Consumed	**Rs. 1,97,000;**	**(*b*) Prime Cost**	**Rs. 3,62,000**
(*c*) Factory Cost	**Rs. 3,77,000;**	**(*d*) Cost of Production**	**Rs. 3,90,000**
(*e*) Cost of Goods sold	**Rs. 3,95,000;**	**(*f*) Cost of Sales**	**Rs. 3,99,500]**

4. Sri Sanjoy Mondal furnishes the following information relating to the manufacture of a standard product during the month of May 1991 :

		Rs.
Raw Material Consumed		40,000
Direct Labour Charges		22,000
Machine hours worked	1,500	
Machine hour rate		5
Office and Administrative Overhead		20% of works cost
Selling overheads		Re. 0·50 per unit sold
Units produced during the month		12,000
Units sold during the month		10,000
Selling price per unit		Rs. 12·00

You are required to prepare a Cost Sheet from the above data, showing (*i*) Cost per unit, (*ii*) Profit for the period, (*iii*) Profit per unit sold.

[Ans. (*i*) Cost per unit Rs. 7·45 (*ii*) Profit for the period Rs. 45,500 (*iii*) Profit per unti sold Rs. 4·55]

5. The Hero Cycle Co. Ltd. manufactured and sold 1,000 bicycles in 1991. Following are the elements obtained from the records of the company :

	Rs.
Materials Consumed	2,00,000
Wages	3,00,000
Manufacturing Expenses	1,25,000
Salaries	1,00,000
Rent, Rates and Insurance	25,000
General Expenses	50,000
Selling Expenses	75,000
Sales	10,00,000

The Company wants to manufacture 1,500 bicycles in 1992. You are required to make a statement showing the price at which these machines would be sold so as to show a profit of 15% on selling price.

Additional information :

(*a*) Cost of materials will rise by 50% on the previous year's level.

(*b*) Wages rates will go up by 20%.

(*c*) Manufacturing expenses will rise in proportion to the Prime Cost.

(*d*) Per unit selling expenses will remain unchanged.

(*e*) Other expenses will remain unchanged.

**[Ans. Profit in 1991 is Rs. 1,25,000; Profit in 1992 is Rs. 2,69,117;
Selling Price in 1992 in Rs. 17,94,117]**

6. From the following particulars you are required to prepare Cost Sheet :

		Rs.
Stock of Raw Materials on 1.1.90		50,000
Stock of Finished goods on 1.1.90		40,000
Purchase of Raw Materials		2,30,000
Wages : Direct	1,50,000	
Indirect	20,000	1,70,000
Factory Rent		5,000
Lubricating Oil, Gas, Mobile		2,000

Car Maintenance	2,000
Office Expenses	5,000
Advertisement	3,000
Administration Expenses	3,500
General Expenses	1,500
Selling Expenses	3,000
Stock of Raw Materials on 31.12.90	30,000
Stock of Finished goods on 31.12.90	50,000

[Ans. Rs. 4,35,000]

7. The following figures are available from the books of Shanti Manufacturing Co. for the year ended 31.12.92. Calculate the (*i*) Raw Materials Consumed, (*ii*) Prime Cost, (*iii*) Works Cost, (*iv*) Cost of Production, (*v*) Cost of goods sold, (*vi*) Cost of Sales and (*vii*) Profit :

	1.1.92	*31.12.92*
Raw Materials	50,000	60,000
Work-in-progress	15,000	17,000
Finished Goods	28,000	22,000
Consumable Stores	5,000	3,000
		Rs.
Purchase of Raw Materials		5,00,000
Purchase of Finished Goods		1,50,000
Purchase of Consumable Stores		25,000
Direct Wages		1,50,000
Chargeable Expenses		15,000
Purchase Return of Raw Materials		40,000
Purchase Return of Finished Goods		8,000
Purchase Return of Consumable Stores		5,000

The factory overhead is estimated 25% of direct wages, office and administration overhead 15% of Prime Cost and Selling and Distribution overhead—10% of cost of goods sold. The company wants to make a profit of 20% on Total Cost.

[Ans. (*i*) **Raw Material Consumed Rs. 4,50,000;** (*ii*) **Prime Cost Rs. 6,15,000;**
(*iii*) **Works Cost Rs. 6,72,500;** (*iv*) **Cost of Production Rs. 7,64,750;**
(*v*) **Cost of goods sold Rs. 7,78,750;** (*vi*) **Cost of Sales Rs. 8,56,625;**
(*vii*) **Profit Rs. 1,71,325]**

8. The following figures for the month of April 1990 were extracted from the records of a factory :

	Rs.
Opening Stock of Finished Goods (5,000 units)	45,000
Purchase of raw materials	2,57,100
Direct Wages	1,05,000
Factory overhead	120% of Direct Wages
Administrative overhead	Rs. 1·10 per unit
Selling & Distribution overhead	10% of Sales
Closing Stock of finished goods (10,000 units)	?
Sales (45,000 units)	6,60,000

Prepare a Cost Sheet for the month of April 1990, assuming that sales are made on the basis of 'FIFO' principle. [*C.U. B.Com. (Hons.), Adopted*]

[Ans. Profit Rs. 1,14,526]

9. A factory uses Job Costing Method. The following cost information is obatined from its books for the year ended 31.12.91 :

	Rs.
Direct Materials	2,00,000
Direct Wages	1,80,000
Factory overhead	90,000
Administrative overhead	94,000
Selling and Distribution overhead	1,03,400
Profit	1,66,850

(*i*) Prepare a Job Cost Sheet, indicating the Prime Cost, Works Cost, Cost of Production, Cost of Sales and the Selling Price.

(*ii*) In 1992 the factory receives an order for a number of jobs. It is estimated that direct materials and direct wages will be Rs. 2,50,000 and Rs. 2,20,000, respectively. Assume that in 1992 Administration overhead has increased by 20%. What price should the product be sold so as to earn the same rate of profit on sales ? The factory recovers works overhead as a % of direct wages and administration, selling and distribution overhead as a % of works cost, based on cost rates prevailing in the previous year.

[Ans. Prime cost Rs. 3,80,000; Works cost Rs. 4,70,000; Cost of Production Rs. 5,64,000; Cost of Sales Rs. 6,67,400; Selling Price Rs. 8,34,250]

10. Your company is exporting 'Madras Checks' to the USA. It has received an enquiry from M/s Philby Incorporation, Boston. The Export Manager seeks the advice of the Cost Accounting department (of which you are the Head) to send a suitable quotation.

From the following figures relating to the last 3 months, you are to suggest a suitable price after preparing a COST SHEET :

Total Production (in metres)	2,00,000
	Rs.
Cost of raw materials	2,00,000
Direct Labour (in factory)	2,50,000
Indirect Labour (in factory)	50,000
Expenses of Storage	10,000
Office Expenses (Direct)	50,000
Selling Expenses	30,000
Expenses for packing, forwarding etc.	20,000
Fees of the Directors	10,000
Salary of the Managing Director for 3 months	15,000

It is to be noted that the depreciation on plant and machinery amounts to Rs. 1,20,000 per year and a profit margin of 20% is kept on sales. **[*B.Com. (Hons.) Delhi*]**

[Ans. Rs. 4·156 per metre]

11. The World Bank has invited global tenders for the supply of structural material. You are the head of the Costing Department of Infrastructures Ltd. Your firm also wants to submit a tender and you have been instructed to prepare a Cost Sheet to find out the cost per tonne for this purpose with the help of the following information for the year 1982 :

Total Production	1,000 tonnes
	Rs.
Cost of raw materials	20,00,000
Carriage Inwards	20,000
Direct Wages	10,00,000
Indirect Wages (in works)	1,00,000
Salary of Works Director	5,000
Office Expenses	2,00,000

Salary etc. of Managing Director	20,000
Directors' fees etc.	15,000
Selling and Distribution of overhead	2,00,000
Expenses for Testing—	
Laboratory for works	10,000
Payment for Income Tax	3,00,000
Dividend paid	4,00,000

[*Delhi, B.Com. (H) adopted*]

[Ans. *Per Tonne Rs. 4,998*]

12. Mohit Ltd. furnished the following information in relation to the production of 2,000 units of product "N" for the year 2001 :

	Rs.
Direct Materials	2,00,000
Direct Labour	1,50,000
Indirect Wages 50% fixed	40,000
Consumable stores (70% variable)	30,000
Office rent (100% fixed)	60,000
Selling expense (40% variable)	80,000

In the year 2002, it is estimated that the production will increase by 50%. The price of materials and labour will go up by 10% and 20%, respectively.

You are required to compute selling price per unit of Product 'N' for the year 2002, if the company wishes to maintain profit @ 10% on cost. [*C.U. B.Com. (H) 2001*]

[Ans. Estimated sales in 2002 : Rs. 9,31,150. Sales price per unit : Rs. 310·39]

13. Music India Ltd. has furnished the following information in relation to the production of 1000 compact discs manufactured by it during the year 2001 :

	Rs.
Cost of Materials	1,00,000
Direct wages paid	70,000
Cost of power and cosumable stores (20% fixed)	15,000
Factory indirect wages paid (40% fixed)	20,000
Cost of lighting in the factory (fixed)	10,000
Office expenses incurred (fixed)	30,000
Selling expenses paid (70% variable)	50,000
Depreciation of plant (under Straight Line Method)	10,000

The entire output were sold at Rs. 350 per unit.

For the year 2002, it is estimated that the production will be increased by 50% by utilizing the spare capacity and the rates for materials and direct wages will increase by 10% and 20% respectively.

The expenses of the company are either fixed or variable and the company assumes that the nature of the expenses will not change in the coming days.

You are required to prepare :

I. A cost sheet for the year 2001 showing the cost per unit.

II. A statement showing estimated cost and profit for the year 2002, assuming that all the goods produced would be sold at a price of Rs. 340 per unit.

[*C.U. B.Com. (H) 1999*]

[Ans. I. Cost for 1,000 units Rs. 3,05,000; per unit cost : Rs. 305
II. Estimated cost for 1,500 units Rs. 4,55,500; P.U. Cost 303·67]

14. The cost structure of an article, the selling price of which is Rs. 500, is as follows :

	Rs.
Direct Materials	50% of the total cost
Direct Labour	30% of the total cost
Overhead	Balance amount

Due to anticipated increase in existing material price by 20% and in the existing labour rate by 10% the existing profit would come down by 30% if the selling price remains unchanged.

Prepare a comparative statement showing the cost, profit and sale price under the present conditions and with the increase expected for future, assuming the same percentage of profit on cost as at present had to be earned. (Calculations may be made to the nearest rupee). **[I.C.W.A. Inter]**

[Ans. Cost Rs. 395; Profit Rs. 171; Sales Rs. 566]

15. The following figures are extracted from the Trial Balance fo Together Co. on 30th September 2002 :

	Rs.
Inventory :	
Finished stock	80,000
Raw materials	1,40,000
Work-in-Progress	2,00,000
Office appliances	17,400
Plant & Machinery	4,60,000
Building	2,00,000
Indirect labour	18,000
Factory supervision	10,000
Repair & Upkeep of factory	14,000
Heat, light & Power	65,000
Rates & Taxes	6,300
Misc. factory expenses	18,700
Sale Commission	33,600
Sales (Cr.)	7,68,000
Sales Returns and rebates	14,000
Materials purchased	3,20,000
Return (Cr.)	4,800
Direct labour	1,60,000
Sales Travelling	11,000
Sales Promotion	22,500
Distribution Deptt. Salaries and expenses	18,000
Office salaries and expenses	8,600
Interest on Borrowed funds	2,000

Further details are available as follows :

1. Closing inventories : Finished Goods Rs. 1,15,000, Raw materials Rs. 1,80,000, Work-in-Progress Rs. 1,92,000.
2. Accrued expenses on : Direct labour Rs. 8,000, Indirect labour Rs. 1,200, Interest on borrowed fund Rs. 200.
3. Depreciation to be provided on : Office appliances 5%, Plant & Machinery 10%, Building 4%.
4. Distribution of the following cost :
   i. Heat, light and power to factory, office and distribution in the ratio 8 : 1 : 1.
   ii. Rates and Taxes two-thirds to factory and one-third to office.
   iii. Depreciation on building to factory, office and selling in the ratio 8 : 1 : 1.

With the help of the above information you are required to prepare : (i) a statement of cost showing various elements of cost; and (ii) a statement of profit. [*C.A. Inter*]

[Ans. Works Cost : Rs. 637·750; C.G.S : 6,21,620; Total Cost : Rs. 7,14,020; Profit : Rs. 35,980]

16. The following data are available from the cost ledger of Acme Industries for the year 2001 :

	Rs.
Plant maintenance	25,000
Lightning	6,300
Depreciation on Plant	8,100
Rates & Taxes for the works	3,900
Staff salaries	32,000
Management salaries	22,000
Power (for the plant)	10,600
Rental for leasehold equipments	9,600
Indirect wages	37,100
Rectification cost of defective (normal)	8,400
Consumable stores	17,600
Selling expenses	30,000
General charges	15,600
Sale proceeds from scrap	4,200

During the year total production was 1,20,000 units. The break up of Prime cost per unit was Materials Rs. 2·20 and Wages Rs. 1·80. The average selling price was Rs. 6·75 per unit and the entire quantity produced during the year was sold out.

With effect from 1 January 2002 the selling price was reduced to Rs. 6·40 per unit. It was envisaged that production could be enhanced during 2002 by $33\frac{1}{3}$ without incurring any overtime or extra shift work or additional selling expense.

You are required to prepare statements showing (i) Actual cost and profit for 2001 ; (ii) Estimated cost and profit for 2002 assuming that the entire production will be sold during the year.

Assumption, if any, required to be made in the above exercise, should be clearly stated.

[*I.C.W.A. Inter*]

[Ans. (*i*) Cost of Sales 7,02,000; Profit : Rs. 1,08,000.
(ii) Estimated Cost and Profit : Rs. 8,72,800; Rs. 1,51,200]

17. From the following particulars of a manufacturing firm prepare a statement showing :

(*i*) Cost of Materials used.
(*ii*) Works Cost
(*iii*) Cost of Production
(*iv*) % of works overhead to productive wages.
(*v*) % of General Overhead to Works Cost.

	Rs.
Stock of Materials on 1st November 1988	40,000
Purchase of Raw Materials in November 1988	11,00,000
Stock of F. Goods on 1st November 1988	50,000
Productive Wages	5,00,000
Finished Goods Sold	24,00,000
Works overheads charges	1,50,000
Office & General Expenses	1,00,000
Stock of Materials on 30th November 1988	1,40,000
Stock of Finished goods on 30th November 1988	60,000

[*I.C.S.I. Inter*]

[Ans. (*i*) Rs. 10,00,000; (*ii*) Rs. 16,50,000; (*iii*) 17,50,000; (*iv*) 30%; (*v*) 6·06%]

18. From the following figures you are required to prepare a production account for the quarter ended 31st March 1984, assuming stock of finished goods at the end of the period to be valued at cost showing : Analysis and classification of Cost :

(*a*) Value of material consumed, (*b*) Cost of Production, (*c*) Cost of goods sold, (*d*) Profit on goods sold and (*e*) Net profit for the period.

	Rs.
Raw Materials on 1.1.84	1,00,000
Raw Materials on 31.3.84	1,23,500
Finished goods on 1.1.84	71,500
Finished goods on 31.3.84	42,000
Work-in-progress on 1.1.84	31,000
Purchase of Raw Materials	88,000
Wages—Direct	70,000
Wages—Indirect	2,500
Work Charges	37,000
Administration Expenses	13,000
Selling Expenses	15,000
Sales	2,84,000

[I.C.S.I. Inter]

[Ans. (*a*) Rs. 64,500, (*b*) Rs. 2,18,000 (*c*) Rs. 2,47,500 (*d*) Rs. 21,500 (*e*) Rs. 56,000.]

19. Bharat Electronics Ltd. furnishes the following information for 10,000 T.V. valves manufactured during the year 1991 :

	Rs.
Materials	90,000
Direct Wages	60,000
Power and Consumable Stores	11,000
Factory Indirect Wages	13,500
Lighting of factory	6,000
Defective work (cost of rectification)	2,000
Clerical Salaries and Management Expenses	33,000
Selling Expenses	5,400
Sale proceeds of Scraps	2,000
Plant Repairs, Maintenance and Depreciation	11,500

The net selling price was Rs. 32 per unit sold and all the units were sold.

As from 1st January 1992, the selling price was reduced to Rs. 31·00 per unit. It was estimated that production could be increased in 1992 by 50% utilising spare capacity. Rates for materials and direct wages will increase by 10%.

You are required to prepare :

(*a*) Cost Sheet for the year 1991, showing various elements of cost per unit, and

(*b*) Estimated Cost and Profit for 1992 assuming that 15,000 units will be produced and sold during the year and factory overheads will be recovered as a percentage of direct wages and office and selling expenses as a percentage of works cost. *[C.A. Inter Adopted]*

[Ans. Cost of Sales in 1991—Rs. 2,30,400; Profit in 1991—Rs. 89,600; Cost of Sales in 1992—Rs. 3,80; 160 & Profit—84,840]

20. The details of expenses incurred on the manufacture of two kinds of drums in the past are given below :

Expenses incurred on the manufacture of drums :

	Type 1	*Type 2*
	Rs.	*Rs.*
Direct Materials	3·50	6·50
Direct Wages	1·00	1·50

Plant and machine usage allocated on hourly basis	3·00	2·00
General Overheads apportioned at 20% of direct wages	2·00	3·00
	9·50	13·00

Cost records for the month of April 1987 show :

Direct materials used	26,500
Direct Wages	5,850
Expenses on Plant & Machinery	16,250
No. of drums manufactured :	
Type 1 2,000	
Type 2 3,000	

Prepare a Consolidated Cost Sheet showing the total Cost of Production of each type according to different elements of cost showing also cost per drum. **[*B.Com. Andhra*]**

[Ans. Total Cost of Type 1 = Rs. 20,525; Total cost of Type 2 = Rs. 39,775; Cost per unit of Type 1 = Rs. 10·26; Cost per unit of Type 2 = Rs. 13·25]

21. A factory has undertaken a contract for the manufacture of 4,000 articles and the following information has been obtained :

For each article	Rs.
Material Cost	12
Direct Wages	10
Selling Price	35

The overhead charges consist of (*a*) Fixed Rs. 6,000 ; (*b*) Variable Rs. 3,600 and (*c*) Semi-variable (out of which 60% is fixed) Rs. 2,400.

Calculate the profit per unit.

What would be the profit per article if the number of articles manufactured were 5,000 and the total fixed overhead charges remain unchanged ? **[*M.Com. C.U.*]**

[Ans. Profit per article 35·00]

22. The following figures are extracted from the books of Fashions Ltd. for the year ended 30.9.87. Prepare a Cost Sheet showing the cost per unit under various elements, and also profit or loss per unit :

		Rs.
Direct Materials		24,00,000
Direct Labour		5,00,000
Depreciation of factory building		15,000
Branch offices expenses		40,000
Depreciation of office building		8,000
Depreciation of Staff Cars		12,000
Insurance of Staff Cars		1,500
Insurance for office building		1,200
Insurance for factory building		1,500
Delivery Van maintenance and running expenses		10,000
Salaries including		3,00,000
Sales Manager	Rs. 25,000	
Factory Chief Engineer	Rs. 25,000	
Finished goods—warehouse expenses		20,000
Electricity (including Rs. 4,000 for administrative office)		40,000
Advertisement		20,000

Sundry factory expenses	3,40,000	
Sales promotion	5,000	
Office administration expenses	50,000	
Expenses for participating in industrial exhibition	10,000	
Sales	42,00,000	
Units produced	10,000	

[*I.C.W.A. Inter*]

[Ans. (*i*) Prime Cost = Rs. 29,00,000; (*ii*) Factory Cost = Rs. 33,17,500; (*iii*) Total Cost = Rs. 37,74,200; (*iv*) Profit = Rs. 4,25,800]

23. The Modern Manufacturing Company submits the following information on the 30th November, 1989 : Analysis & Classification of Cost :

	Rs.	*Rs.*
Sales for the year		2,75,000
Inventories at the beginning of the year :		
Finished Goods	7,000	
Work-in-progress	4,000	
Purchase of materials for the year were		1,10,000
Materials inventory at the beginning of the year : Rs. 3,000 and at the end of the year Rs. 4,000.		
Direct Labour		65,000
Factory overhead was 60% of the Direct Labour Cost		
Inventories at the end of the year :		
Work-in-progress		6,000
Finished Goods		8,000
Other Expenses for the year :		
Selling Expenses		10% of Sales
Administrative Expenses		5% of Sales

[*C.A. Inter*]

[Ans. Total Cost = Rs. 2,51,250 and Profit = Rs. 23,750]

24. A company is manufacturing refrigerators and the following details are furnished in respect of its factory operations for the year ended 31st December 1989 :

	Rs.	*Rs.*
Work-in-progress on 1st. Jan 1989		
At Prime Cost	51,000	
Manufacturing Expenses	15,000	66,000
Work-in-progress on 31st December 1989		
At Prime Cost	45,000	
Manufacturing Expenses	9,000	54,000
Stock of Raw Materials on 1st January 1989		2,25,000
Purchase of Raw Materials		4,77,000
Direct Labour		1,71,000
Stock of Raw Materials on 31st December 1989		2,04,000
Manufacturing Expenses		84,000

On the basis of the above data prepare a statement showing the Cost of Production. Also indicate separately the amount of Manufacturing expenses which enter into the Cost of Production.

[*C.A. Final*]

[Ans. Cost of Production = Rs. 7,65,000; Manufacturing Expenses = Rs. 90,000]

[Hints : Manufacturing Expenses = Manufacturing Expenses + Opening Stock of Work-in-progress (M.E.) – Closing Stock of Work-in-progress (M.E.).]

25. The following data relate to the manufacture of a standard product during the four weeks to July 27, 1996 :

	Rs.
Raw Materials Consumed	25,000
Manual and machine labour wages (directly chargeable)	15,000
Chargeable expenses	4,500
Machine hours worked	1,000
Establishment and general expenses	4,700
Selling and distribution overhead per unit 8 paise	
Units produced	10,000
Units sold	8,000
Selling price per unit	6

(a) You are required to prepare a cost sheet in respect of the above showing therein the cost per unit under each element of cost and the profit for the period.

Also show the percentage that the works overhead cost bears to the Manual and Machine Labour Wages and the percentage that the Establishment & General Expenses bears to the Works Cost.

(b) What price should the Company quote to produce 1,000 units of another which will require an expenditure of Rs. 8,000 for raw materials and Rs. 6,000 for direct wages, so that it will yield a profit of 25% on the Cost of Sales ? *[C.U. B.Com. (H) (1997)]*

[Ans. (a) **Prime cost Rs. 44,500; Works cost Rs. 47,000; Cost of production Rs. 51,700; Cost of goods sold Rs. 41,360; Cost of sales Rs. 42,000; Profit Rs. 6,000. Works overhead to manual and machine labour wages. $16\frac{2}{3}$%. Establishment and general expenses to Works cost 10%.**
(b) Price to be quoted Rs. 20,725]

26. An electric computer manufacturer desired to quote for a contract for the supply of 5,000 computers on 31st July 1990. From the following data prepare statement showing the price to be quoted to give the same percentage of net profit on turnover as was realised during the six months to 30th June 1990 :

	Rs.
Stock of Raw Materials on 1st January 1990	50,000
Stock of Raw Materials 30th June 1990	7,000
Purchase of Raw Materials (six months)	75,000
Factory Wages	1,50,000
Indirect Charges	25,000
Sales	2,70,000
Finished Stock on 1st January 1990	Nil
Finished Stock on 30th June 1990	50,000

The number of computers manufactured during six months was 2,000, including those sold and those in stock at the close of the period. The computers to be quoted for are of uniform size and quality and are similar to those manufactured during the six month period. As from 1st July 1990, the cost of factory labour increased by 10% and that of material by 15%.

[Adopted M.Com. Agra]

Hints : Profit on Sale—10%. Indirect charges have been taken as a percentage of Direct Wages.

[Ans. The Tender price Rs. 1,44,756 (Approx.)]

27. Modern Manufacturing Company Kolkata, purchased a material of 20 tonnes from a mining company. The following data is available for the lot of material purchased :

(*i*) Invoice Price of Material @ Rs. 2,000 per tonne.

(*ii*) Trade discount @ 20% on Invoice Price.

(*iii*) Excise Duty @10% on Invoice Price.

(*iv*) Sales Tax @10%.
(*v*) Freight & Insurance @2%.
(*vi*) Other charges for delivery @ Re. 100 per tonne.
(*vii*) Cost of containers @ Rs. 20 per box of 1 quintal.
(*viii*) Cost of loading and unloading @1% of total cost.

Compute total Material purchase cost and cost per tonne to Modern Manufacturing Company.

[Ans. Total cost, Rs. 46,783; Cost per tonne Rs. 2,339]

[*C.U. B.Com. (H) 2001*]

28. From the following data prepare a Cost Sheet :

Opening stock of Direct Materials	Rs. 30,000
Closing stock of Direct Materials	Rs. 20,000
Purchase of Direct Materials	Rs. 1,90,000
Sales	Rs. 6,50,000
Prime Cost	Rs. 4,10,000
Administrative expenses	Rs. 90,000
Factory expenses	Rs. 1,20,000

10% of the output remained unsold.
There was no direct expenses.

[*C.U. B.Com. (H) 2004*]

29. From the following particulars prepare a statement in such form as you consider most suitable for showing clearly all elements of cost :

	Rs.
Opening Stock of Raw Materials	26,000
Purchase of Raw Materials	70,000
Raw Materials returned to Suppliers	2,000
Closing Stock of Raw materials	18,800
Wages paid to	
Productive workers	18,000
Non-productive workers	8,000
Salaries paid to Office Staff	5,000
Carriage on Raw Materials Purchased	2,500
Carriage on Goods Sold	1,500
Rent and Rates of workshop	2,500
Fuel, Gas, Water etc.	3,000
Repairs to Plant	1,000
Depreciation on Machinery	1,000
Office Expenses	1,500
Direct Chargeable Expenses	800
Advertising	2,200
Abnormal loss of Raw Materials	2,200

[*N.B.U., B.Com. (Hons.) Adopted*]

[Ans. Cost of Sale = Rs. 1,20,000]

30. Prepare a Cost Sheet (with imaginary figures) showing therein the following :

1. Material used (Opening Stock of Materials, Purchases of Materials and Closing Stock of Materials).
2. Direct Wages paid.
3. Chargeable Expenses incurred
4. Prime Cost
5. Work Cost

7. Office on Cost
8. Cost on Production
9. Selling and Distribution on Cost
10. Cost of Sales

If the normal profit is 25% on the Selling Price, what price would you quote for the article shown in your Cost Sheet ? [*N.B.U. B.Com. (Hons.) Adopted*]

31. Cool Air Fans Ltd. produced, in 1990, 300 fans for which the following expenses were incurred :

	Rs.
Materials used	62,600
Direct Labour Charges	55,400
Works overhead	59,000
Establishment Expenses	23,000
Selling Expenses	12,400

Calculate (*a*) Total Cost, (*b*) Percentage of works cost to prime cost, and (*c*) Percentage of establishment and selling expenses to works cost. [*B.Com. Calicut (Adopted)*]

[Ans. (*a*) Total Cost = Rs. 2,12,400 (*b*) % of Works Cost to Prime Cost = 15% (*c*) % of establishment and selling expenses to works cost = 20%.]

32. There is a small factory which does not keep cost accounts. From the following information, ascertain cost (per unit) of two products *A* and *B* :

(*a*) Extract from the financial accounts for the year 1979 are :

Materials :	*Rs.*
Balance as on 1.1.79	15,000
Purchases during the year	2,10,000
Balance as on 31.12.79	7,500
Wages incurred	67,000
Sale proceeds of chipping	720 (Income)

(*b*) As per production records, total quantities of *A* and *B* produced during the year were 5,000 and 500 units, respectively. The opening and closing balances of the work-in-progress were almost the same and, therefore, ignored.

(*c*) All materials purchased and the balances in stock were direct materials, meant only for the *A* product. The raw material for the product *B* was from borings recovered during the year 20 tonnes and the entire quantity was consumed in the product *B*. The rate may be estimated Rs. 100 per tonne.

(*d*) 75 tonnes of chipping were recovered from production *i.e.,* 70 tonnes from product *A* and 5 tonnes from *B,* out of which 72 tonnes were sold at the rate of Rs. 10 per tonne and the balance of 3 tonnes should be treated as wastage.

(*e*) The total wages of Rs. 67,000 should be analysed as under :

	Percentage
Product *A*	60
Product *B*	5
Overheads	35
	100

[*B.Com. Punjab*]

[Ans.	***Product A***	***Product B***
Prime Cost :	**2,55,700 (Rs. 51·54)**	**5,350 (Rs. 10·70)**
Total Cost :	**2,76,674 (Rs. 55·34)**	**7,106 (Rs. 14·21)**

Calculation of Total overhead :

Amount of Total overhead $= 67{,}000 \times \frac{35}{100} =$ **Rs. 23,450**

***Less* : Sale of chipping 720**

(Divided 14 : 1) 22,730

33. Present the following information in a statement showing (1) Material Consumed, (2) Prime Cost, (3) Factory Cost, (4) Cost of Production, (5) Total Cost, and (6) Net Profit.

	Rs.
Stock of Raw Material on 1.1.90	2,40,000
Stock of Raw Materials on 31.12.90	3,14,000
Purchase of Raw Materials	9,20,000
Drawing Office Salaries	32,000
Counting House Salaries	60,000
Carriage Inward	23,000
Bad Debts written off	20,000
Rent and Taxes—Factory	42,000
Office	15,000
Carriage Outwards	21,000
Productive Wages	6,05,000
Depreciation on Plant & Machinery	32,000
Depreciation on Office Furniture	1,500
Gas and Water— Factory	8,000
Office	3,000
Travellers, Salaries and Commission	24,000
Advertisement and Samples	20,000
Maintenance of Delivery Van	20,000
Rent of Warehouse	18,000
Printing & Stationery	12,000
Telephone Charges— Factory	8,000
Office	12,000
Sales	27,25,000

[*Poona B.Com.—Adopted*]

[Ans. (1) Rs. 8,69,000 ; (2) Rs. 14,74,000 ; (3) Rs. 15,96,000 ; (4) Rs. 16,99,500 ; (5) Rs. 18,22,500 ; (6) Rs. 9,02,500]

34. From the following figures for the month ended 31 October 1984, you are required to prepare a statement of Total Cost, grouping (classifying) therein all costs according to variability :

1. Cost of Materials	Rs. 25,000	
2. Direct Wages	Rs. 12,500	
3. Direct Expenses	Rs. 1,250	
4. Overhead :		
i. Production (30% variable)		Rs. 6,250
ii. Administration (10% variable)		Rs. 3,000
iii. Selling (35% variable)		Rs. 2,000
iv. Distribution (20% variable)		Rs. 2,500
	Total	Rs. 52,500

35. A business has three production departments using materials in the proportion of X : Y : Z = 5·5 : 3 : 1·5. From the following information you are requested to find out the total cost of production of each department for the year 1990 :

	Rs.
Opening Stock of Raw Materials	3,00,000
Opening Finished Stock	4,37,000
Closing Stock of Raw Materials	3,50,000
Closing Finished Stock	5,40,000

Purchase for the year 1990	12,00,000
Productive Wages	9,00,000
Unproductive Wages	97,200
Rent rates etc. upto 31.12.90	78,300
Repairs	34,200
Lighting, Heating and Power	73,800
Depreciation on Plant	83,600
Salaries	1,50,300
General Expenses	1,35,000

The wages of each department are :

X—Rs. 5,00,000 in connection with 6 machines

Y—Rs. 3,00,000 in connection with 4 machines

Z—Rs. 1,00,000 in connection with 1 machine

In the absence of any information all expenses with exception of depreciation are to be charged to the departments in the same proportion as the wages paid, depreciation being apportioned in the same ratio as the numbers of machines in each Dept.

[Ans.	**Total**	**X**	**Y**	**Z**
Prime Cost (Rs.)	**20,50,000**	**11,32,500**	**6,45,000**	**2,72,500**
Work Cost	**25,17,100**	**13,35,600**	**7,69,900**	**3,11,600**
Cost of Production	**27,02,400**	**14,94,100**	**8,65,000**	**4,47,300]**

36. Work out in the appropriate Cost Sheet from the selling rate per ton of special paper manufactured by a paper-mill for the Government in January 1988 under the following categories of Cost (*a*) Prime Cost (*b*) Work Cost (*c*) Total Cost (*d*) Selling Price.

The Cost Sheet is to be prepared from the data given below :

Direct Materials :

Paper 500 reams @ Rs. 50 per ream

Other miscellaneous materials—100 kg @ Rs. 30 per kg.

Direct Labour : 80 skilled workers @ Rs. 75 per month

49 unskilled workers @ 50 per month

Direct Expenses :

Special plant Rs. 3,000

Special equipment Rs. 100.

Works overhead :

Variable @ 100% on direct wages, Fixed—@ 60% on direct wages. Administration overhead @ 10% on work cost. Selling & Distribution overhead @ 15% on work cost. Finished paper manufactured—400 tons. Credit on account of sale of manufacture of waste—Rs. 800. There was no W.I.P. at the beginning or at the end of the month.

The Scrap value of the special plant after utilisation in manufacture is nil. Selling rate should be worked out to the nearest rupee.

[Ans. Total Cost = Rs. 65,000; Profit = Rs. 6,500; Selling Price = Rs. 71,500]

3 Materials

Section I : Purchase and Storage

Authors' Comments and Suggestions :

1. ***Almost in every examination one or more questions have been set from this Chapter. Specially in the area of Stores pricing, EOQ levels of Stock and Stock valuation.***
2. ***Students feel difficulty in the areas like treatment of Return and Shortage of Stores, determination of impact on profit of different valuation methods, pricing issues etc. Thorough treatment of subject-material will help the students to improve their confidence level and proficiency in dealing with different situations.***
3. ***Following points should be given special attention for EOQ :***
   (a) A common mistake is to utilise fixed ordering and holding costs and consider these costs in EOQ formulae. In EOQ calculation variable unit cost should be considered.
   (b) EOQ formulae should not be used when discount is available for purchasing different level of quantity, i.e. when the purchasing cost per unit varies with the quantities ordered. In this case, EOQ should be determined by using a tabular method.
4. ***Reader should be clear about the distinction between material control and inventory control. Consumption reduction of Direct Material at production level does not mean inventory control—rather, it falls under material control.***
5. ***Normal loss is debited to production overhead whereas abnormal loss should be charged to Costing Profit and Loss Account.***

Concept—Purchase Department and its Functions-Purchasing Procedure—Goods Received Note—Stores Department—Duties and Functions of Storeskeeper—Different Stock Levels—Economic Ordering Quantity—Bin Card—Stores Ledger—Difference between Bin Card and Stores Ledger.

The term "materials" refers to the basic items require for the purpose of production or rendering services. It is a major part of current assets as well as working capital. In all the developed and developing countries, about 50% to 80% of total capital is generally invested in material. The average investment in material varies from industry to industry. Hence, control must be exercised during the time of purchase, storage and utilization of materials.

Purchase Department and its Functions

Like all other functions purchasing is an important function of management. In big manufacturing organisations separate purchase departments are being set for conducting purchases. Top management lays down the purchase policy and, accordingly, necessary purchases are made by the purchase department. It is the independent function of the purchase department to decide : (*i*) What to purchase (*ii*) Where to purchase, (*iii*) When to purchase, (*iv*) How to purchase.

Centralised *vs* Decentralised Purchase

When all purchases are made under the control of a purchaser or chief purchaser who ranks level with the top management, the buying is said to be 'centralised'. But, if the buying function is performed by other respective departmental managers, including the chief purchaser, it is said to be decentralised. The decision for centralised or decentralised purchase will depend on (*i*) type and quality of material required, (*ii*) location of the production centres, (*iii*) policy of the firm and (*iv*) urgency of purchasing items.

Although centralised purchase is expensive due to increase in administrative cost, it has the advantage of low price and uniform quality, availability of efficient buying staff, economy in accounting and maintaining optimum stock.

Purchasing Procedure

The main functions of purchase department may include :

(*i*) Receiving properly authorised purchase requisitions.
(*ii*) Exploring the best sources of supply and selecting the supplier.
(*iii*) Placement of purchase order and following up the delivery.
(*iv*) Inspecting and receiving of materials, and
(*v*) Checking inward invoices and passing the vouchers for payments.

Goods Received Note

In case of large manufacturing organisations, goods are received and inspected by two separate departments. After proper inspection, the receiving department enter the goods received by its clerks in a document, which is known as Goods Received Note.

Generally five copies of such note are to be prepared and submitted to the

(*i*) Purchase Department
(*ii*) Accounting Department
(*iii*) Storekeeper
(*iv*) Department which initiated the requisition
(*v*) Own Department for future reference.

A specimen of Goods Received Note is given :

Goods Received Note

From............. Purchase Order No. .... G.R.N. No. ....
Supplier's name ..... Delivery Note No. .... Date.........................
Date of Delivery.......

Serial No.	*Description*	*Code No.*	*Qty. Received*	*Qty. Ordered*	*Qty. Rejected*	*Rate*	*Amount*	*Remarks*

Received by..........
Inspected by.........

Stores Department

For effective product planning systematic storage policy is necessary and that also should be maintained by an independent department named storage. After receiving the delivery of purchase order it is the duty of the storekeeper to take them under charge. He is the main responsible person for placing the materials in their appropriate places inside the store and ensuring that they are maintained in good condition during storage till required for utilisation in production.

There are three types of stores :

(*i*) Centralised (*ii*) Decentralised (*iii*) Centralised store with substores.

Duties/Functions of the Storekeeper

The storekeeper is a person who should be the incharge of the stores department and also responsible for receipt, storage, and issue of materials. His main function may be summarised :

(*i*) Receiving of materials after ensuring quantity and quality.

(*ii*) Placing the materials in an 'organised' manner after entering into Bin Cards in order to reduce storage losses.

(*iii*) Issuing of stores to production departments against properly authorised requisition.

(*iv*) Issuing purchase requisition when re-ordering level is reached.

(*v*) Maintaining proper records and checking the Bin Card balances with physical quantities in Bin.

(*vi*) Receiving back the surplus material returned.

(*vii*) Maintaining different levels of stocks, Mix. level, Min. level etc.

(*viii*) Preventing unauthorised persons to enter into store.

(*ix*) Training and supervising the employees of stores.

(*x*) Submitting reports regularly to the management about every item of stores.

Classification and Codification

In order to ensure greater control, materials should be classified on the basis of some similarity, usage etc. and also assigned some symbols or identification numbers or code numbers. Classification accompanied by a proper codification helps not only in proper maintenance of stores but it also facilitates in mechanised accounting and re-ordering.

Different Stock Levels

In order to ensure scientific control and optimum level of inventory, different levels of stocks are fixed, which are :

(*i*) Reorder level

(*ii*) Maximum level

(*iii*) Minimum level

(*iv*) Danger level

(*v*) Average level

(*i*) **Reorder Level.** It is that level of stock at which new purchase order is placed for fresh supplies of the material. It is fixed somewhere between the maximum and minimum levels to avoid unnecessary storage or shortage.

Formula : Re-order Level = Maximum period required for delivery × Maximum usage or consumption per day/week/month.

(*ii*) **Maximum Level.** The maximum level represents that level of stock above which the stock should not be allowed to rise. This level is to be fixed keeping in mind unnecessary blocking of capital in stores.

Formula : Maximum Level = Re-order level + Re-order quantity − (Minimum consumption × Minimum period of delivery).

(*iii*) **Minimum Level.** It is that level below which the inventory of any item should not be allowed to fall. It is known as safety or buffer stock. The main object of fixing this level is to avoid unnecessary delay or hamperation of production due to shortage of materials.

Formula : Minimum level = Re-order level − (Normal consumption per day/Week/month × Average period required to obtain delivery).

(*iv*) **Danger Level.** Generally, this level is fixed below the minimum level and represents the stage where immediate steps are taken for getting stock replenished. In some cases, danger level of stock is fixed above the minimum level but below the re-ordering level.

(*v*) **Average Level.** It is the average level of stocks that should be maintained throughout the year. The cost of storage depends on this average stock.

Formula : $\frac{1}{2}$(Maximum level + Minimum level)

Economic Ordering Quantity (EOQ)

It refers to that quantity where the total of inventory carrying cost and ordering cost is minimum. This represents the most favourable quantity to be ordered at the time of purchase. EOQ is also known as Re-order quantities.

$$\text{Formula} : EOQ = \sqrt{\frac{2AB}{C}}$$

where, A = Annual consumption/demand.
B = Buying cost per order
C = Carrying cost per unit p.a. *i.e.* % of carrying cost × cost per unit.

Bin Card

The bin card shows physical movement of each item of materials in stores. This is a quantitative record of receipts, issues and closing balance of store items. Separate cards are used for each item of material and are placed in shelves or bins where that material is kept. The special advantage of the card is to disclose at a glance the number of quantity of a particular commodity in store without having refer to the stores ledger or ascertain the information by actual inspection of goods.

The proforma of a Bin Card is given below :

ABC Co. Ltd.
Bin Card

Description.............. Bin No. ....
Maximum Level.......... Code No. ....
Minimum Level.......... Stores Ledger No. ....
Re-order Level............ Unit of measurement........
Re-order Quantity.........

	Rceipts		*Issues*		*Balance*	*Stock verification*		
Date	*G.R. Note No.*	*Qty.*	*S.R. No.*	*Qty.*	*Qty.*	*Date*	*Initials*	*Remarks*

Stores Ledger

It is the basic record in accounting for materials in stores. The record contains, in details, receipts, issues and balances along with the money value of each item. The ledger sheets are generally in loose leaf form in binders, separate binders being used for each class of materials.

The proforma of Stores Ledger is given :

ABC Co. Ltd.
Stores Ledger

Description.............. Max Level...........
Code No. .... Min. Level............
Bin No. .... Re-ordering Level............

Receipts				*Balance*				*Remarks*
G.R. No.	*Qty.*	*Rate*	*Amt.*	*S.R. No.*	*Qty.*	*Rate*	*Amt.*	

Difference between Bin Card and Stores Ledger

The following are the difference between Bin Card and Stores Ledger :

Bin Card	Stores Ledger
(*a*) It is maintained by the Storekeeper.	(*a*) It is maintained by the costing department.
(*b*) It records both the inward and outward movement but in quantities only.	(*b*) It records both the inward and outward movement in quantities and values.
(*c*) Here posting is generally made before the transaction takes place.	(*c*) Here posting is done after the transaction takes place.
(*d*) Each transaction is recorded individually.	(*d*) Transactions are recorded periodically.
(*e*) It is a stock record in true sense.	(*e*) It is a stock control record.
(*f*) It cannot supply inventory value for the preparation of Final Accounts.	(*f*) It can supply inventory value for the preparation of Final Accounts.

Section II : Pricing and Control

Stores Requisition—Bill of Materials—Methods of pricing of issues—Advantages and Disadvantages—Material Control—Tools and Techniques of Material Control—Perpetual Inventory System—ABC Analysis—Stock-turnover.

The main function of a storekeeper is to issue materials to the production department at the right time. Again, one of the methods of controlling inventory is pricing of issues. All the issue procedure are generally under the control of management and materials are issued against authorised documents *viz.* material requisition or bill of materials etc.

Materials Requisition (Stores Requisition)

It is an authorised document of the storekeeper to issue materials or other stores. When materials are required, such requisition should be prepared specifying the quality and quantity of the materials required and the job on which they are to be used. The requisition shall be signed by a responsible officer, *e.g.* the production manager or a foreman, and it is an authority to the storekeeper for issuing the materials specified therein.

Materials requisition are generally prepared in triplicate, two copies are sent to the stores department and the third copy is retained by the requisitioning department for their own reference. A specimen of a material requisition :

Materials Requisition

From Bin No. .... No. ....
For Job No. .... Date........
Bill of Material No. ....

Weight or Quality	*Code No.*	*Grade Size*	*Description*	*Rate*	*Amount*	*Remarks*

Authorised by.............. Received by..........
Issued by............... Priced by............

Bill of Materials (Specification of Materials)

It is a complete schedule of parts and materials required for a job, process or operation. The main object of this document is to provide in advance a complete list of materials required for a given period or job. There will be a separate bill of materials for each individual kind of work. On receipt of bills of materials from different departments the storekeeper makes a review of his stock position every day with regard to the particular materials concerned. If he finds that some of his stocks require further supply, he immediately sends purchase requisitions to the buying department in order that further supplies may be forthcoming in time.

A specimen of Bill of Materials is given :

Bill of Materials

Job/Work Order No. .... No. ....
Date of issue............ Date.........
Dept. authorised.......

				For Departmental use			
Item No.	*Description*	*Code*	*Qty.*	*Mat. Requisition*	*Rate*	*Qty.*	*Remarks*

Prepared by................
Requisitioned by...........

Methods of Pricing of Issues

There are various methods of pricing the materials issued in cost accounting. The choice depending largely on the nature of the materials used and the condition of the business itself.

The principal methods used in costing for pricing stores issues are :

(1) **Cost Price Methods**

(*i*) The actual cost/specific price
(*ii*) First-in, first-out (FIFO) price
(*iii*) Last-in, first-out (LIFO) price
(*iv*) Next-in, first out (NIFO) price
(*v*) Base stock price
(*vi*) High-in-first-out (HIFO) price
(*vii*) First-in, last-out (FILO) price.

(2) **Average Cost Price Methods**

(*i*) Simple average price
(*ii*) Weighted simple average price
(*iii*) Periodic simple average price
(*iv*) Periodic weighted average price
(*v*) Moving simple average price
(*vi*) Moving weighted average price.

(3) **Market Price Methods**

(*i*) Realisable price
(*ii*) Replacement price

(4) **Notional Price Methods**

(*i*) Standard price
(*ii*) Inflated price.

Of the above various methods of pricing some have extensive use, which are :

1. The Actual/Specific Price. Under this method materials are issued at its actual cost. This method of pricing is generally used where job costing is in operation and the materials issued can be identified.

2. First-in, First-out (FIFO). This method is based on the principle that materials received first will be issued first and priced at the cost at which that consignment was placed in the stores.

Advantages

(*a*) This method is very simple and useful when prices are falling.
(*b*) Each job or product is charged with its actual cost of material.
(*c*) Neither profit nor loss is unduly made.
(*d*) Closing stocks are valued at current market price.

Disadvantages

(*a*) It involves completed calculations, hence more chances of clerical errors.
(*b*) More than one price may be charged for the same job.
(*c*) In case of rising prices, the products are charged at lower rate than the current rate.
(*d*) Comparison among similar jobs is very difficult.

3. Last-in First-out (LIFO). By this method the latest purchases are deemed to be the first issued and productions are charged with their current cost of replacement.

Advantages

(*a*) Materials are issued at current cost, hence no element of unrealised profit.
(*b*) Production is charged at the recent price.
(*c*) This method is suitable during rising prices, as materials are issued at a higher rate.

Disadvantages

(*a*) Complicated calculations.
(*b*) Stocks are valued at out-of-date price.
(*c*) Comparison among similar jobs is difficult, as more than one price may be charged for the same job.

4. Base-Stock Price. Under this method a minimum quantity of materials are to be kept in stock, which is known as base stock or safety stock, and are valued at the cost price of the first lot. The base stock can only be used in case of emergency; otherwise it should be carried forward as a fixed asset and the major variable portion of stock are to be valued at any other suitable methods (say LIFO, FIFO etc.).

5. Simple Average Price. Under this method materials are issued at the average price which is calculated by dividing the total of unit purchase prices of different lots in stock on the date of issue by the number of prices used in the calculation and quantity of different lots is not considered.

6. Weighted Average Price. Under this method materials are issued at an average price which is calculated by dividing the total cost of materials in stock by the total quantity of materials in stock. Thus, this method considers both the quantity and respective prices.

Advantages

(*a*) During periods of heavy fluctuation, it tends to smooth out fluctuations in prices.

(*b*) It recovers the cost price of materials from production.

(*c*) It is superior to simple average because the latter considers only rate.

7. Standard Price. It is the predetermined price which is used for issue of materials instead of actual price. This method is mainly used where standard costing is in operation. Any difference between the standard price and the actual price is transferred to Material Price Variance A/c. The method is very easy for application.

8. Inflated Price. Under this method materials are charged by something more than its original cost to cover contingencies and other related losses, wastage etc.

Material Control

A good Material Control system ensures the placement of an order at the right time from the right source to acquire the right quantity at the right price and quality. As materials constitute one of the important factors of production, control of materials means control of total production cost.

Different Tools and Techniques of Materials Control

The various tools and techniques commonly used for inventory control :

1. Perpetual inventory system and continuous stock verification.
2. ABC analysis.
3. Stock turnover analysis.
4. Setting-up various levels of stocks.
5. Codification.
6. Determining the Economic Ordering Quantity (EOQ).
7. Establishment of a budget system.
8. Standardisation.
9. Use of control ratios.
10. Computerisation.
11. Simplification through variety reduction.
12. Application of quantitative techniques, operation research for demand forecasting.
13. Review of slow and non-moving items.
14. Provisioning and purchase procedure.
15. Reporting.

Some of the important techniques are discussed here :

Perpetual Inventory System

"It is a system of records maintained by the Controlling Department which reflects the physical movements of stock and their current balance"—CIMA. This is a method of recording store balances after every receipt and issue, to facilitate regular checking with quantities actually in store, so that it may not be necessary to close down the factory for the purpose of annual stock taking. Thus, the basic object of this system is to make available details about the quantity and value of stock at all times.

Perpetual Inventory *vs* Continuous Stock Taking (verification)

The perpetual inventory is sometimes assisted by a programme of continuous stock-taking which ensures that physical stocks agree with book figures. The two terms are sometimes loosely considered synonymous. But actually this is not so. Perpetual inventory maintains the regular system of records, whereas continuous stock verification means the physical checking of those records with actual stocks.

Advantages

1. It ensures better control over all receipts and issues of stores.
2. The system avoids production bottlenecks.
3. It acts as a system of internal check.
4. It facilitates early detection of errors, mistakes and frauds.
5. The investment in stores is kept at minimum.
6. Discrepancies are readily discovered and localised.
7. Loss of stock due to pilferage can be easily detected.
8. Interim financial accounts may be prepared at any time.
9. Obsolete stocks are more readily revealed and stocks which appear to be little used are kept down to the minimum.
10. Correct stock figures are readily available for insurance purposes.

ABC Analysis

ABC analysis is a form of control of inventories according to its value or nature of importance. Under this method total materials are divided into three categories—*A, B,* and *C. A* category will, include those items which have 75% to 80% of total cost. On the other hand, there is a larger number of items which represent a small percentage, say 5% to 10% of the total cost, which will be under *C* group. In between the two categories there are some items, which constitute 15% to 20% of the total cost and 20% to 25% of the total items, called *B* category. The principles lying under this method is that, a closer attention should be paid on the costly items and all types of material control should be applied in the case of such items (*i.e. A* items). In case of items which fall under *B* category, a routine control is to be followed and for *C* category, an elaborate control method is not required. It is also known as the Always Better Control (ABC) method and also as Proportional Parts Value Analysis method of stock control.

Advantages

1. It ensures greater control for items of high value.
2. It reduced storage cost.
3. It helps to maintain high stock-turnover ratio.
4. It reduces the investment in inventory to the minimum.
5. Working capital can be profitably channelised elsewhere.

Stock Turnover

It is a method used for exercising greater control over inventory. This ratio for various kinds of materials are compared to find out the slow-moving and fast-moving items of the stores. Lower of the ratio indicates that the material is slow-moving or obsolete and in that case it is unnecessary to lock-up capital for that material, and vice versa. If the ratio for any item is zero, this represents that the item had not been used during the period. The formula for Stock Turnover Ratio is :

$$\frac{\text{Cost of materials consumed}}{\text{Cost of average stock held}}$$

Section III : Stores Routine

Types of Stores—Method of Inventory Control—Fixation of Stock Levels and EOQ

In Indian industries about 80 to 90% of total capital is generally invested in material. So, if the stores are not efficiently managed, serious losses may have to be suffered. For the purpose of the effective material control, stores control is very much important. That is why a separate department is maintained by all industries, which is known as stores department.

Types of Stores

There are three types of stores. These are (*a*) Centralised stores, (*b*) Decentralised stores; and (*c*) Control stores with sub-stores.

Methods of Pricing of Materials issues

There are four basic types of pricing of materials issues. In practice, it is very difficult to choose an appropriate method. In the following diagram the method of pricing and their sub-divisions is given :

PRICING OF MATERIALS ISSUES

Based on Cost Price	**Based on Average Price**	**Based on Market Price**	**Based on Notional Price**
(*i*) Specific Price	Simple Average	Replacement Price	Standard Price
(*ii*) FIFO	Weighted Average	Realisable Price	Inflated Price
(*iii*) LIFO	Periodic Average		
(*iv*) HIFO	Moving Simple Average		
(*v*) NIFO	Moving Periodic Average		
(*vi*) Base Stock			

Methods of Inventory Control

The following methods are generally used for the purpose of inventory control :

(*a*) Fixation of Stock Levels
(*b*) Perpetual Inventory System
(*c*) ABC Analysis
(*d*) Inventory Turnover Ratios.

Fixation of Stock Levels. In stores different level of stock may be maintained. The level of stock can be classified into four different levels : (*a*) Maximum level, (*b*) Minimum level, (*c*) Reordering level, (*d*) Average stock level.

Formula for finding out the above level

(*i*) **Maximum level** = [Re-order level + Re-order quantities] – Minimum usage × Mimimum Period

(*ii*) **Minimum level** = [Re-order level – (Normal usage × Normal *i.e.* Average period)]

(*iii*) **Re-ordering level** = Maximum usage × Maximum re-order period

(*iv*) **Average stock level** = $\frac{\text{Maximum level + Minimum level}}{2}$

EOQ. It refers to that quantity where the total of inventory carrying cost and ordering cost is minimum, EOQ is also known as Re-order quantities.

Formula for EOQ

$$EOQ = \sqrt{\frac{2AB}{CS}}$$

where, A = Annual consumption
B = Ordering cost per order
C = Cost per unit
S = Inventory carrying cost or Storage or Holding cost.

Proforma of a Bin Card

ABC Co. Ltd.
BIN CARD

Description....... Bin No. ....
Maximum level........ Code No. ....
Minimum level.......... Store Ledger No. ....
Re-ordering level....... Unit..........
Danger level..........

Receipts			*Issues*			*Balance*		
Date	*G.R. No.*	*Qty.*	*Date*	*S.R. No.*	*Qty.*	*Date*	*Qty.*	*Remarks*

Proforma of Store Ledger

ABC Co. Ltd.
STORE LEDGER

Description....... Re-ordering Level.......
Code No. .... Maximum level...........
Bin No. .... Minimum level...........

Date	*Receipts*				*Issues*				*Balance*			*Remarks*
	G.R. No.	*Qty.*	*Rate*	*Amt.*	*S.R. No.*	*Qty.*	*Rate*	*Amt.*	*S.R. No.*	*Qty.*	*Rate*	*Amt.*

WORKEDOUT PROBLEMS

Problem 1

Calculate Maximum Level, Minimum Level and Reorder Level from the following data :
Re-order Quantity : 1,200 units
Re-order period : 4 to 6 weeks
Maximum Consumption : 300 units per week
Minimum Consumption : 200 units per week
Normal Consumption : 250 units per week

[*C.U. B.Com. (Hons.) 1990*]

Solution

Reorder Level = Maximum Consumption × Maximum Re-order period
= 300 units × 6 weeks
= 1,800 units

Minimum Stock Level = Reorder Stock Level – (Normal Consumption × Normal Reorder period)

$$= 1{,}800 \text{ units} - \left(250 \times \frac{4+6}{2}\right)$$

= 1,800 – 1,250 units
= 550 units

Maximum Level = Re-order level + Re-ordering quantity
– (Minimum Consumption × Minimum Re-order period)
= 1,800 units + 1,200 units – (200 × 4) units
= 3,000 units – 800 units.
= 2,200 units.

Problem 2

The products *A* and *B* are used as follows :

	A	*B*
Normal Consumption	200 units per week	100 units per week
Maximum Consumption	300 units per week	200 units per week
Minimum Consumption	100 units per week	50 units per week
Re-order Quantity	1000 units	500 units
Re-order Period	4 to 5 weeks	2 to 4 weeks

Calculate for each product : (*a*) Re-order Level, (*b*) Maximum Level, (*c*) Minimum level, and (*d*) Average Stock Level. **[*I.C.W.A.I. (Inter)—Adopted*]**

Solution

In the Case of Product A

(*a*) Re-order Level = Maximum Consumption × Maximum Reorder period
= 300 units × 5 weeks
= 1,500 units

(*b*) Maximum Level = Re-order Level + Re-order Quantity
– (Minimum Consumption × Minimum Re-order period)
= 1,500 units + 1000 – (100 × 4)
= 2,500 – 400 = 2,100 units

(*c*) Minimum Level = (Maximum Consumption × Maximum Re-order period)
– (Normal Consumption × Normal Re-order period)

$$= (300 \text{ units} \times 5) - \left(200 \text{ units} \times \frac{4+5}{2}\right)$$

= 1,500 – 900 = 600 units

(*d*) Average Stock Level $= \frac{1}{2}$ (Maximum Level + Minimum Level)

$= \frac{1}{2}$ (2,100 units + 600 units)

= 1,350 units

In the Case of Product B

(*a*) Re-order Level = Maximum Consumption × Maximum Re-order period
= 200 units × 4 = 800 units

(*b*) Maximum Level = Re-order Level + Re-order quantity
– (Minimum Consumption × Minimum Re-order period)
= 800 + 500 – (50 × 2)
= 1,300 – 100 = 1,200 units

(*c*) Minimum Level = Re-order level – (Normal Consumption × Normal Re-order period)

$$= 800 - \left(100 \times \frac{2+4}{2}\right)$$

= 800 – (100 × 3) = 800 – 300
= 500 units

(*d*) Average Stock Level $= \frac{1}{2}$ (Maximum Level + Minimum Level)

$= \frac{1}{2}$ (1,200 + 500)

$= \frac{1}{2} \times 1{,}700 = 850$ units

Problem 3

(a) From the following data for the last 7 days, compute the Average Stock Level for a component :

Maximum usage in a week	600 units
Minimum usage in a week	400 units
Average usage in a week	450 units

Time-lag procurement of materials : Maximum 4 days, Minimum 2 days. Re-order quantity = 1,500 units.

(*b*) You also ascertain the Danger Stock Level from the above information.

[*I.C.W.A. Final—Adopted*]

Solution

(a) Average Stock Level $= \text{Minimum Level}^* + \frac{1}{2}(\text{Re-order quantity})$

$= 1{,}050 \text{ units} + \frac{1}{2} \times 1{,}500 \text{ units}$

$= 1{,}800 \text{ units}$

(*b*) Danger Stock Level $= \text{Average usage} \times \text{Minimum Re-order Period}$

$= 450 \text{ units} \times 2 = 900 \text{ units}$

Working Note

*(*i*) Re-order Level = Maximum usage × Maximum Re-order period

$= 600 \times 4 = 2{,}400$ units

(*ii*) Minimum Level = Re-order Level – (Average usage in a week × Average delivery period)

$$= 2{,}400 - \left(450 \times \frac{4+2}{2}\right)$$

$= 2{,}400 - 1{,}350 = 1{,}050$ units

Problem 3(*a*)

Compute the re-order level, minimum level, maximum level, average stock level for components *A* and *B* based on the following data :

	A	*B*
Maximum Consumption per week	150 units	150 units
Average Consumtion per week	100 units	100 units
Minimum Consumption per week	50 units	50 units
Re-order period	8 to 12 weeks	4 to 8 weeks
Re-order quantity	400 units	600 units

[*I.C.W.A. (Int.)*]

Solution

	Component A	*Component B*
1. Re-order level = Maximum Consumption × Maximum Re-order Period	150 × 12 = 1,800 units	150 × 8 = 1,200 units
2. Minimum level = Re-order point – Average consumption × Average Re-order period)	1,800 – (100 × 10) = 800 units	1,200 – (100 × 6) = 600 units
3. Maximum level = Re-order level – (Minimum consumption × Minimum Re-order period) + Re-order Quantity	1,800 – (50 × 8) + 400 = 1,800 units	1,200 – (50 × 4) + 600 = 1,600 units
4. Average Level = $\frac{\text{Maximum Level} + \text{Minimum Level}}{2}$	$\frac{1{,}800 + 800}{2}$ = 1,300 units	$\frac{600 + 1{,}600}{2}$ = 1,100 units

Problem 3(*b*)

ZEE is a product manufactured out of three raw materials *M, N* and *Q*. Each unit of ZEE requires 10 kg, 8 kg and 6 kg of *M, N* and *Q,* respectively. The re-order levels of *M* and *N* are 15,000 kg and 10,000 kg, respectively, while the minimum level of *Q* is 2,500 kgs. The weekly production of ZEE varies from 300 to 500 units, while the weekly average production is 400 units.

You are required to compute :

(*i*) the minimum stock level of *M*.
(*ii*) the maximum stock level of *N*; and
(*iii*) the re-order level of *Q*.

The following additional data are given :

	M	*N*	*Q*
Re-order quantity (in kg)	20,000	15,000	20,000
Delivery (in weeks)			
Minimum	2	4	3
Average	3	5	4
Maximum	4	6	5

[*I.C.W.A. (Int.), Dec. 1995 (New)*]

Solution

(*i*) **Minimum stock level of *M***

Minimum level = Re-order level – (Normal Consumption × Normal Delivery period)
= 15,000 kg – (400 units × 10 kg × 3 weeks)
= 15,000 – 12,000 = 3,000 kg.

(*ii*) **Maximum Stock Levels of *N***

Maximum level = Re-order level + Re-order Quantity
– (Minimum Consumption × Normal Minimum period)
= 10,000 kg + 15,000 kg. – (300 × 8 × 4) kg
= 25,000 – 9,600 = 15,400 kg.

(*iii*) **Re-order Level of *Q***

Re-order level = (Maximum consumption × Maximum period)
= (500 × 5 × 6) = 15,000 kg.

Problem 3(c)

In a factory component *A* is used as follows :

Normal usage	50 kg per week
Minimum usage	25 kg per week.
Maximum usage	75 kg per week.

Re-order quantity 300 kg.
Re-order period 4 to 6 weeks.

Calculate for component *A* :

(*i*) Re-order level, (*ii*) Maximum level.
(*iii*) Minimum level; and (*iv*) Average stock level.

Solution **[*C.U. B.Com. (Hons.) 1994*]**

(*i*) Re-order level = Maximum usage × Maximum period
= 75 × 6 = 450 kg

(*ii*) Maximum level = Re-order level + Re-order quantity
– (Minimum usage × Minimum time)
= 450 + 300 – (25 × 4) = 650 kg.

(*iii*) Minimum level = Reorder level – (Normal usage × Average time)
$= 450 - (50 \times 5) = 200$ kg.

(*iv*) Average stock level $= \dfrac{\text{Maximum level} + \text{Minimum level}}{2}$

$$= \left(\frac{650 + 200}{2}\right) \text{kg} = 425 \text{ kg.}$$

Problem 4

From the following information calculate the Economic Order Quantity :

Annual usage	20,000 units
Cost of Materials (per unit)	Rs. 250
Cost of placing and receiving order	Rs. 2,000

Annual cost of carrying inventory (including interest) – 10% of cost.

Solution

$$\text{EOQ} = \sqrt{\frac{2AB}{CS}}$$

EOQ = Economic Order Quantity :

where, A = Annual Consumption
B = Cost of placing and receiving order
C = Cost per unit
S = Carrying Cost of inventory.

$$= \sqrt{\frac{2 \times 20{,}000 \times 2{,}000}{250 \times \frac{10}{100}}}$$

$$= \sqrt{\frac{2 \times 20{,}000 \times 2{,}000 \times 100}{250 \times 10}}$$

$$= \sqrt{\frac{8{,}00{,}00{,}00{,}000}{2{,}500}}$$

$$= \sqrt{32{,}00{,}000}$$

= 1,788·85 units (approx.)

Problem 4(*a*)

A manufacturer uses 75,000 units of a particualr material per year. The material cost is Rs. 1·50 per unit and the carrying cost is estimated to be 25% p.a. of average inventory cost. The cost of placing an order is Rs. 18.

You are required to determine the Economic Order Quantity and frequency of orders p.a.

[*C.U. B.Com. (Hons.) 1995*]

Solution

We know $\text{EOQ} = \sqrt{\dfrac{2AO}{C}}$

A = Annual consumption = 75,000 units
O = Ordering cost per unit = Rs. 18.
C = Carrying cost per unit = 25% of Rs. 1·5 = 0·375

$$\therefore \text{EOQ} = \sqrt{\frac{2 \times 75{,}000 \times 18}{0{\cdot}375}} = 2{,}691 \text{ units (approx).}$$

$$\text{Frequency of order p.a.} = \frac{75{,}000}{2{,}691} = 28 \text{ (approx.)}$$

Problem 5

From the following particulars determine the Economic Order Quantity :

Ordering Quantity (tonnes)	*Price per tonne (Rs.)*
Less than 100	10·00
Between 100 and 199	9·90
Between 200 and 499	9·80
Between 500 and 999	9·70
Between 1,000 and 1,999	9·60
Between 2,000 and above	9·50

Additional information : (*i*) Annual consumption of materials = 2,000 tonnes ; (*ii*) Carrying cost 10%, (*iii*) Ordering cost Rs. 5 per order. **[*C.U. M.Com.*]**

Solution

Statement Showing Economic Order Quantity

Annual Consumption : 2,000 tonnes

Particulars							
1. Quantity of order (in tonnes) [Multiples of 2,000 units]	80	125	250	400	500	1,000	2,000
2. No. of orders [Total Quantity ÷ Quantity per order]	25	16	8	5	4	2	1
3. Value per order [Serial No. 1 × Price in Rs.]	800	1,237·50	2,450	3,920	4,850	9,000	19,000
4. Average inventory in Rs. [Serial No. 3 ÷ 2]	400	618·75	1,225	1,960	2,425	4,500	8,500
	Rs.	*Rs.*	*Rs.*	*Rs.*	*Rs.*	*Rs.*	*Rs.*
5. Cost of Materials [Annual usage × Rate per unit]	20,000	19,800	19,600	19,600	19,400	19,200	19,000
6. Ordering Cost [No. of orders × Rate per order]	125	80	40	25	20	10	5
7. Carrying Cost [10% of Average Inventory]	40	61·88	122·50	196	242·50	480	950
Total Cost Sl. No. [5 + 6 + 7]	20,165	19,941·88	19,762·50	19,821	19,662·50*	19,690	19,955

* The total cost of the inventory is minimum, when the ordering quantity is 500 units. *i.e.* Rs. 19,662·50.

Therefore Economic Order Quantity = 500 units.

Problem 6

Find the Economic Order Quantity from the following data :

Actual consumption	18,000 units (per annum)
Cost per unit	Rs. 1·50
Cost of placing order and processing the delivery	Rs. 12 per order
Inventory carrying cost	20% of unit value.

[*C.U. B.Com. (Hons.) 1990*]

Solution

$$EOQ = \sqrt{\frac{2AB}{CS}}$$

where, *EOQ* = *Economic Order Quantity*
A = *Annual Consumption*
B = *Ordering Cost*
C = *Cost per unit*
S = *Inventory* Carrying Cost.

$$= \sqrt{\frac{2 \times 18{,}000 \times 12 \times 100}{1{\cdot}50 \times 20}}$$

$$= \sqrt{\frac{4{,}32{,}00{,}000}{30}}$$

$$= \sqrt{14{,}40{,}000} = 1{,}200 \text{ units}$$

Problem 7

Find out the Economic Order Quantity and Order Schedule for raw materials and packing materials with the following data given to you :

1. Cost of ordering : Raw Materials = Rs. 1,000 per order
   Packing Materials = Rs. 5,000 per order
2. Cost of holding inventory : Raw Materials = 1 paisa per unit p.m.
   Packing Materials = 5 paise per unit p.m.
3. Production rate : 2,00,000 units per month **[*C.S. Final*]**

Solution

(*i*) In the case of Raw Materials

$$EOQ = \sqrt{\frac{2AB}{CS}}$$

where, *EOQ* = Economic Order Quantity
A = Annual Consumption
B = Ordering or buying Cost per order
C = Cost per unit
S = Carrying Cost or Storage Cost

$$= \sqrt{\frac{2 \times 2{,}00{,}000 \times 1{,}000 \times 100}{1}}$$

= 2,00,000 units

One order per month = 2,00,000 units

(*ii*) In the case of Packing Materials :

$$EOQ = \sqrt{\frac{2AB}{CS}} = \sqrt{\frac{2 \times 2{,}00{,}000 \times 5{,}000 \times 100}{5}}$$

= 2,00,000 units

One order per month = 2,00,000 units.

Problem 8

Company uses 5,120 units of a component in a year. The purchase price per unit of the component is Rs. 5·00 and the carrying cost including interest is estimated at 20% of the average inventory investment on annual basis. The cost of placing an order and processing the delivery is Rs. 10.

(a) Ascertain the economic order quantity and the number of orders each of the economic order quantity, to be placed for the component in a year.

(*b*) Assuming that the average daily consumption of the above component is 14 units and that the normal lead time is 15 days, calculate the ordering level for the component, where safety stock is considered to be equal to 25 days' consumption. State why ordering level is fixed.

[*C.U. B.Com. (Hons.)*]

Solution

$$EOQ = \sqrt{\frac{2AB}{CS}} = \sqrt{\frac{2 \times 5{,}120 \times 10 \times 100}{5 \times 20}} = 320 \text{ units}$$

where, EOQ = Economic Order Quantity
A = Annual usage = 5,120 units
B = Cost of placing an order and processing delivery = Rs. 10
C = Cost per unit = Rs. 5
S = Carrying cost including interest = 20%

$$\text{No. of orders} = \frac{\text{Annual usage}}{\text{Economic Order Quantity}}$$

$$= \frac{5{,}120 \text{ units}}{320 \text{ units}} = 16 \text{ times}$$

Cost per order of EOQ = 320 units × Rs. 5 + Rs. 10 + 20% of (320 units × Rs. 5 + Rs. 10)
= Rs. 1,932

(b) Ordering Level = Minimum Stock Level + Average consumption day × Normal lead time
= (14 × 25) + (14 × 15)
= 350 + 210 = 560 units.

Problem 9

A Purchase Manager has decided to place orders for minimum quantity of 500 Nos. of a particular item in order to get a discount of 10%. From the records, it was found out that in the last year, 8 orders each of size 200 Nos. had been placed. Given ordering cost = Rs. 500 per order, inventory carrying cost = 40% of the inventory value and the cost per unit = Rs. 400.

Is the Purchase Manager justified in his decision ?

What will be the effect of his decision on the company ?

[*C.A. Final*]

Solution

$$\text{EOQ} = \sqrt{\frac{2AB}{CS}}$$

$$= \sqrt{\frac{2 \times (200 \times 8) \times 500 \times 100}{400 \times 40}}$$

$$= \sqrt{\frac{16{,}00{,}00{,}000}{16{,}000}}$$

= 100 Nos.

where, EOQ = Economic Order Quantity
A = Annual Consumption
B = Buying Cost
C = Cost per order
S = Carrying Cost.

Number of orders = 1,600 ÷ 100 = 16 orders p.a.

(*i*) Total cost of 16 orders :

	Rs.
Ordering cost (16 × Rs. 500)	8,000
Carrying Cost of Average Inventory (100 × 160) ÷ 2	8,000
Purcahse Cost (Rs. 400 × 1,600 units)	6,40,000
Total Cost of Inventory	6,56,000

(*ii*) Total Inventory Cost of last year :

	Rs.
Ordering Cost (Rs. 500 × 8)	4,000
Carrying Cost (Rs. 400 × 40% × 200 Nos.) ÷ 2	16,000
Purchase Cost (Rs. 400 × 1,600 units)	6,40,000
Total Cost of Inventory	6,60,000

(*iii*) Total Inventory Cost due to Purchase Manager's decision :

	Rs.
Ordering Cost (Rs. 500 × 4*)	2,000
Carrying Cost of Average inventory $\left[\text{Rs.}\left(360\times\frac{40}{100}\right)\times 500\text{ Nos.}\right]\div 2$	36,000
Purchase Cost (Rs. 360** × 1,600 Nos.)	5,76,000
Total Cost of Inventory	6,14,000

$$\text{*No. of orders} = \frac{\text{Annual Consumption}}{\text{Minimum quantity of Nos. to place at a time}}$$

$$= \frac{1,600}{500} = 3{\cdot}2, \text{ i.e. } 4 \text{ orders.}$$

** (Rs. 400 – 10% of Rs. 400) = 360

Effect of the decision of Purchase Manager to the company :

(*i*) Total Inventory Cost at EOQ Level = Rs. 6,56,000

(*ii*) Total Inventory Cost of last year = Rs. 6,60,000

(*iii*) Total Inventory Cost due to Purchase Manager's decision = Rs. 6,14,000

∴ Savings (Rs. 6,60,000 – Rs. 6,14,000) = Rs. 46,000

Purchase Manager is justified in his decision as it resulted in maximum savings, *i.e.* Rs. 46,000.

Problem 10

Following information in an inventory problem is available :

Annual demand 2,400 units; Unit price Rs. 2·40; Ordering cost Rs. 4·00; Storage cost 2% per year; Interest rate 10% per annum; Lead time $\frac{1}{2}$ month.

Calculate EOQ; Reorder Level and Total Annual Inventory Cost.

How much does the total inventory cost vary if the unit price is changed to Rs. 5 ?

[*I.C.W.A. (Final)*]

Solution

$$EOQ = \sqrt{\frac{2AB}{CS}}$$

where, *EOQ* = Economic Order Quantity
A = Annual Consumption
B = Ordering Cost
C = Cost per unit
S = Storage cost including interest.

$$= \sqrt{\frac{2\times 2,400\times 4}{\left(2{\cdot}40\times\frac{10}{100}\right)+\left(2{\cdot}40\times\frac{2}{100}\right)}}$$

$$= \sqrt{\frac{19,200}{0{\cdot}288}} = 258{\cdot}19$$

or, 258 units (approx.)

Reorder Level : Maximum Consumption per unit of time × Maximum period required for delivery

$$= \frac{2,400}{12}\times\frac{1}{2} = 100 \text{ units.}$$

Working Notes :

Calculation of Annual Inventory Cost [when cost per unit Rs. 2·40]

	Rs.
Cost of Inventory [2,400 units × Rs. 2·40]	5,760·00
Ordering Cost [No. of Orders × Rs. 4]	40·00
Storage Cost (Average) [2% of Rs. 5,760 × $\frac{1}{2}$]	57·60
Interest (Average) [10% of Rs. 5,760 × $\frac{1}{2}$]	288·00
Total Annual Inventory Cost	6,145·60

Calculation of Annual Inventory Cost [when cost per unit Rs. 5·00]

	Rs.
Cost of Inventory [2,400 units × Rs. 5]	12,000
Ordering Cost [10* × Rs. 4]	40
Storage Cost (Average) [2% of Rs. 12,000] × $\frac{1}{2}$	120
Interest (Average) [10% of Rs. 12,000] × $\frac{1}{2}$	600
Total Annual Inventory Cost	12,760

When Material Cost per unit is Rs. 5·00 the Inventory Cost increases
= Rs. 12,760 – Rs. 6,145·60
= Rs. 6,614·40

Working Notes :

No. of orders for a year $= \frac{2,400 \text{ units}}{258}$
= 9·31 or 10 (approx.)

Problem 11

The following relations to inventory costs have been established for PQR Ltd. :

(*i*) Orders must be placed in multiples of 100 units.
(*ii*) Requirements for the years are 4,00,000 units.
(*iii*) The purchase price per unit is Rs. 4·00.
(*iv*) Carrying cost is 20% of the purchase price of goods.
(*v*) Cost per order placed is Rs. 25·00.
(*vi*) Desired safety stock is 10,000 units. This quantity is on hand initially.
(*vii*) Three days are required for delivery.

Calculate (*i*) EOQ, (*ii*) how many order should the company place each year ? (*iii*) At what inventory level should an order be placed ? **[*I.C.W.A. (Final) Adopted*]**

Solution

(*i*) EOQ $= \sqrt{\frac{2AB}{CS}}$

where, *EOQ* = Economic Order Quantity.
A = Annual Consumption
B = Ordering per Order
C = Cost per Order
S = Storage Cost.

$$= \sqrt{\frac{2 \times 4,00,000 \times 25 \times 100}{4 \times 20}}$$

$$= \sqrt{\frac{2,00,00,00,000}{80}}$$

$$= \sqrt{2,50,00,000}$$

$$= 5,000$$

(*ii*) No. of order $= \frac{\text{Annual Consumption}}{\text{EOQ}} = \frac{4,00,000 \text{ units}}{5,000 \text{ units}} = 80$

(*iii*) Re-order Level = Minimum Stock + Average Consumption per unit of time × Average lead time

$$= 10{,}000 \text{ units} + \left(\frac{4{,}00{,}000}{300} \times 4\right) \text{ units}$$

$$= 10{,}000 \text{ units} + 5{,}333 \text{ units}$$

$$= 15{,}333 \text{ units (approx.)}$$

Note. (1) Assumed that 300 working days during the year.

(2) Lead time = Date of placing an order + 3 days required for delivery *i.e.* 1 + 3 = 4 days.

Problem 12

A company is trying to establish a control policy to reduce inventory costs. The financial manager estimated that a two months' delivery schedule can be expected. The total purchase requirement is estimated to be 3,000 units for the year. The purchase price per unit is Rs. 6 and ordering cost per order is Rs. 20. However, for the company the inventory usage does not remain constant. Suppose the inventory usage during two months lead time is expected to be :

Demand (units) :	80	120	160	200	240	280	320
Probability :	0·04	0·06	0·20	0·40	0·20	0·06	0·04

If the stock out cost is Rs. 4 per unit and the carrying cost is 50% of cost of inventory per unit per year, determine optimal safety stock. **[*C.U. M.Com.—Adopted*]**

Solution

The decision is for maintaining a safety stock with an eye to minimise stock out cost of carrying additional inventory. Here we assume that the average demand varies with the total demand accordingly and uniformly.

From probability distribution expected demand for two months (*i.e.* one of the seven different levels of demand for two months will occur), we find that 200 is the most likely level of demand for lead time (two months), because it is assigned the highest probability *i.e.* 0·04.

We also find that there is a 0·30 probability that demand will be between 240 and 320 units.

If we decide to use re-order point equal to 200 units stock outs would occur only if demand is for 240, 280 or 320.

Now, we construct a table showing probability of a stock-out with a reorder point of 200 units and Safety Stock of 0, 40, 80 and 120 units :

Probability of Stock-out	0·40	0·20	0·06	0·04
Demand during lead time	200	240	280	320
Stock out if safety stock is made for :				
0 units	0	40	80	120
40 units	0	0	40	80
80 units	0	0	0	40
120 units		0	0	0

Here, $\text{EOQ} = \sqrt{\frac{2AO}{C}} = \sqrt{\frac{2 \times 3{,}000 \times 20}{3}}$ [∴ C = 50% of Rs. 6]

$$= \sqrt{40{,}000} = 200 \text{ units}$$

$$\therefore \text{ No. of orders} = \frac{3{,}000}{200} = 15$$

Computation of Optimal Safety Stock

Safety Stock (units) (1)	*Stock out (units)* (2)	*Stock out cost @ Rs. 4 per unit* (3)	*Probability* (4)	*No. of orders p.a.* (5)	*Expected Stock out cost* (6) = (3)×(4)×(5)	*Carrying Cost* (7)	*Total Cost* (8) = (6) + (7)
0	40	160	0·20	15	480		
	80	320	0·06	15	288		
	120	480	0·04	15	288		
					1,056	0	1,056
40	40	160	0·06	15	144		
	80	320	0·04	15	192		
					336	120	456
80	40	160	0·04	15	96	240	336
120	0	0	0·00	15	0	360	360

Now at Safety Stock of 80 units, the total cost is minimum. Hence the Optimal Safety Stock is 80 units.

Problem 13

The following information regarding receipts and issues of material A has been obtained from store records of a concern :

2007			
Jan.	1	Balance	500 units
"	2	Issued S.R. No. 101	100 units
"	5	Received G.R. No. 51	200 units
"	7	Issued S.R. No. 111	240 units
"	10	Returned to Stores S.C. No. 10	20 units
"	12	Received G.R. No. 57	150 units
"	15	Issued S.R. No. 121	210 units
"	18	Received G.R. No. 60	330 units
"	20	Returned to vendor M.D. No. 184	30 units
"	25	Received G.R. No. 63	50 units
"	30	Issued S.R. No. 131	100 units

Other Information

(*i*) Stock verification on January 31 reveals a shortage of 20 units

(*ii*) Bin Card No. 234; Code No. AB 555; Minimum Level 300 units; Reorder Level 350 units; Reorder quantity 325 units; Maximum level 800 units.

Prepare a Bin Card for the month ended 31 January 2007.

Solution

BIN CARD

Description—A........	Bin Card No. 234
Stores Ledger Folio........	Code No. AB 555
Maximum level......800	Unit........Number
Reorder level..........350	Reorder Quantity 325 units
Minimum level......300	

Date	Receipts		Issues		Balance	Remarks
2007	Ref. No.	Quantity	Ref. No.	Quantity	Quantity	
Jan. 1					500	
" 2			S.R. No. 101	100	400	
" 5	G.R. No. 51	200			600	
" 7			S.R. No. 111	240	360	
" 10	S.C. NO. 10	20			380	
" 12	G.R. NO. 57	150			530	
" 15			S.R. NO. 121	210	320	
" 18	G.R. NO. 60	330			650	
" 20			M.D. NO. 184	30	620	
" 25	G.R. NO. 63	50			670	
" 30			S.R. No. 131	100	570	
" 31			Shortage	20	550	

Problem 14

From the following particulars find out the value of closing stock when materials are issued under Simple Average Method :

2007			
Jan.	1	Balance	2,000 units Rs. 10,000
"	5	Received	3,000 units @ Rs. 6 per unit
"	10	Issues	3,500 units
"	15	Issues	500 units
"	20	Received	2,000 units @ Rs. 7 per unit

Solution

Balance of Stock on 5th January 2007 : 5,000 units at Rs. 28,000

Issues on 10th January, Stock to be valued at $\frac{\text{Rs. } 6{\cdot}00 + \text{Rs. } 5{\cdot}00}{2}$ = Rs. 5·50 per unit.

Balance on 15th =	5,000 units at	Rs. 28,000
Less : Issues [3,500 + 500]	4,000 units @ Rs. 5·50 =	Rs. 22,000
	1,000 units	Rs. 6,000

Balance on 20th January 1,000 units + 2,000 units = 3,000 units = Rs. 6,000 + Rs. 21,000
= Rs. 27,000

Problem 15

From the following details write Store Ledger under simple average method :

2006.			
Dec.	1	Opening Balance	100 kg @ Rs. 5·00
"	5	Received	50 kg @ Rs. 5·20
"	8	Issued	120 kg
"	10	Issued	10 kg
"	15	Received	80 kg @ Rs. 5·40
"	18	Issued	50 kg
"	20	Received	100 kg @ Rs. 5·60
"	25	Issued	40 kg
"	29	Issued	60 kg

The stock verifier found a shortage of 10 kg. on 16.12.06 and another shortage of 10 kg on 26.12.06. *[C.U. B.Com. (Hons.) Adopted]*

Solution

Stores Ledger under Simple Average Method

Date	Receipts				Issues				Balance			Remarks
	G.R. No.	Qty. Kg.	Rate Rs.	Amount Rs.	S.R. No.	Qty. kg.	Rate Rs.	Amount Rs.	Qty. kg.	Rate Rs.	Amount Rs.	
2006												
Dec. 1		—	—	—		—	—	—	100	5·00	500	
" 5		50	5·20	266		—	—	—	150		760	
" 8		—	—	—		120	5·10	612	30		148	
" 10		—	—	—		10	5·20	52	20		96	
" 15		80	5·40	432		—	—	—	100		528	
" 16		—	—	—		10	5·30	53	90		475	Shortage
" 18		—	—	—		50	5·30	265	40		210	
" 20		100	5·60	560		—	—	—	140		770	
" 25		—	—	—		40	5·50	220	100		550	
" 26		—	—	—		10	5·60	56	90		494	Shortage
" 29		—	—	—		60	5·60	336	30		158	

Problem 16

The particulars of receipts and issues of materials in a factory in January 2007 are :

Jan. 1	Opening Balance	1,500 kg @ Rs. 12 per kg
" 2	Issued	650 kg
" 5	Purchased	400 kg @ Rs. 12·50 per kg
" 9	Issued	300 kg
" 10	Purchased	200 kg @ Rs. 12·50 per kg
" 11	Issued	300 kg
" 12	Returned from workshop issued on 2nd January	20 kg
" 13	Issued	450 kg
" 16	Purchased	500 kg @ Rs. 13·00 per kg
" 18	Issued	400 kg
" 22	Purchased	300 kg @ Rs. 12·00 per kg
" 30	Issued	200 kg

Pricing of issues is to be done on FIFO basis. A shortage of 10 kg was noticed on 16th January. Prepare the Store Ledger for the month of January 2007. [*C.U. B.Com. (Hons.) Adopted*]

Solution

Stores Ledger Accounting—FIFO Method

Date	Receipts				Issues				Balance			Remarks
	G.R. No.	Qty. Kg	Rate Rs.	Amount Rs.	S.R. No.	Qty. kg	Rate Rs.	Amount Rs.	Qty. kg	Rate Rs.	Amount Rs.	
1.1.07		—	—	—		—	—	—	1,500	12·00	18,000	
2.1.07		—	—	—		650	12·00	7,800	850	12·00	10,200	
5.1.07		400	12·50	5,000		—	—	—	850	12·00	10,200	
									400	12·50	5,000	

9.1.07		—	—	—		300	12·00	3,600	550	12·00	6,600	
									400	12·50	5,000	
10.1.07		200	12·50	2,500		—	—	—	550	12·00	6,600	
									600	12·50	7,500	
11.1.07		—		—		300	12·00	3,600	250	12·00	3,000	
									600	12·50	7,500	
12.1.07		20	12·00	240		—	—	—	270	12·00	3,240	Returned
									600	12·50	7,500	from workshop
13.1.07		—	—	—		270	12·00	3,240	420	12·50	5,250	
						180	12·50	2,250				
16.1.07		500	13·00	6,500		10	12·50	125	410	12·50	5,125	Shortage
									500	13·00	6,500	
18.1.07		—	—	—		400	12·00	4,800	10	12·50	125	
									500	13·00	6,500	
22.1.07		300	12·00	3,600		—	—	—	10	12·50	125	
									500	13·00	6,500	
									300	12·00	3,600	
30.1.07		—	—	—		10	12·50	125	310	13·00	4,030	
						190	13·00	2,470	300	12·00	3,600	

Problem 17

The following is an extract of the record of receipts and issues of sulphur in a chemical factory during June 1992 :

1992	June	1	Opening Balance 50 tons @ Rs. 200
	”	9	Issued : 25 tons
	”	14	Received from supplier 20 tons @ Rs. 190
	”	17	Issued : 18 tons
	”	21	Received from supplier 24 tons @ Rs. 180
	”	25	Issued : 30 tons
	”	26	Received from supplier 32 tons @ Rs. 190
	”	29	Issued : 20 tons
	”	30	Returned from department 3 tons @ Rs. 190

Issues are to be priced on the principle of FIFO. The stock verifier of the factory had found a shortage of 1 ton on 23rd June and left a note accordingly.

Draw up a priced stores ledger card for the materials, showing the above transactions.

[*C.U. B.Com.—Adopted*]

Solution *(see next page)*

Solution (Problem 17)

STORES LEDGER UNDER FIFO METHOD

Meterial Name..........
Code No. ....
Bin No. ....

Maximum Level.........
Reorder Level.........
Minimum Level.........
Reorder Quantity........

Date	Receipts				Issues				Balances			Remarks
	G.R. No.	Qty. Tons	Rate Rs.	Amount Rs.	S.R. No.	Qty. Tons	Rate Rs.	Amount Rs.	Qty. Tons	Rate Rs.	Amount Rs.	
1992 June 1		—	—	—		—	—	—	50	200	10,000	
" 9		—	—	—		25	200	5,000	25	200	5,000	
" 14		20	190	3,800		—		—	45 { 25 20	200 190	8,800 { 5,000 3,800	
" 17		—	—	—		18	200	3,600	27 { 7 20	200 190	5,200 { 1,400 3,800	
" 21		24	180	4,320		—	—	—	51 { 7 20 24	200 190 180	9,520 { 1,400 3,800 4,320	
" 23		—	—	—		1	200	200	50 { 6 20 24	200 190 180	9,320 { 1,200 3,800 4,320	Shortage
" 25		—	—	—		30 { 6 20 4	200 190 180	5,720 { 1,200 3,800 720	20	180	3,600	
" 27		32	190	6,080		—	—	—	52 { 20 32	180 190	9,680 { 3,600 6,080	
" 29		—	—	—		20	180	3,600	32	190	6,080	
" 30		3	190	570		—	—	—	35 { 32 3	190 190	6,650 { 6,080 570	Returns

Problem 18

Prepare a Stores Ledger under the LIFO method of pricing the issues of Stores, using the following information :

1991			Units
Jan.	1	Balance in hand @ Rs. 1·10 per unit	100
"	2	Received @ Rs. 1·20 per unit	200
"	10	Issued	150
"	14	Received @ 1·30 per unit	100
"	18	Issued	150
"	23	Returned from the issues on 10th January	20
"	26	Received @ Rs. 1·20 per unit	100
"	30	Wastage	10
"	31	Issued	110

[*C.U. B.Com. (Hons.)*]

Solution *(see next page)*

Problem 19

The particulars of receipts and issues of a certain material during January 1987 are given below :

Date	*Receipts*	*Units*	*Rate Per unit*	*Issues*	
				Date	*Units*
Jan. 6	Purchased	450	Rs. 25·00	Jan. 3	600
" 12	Purchased	600	Rs. 24·50	Jan. 8	500
" 15	Returned from workshop (Issued on Jan. 3)	50		Jan. 13	250
" 22	Purchased	350	Rs. 26·00	Jan. 27	500
" 28	Purchased	500	Rs. 27·00	Jan. 31	300

Further information :

Opening balance on January 1, 1987—1,000 @ 24·00 per unit.

A shortage of 15 units was noticed and recorded on January 9, 1987.

Prapare Store Ledger in respect of the materials for the month of January 1987 under the LIFO system. [*C.U. B.Com. (Hons.) 1987*]

Sol. (*see page 115*)

Solution (Problem 18)

STORES LEDGER ACCOUNT UNDER LIFO METHOD

Date	Receipts				Issues				Balances			Remarks
	G.R. No.	Qty. (Units)	Rate Rs.	Amount Rs.	S.R. No.	Qty. (Units)	Rate Rs.	Amount Rs.	Qty. (Units)	Rate Rs.	Amount Rs.	
	1992											
June 1		—	—	—		—	—	—	100	1·10	110	
" 2		200	1·20	240		—	—	—	300 {100, 200}	1·10, 1·20	350 {110, 240}	
" 10		—	—	—		150	1·20	180	150 {100, 50}	1·10, 1·20	170 {110, 60}	
" 14		100	1·30	130		—	—	—	250 {100, 50, 100}	1·10, 1·20, 1·30	300 {110, 60, 130}	
" 18		—	—	—		150 {100, 50}	1·30, 1·20	190 {130, 60}	100	1·10	110	
" 23		20	1·20	24		—	—	—	120 {100, 20}	1·10, 1·20	134 {110, 24}	Returns
" 26		100	1·20	120		—	—	—	220 {100, 120}	1·10, 1·20	254 {110, 144}	
" 30		—	—	—		10	1·20	12	210 {100, 110}	1·10, 1·20	242 {110, 132}	Wastage
" 31		—	—	—		110	1·20	132	100	1·10	110	

Solution (Problem 19)

Stores Ledger Account—FIFO Method

Date	Receipts				Issues				Balance		
	G.R. No.	*Qty. Kg.*	*Rate Rs.*	*Amount Rs.*	*S.R. No.*	*Qty. kg.*	*Rate Rs.*	*Amount Rs.*	*Qty kg.*	*Rate Rs.*	*Amount Rs.*
1.1.87		—	—	—		—	—	—	1,000	24	24,000
3.1.87		—	—	—		600	24	14,400	400	24	9,600
6.1.87		450	25	11,250		—	—	—	400	24	9,600
									450	25	11,250
8.1.87		—	—	—		450	25	11,250			
						50	24	1,200	350	24	8,400
9.1.87		—	—	—		15	24	360	335	24	8,040
12.1.87		600	24·50	14,700		—	—	—	335	24	8,040
									600	24·50	14,700
13.1.87		—	—	—		250	2,450	6,125	335	24	8,040
									350	24·50	8,575
15.1,87		50	24	1,200		—	—	—	385	24	9,240
									350	24·50	8,575
22.1.87		350	26	9,100		—	—	—	385	24	9,240
									350	24·50	8,575
									350	26	9,100
24.1.87		—	—	—		300	26	7,800	385	24	9,240
									350	24·50	8,575
									50	26	1,300
27.1.87		—	—	—		50	26	1,300			
						350	24·50	8,575			
						100	24	2,400	285	24	6,840
28.1.87		500	27	13,500		—	—	—	285	24	6,840
									500	27	13,500
31.1.87		—	—	—		300	27	8,100	285	24	6,840
									200	27	5,400

Problem 20

The following are the details supplied by J.K. Corporation in respect of its raw materials for the month of December 1988 :

Date	Receipts (units)	Price Per unit (Rs.)	Issued (units)
1.12.88	2,000 (opening)	5·00	
7.12.88	1,000	6·00	
10·12.88			2,500
15.12.88	2,000	6·50	
31.12.88			2,200

On 31.12.88 a shortage of 100 units was found. Find the values of issues and resulting stocks on different dates using (*i*) LIFO, (*ii*) FIFO; and (*iii*) Simple Average methods.

[*C.U. B.Com. (Hons.)*]

Solution

Stores Ledger Account—LIFO Method

Date	Receipts				Issues				Balance		
	G.R. No.	*Qty. Kg.*	*Rate Rs.*	*Amount Rs.*	*S.R. No.*	*Qty. kg.*	*Rate Rs.*	*Amount Rs.*	*Qty. kg.*	*Rate Rs.*	*Amount Rs.*
1.12.88		—	—	—		—	—	—	2,000	5·00	10,000
7.12.88		1,000	6·00	6,000		—	—	—	3000 {2,000 1,000	5·00 6·00	10,000 6,000 } 16,000
10.12.88		—	—	—		2,500 {1,000 1,500	6·00 5·00	6,000 7,500 } 13,500	500	5·00	2,500
15.12.88		2,000	6·50	13,000		—	—	—	2,500 {500 2,000	5·00 6·50	2,500 13,000 } 15,500
31.12.88		—	—	—		2,200 {2,000 200	6·50 5·00	13,000 1,000 } 14,000			
						100	5·00	500	200	5·00	1,000

Stores Ledger Account—FIFO Method

Date	Receipts				Issues				Balance		
	G.R. No.	*Qty. Kg.*	*Rate Rs.*	*Amount Rs.*	*S.R. No.*	*Qty. kg.*	*Rate Rs.*	*Amount Rs.*	*Qty. kg.*	*Rate Rs.*	*Amount Rs.*
1.12.88		—	—	—		—	—	—	2,000	5·00	10,000
7.12.88		1,000	6·00	6,000		—	—	—	2,000	5·00	10,000
									1,000	6·00	6,000
10.12.88		—	—	—		2,000	5·00	10,000			
						500	6·00	3,000	500	6·00	3,000
15.12.88		2,000	6·50	13,000		—	—	—	500	6·00	3,000
									2,000	6·50	13,000
31.12.88		—	—	—		500	6·00	3,000			
						1,700	6·50	11,050			
						100	6·50	650	200	6·50	1,300

Stores Ledger Account—Simple Average Method

Date	Receipts				Issues				Balance		
	G.R. No.	*Qty. kg.*	*Rate Rs.*	*Amount Rs.*	*S.R. No.*	*Qty. kg.*	*Rate Rs.*	*Amount Rs.*	*Qty. kg.*	*Rate Rs.*	*Amount Rs.*
1.12.88		—	—	—		—	—	—	2,000	5·00	10,000
7.12.88		1,000	6·00	6,000		—	—	—	3,000	—	16,000
10.12.88		—	—	—		2,500	5·50[1]	13,750	500	—	2,250
15.12.88		2,000	6·50	13,000		—	—	—	2,500	—	15,250
31.12.88		—	—	—		2,200	6·25[2]	13,750	200	6·50	1,300
						100	6·50	650			

Working Notes :

[1. Rate of stock issued on 10.12.88 = $\frac{\text{Rs. } 5{\cdot}00 + \text{Rs. } 6{\cdot}00}{2}$ = Rs.5·50

[2. Value of stock issued on 31.12.88 = $\frac{\text{Rs. } 6{\cdot}00 + \text{Rs. } 6{\cdot}50}{2}$ = Rs. 6·25 (Here opening Stock rate *i.e.* Rs. 5 will not be considered as it has already been exhausted).

Problem 21

The following are the details supplied by AB Ltd. in respect of its raw materials for the month of December 1988 :

	Receipts		*Issues*
Date	*Units*	*Amount (Rs.)*	*Issues (units)*
1.11.90	1,000 (opening)	6,000	
10.11.90	500	3,500	
15.11.90			1,200
20.11.90	1,000	8,000	
30.11.90			1,100

On 30th November 1990 a shortage of 50 units was found. Find the values of issues and resulting stocks on different dates using (*a*) LIFO, (*b*) Simple Average and (*c*) Weighted Average.

[*C.U. B.Com. (Hons.) 1991*]

Solution

Stores Ledger Account—LIFO Method
AB Limited

	Receipts				*Issues*				*Balance*		
Date	*G.R. No.*	*Qty. kg*	*Rate Rs.*	*Amount Rs.*	*S.R. No.*	*Qty. kg*	*Rate Rs.*	*Amount Rs.*	*Qty. kg*	*Rate Rs.*	*Amount Rs.*
1.11.90		—	—	—		—	—	—	1,000	6·00	6,000
10.11.90		500	7·00	3,500		—	—	—	1,000	6·00	6,000
									500	7·00	3,500
15.11.90		—	—	—		500	7·00	3,500			
						700	6·00	4,200	300	6·00	1,800
20.11.90		1,000	8·00	8,000		—	—	—	300	6·00	1,800
									1,000	8·00	8,000
30.11.90		—	—	—		1,000	8·00	8,000			
						100	6·00	600			
						50	6·00	300	150	6·00	900

Stores Ledger Account—Simple Average

	Receipts				*Issues*				*Balance*		
Date	*G.R. No.*	*Qty. kg*	*Rate Rs.*	*Amount Rs.*	*S.R. No.*	*Qty. kg*	*Rate Rs.*	*Amount Rs.*	*Qty. kg*	*Rate Rs.*	*Amount Rs.*
1.11.90		—	—	—		—	—	—	1,000	6·00	6,000
10.11.90		500	7·00	3,500		—	—	—	1,500	—	9,500
15.11.90		—	—	—		1,200	6·50	7,800	300	—	1,700
20.11.90		1,000	8·00	8,000		—	—	—	1,300	—	9,700
30.11.90		—	—	—		1,100	7·50	8,250	200	—	1,450
						50	8·00	400	150	—	1,050

Stores Ledger Account—Weighted Average

Date	Receipts				Issues				Balance		
	G.R. No.	Qty. kg	Rate Rs.	Amount Rs.	S.R. No.	Qty. kg	Rate Rs.	Amount Rs.	Qty. kg	Rate Rs.	Amount Rs.
1.11.90		—	—	—		—	—	—	1,000	6·000	6,000
10.11.90		500	7·00	3,500		—	—	—	1,500	6·330	9,500
15.11.90		—	—	—		1,200	6·33[1]	7,600	300	6·330	1,900
20.11.90		1,000	8·00	8,000		—	—	—	1,300	7·615	9,900
30.11.90		—	—	—		1,100	7·615[2]	8,377			
						50	7·615	381	150	7·615	1,142

Working Notes :

(*i*) Rate of material issued on 15.11.90 $= \dfrac{6{,}000 + 3{,}500}{1{,}000 + 500} = \dfrac{9{,}500}{1{,}500} =$ Rs. 6·33.

(*ii*) Rate of material issued on 30.11.90 $= \dfrac{1{,}900 + 8{,}000}{300 + 1{,}000}$

$= \dfrac{9{,}900}{1{,}300} =$ Rs. 7,615

Problem 22

The stock of materials of a company on 1.7.90 was 1,000 units at Rs. 2 per unit. Further purchases were made during the month as follows :

4th July 200 units @ Rs. 2·50 per unit
10 " 500 " @ Rs. 3·00 " "
20 " 1,000 " @ Rs. 3·50 " "

The issues during the period were as follows :

12th July 1,600 units
28th July 900 units.

What would be the value of the closing stock at the end of the month on the basis of materials being treated to have been issued according to :

(*i*) First-in-first out method ?
(*ii*) Weighted average method ?
(*iii*) Last-in-first-out method ?

[*C.U. B.Com. (Hons.)—Adopted*]

Solution

(*i*) **First-in-first out Method**

Opening stock of material		1,000 units
Purchases of materials :		
on 4.7.90	200 units	
on 10.7.90	500 units	
on 20.7.90	1,000 units	
		1,700 units
		2,700 units
Consumption :		
on 12.7.90	1,600 units	
on 28.7.90	900 units	
		2,500 units
		200 units

∴ Valuation of closing stock :

200 units @ Rs. 3·50 per unit = Rs. 700

(The per unit rate of closing stock at Rs. 3·50, because the last purchase was 1,000 units; it is more than 200 units).

(*ii*) **Weighted-Average Method**

		Qty. (units)	Rate (Rs.)	Amount (Rs.)
1.7.90	Opening Stock of Materials	1,000	2·00	2,000
4.7.90	Purchases of Materials	200	2·50	500
10.7.90	Purchases of Materials	500	3·00	1,500
		1,700	2·353*	4,000
12.7.90	Issues of Materials	1,600	2·353	3,765
		100		235
20.7.90	Purchases of Materials	1,000	3·50	3,500
		1,100	3·395**	3,735
28.7.90	Issues of Materials	900	3·395	3,056
		200	3·395	679

Working Notes

$$* \frac{\text{Rs. } 4{,}000}{1{,}700} = \text{Rs. } 2{\cdot}353$$

$$** \frac{\text{Rs. } 3{,}735}{1{,}100} = \text{Rs. } 3{\cdot}395$$

(*iii*) **Last-in-first out Method**

		Per unit Rs. 2·00	Rs. 2·50	Rs. 3·00	Rs. 3·50
1.7.90	Opening Stock of Materials	1,000	—	—	—
4.7.90	Purchases of Materials	—	200	—	—
10.7.90	Purchases of Materials	—	—	500	—
12.7.90	Issues of Materials	900	200	500	—
		100	—	—	—
20.7.90	Purchases of Materials	—	—	—	1,000
28.7.90	Issues of Materials	—	—	—	900
Balance on 31.7.90		100	—	—	100

∴ Valuation of Closing Stock

	Rs.
100 units @ Rs. 2·00	200
100 units @ Rs. 3·50	350
	550

Comparative Statement

Method	Valuation of Closing Stock of 200 units
(i) First-in-first-out	Rs. 700
(*ii*) Weighted Average	Rs. 679
(*iii*) Last-in-first-out	Rs. 550

Problem 23

Following information about materials is available in respect of a manufacturing company :

(*i*) January 1, 1988 purchased 6,000 kg @ Rs. 15 per kg

(*ii*) January 2, 1988 purchased 10,000 kg @ Rs. 16 per kg

(*iii*) January 3, 1988 issued 10,000 kg

(*iv*) January 4, 1988 purchased 4,000 kg @ Rs. 18 per kg

Determine the value of stock on 4.1.1988 (at closing hour) under : (1) FIFO Method; (2) LIFO Method; (3) Simple Average Method; (4) Weighted Average Method.

(The answer is not required to be given in normal Stores Ledger form; but calculation procedure in detail should be clearly shown.) ***[B.U. B.Com. (Hons.) 1987—Adopted]***

Solution

(1) **Under FIFO Method**

On 3rd January 1988, 6,000 kg of materials @ Rs. 15 per kg and 4,000 kg of materials @ Rs. 16 per kg are issued to manufacturing centre.

On 4th January 1988, there is closing stock 6,000 kg of materials @ Rs. 16 per kg and 4,000 kg of materials @ Rs. 18 per kg *i.e.,* 10,000 kg for Rs. 1,68,000.

(2) **Under LIFO Method**

On 3rd January 1988, 10,000 kg @ Rs. 16 per kg are issued to manufacturing centre. On 4th January 1988, there is a closing stock of 6,000 kg @ 15 per kg and 4,000 kg @ Rs. 18 per kg *i.e.,* 10,000 kg for Rs. 1,62,000.

(3) **Under Simple Average Price Method**

This method is based on FIFO Principle. On 3rd January 1988, 10,000 kg of materials are issued to manufacturing centre @ Rs. $\left(\frac{15+16}{2}\right)$ or Rs. 15·50 per kg. So the purchase of 6,000 kg materials on 1st January 1988 are fully issued. For this reason, the closing stock on 4th January 1988, 10,000 kg (6,000 + 4,000), are valued @ Rs. $\left(\frac{16+18}{2}\right)$ or Rs. 17 per kg *i.e.* 10,000 kg for Rs. 1,70,000.

(4) **Under Weighted Average Method**

On 3rd January 1988 10,000 kg of materials are issued @

$$\frac{6{,}000 \text{ kg} \times \text{Rs. } 15 + 10{,}000 \text{ kg} \times \text{Rs.}16}{(6{,}000 + 10{,}000) \text{ kg}} \text{ or Rs. } 15{\cdot}625 \text{ per kg.}$$

On 4th January, 1988, Closing Stock of materials is in valued at

$$\frac{6{,}000 \text{ kg} \times \text{Rs. } 15{\cdot}625 + 4{,}000 \text{ kg} \times \text{Rs. } 18}{(6{,}000 + 4{,}000) \text{ kg}} \text{ or Rs. } 16{\cdot}575 \text{ per kg.}$$

i.e., value of closing stock of 10,000 kg as on 4th January 1988, is Rs. 1,65,750.

Problem 24

The following transactions took place in respect of an item of raw material used in a factory, during the month of December 1989 :

Date 1989	*Quantity*	*Purchase*	*Issued Quantity*
Dec. 1	500 kg	Rs. 2·00	
" 10	300 kg	Rs. 2·10	—
" 15	—	—	600 kg
" 20	400 kg	Rs. 2·20	—
" 25	—	—	300 kg
" 27	500 kg	Rs. 2·10	—
" 31	—	—	200 kg

Write-up the Stores Ledger Account showing therein the above transactions assuming that the factory always maintains a Base Stock of 200 kg @ Rs. 2·00 per kg and follows the 'first-in-first-out' method of pricing.

Sol. (*see next page*)

Solution. (Problem 24)

STORES LEDGER ACCOUNT (Base Stock Method)

Material's Name .... Maximum Level.........
Code No. .... Re-order Level.............
Location .... Minimum Level..........

Date	Receipts				Issues				Balances			Remarks
	G.R. No.	*Qty. kg.*	*Rate Rs.*	*Amount Rs.*	*S.R. No.*	*Qty. kg.*	*Rate Rs.*	*Amount Rs.*	*Qty. kg.*	*Rate Rs.*	*Amount Rs.*	
1989 Dec. 1		500	2·00	1,000		—	—	—	500	200	10,000	
" 10		300	2·10	630		—	—	—	800 {500 300}	2·00 2·10	1,000 630} 1,630	
" 15		—	—	—		600 {300 300}	2·00 2·10	600 630} 1,230	200	200	400	
" 20		400	2·20	880		—	—	—	600 {200 400}	2·00 2·20	400 880} 1,280	
" 25		—	—	—		300	2·20	660	300 {200 100}	2·00 2·20	400 220} 620	
" 27		500	2·10	1,050		—	—	—	800 {200 100 500}	2·00 2·20 2·10	400 220 1,050} 1,670	
" 31		—	—	—		200 {100 100}	2·20 2·10	220 210} 430	600 {200 400}	2·00 2·10	400 840} 1,240	

Problem 25

From the following particulars in respect of a certain material during April 1992, you are required to draw up Store Ledger under Periodic *Simple* and Periodic *Weighted* Average Method :

1992		
April 1	Stock in hand	200 units @ Rs. 5·00
" 4	Purchases	400 units @ Rs. 6·00
" 7	Issued	300 units
" 12	Purchases	100 units @ Rs. 7·00
" 16	Returned to Stores	50 units [which were issued out of opening stock]
" 20	Purchases	200 units @ Rs. 8·00
" 25	Issued	400 units
" 28	Returned to vendors	50 units

A shortage of 50 units was noticed and recorded on 26th April.

Solution

Stores Ledger (Under Periodic Simple Average Method)

Date	Receipts				Issues				Balance		Remarks
	G.R. No.	*Qty. Units*	*Rate Rs.*	*Amount Rs.*	*S.R. No.*	*Qty. Units*	*Rate Rs.*	*Amount Rs.*	*Qty. Units*	*Amount Rs.*	
1990											
April 1		—	—	—		—	—	—	200	1,000	
" 4		400	6	2,400		—	—	—	600	3,400	
" 7		—	—	—		300	7	2,100	300	1,300	
" 12		100	7	700		—	—	—	400	2,000	
" 16		50	5	250		—	—	—	450	2,250	Returned
" 20		200	8	1,600		—	—	—	650	3,850	
" 25		—	—	—		400	7	2,800	250	1,050	
" 26		—	—	—		50	7	350	200	700	Shortage
" 28		—	—	—		50	7	350	150	350	Returned

Working Notes :

$$\text{Periodic Simple Average Rate} = \frac{\text{Total of the unit price during the period}}{\text{Frequency of purchase}}$$

$$= \frac{\text{Rs. }(6+7+8)}{3} = \frac{21}{3} = \text{Rs. } 7$$

Stores Ledger Under Periodic Weighted Average Method

Date	Receipts				Issues				Balance		Remarks
	G.R. No.	*Qty. Units*	*Rate Rs.*	*Amount Rs.*	*S.R. No.*	*Qty. Units*	*Rate Rs.*	*Amount Rs.*	*Qty. Units*	*Amount Rs.*	
1990											
April 1		—	—	—		—	—	—	200	1,000	
" 4		400	6	2,400		—	—	—	600	3,400	
" 7		—	—	—		300	6·72	2,016	300	1,384	
" 12		100	7	700		—	—	—	400	2,084	
" 16		50	5	250		—	—	—	450	2,334	Returned
" 20		200	8	1,600		—	—	—	650	3,934	
" 25		—	—	—		400	6·72	2,688	250	1,246	
" 26		—	—	—		50	6·72	336	200	910	Shortage
" 28		—	—	—		50	6·72	336	150	574	Returned

Working Notes :

$$\text{Weighted Periodic Average Method} = \frac{\text{Value of goods purchased during the period}}{\text{Total units of purchase}}$$

$$= \frac{\text{Rs. } (2{,}400 + 700 + 1{,}600)}{400 + 100 + 200} = \frac{4{,}700}{700} = \text{Rs. } 6{\cdot}72$$

Problem 26

New Cycle House is a distributor of bicycles. On 30.6.07 stock-in-hand was 200 units which had a value of Rs. 8,400.

Transaction for the six months to 31st December were as follows :

Month	*Purchase Quantity (Units)*	*Cost per unit Rs.*
July	200	46·00
August	500	49·40
September	1,000	52·50

The purchase manager obatined a bulk purchase discount of Rs. 7·50 per unit on the September purchases :

Month	*Sale Quantity (Units)*	*Unit Sale Price (Rs.)*
October	500	66·00
November	700	70·00
December	500	75·00

There were no sales during the first three months of the period. Using the FIFO, LIFO and Cumulative weighted average methods of stock valuation, you are required to :

(*a*) Prepare the Store Ledger.

(*b*) Prepare trading accounts for the six months period using each of the three valuation methods; and

(*c*) Indicate which valuation method is the best measure of profit and why ?

Solution

Stores Ledger Under FIFO Method

Month	*Receipts*			*Issues*			*Balance*		
2007	*Units*	*Rate*	*Amount*	*Units*	*Rate*	*Amount*	*Units*	*Rate*	*Amount*
30th June (Op. Bal.)	—	—	—	—	—	—	200	42·00	8,400
July	200	46	9,200	—	—	—	200 200 } 400	42 46	17,600
Aug.	500	49·40	24,700	—	—	—	200 200 500	42 46 49·40	42,300
Sept.	1,000	52·50	52,500	—	—	—	200 200 500 1,000	42 46 49·40 52·50	94,800
Oct.	—	—	—	200 200 100	42 46 49·40	8,400 9,200 4,940	400 1,000	49·40 52·50	72,260
Nov.	—	—	—	400 300	49·40 52·50	19,760 15,750	700	52·50	36,750
Dec.	—	—	—	500	52·50	26,250	200	52·50	10,500

Stores Ledger Under LIFO Method

Month	Receipts			Issues			Balance		
2007	*Units*	*Rate*	*Amount*	*Units*	*Rate*	*Amount*	*Units*	*Rate*	*Amount*
30th June (Op. Bal.)	—	—	—	—	—	—	200	42·00	8,400
July	200	46	9,200	—	—	—	200 200	42 46	17,600
Aug.	500	49·40	24,700	—	—	—	200 200 500	42 46 49·40	42,300
Sept.	1,000	52·50	52,500	—	—	—	200 200 500 1,000	42 46 49·4 52·5	94,800
Oct.	—	—	—	500	52·5	26,250	200 200 500 500	42 46 49·4 52·5	68,550
Nov.	—	—	—	500 200	52·5 49·4	36,130	200 200 300	42 46 49·4	32,240
Dec.	—	—	—	300 200	49·4 46	24,020	200	42	8,400

Stores Ledger Under Cumulative Weighted Average Method

Month	Receipts			Issues			Balance		
2007	*Units*	*Rate*	*Amount*	*Units*	*Rate*	*Amount*	*Units*	*Rate*	*Amount*
30th June (Op. Bal.)	—	—	—	—	—	–	200	42	8,400
July	200	46	9,200	—	—	—	400	—	17,600
Aug.	500	49·40	24,700	—	—	—	900	—	42,300
Sept.	1,000	52·50	52,500	—	—	—	1,900	—	94,800
Oct.	—	—	—	500	49·8947*	24,947	1,400	—	69,853
Nov.	—	—	—	700	49·8947	34,926	700	—	34,927
Dec.	—	—	—	500	49·8947	24,947	200	—	9,980

* Calculation to Weighted Average Rate $= \frac{\text{Rs. } 94,800}{1,900} =$ Rs. 49·89

(*b*) (*i*) **Calculation for purchases during the period**

	Rs.
July	9,200
Aug.	24,700
Sept.	52,500
	86,400

(*ii*) **Calculation for Total Sales during the period**

Oct. = 500 × Rs. 66	33,000
Nov. = 700 × Rs. 70	49,000
Dec. = 500 × Rs. 75	37,500
	1,19,500

Trading A/c for 6 Months

Particular	*FIFO*	*LIFO*	*Weighted Average*	*Particulars*	*FIFO*	*LIFO*	*Weighted Average*
To Op. Stock	8,400	8,400	8,400	By Sales	1,19,500	1,19,500	1,19,500
To Purchase	86,400	86,400	86,400	By Cl. Stock	10,500	8,400	9,980
To Gross Profit	35,200	33,100	34,680				
	1,30,000	1,27,900	1,29,480		1,30,000	1,27,900	1,29,480

(*c*) In this case prices are on increasing trend. Hence LIFO method is better, because in this method issues are valued at current prices. Price arrived will be lower and more accurate as the replacement material will be at current price.

EXERCISES

1. *State which of the following statements are wrong and which are correct :*

(*a*) Original copy of the purchase order is retained by the purchasing department.
(*b*) Goods Received note is prepared by the goods receiving clerk.
(*c*) Purchase control is exercised by the storekeeper.
(*d*) Purchase requisition is sent by the purchasing department.
(*e*) Tender form is issued by the purchasing department.
(*f*) Purchase order is prepared by the purchasing department.
(*g*) Material turnover ratio is calculated by dividing the cost of material consumed by cost of average stock held.
(*h*) Under the ABC analysis of material control, 'A' stands for high value items.
(*i*) Bin card makes a record of the quantity and value of material kept in stores.
(*j*) The perpetual inventory system enables management to ascertain stock without physical verification.
(*k*) The perpetual inventory system means a continuous stock taking system.
(*l*) Orders should automatically be placed with the supplier quoting the lowest price.
(*m*) The purchase department is a service department.
(*n*) Centralisation or decentralisation of purchases is only a matter of managerial policy which need not be taken much cognisance of.
(*o*) Routing the purchase requisition through the purchase department entails unnecessary delay in receiving the required materials.
(*p*) The purchase manager is himself the controller of materials.
(*q*) Lack of an efficient material control system increases the material cost component of the end product.
(*r*) Material control is a term used to control the prices of scarce materials.

[Ans. Correct : (*b*), (*e*), (*f*), (*h*), (*j*), (*k*), (*m*), (*q*).
Wrong : (*a*), (*c*), (*d*), (*g*), (*i*), (*l*), (*n*), (*o*), (*p*), (*r*).]

2. *Which of the following is correct (C)/False (F) :*

(*a*) Valuation of closing stock is same under FIFO and LIFO method.
(*b*) The cost of primary packing is a part of prime cost, whereas cost of secondary packing is a selling and distribution overhead.
(*c*) Loss in the value of returnable containers is treated as selling and distribution overhead.
(*d*) Defectives are that portion of production which can be rectified at some extra cost.
(*e*) Wastage can be realised, whereas scrap cannot be realised.
(*f*) Abnormal wastage should be a part of the cost of production.
(*g*) Normal wastage is avoidable.
(*h*) A bill of material gives a complete list of all materials required with quantities for a particular job.

[Ans. (*a*) F, (*b*) C, (*c*) C, (*d*) C, (*e*) F, (f) F, (*g*) F, (*h*) C.]

3. *Which of the following is correct ?*

A. Which of the following is the correct valuation base for finished goods stock for balance sheet valuation purpose ?

(*i*) Prime cost per unit (*ii*) Production cost per unit
(*iii*) Production margin per unit (*iv*) Total cost per unit.

B. A perpetual inventory system may be defined as :

(*i*) The checking of physical stock against the bin card information on a continuous basic.
(*ii*) The documentation system which records all stores transaction on a continuous basic.
(*iii*) The checking of stock on the same date in each accounting period.
(*iv*) Ensuring that stock taking procedures conform to a previously agreed procedure.

C. Which of the following does not usually appear on a GRN ?

(*i*) Date received (*ii*) Price of goods
(*iii*) Quantity received (*iv*) Description of goods

D. A purchase requisition is raised :

(*i*) To intimate to the supplier the quantity and quality of new material required.
(*ii*) When the stock of a raw material has fallen to the re-order level.
(*iii*) When goods are received from a supplier.
(*iv*) To let the accounts department know that an invoice should be expected from a supplier.

E. If the raw materials prices are suffering from inflation, which of the following methods of valuing stocks will give the lowest gross profit ?

(*i*) LIFO (*ii*) FIFO
(*iii*) Replacement cost (*iv*) Simple average.

F. Which of the following is disadvantage of the FIFO method of stock valuation ?

(*i*) Physical issue must follow the same order as physical receipts.
(*ii*) One issue may be split between two or more different deliveries for costing purpose.
(*iii*) Jobs started on the same day must be issued with stock from the same delivery.
(*iv*) It is necessary to analyse deliveries particular issues have been obtained from.

G. Re-ordering quantity may be measured is :

(*i*) Weighted average cost (*ii*) FIFO (First-in-first-out)
(*iii*) Standard cost (*iv*) LIFO (Last-in-First-out)

H. Which of the following source documents in a cost accounting system is designed to exercise control over the delivery of and accurate recording of the receipts of goods ?

(*i*) Goods received note (*ii*) Material requisition
(*iii*) Order to the supplier (*iv*) Purchase requisition.

I. A written request to a supplier for specified goods at an agreed upon price is called a :

(*i*) Purchase order (*ii*) Receiving report
(*iii*) Purchase requisition (*iv*) Materials requisition form

J. The total of the materials subsidiary ledger inventory cards must be equal to the amount in the following account :

(*i*) Cost of goods sold (*ii*) Material inventory
(*iii*) Purchase of raw materials (*iv*) Work-in-process inventory.

K. Under a periodic inventory system, the purchase of materials is recorded in an account entitled :

(*i*) Cost of goods sold (*ii*) Purchase of raw materials
(*iii*) Material inventory (*iv*) Work-in-process inventory.

L. Under a perpetual inventory system, the purchase of raw materials is recorded in an account entitled :

(*i*) Cost of goods sold (*ii*) Purchase of raw materials
(iii) Work-in-process inventory (*iv*) Material inventory.

M. Which of the following forms must be filled out when an inventory is to be removed from the materials inventory to be placed into production ?

(*i*) Purchase order (*ii*) Receiving report
(*iii*) Purchase requisition (*iv*) Material requisition form

N. A written request to a supplier for specified goods at an agreed upon price is called a :
(i) Purchase order (ii) Purchase requisition
(iii) Receiving report (iv) Material requisition.

[Ans. A (*ii*) ; B (*ii*) ; C (*ii*) ; D (*ii*) ; (E) (*i*) ; F (*ii*) ; G (*iv*) ; H (*i*) ; I (*i*) ; J (*ii*) ; K (*iii*) ; L (*iv*) ; M (*ii*) ; N (*i*).]

THEORETICAL QUESTIONS

(*a*) Pricing & Storing

1. State in brief the advantages and disadvantages of centralised and decentralised stores. **[*I.C.W.A. (Int.)*]**

2. What do you understand by Economic Order Quantity ? Discuss what factors are to be taken into consideration for deciding this quantity.

3. What do you mean by the expressions 'Maximum Level', 'Minimum Level' and 'Re-ordering Level' ? What factors are to be taken into account in fixing these levels ? **[*I.C.W.A. (Int.)*] [*C.U. B.Com. (Hons.)*]**

4. Distinguish between Bin Card and Stores Ledger. Give a specimen of Bin Card with four imaginary transactions. **[*C.U. B.Com. (Hons.)*]**

5. In material management, what do you understand by (*i*) Maximum Level (*ii*) Minimum Level; and (*iii*) Ordering Level ? **[*I.C.W.A. Dec. 1994*]**

(*b*) Issues and Control

1. What are the methods of pricing materials issues ? When do you advocate pricing the issues at the highest purchase price ?

2. Describe the various methods of pricing materials issued for production and point out their advantages and disadvantages.

3. It is often suggested that the proper control of inventories can make a substantial contribution to the efficiency of a business. Discuss this and suggest control measures which might be applied. **[*I.C.W.A. (Int.)*]**

4. What do you mean by Perpetual Inventory System ? How does it differ from continuous stock-taking ? State the advantages of the Perpetual Inventory System. **[*C.U. B.Com. (Hons.)*]**

5. Define a 'Bill of Materials' and explain fully the purpose it serves. Give the specimen of 'Bill of a Materials'. **[*C.U. B.Com. (Hons.)*]**

6. Write short notes on :
(*a*) Bin card (*b*) Perpetual Inventory (*c*) Weighted Average Price (*d*) Bill of Materials
(*e*) Purchase Requisition (*f*) Stores Ledger (*g*) Stock Turnover. **[*C.U. B.Com. (Hons.)*]**

PROBLEMS

1. Two components *A* and *B* are used as below :
Minimum usage : 25 units per week each
Maximum usage : 7·5 units per week each
Maximum stock levels : *A* = 650 units
B = 750 units
Re-order period : *A* = 4 to 6 weeks.
B = 2 to 4 weeks.

Calculate for each component : (*i*) Re-order level, (*ii*) Minimum level, (*iii*) Re-order quantity. **[*B.U. B.Com. (Hons.) 1988*]**

[Ans.

	A	*B*
(*i*) Re-order level	**450 units**	**300 units**
(*ii*) Minimum level	**200 units**	**150 units**
(*iii*) Re-order quantity	**300 units**	**500 units]**

2. The following information is available in respect of component 20 :
Maximum Stock Level : 8,000 units
Budget Consumption : Maximum 1,500 units per month
Minimum 800 units per month

Estimated delivery period : Maximum 4 months
Minimum 2 months

You are required to calculate : (*i*) re-order level, and (*ii*) re-order quantity. [*I.C.W.A. Inter*

[Ans. (*i*) 6,000 units (*ii*) 4,000 units

3. From the following information you are required to calculate maximum level, minimum level and ordering level for materials *X* and *Y* :

	X	*Y*
Normal usage per week	150	200
Reordering Quantity	900	1,500
Maximum usage per week	225	250
Minimum usage per week	75	100
Re-ordering Period (weeks)	12 to 18	6 to 12

[*I.C.W.A. (Int.) Dec. 1994*

4. In a factory component *A* is used as follows :

Normal usage	50 kg per week
Minimum usage	25 kg per week
Maximum usage	75 kg per week
Re-order quantity	300 kg.
Re-order period	4 to 6 weeks.

Calculate for component *A* :

(*i*) Re-order level ; (*ii*) Maximum level ; (*iii*) Minimum level and (*iv*) Average stock level.

[*C.U. B.Com. (Hons.) 1994*

[Ans. (*i*) 450; (*ii*) 650; (*iii*) 200; (*iv*) 425

5. A company, for one of the *A* class items, placed 6 orders each of size 200 in a year. Given orderin cost Rs. 600, holding cost 40%, cost per unit Rs. 40. Find out the loss to the company because i is not operating scientific inventory policy.

What are your recommendations for the future ?

[*C.A. Final, Nov. 1985*

[Ans. EOQ—300 units; Loss on Materials = 400

6. A publishing house purchases 200 units of a particular item per year at an unit cost of Rs. 20, th ordering cost per order is Rs. 50 and the inventory carrying cost is 25 per cent.

Find the optimal order quantity and minimum total cost including purchase cost.

If a 3 per cent discount is offered by the supplier for purchases in lots of 1,000 or more, shoul the publishing house accept the proposal ? [*I.C.W.A. (Final), June 198*

[Ans. EOQ = 200 units; Total Cost = Rs. 41,000; (without Discount) = Rs. 41,325; (wit 3% Discount

7. A company uses 2,500 units of a component having a constant usage are usually which it purchase from an outside supplier under the following terms :

Order Quantity :	100-499	500-2,499	2,500-4,999	5000-over
Price per unit :	Rs. 5·00	Rs. 4·75	Rs. 4·06	Rs. 4·05

The ordering cost is Rs. 100 and the holding cost, expressed as a percentage of unit price, is 1 per cent per year. No safety stock is held.

If the component is used at a uniform rate, calculate the economic order size and the total annu cost to the company. [*I.C.W.A.I. Fina*

[Ans. EOQ= 2,500 untis; Total annual cost = Rs. 10,757·5

8. Annual consumption of a material of a company is 1,00,000 units at Rs. 2·40 per unit. Each ord costs Rs. 90 and carrying cost is 15% of the annual average inventory value. The company operat 250 days per year. The procurement time is 10 days and safety stock is 1,000 units.

Calculate Maximum Stock Level. [*C.U. B.Com. (Hons.) 200*

[Ans. 8,071 units

9. Two materials, *X* and *Y*, are used as follows :

Minimum usage	50 units per week each
Maximum usage	150 units per week each
Normal usage	100 units per week each

Ordering quantity : X = 600 units and Y = 1,000 units

Delivery period : X = 4 to 6 weeks, Y = 2 to 4 weeks

Calculate for each material : (*a*) Minimum level, (*b*) Maximum level ; and (*c*) Ordering level.

[*C.A. Inter*]

[Ans.	***X***	***Y***
(*a*) Minimum level	**4000 units**	**300 units**
(*b*) Maximum level	**1,300 units**	**600 units**
(*c*) Ordering level	**900 units**	**600 units]**

10. A company uses 10,000 units per year of an item costing Rs. 5 each. The cost of processing a purchase order is Rs. 100 and the stock holding cost amounts to 20% per year of the money value of inventory.

How much should the company buy at a time (in a single order) in order to minimise the inventory cost ? [*I.C.W.A. (Final)*]

[Ans. 1,414 units (approx.)]

11. A company is trying to establish a control policy to reduce inventory costs of a spare part no. 003-04-117. The financial manager estimates that a three week delivery schedule can be expected. The purchase price per unit is Rs. 6 and purchase order cost is Rs. 24. The total purchase requirement for a 50 week year is estimated to be 4,000 units and carrying costs are estimated at 20% of average inventory value.

You are required to compute : (*i*) The EOQ ; (*ii*) the optional number of orders to be placed ; and (*iii*) the minimum level of inventory before re-ordering.

[*C.U. M.Com.*]

[Ans. (*i*) EOQ = 400 units (*ii*) Optional No. of orders = 10 times (*iii*) Minimum level of inventory before reordering = 240 units]

12. A company's monthly requirement of an inventory item is 1,800 units. The cost of processing an order is Rs. 5 and the carrying cost per unit is 20 paise.

The company's supplier agrees to offer quantity discount as under :

Lot Size (in units)	up to 400	401-600	601-800	801-1,000	1,000-Above
Discount (in Rs.)	Nil	6	10	15	20

Lead time is 2 days and the company wishes to keep a safety stock equal to 50% of the usage in the lead time :

(*a*) Find the Economic Ordering Quantity (EOQ) with considering the offer of discount.

(*b*) Explain the reasons for your calculations.

(*c*) Calculate re-ordering point taking 30 working days in month.

(*d*) Tabulate different types of cost as also effect of discount on different order sizes taking 1, 2, 3.....7 orders a month and indicate the EOQ. [*C.A. (Final)*]

[Ans. EOQ = 1,000 units; (approx.) safety stock = 60 units; Re-order point = 180 units; EOQ = 450 units]

13. A manufacturer requires 1,80,000 unit component for use during the next year which is assumed to consist of 250 working days. The cost per unit of component is Rs. 20 and ordering cost per order is Rs. 100. The manufacturer maintains safety stock of one month's requirement to meet emergency. The cost of storing one component is supposed to be 10% per unit of average inventory. Find out reordering quantity and total cost.

What will be your decision if the manufacturer gets concession of 5% on purchase price, if (*i*) it orders 15,000 units or more but less than 20,000 units. (*iii*) on order of 20,000 units or more it gets 2% concession in addition to 5%.

[Ans. EOQ = 4,243 units (approx.)
Total cost = at EOQ unit = 36,42,686
at 15,000 units lot = 34,78,200
at 20,000 units lot = 34,14,000
Purchase at 20,000 units lot is more economical.]

14. A company plans to consume for a particular production 1,520 units of a particular component. Last year's record indicates that the purchase department spent Rs. 25,110 for placing 7,750 orders. The average inventory was valued at Rs. 45,000 and the total storage cost was Rs. 9,000 which included wages, rent, taxes, insurance etc. relating to store department. The company borrows capital at the rate of 10% p.a.

The Safety Stock level is one month's consumption. Purchase price per unit = Rs. 10.

Find out (*i*) EOQ units (*ii*) Total cost per year. (*iii*) What inventory level should an order be placed.

[Ans. (*i*) EOQ = 70 units (approx.) (*ii*) Total cost = Rs. 15,396·28
(*iii*) Inventory level when fresh order should be placed = 197 units (approx.)]

15. M/s T.P. Limited, manufacturers of a special product, follows the policy of EOQ (Economic Order Quantity) for one of its components. The components details are as follows :

Purchase price per component	200
Cost of an order	100
Annual cost of carrying one unit	10% of purchase price
Total cost of inventory carrying and ordering per annum	4,000

The company has been offered a discount of 2% on the price of the component provided the lot size is 2,000 components at a time.

You are required to : (*a*) Compute the EOQ.

(*b*) Advise whether the quantity discount offer can be accepted.

(*c*) Would your advice differ if the company is offered 5% discount on a single order ?

[*C.S. Nov. 1994*]

[Ans. (*a*) EOQ : 200 units.
(*b*) Discount policy not to be followed. Then increases in composition.
(*c*) May be accepted. Fall in cost Rs. 3,900]

16. Eats Ltd. supplies a number of products to bakers and confectioneries. One of their products is packets of cake decoration. The cake decorations are sold in packets of twelve decorations for Rs. 20 per packet. The demand for cake decorations is very constant over a long period of time at the rate of 2,000 packets per month. The packets cost Eats Ltd. Rs. 10 each from the manufacturer and a lead time of four days is required. Ordering cost is 1·20 per order and the holding cost is 10 per cent per annum.

Calculate (*a*) (*i*) the economic order quantity; (*ii*) the total cost of ordering and carrying cake decorations per annum; (*b*) Assuming that the present stock level is 200 packets and that no buffer stocks are kept, when must the next order be placed ? Assume 360 days a year.

[C.U. M.Com]

[Ans. 240 packets.]

17. A manufacturer uses 75,000 units of a particular material per year. The material cost is Rs. 1·50 per unit and the carrying cost is estimated to be 25% p.a. of average inventory cost. The cost of placing an order is Rs. 18.

You are required to determine the economic order quantity and frequency of orders p.a.

[*C.U. B.Com. (H) 1995*]

[Ans. Economic order quantity 2,683 units Frequency of order per annum 28]

18. Sachin Ltd. furnishes the following information :

(*i*) Consumption—300 units per quarter;
(*ii*) Cost per unit Rs. 40;
(*iii*) Cost of processing an order Rs. 600;
(*iv*) Obsolescence 15%;
(*v*) Insurance on inventory 25%.

Compute :

(*a*) Economic Order Quantiy ;
(*b*) No. of orders per year ;
(*c*) Time between two consecutive orders.

A supplier offers a discount of 2% on a purchase of 600 units. Should it be accepted ? **[*C.U. B.Com. (Hons.) 1998*]**

[Ans. (*a*) 300 units ; (*b*) 4 ; (*c*) 3 months.

Total cost without discount Rs. 52,800 and with discount Rs. 52,944. Hence, the offer is not acceptable.]

19. The following data are available in respect of a material used in the production of a product of M/s Bright Ltd. for the year 2001 :

Cost of the Materials per unit—Rs. 50;

Weekly consumption—300 units;

Ordering cost per order—Rs. 650;

Stock holding cost—2% per month (on cost)

Compute (a) Economic Ordering Quantity, (b) Optimum No. of orders per year, and (c) Time lag between two consecutive orders. [*C.U. B.Com. (Hons.) 2002*]

[Ans. (*a*) 1,300 units; (*b*) 12; (*c*) 1 month.]

20. Prepare the Stores Account for the month of April 1990 from the following transactions relating to the receipt and supply of material on the basis of : (*a*) Simple Average Price; (*b*) Weighted Average Price :

Date of Receipt	*Quantity of Material*	*Rate*
5.4.90	2,000 kg	Rs. 1 per kg
15.4.90	3,000 kg	Rs. 1·2 per kg
25.4.90	1,000 kg	Rs. 1·6 per kg
Date of Issue		
8.4.90	1,000 kg	
20.4.90	2,000 kg	
28.4.90	2,000 kg	

[Ans. : (*a*) *Simple Average Price* : Value of issues : Rs. 1,000; Rs. 2,200; Rs. 2,800; Value of closing stock Rs. 1,200.

(*b*) *Weighted Average Price* : Value of issues : Rs. 1,000; Rs. 2,300; Rs. 2,600; Value of closing stock Rs. 1,300.]

21. The following is an extact of the record of receipts and issues of an item of product used in the factory during the month of July 1991 :

Date	*Particulars*	*Quantity* *kgs*	*Rate per kg.* *Rs.*
July 1	Opening Balance	500	20·08
" 2	Purchased	200	19·00
" 5	Issued	250	—
" 10	Purchased	300	19·00
" 15	Issued	100	—
" 20	Received from Production Department	20	20·00
" 25	Shortage	10	—
" 28	Received from vendor	300	18·00
" 30	Issued	200	—

Draw up a Priced Stores Ledger Card for the product showing therein the abvoe transactions. Assume that the Weighted Average Method of a pricing is adopted by the factory.

[Ans. 760 kg. Rs. 14,460]

22. Following information about material is available in respect of a manufacturing company :

(*i*) March 1, 1989 Purchase 300 kg @ Rs. 15 per kg

(*ii*) March 12, 1989 Purchase 500 kg @ Rs. 16 per kg

(*iii*) March 23, 1989 Issued 500 kg

(*iv*) March 24, 1989 Purchased 200 kg. @ Rs. 18 per kg.

Determine the value of stock on 31.3.1989 under :

(*i*) First-in-first-out method ; (*ii*) Last-in-first out method ;
(*iii*) Simple average method and (*iv*) Weighted average method.

[Ans. (*i*) FIFO = Rs. 8,400 (*ii*) LIFO = Rs. 8,100 (*iii*) Simple Average = Rs. 8,350 (*iv*) Weighted Average = Rs. 8,288]

23. The following transactions took place in respect of a raw material during the month of January, 1993 :—

Date	*Particulars*	*kg.* (Rs.)	*Rate per kg.*
Jan.			
1	Balance	1,000	9
2	Purchased	1,500	10
5	Issued	390	—
8	Shortage	10	—
15	Surplus returned by a Production Department	200	12
20	Issued	1,000	—
25	Received from Vendor	300	14
28	Issued	1,200	—
31	Issued	100	—

You are required to write up the Stores Ledger Account applying the Simple Average Method of pricing issues. ***[C.U. B.Com. (H) 1993]***

[Ans. Value of issues Rs. 3,705; Rs. 10,600; Rs. 14,500; Rs. 1,300 Value of shortage Rs. 95; Value of closing balance Rs. 400]

Note : (1) Calculation of simple average price :

For issue on 5th Jan. $\frac{9+10}{2}$ = Rs. 9·50

For shortage on 8th Jan. Rs. 9·50

For issue on 20th Jan. $\frac{9+10+12}{3}$ = Rs. 10·333 for 600 kg.

$\frac{10+12}{2}$ = Rs. 11·00 for 400 kg.

(Rs. 9 has been excluded as the stock purchased at that price has been exhausted)

For issue on 28th Jan. $\frac{10+12+14}{3}$ = Rs. 12·00 for 1,100 kg.

$\frac{10+14}{2}$ = Rs. 13·00 for 100 kg.

For issue on 31st January Rs. 13·00

(2) Surplus returned by a production department on 15th January has been treated as a new receipt.

24. From the following information select the most suitable method of pricing material issues and write up a Stores Ledger Card based on that method :

1996		
Jan. 1	Opening Balance	24,000 kg. @ Rs. 7,500 per tonne.
1	Purchased	44,000 kg. @ Rs. 7,600 per tonne.
3	Issued	10,000 kg.
5	Issued	16,000 kg.
12	Purchased	10,000 kg. @ Rs. 7,800 per tonne.
13	Issued	24,000 kg.
18	Issued	25,000 kg.
22	Purchased	50,000 kg. @ Rs. 8,000 per tonne.
28	Issued	20,000 kg.
31	Issued	22,000 kg.

On 24th January 1996 a shortage of 200 kg. was noticed in stock-taking.

[C.U. B.Com. (Hons.) (1996)]

[Ans. When prices are rising, LIFO method is the most appropriate to apply because it matches the latest cost price with each sale.
Value of issues Rs. 76,000; Rs. 1,21,600; Rs. 1,84,400; Rs. 1,87,900; Rs. 1,60,000; Rs. 1,600 (shortage); Rs. 1,76,000. Value of closing balances Rs. 84,900]

25. Record the following transactions in a specimen stores ledger using : (*a*) Weighted average method ; and (*b*) The LIFO method of pricing issues.

			Units	*Price* Rs.
March	1	Opening Balance in hand	3,000	2
	2	Purchased	2,000	2·20
	3	Issued	1,500	?
	5	Purchased	2,000	2·30
	10	Issued	1,500	?
	15	Issued	2,000	?
	20	Purchased	2,000	2·40
	31	Issued	1,500	?

In the above situation, what are the effects of each method ? [*C.U.B.Com. (Hons.) 2002*]

[Ans. (*a*) Weighted average method :
Value of issues : Rs. 3,120; Rs. 3,240; Rs. 4,320; Rs. 3,420;
Value of closing stock Rs. 5,700
(*b*) LIFO method :
Value of issues : Rs. 3,300; Rs. 3,450; Rs. 4,250; Rs. 3,600
Value of closing stock Rs. 5,200]

26. From the following particulars relating to material 'ESS', prepare a 'Stores Ledger Account' under FIFO System :

1989			
July	1	Balance b/f	900 units @ Rs. 3·30
"	5	Purchased	400 units @ Rs. 4·20
"	10	Issued	1,000 units
"	16	Issued	200 units
"	19	Returned from Production centre issued or 10-7-89	80 units
"	25	Purchased	800 units @ Rs. 4·50
"	30	Issued	500 units

A surplus of 20 units was noticed on 21.7.89.

[*C.U. B.Com. (Pass)*]

[Ans. Balance on 30.7.89 500 units of Rs. 2,250]

27. From the following particulars relating to material 'K', prepare a 'Stores Ledger Account' under 'LIFO' System :

1990			
July	1	Balance	600 units @ Rs. 3·00
"	5	Purchased	1,100 units @ Rs. 3·30
"	10	Purchased	800 units @ Rs. 3·60
"	14	Issued	1,200 units
"	19	Purchased	1,000 units @ Rs. 3·30
"	25	Issued	900 units
"	31	Issued	700 units

A surplus of 10 units and a shortage of 20 units were noticed on 16.7.90 and 30.7.90, respectively.

[*C.U. B.Com. (Pass) Adopted*]

[Ans. Rs. 2,094]

28. Show the year-end value of stock under 'First-in-first-out' method and 'Last-in-first-out' method from the following data :

Opening balance 24,000 units @ Rs. 1·00 per unit.

	Received (units)	*Issued (units)*
1st Quarter	40,000 @ Rs. 1·10	32,000
2nd Quarter	60,000 @ Rs. 1·20	52,000
3rd Quarter	50,000 @ Rs. 1·15	64,000
4th Quarter	20,000 @ Rs. 1·125	16,000

Assume that all the purchases were made on the first day of the quarter.

[Ans. FIFO : Balance after 4th Quarter 34,000; LIFO : Balance after 4th Quarter 30,700]

29. The following are the particulars of receipts and issues of a material in a factory during March 1992 :

July	1	Opening Balance	1,000 kg @ Rs. 20 per kg
"	9	Issued to jobs	500 kg
"	13	Received from supplier	400 kg @ Rs. 30 per kg
"	14	Return of surplus from a job	30 kg @ Rs. 25 per kg
"	16	Issued to jobs	305 kg
"	21	Received from supplier	600 kg @ Rs. 34 per kg
"	25	Issued to jobs	550 kg
"	29	Received from supplier	600 kg @ Rs. 35 per kg
"	31	Issued to jobs	350 kg

You are required to prepare statements to show how the values of the issues and balances of materials should be arrived at under the FIFO and LIFO systems.

[*N.B.U.B.B.Com. (Hons.)—Adopted*]

[Ans. Value of Closing Stock : Under FIFO = Rs. 32,050; Under LIFO = Rs. 24,200]

30. X Ltd. has purchased and issued the material in the following order :

April	1	Purchased	3,000 units @ Rs. 3 per unit
"	4	Purchased	6,000 units @ Rs. 4 per unit
"	6	Issued	5,000 units
"	12	Purchased	7,000 units @ Rs. 4 per unit
"	17	Issued	8,000 units
"	22	Purchased	3,000 units @ Rs. 5 per unit
"	25	Issued	1,000 units.

Ascertain the quantity of closing stock as on 30th April and state its value (in each case) if issues are made under the following methods : (*a*) Average Cost, (*b*) FIFO, (*c*) LIFO.

[*C.A. Inter—Adopted*]

[Ans. 5,000 units, (*a*) Rs. 22,200, (*b*) Rs. 23,000, (*c*) Rs. 19,000]

31. The following information regarding the receipts and issues of an item of Raw Material are available :

Date		*Receipts*	*Cost*	*Issues*
1990		Quantity (units)	*(Rs.)*	*(units)*
March	1	500	500	—
"	10	400	600	—
"	15	—	—	500
"	25	400	500	—
"	29	—	—	500

Find out the values of : (*a*) Issues made on 15th March and resulting inventory on that date; (*b*) Issues made on 29 March and the resulting inventory on that date, if the issues are made according to the (*i*) FIFO, (*ii*) LIFO, (*iii*) Simple Average Methods and (*iv*) Weighted Average Methods.

[Ans. (*i*) Stocks under FIFO : Rs. 600 & Rs. 375 (*ii*) Stocks under LIFO : Rs. 400 & Rs. 300 (*iii*) Stocks under Simple Average Method : Rs. 475 & Rs. 366 (*iv*) Stocks under Weighted Average Method : Rs. 489 & Rs. 371]

32. From the following monthly simple average prices relating to two different cases, you are required to calculate 4 monthly Moving Simple Average prices. Compare the prices calculated and give your comments :

Case I

Months	Jan	Feb.	Mar.	Apr.	May.	June	July	Aug.
Prices (Rs.)	30	32	33	36	37	39	40	42

Case II

Months	Jan.	Feb.	Mar.	Apr.	May.	June	July	Aug.
Prices (Rs.)	40	38	35	32	30	29	27	26

[Ans. Case I *From April.* Rs. 32·75; Rs. 34·50; Rs. 36·25; Rs. 38; Rs. 39·5
Case II *From April.* Rs. 36·25; Rs. 33·75; Rs. 31·50; Rs. 29·50; Rs. 28]

33. From the following transactions extracted from the books of accounts of a manufacturing concern as on 31st December 1990. Work out (*a*) consumption value of raw materials in the month and (*b*) value of closing stock as on 31st December, 1990, under following four methods of pricing issues :

(*i*) First-in-first-out (*ii*) Last-in-first-out
(*iii*) Moving Average Cost (*iv*) Weighted Average Cost (end of month)

Show the results in a tabular form.

1990			Quantity in units	*Rate per unit* *Rs.*
Dec.	1	Opening Stock	3,000	9·70
"	4	Purchases	2,500	9·80
"	12	Issues	4,000	
"	16	Purchases	3,000	10·05
"	21	Issues	2,100	
"	26	Purchases	1,500	10·30
"	31	Issues	1,000	

[Ans. ***Consumption value of R/M. Value of closing stock :***

		Rs.	*Rs.*
(*i*)	**FIFO**	**69,680**	**29,520**
(*ii*)	**LIFO**	**70,455**	**28,745**
(*iii*)	**Moving Average Cost**	**69,954**	**29,246**
(*iv*)	**Weighted Average Cost**	**70,432**	**28,768]**

34. The following is the information regarding receipts and issues of pigments and the stores record of a paint manufacturing factory :

			Kg
Sept.	1	Opening Stock of pigments (there were no issues or receipts during the last week of August)	25,000
"	2	Issues of Requisition No. 1	13,000
"	3	Received from supplier by Challan No. 15 of 3-9-80 as per stipulated date of delivery	30,000
"	3	Issue on Requisition No. 3	10,000
"	4	Issue on Requisition No. 4	5,000
"	6	Received from supplier by Challan No. 82	10,000
"	7	Issue on Requisition No. 5	4,500

Examination by the store verification on 6th morning recorded a shortage of 500 kg.

Maximum Limit was 50,000 kg
Minimum Limit was 8,000 kg
Ordering Level was 25,000 kg

You are required to prepare Bin Card No. 36 for the item of pigment for which the symbol allotted is $X = 40$.

[*C.A. Inter*]

[Ans. Balance : 30,000 kg]

35. From the following data in respect of a particular material during the month of August 1989, you are required to draw up a Store Ledger under (*i*) Simple Periodic Average Method; and (*ii*) Weighted Periodic Average Method :

1989			
August	1	Opening Stock	500 units @ Rs. 10
"	3	Receipts	200 units @ Rs. 14
"	8	Issued	400 units
"	10	Receipts	300 units @ Rs. 16
"	15	Returned to stores	100 units [which were issued on 8.8.89]
"	18	Receipts	100 units @ Rs. 18
"	20	Returned to vendors	50 units
"	25	Shortage	60 units
"	29	Issued	300 units

[Ans. Simple Periodic Average Method : Closing Balance 390 units; Value Rs. 3,040; Weighted Periodic Average Method : Closing Balance 390 units; Value Rs. 3,274·90]

36. The following is an extract of the record of receipts and issues of a chemical factory during the month of March 1993 :

March	1	Opening Balances 500 kg @ Rs. 20
"	2	Issue 70 kg
"	4	Issue 100 kg
"	8	Issue 80 kg
"	13	Received from supplier 200 kgs @ Rs. 19
"	14	Received from Job No. 008, 15 kg
"	16	Issue 180 kg
"	20	Received from suppliers 240 kg @ 19
"	22	Issue 300 kg
"	25	Received from suppliers 320 kg @ Rs. 19
"	26	Issue 115 kg
"	27	Returned from customers 35 kg
"	28	Received from Suppliers 100 kg @ Rs. 19

Additional Information : (1) The stock verifier of the factory has found shortage of 10 kg on 18th and 20 kg damaged on 2nd. Draw up a priced stores ledger under (*a*) LIFO (*b*) FIFO methods.
(*b*) Which method would you consider more economical at the time of price inflation ?

[Ans. Closing Balance 555 tons; Rs. 11,545]

37. S. Ltd. uses large quantities of components for its products. The following figures relate to this material during the year 1992 :

Quarter	*Qty. of Purchase (kg)*	*Price per kg*	*Consumption (kg)*
1st Qr.	1,000	6·20	600
2nd Qr.	2,100	6·30	1,200
3rd Qr.	700	6·40	1,500
4th Qr.	1,200	6·70	1,350

Market replacement cost :

31.12.92	6·60
31.12.91	6·10

The stock of material on 31.12.91, was 1,000 kg valued for accounting purpose at cost of Rs. 6 per kg. Delivery of goods to the factory is made on the first day of each quarter.

You are required

(*a*) to compute the value of stock of material as on 31.12.92 applying
(*i*) LIFO; and (*ii*) FIFO

(*b*) for internal accounting purpose to compare the effect on the profit of 1992 of adopting each of the above method for valuation in place of market replacement cost method.

**[Ans. Under LIFO = Rs. 8,170; Under FIFO = Rs. 9,000;
Reduction in Profits for 1992 if LIFO method is Applied = Rs. 640
Additional Profits for 1992 if FIFO = Rs. 190]**

38. AB & Co. manufactures two types of pens *P* and *Q*. The cost data for the year ended 30th September 1990 is as follows :

	Rs.
Direct materials	4,00,000
Direct wages	2,24,000
Production overhead	96,000
	7,20,000

It is further ascertained that :

(*a*) Direct materials in type *P* cost twice as much direct materials in type *Q*.

(*b*) Direct wages for type *Q* were 60% of those for type *P*.

(*c*) Product overhead was of same rate for both types.

(*d*) Administration overhead for each was 200% of direct labour.

(*e*) Selling cost were 50 paise per pen for both types.

(*f*) Production during the year :

Type *P*	40,000
Type *Q*	1,20,000

(*g*) Sales during the year :

Type *P*	36,000
Type *Q*	1,00,000

(*h*) Selling prices were Rs. 14 per pen for type *P* and Rs. 10 per pen for type *Q*.

Prepare a statement showing per unit cost of production, Total cost, profit and also total sales value and profit separately for two types of pens *P* and *Q*.

[*I.C.W.A. (Inter) Dec. 1990*]

[Ans. (*i*) P—10·60 per unit, Q—6·20 per unit (*ii*) 10,69,600; 4,34,400; 15,04,000 (*iii*) P—1,04,400 (*iv*) 3,30,000]

4 Labour

Section I : Cost and Control

Authors' Comments and Suggestions :

1. ***Generally, the questions from this chapter have been set relating to the methods of remuneration and evaluation of incentive schemes.***
2. ***Ambiguity in the application of different formulae should be avoided.***
3. ***The cost of normal idle time should be considered as a part of cost of product or service.***
4. ***Sometimes special factors like labour efficiency factor etc. are given in the question. In this case, efficiency factor should be duly considered.***
5. ***A number of short notes are set in the examination from this chapter.***
6. ***Regarding group bonus schemes sometime the students feel difficulty to find out the clue to solve the problem in this situation lead should be given in the language of the question.***

Concept—Control—Direct Labour and Indirect Labour—Labour Turnover—Treatment of Labour Turnover, Idle Time, Overtime and Idle facilities.

Concept of Labour Cost

Labour cost represents the related cost of converting raw materials into finished products. It represents an important item of total cost. Labour cost relates to human behaviour, hence most sensitive. So labour cost not only means wages but also includes cost of recruitment and training, cost of idle time, cost of labour turnover, cost of overtime and shift work, cost of labour inefficiency, cost of wastage and spoilage etc. According to Matz, Curry and Frank : "labour cost, representing the human contribution to production, is an important cost factor which requires constant control, measurement and analysis." This may be basically divided into direct and indirect costs.

Control of Labour Cost

Controlling of labour cost is the most important function of administrative management. It is not like material which can be stored for future. If a day's labour is not utilised efficiently on the same day, idle time will occur with a loss to the department concerned. Again, if the management takes any action without recognising the human element, it may result to strike or close down of the business. So it is a difficult task for management to exercise control over labour cost.

There are various *techniques* for effective control of labour costs :

(*i*) Planning of production.
(*ii*) Budgeting of labour forces.
(*iii*) Standardisation of labour hour and labour cost.
(*iv*) Labour performance reports.

(*v*) Time booking through automatic time-recorder.
(*vi*) Suitable system of wage payment coupled with various incentive schemes.

Direct Labour Cost

According to I.C.M.A., England : "Direct labour cost is that cost which can be identified with and allocated to cost centres or cost units." Thus, direct labour has a linear relationship with the volume of production—varying with the movement of output and, hence, is a variable element of cost and controllable. It forms part of prime cost.

Indirect Labour Cost

According to I.C.M.A., England : "Wages which cannot be apportioned to or absorbed by cost centres or cost units" is indirect labour cost. Thus those labour who are not directly engaged in altering the composition or condition of the product provide various types of services. They are helpers, maintenance personnel etc. Indirect labour cost is part of overhead.

Importance of Distinction between Direct and Indirect Labour Cost

The distinction between direct and indirect labour cost is necessary :

(*i*) To allocate the overhead expenses correctly.
(*ii*) To charge the labour cost on the various products—directly and proportionately.
(*iii*) To provide more accurate product cost.
(*iv*) To provide strict control over labour costs.
(*v*) To assist in various managerial decision-making.

Labour Turnover

Labour turnover may be defined as the rate of change in composition of the labour force of an organisation during a specified period. Labour turnover is a peculiar problem of industry and leads to high costs and low productivity. It is the ratio represented by :

$$\text{Labour Turnover} = \frac{\text{Number of workers leaving in a particular period}}{\text{Average number of workers employed during the period}}$$

Causes of Labour Turnover

The causes of labour turnover may be divided as : (a) Avoidable causes; and (b) Unavoidable causes.

(*a*) **Avoidable causes :**

(*i*) Redundancy, *i.e.* lack of planning and foresight
(*ii*) Dissatisfaction with job
(*iii*) Dissatisfaction with remuneration
(*iv*) Unhealthy working condition
(*v*) Lack of proper recreational facilities
(*vi*) Dissatisfaction with hours of work
(*vii*) Bad relationship with supervisor and fellow-workers
(*viii*) Lack of promotional opportunities
(*ix*) Lack of transport, accommodation etc.
(*x*) Disputes between rival trade unions.

(*b*) **Unavoidable causes** include :

(*i*) Individual betterement
(*ii*) Illness or accidents
(*iii*) Retirement and death
(*iv*) Domestic responsibilities — to look after children
(*v*) Discharge due to unsuitability or inefficiency

(*vi*) Marriage and pregnancy in case of female workers
(*vii*) Moving elsewhere from locality
(*viii*) National service.

Effects of Labour Turnover

Normally, labour turnover is unavoidable. To some extent it is desirable also, as it injects fresh blood to adjust its labour force according to the workload. Too low labour turnover is not a good sign, particularly in Senior Grades. Again, too high labour turnover results in increased cost of production for the following reasons :

(*i*) Cost of replacing workers — *i.e.* selection, training etc.
(*ii*) Additional cost of tools, gigs etc.
(*iii*) Losses due to wastage, spoilage and defectives etc.
(*iv*) Decrease in overall production due to lack of desired efficiency of new workers.

Measurement of Labour Turnover

There are three distinct methods for measurement of labour turnover. The choice of a particular method will depend upon the organisation.

(*i*) **Separation Method**

Under this method labour turnover is measured by dividing the total number of separations (*i.e.* workers left) during a period by the average number of workers on the pay roll and multiplying by 100. Thus

$$\text{L.T.} = \frac{\text{Number of separations during a period}}{\text{Average number of workers during the period}} \times 100$$

(*ii*) **Replacement Method (or Net Labour Turnover Method)**

This method takes into consideration only the actual replacement irrespective of the number of workers leaving. In other words

$$\text{L.T.} = \frac{\text{Number of workers replaced in a period}}{\text{Average number of workers during the period}} \times 100$$

Illustration

From the following information calculate labour turnover rate using different methods :
Number of workers on the pay roll :

On 1.1.94	1,000
On 31.1.94	1,200

During the month 20 persons quit while 80 persons are discharged. 300 workers are required during the month, of these 50 workers are recruited in the vacancies of those leaving while the rest were engaged in accordance with an expansion scheme.

Solution

Average number of workers during the month :

$$\frac{1{,}000 + 1{,}200}{2} = 1{,}100$$

Labour Turnover Rate :

(*i*) Separation Method :

$$\left(\frac{20 + 80}{1{,}100}\right) \times 100 = \frac{100 \times 100}{1{,}100} = 9.09\%$$

(*ii*) Replacement Method :

$$\frac{50}{1{,}100} \times 100 = 4.55\%$$

(*iii*) Flux Method :

$$\left(\frac{100+50}{1{,}100}\right) \times 100 = \frac{150 \times 100}{1{,}100}\% = 13.63\%$$

(*iv*) Flux or Separation-cum-Replacement Method

Under this method both separation and replacement are being considered. Thus

$$\text{L.T.} = \frac{\text{Number or separations + Number of replacements}}{\text{Average number of workers during the period}} \times 100$$

Treatment of L.T. in Cost Accounts

Cost of labour turnover is treated as an overhead expense and should be charged directly to production.

Job Evaluation and Merit Rating

Job evaluation represents an effort to determine the relative value of every job. The evaluation may be achieved through the assignments of points or the use of some other systematic rating method for essential job requirements, such as skill, experience and responsibility.

Merit rating, on the other hand, refers to the evaluation of merit of an employee in terms of the requirements of the job. It is actually the evaluation of the performance of an employee. In merit rating, the personal qualities of an individual are taken into account.

The main difference between the two is — job evaluation is an objective assessment of the worth of job, while merit rating is a subjective technique.

Treatment of Idle time, Overtime, Idle Facilities etc.

(A) Idle Time

Idle time refers to such a time for which wages are paid without any production. It is the difference between the time as per attendance records and the time booked for different jobs or workorders. The idle time may arise mainly due to two causes. : (*i*) Normal causes, and (*ii*) Abnormal causes.

(1) Normal Causes

(*a*) Time lost from factory gate to the place of work and return.
(*b*) Time wasted in changing from one job to another.
(*c*) Time taken for packing up the work.
(*d*) Time lost for allotment of the job to workers.
(*e*) Time lost due to normal fatigue.
(*f*) Time taken for personal needs.
(*g*) Setting-up time for the machine.

(2) Abnormal Causes

(*a*) Time lost on account of accidents etc.
(*b*) Time lost due to bad planning and poor supervision.
(*c*) Lack of proper coordination and control.
(*d*) Breakdown and power failure.
(*e*) Lost time due to lockouts, strikes, fire, flood, storm etc.
(*f*) Loss of time arising out of inefficient managements.
(*g*) Non-availability of raw materials, working environment etc.

The above causes may also be grouped into : (*i*) Productive, (*ii*) Administrative and (*iii*) Economic, depending upon its nature and the department to which it is related.

Treatment of Idle time

Cost of idle time has an adverse effect on product costing. The control and treatment of idle time in cost accounting depends on the types of idle time.

(*i*) **Normal and Controllable Idle Time.** Such type of idle time should be charged to production as Factory Overhead. If responsibility for such idle time can be identified with a particular department, the cost should be charged to that particular department.

(*ii*) **Normal and Uncontrolable Idle Time.** Cost of this type of idle time should be charged to the job or workorder at an inflated rate. Normal idle time for direct workers should be treated as direct wages.

(*iii*) **Abnormal Idle Time.** Cost of abnormal idle time should not be included in product cost but should be charged direct to Costing Profit and Loss A/c.

(B) Overtime

If a worker spends more time over and above the normal working hours, it is known as overtime. Generally, rate of overtime is higher than the normal rate. The extra payment required to be paid for overtime work is known as overtime premium.

Treatment of Overtime Cost

For proper treatment and control of overtime cost, one should know the circumstances under which overtime work is done. Following are three circumstances where overtime work is generally required :

(*i*) In order to complete a job or workorder within a specific date as per request of a specific customer.

(*ii*) In order to make up the production shortage due to unavoidable reasons, such as breakdown, power failure etc.

(*iii*) In order to solve the problem of labour shortage, workers are engaged as a matter of administrative policy.

Though overtime work cannot be completely eliminated, it is essential that proper control should be exercised to keep it to a minimum.

For above case (*i*), overtime cost should be charged to the job as direct product cost.

For the above case (*ii*), overtime cost should be treated as overhead and recovered from jobs completed during the period.

For the above case (*iii*), the overtime cost may be treated as part of labour cost by spreading the extra cost over the number of jobs completed during the hours worked.

Cost of overtime due to abnormal reasons such as flood, strike etc. should be charged to Costing Profit and Loss A/c.

(C) Idle Facilities

Idle facilities means the plant and machinery facilities available for utilisation but which are not used fully due to normal or abnormal reasons. This generally arises from market constraint or defective management policy. The normal reasons of idle facilities are, generally, preventive maintenance, intermittent use of machine during process, and the abnormal reasons may be trade depression, flood, recession etc. The cost of normal idle facilities should be charged as overhead expense and the abnormal idle time cost should be charged to Costing Profit and Loss Account.

(D) Idle Capacity and Excess Capacity

The term idle capacity refers to temporary idleness because of shortage of production due to lack of orders or any other causes. This is the difference between practical capacity and the capacity based on expected sales or actual capacity. The main logic behind this is that as soon as the difficulties in achieving production are removed, idle capacity is wiped out and full capacity is restored. Idle capacity cost is treated as an overhead cost under normal circumstances but such cost may be directly charged to Costing Profit and Loss Account if idle capacity arises due to abnormal reasons.

Excess capacity represents the surplus capacity over what can be expected to be utilised at present due to unbalanced machines and equipments within the departments. The cost of excess capacity should be excluded in computing overhead rates and charged to Costing Profit and Loss Account.

Section II : Remuneration and Incentives

Introductions—Needs—Factors—Methods—Comparison between Halsey and Rowan—Different Bonus Schemes—Workedout Problems—Exercise.

Introduction

Selection of the method of remuneration to the workers is the most complex problem nowadays —from the viewpoint of both the workers as well as employers. There is not any single method which is acceptable to both. Hence, prosperity of a concern depends on the joint and co-ordinated efforts of both the employers and employees. There are various methods of wage payment, but they can be grouped under two main heads : (*i*) Remuneration on time basis, and (*ii*) Remuneration on result basis. There are also various monetary and non-monetary incentive schemes.

Requisites of a Satisfactory Wages Payment System

Following are the factors that should be considered for a satisfactory wage payment system :

(*i*) The method of remuneration should be fair to all.

(*ii*) There should be a guaranteed minimum wage.

(*iii*) The plan should be based on scientific time and motion study.

(*iv*) The plan should provide suitable incentives.

(*v*) The plan should be simple and flexible to premit any necessary changes which may arise time to time.

(*vi*) The wage plan should be in conformity with various labour laws and regulations—both local and national.

(*vii*) The cost of operation and administration of the system should be kept at the minimum.

(*viii*) There should be an escalation clause, providing for an automatic rise in wages and attendances as cost of living index increases.

(*ix*) The scheme should aim at increasing the morale of the workers and reducing labour turnover.

(*x*) Finally, the plan should be such as to encourage the workers for improvement of production—both quantitatively and qualitatively.

Need (or Objective) for Incentive Schemes

It is true that low wages do not necessarily mean low costs, again, higher wages also need not necessarily mean a high wage cost per unit. In fact, it is widely recognised that efficiently organised manufacturing concerns may pay the highest wages, and yet have lowest labour cost. Incentive schemes are necessary for the following reasons :

(*i*) To induce the employees to earn more by producing more.

(*ii*) To reduce cost of production per unit by increasing production.

(*iii*) To reduce production time, which increases efficiency of a worker.

(*iv*) To provide better standard of living of employees by allowing more scope of earning.

(*v*) To enhance the economic condition of a country by increasing per-capita income of the workers.

Factors for Selecting Successful Incentive Schemes

For selecting a successful incentive scheme the following factors should be considered :

(*a*) **Simplicity.** The system should be simple and unambiguous so that it can be easily understood by all the workers.

(*b*) **Productivity.** The ultimate aim of an organisation is to increase productivity. Hence, the incentive plan should be such that it can increase productivity.

(*c*) **Effect on Workers.** The incentive scheme should be such that it has no adverse effect on the workers. Any adverse effect may increase labour turnover which means increase in cost of production. A good incentive plan will attract efficient workers from outside as also retain those who are already in employment.

(*d*) **Incidence of overhead.** Due to increase of production, fixed cost are allocated over a greater number of units, resulting in lesser share of overhead cost per unit. Hence, increased volume of production means lower unit fixed cost.

(*e*) **Quantity and Quality of output.** When quantity of production is more important than quality, the method of remuneration should be such as to encourage increased production. On the other hand, if quality is more important than the quantity produced, wage payment should be based preferably on time.

Methods of Remuneration

Basically, there are two principal systems of wages payment :

(1) Time Rate System (2) Payment by results.

1. Time Rate System. Under this system a worker is paid on the basis of time spent by him, regardless of the output produced. The unit of time may be an hour, a day, a week or a month. The formula is :

$$\text{Time Wages} = \text{Hours worked} \times \text{Rate per hour}$$

This method is suitable mainly where the production cannot be measured in terms of units, quality of the output is of utmost importance and a considerable degree of skill is needed.

The main *advantages* of the method are :

(*a*) The method is very simple and easy to understand.

(*b*) The workers are assured of steady income.

(*c*) It is helpful to average and below-average workers.

(*d*) It avoids many complex negotiations necessary for most incentive schemes.

(*e*) This method does justice to the skilled workers.

The main *disadvantages* of the system is that it discourages efficiency. Further greater supervision is necessary to get the desired output.

2. Payment by Results. Under this system a worker is paid on the basis of the quantity of work done without any consideration to the time taken by him to perform the work. The formula is :

$$\text{Wages} = \text{Units produced} \times \text{Rate per unit}$$

This method is suitable mainly where the production is of repetitive nature, can be measured in term of units and quantity of output is of utmost importance due to limitation of time.

The main advantages of this method is that efficient workers are being rewarded by producing more within a given time, which reduces the fixed cost per unit.

Some Important Incentive Schemes

Some of the important incentive schemes are briefly discussed here :

(1) Halsey Premium Plan

(2) Halsey-Weir Premium Scheme

(3) Rowan Plan

(4) Taylor's Differential Piece Rate System

(5) Gantt Task and Bonus Plan

(6) Merrick Differential Piece Rate Plan

(7) Bedaux Point Premium System

(8) Emerson's Efficiency Plan.

1. Halsey Premium Plan. This plan was introduced by F. A. Halsey, an American engineer, in 1891. It recognises individual efficiency and pays bonus on the basis of time saved. Under the method a worker is given wages at the time rate for the time he actually worked and also paid a bonus if he can complete the work in less than the time allotted to do the work. The bonus is paid at a fixed percentage of the time saved, usually 50%, (though the percentage varies from 30% to 70% of time saved). The remaining 50% of the time saved is shared by the employer. Thus,

Total Earnings = T.T. × H.R. + 50% (T.S. × H.R.)

where, T.T. = Time Taken
H.R. = Hourly Rate
T.S. = Time Saved

The main *advantages* of the method are :

(*i*) The method is simple to operate and easy to understand.
(*ii*) The slow workers are not penalised, as time wage is guaranteed.
(*iii*) It provides incentives to more efficient workers.
(*iv*) Worker's efficiency means reduction in cost per unit.
(*v*) The benefit of time saved is shared between employer and employee equally.

The main *disadvantages* of the method are :

(*i*) Many employees' organisations do not like to share the benefit of time saved equally.
(*ii*) Attraction of bonus reduces the quality of work.
(*iii*) Reduction of quality means chances of more wastage, spoilage, defective and break down etc. and more supervision cost.
(*iv*) It is not so much attractive as in the case of piece rate payments.
(*v*) It offers less incentive to the workers as compared to other incentive plans.
(*vi*) If the time rate is not fixed properly, this may lead to a higher bonus.

2. Halsey-Weir Premium Scheme. The scheme was introduced by Weir Ltd. of Glasgow in about 1900. It is similar to Halsey Scheme except that under this scheme the employee gets $33^1/_3$% (often 30%) of the time saved as bonus and the remaining $66^2/_3$% goes to the employer. Thus :

Total Earnings = T.T. × H.R. + $33^1/_3$% (T.S. × H.R.)

where, T.T. = Time Taken
H.R. = Hourly Rate
T.S. = Time Saved

3. Rowan Plan. Grames Rowan first introduced this plan in Glasgow in 1898. Under this scheme also the worker gets his guaranteed time wages for the hours of his actual work, like Halsey Scheme. But here the premium is calculated by a different method. If the worker can complete the job in less than the time allowed, his bonus becomes equal to his *time wages for that proportion of the time taken as the time saved bears to the time allowed.*

Thus, the bonus is calculated as :

$$\frac{\text{Hourly Rate} \times \text{Time taken} \times \text{Time saved}}{\text{Time Allowed}}$$

and, Total Earnings = T.T. × H.R. + (T.T. × H.R.) × $\frac{\text{T.S.}}{\text{T.A.}}$

where, T.T. = Time Taken
H.R. = Hourly Rate
T.S. = Time Saved
T.A. = Time Allowed

The following are the main *advantages* of the scheme :

(*i*) It provides incentives to learners and slow workers.
(*ii*) Since the premium is proportionate to the time saved, the employers get protection if the rate is not fixed properly.

(*iii*) From the point of view of employer the Rowan Scheme is safer than the Halsey Scheme.

(*iv*) Up to 50% of the time saved, bonus under the scheme is higher than that under Halsey Scheme.

(*v*) As the bonus increases at a decreasing rate; the employees do not rush for rapid completion of job, hence lesser chances of wastage etc.

(*vi*) Due to higher output, fixed overhead per unit will be lower.

The main *disadvantages* are :

(*i*) Method is complicated.

(*ii*) At the level of higher production, incentive is low.

(*iii*) Employees are not willing to share their time savings with their employers.

Comparison between Halsey and Rowan Scheme

(1) Up to 50% of time saved, the premium will be same under the two schemes.

(2) Under Rowan Scheme bonus rises faster than Halsey Scheme until the job performed in half than the standard time.

(3) But when the time taken to perform the work is less than half of the standard time, premium and total earnings under the Halsey Scheme are both greater than those under Rowan Scheme.

(4) On the other hand, when the time taken to perform the work is more than half of the standard time, bonus and total earning under the Rowan Scheme are both greater than those under the Halsey Scheme.

(5) The Halsey Scheme provides more incentive to speed up production but there is an automatic check under the Rowan Scheme after certain stage.

(6) Halsey Scheme proves to be costlier if more than half the time is saved, while Rowan Scheme is costlier if less than half the standard time is saved.

4. Differential Piece Rates. The main object of the system is to reward the efficient workers automatically. There are various differential piece rate plans. Some of the differential schemes are :

(*i*) Taylor's Differential Piece Rate System.

(*ii*) Merrick Differential Piece Rate Plan.

(*iii*) Gantt Task and Bonus Plan.

(*i*) **Taylor's Differential Piece Rate System.** This system was first introduced by F. W. Taylor, the Father of Scientific Management. This system provides no minimum guaranteed time wages. But under the system two piece rates are fixed : (*a*) a low piece rate for output below the standard is paid to the workers, and (*b*) a higher rate is paid to the workers who produce equal or more than the standard. Thus, this system penalises the inefficient workers and rewards the efficient workers.

The efficiency of a worker may be determined as a percentage, either : (*i*) of the time allowed for a job to the actual time taken, or (*ii*) of actual output to the standard output, within a specified time.

(*ii*) **Merrick Differential Piece Rate Plan.** This is a slight modification of Taylor's System and uses three rates instead of two. Under this system also day wages are not guaranteed. The three piece rates are :

Efficiency	*Piece rate applicable*
Up to 83%	Normal rate
Up to 100%	10% above normal rate
Above 100%	20% above normal rate

The main feature of this system is that it does not penalise the workers who produce below the standard output up to 83% and the earnings increase with increased efficiency at two stages.

(*iii*) **Gantt Task and Bonus Plan.** The plan is a good combination of time-work and piecework. Under the scheme the day wages of the worker are guaranteed. The main features of the bonus scheme are :

Output	*Bonus*
At 100%	20% on the total output.
Above 100%	20% of the wages of the standard time, or High piece rate on the worker's whole output.

This scheme protects and encourages the less efficient workers who cannot produce the standard output. It offers a good incentive to the efficient workers.

5. **Emerson's Efficiency Plan.** This scheme is also a combination of time wage, piece rate wage and bonus plans. Under this method a standard time is set for each job, or task, or volume of output is fixed as the standard. The standard efficiency is set at $66^2/_3$ or 67%. For efficiency up to 67% the worker gets his day wage only. If he crosses the standard task, he becomes entitled to bonus and the rate of bonus increases with the increase in efficiency. At 100% level of efficiency, the bonus becomes 20%. Again, if the efficiency exceeds 100%, bonus increases by 1% for every 1% increase of a efficiency above 100%.

Group Bonus Plans

The incentive schemes explained so far are applicable to individual workers only. But, sometimes it becomes necessary to introduce Group Bonus Scheme. Under the scheme bonus is paid to the group as a whole, depending upon the performance of the group and the amount of bonus is shared by themselves equally or at an agreed proportion.

The group bonus is suitable in the following circumstances :

(*a*) When it is very difficult to measure the performance of individual worker, but the production through collective efforts of a group of workers can be measured.

(*b*) The nature of the work requires collective effort.

(*c*) Where it is desirable to dvelop a team spirit.

(*d*) Where both the direct and indirect workers are to be rewarded.

(*e*) When bonus scheme cannot be operated successfully for individual workers.

However, before introducing a group bonus scheme, following points must be considered very carefully :

(*i*) Well combination among the group.

(*ii*) The size of the group should be economic.

(*iii*) The group should be homogeneous.

(*iv*) The production of the group should be within its control.

Thus, group bonus schemes encourages team spirit, reduces wastage, assures cooperation, lessens supervisory work and reduces overall costs.

Illustration

Time allowed for a job = 5 hrs

Time taken to complete the job = 4 hrs

Rate Per hour = Rs. 1

Calculate the total earnings of a worker under the Halsey Premium Scheme.

Solution

$$\text{Total Earnings} = \text{Hours worked} \times \text{Rate per hour} + \frac{50}{100} \times (\text{time saved} \times \text{hourly rate})$$

$$= \text{Rs. } 4 \times 1 + \left(\frac{50}{100} \times 1\right) \times 1$$

$$= \text{Rs. } \left(4 + \frac{1}{2}\right) = \text{Rs. } \mathbf{4.50}$$

Illustration

Time allowed for a work = 10 hrs

Time taken to complete the job = 8 hrs

Rate per hour = Rs. 2

Calculate the total earnings of a worker under the Halsey Premium Scheme.

Solution

Total Earnings = Time Taken × Hourly Rate + $33\frac{1}{3}$ (T.S. × H.R.)

Where T.S. = Time Saved, H.R. = Hourly Rate

$$\text{Total Earnings} = 8 \times \text{Rs. } 2 + \frac{33\frac{1}{3}}{100} \times 2 \times \text{Rs. } 2$$

$$= \text{Rs. } 16 + \text{Rs. } \tfrac{1}{3} \times 4 = \text{Rs. } 16 + \text{Rs. } 1.33 = \text{Rs. } \mathbf{17.33}$$

Illustration

Standard time is 20 hrs, Time taken is 16 hrs, Hourly Rate is Re. 0.50

Find out total earnings under Rowan Plan.

Solution

$$\text{Total Earnings} = \text{Time Taken} \times \text{Hourly Rate} + (\text{Time Taken} \times \text{Hourly Rate}) \times \frac{\text{Time Saved}}{\text{Time Taken}}$$

Time Saved = Time Allowed – Time Taken

= (20 – 16) hrs. = 4 hrs

$$\therefore \text{Total Earnings} = 16 \times \text{Re. } 0.50 + (\text{Re. } 0.50 \times 16) \times \frac{4 \times \text{Re. } 0.50}{20}$$

$$= \text{Rs. } 8 + \text{Rs. } \frac{8 \times 2}{20} = \text{Rs. } (8 + 0.80)$$

$$= \textbf{Rs. 8.80}$$

A factory works 8 hours a day. The standard output is 10 units per hour and normal rate is Rs. 5 per hour. The factory has introduced the following differentials in the matter of wage payment :

80% of piece rate when below standard.

120% of piece rate when at or above standard.

Find out piece rate at below and above standard.

Solution

$$\text{Normal piece rate} = \frac{\text{Rs. } 5}{10} = 0.50$$

$$\text{When below standard the piece rate will be} = 0.50 \times \frac{80}{100} = \text{Re. } 0.40$$

$$\text{When above standard the piece rate will be} = \frac{120}{100} \times 0.5 = \text{Re. } \mathbf{0.60}$$

Standard Production : 80 units per week. No. of men working in the group = 10. Bonus for every 25% increase in production, a bonus of Rs. 10 will be shared prorata among the 10 members of the group.

Actual production during a week = 110 units.

Solution

Increase in production over standard = (110 – 80) units = 30 units

i.e. $\frac{30}{80} \times 100$ or 37.5%

$\therefore$ Bonus = Rs 10 + $\frac{12.5}{25} \times$ Rs. 10

= Rs. 10 + 5 = Rs. 15

Each member of the group, therefore, receives = Rs. 15 ÷ 10 = **Rs. 1.50**

WORKEDOUT PROBLEMS

Problem 1

Calculate by the Halsey Premium Plan and determine on this basis the total earnings of a worker by the given data :

Standard time for work	20 hours
Actual time taken	16 hours
Rate per hour	Rs. 2

Solution

Total Earnings = Time taken × Rate per hour + 50% (Time saved × Rate per hour).

Standard time = 20 hours

Time taken = 16 hours

$\therefore$ Time Saved = Standard time – Time taken *i.e.* 20 hours – 16 hours = 4 hours.

$\therefore$ Total Earnings = $16 \times 2 + \frac{50}{100}(4 \times 2) = 32 + 4 =$ Rs. 36

Total Earnings under Halsey Premium Plan = Rs. **36**

Problem 2

Calculate total monthly remuneration of workers *A, B, C* and *D* on the basis of the following information for the month of January 2007 :

(i) Standard Production for each worker = 1,000 units

(ii) Rate of wages = 10 paise per unit

(iii) Bonus = Rs. 5 for each 1% increase over 90% of the standard.

(iv) Dearness Allowance per month = 100% of piece wage.

The units completed by the four workers were as under :

A = 950 units, *B* = 900 units, *C* = 960 units, *D* = 850 units.

[C.U. B.Com. (Hons.)]

Solution

% of work done by the workers :

$A = \frac{950}{1,000} \times 100 = 95\%$ $B = \frac{900}{1,000} \times 100 = 90\%$

$C = \frac{960}{1,000} \times 100 = 96\%$ $D = \frac{850}{1,000} \times 100 = 85\%$

Statement showing Calculation of Remuneration
for the month of January 2007

Particulars	*A* Rs.	*B* Rs.	*C* Rs.	*D* Rs.
Piece wages [Units produced × Rate per unit]	95	90	96	85
D.A. [100% of piece wages]	95	90	96	85
Bonus [Rs. 5 for each 1% increase over 90% of the standard]	25	—	30	—
Total Earnings	215	180	222	170

Problem 3

From the following particulars, calculate the cash required for wages in a company, during the month of January 2007 :

		Rs.
(*i*)	Wages for normal hours worked	40,000
(*ii*)	Overtime	5,000
(*iii*)	Employees, contribution to Provident Fund	1,800
(*iv*)	Deduction of employees, share of State Insurance	1,000
(*v*)	Leave Wages	3,000

(*vi*) House rent is to be recovered from 60 employees @ Rs. 20 per month.

Solution

Statement showing the Payment of Wages

Particulars	*Amount* Rs.	*Amount* Rs.
Normal Wages		40,000
Overtime		5,000
Leave Wages		3,000
		48,000
Less : Employees, contribution to Provident Fund	1,800	
Employees, contribution to State Insurance	1,000	
House Rent @ Rs. 20 P.M. for 60 employees = 60 × 20 × 12	14,400	17,200
Total Cash required		30,800

Problem 4

A worker takes 12 hours to complete a work on daily wages and 8 hours on a scheme of payment by results. The worker's day rate is Rs. 6.00 per hour. The cost of material of the product is Rs. 20 and the overheads are recovered at 200% of the total wages.

Calculate the factory works cost of the product under : (*i*) Rowan Plan (*ii*) Halsey Scheme.

Solution

Rs.

(*i*) **Rowan Plan :**

Direct wages
[Time taken × Rate per hour]
i.e. 8 × Rs. 6.00 — 48.00

$$\text{Bonus} = \frac{\text{Time saved}}{\text{Time Allowed}} \times \text{Time taken} \times \text{Rate per hour}$$

i.e. $\frac{4}{12} \times 8 \times 6$ = 16.00

64.00

Computation of Works Cost

	Rs.
Material Cost	20.00
Add : Wages	64.00
Add : Overhead @ 200% of wages	128.00
	212.00

(*ii*) **Halsey Scheme**

	Rs.
Direct Wages	48.00
Bonus 50% of (Time Saved × Rate per hour)	
i.e. $\frac{50}{100} \times 4 \times 6$	12.00
	60.00

Computation of Works Cost

	Rs.
Material Cost	20.00
Add : Wages	60.00
Add : Overhead @ 200% of wages	120.00
	200.00

Problem 5

Production department of a company pays its workers standard wages @ Rs. 2.00 per hour plus a bonus under the Rowan Premium Bonus Scheme and Dearness Allowance of Rs. 50 per week of 55 hours. At the end of a particular week the time sheet of a worker is summarised below :

Job No.	Time Allowed	Time taken by the worker
205	30 hrs	25 hrs
108	25 hrs	20 hrs
12	5 hrs	3 hrs
Idle Time (waiting)		7 hrs
		55 hours

Calculate the gross wages (including bonus and D.A.) of the worker of the week.

[N.B.U. B.Com. (Hons.)]

Solution

Statement showing Calculation of Gross Wages for a Week

Items	*Details*	*Amount* Rs.
Basic wages (Time Rate)	48 × Rs. 2	96.00
Idle time Wages	7 × Rs. 2	14.00
Dearness Allowance (Fixed)	—	50.00
Bonus	18.73	
Gross Wages		178.73

Working Notes :

(*i*) Time Saved

Job No. 205 = (30 – 25) hours = 5 hours

Job No. 108 = (25 – 20) hours = 5 hours

Job No. 12 = (5 – 3) hours = 2 hours

(*ii*) Total Amount of Bonus

		Rs.
Job No. 205	= $^5/_{30}$ × (Rs. 2 × 25 hours) =	8.33
Job No. 108	= $^5/_{25}$ × (Rs. 2 × 20 hours) =	8.00
Job No. 12	= $^2/_5$ × (Rs. 2 × 3 hours) =	2.40
	Total Bonus	18.73

Problem 6

From the following calculate the total monthly remuneration of each of three workers *A*, *B* and *C* :

(*i*) Standard production per month per worker = 1,000 units

(*ii*) Actual production during a month : *A* = 890 units, *B* = 720 units, *C* = 960 units.

(*iii*) Piece work rate per unit of actual production = 20 paise

(*iv*) Dearness wages Rs. 50 per month (fixed)

(*v*) House Rent allowance Rs. 20 per month (fixed)

(*vi*) Additional production bonus at the rate of Rs. 5 for each percentage of actual production exceeding 80% of the standard. *[C.U. B.Com. (Hons.)]*

Solution

Statement showing calculation of Total Monthly Remuneration of A, B and C

Items	*A* Rs.	*B* Rs.	*C* Rs.
Basic Wages [Units produced × Rate per unit]	178	144	192
Dearness Wages	50	50	50
Bonus[1]	45	—	80
House Rent Allowance	20	20	20
Total Remuneration	293	214	342

Working Notes :

1. Calculation of Bonus :

(*i*) *Worker A* :

Actual Production = 890 units *i.e.* $\frac{890}{1,000} \times 100 = 89\%$ efficiency

∴ Bonus = (89 – 80) × Rs. 5 = Rs. 45

(*ii*) *Worker B* :

Actual Production = 720 units *i.e.* $\frac{720}{1,000} \times 100 = 72\%$ efficiency

∴ Bonus = Nil

(*iii*) *Worker C* :

Actual Production = 960 units *i.e.* $\frac{960}{1,000} \times 100 = 96\%$ efficiency

∴ Bonus = (96 – 80) × Rs. 5 = Rs. **80**

Problem 7

During a certain week in September 2006, a worker manufactured 240 articles. Working hours during a week are 48 hours, standard rate Rs. 5 per hour and standard time to manufacture an article is 15 minutes.

Calculate his gross wages for the week according to (*a*) Piece work with guaranteed weekly wages, (*b*) Rowan Premium Bonus Plan, (*c*) Halsey Premium Bonus Plan.

[C.U. B.Com. (Hons.) Adopted]

Solution

(*a*) **Under Piece work with guaranteed weekly wages**

Actual Wages = Time Taken × Rate per hour
= 48 hours × Rs. 5 = Rs. 240

Guaranteed weekly wages = Standard Time × Rate per hour
= 60 hours × Rs. 5 = Rs. 300

Therefore, actual wages is less than guaranteed wages. So the worker will receive guaranteed wages Rs. 300 for the week.

$\therefore$ Rate per hour = $\frac{\text{Rs. } 300}{48 \text{ hrs.}}$ = Rs. 6.25

	Rs.
(*b*) **Time wages** *i.e.* [Time taken × Rate per hour] (48 hrs × Rs. 5)	240.00
Bonus $\left[\frac{\text{Time Saved}}{\text{Time Allowed}} \times \text{Time wages}\right]$ $\left[\frac{(60-48)}{60} \times \text{Rs. } 240\right]$	48.00
	288.00

$\therefore$ Rate per hour = $\frac{\text{Rs. } 288}{48 \text{ hrs}}$ = Rs. 6.00

(*c*) **Halsey Premium Bonus Plan**	*Rs.*
Time Wages = Time Taken × Rate per hour [48 hours × Rs. 5]	240
Bonus $\left[\frac{1}{2} \times \text{Time Saved} \times \text{Rate per hour}\right]$ $\left[\frac{1}{2} \times 12 \text{ hrs} \times \text{Rs. } 5\right]$	30
	270

Rate per hour = $\frac{\text{Rs. } 270}{48 \text{ hrs.}}$ = Rs. 5.63 (Approx.)

Working Notes :

(*i*) Standard time for 240 articles = 240 × 15 minutes
= 3,600 minutes or 60 hours.

Problem 8

From the following data ascertain the total earnings of each worker separable under (i) Halsey Scheme (50%), (ii) Rowan Scheme. Also calculate the effective hourly rate of wages of the workers under both the schemes :

Name of Worker	*Amal*	*Bimal*
Time Allowed (Hours)	5	5
Actual time taken (Hours)	4	6
Basic rate of wages per hour	Rs. 3.00	Rs. 3.00

[C.U. B.Com. (Hons.), 1990]

Solution

(*i*) **Under Halsey Scheme : Amal :**	*Rs.*
Time Wages = 4 hours × Rs. 3.00	12.00
Bonus [50% × Time Saved × Rate per hour] [50% × 1 hour × Rs. 3.00]	1.50
Total Wages	13.50

Effective hourly rate of wage = $\frac{\text{Rs. } 13.50}{4 \text{ hrs}}$ = Rs. 3.38 (approx.)

Bimal : *Rs.*

Time Wages = 6 hours × Rs. 3.00 18.00

Bonus Nil

Total Wages 18.00

$$\text{Effective hourly rate of wages} = \frac{\text{Rs. } 18.00}{6 \text{ hrs}} = \text{Rs. } 3.00$$

(*ii*) **Under Rowan Scheme : Amal**

Time wages = 4 hrs × Rs. 3.00 12.00

$$\text{Bonus} = \frac{\text{Time Saved}}{\text{Time Allowed}} \times \text{Time Wages}$$

$$= \frac{1}{5} \times \text{Rs. } 12.00 \qquad 2.40$$

Total Wages 14.40

$$\text{Effective hourly rate of wages} = \frac{\text{Rs. } 14.40}{4 \text{ hrs}} = \text{Rs. } 3.60$$

Bimal :

Time Wages = 6 hours × Rs. 3.00 18.00

Bonus Nil

Total Wages 18.00

$$\text{Effective hourly rate of Wages} = \frac{\text{Rs. } 18.00}{6 \text{ hrs}} = \text{Rs. } 3.00$$

Problem 9

From the following particulars you are required to calculate under 'Average Wage Rate' the labour cost chargeable to Job No. 'A' which was completed in 1990 :

Basic Wage Rate is Rs. 2 per hour and overtime rates are :

Before or after working hours 150% of basic wage rate.

Sundays and holidays – 200% of basic wage rate.

During the year 1990 the following hours were worked :

Normal time	2,00,000 hours
Overtime before or after working hours	30,000 hours
Overtime on Sundays and holidays	20,000 hours
Total	2,50,000 hours

For Job 'A' 3,500 hours were spent as follows :

Normal time	3,000 hours
Before and after working hours	300 hours
Sundays and Holidays	200 hours

[C.U. B.Com. (Hons.), 1991]

Solution

Average Wage Rate

Particulars	*Hours worked*	*Rate per hour Rs.*	*Wages Paid Rs.*
Normal Time	2,00,000	2	4,00,000
Overtime before or after working hours	30,000	3	90,000
Overtime on Sundays and other holidays	20,000	4	80,000
	2,50,000		5,70,000

$$\therefore \text{ Average Wage Rate} = \frac{5,70,000}{2,50,000} = \text{Rs. } 2.28$$

Now, computation of labour cost under 'Average Wage Rate'

Items	Job No. 'A'
Hours Spent	3,500
Average Wage Rate	Rs. 2.28

∴ Labour Cost Chargeable = 3,500 hours × Rs. 2.28 = Rs. 7,980

Problem 10

In an assembly shop four workmen *A, B, C, D* work together as a team and are paid on group piece rate. They also work individually on hourly rate jobs. In a 44 hour week, the following hours have been spent by them on group piece-work : *A*—40 hours, *B*—40 hours, *C*—30 hours and *D*—20 hours. The balance of the time in the week has been booked by each worker on day work jobs. Their hourly rates are as follows :

A = Rs. 3.00, B = Rs. 4.50, C = Rs. 6.00, D = Rs. 6.00

The group piece rate is Rs. 6.00 per unit and the team has produced 150 units.

Calculate the gross weekly earnings of each workman taking into consideration that each individual is entitled to Dearness Allowance of Rs. 50 per week. *[C.U. B.Com. (Hons.)]*

Solution

Total piece earnings of the group = Rs. 6 × 150 = Rs. 900

Time wages of the workers for the time of group works = Time Rate × Hours Spent

∴ A = 40 × Rs. 3 = Rs. 120

B = 40 × Rs. 4.50 = Rs. 180

C = 30 × Rs. 6 = Rs. 180

D = 20 × Rs. 6 = Rs. 120

Now the group earnings will be apportioned by the workers in the ratio of

A : B : C : D = 12 : 18 : 18 : 12 = 2 : 3 : 3 : 2

Statement showing Gross Weekly Earnings of the Workmen

Particulars	*A*	*B*	*C*	*D*
Time Allowed (hours)	44	44	44	44
Time spent for group works	40	40	30	20
Time booked for another job work	4	4	14	24
Time Wage (Individual job work) [Individual Time × Individual Rate]	12	18	84	144
Share of group wages of Rs. 900 in the ratio of 2 : 3 : 3 : 2	180	270	270	180
D.A.	50	50	50	50
Total Weekly Earnings	242	338	404	374

Problem 11

A worker takes 80 hours to do a job for which the time allowed is 100 hours. His daily rate is Rs. 2.50 per hour.

Calculate the works cost of the job under the following methods of payment of wages : (*i*) Time rate, (*ii*) Halsey Plan; and (*iii*) Rowan Plan.

Additional information : (*i*) Material cost Rs. 120; (*ii*) Factory overhead 125% of wages. *[C.U. B.Com. (Hons.)]*

Solution

Payment of Wages of the Worker

(i) Under Time Rate = Hours worked × Rate per hour

= 80 hours × Rs. 2.50 = Rs. 200

(*ii*) Under Halsey Plan = (Hours worked × Rate per hour) + 50% (Time saved × Rate per hour)

$$= (80 \text{ hours} \times \text{Rs. } 2.50) + \frac{50}{100}(20 \times 2.50)$$

= Rs. 200 + Rs. 25 = Rs. 225

(*iii*) Under Rowan Plan = (Hours worked × Rate per hour)

$$+ \frac{\text{Time Saved}}{\text{Time Allowed}} \times (\text{Hours worked} \times \text{Rate per hour})$$

$$= (80 \text{ hrs.} \times \text{Rs. } 2.50) + \frac{20}{100}(80 \text{ hrs.} \times \text{Rs. } 2.50)$$

= Rs. 200 + Rs. 40 = Rs. 240

Statement of Works Cost for a Job

for the period ended ......

Particulars	*Time Rate worked*	*Halsey Plan Rs.*	*Rowan Plan Rs.*
Direct Material	120	120	120
Direct Wages	200	225	240
PRIME COST	320	345	360
Add : Factory overhead @ 125% of Direct Wages	250	281.25	300
WORKS COST	570	626.25	660

Problem 12

In a factory two workmen *X* and *Y* produce the same product using the same materials. Their normal wages rate is also the same. They are paid bonus under Rowan System. The time allowed for the product is 50 hours.

X takes 30 hours and Y takes 40 hours to finish the product. The factory cost of the product for X is Rs. 200 and for Y Rs. 222. The factory overhead rate is Re. 1 per man hour.

Find the normal rate of wages and the cost of materials used for the product.

[I.C.W.A. (Inter) Adopted]

Solution

We know that

Factory Cost = Material + Direct Wages + Factory Overheads

Assume, M = Amount of Materials

and W = Rate of Wages

So, the amount of Factory Cost of X : $= M + \left(30 + \frac{20}{50} \times 30\right) W + 30 = \text{Rs. } 200$

and the amount of Factory Cost of Y : $= M + \left(40 + \frac{10}{50} \times 40\right) W + 40 = \text{Rs. } 222.$

as, $M + 42\ W = 170$ ... (*i*)

$M + 48\ W = 182$ ... (*ii*)

Solving equations (i) and (ii), we get

W = Rs. 2 and M = Rs. 86

i.e. Rate of Wages = Rs. 2

and Material Cost = Rs. 86

Problem 13

In a factory bonus system, bonus hours are credited to the employee in the production of time taken which time saved bears to time allowed. Jobs carried forward from one week to another. No overtime is worked and payment is made in full for all units worked on, including those subsequently rejected.

From the following, you are required to calculate for each employee : (*a*) the bonus hours and amount of bonus earned ; (*b*) total wage cost ; (*c*) the wage cost of each good unit produced.

Name of employees	A	B	C
Basic wage rate per hour	Rs. 5	Rs. 8	Rs. 10
Units issued for production	2,500	2,200	3,600
Time allowed for 100 units	2 hrs	3 hrs	4 hrs
Time Taken	40 hrs	60 hrs	140 hrs
Rejects	100 units	50 units	100 units

[I.C.W.A. Adopted]

Solution

(*a*) **Statement of Calculation of Bonus**

Name of the Employees	A	B	C
Time taken	40 hrs	60 hrs	140 hrs
Time allowed [Time allowed × Units produced]	50 hrs	66 hrs	144 hrs
Time saved [Time allowed – Time taken]	10 hrs	6 hrs	4 hrs
∴ Bonus $\left[\text{Time saved} \times \frac{\text{Time taken}}{\text{Time allowed}} \times \text{Rate}\right]$	Rs. 40	Rs. 43.64	Rs. 38.89

(*b*) **Statement of Calculation of Units of Goods Produced by A, B and C**

Name of the Employees	A *units*	B *units*	C *units*
Production	2,500	2,200	3,600
Rejection	100	50	100
Production of goods units [Production – Rejection]	2,400	2,150	3,500

(*c*) **Statement of Calculation of Earnings of A, B and C**

Name of the Employees	A *(Rs.)*	B *(Rs.)*	C *(Rs.)*
Basic Wages [Time taken × Rate per hour]	200	480	1,400
Bonus	40	43.64	38.89
Total Earnings [Wages + Bonus]	240	523.64	1,438.89
Wage Rate per unit of goods output $\left[\frac{\text{Time Earnings}}{\text{No. of goods units}}\right]$	0.10	0.24	0.41

Problem 14

In a factory, two workers *A* and *B* produce the same product using the same material. Their normal wage rate is also the same. They are paid bonus according to Rowan System. The time allocated to the product is 40 hours. *A* takes 25 hours and *B* takes 30 hours to finish the product. The factory cost of the product for *A* is Rs. 193.75 and for *B* Rs. 205.00. The factory overhead rate is one rupee per man hour.

Find out the normal rate of wages and the cost of materials used for the product.

[I.C.W.A. Inter]

Solution

Remuneration of A

Let, Rate of wage is W and Cost of Material = M

Factory Cost = 25 hrs. × Re. 1.00 = Rs. 25.00

Time Saved = 40 hours – 25 hours = 15 hours.

$$\therefore \quad \text{Earnings} = 25\ W + \left(\frac{15}{40} \times 25 \times W\right) + 25 = 193.75 \quad \ldots \text{(i)}$$

For B : Factory Cost = 30 hrs × Re. 1.00 = Rs. 30.00

Time Saved = 40 hrs – 30 hrs = 10 hrs

$$\therefore \quad \text{Earnings} = 30\ W + \frac{10}{40} \times 30\ W + 30 = 205$$

$$\therefore \quad M + 25\ W + \frac{15}{40} \times 25 \times W + 25 \times W + 25 = 193.75$$

$$M + 30\ W + \frac{10}{40} \times 30 \times W + 30 = 205$$

$$\text{or,} \quad M + 25\ W + \left(\frac{75}{8}\right) W = 193.75 - 25$$

$$M + 30\ W + \left(\frac{15}{2}\right) W = 205 - 30$$

$$\text{or,} \quad M + \frac{275}{8} W = 168.75$$

$$M + \frac{75}{2} W = 175.00$$

$$\text{or,} \quad \frac{25}{8} W = 6.25$$

$$\therefore \quad W = \frac{6.25 \times 8}{25} = \text{Rs. 2 per hour}$$

∴ Normal rate of wages Rs. 2 per hour.

Material :

Putting the value of W in equation (*i*) we get,

$$M + \frac{275}{8} \times 2 = 168.75$$

$$\text{or,} \quad M = 168.75 - 68.75 = \text{Rs. } 100$$

∴ Cost of materials = Rs. 100

Problem 15

Calculate the earnings of workers *A* and *B* from the following particulars for a month and allocate the earnings to each job *P, Q* and *R* :

	A	*B*
(a) Basic Wages	Rs. 200	Rs. 200
(b) Dearness Allowance	50%	50%
(c) Provident Fund (basic wages)	10%	10%
(d) Employees' State Insurance (on basic wages)	$2\frac{1}{2}\%$	$2\frac{1}{2}\%$
(e) Overtime	10 hours	—
(f) Idle time and leave	—	16 hours

The normal working hours for the month is 192. Overtime is paid for @ double the normal wages with dearness allowance. Employer's contribution to State Insurance and Provident Fund are at equal rates with employees' contribution. The month contain 24 working days and one paid-holiday. The two workers were employed on jobs *P, Q* and *R* in the following proportion :

Job	*P*	*Q*	*R*
Worker *A*	50	30	20
Worker *B*	40	30	30

Overtime was done on job *R*. ***[I.C.W.A. (Inter) Adopted]***

Solution

Statement showing the Earnings of Workers A and B

Particulars	*A* Details Rs.	*A* Amount Rs.	*B* Details Rs.	*B* Amount Rs.
Basic Wages	—	200	—	200
Dearness Allowance	—	100	—	100
Overtime Wages (200% of Basic Wages + D.A.)	—	31.25	—	—
Gross Wages	—	331.25	—	300
Less : Contribution to P.F. @ 10%	20	—	20	—
E.S.I. Contribution @ $2\frac{1}{2}$%	5	25.00	5	25
Net Wages		306.25		275

Statement showing Calculation of Labour Cost per Hour

Particulars	*A* Rs.	*B* Rs.
Gross Wages (excluding overtime wages)	300	300
Employer's contribution to P.F. and E.S.I.	25	25
Total Labour Cost	325	325
Labour Cost per hour = $\frac{\text{Total Labour Cost}}{\text{192 hours}}$	1.69 (approx.)	1.69 (approx.)

Statement showing Allocation of Wages to Jobs

Items	*P* Rs.	*Q* Rs.	*R* Rs.	*Total* Rs.
Worker *A* :				
Ordinary Wages	162.50	97.50	65	325
Overtime Wages			31.25	15.62
Worker *B* :				
Ordinary Wages	130.00	97.50	97.50	325
	292.50	195.00	193.75	665.62

Working Notes :

(*i*) Normal rate of wages $= \frac{\text{Total Basic Wages}}{\text{Total working hours}}$

$= \frac{\text{Rs. } 300}{192} = \text{Rs. } 1.5625$

(*ii*) Overtime Wages = Rs. 1.5625 × 2 = Rs. 3.125

(*iii*) Idle time and leave time have been taken as normal

Problem 16

Find out the normal and overtime wages payable to a worker from the following particulars :

Days	*Hours Worked*
Monday	10
Tuesday	8
Wednesday	11
Thursday	9
Friday	9
Saturday	5
	52

Normal working hours = Per day 8 hours
Normal rate = Re. 1 per hour
Overtime rate = up to 9 hours in a day at single rate and over 9 hours in a day at double rate.

Or

up to 48 hours in a week at single rate, whichever is more beneficial to the workman.

Solution

(*a*) **Calculation of Normal and Overtime Wages under Daily Basis**

Days	*Hours worked*	*Normal Hours*	*Overtime Hours*	
			Single Rate	*Double Rate*
Monday	10	8	1	1
Tuesday	8	8	—	—
Wednesday	11	8	1	2
Thursday	9	8	1	—
Friday	9	8	1	—
Saturday	5	4	1	—
Total	52	44	5	3

Normal Wages for 44 hours @ Re. 1 per hour =	Rs. 44
Overtime Wages :	
5 hours @ Re. 1 per hour	Rs. 5
3 hours @ Rs. 2 per hour	Rs. 6
Total Wages	Rs. 55

(*b*) **Calculation of Normal and Overtime Wages under Weekly Basis**

Total hours worked during this week = 52 hours

Normal Wages for 48 hours @ Re. 1 per hour	Rs. 48
Overtime wages for 4 hours @ Rs. 2 per hour	Rs. 8
Total Wages	Rs. 56

Problem 17

In a manufacturing concern bonus to workers are given on a slab rate based on cost saving towards labour and overhead. The following are the slab rates :

(*i*) up to 10% saving 5% of the earning.
(*ii*) up to 15% saving 9% of the earning.
(*iii*) up to 20% saving 13% of the earning.
(*iv*) up to 30% saving 21% of the earning.

(*v*) up to 40% saving 28% of the earning.

(*vi*) Above 40% saving 32% of the earning.

The wage rates per hour of four workers, namely *P, Q, R* and *S*, are, respectively, Re. 1.00, Rs. 1.10, Rs. 1.20 and Rs. 1.40. Overhead is recovered on direct wages @ 200%. Standard cost under wages and overhead per unit is fixed at Rs. 30. The workers have completed one unit each in 8, 7, 5.5 and 5 hrs, respectively.

Calculate in respect of each worker :

(*a*) Amount of bonus earned

(*b*) Total earnings

(*c*) Total earnings per hour.

Solution

Statement showing Bonus Earned, Total Earnings and Earnings per hour

Particulars	*P*	*Q*	*R*	*S*
Time taken (hrs)	8	7	5.5	5
Hourly Rate (Rs.)	1.00	1.10	1.20	1.40
(*i*) Time wages = (Time Taken × Hr.)	8.00	7.70	6.60	7.00
(*ii*) Overhead (@ 200% or D/W)	16.00	15.40	13.20	14.00
(*iii*) Total Cost (*i* + *ii*)	24.00	23.10	19.80	21.00
(*iv*) Standard Cost	30.00	30.00	30.00	30.00
(*v*) Savings in Cost (*iv* – *iii*)	6.00	6.90	10.20	9.00
∴ Savings in Cost = $\left[\frac{\text{Saving in cost}}{30} \times 100\right]$	$\frac{6}{30} \times 100$ = 20%	$\frac{6.9}{30} \times 100$ 23%	$\frac{10.20}{30} \times 100$ = 34%	$\frac{9}{30} \times 100$ = 30%
∴ Bonus Payable [according to slab rate]	13%	21%	28%	21%
(*vi*) Bonus earned	$\left[\frac{13}{100} \times 8\right]$ = 1.04	$\frac{7.70 \times 21}{100}$ 1.62	$\frac{6.60 \times 28}{100}$ 1.85	$\frac{7 \times 21}{100}$ = 1.47
∴ Total earnings (Time Wages + Bonus)	8.00 + 1.04 = 9.04	7.70 + 1.62 = 9.32	6.60 + 1.85 = 8.45	7 + 1.47 = 8.47
Total earnings per hr. $\left[\frac{\text{Total earnings}}{\text{Time taken}}\right]$	$\frac{9.04}{8}$ = 1.13	$\frac{9.32}{7}$ = 1.33	$\frac{8.45}{5.5}$ = 1.54	$\frac{8.47}{5}$ = 1.69

Problem 18

An enterprise has introduced a bonus system of wage payment of a slab rate based on cost of reduction towards wages and overhead, the slab rates are as follows :

Up to 10% of saving in cost bonus is 5% of the earning
" " 20% " " " " " 10% " "
" " 40% " " " " " 20% " "
" " 50% " " " " " 30% " "
" " 75% " " " " " 40% " "
Above 75% " " " " " 50% " "

The wage rate of the workers Utpal, Sumit and Bikash are Re. 1, Rs. 1.25 and Rs. 1.30, respectively. The overhead recovery rate is 300% on productive wages. The standard cost towards wages and overhead per unit is Rs. 1.50 per unit.

If the time taken by Utpal, Sumit and Bikash to finish 100 units is 25 hours, 30 hours and 20 hours, respectively, how much bonus will be due to the three workers ?

Solution

	Utpal	*Sumit*	*Bikash*
Time taken (hours)	25	30	20
Wage Rate (Rs.)	1	1.25	1.30
∴ Wage Payable (Rs.) (*a*)	25	37.50	26.00
Overhead (300%) (b)	75	112.50	78.00
∴ Total wages and overhead [(a) + (b)]	100	150	104
Standard Cost [100 × Rs. 1.50]	150	150	150
∴ Cost reduction (Saving)	50	—	46
Percentage of reduction on standard	$33\frac{1}{3}\%$	—	$30\frac{2}{3}\%$
∴ Percentage of Bonus on earnings (as per slab)	20%	—	20%
Wages	25	37.50	26

∴ Amount of Bonus due :

Utpal = Rs. 25 × 20% = Rs. 5
Sumit = Nil
Bikash = Rs. 26 × 20% = Rs. 5.20

Problem 19

The standard hours of Job No. 10 is 200 hrs. The job has been completed by a worker in 120 hrs.

The bonus system applicable to the job is as follows :

Percentage of time saved to time allowed	Bonus
Up to 10%	10% of time saved
Next 10%	15% " "
Next 20%	20% " "
Balance	25% " "

The rate of pay is Rs. 2 per hour.

Calculate the total earnings of the worker; and also the rate of earnings per hour.

Solution

	hrs
Standard time	200
Time Taken	120
∴ Time Saved	80

∴ % of Time Saved to Time Allowed $= \frac{80}{200} \times 100 = 40\%$

			Bonus hrs
10% of 200 hrs	*i.e.,* 20 hrs	= 10% of 20 hrs	2
10% of 200 hrs	*i.e.,* 20 hrs	= 15% of 20 hrs	3
20% of 400 hrs	*i.e.,* 40 hrs	= 20% of 40 hrs	8
40%	80 hrs		13

	Rs.
∴ Time Wages = 120 × Rs. 2	240
Add : Bonus = Rs. 2 × 13	26
∴ Total Earnings	266

∴ Earnings per hour $= \frac{266}{120}$ = Rs. 2.217

Problem 20

For a certain work order, the standard time is 25 hrs, wages Rs. 5 per hr, the actual time taken is 18 hrs. and factory overhead rate is 75% of standard time.

Prepare a comparative statement showing the effect on paying wages on (*i*) Halsey; and (ii) Rowan Scheme.

Solution

	Rs.
Normal Wages : Time taken × Hr. Rate = 18 × Rs. 5	90
Bonus : Halsey Scheme	
$= \frac{1}{2} \times$ Time Save × H.R. $= \frac{1}{2} \times (25 - 18) \times 5$	= 17.50
Rowan Scheme : $\frac{\text{Time Saved}}{\text{Time Allowed}} \times$ Time Taken × H.R.	
$= \frac{7}{25} \times 18 \times 5$	= 23.20

Employer's Saving

Particulars	*Halsey*	*Rowan*
Labour Savings :		
Standard Wages (1)	125.00	125.00
Less : Wages payable (2)		
Time wage	90.00	90.00
Bonus	17.50	23.20
	107.50	113.20
∴ Labour Savings (1 – 2)	17.50	21.80
Overhead Savings (75% of Standard time) $\left[\frac{75}{100} \times 35\right]$	26.25	26.25
	43.75	48.05

Statement showing the Effect of Paying Wages Under Different Schemes

Incentive System	*Normal Wages*	*Bonus*	*Total Earnings*	*Effective Hourly Rate*	*Employees' Savings*
Halsey	90.00	17.50	107.50	5.972	43.75
Rowan	90.00	23.20	113.20	6.289	48.05

Problem 21

A worker worked in a factory under the Halsey method of remuneration. His weekly wage is Rs. 120 for 48 hrs plus a cost of living bonus is Re. 1 per hr He is given an 8 hr task to perform. He completed the task in 6 hrs. He is allowed 30% of the time saved as premium bonus.

What would be his total hourly rate of earnings and what difference would it make if he was paid under the Rowan method ?

Solution

Hourly Rate $= \frac{120}{48}$ = Rs. 2.50

Cost of living bonus per hr. = Re. 1

Total earnings under Halsey Method :

	Rs.
Time Wages = Rs. 2.50 × 6	15.00
Add : Cost of living bonus = 6 × Re. 1	6.00
Add : Bonus Premium : $(8-6) \times \frac{3}{100} \times 2.50$	1.50
	22.50

∴ Effective hourly Rate = Rs. $\frac{22.50}{6}$ = Rs. 3.75

Under Rowan Plan :

Wages for 6 hrs = (2.50 × 6)	15.00
Cost of living Bonus (1 × 6)	6.00
Bonus = $\frac{2}{8} \times 6 \times 2.5$	3.75
	24.75

∴ Effective hourly Rate = Rs. $\frac{24.75}{6}$ = Rs. **4.12**

Problem 22

From the following particulars calculate the Group Bonus payable in this case and the amounts that will be paid to each member of the group.

Standard production in a week 120 units.

It is agreed that for every 10% increase in production bonus of 5% of the total wages payable of the week will be paid and the same will be shared by the group consisting of members in proportion to their total wages of the week.

Total production for the week 145 units wages earned by the four members of the group (*A*, *B*, *C* and *D*) are, respectively, Rs. 80, Rs. 78, Rs. 72 and Rs. 68. ***[I.C.W.A. Inter]***

Solution

		Units
	Actual Production	145
	Standard Production	120
∴	Increase in Production	25

∴ % of increase in production = $\frac{25}{120} \times 100 = 20\frac{5}{6}\%$

Bonus = 10% of total wages

As 5% bonus is available for every 10% increase, here increase is $20\frac{5}{6}\%$, *i.e.* 20% approx.

Name of Workers	*Wages*	*Bonus (10% of Wages)*	*Total*
A	80.00	8.00	88.00
B	78.00	7.80	85.80
C	72.00	7.20	79.20
D	68.00	6.80	74.80
Total	298.00	29.80	327.80

Problem 23

There are two piece workers, Rakhal and Upendra, who are paid Rs. 5 for each piece work executed which costs Rs. 15 per piece in material.

In a working day of 8 hours, Rakhal can complete 4 pieces and Upendra only 3.

If the overhead charges be Rs. 1.50 per hour, show which of the two piece workers is more useful to the factory.

In what circumstance would it be justifiable to employ even the less efficient worker ?

[I.C.W.A. Inter]

Solution

Calculation of Wages

Rakhal = Number of piece produced × Rate = 4 × Rs. 5 = Rs. 20
Upendra = Number of piece produced × Rate = 3 × Rs. 5 = Rs. 15

Statement of Cost of Production for a Particular Day

Items	*Rakhal* Rs.	*Upendra* Rs.
Materials	60	45
Wages	20	15
PRIME COST	80	60
Overhead of 8 hours @ Rs. 1.50 per hour	12	12
Total cost of production	92	72
Per unit cost of production = $\frac{\text{Total cost of production}}{\text{No. of pieces produced}}$	23	24

The cost of production (per unit) of goods produced by Upendra is higher than that of Rakhal. So, Rakhal is the most efficient worker. But Upendra may be appointed if his wages is to be reduced to equalise the cost of production.

Problem 24

From the following data calculate total monthly remuneration of three workers *A*, *B* and *C* :

(*i*) Standard production per month per worker is 1,000 units
(*ii*) Actual production during a month :
A—800 units, *B*—700 units and *C*—900 units ;
(*iii*) Piece work rate per unit produced—15 paise ;
(*iv*) Dearness wages Rs. 40 per month (fixed) ;
(*v*) House rent allowance—Rs. 20 per month (fixed) ;
(*vi*) Additional production bonus at the rate of Rs. 5 for each percentage of actual production exceeding 75 per cent of actual production Over standard. ***[I.C.W.A Inter]***

Solution

Calculation of Monthly Remuneration of A, B and C

Particulars	A	B	C	Total
Actual Production (in units)	800 units	700 units	900 units	2,400 units
Efficiency of work done = $\left(\frac{\text{Actual Production}}{\text{Standard Production}} \times 100\right)$	80%	70%	90%	
Piece rate wages = [Actual Production × Rate]	120	105	135	360
Production Bonus = [Rs. 5 × excess over 75% of efficiency]	25	—	75	100
Dearness Wages [Fixed]	40	40	40	120
House Rent Allowance	20	20	20	60
Total	205	165	270	640

Problem 25

Payment of wage bonus is made in a concern on the following scale on the basis of the percentage of time saved to time allowed :

Time Saved (% of standard)	*Bonus (% of time saved)*
up to 25%	10%
Above 25% and up to 35%	(i) Plus 20% time saved above 25% and 35%
Above 35%	(ii) Plus 30% of time saved beyond 35%

Calculate the earnings of a worker (wage rate Rs. 1.20 per hour) who takes 50 hours to complete a job, the standard allowed time for which is 100 hours. **[I.C.W.A. Inter]**

Solution

Calculation of Bonus

$$\% \text{ of time saved to time allowed} = \frac{\text{Time Saved}}{\text{Time Allowed}} \times 100$$

$$= \frac{50}{100} \times 100 = 50\%$$

% of Time Saved to time allowed	*Time Saved (hours)*	*Bonus Time*	*Rate Rs.*	*Bonus Rs.*
25%	25	10% of 25 hrs = 2.5 hrs	1.20	3.00
10%	10	20% of 10 hrs = 2 hrs	1.20	2.40
15%	15	30% of 15 hrs = 4.5 hrs	1.20	5.40
				10.80

Statement of Total Earnings

Actual Wages [Time worked × Rate per hour]	
i.e. 50 hrs × Rs. 1.20	60.00
Bonus	10.80
Total Earnings	70.80

Problem 26

A worker, whose day-work wages is Rs. 2.50 per hour, received production bonus under the Rowan Plan. He carried out the following work in a 48 hour week :

Job. 1. 1,500 items at 4 hours per 1,000.

Job. 2, 1,800 items at 3 hours per 1,000.

Job. 3, 9,000 items at 6 hours per 1,000.

Job. 4, 1,500 items for which no standard time was fixed and it was arranged that the worker would be paid a bonus of 25%. Actual time on the job was 4 hours.

Job 5, 2,000 items at 8 hours each item was estimated to be half finished.

Job 2 was carried out on a machine running at 90% efficiency and an extra allowance of $^1/_9$th of actual time was given to compensate the worker..

4 hours were lost due to power cut.

Calculate the earnings of the worker, clearly stating your assumptions for the treatment given by you for the hours lost due to power cut.

[I.C.W.A. Inter]

Solution

Calculation of Standard Time

		Hours
Job 1	1,500 items at 4 hours per 1,000	6.00
Job 2	1,800 items at 3 hours per 1,000	5.40
	and extra time $^1/_9$th	0.60
Job 3	9,000 items at 6 hours per 1,000	54.00
Job 4	1,500 items actual time 4 hours plus bonus 25% of actual	5.00
Job 5	1,000 items (50% of 2,000) at 8 hours per 1,000	8.00
		79.00

∴ Standard Time = 79 hours

Time taken :

Total time	48 hours
Less : Time lost due to power cut	4 hours
	44 hours

$\therefore$ Time Saved = Standard time – Time taken
= 79 hours – 44 hours
= 35 hours

$$\text{Total earnings of worker} = \text{Total time} \times \text{Rate per hour} + \frac{\text{Standard time} - \text{Time taken}}{\text{Standard time}} \times \text{Time taken} \times \text{Rate per hour}$$

$$= 48 \text{ hrs} \times \text{Rs. } 2.50 + \frac{79 \text{ hrs} - 44 \text{ hrs}}{79 \text{ hrs}} \times 44 \text{ hrs} \times \text{Rs. } 2.50$$

$$= \text{Rs. } 120 + \frac{35 \text{ hrs}}{79 \text{ hrs}} \times 44 \text{ hrs} \times \text{Rs. } 2.50$$

$$= \text{Rs. } 120 + \text{Rs. } 48.73 = \text{Rs. } 168.73$$

The worker is entitled to bonus for the time lost due to power cut.

Problem 27

In a workshop, bonus hours are calculated to its worker by the following formula :

$$\text{Time Saved} \times \frac{\text{Time taken}}{\text{Time allowed}}$$

The works are carried forward from one period to another. There is no provision for overtimes. Workers are paid for all units produced including rejected units.

From the following data you are requested to calculate for each employee :

(*a*) the total earnings

(*b*) the wages cost of each good unit produced.

Particulars	*Ram*	*Rahim*	*John*
Hourly Rate	2.50	4.00	3.75
Units issued for production	2,600	2,250	3,600
Time allowed for 100 hours	50	60	80
Time taken	48	38	42
Rejects	100	80	400

Solution

Statement Showing Total Earnings of the Employee

Particulars	*Ram*	*Rahim*	*John*
Time wages (Time taken × Hourly Rate)	48 × Rs. 2.5 = 120.00	38 × Rs. 4 = 152.00	42 × Rs. 3.75 =157.50
Add : Bonus[1] $\left[\frac{\text{Time Saved} \times \text{Time Taken}}{\text{Time Allowed}} \times \text{Hourly Rate}\right]$	9.23	—	10.50
Total Earnings	129.23	152.00	168.00
Good units product (Total units – Rejects units)	(2,600 – 100) = 2,500	(2,280 – 80) = 2,200	(3,600 – 400) = 3,200
$\therefore$ Cost of wages per unit of good units	$\frac{129.23}{2{,}500}$ = 0.0517	$\frac{152.00}{2{,}200}$ = 0.0691	$\frac{168.00}{3{,}200}$ = 0.0525

Working Notes :

Calculation for Bonus

Particulars	*Ram*	*Rahim*	*John*
Time allowed (hours)	$\frac{2,600}{50} = 52$	$\frac{2,280}{60} = 38$	$\frac{3,600}{80} = 45$
Time taken	48	38	42
∴ Time Saved	4	—	3
Bonus :	$\frac{4}{52} \times 48 \times 2.5 = 9.23$	—	$\frac{3}{45} \times 42 \times 3.75 = 10.50$

Problem 28

Two workwomen, Mita and Kakoli, produce the same product using the same material. Their normal wage rate is also the same. Mita is paid bonus according to Rowan System, while Kakoli is paid bonus according to the Halsey System. The time allowed to make the product is 200 hours. Mita takes 120 hours while Kakoli takes 160 hours to complete the product. The factory overhead rate is Rs. 5 per woman hour actually worked. The factory cost for the product for Mita is Rs. 14,560 and for Kakoli it is Rs. 15,200.

You are required to

(*a*) find the normal rate of wages

(*b*) find the cost of materials

(*c*) prepare a statement comparing the factory cost of the products as made by the two workwomen. ***[C.A. Inter Adopted]***

Solution

Factory overhead :

Mita = 120 hrs × Rs. 5 = Rs. 600

Kakoli = 160 hrs × Rs. 5 = Rs. 800

Assumed that :

Cost of Material = M

Cost of Labour = W

∴ Factory Cost = M + W + 1,400 = 14,560 + 15,200

Labour Cost :

$$\text{Mita} = \text{Hours worked} \times \text{Rate per hour} + \frac{\text{Time Saved}}{\text{Time Allowed}} \times \text{Hours worked} \times \text{Rate per hour}$$

$$= \left(120 + \frac{80}{200} \times 120\right) \text{Rate per hour}$$

= (120 + 48) Rate per hour (RH) = 168 RH

Kakoli = Hours worked + 50% (Time Save × Rate per hour)

$$= 160 + \frac{50}{100}(40 \times RH) = 180\ RH$$

(*a*) So, M + 168 RH + 600 = 14,560 ... (i)

M + 180 RH + 800 = 15,200 ... (ii)

or, M + 168 RH = 13,960

M + 180 RH = 14,400

or, 12 RH = 440

∴ RH = 440/12 = Rs. 36.67

(*b*) Material Cost = M + 168 × 36.67 = 13,960

or, M + 6,160 = 13,960

or, M = 7,800

Mita : $E = HW \times RH + \frac{TS}{TA} \times HW \times RH$

$= 120 \times 36.67 + \frac{80}{200} \times 120 \times 36.67 = 6{,}160$

Kakoli : $K = HW \times RH + 50\% \ (TS \times RH)$

$= 160 \times 36.67 + \frac{50}{100} \ (40 \times 36.67) = 6{,}600$

Statement of Cost of Products

	Mita	*Kakoli*
Cost of Material	Rs. 7,800	Rs. 7,800
Labour Cost	Rs. 6,160	Rs. 6,600
Factory overhead	Rs. 600	Rs. 800
	Rs. 14,560	Rs. 15,200

Problem 29

In a factory guaranteed wages are paid @ Rs. 4 per hour and the payment is made on a weekly basis of 48 hrs per week. It is estimated that 25 minutes are required to produce a product. To this, personal time and contingency allowance of 20% is to be added. During one week Miss Rekha produced 110 products.

Calculate her wages under :

(*i*) Time rate
(*ii*) Piece rate with guaranteed weekly wage
(*iii*) Rowan Premium Bonus
(*iv*) Halsey Premium Bonus

Solution

(*i*) **Time Rate**

Hourly Rate = Rs. 4
Hours per week = 48 hrs
Time Rate = Rs. 4 × 48 = Rs. 192

(*ii*) **Piece Rate**

	Time taken per unit	= 25 minutes
Add :	Contingency time (20% of 25)	= 5 minutes
	Standard time per unit	= 30 minutes

$\therefore$ Piece Rate $= \frac{\text{Rs. } 4 \times 30}{60} = \text{Rs. } 2$

$\therefore$ Piece Rate Wages = Rs. 2 × 110 = Rs. 220

(*iii*) **Rowan Premium Bonus**

Standard time for 110 units

$= \frac{110 \times 30}{60} = 55 \text{ hrs}$

Time Taken = 48 hrs
Time Saved = (55 − 48) = 7 hrs

Time Wages = 48 × Rs. 4 = 192

Add : Bonus $= \frac{\text{Time saved}}{\text{Time allowed}} \times \text{Time taken} \times \text{hr Rate}$

$= \frac{7}{55} \times 48 \times 4$ = 24.44

= 216.44

(*iv*) **Halsey Premium Bonus**

			Rs.
	Time Wages = 48 × Rs. 4	=	192
Add :	Bonus $= \frac{1}{2} \times 7 \times 4$	=	14
			206.00

Problem 30

The time allowed for a work order is 80 hrs. The hourly rate guaranteed wage is Re. 1.00. But due to the saving in time, Rahim, a worker gets an hourly wage is Rs. 1.25. The bonus due to savings in time is calculated under Rowan Scheme.

You are requested to calculate the hourly rate of wages if Rahim will get bonus under Halsey Weir Premium bonus system (50% of works).

Solution

Let the time taken by Rahim = x hours

Now the total earnings under Rowan Scheme will be :

$$\text{Total Wage} = x \times \text{Re. } 1 + \frac{(80-x)}{80} \times x \times \text{Re. } 1$$

$$= x + \frac{(80-x)}{80}\, x$$

∴ Now effective hourly Rate is Rs. 1.25

Hence we can say

$$\text{Rs. } 1.25 = \frac{x + \frac{(80-x)}{80} x}{x}$$

or $$1.25 = \frac{x\left[1 + \frac{(80-x)}{80}\right]}{x}$$

or $$1.25 = 1 + \frac{(80-x)}{80}$$

or $$1.25 - 1 = \frac{(80-x)}{80}$$

or $$1.25 - 1 = \frac{80-x}{80}$$

or $$0.25 \times 80 = 80 - x$$

or $$20 = 80 - x$$

∴ $$x = 60$$

Now if Rahim is paid under Halsey Scheme, his total earnings will be :

	Rs.
Time wages = 60 × Re. 1	60.00
Add : Bonus $= \frac{1}{2}(80 - 60) \times$ Re. 1	10.00
Total Earnings	70.00

∴ Effective Hourly Rate $= \frac{\text{Rs. } 70}{60}$ = Rs. 1.167

Problem 31

The Alpha Corporation has filed the following income statement for the year ending 31st March 2007 :

	Sales		Rs. 24,00,000
Less :	Variable Costs		
	Material	Rs. 6,01,000	
	Direct Labour	5,19,000	
	Variable factory overheads	3,20,000	
	Variable selling and distribution overhead	1,90,000	16,30,000
	Contribution		7,70,000
Less :	Fixed overheads		5,30,000
	Net income before tax		2,40,000
	Capital employed		12,00,000

The actual number of hours for direct labour worked in the year under review was 2,06,000. As a consequence of delays in filling vacancies of employees who quit, 6,000 potential direct hours were not worked and included in the actual hours worked were 4,000 hours of trainees, half of which time was unproductive.

The costs incurred in consequence of re-employment were as follows :

(*a*) Separation costs Rs. 25,630 (*b*) Selection costs Rs. 32,080

(*c*) Recruitment costs Rs. 23,140 and (*d*) Training costs Rs. 31,160

Calculate the profits lost or forgone on account of labour turnover (round off to the nearest rupee) and the potential return on capital and sales and turnover ratio. ***[I.C.W.A. Final Adopted]***

Solution

Cost of labour turnover can be broadly grouped under two categories :

(*a*) Preventive Cost (*b*) Replacement Cost

This particular question deals with the replacement cost only. Profit cost on account of labour turnover may be due to :

(*i*) Saving in cost provided there was no labour turnover.

(*ii*) Loss in contribution due to under-utilisation of capacity.

(*i*) Saving in cost, if no replacement cost is incurred :

	Rs.
Separation Costs	25,630
Selection Costs	32,080
Recruitment	23,140
Training	31,160
Total Replacement Costs	1,12,010

(*ii*) **Loss in Contribution**

Actual effective direct labour hours = Actual direct labour hrs worked − trainees' unproductive hours

$$= 2{,}06{,}000 - \left(4{,}000 \times \frac{50}{100}\right) = 2{,}04{,}000 \text{ hrs}$$

Potential effective labour hours = Actual direct labour hrs. worked − potential direct hours not worked

$$= 2{,}06{,}000 + 6{,}000 = 2{,}12{,}000 \text{ hours}$$

Effective labour hours Cost = Potential effective labour hours − Actual effective labour hours.

$$= 2{,}12{,}000 - 2{,}04{,}000 = 8{,}000 \text{ hrs}$$

$$= \frac{8{,}000}{2{,}04{,}000} \times 100 = 3.9216\%$$

Had there been no loss of effective hours, production and sales would have gone up by 3.9216%. The following losses can now be worked out

(a) Loss in contribution = Rs. 7,70,000 × 3.9216%
= Rs. 30,196

(b) Total profit lost = Loss in saving + Loss in contribution
= 1,12,010 + 30,196
= Rs. 1,42,206

(c) Potential Profit = Net profit before tax + Profit forgone at (b)
= 2,40,000 + 1,42,206
= Rs. 3,82,206

(d) Potential Sales = Existing Sales + Sales lost
= 24,00,000 + (24,00,000 × 3.9216%)
= 24,00,000 + 94,118 = 24,94,118

(e) Potential on capital invested $= \frac{\text{Potential profit}}{\text{Capital invested}}$

$= \frac{3,82,206}{12,00,000} \times 100 = 31.851\%$

(f) Potential return on sales $= \frac{\text{Potential profit}}{\text{Potential sales}} \times 100$

$= \frac{3,82,206}{24,94,118} \times 100 = 15.326\%$

(g) Turnover ratio $= \frac{\text{Labour hours lost}}{\text{Potential labour hours}} \times 100$

$= \frac{8,000}{2,12,000} \times 100 = 3.774\%$

Problem 32

The Managing Director of All Found Limited is very much perturbed to see that labour turnover is increasing every year. Before taking appropriate action, he desires to know the profit forgone on account of labour turnover.

You are required to calculate the profit forgone on account of labour turnover from the following :

ALL FOUND LTD.
Income Statement for the Year Ended 31.12.06

	Rs.	*Rs.*
Sales		2,00,000
Variable cost :		
Material	50,000	
Direct Labour	40,000	
Variable Overhead	40,000	1,30,000
Contribution		70,000
Less : Fixed Overhead		20,000
Profit before tax		50,000

The direct labour hours worked in the concern during the period were 20,300 of which 500 hours pertained to the new workers on training. Only 40% of the trainees' time was productive. As replacement for the worker left was delayed for some time, 600 productive hours were lost.

The direct costs incurred by the company as a consequence of labour separation and replacements were as follows :

Separation Costs	Rs. 2,000
Selection Costs	Rs. 3,000
and Training Costs	Rs. 5,000.

[I.C.W.A. Final Adopted

Solution

	Direct Labour hours worked	20,300
Less :	Unproductive time of new workers [500 hours × 60%]	300
	Productive Hours	20,000

Lost Labour Hours 600 (Replacement) + 300 (Training) = 900

Unit sales per Productive Labour Hour

$$\text{Rs. } \frac{2,00,000}{20,000} = \text{Rs. } 10$$

(*a*) Loss of potential sales = 900 hours × Rs. 10 = Rs. 9,000

Direct Labour Cost per hour worked = $\frac{\text{Rs. } 40,000}{20,300}$ = Rs. 1.97

(*b*) Increase in Direct labour cost of lost hours due to replacement = 600 × Rs. 1.97 = Rs. 1,182

[300 hours already included while calculating the hourly rate]

(*c*) Increase in material and variable overhead due to increase in potential sales = $\frac{90,000}{2,00,000} \times 9,000$ = Rs. 4,050

Total increase in cost (*b* + *c*) = 1,182 + 4,050

Contribution forgone (*a* – *c*)	=	Rs. 5,232
Add : Separation, selection and training costs		3,768
		10,000
Profit forgone due to labour turnover		13,768

Problem 33

Manpower planning is an important exercise in personal policy of any company. From the following details, calculate the estimated recruitment of company over the next two years. The company has 1,000 staff in clerical grade I, the lowest clerical grade in the company, with the following age structure :

Under 20	600
20 — 30	300
Over 30	100
	1,000

Wastage rates and promotion prospects in the next two years are expected to be :

Age	*Wastage*	*Promotion to next higher grade*
Under 20	30%	10%
20 — 30	10%	40%
Over 30	5%	20%

The demand forecast shows that 1,200 clerical grade I staff will be required in two years time. Assume that no promotion will be made from lower grade to clerical grade I. ***[I.C.W.A. Final]***

Solution

Manpower in the beginning			1,000
(*A*) *Wastages*			
(*i*) 30% of 600	= 180		
(*ii*) 10% of 300	= 30		
(*iii*) 5% of 100	= 5	215	
(B) *Promotions*			
(*i*) 10% of 600	= 60		
(*ii*) 40% of 300	= 120		
(*iii*) 20% of 100	= 20	200	415
			585
Staff requirement			1,200
Estimated recruitment over 2 years			615

Problem 34

Calculate normal overtime and total wages payable to a worker from the particular given below :

Day	Hrs worked
Monday	10
Tuesday	9
Wednesday	8
Thursday	12
Friday	9
Saturday	4

Normal working hour = 8 per day.
Normal Rate = Rs. 5 per day.
Overtime Rate = up to 9 hrs per day – single rate and beyond 9 hrs a day—Double rate.

[I.C.W.A. (Int.) Dec. 1995]

Solution

Statement Showing Normal Overtime

Day	*Normal Working hrs*	*Hours Worked*	*At Normal Rate*	*Overtime*	
				Single Rate	*Double Rate*
Monday	8	10	8	1	1
Tuesday	8	9	8	1	—
Wednesday	8	8	8	—	—
Thursday	8	12	8	1	3
Friday	8	9	8	1	—
Saturday	4	4	4	—	—
		52	44	4	4

Calculation of total wages payable :

Normal wages on time rate basis	= 44 × 5 = Rs. 220
Overtime Wages Single Rate	= 4 × 5 = Rs. 20
Double Rate	= 4 × 10 = Rs. 40
Total Wages	280

Problem 35

Wage negotiations are going on in a company with the Recognised Labour Union and the Management requests you, as the Cost Accountant of the Company, to formulate an incentive wage scheme with a view to increasing productivity.

The case of three representatives *X*, *Y* and *Z*—who produce, respectively, 1,500, 1,200 and 900 units in a normal week of 40 hrs is taken up for study.

Assume that day wages would be guaranteed at Rs. 6 per hour and the piece rate would be based on a standard hourly output of 25 units.

Calculate the earnings and labour cost per 100 pieces of each of the above three workers under (i) Piece-work with a guaranteed weekly wage, (ii) Halsey-Premium Plan and (iii) Rowan Premium Plan.

Also calculate the average wage cost for the company to produce 100 pieces under each of the above methods. ***[C.U. B.Com. (Hons.) 1995]***

Solution

Working Notes :

Hourly Rate = Rs. 6

Per hour production = 25 units

$\therefore$ Piece Rate = $\frac{\text{Rs. } 6}{25}$ = 0.24

Statement showing Weekly Wages of Workers

Particulars	X	Y	Z
Units Produced	1,500	1,200	900
St. hours for production = $\frac{\text{(Actual Production)}}{25}$	60	48	36
Actual Time Taken	40	40	40
$\therefore$ Time Saved (hrs) (St. hrs – Time Taken)	20	8	—
Hourly Rate (Rs.)	6	6	6
Piece Rate (Rs.)	0.24	0.24	0.24
Wages under Time Rate (Actual Time × Hourly Rate (Rs.)	240	240	240
Wages under Piece Rate (Rs.) (Piece Rate × Production units)	360	288	216
(i) Wages under piece work with guaranteed wage	360	288	240
(ii) Wages under Halsey Premium Plan : Time wages (Rs.)	240	240	240
Add : Bonus $\left(\frac{1}{2} \times \text{Time saved} \times \text{Hourly Rate}\right)$	$\left(\frac{1}{2} \times 20 \times 6\right)$ = 60	$\left(\frac{1}{2} \times 8 \times 6\right)$ = 24	—
$\therefore$ Total Wages under Halsey Plan	300	264	240
(ii) Wages under Rowan Plan Time Wages (Rs.)	240	240	240
Add : Bonus $\left(\frac{\text{Time Saved}}{\text{Time allowed}} \times \text{Time Taken} \times \text{Hourly Rate}\right)$	$\frac{20}{60} \times 40 \times 6$ = 80	$\frac{8}{48} \times 40 \times 6$ = 40	—
Total Wages under Rowan Plan	320	280	240

Statement showing Average Wages Cost for 100 Piece under each of the above methods

Methods	X	Y	Z	*Average*
No. of units produced	1,500	1,200	900	
Wages under piece work with a guaranteed weekly wage (Rs.)	360	288	240	
$\therefore$ Per unit wage	$\frac{\text{Rs. } 360}{1{,}500} = 0.24$	$\frac{\text{Rs. } 288}{1{,}200} = 0.24$	$\frac{\text{Rs. } 240}{900} = 0.267$	0.25
Wages under Halsey Plan (Rs.)	300	264	240	
$\therefore$ Per unit wage	0.20	0.22	0.267	0.23
Wages under Rowan Plan (Rs.)	320	280	240	
$\therefore$ Per unit wage	$\frac{\text{Rs. } 320}{1{,}500} = 0.213$	$\frac{\text{Rs. } 280}{1{,}200} = 0.20$	$\frac{\text{Rs. } 240}{1{,}200} = 0.267$	0.227

$\therefore$ Average wage cost for 100 pieces under each method will be as follows :

(i) Under piece work with guaranteed wage = 0.25 × 100 = Rs. 25

(ii) Under Halsey Plan = Rs. 0.23 × 100 = Rs. 23

(iii) Under Rowan Plan = Rs. 0.227 × 100 = Rs. 22.70.

Problem 36

The normal working hours per week are fixed at 44 hours in a factory. An analysis of the time card of a worker shows that during a week he actually worked 43 hours (including 4 hours overtime). On production and remained idle for the remaining 5 hrs due to machine breakdown.

Normal rate per hour is Rs. 5 Overtime rate is 150% of the normal and the rate of wage for idle time is 80% of the normal.

Calculate total wages payable to the worker and show how the total amount shall be treated in Cost Accounts. ***[C.U. B.Com. (Hons.) 1994]***

Solution

Normal rate per hour = Rs. 5

Overtime Rate per hour $= 5 \times \frac{150}{100}$ = Rs. 7.50

Idle Time Rate = 80% of Rs. 5 = Rs. 4

Total Hours fixed during the week = 44 hrs

	hrs
Total hours worked =	43
Less : Overtime hours =	4
∴ Normal hours worked =	39

∴ Idle time hours = (44 – 39) = 5 hrs

Total wages per week		*Rs.*
Normal time wages	= 39 × Rs. 5 =	195
Overtime wages	= 4 × Rs. 7.50 =	30
Idle time wages	= 5 × Rs. 4 =	20
		245

Treatment of Total Wages in Cost Accounts

(*i*) Normal wages should be treated as a component of Prime Cost charged directly to such Job or work.

(*ii*) Overtime wages, here, is due to fault of management, hence it should be charged directly to the departmental overhead.

(*iii*) Wages for Idle Time—This can be treated as normal 'Idle Time', hence the cost of wage paid should be treated as an item of general overhead.

EXERCISES

1.A. *State which statements are correct (C) and which are wrong (W) :*

(*i*) The cost of labour turnover is recovered through departmental overhead recovery rates.

(*ii*) Measurement of labour turnover gives an idea of the degree of mobility of labour.

(*iii*) Labour mobility being purely personal, nothing can be done to reduce high labour turnover

(*iv*) Defection of workers is one of the reasons for labour turnover.

(*v*) The cost of abnormal idle time may be recovered by inflating the hourly rate.

(*vi*) The cost of normal idle time may be charged to departmental overhead.

(*vii*) The treatment of idle time in cost accounting depends upon the destination between normal an abnormal idle time.

(*viii*) The difference between time clocked and time booked is known as idle time.

(*ix*) Time booking is the recording of time spent by a worker on a specific job or work order

(*x*) Time booking is not necessary when time keeping is accomplished.

(*xi*) Time keeping facilitates the preparation of payroll.

(*xii*) Labour cost can be reduced by recruiting cheap labour.

(*xiii*) A well-satisfied team of workers can raise productivity to a large extent.

(*xiv*) Productivity of workers can be improved only if they are supervised closely.

[Ans. Correct (C) : (*i*), (*ii*), (*iv*), (*vi*), (*vii*), (*viii*), (*ix*), (*xi*), (*xiii*)

Wrong (W) : (*iii*), (*v*), (*x*), (*xii*), (*xiv*)]

B. *State which statements are correct and which are wrong* :

(*i*) The Halsey Plan protects workers against loose premium rate setting.

(*ii*) Piece rate system cannot be successfully applied when the work is of repetitive type.

(*iii*) Time wages system is suitable where output cannot be measured.

(*iv*) Piece rate system is suitable when quality of goods produced is of extreme importance.

(*v*) There are two principal wage system.

(*vi*) Low time wages do not necessarily mean low cost of production and high wages mean high cost of production.

[Ans. Correct (C) : (*iii*), (*v*), (*vi*).
Wrong (W) : (*i*), (*ii*), (*iv*).]

C. *State which statements are correct and which are wrong* :

(*i*) Muster roll is necessary for the preparation of the payroll.

(*ii*) High wages need not necessarily mean high cost per unit.

(*iii*) Non-financial incentive or labour-based costs are also fringe benefits.

(*iv*) Fringe benefits are labour-related costs.

(*v*) Group Bonus plans distinguish between efficient and inefficient workers.

(*vi*) Under the Rowan Plan bonus is a fixed percentage.

(*vii*) The Halsey Plan guarantees a minimum hourly wage.

(*viii*) Incentive plans benefit only the employees.

(*ix*) Premium Bonus plans induce workers to increased efficiency and greater output.

(*x*) Payment by result method lowers the cost of production through their impact on fixed costs.

(*xi*) Time and Motion study, which is a function of the Engineering department, is useless for the determination of wages.

[Ans. Correct (C) : (*i*), (*ii*), (*iv*), (*vi*), (*ix*), (*x*).
Wrong (W) : (*iii*), (*v*), (*vii*), (*viii*), (*xi*).]

2. *Which of the following statements is correct in each of the following questions* :

A. The wages paid to a joiner who constructs wooden mould for concrete laying on a building contract should be as :

(*i*) Direct labour cost of the contract. (*ii*) Indirect labour cost of the contract.
(*iii*) Fixed labour cost of the contract. (*iv*) Non-controllable cost of the contract.

B. Overtime premium pay may be correctly defined as :

(*i*) The bonus paid to skilled workers.

(*ii*) The increased payment during overtime hours because of increased rates of pay.

(*iii*) The payment for all hours in excess of the basic working week.

(*iv*) A premium paid to workers to compensate for fatigue.

C. Vacation pay for factory workers should be charged to :

(*i*) Work-in-process inventory. (*ii*) Direct labour.
(*iii*) Administrative expenses. (*iv*) Factory overhead.

D. Labour turnover rate is best defined as :

(*i*) The number of employees successfully completing the required job training programme.

(*ii*) The degree of mobility of employees from one department to another.

(*iii*) The number of the employees recruited each week.

(*iv*) The number of labourers replaced divided by the average number of employees on the payroll.

E. Which of the following method of remuneration is most likely to give stability of labour cost of the employer :

(*i*) Straight piecework. (*ii*) Premium bonus scheme.
(*iii*) Measured day work. (*iv*) Group bonus scheme.

F. Which of the following is the most relevant use of the clock card :

(*i*) To measure employee efficiency.

(*ii*) To facilitate payment for time spent on the work premises.

(*iii*) To allow labour time to be charged to individual job.

(*iv*) To allow calculation of bonus payment.

G. Which of the following is usually prepared daily by employees for each job worked on ?

(*i*) Labour job ticket. (*ii*) Punch card.
(*iii*) Time card. (*iv*) Cost control card.

[Ans. A (*i*) ; B (*ii*) ; C (*iv*) ; D (*iv*) ; E (*iii*) ; F (*ii*) ; G (*i*).]

THEORETICAL QUESTIONS

(a) *Cost and control*

1. What is meant by idle time ? How is it treated in costing ? Distinguish it from 'idle facility' and 'idle capacity'. ***[I.C.W.A. Inter]***

2. What is labour turnover ? How is it measured ? What are its causes and its effects on labour cost ? How can it be reduced ? ***[I.C.W.A. Inter, C.U. B.Com. (H)]***

3. Describe the essential characteristics of a good system of wage payment.

4. What do you mean by 'overtime premium' ? How overtime premium paid to Direct Labour should be treated in cost accounts ? ***[C.U. B.Com. (H)]***

5. Discuss the importance of the following :

(*a*) Time booking (*b*) Time keeping (*c*) Group incentive.

6. Distinguish between time keeping and time booking. ***[I.C.W.A. Inter, Dec 1995]***

7. Explain the difference between Direct Labour and Indirect Labour, highlighting the importance of such distinction. ***[I.C.W.A. Inter, 1992]***

(b) *Remuneration and Incentives*

1. Discuss the principles of "Premium Bonus Plans'. Describe the salient features of 'Rowan Plan' and 'Halsey Plan' with illustration.

2. What is the principal justification of labour incentive schemes in current Indian conditions ? Describe the essential features of a successful incentive scheme with which you are familiar, or suggest a suitable scheme for an industry which you have studied. ***[I.C.W.A. (Inter)]***

3. Explain the fundamental differences between :

(*a*) Straight piece work ; (*b*) Differential piece work ; (*c*) the Rowan system of premium bonus. In what circumstances would you recommend the use of each of the three systems ?

[I.C.W.A.]

4. What do you mean by "Group Bonus Scheme" ? Discuss its advantages.***[C.U. B.Com. (H)]***

(*a*) Your organisation is experiencing a high labour turnover in recent year and management would like you to submit a report on the loss suffered by the company due to such labour turnover. Following figures are available for your consideration :

Sale	Rs. 600 lakhs
Direct materials	Rs. 150 lakhs
Direct labour 48 lakhs on	4,80,000 man hours
Other variable expenses	60 lakhs
Fixed overheads	80 lakhs

The direct man-hour includes 9,000 man-hours spent on trainees and replacement only 50% of which were productive. Further, during the year, 12,000 man-hours of potential work could not be availed of because of delay replacement. The cost incurred due to separations and replacements amounted to Rs. 1 lakh.

On the basis of the above data, prepare a comparative statement showing actual profit vis-a-vis the profit which would have been realised had there been no labour turnover.

(*b*) What are the important factors to be considered for deciding upon suitability of a particular method of overhead recovery ? ***[I.C.W.A. (Inter) Dec. 1994]***

Following particulars have been extracted from the books of Supreme Engineers Ltd. :

Time allowed for the Job	15 hrs	15 hrs	15 hrs
Time taken	15 hrs	12 hrs	9 hrs
Bonus ratio for Halsey		50%	
Rate per hour		Rs. 2	

(*i*) You are required to compute the quantum of wages under Halsey scheme and Rowan scheme. Which of these schemes would you like to introduce in this company if the time taken to complete the job is likely to reduce to 6 hours after three months ?

(*ii*) An alternative method of payment by results by a straight piece work rate for completion of the job in 7 hours is feasible.

Would you like to switch over to this method of payment given further that hourly rate would be rackoned at Rs. 1.50 for fixation of the piece rate ? Please give reasons for your advice. ***[I.C.W.A. (Inter) Dec. 1994]***

5. Distinguish between (*a*) Taylor Differential Rate and Emerson Efficiency Plan. (*b*) Idle Time and Overtime.

6. Define overtime. Why is it necessary ? Is it desirable to have overtime ? How can overtime be controlled ? How is overtime treated in cost accounts ? ***[I.C.W.A. Inter]***

7. Discuss the advantages and disadvantages of piece work system of payment of wages. Distinguish between time rate wages and piece rate wages. ***[I.C.W.A. Inter, June '90]***

PROBLEMS

1. In a factory, two workers produce the same product from the same material and use the same machine. Their normal wages rate is also the same. They are entitled to bonus under Rowan System. The time allowed to the product is 60 hours. But A takes 40 hours and B takes 50 hours to finish the product. The factory cost of the product for A is Rs. 240 and for B is Rs. 206.67. The factory overhead is Re. 1 per man hour.

   Find out the normal wage rate of the workers and cost of material used.

   [Ans. Cost of material used = Rs. 40; Wage Rate of A = Rs. 3; Wage Rate of B = Rs. 2]

2. For a certain product the standard time is 40 hours. Hourly Rate is Rs. 10, the actual time taken is 26 hours and factory overhead charges 80% of direct wages for standard time.

   Prepare a comparative statement showing the effect of paying wages and employer's savings on (*a*) Halsey and (*b*) Rowan System.

   [Ans. (*a*) Effective hourly Rate—under Halsey Rs. 12.692; under Rowan Rs. 13.50
   (*b*) Employer's Savings—under Halsey Rs. 56.00; under Rowan Rs. 39.20]

3. From the following particulars, calculate the labour cost per man-day of 8 hours :

   (*i*) Basic Salary—Rs. 20 per day.
   (*ii*) Dearness Allowance—Rs. 125 per month plus 50% of Basic Salary.
   (*iii*) Leave Salary—20% of Basic plus D.A.
   (*iv*) Employer's contribution to Provident Fund—Rs. 20 per month plus 10% of Basic + D.A. + Leave Salary.
   (*v*) Expenditure on amenities to labour—Rs. 75,000 per month.
   (*vi*) Number of labour—200
   (*vii*) Number of working days in a month—25 days of 8 hours each.

   [C.U. B.Com. (Pass) 1990]

   [Ans. Rs. 65.40]

4. From the following data ascertain the total earnings of each worker separately under (*i*) Halsey, and (*ii*) Rowan Schemes of incentive payment :

	A	*B*	*C*
(*a*) Worker	*A*	*B*	*C*
(*b*) Time allowed (hours)	3	4	5
(*c*) Actual time taken (hours)	5	3	3
(*d*) Basic rate of wages per hour (Rs.)	2	2	2

   [C.U., B.Com. (Pass)]

   [Ans. (*i*) *A* = Rs. 10; *B* = Rs. 7; *C* = Rs. 8, (*ii*) *A* = Rs. 10; *B* = Rs. 7.50; *C* = Rs. 8.40]

5. A workman is paid at the rate of Rs. 2 per hour under Halsey Premium Plan. He also gets dearness allowance of Rs. 40 per week plus a house rent allowance @ $12^1/_2$% of pay excluding incentive bonus but including dearness allowance.

From the following details, calculate the workman's earning for the week :

Job No.	*Time allowed*	*Time taken*
106	36 hours	24 hours
192	33 hours	22 hours
Waiting time		2 hours

[C.U. B.Com. Pass]

[Ans. Total earnings for the weak Rs. 1.76]

Notes. Bonus = Rs. 23.23 and H.R.A. = Rs. 17

6. A worker takes 80 hours to do a job for which time allowed is 100 hours. His daily rate is Rs. 6.00 per hour.

Calculate the works cost of the job under the following methods of payment of wages :

(*i*) Time rate (*ii*) Piece rate

(*iii*) Halsey Plan; and (*iv*) Rowan Plan

Additional information :

(*a*) Materials Cost = Rs. 800

(*b*) Factory Overhead = 125% of wages. *[C.U. B.Com. Pass, 1989]*

[Ans. (*i*) Rs. 1,880 (*ii*) Rs. 2,150 (*iii*) Rs. 2,015 (*iv*) Rs. 2,096]

7. In an engineering concern, the employees are paid incentive bonus in addition to their normal wages at hourly rates. Incentive bonus is calculated in proportion of time taken to time allowed, or the time saved.

The following details are made available in respect of employees Ajoy, Bijay and Sujay for a particular week :

	Ajoy	*Bijay*	*Sujay*
Normal wages (Rs. per hour)	4.00	5.00	6.00
Completed units of production	6,000	3,000	4,800
Time allowed (per 100 units)	0.8 hrs	1.5 hrs	1 hr
Actual time taken (hours)	42	40	48

You are required to work out for each employee :

(*i*) the amount of bonus earned

(*ii*) the total amount of wages received

(*iii*) the total wages cost per 100 units of output. *[I.C.W.A. Inter]*

[Ans.

	Ajoy Rs.	**Bijoy Rs.**	**Sujay Rs.**
(*i*) Bonus	**21**	**22.22**	**—**
(*ii*) Total wages	**189**	**222.22**	**288**
(*iii*) Wages cost per 100 unit	**3.15**	**7.41**	**6.001]**

8. From the following data, calculate the remuneration of each of the 3 workers, A, B and C for the month :

(*i*) Standard production per month per worker is 10,000 units.

(ii) Actual production during the month were :

A = 8,000 units, B = 7,000 units, C = 9,000 units.

(*iii*) Piece rate per unit produced is Rs. 2.50.

(*iv*) D.A. Rs. 400 p.m. for each (fixed).

(*v*) House Rent Allowance Rs. 300 p.m. for each (fixed).

(*vi*) Additional production bonus at Rs. 2.00 for each produced, which will be in excess of 75% over the standard production.

(*vii*) Calculate the effective Direct Labour Cost per unit under each of the 3 workers above.

[Audit and Acct. Service Examination Adopted]

[Ans. A = Rs. 2.7125 B = Rs. 2.60 C = Rs. 2.911]

9. From the following particulars tabulate the total earnings per hour of each worker separately under (*i*) 'Halsey'; and (*ii*) 'Rowan' Schemes of incentive payment :

(*a*) Workers	A	B	C	D	E	F
(*b*) Time Allowed (hrs)	3	4	5	6	7	8

(*c*) Actual time (hrs)	5	3	4	5	3	3
(*d*) basic wages per hour (Rs.)	2	2	2	2	2	2

[*I.C.W.A. Inter]*

**[Ans. A : (*i*) Rs. 10; (*ii*) Rs. 10; B : (*i*) Rs. 7; (*ii*) Rs. 7.50;
C : (*i*) Rs. 9; (*ii*) Rs. 9.60; D : (*i*) Rs. 11; (*ii*) Rs. 11.67;
E : (*i*) Rs. 10; (*ii*) Rs. 9.43; F : (*i*) Rs. 11; (*ii*) Rs. 9.75]**

10. From the following data, you are required to calculate the earnings of a worker for a month under :

(*i*) Straight price rate, (*ii*) Differential piece-rate
(*iii*) Halsey premium scheme (50% Sharing); and (*iv*) Rowan Premium Scheme

Monthly working hours 192
Hourly Wage Rate Rs. 7.50
Normal time taken per piece 20 minutes
Normal output per month 480 pieces
Actual output for the month 600 pieces
Differential piece rate—when output is below normal, 80% of piece rate and when output is at or above normal 120% of piece rate.

**[Ans. (*i*) Straight piece rate = Rs. 1,500; (*ii*) Differential piece rate = Rs. 1,800;
(*iii*) Halsey Premium Scheme = Rs. 1,620; (*iv*) Rowan Premium Scheme = Rs. 1,728]**

11. From the following information, you are requested to calculate the amount earned by each employee under the following remuneration method :

(*a*) Piecework (with guaranteed hourly rate)
(*b*) Hourly rate
(*c*) Bonus system (under which the employees receives $^2/_3$rd of time saved) :

Name of employee	Ram	Shyam	Jadu
Standard time for 100 units	48	64	76
Price per unit (Paise)	12.5	10	15
Guaranteed hourly rate (Paise)	60	75	50
Time taken (hours)	80	84	78
Units produced	400	250	300

You are also asked to calculate the gross wages paid to each employee under each of the above methods.

**[Ans. Ram (*a*) Rs. 25; (*b*) Rs. 24; (*c*) Rs. 26.40
Shyam : (*a*) Rs. 31.50 (Guaranteed minimum); (*b*) Rs. 31.50, (*c*) 31.50;
Jadu : (*a*) Rs. 22.50; (*b*) Rs. 19.50; (*c*) Rs. 25.50]**

12. Calculate the earnings of Ram, Rahim and John from the following data :

(*a*) Time Rate (*b*) Straight Piece Rate
(*c*) Different Piece Rate (*d*) Straight Piece Rate based on Standard hours.
(*e*) Halsey Scheme (*f*) Rowan Scheme

Total hours worked in a particular week 45 hours.

	Hours Actually Worked	*No. of unit Produced*
Ram	42	400
Rahim	37.5	420
John	33	350

Standard Production per hour 7.5 hours
Rate per hour Rs. 3
Rate per piece 30 paise

Different Piece Rate :

Production below std.	80% of Normal Rate
100% of efficiency	Normal Rate
100%—110%	106% of Normal Rate
110%—125%	115% of Normal Rate
Above—125%	120% of Normal Rate

[Ans. (*a*) Ram = Rs. 126; Rahim = Rs. 112.50; John = Rs. 99
(*b*) Ram = Rs. 120; Rahim = Rs. 126; John = Rs. 105
(*c*) Ram = Rs. 142.21; Rahim = Rs. 156.79; John = Rs. 108.88
(*d*) Ram = Rs. 160; Rahim = Rs. 168; John = Rs. 140
(*e*) Ram = Rs. 143; Rahim = Rs. 140.25; John = Rs. 119.50
(*f*) Ram = Rs. 152.77; Rahim = Rs. 149.67; John = Rs. 128]

13. From the data given below, calculate the comparative works cost for a job in Factory A and Factory B :

	Factory A	*Factory B*
Methods of payment of wages	Halsey Plan (50%)	Rowan Plan
Standard time for the job	250 hours	240 hours
Actual time taken	200 hours	210 hours
Hourly rate of wages	Rs 2.50	Rs. 3.00
Material cost for the job	Rs. 1,000	Rs. 900
Factory overhead	150% of wages	$133^1/_3$% of wages

[C.U. B.Com. (Hons.)]

[Ans. Works cost : *Factory A* Rs. 2,406.25; *Factory B.* Rs. 2,553.75]

14. A worker under the Halsey method of remuneration has a day rate of Rs. 12 per week of 48 hours plus a cost of living bonus of 10 paise per hour worked. He is given an 8 hour task to perform, which he accomplishes in 6 hours. He is allowed 30% of the time saved as premium bonus. What would be his total hourly rate of earnings and what difference would it make if he was paid under the Rowan method ? ***[B.Com. Rajasthan]***

[Ans. Halsey—Re. 0.375; Rowan—Re. 0.225]

15. In a light engineering concern, the standard time fixed for a job is 20 hours and basic wages Re. 1.00 per hour. A bonus scheme has been introduced so that the worker may get his normal rate for the hours actually worked and for half the hours saved.

What will be the earnings of the worker and his effective earnings per hour if the job is completed in : (a) 15 hours, and (b) 18 hours. If the material of the job costs Rs. 50.00 and the factory overhead is to be charged at Rs. 2.00 per hour, calculate the factory costs of the job in both the above cases. ***[B.Com. Bangalore]***

[Ans. (*a*) Rs. 17.50 and Rs. 19.00; (*b*) Earnings per hour : Rs. 1.66 and Rs. 1.05;
(*c*) Factory cost : (*a*) Rs. 97.50 (*ii*) Rs. 105.00]

16. In an Assembly shop of a motor cycle factory 4 workmen A, B, C and D work together as a team and are paid on group piece rate, they also work individually on day rate jobs. In a 44 hour week the following hours have been spent by A, B, C and D on group piece work, *viz,* A = 40 hours, B = 40 hours, C = 30 hours, and D = 20 hours. The balance of the time has been booked by each worker on day work jobs. Their hourly rates are :

A	=	0.50 paise ;	B	=	0.75 paise
C	=	Re. 1.00 ;	D	=	Re. 1.00

The group piece rate is Re. 1.00 per unit and the team has produced 150 units.

Calculate the gross weekly earnings of each workman taking into consideration that each individual is entitled to Dearness Allowance of Rs. 20 per week. ***[C.U. B. Com. Hons.]***

[Ans. A = Rs. 52; B = Rs. 68; C = Rs. 79; D = Rs. 74]

17. The guaranteed wages for workers in a factory is Rs. 16 per day of 8 hours. Calculate the total earnings and effective rate per hour of the following workers under (*a*) Emersion Efficiency Bonus Plan, (*b*) Halsey Plan, and (*c*) Rowan Plan.

The workers finish their day's work as Rama 12 hours, Bhima 14 hours, Soma 6 hours, and Thima in 4 hours. ***[Mysore, B.Com. 1987]***

[Ans. Earnings :

Rama : (*a*) Rs. 16.00, Rs. 2.00; (*b*) Rs. 16.00, Rs. 2.00; (*c*) Rs. 16.00, Rs. 2.00
Bhima : (*a*) Rs. 18.00, Rs. 2.00; (*b*) Rs. 16.00, Rs. 2.00; (*c*) Rs. 16.00, Rs. 2.00
Soma : (*a*) Rs. 24.53, Rs. 3.067; (*b*) Rs. 18.66, Rs. 2.33; (*c*) Rs. 20.00, Rs. 2.50
Thima : (*a*) Rs. 35.20, Rs. 4.40; (*b*) Rs. 24.00, Rs. 3.00; (*c*) Rs. 24.00, Rs. 2.00]

18. An analysis of the time card of a workman on a particular machine of the factory shows that of the total 96 hours, he worked 90 hours (out of 90 hours, 8 hours overtime) on production and that 6 hours were idle time due to power cut.

The rate of worker is Re. 1 per hour, but overtime is paid at 50% extra.

You are required to calculate the total wages paid to the workman between 'Direct' and 'Indirect' labour, indicating reasons therefore.

[Ans. Direct wages = Rs. 94 and Indirect wages = Rs. 6]

19. In a manufacturing company the daily wage rate guaranteed for a worker is Rs. 1.87 and the standard output fixed for the month is 1,000 articles, representing 100% efficiency. The daily wage rate is paid without bonus to those workers who show up to $66\frac{2}{3}$% of the efficiency standard. Beyond this, there is a bonus payable in a graded scale in a fixed ratio to the increased output as :

Efficiency	*Bonus Payable*
90%	10%
100%	20%

Further increase of 1% is given for every 1% further rise in efficiency.

Find out the total earnings of A, B, C and D who have worked for 26 days in a month.

The workers' output are

A = 500 articles ; B = 900 articles ; C = 1,000 articles ; D 1,300 articles.

[B.Com. Punjab]

[Ans. A = Rs. 48.62; B = Rs. 53.48; C = Rs. 58.34; D = Rs. 72.93]

20. A workman whose basic rate of pay is Rs. 2.00 per hour is working under the 'Rowan System' of premium bonus. In addition, he receives a cost of living bonus of Rs. 33 per week of 44 hours. During the week he does the following jobs : (*i*) Job 'A' for which 30 hours are allowed, in 20 hours ; (ii) Job 'B' for which 36 hours allowed, in 20 hours. During the week his waiting time amounts to 4 hours.

Calculate the workman's earnings and the amounts to be charged to each job and to overhead.

[I.C.W.A. U.K.]

[Ans. Job A Rs. 68.33; Job B Rs. 75.77; Overhead Rs. 8.00; Total Earnings Rs. 152.10]

21. An employee working under a bonus scheme saves 4 hours in a job for which the standard time is 32 hours. Calculate the rate per hour worked and wages payable for the time taken under the following alternative scheme (award rate is Re. 1 per hour) :

(*i*) Employee receives an increase in the hourly rate based on percentage.

(*ii*) A bonus of 10% on award rate is payable when standard time (namely 100% efficiency) is achieved plus a further bonus of 1%, award rate for each 1% in excess of 100% efficiency.

[I.C.W.A. Inter]

[Ans. (*i*) Wages = Rs. 31.50 (*ii*) Rate per hour = Rs. 1.24]

22. In a factory, the employees are paid a bonus on hours saved at the basic wage rates. The bonus hours are calculated on the hours saved multiplied by the hours saved divided by time allowed. Works are carried forward from one month to another and no overtime is required. Payment is made in full for total units produced. The data relating to the production are as follows :

Name of the Employee	Arup	Anup	Ashim
Unit issued to worker (dozen)	160	224	140
Time Allowed (hours)	432	500	300
Basic wage rates per hour	Re. 0.70	Re. 0.50	Re. 0.80
Time taken (hours)	288	300	320
Rejects (units)	128	272	80

You are required to calculate for each employee :

(*i*) bonus hours and bonus earned ;

(*ii*) Gross wages earned ;

(*iii*) Wage cost per good unit produced.

[Ans.	Arup	Anup	Ashim
Bonus hours	**48 hours**	**80 hours**	**Nil**
Bonus earned	**Rs. 33.60**	**Rs. 40**	**Nil**
Gross wages	**Rs. 235.20**	**Rs. 190**	**Rs. 256**
Wages cost per unit	**13 Paise**	**8 Paise**	**16 Paise]**

23. In a factory's bonus system bonus hours are credited to the employee in the proportion of time taken, which time saved bears to the time allowed. No overtime is worked and payment is made in full for all units worked on, including those subsequently rejected.

From the following, you are required to calculate for each employee :

(*a*) The bonus hours and amount of bonus earned

(*b*) Total wages cost

(*c*) Wages cost of each good unit produced.

Employee	Ami	Tumi	Se
Basic Wages/hour	Rs. 10	Rs. 16	Rs. 15
Units issued for production	5,000	4,400	1,200
Time allowed for 200 units	1 hour 18 mts	$1\frac{1}{2}$ hrs	45 mts
Time taken	52 hrs	75 hrs	48 hrs
Rejects	200 units	80 units	800 units

[Ans.	Ami	Tumi	Se
(*a*) **Bonus hrs and Bonus**	**Nil**	**Nil**	**Nil**
(*b*) **Total Wages Cost**	**Rs. 520**	**Rs. 1,200**	**Rs. 720**
(*c*) **Wages Cost of each good unit produced**	**Re. 0.11**	**Re. 0.28**	**Rs. 1.80]**

24. Two fitters, a labourer and a boy, undertake a job on piece rate basis for Rs. 1,290. The time spent by each of them is 220 ordinary working hours. The rates of pay on time rate basis, are Rs. 1.50 per hour for each of the two fitters, Re. 1 per hour for the labourer and Re. 0.50 per hour for the boy. Calculate :

(*a*) The amount of piecework premium and the share of each worker, when the piecework premium is divided proportionately to the wages paid.

(*b*) The selling price of the above job on the basis of the following additional data :

Cost of direct material	Rs. 2,010
Works overhead	20% of prime cost
Selling overhead	10% of works cost
Profit	20% on cost of sales.

[I.C.W.A. Inter]

[Ans. Piecework Premium Rs. 300; Share of 2/5 Rs. 200; One labourer Rs. 66.67; One boy Rs. 33.33; Selling Price Rs. 5,445]

25. An employee working under a bonus scheme saves 10 hours in a job for which the standard time is 60 hours. Calculate the rate per hour worked and wages payable to him, if incentive bonus of 10% on the hourly rate is payable when standard time (namely 100% efficiency) is achieved, and a further incentive bonus of 1% on hourly rate for each 1% excess of that 100% efficiency is payable. Assume that normal rate of payment is Rs. 5 per hour. ***[C.A. Inter]***

[Ans. Rate per hour = Rs. 6.50 ; Wages payable = Rs. 325.]

26. Calculate the earnings of the workers Ajay and Bijay from the following data for a month :

	Ajay	*Bijay*
Basic wages (Rs.)	200	200
D.A. (on basic wage)	50%	50%
Provident Fund (on basic wage)	8%	8%
E.S.I. (on basic wage)	2%	2%
Overtime (at double the normal Wage and D.A.)	10 hours.	
Leave		10 hours
Units produced	5	5
Standard time fixed for per unit of product	50 hours	50 hours
Bonus paid (at normal basic wage)	Halsey	Rowan

A month consists of 200 working hours. ***[C.U. B.Com. (Hons.) Adopted]***

[Ans. Net earnings : Ajay = Rs. 160 ; Bijay = Rs. 175]

27. In an organisation 10 workers work as a group when weekly production of the group exceeds standard product units 200 per hour. Each man of the group is paid bonus for the excess production in addition to his wages rate of Rs. 2 per hour. There is no relationship between the individuals hourly rate and the bonus rate.

The following is the work record for the week ended on 31.12.92. It is also considered that 50% of the percentage of excess production will be the worker's share.

Day	Hours Worked	Production
Monday	100	25,000
Tuesday	80	20,000
Wednesday	100	22,000
Thursday	85	18,000
Friday	95	23,500
Saturday	40	11,500
	500	1,20,000

(*a*) Compute the rate and amount of bonus for the week.

(*b*) Compute the total pay of Shyamal, who worked 45 hours and was paid Rs. 2.25 per hour and Kamal, who worked 48 hours and was paid @ Rs. 2.00 per hour.

[Ans. Bonus Rate = 20 per hour; Amount of Bonus = Rs. 100;
Total Wages Payable : Shyamal = Rs. 105.60; Kamal = Rs. 110.25]

28. 20 men formed a group. They worked as a group to produce a special type of product. The scheme for group bonus provides the following :

(*a*) Standard output per hour per worker is fixed at 500 units. Bonus is calculated @ 50% of actual production exceeding the standard production.

(*b*) Payment of bonus will be made at the above rate applied on average wage rate of Rs. 4 per hour per worker. There is no relationship between individual worker's hourly rate and the bonus rate.

Assuming that the group produced 80,000 units in 7 hrs.

Compute the rate and the amount of bonus payable to the group.

Also compute the total pay of A if he has worked for 7 hrs and paid a basic wage @ Rs. 4.10 per hour.

[Ans. Bonus rate 7.15% of Actual Production; Amount of bonus payable to the group = Rs. 40.04; Wages payable to A = Rs. 30.70]

29. Both Direct and Indirect labour of a concern are entitled to production bonus in accordance with group bonus scheme. The procedure of which are as follows :

(*i*) For any production in excess of the standard rate fixed at 10,000 units per month of 25 days, a general incentive of Rs. 10 per unit is paid in aggregate. The total amount payable to each group is determined on the basis of an assumed percentage of such excess production being contributed by it, namely 70% by Direct Labour @ 10% by Inspection Staff and @ 12% by Maintenance Staff and 8% by Supervisory Staff.

(*ii*) Again, if the excess production is more than 20% above the standard, direct labour also gets a special bonus @ Rs. 5 per unit for all production in excess of 120% standard.

(*iii*) Inspection staff are penalised @ Rs. 20 per unit for any rejection by customer in excess of 1% of production.

(*iv*) Maintenance staff are also penalised @ Rs. 20 per hour of machine breakdown from the following information find out the production bonus earned by each group. Information :

Actual working days	20
Production	11,000 units
Rejection	200 units
Machine breakdown	40 hrs

[Ans. Direct labour = Rs. 28,000; Inspection staff = Rs. 1,200; Maintenance staff = Rs. 2,800; Supervisory staff = Rs. 2,400; Penalty—Inspection staff = Rs. 1,800; Maintenance Staff = Rs. 800]

30. Using the following data find the earning of a worker under (*a*) Rowan, and (*b*) Halsey premium bonus systems :

Time allowed	48 hours
Time taken	40 hours
Rate per hour	Re. 1.00

[B.Com. Andhra]

[Ans. (*a*) Rs. 46.67, (*b*) Rs. 44.00]

31. Bright Future Co. Ltd. pays its direct factory workers a guaranteed minimum wage of Rs. 2 per hour. In addition, a bonus is paid for effective production time saved at the rate of Rs. 2 per hour. What amount would be earned by each of the following workers :

Worker	*Hours worked*	*Standard hourly output*	*Actual output*
A	40	80 units	3,360 units
B	38	80 units	3,648 units
C	40	80 units	3,000 units

[Ans. A = Rs. 48; B = Rs. 91.20; C = Rs. 80]

32. A worker takes 18 hours to complete a job on daily wages and 12 hours on a scheme of payment by results. His day rate is 75 paise per hour. The material cost of the product is Rs. 6 and the overheads are recovered at 150% of total direct wages.

Calculate the factory cost of the product under (*i*) Piecework plan, (*ii*) Halsey Plan, and (*iii*) Rowan Plan. *[B.Com. Bangalore]*

[Ans. Rs. 9.00, Rs. 11.25 and Rs. 12.00, Factory cost : Rs. 28.50, Rs. 34. 13 and Rs. 36.00]

33. A workman whose basic rate of pay is Rs. 2 per hour is working under the "Rowan System" of premium bonus. In addition, he receives a cost of living bonus of Rs. 33 per week of 44 hours. During the week he does the following jobs : (*i*) Job 'A' for which 30 hours are allowed. in 20 hours. (*ii*) Job 'B' for which 36 hours are allowed, in 20 hours. During the week his waiting time amounts to 4 hours.

Calculate the workman's earnings and the amounts to be charged to each job and to overhead.

[I.C.M.A. London]

[Ans. Job A = Rs. 68.33; Job B = Rs. 75.77; Overhead = Rs. 800; Total earnings Rs. 152.10]

34. A worker is paid 50 paise per hour and the 5 day working week contains 42 hours. The daily allowance for approved absence from his place of work, maintenance of machine, etc. is 12 minutes, and his job cards show that his time chargeable during the week to various cost centres is as follows : Job No. 305 = 20 hours; Job No 310 = 10 hours; Job No 320 = 8 hours.

Time unaccounted for is caused by a power failure.

Show how his wages for the week would be dealt with in cost accounts.

[B.Com. (Hons.) Delhi]

[Ans. Rs. 21.00]

35. Time allowed for the production of 100 "Bolt" is 2 hours and hourly rate of wage payment is Rs. 12. M and N produced 600 and 500 pieces of "Bolt", respectively, in a particular day of 8 hours. Calculate their earnings under Halsey Premium Bonus and Rowan Premium Bonus method.

[C.U. B.Com. (H) 2003]

[Ans.

		Halsey	*Rowan*
		Rs.	*Rs.*
M :	**Basic wages**	**96.00**	**96.00**
	Bonus	**24.00**	**32.00**
		120.00	**128.00**
N :	**Basic wages**	**96.00**	**96.00**
	Bonus	**12.00**	**19.00**
		180.00	**115.00]**

36. A worker produced 180 units in a week, the guaranteed weekly wage payment for 44 hrs. is Rs. 77. The expected time to produce one unit is 16 minutes which is further raised by 25% under the incentive scheme.

What will be the earnings per hour of the worker under the Halsey and Rowan Schemes ?

[C.U. B.Com. (Hons.) 2000]

[Ans. Halsey Scheme : Total earning = Rs. 91.00
Earnings per hour = Rs. 2.07
Rowan Scheme : Total earnings = Rs. 97.53
Earnings per hour = Rs. 2.22]

37. From the following data, calculate works cost for jobs performed by Ajay and Saurav :

	Ajay	*Saurav*
Time allowed (per 100 units)	40 hrs	42 hrs
Rate per unit	Rs. 3	Rs. 4
Rate per hour	Rs. 8	Rs. 12
Actual time taken	48 hrs.	70 hrs.
Actual units produced	150 units	200 units
Material cost for jobs	Rs. 668	Rs. 1,020
Bonus plan	Halsey	Rowan
Factory overhead	150% of wages	100% of wages

[C.U. B.Com. (Hons.) 1998]

[Ans. Ajay : Bonus Rs. 48; Total wages Rs. 432; Prime cost Rs. 1,100; Works cost Rs. 1,748
Saurav : Bonus Rs. 140; Total wages Rs. 980; Prime cost Rs. 2,000; Works cost Rs. 2,980]

38. In a factory, 20 workers are employed in the production of a commodity.
From the following particulars compute the Wages Bill for the workers for January 2002 :
Basic wages—@ Rs. 1,000 p.m. per worker;
Dearness allowance—@ Rs. 900 p.m. per worker;
Bonus for the month—@ 20% of basic wages plus D.A.;
Other allowances—@ Rs. 200 p.m.;
Own and employer's contribution to P.F.—@ 10% of basic wages;
Own and employer's contribution to ESI—@ 2% of basic wages;
Professional Tax deducted from salary—Rs. 20 p.m. *[C.U. 2002]*

[Ans. Gross wages for the month Rs. 49,600; Net wages payable for the month Rs. 46,800; Wages cost for the month Rs. 52,000]

39. From the following particulars you are required to calculate according to 'Average Wage Rate' the labour cost chargeable to Job. No. P-301 which was completed in 1998 :
Basic wage rate is Rs. 15 per hour and overtime rates are as follows :
Before or after working hours—150% of basic wage rate
Sundays and other holidays—200% of basic wage rate

During the year 1998 the following labour hours were worked :

Normal time	4,00,000 hours
Overtime before or after working hours	50,000 hours
Overtime on Sundays and holidays	40,000 hours
Total	4,90,000 hours

For Job. No. P-301, 4,000 hours were spent as follows :

Normal time	3,000 hours
Before or after working hours	700 hours
Sundays and holidays	300 hours

[C.U. B.Com. (Hons.) 1999]

[Ans. Average wage rate for the year Rs. 16.9898 per hr. Labour cost chargeable to job No. P-301, Rs. 67,959.20 (i.e., 4,000 hours @ Rs. 16.9898]

40. (*a*) In a factory a job can be executed either through workman Pradip or Arindam. Pradip takes 32 hours to complete the job while Arindam finishes it in 30 hours. The standard time to finish the job is 40 hours.

The raw material input cost and hourly wage rate are same for both the workers. Pradip is entitled to receive bonus according to Halsey Plan while Arindam is paid bonus as per Rowan Plan. Works overheads are recovered on the job at Rs. 15 per labour hour worked. The factory cost of the job comes to Rs. 5,200 irrespective of the workmen engaged.

Find out hourly wage rate and cost of raw materials input.

(*b*) During the same period, the factory received a job order the detail of which are given below :

Raw material cost	Rs. 5,000
Standard labour time	200 hours
Actual Time (job done by Arindam)	150 hours
Administration overhead	15% of works cost
Selling and Distribution Overhead	10% of total cost
Profit margin	20% on sales

What price do you recommend for the job ? *[C.U. B.Com (H) 2001]*

[Ans. (*a*) Wage rate Rs. 20 per hour; Cost of raw materials input Rs. 4,000. (*b*) Rs. 17,393.75]

41. On the basis of the following information calculate the earnings of A and B under straight piece rate system and Taylor's differential piece rate system :

Standard Production	8 units per hour
Normal time rate	Re. 0.40 per hour

Differential to be applied : 80% of piece rate below standard : 120% of piece rate at or above standard.

In a nine hour day, A produces 54 units and B produces 75 units. *[B. Com. Kerala]*

[Ans. A = Rs. 2.16; B = Rs. 4.50]

[**Hints** : Standard production per day = 9 × 8 = 72 units

Normal, piece rate = Re. $\frac{0.40}{8}$ = 0.5 Paise.

Lower piece rate below standard = 0.5 × $\frac{80}{100}$ = 0.4 Paise

Higher piece rate = 0.5 × $\frac{120}{100}$ × 0.6 Paise]

42. Jobs are issued to operative X to make 189 units and to operative Y to make 204 units, for which a time allowance 20 standard minutes and 15 standard minutes per unit, respectively, is credited. For every hour saved bonus is paid at 50% of basic rate, which is Rs. 6 per hour for both employees. The basic working week is 42 hours. Hours in excess are paid at time plus one-third. X completes his units in 45 hours and Y completes his units in 39 hours, (but works a full week) due to defective material. Six of X's units and four of Y's units are subsequently scrapped, although all units produced are paid for.

You are required to calculate for each of X and Y :

(*a*) The amount of bonus payable; (b) The total gross wages payable; (c) The wages cost per good unit made. *[I.C.M.A. (London)]*

[Ans. (*a*) Bonus X = Rs. 54; Y = Rs. 36; (*b*) Wages : X = Rs. 330; Y = Rs. 270 (*c*) Labour cost per unit : X = Rs. 1.80; Y = Rs. 1.35]

[Hints : X : 189 − 6 = 183 units; Y : 204 − 4 = 200, Rs. 270 ÷ 200]

43. Bharat machine Works paid Rs. 4 per day of 8 hours to its workers in the assembly shop and those who assembled more than 2 assemblies per day were paid at a piecework rate of Rs. 2.50 per assembly. Overhead rate per direct labour hour in this shop was Rs. 4 per labour and will remain so even if output is increased to 4 assemblies per day of 8 hours.

Managements and workers agreed on a new system of payment of wages on output basis so that a worker will get : (*i*) Rs. 2.50 per assembly completed in 4 hours, (*ii*) Rs. 2.72 per assembly completed in $3^1/_2$ hours, (*iii*) Rs. 3.00 per assembly completed in 3 hours, (*iv*) Rs. 3.50 per assembly completed in $2^1/_2$ hours.

Prepare a statement showing the advantage or disadvantage to the worker and the employer in each of the above cases as compared to the old system. *[C.A. (Final)]*

[Ans. Gain in wages under new system (*i*) Re. 1, (*ii*) Re. 0.50 (*iii*) Rs. 1.33 (*iv*) Rs. 3.20 Cost per unit of output is higher under the new system. However, it is likely that employer would gain in the long run since the employee would try to produce 3.20 (8 × 2/5) assemblies per day on account of sharp increase in his wage. Thus the unit cost would be less.]

44. The Alpha Corporation has filed the following income statement for the year ended 31.3.95 :

			Rs.
	Sales		24,00,000
Less :	Variable costs :		
	Materials	6,01,000	
	D/Labour	5,19,000	
	V. Overhead	3,20,000	
	V. Selling and Distribution Overhead	1,90,000	
		16,30,000	
	Contribution	7,70,000	
Less :	Fixed Overhead	5,30,000	
	Net income before tax	2,40,000	
	Capital invested	12,00,000	

The actual number of hours of direct labour worked in the year under review was Rs. 2,06,000. As a consequence of delays in filling vacancies of employees who quit, 6,000 potential direct hours were not worked, and included in the actual hours worked were 4,000 hours of trainees, half of which time was unproductive.

The costs incurred in consequence of re-employment was as follows :

(*a*) Separation costs Rs. 25,630 ; (*b*) Selection cost Rs. 32,080 ;
(*c*) Recruitment costs Rs. 23,140 ; and (*d*) Training costs Rs. 31,160.

Calculate the profits lost or forgone on account of labour turnover (round off to the nearest rupee) ; and the potential return on capital and sales; and turnover ratio. *[I.C.W.A. (Final)]*

[Ans. Loss of Profit = Rs. 1,42,206; ROCE = 31.85%; ROS = 15.32%; Labour Turnover Ratio = 3.77]

[Hints. 1. Profit forgone/Lost = Cost which have been avoided.
(i.e. Separation, Selection, Recruitment, Training) + Loss in contribution for under-utilisation.

2. Effective labour hours lost = Potential labour hour – Actual labour hour
[(2,06,000 + 6,000) – 2 (2,06,000 – 2,000)] = 8,000 or 3.9215%

3. Loss in Contribution = $7,70,000 \times \frac{3.9215}{100}$ = Rs. 30,196]

45. From the following information, determine the estimated recruitment of XYZ Ltd. over the next five years :

The company has 10,000 staff in lower division clerk grade in the company with the following age group :

Under 20	2,000
20-30	3,000
Above 30	5,000
	10,000

Wastage rates and Promotion prospects in the next Five Years are expected to be :

Age	% wastage	% of Promotion to next higher grade
Under 20	25%	5%
20-30	10%	30%
Above 30	5%	20%

The demand for a cost shows that 14,000 clerical grade of lower division clerk will be required in next five years time. Assume that there is no scope of getting higher promotion other than from lower clerical grade.

[Ans. 7050]

46. The budgeted annual production of a company is 1,20,000 units, each unit requiring $2\frac{1}{2}$ hours at an hourly wage rate of Rs. 15. Currently the average efficiency of the production workers is only 60%. The management has a scheme to raise this to 75%. The scheme involves realigning the machinery and intensive training of the production workers, at an one time cost of Rs. 10 lakhs. The scheme also proposes to raise the wage rate to Rs. 16 to enlist the full cooperation of the workers. Examine the scheme and state whether it can be accepted.

[I.C.W.A. Dec. 04]

[Ans. Saving in Labour Cost per Unit : Rs. 5.50
Total Savings : Rs. 6,60,000
Hence the scheme can not be accepted.]

47. Rowan and Halsey Incentive Scheme.

A skilled worker in XYZ Ltd. is paid a guaranteed wage rate of Rs. 30 per hour. The standard time per unit for a particular product is 4 hours. P, a machine man, has been paid wages under the Rowan Incentive Plan and he had earned an effective hourly rate of Rs. 37.50 on the manufacture of that particular product.

What would have been his total earnings and effective hourly rate, had he been put on Halsey Incentive Scheme ?

[C.A. Inter, Nov. 1999]

[Ans. Earning : Rs. 105; Effective hourly rate : Rs. 35]

48. Straight Piecework and Emerson Plan.

During audit of accounts of the Company, your assistant found errors in the calculation of the wages of factory workers and he wants you to verify his work.

He has extracted the following information :

I. The contract provides that the minimum wage for a worker is his base rate. It is also paid for downtimes i.e. the machine is under repair or the worker is without work. The standard work week is 40 hours. For overtime production, workers are paid 150 percent of base rate.

II. Straight Piecework—the worker is paid at the rate of 20 paise per piece.

III. Percentage Bonus Plan—Standard quantities of production per hour are established by the engineering department. The worker's average hourly production, determined from his total hours worked and his production, is divided by the standard quantity of production to determine his efficiency ratio. The efficiency ratio is then applied to his base to determine his hourly earnings for the period.

IV. Emerson's Efficiency Plan—A minimum wage is paid for production up to $60^2/_3$% of the standard output or efficiency. When the worker's production :

Efficiency Level	Bonus
Up to $66\frac{2}{3}$%	Nil
Above $66\frac{2}{3}$% to 79%	10%
80%-99%	20%
100%-125%	45%

Your assistant has produced the following schedule pertaining to certain workers of a weekly pay roll :

Workers	Wage Incentive Plan	Total Hours	Down Time Hours	Units Produced	Standard units	Base Rate Rs.	Gross Wages as per book. Rs.
Rajesh	Straight piecework	40	5	400		1.80	85
Mohan**	Straight piecework	46		455		1.80	95
John	Straight piecework	44		425		1.80	85
Harish	Percentage bonus plan	40	4	250	200	2.20	120
Mahesh	Emerson	40		240	300	2.10	93
Anil	Emerson (40 hours production)	40		600	500	2.00	126

** Total hours of Mohan include 6 overtime hours.

Prepare a schedule showing whether the above computation of workers' wages are correct or not. Give details. ***[C.A. Inter, May 1999]***

[Ans. Rajesh : Rs. 80; Mohan : Rs. 91; John : Rs. 85; Harish : Rs. 110; Mahesh : 100.80; Anil : 116]

49. XYZ Ltd. employs its workers for a single shift of 8 hours for 25 days in a month. The company has recently fixed the standard output for a mass production item and introduced an incentive to boost output.

Details of wages payable to the workers are as follows :

(*i*) Basic wages/piece work wages @ Rs. 2 per unit subject to a guaranteed minimum wage of Rs. 60 per day.

(*ii*) Dearness Allowance at Rs. 40 per day.

(*iii*) Incentive bonus :

Standard output per day per worker	: 40 units
Incentive bonus up to 80% efficiency	: Nil
Incentive bonus for efficiency above 80% above 80%.	Rs. 50 per every 1% increase

The deatils of performance of four workers for the month of April 1998 are :

Workers	No. of days worked	Output (units)
A	25	820
B	18	500
C	25	910
D	24	780

Calculate the total earnings of each of these workers. ***[I.C.W.A. Inter, Dec. 1998]***

[Ans. A : Rs. 2,740; B : 1,800; C : Rs. 3,370; D : Rs. 2,570]

50. Straight Piece Rate and Merrick's Multiple Piece Rate.

Calculate the earnings of workers A, B and C under straight piece rate system and Merrick's Multiple Rate System from the following particulars :

Normal Rate per hour	Rs. 5.40
Standard Time per unit	1 minute

Output per day is as follows :
Worker A—390 units
Worker B—450 units
Worker C—600 units
Working hours per day are 8. *[C.A. Inter, May 1998]*

[Ans. A : Rs. 35.10; B : 40.50; C : 54.00
A : Rs. 35.10; B : Rs. 44.55; C : 64.80]

51. Halsey/Rowan Systems of Wage payment :

(*a*) Bonus paid under the Halsey Plan with bonus at 50% for the time saved equals the bonus paid under the Rowan System.
When will this statement hold good ? (Your answer should contain the proof).

(*b*) The time allowed for the job is 8 hours. The hourly rate is Rs. 8.
Prepare a statement showing :
(*i*) The bonus earned (*ii*) total earnings of labour and (*iii*) Hourly earnings.

Under the Halsey System with 50% bonus for time saved and Rowan System for each hour saved progressively. *[C.A. Inter, May 1991]*

[Ans. (a) At 50% savings in standard time bonus will be equal.
(b) For 1 hour saved :
Halsey (i) Rs. 4.00 (ii) Rs. 60.00 (iii) Rs. 8.57 (iv) Rs. 7.00 (v) Rs. 63.00 (vi) Rs. 9.00.

52. Total Earning and Rate of Earning.

The standard hours of job X are 100 hours. The job has been completed by Amar in 60 hours, Akbar in 70 hours and Anthony in 95 hours.
The bonus system applicable to the job is as follows :

Percentage of time saved to time allowed	Bonus
Savings upto 10%	10% of time saved
From 11% to 20%	15% of time saved
From 21% to 40%	20% of time saved
From 41% to 100%	25% of time saved

The rate of pay is Re. 1 per hour.
Calculate the total earnings of each worker and also the rate of earnings per hour.
[C.A. Inter; I.C.W.A. Inter]

[Ans. Rate of earning per hour : Amar Rs. 1.133; Akbar : Rs. 1.086; Anthony : 1.005]

53. Rowan and Halsey Schemes.

The workmen, Vishnu and Shiva, produce the same product using the same materials. Their normal wage rate is also the same. Vishnu is paid bonus according to the Rowan System, while Shiva is paid bonus according to the Halsey System. The time allowed to make the product is 100 hours. Vishnu takes 60 hours while Shiva takes 80 hours to complete the product. The factory overhead rate is Rs. 10 per man-hour actually worked. The factory cost for the product for Vishnu is Rs. 7,280 and for Shiva it is Rs. 7,600.
You are required :
(*a*) To find the normal rate of wages
(*b*) to find the cost of materials
(*c*) to prepare a statement comparing the factory cost of the products as made by the two workmen.
[C.A. Inter, May 1988; November 1997]

[Ans. Factory cost : Visnu Rs. 7,280; Shiva : Rs. 7,600]

54. Loss of profit due to loss of production from labour turnover.

The profitability position of M/s. Pioneer Industries Ltd. for a year is as under :

	Rs. (lakhs)	Rs. (lakhs)
Annual Turnover		200
Variable costs :		
Direct material	60	
Direct labour	40	
Variable overheads	50	150
Marginal contribution		50
Fixed overheads		10
Profit for the year		40

Profit for the year did not match with company's expectation and works management attributed it to labour turnover.

Analysis of the data revealed the following :

Permanent workmen worked during the year	:	9,60,000 direct labour hours
Apprentice workmen worked	:	80,000 direct labour hours
	:	10,40,000 direct labour hours

The effectiveness of direct labour hours put in by apprentice workmen was 50% and delay in replacing against separations during the year resulted in loss of 20,000 direct labour hours.

Calculate the loss of profit on account of loss of production from labour turnover.

[I.C.W.A. Inter, Dec. 1999]

[Ans. Loss of Profit : Rs. 4,63,077]

55. Production Bonus for direct and indirect labour based on excess production—Penalty.

Both direct and indirect labour of a department in a factory are entitled to production bonus in accordance with a Group Incentive Scheme, the outlines of which are as follows :

(*a*) For any production in excess of the standard rate fixed at 10,000 tonnes per month (of 25 days), a general incentive of Rs. 10 per tonne is paid in aggregate. The total amount payable to each separate group is determined on the basis of an assumed percentage of such excess production being contributed by it, namely @70% by direct labour, @ 10% by inspection staff, @ 12% by maintenance staff and @ 8% by supervisory staff.

(*b*) Moreover, if the excess production is more than 20% above the standard, direct labour also gets a special bonus @ Rs. 5 per tonne for all production in excess of 120% of standard.

(*c*) Inspection staff are penalised @ Rs. 20 per tonne for rejection by customer in excess of 10% of production.

(*d*) Maintenance staff are also penalised @ Rs. 20 per hour of breakdown.

From the following particulars for a month, work out the production bonus earned by each group :

(*a*) Actual working days 20

(*b*) Production 11,000 tonnes

(*c*) Rejection by customer 200 tonnes

(*d*) Machine breakdown 40 hours. *[I.C.W.A. Inter]*

[Ans. Rs. 28,000; Rs. 1,200; Rs. 2,800; Rs. 2,400]

56. Labour turnover—Actual profit vis-a-vis Notional profit.

Your organisation is experiencing a high labour turnover in recent years and management would like you to submit a report on the loss suffered by the company due to such labour turnover. Following figures are available for your consideration :

Sales	Rs. 600 lakhs
Direct Materials	Rs. 150 lakhs
Direct Labour	Rs. 48 lakhs on 4,80,000 man-hours
Other Variable Expenses	Rs. 60 lakhs
Fixed Overheads	Rs. 80 lakhs

The direct man-hours included 9,000 man-hours spent on trainees and replacement, only 50% of which were productive. Further, during the year 12,000 man-hours of potential work could not be availed of because of delayed replacement. The cost incurred due to separations and replacements amounted to Rs. 1 lakh.

On the basis of above data prepare a comparative statement showing actual profit vis-a-vis the profit which would have been realized had there been no labour turnover.

[I.C.W.A. Inter, Dec. 1994]

[Ans. Loss of Profit Rs. 13,33,312]

57. Profit forgone due to labour turnover.

The management of In and Out Ltd. are worried about their increasing labour turnover in the factory and before analysing the causes and taking remedial steps, they want to have an idea of the profit forgone as a result of labour turnover in the last year :

Last year sales amounted to Rs. 83,03,300 and the P/V ratio was 20 per cent. The total number of actual hours worked by the Direct Labour force was 4.45 lakhs. As a result of the delays by the Personnel Department in filling vacancies due to labour turnover, 1,00,000 potentially productive hours were lost. The actual direct labour hours included 30,000 hours attributable to training new recruits, out of which half of the hours were unproductive.

The costs incurred consequent on labour turnover revealed on analysis the following :

Settlement cost due to leaving	Rs. 43,820
Recruitment costs	Rs. 26,740
Selection costs	Rs. 12,750
Training costs	Rs. 30,490

Assuming that the potential production lost as a consequence of labour turnover could have been sold at prevailing prices, find the profit forgone last year on account of labour turnover.

[C.A. Inter, Nov. 1986; May 1998]

[Ans. Profit forgone Rs. 5,00,000]

5 Overhead

Section I : Definition and Classification

Authors' Comments and Suggestions :

1. ***In all examinations at least one question either for overhead apportionment or for computation of M.H.R. is set up. These questions involve a lot of calculations and students normally commit computational errors.***
2. ***Direct cost of service departments should be distributed amongst production department as it is an indirect cost of Production Department.***
3. ***Students should be well-versed with the methodology of disposal of under/over absorbed overheads.***
4. ***Difference between primary distribution and secondary distribution should be properly understood. Clues given should be properly used.***
5. ***At the time of absorption of overhead, it should be ascertained whether the cost is to be absorbed based on machine hours or on labour hours. In this case, the production process—i.e., whether it is capital intensive or labour intensive—should be considered, in absence of any information relating to the absorption basis.***
6. ***Before computing the comprehensive machine-hour rate, it is necessary to find out the total effective machine-hour and total wages paid to operators. In finding out effective machine-hours, due consideration should be given to normal and abnormal idle time.***

Definition—Chargeable Expenses and Overhead—Different Classifications.

Like direct costs, each and every organisation does incur some indirect costs which are called Common Costs—those which cannot be related to specific units of production. Because of several influences (such as automation, specialisation, large-scales-operations, diversification of products, expansion of markets, improvement of technology, investment and supervision) such costs are becoming more or less equal to (even sometimes more) the prime costs. Since they are as much a part of the cost of producing the end-product of the firm and doing business as direct costs, they must be recognised and treated in some sensible manner.

Definition

Overheads comprise those costs which the cost accountant is either unable or unwilling to allocate to a particular product, job or process. The C.I.M.A., London, terminology defines the term as "the aggregate of indirect material, indirect wages and indirect expenses." Broadly speaking, any expenditure over and above the prime cost is known as Overhead.

According to the terminology mentioned above, overheads consist of the cost of indirect material, indirect labour and indirect expenses. But, overheads sometimes include even the direct material cost, direct labour cost and chargeable expenses, when they cannot be identified with a particular job. Nails, glue, thread etc. are examples of such cases. Various terms that are generally used to denote overhead are : overhead charges, on cost, overhead expenses, non-productive costs, loading, burden, supplementary costs etc.

Chargeable Expenses and Overhead

Expenses which are neither direct material cost nor direct labour cost, but which are chargeable or related to a specific job or work order are called Chargeable Expenses. These expenses can also be called Direct Expenses. On the other hand, expenses which cannot be allocated but can only be apportioned to or absorbed by cost centres or cost units are known as Indirect Expenses and these are called Overheads. These two terms may be distinguished on the basis of their being capable of getting identified with the specific job or work order.

Classification of Overheads

According to CIMA London, Terminology, cost classification means "(*i*) the process of grouping costs according to their common characteristics, and (*ii*) establishing a series of special groups according to which costs are classified." Thus, on the one hand, it is the determination of definite groups in which the expenses should be classified and the placing of various items into one or the other of these groups according to their common characteristics.

Overheads may be classified according to their functions, elements, behaviours, normality and controllability. The following chart shows their classification at a glance :

OVERHEAD

Functions	***Elements***	***Behaviour or Variability***	***Normality***	***Controllability***
(*i*) Production	(*i*) Indirect Material	(*i*) Fixed	(*i*) Normal	(*i*) Controllable
(*ii*) Administration	(*ii*) Indirect Labour	(*ii*) Variable	(*ii*) Abnormal	(*ii*) Uncontrollable
(*iii*) Selling	(*iii*) Indirect Expenses	(*iii*) Semi-variable		
(*iv*) Distribution				

(A) Functional Classification

(*i*) **Manufacturing or Production Overhead.** It is the indirect cost incurred for maintaining and operating the manufacturing division of an organisation. It includes all such expenses incurred by the factory from the receipt of raw material until production is completed. It is also known as works overhead, factory overhead etc. Some common examples are : Depreciation of plant and factory premises, cotton waste, oil, grease, electricity, fuel, salaries and wages of supervisors etc.

(*ii*) **Administrative Overhead.** The term includes all expenses incurred in the direction, control and administration, including secretarial, accounting and financial control, of an undertaking. These are also known as general or office overheads. Some common examples are : Salaries of office staffs, Directors etc., office rent, depreciation of office plant and buildings, telephone expense etc.

(*iii*) **Selling Overhead.** This is the expenditure incurred in promoting sales and retaining customers. The examples are : Advertising, salaries and commission of selling agents, salesmen, bad debts etc.

(*iv*) **Distribution Overhead.** This expenditure is incurred in the process which begins with making the product produced available for despatch and ends with making the reconditioned empty package available for reissue. Some of the examples are : transport expenses, packing, warehousing, staff salaries, normal loss of finished goods etc.

(B) Elementwise Classification

(*i*) **Indirect Material.** This is a part of material cost which cannot be allocated to a particular job or production but is absorbed by cost centre or cost units indirectly. Some examples are : fuel, consumable stores, small tools, cotton waste etc.

(*ii*) **Indirect Labour.** This includes such wages which cannot be allocated, but can only be apportioned to cost centres or cost units. Some examples are : wages for maintenance staff, salary of storekeeper and foreman, idle time cost etc.

(*iii*) **Indirect Expenses.** The expenses which cannot be allocated directly but can only be apportioned to or absorbed by cost centres or cost units. The common examples are : salary to factory staff, training expenses, taxes, insurance, rents and rates of factory, hospital and dispensary, canteen etc.

(C) Behavioural Classification

(*i*) **Fixed Overhead.** Fixed overhead cost represents those costs which tend to remain fixed by variation in volume of output. In fact this is a period cost and remains unaffected for a given period. The examples of such costs are rent and taxes, salaries of staff etc.

(*ii*) **Variable Overhead.** This is a cost which tends to vary directly with the change in output. Thus the cost changes in direct proportion to output. The examples of such costs are power, selling commission, repair, fuel etc.

(*iii*) **Semi-variable Overhead.** These costs are partly fixed and partly variable. Those expenses which neither remain fixed nor they vary directly with the output are called semi-variable overhead. They do not vary in the same ratio in which the output changes. The main examples of such costs are depreciation, repairs and maintenance etc.

COST PER UNIT GRAPH

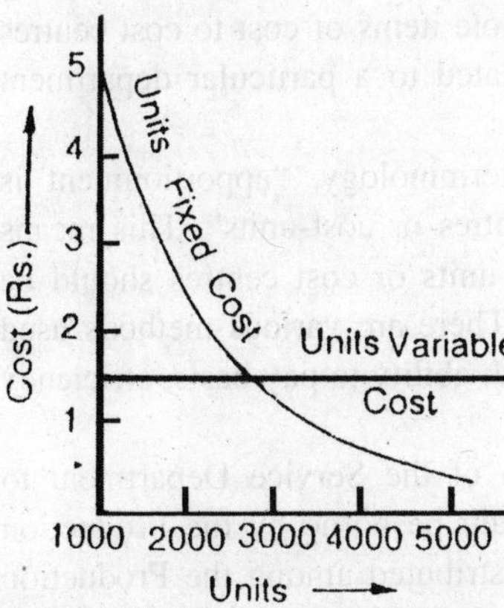

TOTAL COST GRAPH

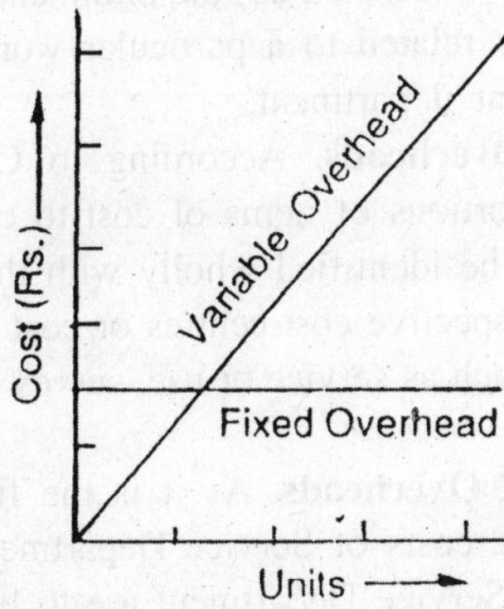

SEMI-VARIABLE COST GRAPH

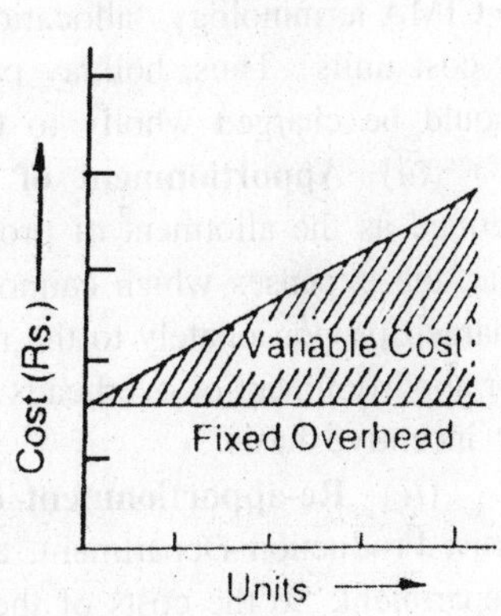

(D) Classification according to Normality

(*i*) **Normal Overhead.** These represent such overheads which are expected to be incurred in attaining a given output. These overheads are essential and unavoidable. Thus, these costs should be included in product costs.

(*ii*) **Abnormal Overhead.** These represent such overheads which are not expected to be incurred in attaining a given output, *e.g.* cost of abnormal idle time. Hence these costs should be excluded from total cost and to be charged to Costing Profit and Loss Account.

(E) Classification according to Controllability

(*i*) **Controllable Overhead.** These overhead costs are those costs which can be controlled by executive action at the point of their incurrence. Generally speaking, all direct costs including direct material, direct labour, direct expenses and some of the oveheads are controllable costs.

(*ii*) **Uncontrollable Overhead.** These are overhead costs which are not controllable by management. They are incurred on time basis. All fixed costs are uncontrollable.

Section II : Allocation, Apportionment and Absorption

Accounting and Control of overhead—Distinction between allocation and apportionment bases of absorption—Predetermined overhead rates—Primary and secondary distribution—Under and over absorption of overhead—Concept of capacity—Workout Problems.

Introduction

Charging the overhead to cost centres and cost units is the most important consideration in the operation of a cost accounting system. Even though the cost cannot be identified directly with specific product/job, they are essentially part of cost of manufacturing products and must be included with prime cost for product pricing, performance evaluation and decision-making.

Steps for Accounting and Control of Overhead Costs

The procedure for accounting and control of overhead costs involve following steps :

(*i*) **Classification and Collection of Oveheads.** After classification (grouping) of overhead on some scientific and consistent basis, overhead should be regularly collected under separate headings. For the collection of overheads the documents, *viz.*, stores or pay-bills, subsidiary records, cash book etc. are used. Various sources are used for collecting different types of expenses.

(*ii*) **Departmentalisation/Allocation of Overheads.** This refers to distribution of overhead cost among two or more products, departments or cost centres. Allocation consists in tracing and assigning the whole amount of overhead costs to a particular department or cost centre. According to CIMA terminology, 'allocation' is defined as 'the allotment of whole items of cost to cost centres or cost units'. Thus, holiday pay related to a particular worker related to a particular department should be charged wholly to that department.

(*iii*) **Apportionment of Overheads.** According to CIMA terminology, "apportionment is defined as the allotment of proportions of items of cost to cost centres or cost-units". This means that, the expenses which cannot be identified wholly with the cost-units or cost centres should be charged proportionately to the respective cost-centres or cost units. There are various methods used for apportionment of overheads such as service or use, survey method, ability to pay basis, efficiency or incentive basis.

(*iv*) **Re-apportionment of Overheads.** As it is the function of the Service Department to assist Production Department, the costs of Service Department should be borne by the Production Department. So the costs of the Service Department are to be re-distributed among the Production Department on some equitable basis. This process of re-distribution is known as re-apportionment or secondary distribution.

(*v*) **Absorption of Overheads.** Charging overheads to individual products or jobs is known as overhead absorption. According to the terminology of CIMA, "the allotment of overhead to cost units is known as overhead absorption". The main object of overhead absorption is that the total of the departmental overhead is to be distributed over the units produced in that department. Thus, total overhead of each production cost centre should be absorbed in such a way that each job or cost unit gets due share of it to the departments through which it passes. There are various methods of absorption of overheads such as actual rate, pre-determined rate, standard rate etc.

Distinction between Allocation and Apportionment

Allocation and apportionment represent two successive stages in the process of distribution, although the purpose of the concern is to determine the cost per unit.

The main difference between the two are :

(1) Allocation denotes the allotment of whole items of cost, whereas apportionment involves allotment of proportions of items of cost.

(2) Allocation is a direct process but apportionment is an indirect method for which equitable bases are to be selected.

(3) Allocation ends with a cost centre, but the process of apportionment is carried further down.

(4) Allocation refers to distribution of overhead expenses on departmental basis, while apportionment means the method of distribution of the overhead of one department to the other department.

(5) Allocation is much wider and accurate than apportionment.

Methods of Absorption or Bases for Absorption

(1) Product Unit Method

(2) Percentage Methods :

- (*i*) Percentage of Direct Material Cost
- (*ii*) Percentage of Direct Labour Cost
- (*iii*) Percentage of Prime Cost.

(3) Hourly Rate Methods :

- (*i*) Direct Labour Hour Rate
- (*ii*) Machine Hour Rate
- (*iii*) Combined Machine and Direct Labour Hour Rate.

1. Production Unit Method

Under this method, the total overhead costs should be divided by the number of units produced in order to get the rate per unit. Each unit of production is charged with this rate for the absorption of overhead. This method is simple and easy to calculate. The method can be conveniently used where only one product is produced or where the units are of uniform size, quality and standard.

2. Percentage Methods

(*i*) **Percentage of Direct Material Cost.** Under this method, actual, or predetermined rate is calculated by dividing overhead cost by the material cost and expressing as a percentage.

Thus, $\%\text{ of Overhead to Material} = \dfrac{\text{Overhead Cost}}{\text{D. Material Cost}} \times 100$

This method is suitable only where material cost forms the major part of the total cost.

(*ii*) **Percentage of Direct Labour Cost.** Under this method also actual or predetermined rate is calculated by dividing the Overhead Cost by the labour cost and expressing the result as a percentage.

Thus, $\%\text{ of Overhead Cost to Labour} = \dfrac{\text{Overhead Cost}}{\text{D. Labour Cost}} \times 100$

This method is suitable only when wages form the greater part of the total cost.

(*iii*) **Percentage of Prime Cost.** This method is based on Prime Cost. An actual or predetermined rate is calculated by dividing the overhead cost by the prime cost and expressing the result as a percentage.

Thus, $\%\text{ of Overhead Cost to Prime Cost} = \dfrac{\text{Overhead Cost}}{\text{Prime Cost}} \times 100$

The main logic behind this method is that, both the material and labour costs are considered here.

3. Hourly Rate Methods

(*i*) **Direct Labour Hour Rate.** Under the method, labour hours are taken as the base for absorption of overhead. The actual or predetermined rate is calculated by dividing the overhead of a department for a particular period to the total number of direct labour hours of that department for the same period. Thus,

$$\text{Direct Labour Hour Rate} = \frac{\text{Total Overhead for a period}}{\text{Total Labour hours for the period}}$$

This method attempts to allocate various types of overhead to the various categories of workers according to direct labour hours involved. This is an improved method than percentage of direct wages bases as it gives due recognition of time factor.

(*ii*) **Machine Hour Rate.** It is the cost of running a machine per hour. Machine hour rate is an actual or predetermined rate which is calculated by dividing the overhead by the number of machine hours. Thus,

$$\text{Machine Hour Rate} = \frac{\text{Overhead Cost}}{\text{Machine hours during the period}}$$

When machine plays a predominant role than the labourers, this method is most suitable for absorption of overheads.

There are three types of machine hour rate :

(*i*) Ordinary Machine Hour Rate

(*ii*) Composite or Comprehensive Machine Hour Rate

(*iii*) Group Machine Hour Rate.

(*i*) **The Ordinary Machine Hour Rate.** Under this method, those indirect expenses are taken into consideration which can be directly allocated to the machine (*i.e.* directly related to operate the machine). Some of these expenses vary in proportion to the operating time of machines (*viz.* power, fuel, depreciation, repair etc.), while some others change disproportionately (*viz.* insurance, taxes, wastages, cleaning etc.). It is not difficult to calculate the rate for expenses which are proportional to operating hours. But for disproportional expenses, estimated expenses related to a machine should be located first. Then it should be divided by the number of working hours of the machine to find out the hourly rate. The total of these two rates gives the Ordinary Machine Hour Rate.

(*ii*) **Composite or Comprehensive Machine Hour Rate.** This method takes into account not only expenses directly allocated to machine as mentioned above, but also other expenses which cannot be directly allocated to machine, such as supervisory charges, heating, lighting, rent etc. These indirect expenses are known as Standing Charges or Fixed Charges. This fixed or standing charges are then apportioned among the various departments first. Expenses apportioned to each department are then apportioned among all the machines in that department on some equitable basis. The share of overhead for each machine is then divided by the estimated normal working hours of the machine to calculate the cost of standing charges per machine hour. When this rate is added to the ordinary machine hour rate, the Composite Machine Hour Rate is obtained.

(*iii*) **The Group Machine Hour Rate.** In a factory where there are number of identical machines, a group machine hour rate can be calculated for charging to the output of each machine in respect to a particular group. All direct expenses like power, fuel, operator's wages, etc. are allocated. The indirect expenses such as rent, rates, insurance, electricity etc. are apportioned to each group of machine on appropriate basis. The aggregate cost of those allocated and apportioned expenses is then divided by the total number of machine hours available for use to find out the rate per hour for each group of machines.

Notes :

1. There are certain workers whose wages are directly connected with the machines, such as machine operators, turners, fitters etc. and this type of wages are direct wages. But, if the operators, turners or fitters cannot be retrenched due to fall in production, the wages payable to such workers may be treated as indirect wages and should be included in computing Comprehensive or Composite Machine Hour Rate.

2. If the machine is hired for production for a specified period, the hire-charge should normally be charged as fixed overhead. But if the charges are to be paid on the basis of production the hire-charge may be treated as variable expenses.

3. Depreciation of a machine may be caused due to two reasons : (i) lapse of time (ii) use of the machine. Cost of depreciation due to lapse of time may be treated as fixed charge, again, cost of depreciation due to use should be treated as variable charge.

Actual or Pre-determined Overhead Rate

Actual rate is calculated by dividing the actual overheads by the actual quantity produced or any other base selected. It is known as historical rate. Thus,

$$\text{Actual Rate} = \frac{\text{Actual Overhead}}{\text{Actual Quantity/or any other Base}}$$

On the other hand, predetermined rate is calculated by dividing the budgeted overhead for a period by the budgeted base. Thus

$$\text{Predetermined Rate} = \frac{\text{Estimated or Budgeted Overhead}}{\text{Estimated or Budgeted Base or Quantity}}$$

Needs/Uses of Predetermined Overhead Rate

Predetermined overhead rate is necessary due to following reasons :

(*a*) It helps to find out estimated cost of a product.

(*b*) It helps in preparing quotations and fixing prices.

(*c*) It enables costing of products before the product starts.

(*d*) It helps in cost analysis and cost control.

Stages of Apportionment

Apportionment of overhead expenses can be made in two stages :

(*i*) Primary Distribution

(*ii*) Secondary Distribution.

(*i*) **Primary Distribution.** When overhead costs are apportioned to all production as well as service departments, it is called Primary Distribution. Service departments are those departments which render services towards production departments.

The following are some of the *common bases used for primary distribution* :

Items of Expenditure	*Basis of Apportionment*
1. Rent, rates, heat and lighting	Area occupied
2. Depreciation of plants, machinery, building and equipment, Fire Insurance	Book value
3. Repairs to plant and machinery	Book value
4. Lighting, Electricity, Air-conditioning	No. of light points or area
5. Power	Horse power or (Horse Power × Machine Hours)
6. Insurance of Stock	Stock value
7. Personnel Office, Welfare, Canteen, Supervision, Time and Wage Office, ESI contribution, administration, safety, compensation etc.	No. of employees

8. Material handling, Store keeping, Delivery expenses	Weight or value of material consumed or material requisitions
9. Audit fees	Sales or total cost
10. Delivery vans	Weight, volume, tonne-mile
11. General expenses	Direct wages or number of employees.

(*ii*) **Secondary Distribution.** If total overhead allocated and apportioned to service departments are further apportioned to the production departments, it is called secondary distribution. It is actually the re-distribution of service department, cost to production departments where production is going on. The following are some of the *common bases used for redistribution* (or secondary distribution) :

Items of Expenditure	*Basis of Apportionment*
1. Repairs and maintenance	Hours worked or (Asset value × Hrs. worked)
2. Canteen, Cafeteria, Medical	No. of employees
3. Stores	No. of stores requisition or value of stores issued
4. Accounts, personnel and training	No. of employees or Their Earnings
5. Purchasing, Receiving, Shopping	Volume handled
6. Production Control, Utilities, Quality Control	Material usage
7. Inspection, Crane service	Hours spent or Material handled
8. Tool Room Cost	Direct Labour hours or Machine hours.

Under and Over-Absorption of Overheads

Overhead may be absorbed either at the actual rate or at the predetermined rate. When actual rate is applied for absorption, then there should not be any chance of difference between actual and overhead absorbed. But, if the pre-determined rate is applied there is every possibility of such difference. This "difference between the overhead charged and the overhead incurred is called the under and over-absorption of overheads". If the actual overhead is more than the absorbed overhead, then it is called "under-absorption". On the other hand, if overhead absorbed exceeds the actual overhead, then it is called 'over-absorption'.

Reasons for Under and Over-absorption

Under or Over-absorption may arise due to the following reasons :

(*a*) The actual overhead may be different from budgeted.

(*b*) The actual production may be different from anticipated.

(*c*) The overhead absorption rate may have been wrongly computed.

(*d*) Seasonal fluctuations in overhead costs due to seasonal variation of production.

(*e*) Unutilization of available capacity and unexpected change in output.

(*f*) Due to changes in the methods and techniques of operation.

(*g*) Some non-recurring expenses may be incurred during the period.

(*h*) Valuation of W.I.P. without including proportionate overhead cost in it.

Treatment of Under or Over-absorption

The under or over-absorption of overhead may be treated by one or more of the following reasons :

(*i*) **Use of Supplementary Rates.** When the amount of under or over-absorption is quite large, it is necessary to adjust the difference by using a supplementary rate, calculated by dividing the under/over-absorbed overheads by the actual base. Such rates should be positive for under-absorption while negative for over-absorption.

(*ii*) **Write off to Costing Profit and Loss A/c.** If the under or over-absorption of overheads is not so large or caused by any abnormal reasons (such as surplus or idle capacity), the difference should be transferred to the Costing Profit and Loss A/c.

(*iii*) **Carry over to the next year.** If the normal business cycles extends over more than a year then the under, or over-absorbed overhead may be carried forward to the next year through an overhead reserve or suspense account.

Concept of Capacity

Capacity is the ability to produce output or render services. The capacity of a plant or factory means its ability to produce with the available resources and facilities. This capacity is usually expressed in terms of : (*i*) units of output, (*ii*) productive hours, and (*iii*) monetary values. In computing a pre-determined rate, a decision is required to be taken as to the most suitable level or capacity to be adopted. There are various types of capacities which are :

1. Maximum Capacity or Theoretical Capacity or Rated Capacity. It is the maximum productive capacity of a plant/machinery/department when there is no loss of operating time. But in practice it is very difficult to utilize maximum capacity as some loss of time is inevitable due to repair and maintenance.

2. Practical Capacity or Operating Capacity. Practical capacity is that capacity which is practically attainable. Hence, it is the maximum productive capacity of a plant or factory less the inevitable interruptions due to unavoidable loss of time (such as repairs, maintenance, breakdown, Sundays, holidays, etc.). But, it should be kept in mind that the practical capacity does not take into account the external factors (such as delay in receiving orders, unbalanced capacity in certain departments etc.).

3. Capacity based on sales expectancy. It represents that portion of practical capacity which is based on sales expectancy. It is determined after careful study of the present market situation.

4. Normal Capacity. Normal capacity is the long-term average capacity based on expected sales. But, according to one group, normal capacity equals to the practical capacity. Accordingly, normal capacity is the capacity which will be worked if there is no lack of orders. In rare cases it is regarded as equivalent to the maximum capacity.

5. Ideal Capacity. It is that part of productive capacity which is attainable under ideal conditions. It is very difficult to achieve ideal capacity as an allowance should be made for normal losses to determine the normal capacity which can be attained.

6. Idle Capacity. It is that part of productive capacity which cannot be profitably utilised. In other words, it is the unused productive potential. It is the difference between practical capacity and the actual capacity utilised base on sales. Thus, it is a capital wastage and burden on the productive activities of any concern.

Causes of Idle Capacity

The idle capacity may arise due to three main causes :

(*a*) **Productive Causes**

- (*i*) Non-availability of materials, tools, power.
- (*ii*) Lack of supervision, inspection, instructions.
- (*iii*) Repetitive machine adjustments.
- (*iv*) Machine breakdown.

(*b*) **Administrative Causes**

- (*i*) Lack of proper planning.
- (*ii*) Excess plant for anticipated expansion.
- (*iii*) Strike, lock-out etc.
- (*iv*) Special machines used for one or two jobs.

(*c*) **Economic Causes**

- (*i*) Seasonal demand.
- (*ii*) Cyclical fluctuations.
- (*iii*) Industrial, occurring on account of general shifts in demand.

Idle Capacity Cost and its Treatments

It is the cost (mostly fixed), which remain unabsorbed due to under-utilization of capacity. This is a loss to the organisation and such cost should be kept as minimum as possible.

Treatment

The term idle capacity may be caused due to : (*i*) normal, or (*ii*) abnormal reasons.

(*i*) If it is normal, and cannot be avoided, a supplementary rate may be charged.

$$\text{Supplementary rate} = \frac{\text{Actual Overhead} - \text{Absorbed Overhead}}{\text{Units or Hours (base used)}}$$

(*ii*) If the idle capacity is due to abnormal reasons, it should be charged to Costing Profit and Loss A/c

(*iii*) If it is due to seasonal fluctuations, then the idle capacity cost should be charged in cost of production by inflating overhead rate.

Illustration

Range of output 100-500 units
Average Variable overhead per unit Rs. 40
Total Fixed overhead Rs. 1,500
The following table will explain the nature of variable and fixed overheads :

Units	*Total Variable Overhead*	*Total Fixed Overhead*	*Overhead Cost per unit*	
			Variable Rs.	*Fixed* Rs.
100	4,000	1,500	40	15
200	8,000	1,500	40	7.50
300	12,000	1,500	40	5.00
400	16,000	1,500	40	3.75
500	20,000	1,500	40	3.00

The method of primary distribution of overhead can be explained with the help of the following illustration :

Illustration

XYZ Ltd. has three production departments and one service department, namely P_1, P_2, P_3, and S_1, respectively. The actual expenses incurred during the period ended on 31.3.93 are as follows :

	Rs.
Rent, Rates and Taxes	5,000
Repairs and Maintenance	3,000
Depreciation of Plant and Machinery	2,250
Supervisor's remuneration	7,500
Insurance Premium	2,500
Power	4,500
Light and Electrical Points	1,000
Employees' welfare expenses	750

Additional information in respect of 4 departments :

Particulars	*Dept.* P_1	*Dept.* P_2	*Dept.* P_3	*Dept* S_1
Area (sq. ft.)	750	550	450	250
No. of Employees	20	15	10	15
H.P. of Machines	8	5	2	—
Value of Plant and Machinery (Rs. Lakh)	2.4	1.8	1.2	0.6
Direct Wages	60,000	40,000	30,000	20,000
Value of Stock	1,50,000	90,000	60,000	—
No. of light points	4	3	2	1

Apportion the costs among the above departments (Primary distribution)

Statement showing Primary Distribution of Overhead

Particulars	*Basis*	*Total Rs.*	*Production Depts*			*Service Dept.*
			P_1 *Rs.*	P_2 *Rs.*	P_3 *Rs.*	S_1 *Rs.*
Direct Wages	Given	20,000				20,000
Rent, Rates & Taxes	Floor Area (15 : 11 : 9 : 5)	5,000	1,875	1,375	1,125	625
Repairs & Maint.	Value of P/M (4 : 3 : 2 : 1)	3,000	1,200	900	600	300
Depreciation	—do—	2,250	900	675	450	225
Supervisor's Remuneration	Wages of Employees (6 : 4 : 3 : 2)	7,500	3,000	2,000	1,500	1,000
Insurance Premium	Value of Stock (5 : 3 : 2)	2,500	1,250	750	500	—
Power	H.P. of Machine (8 : 5 : 2)	4,500	2,400	1,500	600	—
Light & Electricity	No. of Light Points (4 : 3 : 2 : 1)	1,000	400	300	200	100
Employees' Welfare Expenses	No. of Employees (4 : 3 : 3)	750	250	187	125	188
Total		46,500	11,275	7,687	5,100	22,438

Direct Redistribution. In this method service department costs are apportioned directly to the production departments only, inter-departmental services are ignored here.

Illustration.

S. Company Ltd. has two production departments and two service departments. The Departmental expenses as per Primary Distribution were as follows :

Production Departments			
X	Rs.	20,000	
Y	Rs.	15,000	35,000
Service Departments			
Stores	Rs.	6,000	
Time Keeping	Rs.	8,000	14,000

The following information are also available in respect of Production Departments :

	Dept. X	*Dept. Y*
No. of workers	500	300
Value of Stores requisitioned (Rs.)	4,000	2,000

Apportion the cost of the service depts. to the production depts.

Statement showing Secondary Distribution of Overhead

Particulars	*Basis*	*Total*	*Production Dept.*	
		Rs.	*X Rs.*	*Y Rs.*
As per Primary Distribution		35,000	20,000	15,000
Secondary Distribution				
Service Dept. Stores	Value of Stores requisitioned (2 : 1)	6,000	4,000	2,000
Time keeping	No. of workers (5 : 3)	8,000	5,000	3,000
Total		49,000	29,000	20,000

Step Method. This method partly recognises the services rendered by one service department to other service departments. Here the cost of the most serviceable department are considered at first for apportionment among the production departments and other service departments. It continues in step by step fashion and ends with the apportionment of cost of that service department which renders least service to the other service departments.

Illustration

A manufacturing company has two production departments *X* and *Y* and three service departments : Store, Maintenance and Time Keeping. The deparmental distribution summary showed the following expenses for June 2007 :

Production Departments :

		Rs.	Rs.
	X	30,000	
	Y	10,000	40,000
Service Departments			
Stores		5,000	
Maintenance		3,000	
Time Keeping		4,000	12,000
	Total		52,000

The other information regarding these departments were :

	X	Y	Stores	Maintenance	Time Keeping
No. of Employees	20	15	10	5	6
No. of stores requisition	24	20	—	6	—
Machine hours	1,200	800	—	—	—

Apportion the service departments' cost to production departments.

Solution

Department	As per Dept. Distribution Summary				
Time keeping	4,000	(–) 4,000			
Stores	5,000	800	(–) 5,800		
Maintenance	3,000	400	696	(–) 4,096	
X	30,000	1,600	2,784	2,458	36,842
Y	10,000	1,200	2,320	1,638	15,158
	52,000	—	—	—	52,000

Section III : Administration and Selling & Distribution Overhead

Definition and Classification—Treatments—Charts for Allocation of Administration and Selling and Distribution Overhead—Workedout Problems and Solutions, Exercises.

(A) Administration Overhead

The main function of office and administrative division is planning and controlling the activities of an organisation. The ICMA defines the term 'Administration Overhead' as "the cost of formulating the policy, directing the organisation, and controlling the operations of an undertaking, which is not related directly to a production, selling, distribution, research or development activity or function." Thus, these costs are general in nature and related to the business as a whole, and, as such, all other functions depend upon the administration function for their successful operation. Some of the expenses which can be termed as administration expenses are office rent, rates, lighting, heating, depreciation, salaries and allowances, postage, law charges, audit fees, bank charges, accounting etc.

Classification

Like manufacturing, administrative overheads may also be classified according to their type, nature, or purpose of expenditure. Each type of expenditure is represented by a separate Standing Order Number which is known as Cost Account Number also.

Accounting Treatment of Administration Ovehead

There are three important methods of accounting administration overhead :

1. Transfer to Profit and Loss A/c. Under the method, administrative cost should be treated as fixed/period cost and have no relationship with production or sales as these are dependent upon the decision of the management. This method is based on the principle that administration overheads are concerned with the formulation of policies and have no direct relationship with production. So in view of these arguments this cost should be transferred to the Profit and Loss A/c.

2. Apportionment to Production and Sales. This method is based on the idea that there are only two main functions : (*i*) Production, and (*ii*) Selling and Distribution, and administration overheads are incurred for the benefit of these two main functions. Hence, administration overhead are distributed to two basic decisions (*i.e.*, production and selling and distribution) and no existence of separate administrative overhead cost. This type of inclusion avoids understatement of product cost. But selection of a reasonable base for apportionment is a difficult task.

The two main necessary journal entries required are :

(*a*)	Adm. O/H A/c	... Dr.
	To G.L. Adj. A/c	
(*b*)	Prodn./Fty. OH A/c	... Dr.
	Selling & Dist. OH	... Dr.
	To Adm. O/H A/c.	

3. Separate Item of Cost. Like production and sales, this method recognises administration as a separate function ; hence added separately to the cost of the job of the product sold on some suitable basis. The bases usually selected for the purpose are :

(*a*) Product Cost/Works Cost,

(*b*) Conversion Cost,

(*c*) Sales Value or Quantity,

(*d*) Gross Profit,

(*e*) Selling Cost,

(*f*) Quantity manufactured.

Out of the above six, method (*i*) or Product Cost/Works Cost is mostly used.

Control of Administration Overhead

In most cases administration cost is a policy cost, hence uncontrollable. However, such cost can be controlled to some extent by means of budgetary control and standard costing system. For this purpose budget should be fixed for each administrative overhead cost and regular comparison with actuals should be made to find out the causes of variances. Finally, corrective actions should be made to rectify the adverse variances.

(B) Selling and Distribution Overheads

Selling Overhead. As per terminology of CIMA this can be defined as "the cost of seeking to create and stimulate demand (sometimes termed as marketing) and of securing orders." So these expenses are incurred for the purpose of selling to the existing customers or for increasing sales to the existing and potential customers. It is incurred for the purpose of promoting sales and retaining customers. Some examples of selling overheads are : salesmen's salaries, commissions, travelling expenses, advertising, catalogues, samples, market research, royalties and rent for sales department, sales office expenses, collection charges, bad debts etc.

Distribution Overhead. As per terminology of CIMA this can be defined as "the cost of the sequence of operations which begins with making the packed product available for despatch and ends with making the reconditioned, returned empty packages, if any, available for reuses." Hence, this cost is mainly related to the physical movement of product to its customers. Some examples of distribution overheads are cost of packing, warehouse rent, labour and other expenses, carriage for goods despatched, repairing and reconditioning of empty packages etc.

Difference between Selling and Distribution Overheads

1. Selling overhead is related to promoting sales, whereas, distribution overhead is related to cost of despatching finished goods to its customers.

2. The main object of selling overheads is retaining the old customers and findings for new customers, whereas, the distribution overheads is meant for safe storing and also for safe delivery of products.

Analysis and Accounting of Selling and Distribution Cost

As selling and distribution cost is a "post-production costs', it requires proper analysis and accounting for ascertaining profit accurately.

(*i*) **Analysis.** Selling and distribution cost may be analysed in the following different methods :

1. *By Nature.* Here the expenses are classified according to the nature of expenses and are placed under separate headings to which it belongs. For example, (*i*) Remuneration, (*ii*) Packing materials, (*iii*) Freight, (*iv*) Sales promotion, (*v*) Discount and allowances etc.

2. *By Functions.* Here functional classifications are made. For example, (*i*) Direct Selling, (*ii*) Advertising and sales promotion, (*iii*) Warehousing and (*iv*) Credit collection etc.

3. *By Areas.* Here, classifications are made areawise. For example, North, South, East, West etc.

4. *By Products.* Expenses are classified according to various types of products produced. For example Product A, B and C etc.

5. *By Salesmen.* Here expenses are grouped in respect of each salesman.

6. *By Types of Customers.* It is called customerwise classification such as (*i*) State Government, (*ii*) Central Government etc.

7. *By Channels of Distribution.* The main examples are : (*i*) Wholesalers, (*ii*) Retailers, and (*iii*) Consumers etc.

(*ii*) **Absorption of Selling and Distribution Overhead.** Selling and distribution cost which cannot be directly allocated to cost units may be recovered by any one of the following methods :

1. *A rate per article.* Under this method, estimated total selling and distribution cost are to be distributed among the number of units sold.

2. *A percentage on works cost.* Here, selling and distribution overhead are recovered as a percentage (%) on works cost. This method is suitable for apportionment of fixed selling and distribution cost.

3. *A percentage on the selling price.* Under this method selling and distribution cost percentage to total sales is calculated, and this percentage is added to total cost for finding out the selling and distribution costs.

4. *A percentage of value added.* Here, the estimated rate is calculated as a percentage of sales value minus cost of material *i.e.* value added.

5. A percentage of cash collected. Usually, loss due to bad debts and other credit collection expenses are apportioned on this basis.

6. *A percentage of stock of finished goods.*

7. *According to number of orders.*

8. *According to number of invoices.*

Control of Selling and Distribution Overhead

It is very difficult to control selling and distribution overhead because of following reasons :

(*i*) As this cost is generally incurred after production is completed.

(*ii*) As this cost varies depending on the tastes and temperaments of customers which are beyond the control of management.

(*iii*) As the capacity and market potentialities cannot be predicted and controlled.

(*iv*) It is difficult to exercise control over competitors.

(*v*) Sometimes it is very difficult to differentiate between selling and non-selling cost.

(*vi*) Direct control cannot be exercised on sales representatives and other workers related to sales.

However, the selling and distribution cost can be controlled and reduced to minimum if following controlling techniques are adopted :

(*i*) **Comparison with past performance.** Under this method, each of the items of expenditure is compared with the corresponding item of expenditure of the previous period. This is helpful for a small organisation; where it is not difficult to calculate percentages of expenses to sales volumes accurately.

(*ii*) **Budgetary Control.** Under this method, the expenses are to be budgeted and classified into fixed and variable portion. Actual expenses are then compared with the budgeted expenses to find out the variances. Then various corrective actions are taken after analysing the variances. If necessary, flexible budgeting may be implemented.

(*iii*) **Standard Costing.** Under this method, standards should be set in order to compare with actuals and then any deviations may be corrected after analysis and investigation. But it is very difficult to set up a standard costing system for selling and distribution expenses.

Basis for Apportionment of Selling and Distribution Overhead

Expenses	*Base for Apportionment*
Warehousing & Storage	Sales volume
Advertising	Sales value or Physical units
Rent	Floor space
Insurance	Value of property
Remuneration, Freight, Material	Direct allocation
Postage & Stationery	Direct allocation
Depreciation	Value of assets
Sales promotion	Sales turnover or number of units sold
Credit control	No. of orders
Selling	% of sales turnover

WORKEDOUT PROBLEMS

Problem 1

XYZ Ltd. has two production and two Service departments namely P_1 and P_2, and S_1 and S_2, respectively. From the following information prepare a statement showing primary distribution of overhead :

Particulars	P_1	P_2	S_1	S_2
Area occupied (sq. ft.)	500	400	100	200
Asset value (Rs. '000)	100	50	30	10
No. of workers	40	20	20	10
Light Points	10	6	2	2
H.P. of Machine	10	5	4	1
Direct Wages (Rs. '000)	10	8	5	3
Direct material (Rs. '000)	15	10	3	2

Total expenses and charges during the period ended are :

	Rs.
Depreciation	19,000
Rent, Rates & Taxes	9,000
Power	6,250
Insurance	4,750
Canteen Expenses	2,700
Electricity	1,800
Indirect Material	3,000
Indirect Wages	5,200
Repairs & Maintenance	9,500
Sundries	2,600

Solution

Statement showing Primary Distribution of Overhead

Particulars	*Basis*	*Total*	*Production Dept.*		*Service Dept.*	
		Rs.	P_1	P_2	S_1	S_2
Direct Material	Given	5,000	—	—	3,000	2,000
Direct Wages	—do—	8,000	—	—	5,000	3,000
Indirect Wages	D/W (10 : 8 : 5 : 3)	5,200	2,000	1,600	1,000	600
Indirect Material	D/M (15 : 10 : 3 : 2)	3,000	1,500	1,000	300	200
Depreciation	Asset value (10 : 5 : 3 : 1)	19,000	10,000	5,000	3,000	1,000
Rent & Taxes	Floor Spaces (5 : 4 : 1 : 2)	9,000	3,750	3,000	750	1,500
Power	H.P. of Mach. (10 : 5 : 4 : 1)	6,250	3,125	1,562	1,250	313
Insurance	Asset value (10 : 5 : 3 : 1)	4,750	2,500	1,250	750	250
Canteen Expenses	No of workers (4 : 2 : 2 : 1)	2,700	1,200	600	600	300
Electricity	No of Light Points (5 : 3 : 1 : 1)	1,800	900	540	180	180
Repairs & Mainteanance	Asset value (10 : 5 : 3 : 1)	9,500	5,000	2,500	1,500	500
Sundries	D/W (10 : 8 : 5 : 3)	2,600	1,000	800	500	300
Total		76,800	30,975	17,852	17,830	10,143

Problem 2

The Electro Cooling Company is divided into four departments; P, Q & R are Production departments and S is a Service department.

The expenses incurred during the month of July 2007 are :

	Rs.
Supervision	1,500
Fire Insurance	500
Power	900
Light	100
Employees' Liability Insurance	150
Rent & Rates	1,000
Repairs & Maintenance	600
Depreciation of Plant	450

The following information are also available in respect of the above departments :

	P	Q	R	S
Floor space	150	110	90	50
No. of workers	20	15	10	15
H.P. of machine	8	5	2	—
D/W	6,000	4,000	3,000	2,000
Value of Plant	24,000	18,000	12,000	6,000
Value of Stock	15,000	9,000	6,000	—
Light Points	4	3	2	1

Apportion the cost of the various departments by the most equitable method.

Solution

Statement showing Distribution of Overhead

Particulars	*Basis*	*Total*	*Production Dept.*		*Service Dept.*	
		Rs.	P	Q	R	S
D/Wages of S.Dep.	D/W	2,000	—	—	—	2,000
Supervision	No. of Employees (4 : 3 : 2 : 3)	1,500	500	375	250	375
Fire Insurance	Value of stock (5 : 3 : 2)	500	250	150	100	—
Power	H.P. of Machine (8 : 5 : 2)	900	480	300	120	—
Light	Points (4 : 3 : 2 : 1)	100	40	30	20	10
Employees' Liability Insurance	No. of Employees (4 : 3 : 2 : 3)	150	50	37	25	38
Rent & Rates	Floor space (15 : 11 : 9 : 5)	1,000	375	275	225	125
Repairs	Value of Plant (4 : 3 : 2 : 1)	600	240	180	120	60
Depreciation	—do—	450	180	135	90	45
Total		7,200	2,115	1,482	950	2,653

Problem 3

The Overhead expenses of a company are recorded by the cost accountant according to various departments *viz.* Production dept. A & B and Service department S. From the following information :

(*a*) Prepare a Primary Distribution Schedule.

	Rs.
Power	2,000
Lighting	1,600
Rent & Rates	8,000
Indirect Wages	4,000
Depreciation of Machinery	12,000
Sundries	10,000

Additional Information :	*A*	*B*	*S*
Working Hrs	4,000	3,500	3,600
Direct Wages	6,000	2,000	2,000
Cost of Machinery	50,000	40,000	30,000
H.P. of machine	25	15	5
Light Points	9	6	5
Floor Spaces	500	600	400

(*b*) Find out the overhead Recovery Rate. Assuming Service Dept. cost is apportioned to Production Dept. in 3 : 2.

Solution

Statement showing Distribution of Overhead

Particulars	*Basis*	*Total Rs.*	*Production Dept.*		*Service Dept.*
			A	*B*	*S*
Power	H.P. of Mach. (5 : 3 : 1)	2,000	1,111	667	222
Lighting	Light Points (7 : 6 : 5)	1,600	720	480	400
Rent & Rates	Floor Space (5 : 6 : 4)	8,000	2,667	3,200	2,133
Indirect Wages	D/W (6 : 2 : 2)	4,000	2,400	800	800
Sundries	—do—	10,000	6,000	2,000	2,000
Dept. of machines	Cost of machines (5 : 4 : 3)	12,000	5,000	4,000	3,000
D/W	Actual	2,000	—	—	2,000
		39,600	17,898	11,147	10,555
Secondary distribution			6,333	4,222	(–) 10,555
Total		39,600	24,231	15,369	—
Hrs worked			4,000	3,500	
∴ Hourly Rate			6.058	4.391	

Problem 4

Calcutta Engineering Co. has three production departments X, Y and Z and one service department S.

From the following particulars calculate Labour Hour Rate of each of the departments X, Y and Z :

Expenses	*Rs.*
Rent	34,000
Power	18,400
Depreciation on machinery	22,000
Indirect Wages	5,300
Canteen Expenses	5,700
Electricity	4,600

Further Information :

	X	*Y*	*Z*	*S*
Floor area (Sq. mt.)	2,000	3,000	2,500	1,000
Light points	18	12	10	6
Cost of Machines (Rs.)	80,000	50,000	60,000	10,000
Horse-power ratio	3	2	4	1
No. of workers	7	5	5	2
Direct Wages (Rs.)	15,000	16,000	18,000	4,000

There were 125 working days of 8 hours each. Services rendered by the Service Department are to be apportioned to the production departments X 50%, Y 25%, and Z 25%.

[C.U. B.Com. (Hons.)]

Solution

Statement Showing the Overhead Distribution

Expenses	*Basis of Apportionment*	*Total*	*Production Departments*			*Service Department*
		Rs.	*X* *Rs.*	*Y* *Rs.*	*Z* *Rs.*	*S* *Rs.*
Direct Wages	Actual	4,000	—	—	—	4,000
Rent	Floor space (Sq.m) (4 : 6 : 5 : 2)	34,000	8,000	12,000	10,000	4,000
Power	H.P. hours ratio (3 : 2 : 4 : 1)	18,400	5,520	3,680	7,360	1,840
Depreciation on machinery	Cost of machine (8 : 5 : 6 : 1)	22,000	8,800	5,500	6,600	1,100
Indirect wages	Direct wages (15 : 16 : 18 : 4)	5,300	1,500	1,600	1,800	400
Canteen Expenses	No. of workers (7 : 5 : 5 : 2)	5,700	2,100	1,500	1,500	600
Electricity	No. of Light Points (9 : 6 : 5 : 3)	4,600	1,800	1,200	1,000	600
		94,000	27,720	25,480	28,260	12,540
Apportionment of service department expenses	% of service rendered (50 : 25 : 25)	—	6,270	3,135	3,135	–12,540
Total		94,000	33,990	28,615	31,395	—
Labour hours worked[1]			7,000	5,000	5,000	
Labour hour rates[2]			4.855	5.723	6.279	

Working Notes :

1. Labour hours worked = No. of working days × hours of daily work × No. of workers

$$X : 125 \times 8 \times 7 = 7{,}000$$
$$Y : 125 \times 8 \times 5 = 5{,}000$$
$$Z : 125 \times 8 \times 5 = 5{,}000$$

2. Labour hour rates $= \dfrac{\text{Expenses}}{\text{Labour hours worked}}$

Problem 5

Moonlight Engineering Company has three production departments, *A*, *B* and *C* and one service department *S*. Following are the particulars of a month of 25 working days of 8 hours each.

Calculate the labour hour rate for each of the production departments :

	Rs.	*Rs.*
Indirect Material		
Dept. *A*	1,735	
Dept. *B*	930	
Dept. *C*	935	
Dept. *S*	300	
		3,900
Indirect Wages		9,000
Rent		8,800
Canteen Expenses		1,800
Lighting		2,200
Depreciation @ 12% p.a.		

Other information :

	Dept. A	*Dept. B*	*Dept. C*	*Dept. S*
No. of workers	20	25	30	15
Area (Sq. metre)	100	100	150	50
Direct Wages (Rs.)	8,000	10,000	12,000	6,000
No. of Electric points	40	30	20	20
Value of Assets (Rs.)	5,000	6,000	6,000	3,000

Service rendered by the service department to production departments A, B and C is in the ratio of 2 : 2 : 1, respectively. *[C.U. B.Com. (Hons.), 1986]*

Solution

Statement Showing the Overhead Distribution

Expenses	*Basis of Apportionment*	*Total*	*Production Departments*			*Service Department*
		Rs.	*A* *Rs.*	*B* *Rs.*	*C* *Rs.*	*S* *Rs.*
Direct Wages		6,000	—	—	—	6,000
Indirect Material	Actual	3,900	1,735	930	935	300
Indirect Wages	Direct Wages (Rs.) (4 : 5 : 6 : 3)	9,000	2,000	2,500	3,000	1,500
Rent	Area (sq. m.) (2 : 2 : 3 : 1)	8,800	2,200	2,200	3,300	1,100
Canteen Expenses	No. of workers (4 : 5 : 6 : 3)	1,800	400	500	600	300
Lighting	No. of electric points (4 : 3 : 2 : 2)	2,200	800	600	400	400
Depreciation[1] @ 12%	Assets value (5 : 6 : 6 : 3)	2,400	600	720	720	360
		34,100	7,735	7,450	8,955	9,960
Apportionment of service department expenses	Ratio of Service rendered (2 : 2 : 1)	—	3,984	3,984	1,992	–9,960
Total		34,100	11,719	11,434	10,947	—
Labour hours worked[2]			4,000	5,000	6,000	—
Labour hour rates	Total/Labour hours worked		2.929	2.286	1.824	—

Working Notes :

1. Total Assets value = Rs. 5,000 + Rs. 6,000 + Rs. 6,000 + Rs. 3,000
   = Rs. 20,000

   ∴ Depreciation = 12% of Rs. 20,000 = Rs. 2,400

2. Labour hours worked = No. of working days × Hours of daily work × No. of workers :

   X : 25 × 8 × 20 = 4,000

   Y : 25 × 8 × 25 = 5,000

   Z : 25 × 8 × 30 = 6,000.

Problem 6

In a certain factory, there are two production departments X and Y, two service departments A and B. Total expenses of the service department A are apportioned between X, Y and B in the ratio 3 : 2 : 1, and the expenses of the service department B are allocated between X and Y equally.

From the following particulars, calculate the overheads to be calculated to Production Departments X and Y :

	X	*Y*	*A*	*B*
Floor space (sq. ft.)	5,000	4,000	1,000	2,000
Assets (Rs. in Lakhs)	10	5	3	1
H.P. of Machine	100	50	40	10
No. of workers	100	50	50	25
Light Points	25	15	10	10
Direct Wages (Rs.)	10,000	8,000	5,000	3,000
Direct Materials (Rs.)	15,000	10,000	4,000	—

Total expenses and charges are :

	Rs.
Depreciation	38,000
Rent, Rates & Taxes	18,000
Power	12,500

Insurance on Assets	9,500
Canteen Expenses	5,400
Electricity	3,600

[C.U. B.Com. (Hons.), 1988]

Solution

Statement showing the Overhead Distribution

Expenses	*Basis of Apportionment*	*Total Rs.*	*Production Dept.*		*Service Dept.*	
			X Rs.	*Y Rs.*	*A Rs.*	*B Rs.*
Direct Material	Actual	4,000	—	—	4,000	—
Direct Wages	Actual	8,000	—	—	5,000	3,000
Rent, Rates & Taxes	Floor Area (5 : 4 : 1 : 2)	18,000	7,500	6,000	1,500	3,000
Depreciation	Cost of Assets (10 : 5 : 3 : 1)	38,000	20,000	10,000	6,000	2,000
Power	H.P. of Mach. (10 : 5 : 4 : 1)	12,500	6,250	3,125	2,500	625
Insurance on Assets	Cost of Asset (10 : 5 : 3 : 1)	9,500	5,000	2,500	1,500	500
Canteen Expenses	No. of Workers (4 : 2 : 2 : 1)	5,400	2,400	1,200	1,200	600
Electricity	Light Points (5 : 3 : 2 : 2)	3,600	1,500	900	600	600
Total		99,000	42,650	23,725	22,300	10,325
(*i*) Expenses of Service Dept. A allocated to X, Y and B in 3 : 2 : 1			11,150	7,433	–22,300	3,717
			53,800	31,158	Nil	14,042
(*ii*) Expenses of Service Dept. B allocated to X and Y in 1 : 1			7,021	7,021		–14,042
			60,821	38,179		Nil

Problem 7

Bharat Engineering Works has three production departments A, B & C and one service department S. From the undermentioned particulars calculate labour hour rate for each of production departments. Expenses for the period of 12 months are :

	Rs.
Rent	36,000
Power	8,250
Indirect wages	5,200
Depreciation on machinery	22,000
Electricity	5,600
Canteen Expenses	6,500

Additional information :

	A	*B*	*C*	*S*
Light Points (Nos.)	7	7	9	5
Floor Space (Sq. m.)	300	250	450	200
Horse Power of machine (H.P.)	65	30	30	40
No. of workers (Nos.)	2	3	6	2
Direct Wages (Rs.)	12,000	14,000	18,000	8,000
Cost of Machine (Rs.)	50,000	60,000	80,000	10,000

Working days : 200 days of 8 hours each.

Service rendered by service department S to production departments A, B, C is 30%, 20% and 50%, respectively.

[C.U. B.Com. (Hons.)]

Solution

Statement Showing the Overhead Distribution

Basis of Expenses	Basis of Apportionment	Total	Production Departments			Service Department
		Rs.	A Rs.	B Rs.	C Rs.	S Rs.
Rent	Floor Space (6 : 5 : 9 : 4)	36,000	9,000	7,500	13,500	6,000
Power	H.P. (13 : 6 : 6 : 8)	8,250	3,250	1,500	1,500	2,000
Indirect Wages	Direct Wages (6 : 7 : 9 : 4)	5,200	1,200	1,400	1,800	800
Depreciation	Cost of Machine (5 : 6 : 8 : 1)	22,000	5,500	6,600	8,800	1,100
Electricity	Light Points (7 : 7 : 9 : 5)	5,600	1,400	1,400	1,800	1,000
Canteen Expenses	No. of Workers (2 : 3 : 6 : 2)	6,500	1,000	1,500	3,000	1,000
Direct wages	Allocated	8,000	—	—	—	8,000
		91,550	21,350	19,900	30,400	19,900
Apportionment of service department expenses	% of service rendered (3 : 2 : 5)		5,970	3,980	9,950	–19,900
Total Cost		91,550	27,320	23,880	40,350	Nil
Labour hours Worked[1]			3,200	4,800	9,600	
Labour hour rates	$\frac{\text{Total cost}}{\text{Labour hours worked}}$		8.54	4.98	4.20	

Working Notes :

1. Labour hours worked = No. of working days × hours of daily work × No. of workers :

$$A : 200 \times 8 \times 2 = 3{,}200$$

$$B : 200 \times 8 \times 3 = 4{,}800$$

$$C : 200 \times 8 \times 6 = 9{,}600$$

Problem 8

The costing records of Rahman Engineering Company show the following data for the year ending on 31.12.06 :

Particulars	Production Dept. X	Y	Z	Service Dept. S_1	S_2
Direct Wages	24,500	21,000	17,500	3,500	2,500
Direct Materials	10,500	8,750	7,000	5,250	3,500
No. of Employees	300	225	225	75	75
Electricity	6,000	4,500	4,500	1,500	3,250
No. of Light Points	10	15	15	5	5
Value of Assets	40,000	24,000	16,000	8,000	8,000
Area occupied	200	300	300	100	100

The expenses for the year were :

Lighting Rs. 700, Power Rs. 7,900, Stores expenses Rs. 1,400, Repairs Rs. 4,200, Depreciation Rs. 21,000, Labour welfare Rs. 10,500, General overhead Rs. 35,000, Rent etc. Rs. 2,100.

Calculate the departmental overheads for each of the production depts. assuming that overheads are recovered as percentage of direct wages. Apportion the expenses of dept. S_1 in ratio of 4 : 3 : 3 and that of dept. S_2 in proportion to direct wages to depts. X, Y and Z.

Solution

Statement Showing Departmental Overheads

Particulars	*Basis*	*Total Rs.*	*Production Dept.*			*Service Dept.*	
			X Rs.	*Y Rs.*	*Z Rs.*	S_1 *Rs.*	S_2 *Rs.*
Direct Wages	Given	6,000	—	—	—	3,500	2,500
Direct Mat.	—do—	8,750	—	—	—	5,250	3,500
Lighting	Light Points (2 : 3 : 3 : 1 : 1)	700	140	210	210	70	70
Power	Electricity kWh (24 : 18 : 18 : 6 : 13)	7,900	2,400	1,800	1,800	600	1,300
Stores Exp.	D/Material (6 : 5 : 4 : 3 : 2)	1,400	420	350	280	210	140
Repairs	Asset value (5 : 3 : 2 : 1 : 1)	4,200	1,750	1,050	700	350	350
Depreciation	—do— (5 : 3 : 2 : 1 : 1)	21,000	8,750	5,250	3,500	1,750	1,750
Labour Welfare Exp.	No. of Employees (4 : 3 : 3 : 1 : 1)	10,500	3,500	2,625	2,625	875	875
Rent	Area occupied (2 : 3 : 3 : 1 : 1)	21,000	4,200	6,300	6,300	2,100	2,100
General Overhead	D/Wages (49 : 42 : 35 : 7 : 5)	35,000	12,428	10,652	8,877	1,775	1,268
		1,16,450	33,588	28,237	24,292	16,480	13,853
Secondary distribution Service. Dept. S_2 (7 : 6 : 5)			5,387	4,618	3,848	—	–13,853
Service Depts S_1 (4 : 3 : 3)			6,592	4,944	4,944	–16,480	—
Total		1,16,450	45,567	37,799	33,084	—	—
∴ Overhead Rate as % of Direct Wages			$\frac{45,567}{24,500} \times 100$ = 185.98 %	$\frac{37,799}{21,000} \times 100$ = 179.99 %	$\frac{33,084}{17,500} \times 100$ = 189.05 %	—	—

Problem 9

A manufacturing Co. has three production departments and two service departments. Total expenses after primary distribution are :

Production Departments :	Service Departments :
A Rs. 5,000	1. Rs. 2,000
B Rs. 3,000	2. Rs. 3,000
C Rs. 2,500	

The following percentages are applicable for the apportionment of the costs of the service departments :

Dept.	*A*	*B*	*C*	*1*	*2*
1	40%	30%	10%	—	20%
2	20%	40%	30%	10%	—

Find out the total costs of production departments after apportionment of the costs of the service departments, taking into consideration inter-department services. ***[B.U. B.Com. (Hons.)]***

Solution

Departmental Overhead Distribution Summary

Expenses	Basis of Apportionment	Total Rs.	Production Depatments			Service Dept.	
			A Rs.	B Rs.	C Rs.	1 Rs.	2 Rs.
As per Departmenal Distribution Summary		15,500	5,000	3,000	2,500	2,000	3,000
Service Dept. 1	[40 : 30 : 10 : — : 20]		800	600	200	–2,000	400
Service Dept. 2	[20 : 40 : 30 : 10 : —]		680	1,360	1,020	340	–3,400
Service Dept. 1	[40 : 30 : 10 : — : 20]		136	102	34	–340	68
Service Dept. 2	20 : 40 : 30 : 10 : —]		13.60	27.20	20.40	6.80	–68
Service Dept. 1	[40 : 30 : 10 : — : 20]		2.72	2.04	0.68	–6.80	1.36
Service Dept. 2	20 : 40 : 30 : 10 : —]		0.30	0.61	0.45	—	–1.36
			6,632.62	5,091.85	3,775.53		

Problem 10

The New Enterprises Ltd. has three production departments A, B and C and two service departments D and E. The following figures are extracted from the records of the company :

	Rs.		Rs.
Rent and Rates	5,000	Power	1,500
General Lighting	600	Depreciation of Machinery	10,000
Indirect wages	1,500	Sundries	10,000

The following further details are available :

	Total	A	B	C	D	E
Floor space (sq. ft.)	10,000	2,000	2,500	3,000	2,000	500
Light Points	60	10	15	20	10	5
Direct Wages (Rs.)	10,000	3,000	2,000	3,000	1,500	500
H.P. of Machines	150	60	30	50	10	—
Value of Machinery (Rs.)	2,50,000	60,000	80,000	1,00,000	5,000	5,000
Working Hours	—	6,226	4,028	4,066	—	—

The expenses of D and E are allocated as follows :

	A	B	C	D	E
D	20%	30%	40%	—	10%
E	40%	20%	30%	10%	—

What is the total cost of an article if its raw material cost is Rs. 50, labour cost Rs. 30 and its passes through departments A, B and C for 4, 5 and 3 hours, respectively ?

[Bombay B.Com.]

Solution

New Enterprises Ltd.

Statement Showing Departmental Overhead Distribution Summary

Expenses	Basis of Apportionment	Total Rs.	Production Department			Service Dept.	
			A Rs.	B Rs.	C Rs.	D Rs.	E Rs.
Rent	Floor space (4 : 5 : 6 : 4 : 1)	5,000	1,000	1,250	1,500	1,000	250
Lighting	Light Point (2 : 3 : 4 : 2 : 1)	600	100	150	200	100	50
Indirect Wages	Direct Wages (6 : 4 : 6 : 3 : 1)	1,500	450	300	450	225	75
Power	H.P. of Machines (6 : 3 : 5 : 1 : —)	1,500	600	300	500	100	—
Depreciation	Value of Machinery (12 : 16 : 20 : 1 : 1)	10,000	2,400	3,200	4,000	200	200
Sundries	Direct Wages (6 : 4 : 6 : 3 : 1)	10,000	3,000	2,000	3,000	1,500	500
		28,600	7,550	7,200	9,650	3,125	1,075
Service Dept. D	(2 : 3 : 4 : — : 1)		625	938	1,250	(–) 3,125	312
Service Dept. E	(4 : 2 : 3 : 1 : —)		555	277	416	139	(–) 1,387
Service Dept. D	(2 : 3 : 4 : — : 1)		28	42	55	(–139)	14
Service Dept. E	(4 : 2 : 3 : 1 : –)		6	3	5	—	(–) 14
Total			8,764	8,460	11,376		
Total working hours	Given		6,226	4,028	4,066		
Hourly Rate			1.41	2.10	2.80		

Statement of Cost of Production

Items	Amount Rs.	Amount Rs.
Material Cost	50.00	
Labour Cost	30.00	80.00
Overheads :		
Production Dept. A = 4 hours @ Rs. 1.41	5.64	
Production Dept. B = 5 hours @ Rs. 2.10	10.50	
Production Dept. C = 3 hours @ Rs. 2.80	8.40	24.54
		104.54

Problem 11

Self-help Ltd. has genset and produces its own power. Data for power costs are :

Horse Power Hours	*Production Depts.*		*Service Depts.*	
	A	*B*	*X*	*Y*
Needed Capacity production	10,000	20,000	12,000	8,000
Used during the month of May	8,000	13,000	7,000	6,000

During the month of May costs for generating power amounted to Rs. 9,300, of this Rs. 2,500 was considered to be fixed cost. Service Depts. X renders service to A, B and Y in the ratio of 13 : 6 : 1 while Y renders service to A and B in the ratio of 31 : 3.

Given that direct labour hours in Deptts. A and B are 1,650 hours and 2,175 hours respectively, find the power cost per labour hour in each of these two Deptts.

[C.A. Inter. Nov. 1985]

Solution

Statement showing the Overhead Distribution

Items of Expenses	*Basis*	*Total Rs.*	*Production Dept.*		*Service Dept.*	
			A Rs.	*B Rs.*	*X Rs.*	*Y Rs.*
Fixed Cost	Needed Capacity of H.P. Hours (5 : 10 : 6 : 4)	2,500	500	1,000	600	400
Variable Cost	H.P. Hours used (8 : 13 : 7 : 6)	6,800	1,600	2,600	1,400	1,200
Total Cost		9,300	2,100	3,600	2,000	1,600
Overhead of Service department X allocated to A, B and Y in the ratio of 13 : 6 : 1			1,300	600	–2,000	100
			3,400	4,200	Nil	1,700
Overhead of Service department Y allocated to A & B in the ratio of 31 : 3			1,550	150		–1,700
Total			4,950	4,350	Nil	Nil
Direct Labour hours			1,650	2,175		
Power Cost per Labour hour			3.00	2.00		

Problem 12

Superclass Co. Ltd. has three production departments X, Y and Z and two service departments A and B. The following estimated figures for a certain period have been made available :

	Rs.
Rent & Rates	10,000
Lighting and Electricity	1,200
Indirect Wages	3,000
Power	3,000
Depreciation of Machinery	20,000
Other Expenses and Sundries	20,000

Following are further details which are also available :

	Total	*X*	*Y*	*Z*	*A*	*B*
Floor Space (sq. mts.)	10,000	2,000	2,500	3,000	2,000	500
Light points (Nos.)	120	20	30	40	20	10
Direct Wages (Rs.)	20,000	6,000	4,000	6,000	3,000	1,000
Horse Power of machines	300	120	60	100	20	—
Cost of Machinery (Rs.)	1,00,000	24,000	32,000	40,000	2,000	2,000
Working hours	—	4,670	3,020	3050	—	—

The expenses of the service departments A and B are to be allocated as follows :

	X	*Y*	*Z*	*A*	*B*
A	20%	30%	40%	—	10%
B	40%	20%	30%	10%	

You are required to calculate the overhead absorption rate per hour in respect of the three production departments.

What will be the total cost of an article with material cost of Rs. 80 and direct labour cost Rs. 40 which passes through X, Y and Z for 2, 3 and 4 hours, respectively ?

[I.C.W.A. Inter]

Solution

Super Class Company Ltd.
Departmental Overhead Distribution Summary

Particulars	*Basis of Apportionment*	*Total Rs.*	*Production Department X Rs.*	*Y Rs.*	*Z Rs.*	*Service Dept. A Rs.*	*B Rs.*
Rent, Rates & Taxes	Floor Area (4 : 5 : 6 : 4 : 1)	10,000	2,000	2,500	3,000	2,000	500
Lighting & Electricity	Light Point (2 : 3 : 4 : 2 : 1)	1,200	200	300	400	200	100
Indirect Wages	Direct wages (6 : 4 : 6 : 3 : 1)	3,000	900	600	900	450	150
Power	Horse power of Machines (6 : 3 : 5 : 1 : —)	3,000	1,200	600	1,000	200	—
Depreciation of Machinery	Cost of Machine (12 : 16 : 20 : 1 : 1)	20,000	4,800	6,400	8,000	400	400
Other expenses and Sundries	Direct Wages (6 : 4 : 6 : 3 : 1)	20,000	6,000	4,000	6,000	3,000	1,000
Direct Wages	Only Service Department (— : — : — : 3 : 1)	4,000	—	—	—	3,000	1,000
		61,200	15,100	14,400	19,300	9,250	3,150
Service Dept. A			1,850	2,775	3,700	–9,250	925
Service Dept. B			1,630	815	1,222	408	–4,075
Service Dept. A			82	122	163	–408	41
Service Dept. B			16	8	13	4	–41
Service Dept. A			2	—	2	–4	
Total		61,200	18,680	18,120	24,400	—	—
Working Hours			4,670	3,020	3,050		
Overheads per hour			4	6	8		

Statement of Cost Per Unit

		Rs.
Cost of Material		80
Cost of Labour		40
Prime Cost		120
Overhead. X 2 × Rs. 4 = 8		
Y 3 × Rs. 6 = 18		
Z 4 × Rs. 8 = 32		58
Total Productive Cost		178

Problem 13

A machine shop of a factory has three cost centres having distinct sets of machines. The following estimates are available for the year 2006 :

	Total for the factory	*Centre I*	*Centre II*	*Centre III*
Value of machines (in Rs.)	6,50,000	2,00,000	1,50,000	3,00,000
Direct Wages (in Rs.)	1,60,000	50,000	50,000	60,000
Power (in Rs.)	20,000			
Repairs & Maintenance (in Rs.)	65,000			
Insurance (in Rs.)	1,300			
Rent (in Rs.)	6,000			
Lighting (in Rs.)	3,600			
Labour welfare expenses (in Rs.)	40,000			
Power of Motor (in horse power)		25	25	50
Floor area (in square metres)		100	200	300
Machine hours		11,150	13,000	31,080
Share of Service Expenses (in Rs.)	10,000	2,000	3,000	5,000

Machines are depreciated at 10% per annum.

(*a*) Compute machine hour rate of overhead absorption for each of the centres.

(*b*) Job X passes through all the three cost centres as stated in question (*a*), and the requirement in each centre is Centre I—4 hours, Centre II—3 hours, Centre III—8 hours.

Compute the cost of the job if its direct materials and direct labour cost are estimated at Rs. 500 and Rs. 300, respectively. ***[B.U. B.Com. (Hons.)]***

Solution

(*a*) **Computation of Machine Hour Rate**

Particulars	*Basis of Apportionment*	*Total Rs*	*Production Centres I Rs.*	*II Rs.*	*III Rs.*
Direct Wages	Actual	1,60,000	50,000	50,000	60,000
Share of Service Exp.	Actual	10,000	2,000	3,000	5000
Depreciation [10% of Value of Machines]	Value of machines (4 : 3 : 6)	65,000	20,000	15,000	30,000
Power	Power of Motors (1 : 1 : 2)	20,000	5,000	5,000	10,000
Repairs & Maintenance	Value of Machines (4 : 3 : 6)	65,000	20,000	15,000	30,000
Insurance	Value of Machines (4 : 3 : 6)	1,300	400	300	600
Rent	Floor Area (1 : 2 : 3)	6,000	1,000	2,000	3,000
Lighting	Floor Are (1 : 2 : 3)	3,600	600	1,200	1,800
Labour Welfare Exp.	Direct Wages (5 : 5 : 6)	40,000	12,500	12,500	15,000
Total		3,70,900	1,11,500	1,04,000	1,55,400
Machine hours			11,150	13,000	31,080
Machine Hour Rate			10.00	8.00	5.00

(*b*) **Statement of Cost of Job**

	Rs.	*Rs.*
Direct Material	500	
Direct Labour	300	
PRIME COST		800
Overheads :		
Centre I : 4 hours × Rs. 10	40	
Centre II : 3 hours × Rs. 8	24	
Centre III : 8 hours × Rs. 5	40	
		104
Cost of the Job		904

Problem 14

The following information relating to the productions of Nalanda Fabricators for 2007 at Standard Capacity has been collected :

Direct Labour Cost :

Machining	Rs. 1,00,000
Assembling	Rs. 50,000

Floor Space Occupied :

Machining Department	60 per cent
Assembling Department	30 per cent
Factory Office	10 per cent

Factory overhead traceable of Departments :

Machining Department	Rs. 92,000
Assembling Department	Rs. 53,000
Factory Office	Rs. 41,000

Factory Overheads not traceable to Departments :

Factory Rent, Taxes and Insurance	Rs. 10,000

It has been decided that the costs of Factory office, which is a service department, can be equitably apportioned to other departments on a direct labour cost basis.

The Machining Department operates on a 40 hour week. There are five machines in the department and every machine has remained idle for 280 hours in 2007 for vacations, holidays, repairs, etc.

Calculate overhead absorption rate based on machine hours for Machining Department and overhead absorption rate based on direct labour cost for Assembling Department.

[B.Com. (Hons.)]

Solution

Overhead Distribution Sheet

Particulars		Production Dept.		Service Dept.
		Machining Department *Rs.*	*Assembling Department* *Rs.*	*Factory office* *Rs.*
Factory Overheads		92,000	53,000	41,000
Factory Rent, Taxes & Insurance (6 : 3 : 1) [Floor space occupied basis)		6,000	3,000	1,000
Total		98,000	56,000	42,000
Factory office of service department apportioned among production departments (2 : 1)		28,000	14,000	–42,000
	Rs.	1,26,000	70,000	Nil
Total machine hours = [40 × 5 × 52]	= 10,400			
Less : Idle time for Holidays [280 × 5]	= 1,400			
	9,000			
∴ Machine Hour Rate		$\frac{1,26,000}{9,000}$ = Rs. 14		
Direct Labour Cost			50,000	
Direct Labour Cost percentage			$\frac{70,000}{50,000} \times 100 = 140\%$	

Problem 15

Modern Manufactures Ltd. has three production departments P_1, P_2 and P_3 and two service departments S_1 and S_2 the details pertaining to which are as under :

	P_1	P_2	P_3	S_1	S_2
Direct Wages (Rs.)	3,000	2,000	3,000	1,500	195
Working hours	3,070	4,475	2,419	—	—
Value of Machines (Rs.)	60,000	80,000	1,00,000	5,000	5,000
H.P. of Machines	60	30	50	10	—
Light Points	10	15	20	10	5
Floor space (sq. ft.)	2,000	2,500	3,000	2,000	500

The following figures extracted from the Accounting records are relevant :

Rent and Rates Rs. 5,000 ; General Lighting Rs. 600 ; Indirect wages Rs. 1,939 ; Power Rs. 1,500 ; Depreciation on Machinery Rs. 10,000 and Sundries Rs. 9,695.

The expenses of the Service Departments are allocated as under :

	P_1	P_2	P_3	S_1	S_2
S_1	20%	30%	40%	—	10%
S_2	40%	20%	30%	10%	—

Find out the total cost of product which is processed for manufacture in Departments P_1, P_2 and P_3 for 4, 5 and 3 hours, respectively, given that its Direct Material Cost is Rs. 50 and Direct Labour Cost Rs. 30.

[C.A. Inter (Nov.) 1984]
[C.U. B.Com. (H) 2000]

Solution

Modern Manufacturing Ltd.
Overhead Distribution Summary

Particulars	*Basis of Apportionment*	*Total Rs.*	*Production Department*			*Service Dept.*	
			P_1 *Rs.*	P_2 *Rs.*	P_3 *Rs.*	S_1 *Rs.*	S_2 *Rs.*
Direct Wages	Actual	1,695	—	—	—	1,500	195
Rent & Rates	Area (4 : 5 : 6 : 4 : 1)	5,000	1,000	1,250	1,500	1,000	250
General Lighting	Light Point (2 : 3 : 4 : 2 : 1)	600	100	150	200	100	50
Indirect wages	Direct Wages (1/5 to D. wages) Assumed	1,939	600	400	600	300	39
Power	H.P. of machine (6 : 3 : 5 : 1)	1,500	600	300	500	100	—
Depreciation	Value of machine (12 : 16 : 20 : 1 : 1)	10,000	2,400	3,200	4,000	200	200
Sundries	Direct Wages (100% of Direct Wages)	9,695	3,000	2,000	3,000	1,500	195
Total		30,429	7,700	7,300	9,800	4,700	929
Redistribution of :							
S_1	(20 : 30 : 40 : — : 10)		940	1,410	1,880	(–) 4,700	470
S_2	(40 : 20 : 30 : 10 : —)		559	279	420	140	(–) 1,399
S_1	(20 : 30 : 40 : — : 10)		28	42	56	(–) 140	14
S_2	(40 : 20 : 30 : 10 : —)		6	3	4		(–14)
S_1	(20 : 30 : 40 : — : 10)				1	(–) 1	—
			9,233	9,034	12,161		
Working Hours	Given		3,070	4,475	2,419		
Hourly Rate			3.00	2.02	5.03		

Statement of Cost of Production

	Rs.	*Rs.*
Cost of Direct Material		50.00
Cost of Direct Labour		30.00
Overhead :		
P_1 4 × Rs. 3.00	12.00	
P_2 5 × Rs. 2.02	10.10	
P_3 3 × Rs. 5.03	15.09	37.19
		117.19

Problem 16

A manufacturing Co. has three production departments and two service departments. Overhead allocated for a period to these departments is as follows :

Production Departments :		*Service Departments*
P	Rs. 67,000	1. Rs. 3,000
Q	Rs. 5,000	2. Rs. 4,000
R	Rs. 8,000	

A technical estimate for the apportionment of the costs of the service departments shows the following position :

Departments :	*P*	*Q*	*R*	1	2
1	30%	40%	20%	—	10%
2	20%	30%	30%	20%	—

You are required to show total overhead chargeable to the three production departments after apportionment of costs of the service departments using simultaneous equation method.

[B.U. B.Com. (Hons.), 1983]

Solution

Firstly, the total cost of Service Departments of 1 and 2 are to be determined by the following equations :

Let, a = Total overhead of Service Dept. 1.

b = Total overhead of Service Dept. 2.

So, a = Rs. 3,000 + 20% of b ... (1)

b = Rs. 4,000 + 10% of a ... (2)

or a = Rs. 3,000 + 0.2 b

b = Rs. 4,000 + 0.1 a

or, $10a - 2b = 30{,}000$ ... (3)

$-a + 10b = 40{,}000$ ... (4)

or, a = 3,878 (approximate) [By solving the eqns. 3 and 4]

b = 4,390

The total costs of Service Departments 1 and 2 are to be apportioned among the production departments P, Q and R on the basis of the given percentage of the problem.

Statement Showing the Re-apportionment of Service Departments Costs to Production Departments

Expenses	*Total*	*Production Departments*		
	Rs.	*P Rs.*	*Q Rs.*	*R Rs.*
As per Departmental Distribution Summary	80,000	67,000	5,000	8,000
Service Dept. 1 [90% of Rs. 3,878]	3,490	1,163	1,551	776
Service Dept. 2 [80% of Rs. 4,390]	3,512	878	1,317	1,317
	87,002	69,041	7,868	10,093

Problem 17

Following are the particulars of three machines used in a factory. Compute the machine hour rate for each machine.

Particulars	*Machine No. 1*	*Machine No. 2*	*Machine No. 3*
Anticipated working hrs	2,200	2,200	2,200
Idle time	10%	10%	10%
No. of workers	5	2	10
Cost of Machine	1,00,000	1,50,000	2,00,000
Power	450	800	1,500
Light Points	2	4	6
Area Occupied (sq. ft.)	100	250	400

The expenses incurred during the period were as follows :

	Rs.
Power	2,750
Lighting	4,800
Rent & Taxes	4,500
Depreciation	1,350
Repairs	1,800
Indirect Wages	4,500
Canteen Expenses	5,100
Sundries	3,000

Solution

Computation of Machine Hour Rate

Estimated working hrs = (2,200 – 10% of 2,200) = 1,980 hrs

Particulars	*Basis*	*Total*	*Machines*		
			1	2	*3*
Standing Charges :					
Lighting	No. of light points (1 : 2 : 3)	4,800	800	1,600	2,400
Rent & Taxes	Floor Spaces (2 : 5 : 8)	4,500	600	1,500	2,400
Sundries	Direct Wages (8 : 3 : 4)	3,000	1,600	600	800
Variable Charges :					
Power	Actual	2,750	450	800	1,500
Depreciation	Cost of Machine (2 : 3 : 4)	1,350	300	450	600
Repairs	—do—	1,800	400	600	800
Indirect Wages	Direct Wages (8 : 3 : 4)	4,500	2,400	900	1,200
Canteen Expenses	No. of works (5 : 2 : 10)	5,100	1,500	600	3,000
		27,800	8,050	7,050	12,700
Effective Machine hrs			1,980	1,980	1,980
∴ Machine hour Rate			4.065	3.65	6.414

Problem 18

A machine was purchased for Rs. 55,000. It was installed in a shop over $\frac{1}{5}$th of its floor area at an additional cost of Rs. 5,000. The working life of the machine as also the scrap value were estimated at 10 yrs and Rs. 5,000, respectively. From the following details compute the Machine Hour Rate :

	Rs.
Rent & Rates of the shop p.a.	5,000
General lighting of the shop p.m.	500
Repairs and maintenance for the machine p.a.	3,000
Insurance Premium p.a.	2,400
Supervisor's salary per month	1,000

It is estimated that the supervisor devotes one-fourth of his time for the machine, the cost of power is Rs. 20 per 100 units and the machine consumed 10 units per hour.

Normal working hours of the machine is estimated at 1,200 but during the year it actually worked for 1,000 hrs.

Solution

Computation of Machine Hour Rate

Estimated working hrs = 1,000

Particulars	*Per Annum*	*Per hour*
Standing Charges :		
Rent & Rates $\left(5{,}000 \times \frac{1}{5}\right)$	1,000	
General lighting $\left(500 \times 12 \times \frac{1}{5}\right)$	1,200	
Insurance Premium	2,400	
Supervisor's Salary $\left(1{,}000 \times 12 \times \frac{1}{4}\right)$	3,000	
	7,600	7.60
Variable Expenses :		
Depreciation $\left(\frac{55{,}000 + 5{,}000 - 5{,}000}{10}\right)$	5,500	5.50
Repairs & Maintenance	3,000	3.00
Power $\left(\text{Rs. } 20 \times \frac{10}{100}\right)$	—	2.00
∴ Machine Hour Rate Rs.		18.10

Problem 19

Compute machine hour rate of a machine in a shop consisting of 3 machines occupying equal floor space. Following details are supplied for the machine of which estimated working hours per year are fixed at 2,500 hours in which normal idle time is estimated at 20% of the standard time :

	Rs.
Rent and Taxes of the shop per annum	3,600
General Electricity for the shop per month	200
Repairs and Maintenance Expenses for the machine per annum	600
Rate of Power charges for 100 units (the machine consuming 10 units per hour)	3
Foreman's salary for supervising all the machines, per month	750
Indirect Labour Cost Rs. 2 per hour for the machine.	

The machine costs Rs. 1,30,000 and scrap value is estimated at Rs. 10,000 and estimated life is 10 years. The Foreman devotes equal attention for each machine in the shop.

[C.U. B.Com. (Hons.)]

Solution

Computation of Machine Hour Rate

Dept./Shop ... Date of Installation... Life 10 years.
Machine No. ... Cost Rs. 1,30,000 Scrap value Rs. 10,000

	Per Year *Rs.*	*Per hour* *Rs.*
Fixed Expenses :		
Rent & Taxes (apportioned on area basis) Rs. 3,600 × $\frac{1}{3}$	1,200	
General Electricity (apportioned on area basis) Rs. 200 × 12 months × $\frac{1}{3}$	800	
Foreman's Salary Rs. 750 × 12 months × $\frac{1}{3}$	3,000	
For 2,000 hours	5,000	2.50
Variable Expenses :		
Depreciation $\frac{\text{Rs. }(1{,}30{,}000 - 10{,}000)}{10 \times 2{,}000}$		6.00
Repairs & Maintenance $\frac{\text{Rs. }600}{2{,}000}$		0.30
Power $\frac{10}{100}$ × Rs. 3		0.30
Indirect Labour		2.00
Machine Hour Rate		11.10

Working Notes :

	hours
Normal working hours of the machine	2,500
Less : Idle time 20% of 2,500	500
Effective working hours	2,000

Problem 20

From the following particulars calculate machine hour rate :

	Rs.
Cost of machine (including installation charges)	1,05,000
Rent of shop p.m.	1,000
Lighting of shop p.a.	1,500
Repairs p.a.	1,700
Supervisor's salary p.m.	1,200
Insurance premium of the machine per quarter	375

The life of the machine is 10 years with a scrap value of Rs. 5,000. It occupies $\frac{1}{5}$th of the shop area and consumes 3 units of power per hour @ $33\frac{1}{3}$ p. per unit. Supervisor devotes $\frac{1}{3}$rd of his time to the machine. The machine has the capacity of working 5,000 hours p.a. but it actually worked 90% of the capacity. ***[C.U. B.Com. (Hons.)]***

Solution

Computation of Machine Hour Rate

Dept./Shop ...	Date of installation...	Life 10 years.
Machine No. ...	Cost Rs. 1,05,000 [including installation charge]	Scrap value Rs. 5,000

	Per Year Rs.	Per hour Rs.
Fixed Expenses :		
Rent of shop Rs. 1,000 × 12 months × $\frac{1}{5}$	2,400	
Lighting of shop Rs. 1,500 × $\frac{1}{5}$	300	
Supervisor's salary Rs. 1,200 × 12 months × $\frac{1}{3}$	4,800	
Insurance Premium of the machine Rs. 375 × 4	1,500	
Fixed Expenses for 4,500 [5,000 × 90%] hours	9,000	
	$\frac{9,000}{4,500}$	2.00
Variable Expenses :		
Repairs Rs. 1,700 ÷ 4,500		0.38
Depreciation $\frac{\text{Rs. } 1,05,000 - \text{Rs. } 5,000}{4,500 \times 10}$		2.22
Power Paise $33\frac{1}{3} \times 3$		1.00
Machine hour rate		5.60

Problem 21

From the particulars furnished below compute the machine hour rate :

	Rs.
Cost of Machine	90,000
Cost of installation	10,000
Scrap value at the end of 10 years	5,000
Indirect wages and materials for the machine	500 per year
Supervision cost for four similar machines	16,000 per year
Insurance Premium for the machine	200 per quarter
Rent of the machine shop	400 p.m.
Electricity cost for the machine shop	100 p.m.

Power consumption of the machine is 20 units per actual working hour.

Power cost is 50 paise per unit.

The total area of the machine shop is 600 sq. metres of which this machine occupies only 150 sq. metres. There are 200 light points in the machine shop of equal wattage of which the machine utilises only 40 points.

It is estimated that the machine will normally work for 2,700 hours in a year, but it is apprehended that the machine will remain idle for 200 hours.

[C.U. B.Com. (Hons.) 1985]

Solution

Computation of Machine Hour Rate

Dept./Shop ...	Date of installation...	Life 10 years
Machine No. ...	Cost Rs. 90,000	Scrap value Rs. 5,000
	Installation expenses Rs. 10,000	

	Per Year *Rs.*	*Per hour* *Rs.*
Fixed Expenses :		
Machine Shop's Rent Rs. 400 × 12 months × $\frac{1}{4}$	1,200	
[Occupied area of the machine = $\frac{150}{600} = \frac{1}{4}$]		
Electricity $\frac{\text{Rs. } 100 \times 12 \text{ months}}{200} \times 40$	240	
Insurance Premium Rs. 200 × 4	800	
Supervision cost for similar machines Rs. 16,000 ÷ 4	4,000	
Fixed Expenses for 2,500 (2,700 – 200) hours	6,240	
	$\frac{6,240}{2,500}$	2.50
Variable Expenses :		
Depreciation $\frac{\text{Rs. } 90,000 + \text{Rs. } 10,000 - \text{Rs. } 5,000}{2,500 \times 10}$		3.80
Power 20 × 50 Paise		10.00
Indirect wages and materials $\frac{500}{2,500}$		0.20
Machine hour rate		16.50

Problem 22

From the following particulars calculate the machine hour rate :

	Rs.
Cost of machine	2,00,000
Installation charges	20,000
Rent of the shop per month	3,000
Insurance Premium for the machine per annum 1% of Capital Cost	
Electricity charges for the shop per month	300
Repair and Maintenance per month 0.5% of Capital Cost	
Supervisor's Salary per month	1,800
Rate of power charges for 100 units	55
[The machine consumes 16 units of power per hour.]	

The machine occupies $^1/_3$rd of the shop area. Its life is 10 years and anticipated scrap value is Rs. 10,000. The supervisor devotes $^1/_4$th of his time on the machine.

Estimated idle time : 50 hours in a year. Normal working days during a year : 250 days of 8 hours, 50 days of 5 hours.

[C.U. B.Com. (Hons.) 1987]

Solution

Computation of Machine Hour Rate

Dept./Shop ... Date of Installation... Life 10 years

Machine No. ... Cost Rs. 2,00,000 Scrap value Rs. 10,000

Installation Rs. 20,000

Effective working hours per year 2,200

	Per Year *Rs.*	*Per hour* *Rs.*
Fixed Expenses :		
Rent Rs. 3,000 × 12 months × $\frac{1}{3}$	12,000	
Electricity Rs. 300 × 12 months × $\frac{1}{3}$	1,200	
Supervisor's Salary Rs. 1,800 × 12 months × $\frac{1}{4}$	5,400	
Insurance Premium for the machine p.a. 1% of Capital Cost		
2,00,000 + 20,000 = 2,20,000 × $\frac{1}{100}$	2,200	
Fixed expenses for 2,200 hours[1]	20,800	9.45
Variable Expenses :		
Repair & Maintenance p.m. 0.5% of Capital Cost		
$2{,}20{,}000 \times \frac{5 \times 12}{100 \times 10} \times \frac{1}{2{,}200}$		6.00
Depreciation . $\frac{2{,}20{,}000 - 10{,}000}{2{,}200 \times 10}$		9.55
Power Rs. 55 × $\frac{16}{100}$		8.80
Machine hour rate		33.80

Working Notes :

[1]Effective working hours of the machine :

	Hrs
250 days × 8 hours	2,000
50 days × 5 hours	250
	2,250
Less : Idle time	50
	2,200

Problem 23

From the following particulars compute a comprehensive Machine Hour Rate :

(*i*) Cost of machine : Rs. 1,00,000. Estimated life : 15 years.. Residual value : Rs. 10,000.

(*ii*) Machine Running Hours : 2040 hours per machine per annum including idle time of 40 hours due to routine repairs and maintenance and 20 hours due to break-down of machine.

(*iii*) Power consumption of the machine per hour : 20 units; rate of power per 100 units Rs. 80.

(*iv*) There are two operators in the shop and wages, workmen's compensation insurance etc. of an operator who is in charge of two machines Rs. 12,000 p.a.

(*v*) Rent, rates and taxes of the shop : Rs. 4,800 p.a.

(vi) Insurance premium for the machine : Rs. 400 per quarter.
(vii) General lighting per month : Rs. 600.
(viii) Repairs and maintenance expenses per month : Rs. 400 per machine.
(ix) Shop supervisor's salary per month : 1,500.
(x) Other factory overhead allocated to the shop : Rs. 6,000 p.a.

There are four identical machines in the Machine Shop. The supervisior devotes one-fifth of his time for supervising the machine. **[C.U. B.Com. (Hons.) 1991]**

Solution

Computation of Comprehensive Machine Hour Rate

		Per Year Rs.	Per hour Rs.
Fixed Expenses :			
Rent and Rates	(Rs. $\frac{4,800}{4}$)	1,200	
Insurance Premium	(Rs. 400 × 4)	1,600	
General Lighting	$\left(\frac{\text{Rs. } 600 \times 12}{4}\right)$	1,800	
Supervisor's Salary	$\left(\text{Rs. } 1,500 \times 12 \times \frac{1}{5}\right)$	3,600	
Factory Overhead	(Rs. 6,000 × $\frac{1}{4}$)	1,500	
Total Fixed Cost for 2,000 hours		9,700	
		$\frac{9,700}{2,000}$	4.85
Variable Expenses :			
Depreciation	$\frac{\text{Rs. } (1,00,000 - 10,000)}{15 \times 2,000}$		3.00
Power	Rs. 80 × $\frac{20}{100}$		16.00
Repairs & Maintenance	$\left[\frac{\text{Rs. } 400 \times 12}{2,000}\right]$		2.40
Machine hour rate			26.25
Wages of operator	$\frac{\text{Rs. } 12,000}{2 \times 2,000}$		3.00
Comprehensive Machine hour rate			29.25

Problem 24

From the following details compute the hourly rate of a machine installed in a shop :

	Rs.
Cost of machine	2,00,000
Installation charges	20,000
Estimated scrap value after expiry of its life (15 years)	10,000
Rent and rates of the shop p.a.	7,200
General Lighting of the shop p.m.	800
Insurance Premium for the machine per quarter	720
Estimated repairs and maintenance cost of the machine p.a.	3,000
Power consumption of the machine	20 units per hour

Rate of power per 100 units	20
Estimated working hours of the machine per year	2,300
Shop supervisor's salary per month	1,800

The machine occupies $^1/_4$th of the total floor area of the shop. The supervisor is expected to devote $^1/_5$th of his time for supervising the machine. Normal idle time is expected to be 300 hours per annum. ***[B.U. B.Com. (Hons.)]***

Solution

Computation of Machine Hour Rate

Dept./Shop ...	Date of Installation...	Life 15 years
	Cost Rs. 2,00,000	Scrap value Rs. 10,000
Machine No. ...	Installation Rs. 20,000	

		Per Year *Rs.*	*Per hour* *Rs.*
Fixed Expenses :			
Rent & Rates of the shop $(7{,}200 \times \frac{1}{4})$		1,800	
General Electricity	$[\text{Rs. } 800 \times 12 \text{ months} \times \frac{1}{4}]$	2,400	
Insurance Premium	[Rs. 720 × 4]	2,880	
Supervisor's salary	$[\text{Rs. } 1{,}800 \times 12 \text{ months} \times \frac{1}{5}]$	4,320	
For 2,000 hours		11,400	5.70
Variable Expenses :			
Repair & Maintenance	$\frac{\text{Rs. } 3{,}000}{2{,}000}$		1.50
Power	$\left[20 \text{ units} \times \frac{\text{Rs. } 20}{100}\right]$		4.00
Depreciation	$\left[\frac{\text{Rs. } 2{,}00{,}000 + \text{Rs. } 20{,}000 - \text{Rs. } 10{,}000}{15 \times 2{,}000}\right]$		7.00
Machine Hour Rate			18.20

Working Notes :

		Hours
	Normal working hours of the machine	2,300
Less :	Idle time	300
	Effective working hours	2,000

Problem 25

Machine costing Rs. 28,700 excluding installation costs of Rs. 300, has an anticipated life of 10 years with residual value of Rs. 500.

The straight line method of depreciation is followed.

From the following details, compute machine hour rate on the basis of anticipated working hours.

1. Rent and rates for the factory is Rs. 4,000 per annum and 5% of the effective area is occupied by this machine.

2. Insurance for this machine is Rs. 150 per annum.

3. Repairs and maintenance for the factory is Rs. 1,000, $12^1/_2$% of this amount relates to this machine.

4. Consumable stores etc. attributed to this machine is Rs. 275.
5. Total of production services is Rs. 4,000. 10% of this amount is applicable to this machine.
6. Power cost is 0.50 paise per working hour.

The year contains 250 working days of 8 hours each but it is anticipated that the machine will remain idle 20% of this time. ***[B.Com. Chennai]***

Solution

Computation of Machine Hour Rate

		Rs.	Rs.
Fixed Charges :			
Rent & Rates	Rs. 4,000 × $\frac{5}{100}$	200	
Insurance		150	
Production Services	Rs. 4,000 × $\frac{10}{100}$	400	
		750	
∴ Fixed charges per hour = $\frac{\text{Rs. } 750}{1{,}600}$			.47
Machine Expenses :			
Consumable Stores	(275 ÷ 1,600)		0.17
Depreciation	$\frac{\text{Rs. } 28{,}700 + \text{Rs. } 300 - \text{Rs. } 500}{10 \times 1{,}600}$		1.78
Repairs & maintenance	$\left[1{,}000 \times \frac{125}{1{,}000}\right] = \frac{\text{Rs. } 125}{1{,}600}$		0.08
Power			0.50
Machine Hour Rate			3.00

Working Notes :

	Normal Working Hours of the machine [250 × 8]	2,000
Less :	Idle time 20% of 2,000	400
		1,600

Problem 26

Calculate Machine Hour Rate for recovery of overheads for a group of 4 machines from the following data :

Original cost of the 4 machines Rs. 76,800.

Depreciation at 10% per annum ; Straight line method.

Maintenance cost average Rs. 8 per day of 8 hours for the group of machines.

Power 25 paise per running hour (per machine).

Supervision for the machine group Rs. 640 per month.

Allocation of building depreciation for the 4 machines on a floor area basis, Rs. 80 per month.

Share of manufacturing overheads, Rs. 240 per month, for the group.

Normal working days in the year, 300.

Normal idle time, 20%.

Normal running, 1 shift of 8 hours. ***[C.U. M.Com.]***

Solution

Computation of Machine Hour Rate

		Per Year Rs.	Per hour Rs.
Fixed Expenses :			
Depreciation*	$\left[\frac{\text{Rs. } 76,800 \times 10}{4 \times 100}\right]$	1,920	
Supervision	$\left[\frac{\text{Rs. } 640}{4} \times 12\right]$	1,920	
Depreciation of Building	$\left[\frac{\text{Rs. } 80}{4} \times 12\right]$	240	
Manufacturing Overhead	$\left[\frac{\text{Rs. } 240}{4} \times 12\right]$	720	
For 1,920[1] hours		4,800	2.50
Variable Expenses :			
Power			0.25
Maintenance	$\left[\frac{\text{Rs. } 8}{4 \times (8 - 20\% \text{ of } 8)}\right]$		0.31
	Total		3.06

*Depreciation is treated as a fixed charge.

Working Notes :

		Hours
	[1]Normal working hours (300 × 8)	2,400
Less :	Idle time (20% of 2,400)	480
	Effective working hours	1,920

Problem 27

Compute comprehensive machine hour rate from the following data :

(*i*) Total machine cost of one machine to be depreciated Rs. 2,30,000, Life for 10 years ; Depreciation on Straight Line.

(*ii*) Departmental Overhead (annual) :

Rent	Rs. 50,000
Heat and Light	Rs. 20,000
Supervision	Rs. 1,30,000

(*iii*) Departmental area 70,000 square feet
Machine area 2,500 square feet

(*iv*) 26 machines in the department

(*v*) Annual cost of reserve materials for the machines Rs. 1,500.

(*vi*) Hours run of production 1,800.

(*vii*) Hours for setting and adjusting 200 (Normal).

(*viii*) Power cost Rs. 0.50 per hour of running time.

(*ix*) Labour (*a*) when setting and adjusting, full time attention.
(*b*) when machine is producing, one man can look after 3 machines.

(*x*) Labour rate Rs. 6 per hour. ***[I.C.W.A. (Inter)]***

Solution

Computation of Comprehensive Machine Hour Rate

Dept./Shop ... Date of Installation... Life 10 years.
Machine No. ... Cost Rs. 2,30,000

Particulars		*Basis*	*Per Year Rs.*	*Per hour Rs.*
Fixed Expenses :				
Rent	$\frac{\text{Rs. } 50{,}000 \times 2{,}500}{70{,}000}$	Area	1,786	
Heat & Light	$\frac{\text{Rs. } 20{,}000 \times 2{,}500}{70{,}000}$	Area	714	
Supervision	$\frac{\text{Rs. } 1{,}30{,}000}{26}$	No. of machines	5,000	
Reserve Materials	$\frac{\text{Rs. } 1{,}500}{26}$	No. of machines	58	
Labour cost for setting and adjustment 200 × Rs. 6		Hours × Rate	1,200	
For 1,800 hours			8,758	4.87
Variable Expenses :				
Depreciation	$\frac{\text{Rs. } 2{,}30{,}000}{10 \text{ years} \times 1{,}800 \text{ hrs}}$	Value of Assets		12.78
Power		Direct		0.50
Labour	$\frac{1}{3} \times$ Rs. 6.00	No. of Supervision Machine		2.00
Machine Hour Rate				20.15

Problem 28

A machine shop has 8 identical drilling machines manned by 6 operators. The machines cannot be worked without an operator wholly engaged on it. The original cost of all these 8 machines works out to Rs. 8 lakhs. These particulars are furnished for a 6 month period :

Normal available hours per month	208
Leave (with pay) hours	20
Absenteeism (without pay) hours	18
Normal idle time (unavoidable) hours	10
Average rate of wages per day of 8 hours	Rs. 20
Production bonus estimated	15% on wages
Value of power consumed	Rs. 8,050
Supervision and Indirect Labour	Rs. 3,300
Lighting & Electricity	Rs. 1,200

These particulars are for a year :

Repairs and maintenance including consumables 3% on value of machines.

Insurance	Rs. 40,000
Depreciation 10% on original cost	
Other Sundry works expenses	Rs. 12,000
General management expenses allocated	Rs. 54,530

You are required to work out a comprehensive machine hour rate for the machine shop.

[C.A. (Inter)]

Solution

Computation of Comprehensive Machine Hour Rate

Particulars	*Basis of Apportionment*	*Per Half Year Rs.*	*Per hour Rs.*
Wages for 6 operators	[208 – 18] 190 × 6 × 6 $\frac{\text{Rs. } 20}{8}$	17,100	
Bonus	15% of Rs. 17,100	2,565	
Power	Actual	8,050	
Supervision & Indirect Labour	Actual	3,300	
Lighting & Electricity	Actual	1,200	
Repairs & Maintenance	Rs. 8,00,000 × 3/100 × 6/12	12,000	
Insurance	Rs. 40,000 × 6/12	20,000	
Depreciation	Rs. 8,00,000 × 10/100 × 6/12	40,000	
Other Sundry works exp.	Rs. 12,000 × 6/12	6,000	
General Management exp.	Rs. 54,530 × 6/12	27,265	
For 5,760 hours*		1,37,480	
∴ Machine Hour Rate	Rs. $\frac{1,37,480}{5,760}$		23.87

Working Notes :

			Hours
	*Normal working hours of the machine per month		208
Less :	Idle time :		
	Leave hours	20	
	Absenteeism	18	
	Normal idle time	10	48
			160

∴ Effective working hours = 160 hours × 6 operators × 6 months
= 5,760 hours.

Problem 29

A mcahine costs Rs. 90,000 and is deemed to have a scrap value of 5% at the end of its effective life (19 years). Ordinarily the machine is expected to run for 2400 hours per annum but it is estimated that 150 hours will be lost for normal repairs and maintenance and further 750 hours will be lost due to staggering. The other details in respect of the machine shop are :

(*a*) Wages, bonus and provident fund contribution of each of two operators (each operator is in charge of two machines)	6,000 per year.
(*b*) Rent & rates of the shop	3,000 per year.
(*c*) General Lighting of the shop	250 per month
(*d*) Insurance Premium for the machine	200 per quarter
(*e*) Cost of repairs & maintenance per machine	250 per month
(*f*) Shop Supervisor's Salary	500 per month
(*g*) Power Consumption of the machine per hour 20 units, rate of power per 100 units	Rs. 10
(*h*) Other factory overhead attribute to the shop	4,000 per year

There are four identical machines in the shop. The supervisor is expected to devote one-fifth of his time for supervising the machine. Compute a comprehensive machine hour rate from the above details.

[I.C.W.A. (Inter), C.A. (Inter), Audit & Accounts Service Exam.]

Solution

Statement showing Computation of Machine Hour Rate

Machine No. ... Cost Rs. 90,000 Life of Machine = 19 Years
Scrap value –5% of Rs. 90,000 Working hours = 2,400 hours
Idle time = 150 + 750 = 900

Particulars		Per Year Rs.	Per hour Rs.
Fixed Expenses :			
Rent & Rates	Rs. $\frac{3,000}{4}$	750	
General Lighting	$\frac{\text{Rs. } 250 \times 12}{4}$	750	
Insurance	Rs. 200 × 4	800	
Supervisor's Salary	$\frac{\text{Rs. } 500 \times 12}{5}$	1,200	
Allocated Overheads	$\frac{\text{Rs. } 4,000}{4}$	1,000	
	For 1,500 [2,400 – 900] hours	4,500	3.00
Variable Expenses :			
Wages, Bonus & Provident Fund	$\left(\frac{\text{Rs. } 6,000}{2 \times 1,500}\right)$		2.00
Power	Rs. 10 × $\frac{20}{100}$		2.00
Repairs & Maintenance	$\frac{\text{Rs. } 250 \times 12}{1,500}$		2.00
Depreciation	$\frac{\text{Rs. } (90,000 - 4,500)}{1,500 \times 19}$		3.00
Machine Hour Rate			12.00

Problem 30

From the following data of a cotton industries machine room compute the hourly machine rate. Assuming that the machine room will work on 90% capacity throughout the year and that a breakdown allowance of 10% is reasonable.

There are 3 holidays at Deepavali, 2 at Holi, 2 at Christmas, exclusive of Sundays. The factory works 8 hrs a day on 5 days and 4 hrs on Saturdays.

The Number Of Machines (Each of same time)	40

The following expenses were incurred during the year :

	Rs.
Power	3,120
Lighting	640
Salaries of Foreman	1,200
Lubricating oil	60
Repairs to machine	1,446
Depreciation	785

Solution

Computation of Machine Hour Rate

Estimated effective working hrs 1,814

Particulars	*Per Year* Rs.	*Per hour* Rs.
Standing Charges :		
Lighting ($^{640}/_{40}$)	16.00	
Salaries of Foreman ($^{1,200}/_{40}$)	30.00	
Lubricating oil ($^{60}/_{40}$)	1.50	
	47.50	0.0262
Variable Expenses :		
Power ($^{3,120}/_{40}$)	78.00	
Depreciation ($^{785}/_{40}$)	19.62	
Repairs ($^{1,446}/_{40}$)	36.15	
	133.77	0.0737
∴ Machine Hour Rate Rs.		0.0999

Working Notes :

Calculation for Effective Working hrs

No. of days in a year		365
Less : Sundays	52	
Less : Saturdays (4 hrs. a day)	52	
Less : Holidays (3 + 2 + 2)	7	111
		254

	hrs
∴ Total working hrs on 254 days @ 8 hrs	2,032
Add : Total working hrs on 52 days @ 4 hrs	208
∴ Total Estimated working hrs at full capacity	2,240

∴ Total Estimated working hrs. at 90% capacity

$$= \frac{90}{100} \times 2,240 = 2,016$$

Less : Breakdown Allowance (10%) 202

1,814

Problem 31

A S Ltd., a chemical company having 20 different types of machines, supplied you the following information relating to the year ended on 31.03.07 in respect of a *Machine No. 10* :

	Rs.
(*A*) Cost of the machine	1,20,000
Life	10 yrs.
Scrap value	20,000
(*B*) Overhead Expenses :	
Rent & Rates	1,00,000 p.a.
Heat & Lighting	50,000 p.a.
Supervision	2,00,000 p.a.
Special Equipment for Machine No. 10	5,000 p.a.
Area of the factory	10,000 sq. ft.
Area occupied by Machine No. 10	1,000 sq. ft.

Power cost Re. 0.80 per hr when in operation.

(*C*) Wages of operator is Rs. 32 per day of 8 hrs including all benefits. He can look after one machine when it is under set-up and two machines while under operation.

(*D*) Estimated Production hrs 3,600 p.a.

Set-up time hrs. 400 p.a.

Compute comprehensive machine hour rate and also find out the cost of the following job :

	Job No. 007
Set-up time (hrs)	80
Operation time (hrs)	120

Solution

Computation of Comprehensive Machine Hour Rate

Estimated effective working hrs = (3,600 + 400) = 4,000 hrs

Particulars		*Per Annum Rs.*	*Per Hour Rs.*
Standing Charges :			
Depreciation	$\left(\frac{1{,}20{,}000 - 20{,}000}{10}\right)$	10,000	
Rents & Rates	$\left(\frac{1{,}00{,}000}{10{,}000} \times 1{,}000\right)$	10,000	
Heat & Lighting	$\left(50{,}000 \times \frac{1{,}000}{10{,}000}\right)$	5,000	
Supervision	$\left(\frac{2{,}00{,}000}{20{,}000}\right)$	10,000	
	Special Equipment	5,000	
		40,000	10.00
Variable Expenses :			
Power			0.80
∴ Machine Hour Rate			10.80

Comprehensive Machine hour Rate

	Set up.	*Operation*
Fixed Rate	10.00	10.00
Power		0.80
Wages of Operator	4.00	2.00
Comprehensive MHR	14.00	12.80

Statement showing cost of Job No. 007

Particulars.	*H.R.*	*Hours Taken*	*Amt.*
Set up	14.00	80	1,120.00
Operation	12.80	120	1,536.00
			2,656.00

Problem 32

The Pipe Co. manufactures two products, A and B, during the first year of its operations. For purposes of product costing, an overhead rate of application of Rs. 1.70 per direct labour hour was used, based on budgeted factory overhead of Rs. 3,40,000 and budgeted direct labour hours of 2,00,000 as follows :

	Budgeted Overhead (Rs.)	*Budgeted Hours (Rs.)*
Department 1	2,40,000	1,00,000
Department 2	1,00,000	1,00,000
Total	3,40,000	2,00,000

The number of labour hours required to manufacture each of these products was :

	Product A	*Product B*
Department 1	4	1
Department 2	1	4
	5	5

At the end of the year, there was no WIP. There were, however, 2,000 and 6,000 Finished Units, respectively, of products A and B on hand. Assume that budgeted activity was attained.

(*a*) What was the effect on the company's income of using a plantwise overhead rate instead of departmental overhead rates ?

(*b*) Assume that material and labour cost per unit of Product A were Rs. 10/- and that the selling price was established by adding 40% to cover profit and selling and administrative expenses.

What difference in selling price would result from the use of departmental against plantwise overhead rates ? ***[I.C.W.A. (Int.)]***

Solution

(a) Statement showing the effect of the company's income for using plantwise overhead rate instead of departmental overhead rates :

Overhead rates :

Department 1 = Rs. 2,40,000 ÷ 1,00,000 = Rs. 2.40 Per D.L.H.

Department 2 = Rs. 1,00,000 ÷ 1,00,000 = Rs. 1.00 Per D.L.H.

	Product A	*Product B*
(i) Plant-wise overhead	5 × 1.70 = **Rs. 8.50**	5 × 1.70 = **Rs. 8.50**
(ii) Departmental overhead :		
Dept. 1	4 × 2.40 = 9.60	1 × 2.40 = 2.40
Dept. 2	1 × 1.00 = 1.00	4 × 1.00 = 4.00
	10.60	6.40
(iii) Difference between the two (*i* – *ii*)	(–) 2.10	(+) 2.10
(iv) Difference on finished units	2,000 × (–) 2.10 = (4,200)	6,000 × 2.10 = 12,600

Overall difference between Product A and Product B = + 8,400

Effect on the company : By using plantwise overhead rate, the closing stock of product A was undervalued to the extent of Rs. 4,200 and closing stock of Product B was over-valued to the extent of Rs. 12,600. The overall over-valuation of these products comes to Rs. 8,400. In other words, the Company's income was overstated by Rs. 8,400.

(*b*)

		Product A
(*i*)	Materials and Labour Cost @ Rs. 10 per unit	10.00
	Plantwise Overheads	8.50
	Work Cost	18.50
Add :	40% to cover profit, selling and administration expenses	7.40
	Selling Price	25.90
(*ii*)	Materials and Labour Cost	10.00
	Departmental Overheads	10.60
	Works Cost	20.60
Add :	40% to cover profit, selling and Administration expenses	8.24
	Selling Price	28.84
	Difference between (*i*) & (*ii*)	2.94

Problem 33

A machine was purchased on April 1, 2007 for rupees 5,00,000. The total cost of all machinery inclusive of the new machine was Rs. 75,00,000. The following further information are available :

Expected life of the machine 10 years. Scrap value at the end of 10 years Rs. 5,000. Repairs and maintenance for the machine during the year Rs. 2,000. Expected number of working hours of the machine per year 4,000 hours. Insurance premium annually for all machines Rs. 4,500.

Electricity consumption for the machine per hour (@ 75 paise per unit) 25 units.

Area occupied by the machine 100 sq. ft. Area occupied by other machines 2,500 sq. ft. Rent per month of the department Rs. 800.

Lighting charges for 20 points for the whole department, out of which three points are for the machine, Rs. 120 per month.

Prepare the machine hour rate for the new machine on the basis of data given above.

[C.S. (Inter) Adopted]

Solution

Computation of Machine Hour Rate

Particulars	*Basis of Apportionment*	*Total Exp. Rs.*	*Per hour Rs.*
Standing/Fixed Charges :			
Depreciation	Actual [See Note 1]	49,500	
Insurance Premium	Cost of machine $\left[\frac{4,500 \times 5,00,000}{75,00,000}\right]$	300	
Repairs and Maintenance	Actual	2,000	
Rent	Area Occupied $\left[\frac{9,600 \times 100}{1,600}\right]$	600	
Lighting	No. of points $\left[\frac{120 \times 12 \times 3}{20}\right]$	216	
		52,616	13.154
Variable/Running Expenses :			
Electricity	25 units per hour @ 75 p. per unit [i.e. 25 × 0.75]		18.750
Machine Hour Rate			31.904

Working Notes :

Calculation of Depreciation :

	Rs.
Cost of machine	5,00,000
Less : Scrap value	5,000
	4,95,000

Life of machine = 10 years.

$\therefore$ Depreciation per year = $\frac{4,95,000}{10}$ = Rs. 49,500

Problem 34

The following information has been extracted from the management accounting records of W. Limited :

Budget for the year ended 30th November 2006

	Manufacturing Departments		*Service Departments*	
	Machining	*Finishing*	*Maintenance*	*Administration*
	Rs.	*Rs.*	*Rs.*	*Rs.*
Sales	1,00,000	1,50,000	—	—
Direct Materials	30,000	50,000	—	—
Direct Labour	20,000	30,000	—	—
Variable Overheads	20,000	25,000	—	—
Fixed Overheads	15,000	18,000	7,260	4,000
Budgeted Direct Labour hours	8,000	12,000		

Actual figures for the last year were as follows :

	Machining	*Finishing*	*Maintenance*	*Administration*
Direct Labour hours :	10,400	13,300		
	Rs.	*Rs.*	*Rs.*	*Rs.*
Sales	1,30,000	1,70,000	—	—
Direct Materials	40,000	55,000	—	—
Direct Labour	28,000	35,000	—	—
Variable Overheads	25,000	27,000	—	—
Fixed overheads	15,500	18,200	7,480	4,200

Service department costs are apportioned as follows :

	Maintenance	*Administration*
	%	%
Machining	30	30
Finishing	50	40
Maintenance	—	30
Administration	20	—

Overhead costs in the Machine and Finishing departments are absorbed on a Direct Labour hour rate basis.

Required :

(*a*) Compute (*i*) the overhead cost absorption rates used during the year, and (*ii*) the budgeted trading results.

(*b*) Show the under or over-absorption of overheads during the year.

(*c*) Explain and illustrate the effect of volume on the absorption of fixed overheads.

(*d*) Given that the company is a jobbing engineering concern, explain how standard costing principles might be applied to its products. ***[I.C.W.A. Final]***

Solution

Overhead Cost Absorption Rates

(*i*) Allocation of Service Department overheads to production departments :

Maintenance (M) = 7,260 Administration (A) = 4,000

But a certain percentage of service and production department expenditure is incurred on each other.

So, $M = 7{,}260 + 0.3A$ and $A = 4{,}000 + 0.2M$

Solving the above equations, $M = 9{,}000$ and $A = 5{,}800$, apportioning these expenses to manufacturing departments on basis of given ratio.

	Production Dept. *Maintenance*	*Service Dept.* *Administration*
Machining	2,700	1,740
Finishing	4,500	2,320

	Machining Total Overheads (*a*)	*Machining* Rate per hour (*a*)/8,000	*Finishing* Total Overheads (*b*)	*Finishing* Rate per hour (*b*)/12,000
Variable Overhead	20,000	2.50	25,000	2.08
Fixed Overhead	15,000	1.875	18,000	1.50
Maintenance Overhead	2,700	0.3375	4,500	0.375
Administration Overhead	1,740	0.2175	2,320	0.193
Composite Absorption Rate		4.9300		or 4.148
				or 4.15

(ii) Budgeted trading results

	Machining *Rs.*	*Finishing* *Rs.*	*Total* *Rs.*
Sales	1,00,000	1,50,000	2,50,000
Direct material	30,000	50,000	80,000
Direct Labour	20,000	30,000	50,000
Variable Overhead	20,000	25,000	45,000
Total Variable Cost	70,000	1,05,000	1,75,000
Contribution	30,000	45,000	75,000
Fixed Oveheads including Service Dept. Costs (given)	15,000	18,000	33,000
Share of maintenance	2,700	4,500	7,200
Share of Administration	1,740	2,320	4,060
	19,440	24,820	44,260
∴ Net Profit	10,560	20,180	30,740

(*b*) Allocation of Actually Incurred Service Department Expenditure to Production Department

$M = 7{,}480 + 0.3A$ $A = 4{,}200 + 0.2M$

Solving the above equation

$M = 9{,}298$, $A = 6{,}060$

	Maintenance	*Administration*
Machining	2,789	1,818
Finishing	4,649	2,424

Total actual overheads after allocation to service department costs are :

	Machining	*Finishing*
	Rs.	*Rs.*
Variable Overheads	25,000	27,000
Fixed Overheads	15,500	18,200
Share of Service Department :		
Maintenance	2,789	4,649
Administration	1,818	2,424
Total Overhead incurred	45,107	52,273
Overhead absorbed		
10,400 hrs × Rs. 4.93	51,272	
13,300 × Rs. 4.15		55,195
Overhead over-absorbed during the year	6,165	2,922

Problem 35

Your company uses historical cost system and applies overheads on the basis of 'predetermined' rates. The following are the figures from the Trial Balance as at 30.9.06 :

Manufacturing Overheads	Rs. 4,26,544 Dr.
Manufacturing Overheads applied	Rs. 3,65,904 Cr.
Work-in-progress	Rs. 1,41,480 Dr.
Finished Goods stock	Rs. 2,30,732 Dr.
Cost of Goods Sold	Rs. 8,40,588 Dr.

Give two methods for the disposal of the under-absorbed overheads and show the profit implications of each method. ***[C.A. Inter]***

Solution

Actual Overheads	Rs. 4,26,544
Less : Overhead recovered	Rs. 3,65,904
Overhead Under-absorbed	Rs. 60,640

Following two methods are available here :

(*i*) Adjustment to cost of sales and stocks of work-in-progress and finished goods.

Where first method is followed, amount of Rs. 60,640 will be debited to Costing Profit and Loss Account resulting in the reduction of figure of profit for this year by Rs. 60,640.

Second approach stipulates that under-absorbed overhead should be distributed to three Control Accounts, *i.e.*, Work-in-progress, Finished Goods Stock Account, and Cost of Goods Sold Account. This distribution can be attempted as follows :

	Balances	*Additional Overhead (under-absorbed)*	*Total*
	Rs.	*Rs.*	*Rs.*
Work-in-progress	1,41,480	7,074[1]	1,48,554
Finished goods A/c	2,30,732	11,537[2]	2,42,269
Cost of Sales A/c	8,40,588	42,029[3]	8,82,617
	12,12,800	60,640	12,73,440

Working Notes :

	Rs.
1. (1,41,480 ÷ 12,12,800) × 60,640	7,074
2. (2,30,732 ÷ 12,12,800) × 60,640	11,537
3. (8,40,732 ÷ 12,12,800) × 60,640	42,029

By using this method, profit for this year will be reduced by Rs. 42,029 – (7,074 + 11,537) = 23,418. Amount of Rs. 42,029 will be debited to Profit & Loss A/c with Cost of Sales. Amount of Rs. 70,714 + Rs. 11,537, *i.e.* 18,611, will be credited to Profit and Loss Account as value of closing stock. The amount of Rs. 18,611 will again get debited to Profit & Loss Account next year as value of opening stock.

Problem 36

A company is concerned about the profitability of selling to its small customers. The following data were obtained from its records :

Customer group by annual Sales value	*Total annual Sales*	*No. Of Customers*	*Gross margin*	*No. of Salesmen's Calls p.a.*	*No. of orders p.a.*
Rs. 000	Rs. million	%			
Over 10	0.7	40	20	310	520
5 to 9.999	0.5	68	22	420	740
1.5 to 4.999	0.4	106	24	570	800
0.5 to 1.499	0.35	342	25	1,750	2,140
Under 0.5	0.3	1,800	25	3,750	4,500

	Rs. p.a.
Sales Department Costs :	
Sales Management (central and regional)	60.0
Salesmen's Salaries	72.0
Salesmen's Commission (5% of Sales)	112.5
Salesmen's Expenses	33.0
Sales Office Costs (excluding costs of handling sales ordes)	42.0
	319.5

Work study carried out indicated that the cost of handling sales orders was Rs. 2 per order. During the year there were 1,200 prospective customers on whom the salesmen made 2,200 calls but obtained no orders.

You are required to :

(*a*) Calculate for the year the

(*i*) Cost per Salesman's Call and

(*ii*) Profit per customer group.

(*b*) State with reasons whether the company should stop supplying directly those customers who buy under Rs. 500 of goods per annum from the company.

[C.I.M.A. London, Adopted]

Solution

(*a*) (*i*) Sales Department Cost per annum :

Sales Management	Rs. 60,000
Salesmen's Salaries	Rs. 72,000
Salesmen's Commission	Rs. 1,12,500
Salesmen's Expenses	Rs. 33,000
Sales Office Cost (excluding costs of handling Sales Orders)	Rs. 42,000
	Rs. 3,19,500

No. of Salesmen's calls per annum

= 310 + 420 + 570 + 1,750 + 3,750 + 2,200 for prospective customers

= 9,000

Cost per salesman's call for the year Rs. 3,19,500 ÷ 9,000 = Rs. 35.50

(*ii*) Profit per customer group

Customer group by annual sales value '000	*Sales margin *1*	*Annual Cost of each call *2 @ Rs. 35.50*	*Order cost @ Rs. 2*	*Net Profit (Loss)*
Over 10	Rs. 1,40,000	Rs. 11,005	Rs. 1,040	Rs. 1,27,955
5 to 9.999	Rs. 1,10,000	Rs. 14,910	Rs. 1,480	Rs. 93,610
1.5 to 4.999	Rs. 96,000	Rs. 20,235	Rs. 1,600	Rs. 74,165
0.5 to 1.4999	Rs. 87,500	Rs. 62,125	Rs. 4,280	Rs. 21,095
Under 0.5	Rs. 75,000	Rs. 1,33,125	Rs. 9,000	Rs. (67,125)
Prospective customer	—	Rs. 78,100	—	Rs. (78,100)
	Rs. 5,08,500	Rs. 3,19,500		Rs. 1,71,600

*1 Based on percentage of total annual sales given.

*2 310 × Rs. 35.50 and so on.

(*b*) Based on the above table (*ii*) the company should stop supplying directly those customers who buy under Rs. 500 of goods p.a. from the company.

Problem 37

A machine shop of a factory has 3 cost centres having distinct sets of machines. The following estimates are available for the year 2006 :

	Total for factory	*Centre I*	*Centre II*	*Centre III*
Direct Wages	1,60,000	50,000	50,000	60,000
Share of Service Expenses	5,000	1,000	1,500	2,500
Power	10,000			
Repairs & Maintenance	13,000			
Insurance	3,900			
Rent	3,000			
Lighting	1,800			
Indirect Wages	14,400			
Labour Welfare Expenses	20,000			
Value of Machines	3,25,000	1,00,000	75,000	1,50,000
Floor Area (sq. ft.)		120	240	360
Power of Motor (H.P.)		10	10	20
Machine Hours		5,000	6,000	10,000
No. of workers		12	10	18

(*a*) Compute a suitable machine hour rate of overhead absorption of each of the machine centres.

(*b*) Job No. 201 passes through all the above three cost centres and the time required in each centre is :

Centre I—4 hrs, Centre II—3 hrs, Centre III—8 hrs.

What price should the company quote for Job No. 201 to yield a profit of 20% on cost if its direct materials and direct labour costs are estimated at Rs. 500 and 300, respectively, and other expenses are 20% on work cost ? ***[C.U. B.Com. (Hons.) Adopted]***

Solution

(*a*) **Computation of Suitable Machine Hour Rate**

Particulars	*Basis*	*Total* *Rs.*	*Centre I* *Rs.*	*Centre II* *Rs.*	*Centre III* *Rs.*
Share of Service Exp.	Given	5,000	1,000	1,500	2,500
Power	H.P. of Machine (1 : 1 : 2)	10,000	2,500	2,500	5,000
Repairs & Maintenance	Value of machine (4 : 3 : 6)	13,000	4,000	3,000	6,000
Insurance	—do—	3,900	1,200	900	1,800
Rent	Floor Area (1 : 2 : 3)	3,000	500	1,000	1,500
Lighting	—do—	1,800	300	600	900
Indirect Wages	Direct wages (5 : 5 : 6)	14,400	4,500	4,500	5,400
Labour Welfare Expenses	No. of workers (6 : 5 : 9)	20,000	6,000	5,000	9,000
Total		71,100	20,000	19,000	32,100
Machine Hours			5,000	6,000	10,000
∴ Machine Hour Rate			4	3.167	3.21

(*b*) **Statement showing Quoted Price for Job No. 201**

Particulars	*Amount* *Rs.*	*Amount* *Rs.*
Direct Materials	500	
Direct Labour	300	
PRIME COST		800.00
Add : Factory overhead :		
Centre I—Rs. 4 × 4	16	
Centre II—Rs. 3.167 × 3	9.50	
Centre III—Rs. 3.21 × 8	25.68	
		51.18
Factory Cost		851.18
Add : Other expenses (20% on work cost)		170.24
		1,021.42
Add : Profit (20% on cost)		204.28
Quoted Price		1,226.70

Problem 38

The following data relating to selling and distribution activities of M/s ABC Ltd. are available from its books of accounts :

	Rs.
Direct selling expenses	3,60,000
Advertisement	1,20,000
Sales Overhead (office expense)	4,20,000
Ordering and Billing	60,000
Decorative Packing	5,40,000
Storage (Godown Rent)	1,44,000
Transport	1,80,000

The following additional data relating to the company's operations are also available :

Products	A	B	C
Sales Turnover (Rs.)	60,00,000	90,00,000	1,20,00,000
Units Sold	15,00,000	12,00,000	20,00,000
Advertising space	40%	25%	35%
No. of Invoice	600	400	800
No. of Packages delivered	20,000	30,000	40,000
Average Storage Days	15	10	25
Salesmen's time	30%	25%	45%
Manufacturing Costs :			
Variable (Rs./Unit)	2.00	4.50	3.25
Fixed (Rs./Annum)	6,00,000	24,00,000	30,00,000

Based on the above data, prepare a statement showing cost and profitability of each product.

[I.C.W.A. (Inter)]

Solution

Statement showing Cost & Profitability

Products	A	B	C
Units Sold (in nos.)	15,00,000	12,00,000	20,00,000
Sales Value (in Rs.)	60,00,000	90,00,000	1,20,00,000
Less : Variable Cost			
A ⇒ @ Rs. 2.00	30,00,000		
B ⇒ @ Rs. 4.50		54,00,000	
C ⇒ @ Rs. 3.25			65,00,000
CONTRIBUTION	30,00,000	36,00,000	55,00,000
Less : Fixed Cost (Mfg.)	6,00,000	24,00,000	30,00,000
GROSS MARGIN	24,00,000	12,00,000	25,00,000
Less : Selling and Distribution Cost (See Working Note)	4,72,533	5,42,133	8,09,334
Profit	19,27,467	6,57,867	16,90,666

Working Note : **Apportionment of Selling & Distribution Costs**

Expenses	*Basis of Apportionment*	A *Rs.*	B *Rs.*	C *Rs.*
Direct selling expenses	Salesmen's time	1,08,000	90,000	1,62,000
Advertisement	Advertisement space	48,000	30,000	42,000
Sales Overhead	Sales value	93,333	1,40,000	1,86,667
Ordering & Billing	No. of Invoice	20,000	13,333	26,667
Decorative Packing	Sales Value	1,20,000	1,80,000	2,40,000
Storage (Godown Rent)	Average Storage Days	43,200	28,800	72,000
Transport	No. of Packages	40,000	60,000	80,000
		4,72,533	5,42,133	8,09,334

EXERCISES

1.A. *State which statements are correct (C) and which are wrong (W) ?*

(*i*) Variable overhead cost is a discretionary cost.
(*ii*) Fixed overhead cost is an output cost.
(*iii*) Fixed expenses will move up by jumps if the output exceeds the capacity.
(*iv*) Fixed overhead cost is a committed cost.
(*v*) Variable overhead cost is a period cost.

[Ans. Correct (C) : (*iii*), (*iv*),
Wrong (W) : (*i*), (*ii*), (*v*)]

B. *Which of the following is correct (C) and which are wrong (W) ?*

(*i*) Direct labour hour rate of absorption of overhead is suitable where most of the production is done by using machines.
(*ii*) The time factor is ignored when the cost of material is used as the basis for absorption of overhead.
(*iii*) Predetermined rate of absorption of overhead helps in quick preparation of cost estimates and quoting prices.
(*iv*) Basis of apportionment of depreciation of plants is values of plants in each department.
(*v*) Basis of apportionment of cost of system is wages of each department.

[Ans. Correct (C) : (*ii*), (*iii*), (*iv*).
Wrong (W) : (*i*), (*v*).]

C. *State which statements are correct and which are wrong :*

(*i*) Cost of indirect materials is apportioned to various departments.
(*ii*) The secondary distribution on a reciprocal basis is known as the step-ladder method.
(*iii*) Linking overhead to cost unit is known as overhead absorption.
(*iv*) Blanket rate of overhead is well-suited to a factory which has a number of departments.
(*v*) A pre-determined factory overhead holds up product costing.
(*vi*) Primary distribution is effected on the basis of service rendered to the production departments by service departments.
(*vii*) Factory rent is a direct cost to the factory as a whole but indirect to the departments.
(*viii*) Fixed cost varies with volume rather than time.
(*ix*) Variable overheads vary with time.
(*x*) Variable cost per unit remains constant.
(*xi*) Factory overhead and other expenses are synonymous terms.
(*xii*) Departmentalisation of overhead facilitates the control objective of cost accounting.
(*xiii*) Direct assignment of factory overhead cost to each department is known as apportionment.

[Ans. Correct (C) : (*i*), (*iii*), (*vii*), (*x*), (*xii*).
Wrong (W) : (*ii*), (*iv*), (*v*), (*vi*), (*viii*), (*ix*), (*xi*), (*xiii*).]

2. *Which of the following are correct ?*

A. The wages paid to maintenance department workers who do repair work principally for production departments but also on the vehicles in the distribution department should bé charged as :

(*i*) Distribution costs (*ii*) Service costs
(*iii*) Production costs (*iv*) General costs.

B. Which of the following costs of management is likely to have least control ?

(*i*) Wages cost (*ii*) Machine breakdown cost
(*iii*) Buildings insurance cost (*iv*) Advertising cost.

C. Which of the following costs are most likely to have a cost behaviour pattern described as ... a fixed cost up to an activity level of 1,000 units with a variable cost thereafter which decreases from 10 P to 8 P per unit at 2,000 units ?

(*i*) Photocopying equipment with a fixed hire charge plus a reducing charge per unit.
(*ii*) Wages payment which is fixed for a minimum output quantity after which a bonus per unit is paid which reduces above a certain output level to a smaller bonus per unit.
(*iii*) Royalty payment per unit which reduces after 2,000 units.
(*iv*) Material cost of 12 P per unit for the first 1,000 units followed by 10 P per unit up to 2,000 units and 8 P per unit thereafter.

D. Which of the following is most likely to be an allocated production overhead cost to the finishing cost centre ?
- (*i*) Factory rates.
- (*ii*) Salary of the finishing cost centre supervisor.
- (*iii*) Power used on finishing cost centre machines.
- (*iv*) Salary of the production manager.

E. Which of the following is a valid classification of the salary paid to the foreman in charge of the packing department ?
- (*i*) Indirect departmental cost
- (*ii*) Direct departmental cost
- (*iii*) Direct product cost
- (*iv*) Service department cost.

F. Which of the following methods of charging service cost centres will be compatible with control of the efficiency of the service within the service cost centre ?
- (*i*) No charge to users.
- (*ii*) Charges users with total actual cost incurred.
- (*iii*) Charges users with total (full) absorption cost.
- (*iv*) Charges users with the opportunity cost of the service.

G. Non-production overheads are usually omitted from stock valuation for the following reason :
- (*i*) They are outside the control of production management.
- (*ii*) They are fixed period costs.
- (*iii*) They are incurred after the stock has been brought to its present location and condition.
- (*iv*) They cannot be identified with individual products.

H. If the overhead to be absorbed was the foreman's salary, the most likely appropriate basis for absorption would be :
- (*i*) Weight of material
- (*ii*) Selling price
- (*iii*) Direct labour hours
- (*iv*) Prime cost.

I. Absorption of production overhead cost in unit cost on a marginal cost basis is unacceptable :
- (*i*) As a cost control mechanism.
- (*ii*) As a decision-making aid.
- (*iii*) For stock valuation in compliance with SSAPG.
- (*iv*) For profit measurement in monthly management accounts.

J. Which of the following best describes a fixed cost ? A cost which :
- (*i*) Represents a fixed proportion of total costs.
- (*ii*) Remains at the same level up to a particular level of output.
- (*iii*) Has a direct relationship with output.
- (*iv*) Remains at the same level when output increases.

K. Which of the following would not cause either an under or over-absorption of overheads ?
- (*i*) Actual direct labour time per unit being greater than budget.
- (*ii*) Actual cost of diect labour being greater than budget.
- (*iii*) Actual overheads incurred being less than budget.
- (*iv*) The number of units produced being greater than budget.

[Ans. A (*ii*) ; B (*iii*) ; C (*ii*) ; D (*ii*) E (*ii*) ; F (*iv*) ; G (*iii*) ; H (*iii*) ; I (*iii*) ; J (*ii*) ; K (*ii*).]

THEORETICAL QUESTIONS

(*a*) Classifications of Overhead

1. Define 'Overhead'. State the different methods of classification of overhead with example.
2. What do you mean by 'Fixed Overhead Cost' ? What are the important characteristics of these costs ? Classify 'fixed variable' and 'semi-variable' overhead costs.
3. Why behaviour-wise classification of overhead costs becomes necessary ? What are its limitations ?
4. Costs are not inherently fixed but acquired. This characteristic is as a result of policies established by management. Is this view correct ? ***[I.C.W.A. (Final)]***

(*b*) Allocation, Apportionment and Absorption

1. (*a*) What do you understand by cost allocation, cost apportionment and cost absorption.
   (*b*) Distinguish between—
   (*i*) cost allocation and cost apportionment.
   (*ii*) cost apportionment and cost absorption.

2. What do you mean by overhead ? Discuss the different methods of recovering factory overhead. *[C.U. B.Com. Pass]*

3. Describe various methods of absorption of factory overhead. Which of the methods do you consider most scientific and why ? *[C.U. B.Com. (H)]*

4. Explain the various bases of apportionment of works overheads to departments with illustration as to the items of expenses.

5. Explain the term "applied overhead cost". What are the various methods of treating over or under-applied overheads in Cost Accounts ? *[I.C.W.A. (Int.) De. 1993]*

6. What do you mean by machine-hour-rate ? How is it ascertained ?

7. What factors would you consider for determining the overhead absorption rate ? *[C.A. (Int.)]*

(c) Administration, Selling and Distribution Overheads

1. (*a*) Explain the term "Administrative Overheads" and briefly discuss three methods of treatment thereof in cost accounts.

(*b*) What, according to you, are the steps to be followed in controlling Administrative Overheads ? *[I.C.W.A. (Int.) June 1992]*

2. What are the Administrative Overheads ? How are they treated in Cost Accounts ? *[I.C.W.A. (Int.) June 1986]*

3. In controlling the selling and distribution expenses it is necessary to analyse them under various methods. Examine the fundamental methods and state which method you consider to be the most effective from the view-point of cost control. *[I.C.W.A.I. (F)]*

4. Distinguish between selling and overhead. Give at least two examples of each kind. *[B.U. B.Com. (H) 1986]*

PROBLEMS

1. A factory has two production departments and one service department. The service department (X) renders service to production departments (A and B) in 3 : 2 ratio. The particulars of the departments and the details of expenses are given below.

Determine the amount of factory overheads chargeable to the production departments.

	Rs.
Rent & Rates	5,200
Depreciation	45,000
Power	1,200
Electricity	3,500
Canteen Expenses	11,000
Insurance	2,600

Other information :

	Dept. A	*Dept. B*	*Dept. X*
Direct Wages (Rs.)	30,000	20,000	5,000
H.P. of Machines	200	100	50
Light Points	40	30	10
Floor Space (sq. mt.)	400	200	50
Fixed Assets (Rs. in lakh)	5	3	1
Total Assets (Rs. in lakh)	7	4	2

[Ans. A = Rs. 45,481 ; B = Rs. 28,019].

2. In a Light Engineering factory, the following particulars have been collected for three months' period ended 31.12.91. Compute the departmental overhead rates for each of the production dept. Assuming overhead are recovered as percentage of direct wages.

Particulars	*Production Dept.*			*Service Dept.*	
	A	B	C	X	Y
	Rs.	*Rs.*	*Rs.*	*Rs.*	*Rs.*
Direct Wages	20,000	30,000	40,000	10,000	20,000
Direct Material	10,000	20,000	20,000	15,000	15,000
Staff (Nos.)	100	150	150	50	50
Electricity (kW)	4,000	3,000	2,000	1,000	1,000

Light Points	10	16	4	6	4
Assets Value	60,000	40,000	30,000	10,000	10,000
Area	150	250	50	50	50

The expenses for the period were :

	Rs.
Motive Power	550
Lighting Power	100
Stores Overhead	400
Amenities to staff	1,500
Depreciation (P.A.)	15,000
Repairs & Maintenance	3,000
General Overhead (P.A.)	12,000
General & Taxes (P.A.)	11,000

The expenses of Service Dept. 'X' proportionate to Direct wages and that of Service Dept. 'Y' in the ratio 5 : 3 : 2 for Departments A, B and C, respectively.

[Ans. A = 35, 126 ; B = 29, 249 ; C = 28,175]

3. A company having two production departments and one service department furnishes the following particulars :

	Rs.
Power	900
Lighting	800
Rent & Rates	4,000
Indirect Wages	2,000
Sundries	5,000
Depreciation of machinery	6,000

The other particulars are :

	Production Departments		*Service Departments*
	A	*B*	
Working hours	4,000	3,500	3,600
Direct Wages (Rs.)	3,000	2,500	3,000
Cost of Machinery (Rs.)	25,000	20,000	15,000
H.P. of Machinery	50	30	10
Light Points	18	12	10
Floor space (sq. ft.)	1,000	1,200	800

The expenses of service department are to be allocated between production departments A and B in the ratio of 60 : 40.

You are required to apportion the costs to the various departments on the most equitable basis. *[B.Com. C.U.]*

[Ans. A = Rs. 12,168 ; B = Rs. 9,523]

4. Continuous Distribution Method and Simultaneous Equation Method

A company has three production cost centers A, B and C and two service cost centers X and Y. Costs allocated to service centers are required to be apportioned to the production centers to find out cost of production of different products.

It is found that benefit of service cost centers is also received by each other along with the production cost centers.

Overhead costs as allocated to the five cost centers and estimates of benefit of service cost centers received by each of them are as under :

Cost Centers	Overhead costs as allocated (Rs.)	Estimates of benefits received from service centers in %	
		X	Y
A	80,000	20	20
B	40,000	30	25
C	20,000	40	50
X	20,000		5
Y	10,000	10	—

Required :

Work out final overhead costs of each of the production departments including reapportioned cost of service centers using (a) Continuous distribution method, and (b) Simultaneous equation method.

[I.C.W.A. Inter, June 1994 ; June 1985]

[Ans. A : Rs. 86,533; B : Rs. 49,196; C : Rs. 34,271]

5. **Computation of Overhead Rates—Step Ladder Method.**

Deccan Manufacturing Ltd. has three departments which are regarded as production department, service departments' costs are distributed to these production departments using the "Step Ladder method" of distribution. Estimates of factory overhead costs to be incurred by each department in the forthcoming year are as follows. Data required for distribution is also shown against each department :

Department's Production	Factory Overhead (Rs.)	Direct Labour Hours	No. of Employees	Area in Sq. mt.
X	1,93,000	41,000	100	3,000
Y	64,000	3,000	125	1,500
Z	83,000	4,000	85	1,500
Service				
P	45,000	1,000	10	500
Q	75,000	5,000	50	1,500
R	1,05,000	6,000	40	1,000
S	30,000	3,000	50	1,000

The overhead costs of the four service departments are distributed in the same order viz. P, Q, R and S, respectively, on the following basis :

Departments	Basis
P	Number of Employees
Q	Direct Labour Hours
R	Area in Square Metres
S	Direct Labour Hours

You are required to :

a) prepare a schedule showing the distribution of overhead costs of the four service departments to the three production departments; and

b) calculate the overhead recovery rate per direct labour hour for each of the three production departments.

[C.A. Inter]

[Ans. X : Rs. 75; Y : Rs. 45; Z : Rs. 40]

6. In a factory, the following particulars have been found for a three months' period. Compute the departmental overhead rates for each of the production departments assuming that overheads are recovered as a percentage of Direct Wages :

	Production Dept.			*Service Dept.*	
	A	*B*	*C*	*D*	*E*
Direct Wages (Rs.)	2,000	3,000	4,000	1,000	2,000
Direct Materials (Rs.)	1,000	2,000	2,000	1,500	1,500
No. of employees	100	150	150	50	50
Electricity kwh	4,000	3,000	2,000	1,000	1,000
Light Points	10	16	4	6	4
Assets Value	60,000	40,000	30,000	10,000	10,000
Area (sq. yds.)	150	250	50	50	50

The expenses for the period were :

	Rs.
Motive Power	550
Lighting Power	100
Stores Overhead	400
Amenities to staff	1,500
Depreciation	15,000
Repairs & Maintenance	3,000
General Overheads	6,000
Rent and Taxes	275

Apportion the expenses of the service department E proportionate to Direct wages and that of Service department D in the ratio of 5 : 3 : 2 to departments A, B and C, respectively.

[B.Com. C.U.]

[Ans. A = Rs. 12,444; B = Rs. 10,522; C = Rs. 9,859]

7. Modern Machinists Ltd. has three production departments (A, B and C) and two service departments (D and E). From the following figures extracted from the records of the company, calculate the overhead rate per labour hour :

	Rs.
Indirect Materials	15,000
Indirect Wages	10,000
Depreciation on machinery	25,000
Depreciation on building	5,000
Rent, Rates and Taxes	10,000
Electric Power for Machinery	15,000
Electric Power for Lighting	500
General Expenses	15,000

	A	*B*	*C*	*D*	*E*
Direct materials (Rs.)	20,000	10,000	9,000	6,000	5,000
Direct Wages (Rs.)	15,000	15,000	4,000	2,000	4,000
Value of machinery (Rs.)	60,000	1,00,000	40,000	25,000	25,000
Floor Area (sq. ft.)	15,000	10,000	10,000	5,000	10,000
H.P. of machinery	50	60	30	5	5
No. of Light Points	15	10	10	5	10
Labour hours	5,000	5,000	2,000	1,000	2,000

The expenses of Service departments D and E are to be apportioned as follows :

	A	*B*	*C*	*D*	*E*
D	40	20	30	—	10
E	30	30	40	—	—

Expenses		*Ratio*
Indirect Materials	→	Direct Materials
" Wages	→	Direct Wages
General Expenses	→	"

[I.C.W.A. Inter]

[Ans. A = 8.69; B = Rs. 8.16; C = Rs. 14.12]

8. Kapil Ltd. has 3 production departments P, Q, R and two service departments S_1 and S_2. The following figures are available for the year ended 31.12.92 :

	Rs.
Depreciation	8,000
Lighting	480
Indirect Wages	1,800
Rent and Rates and Taxes	4,000
Power	2,400
Sundry Expenses	1,200

The following further information are available :

	P	*Q*	*R*	S_1	S_2
Direct Wages (Rs.)	1,800	1,200	1,800	900	300
Floor Area (sq. ft.)	1,000	800	1,200	600	400
Light Point (Nos.)	4	2	3	2	1
H.P. of Machines	30	30	20	—	—
Value of Plant (Rs. '000)	20	24	36	—	—
Working Hours	1,600	1,200	2,000		

The service departments' expenses are to be allocated on a percentage basis as follows :

	P	*Q*	*R*	S_1	S_2
Service Department S_1	40	30	10		20
Service Department S_2	25	25	40	10	—

You are required to calculate :

(a) the hourly recovery rates of the three departments.

(b) the overhead that will be absorbed by each unit of product X and Y on the manufacture of which the following hours are spent in the production department :

	P	*Q*	*R*
Product A—per unit	20	—	10
Product B—per unit	—	10	6

[Ans. (*a*) P = Rs. 3.85 per working hour (*b*) X = Rs. 112.75
Q = Rs. 4.80 per working hour Y = Rs. 69.49]
R = Rs. 3.58 per working hour

9. The analysis of overhead costs before the distribution of cost of service departments are as follows :

Service Departments		*Production*	*Departments*
Store Room	Rs. 52,800	Dept. X	Rs. 54,000
Costing Dept.	Rs. 56,400	Dept. Y	Rs. 48,000

The percentage distribution of the cost of each service department is given as follows on the basis of man-hours worked :

	Store room	*Costing*	*Dept. X*	*Dept. Y*
Store Room	—	15%	55%	30%
Costing Dept.	40%	—	25%	35%

Distribution of the costs of service department to the production department according to the continued distribution method. ***[B.Com. Andhra]***

[Ans. X = Rs. 1,15,000 ; Y = Rs. 95,800]

10. In a factory there are two service departments P and Q and three production departments A, B and C. In January 1992, the departmental expenses were :

Departments	*Rs.*
A	62,000
B	60,000
C	50,000
P	12,000
Q	10,000

The service department expenses are allocated on a percentage basis as follows :

Service Dept.	*Production Dept.*			*Service Depts.*	
	A	*B*	*C*	*P*	*Q*
P	30	40	15	—	15
Q	40	30	25	5	—

Prepare a statement showing the distribution of the two service departments' expenses to the three production departments. Method of calculation should be shown clearly.

[Karnataka, B.Com. Adopted]

[Ans. A = Rs. 70,534; B = Rs. 68,604; C = Rs. 54,862]

11. A factory is having three Production departments : A, B, C and two service departments X and Y. The expenses increased are :

Rent and Rates Rs. 5,000 ; Repair Rs. 6,000 ; Depreciation Rs. 30,000 ; Electricity charges Rs. 2,000 ; Power Rs. 12,000 ; Supervision exp. Rs. 3,000 ; General Charges Rs. 1,500.

	Production Dept.			*Service Dept.*	
	A	*B*	*C*	*X*	*Y*
Direct Wages (Rs.)	12,000	8,000	5,000	3,000	2,000
Floor Area (sq. ft)	8,000	6,000	4,000	4,000	3,000
Value of machine (Rs.)	1,00,000	80,000	60,000	40,000	20,000
Horse Power of Machine	50	30	20	20	—
No. of Light Points	80	40	40	30	10

The expenses of service department apportioned to production department as :

	A	*B*	*C*	*X*	*Y*
X Dept.	20%	40%	30%	—	10%
Y Dept.	10%	20%	20%	20%	—

Show clearly how the expenses of the service departments would be apportioned to Production Departments.

[Ans. A = Rs. 26,219; B = Rs. 21,872; C = Rs. 16,409]

12. Calculate the overheads allocated to production departments X and Y. There are also two service departments A and B.

A renders service worth Rs. 15,000 to B and the balance to X and Y as 3 : 2. B renders service to X and Y as 3 : 1.

	X	*Y*	*A*	*B*
Floor space (sq. ft.)	5,000	4,000	1,000	2,000
Assets (Rs. in lakh)	10	5	3	1
H.P. of machines	1,000	500	400	100
No. of workers	100	50	50	25
Light & Fan points	50	30	20	20

Expenses and charges are :

	Rs.
Depreciation	1,90,000
Rent, Rates and Taxes	36,000
Insurance	15,200
Power	20,000
Canteen Expenses	10,800
Electricity	4,800

[M.Com. C.U.]

[Ans. X = Rs. 1,86,780; Y = Rs. 90,020]

13. The following information relates to the activities of a production department of a factory for a certain period :

	Rs.
Materials used	36,000
Direct Wages	30,000
Labour hour worked	24,000
Hours of Machine operation	20,000
Overhead chargeable to the Dept.	25,000

On one order carried out in the department during the period the relevant data was :

	Rs.
Material used	2,000
Direct Wages	1,650
Labour hours	1,650
Machine hours	1,200

Calculate by three different methods the overhead chargeable to the job. *[I.C.W.A. Inter]*

[Ans. Direct Wages Method Rs. 1,375; Labour Hour Method Rs. 1,719; Machine Hour Method Rs. 1,500]

14. Electro Cooling Engineering Co. has three production departments P_1, P_2, P_3 and one service department S. From the following particulars find out the Labour Hour Rate of each of the production departments.

Expenses incurred during the year ended 31st March 1987 :

Expenses	*Rs.*
Rent, Rates & Taxes	17,000
Power	26,500
Depreciation on Machinery	10% p.a.
Indirect Wages	10,600
Canteen Expenses	11,400
Electricity	9,200

Additional information :

	P_1	P_2	P_3	*S*
Floor Area (sq. ft.)	200	300	250	100
Light Points	18	12	10	6
Value of machines (Rs.)	1,60,000	1,00,000	1,20,000	20,000
H.P. of machine	3	2	4	1
No. of workers	7	5	5	2
Direct Wages	40,000	32,000	9,000	8,000
Direct Material	20,000	16,000	10,000	5,000

There were 250 working days of 8 hours each. Service rendered by the service department are to be apportioned to the production departments in 2 : 1 : 1 ratio.

[Ans. $P_1 \rightarrow$ 3.715; $P_2 \rightarrow$ 3.626; $P_3 \rightarrow$ 3.942]

15. A company makes two distinct types of electronic toys *X* and *Y*. The total expenses during a period as shown by the books for assembly of 600 of *X* and 800 of *Y* are as under :

	Rs.		Rs.
Materials	1,98,000	Depreciation	2,200
Direct wages	12,000	Labour amenities	1,500
Stores overhead	19,000	Works—general	30,000
Running expenses of machines	4,400	Administration and Selling	26,800

Other data available to you are :	X : Y
Materials cost ratio per unit	1 : 2
Direct Labour ratio per unit	2 : 3
Machine utilisation ratio per unit	1 : 2

Calculate the cost of each toy per unit giving reasons for the basis of apportionment of expenses adopted by you. *[C.U. B.Com. (H)]*

**[Ans. X : Works cost Rs. 75,482; Total cost Rs. 83,056 Cost per unit Rs. 138.43
Y : Works cost Rs. 1,91,618; Total cost Rs. 2,10,844 Cost per unit Rs. 263.56]**

Note : Basis of apportionments—

(*i*) Materials : No. of units × cost ratio per unit.
(*ii*) Direct wages : No. of units × cost ratio per unit.
(*iii*) Stores Overhead : On the basis of material cost.
(*iv*) Running expenses of machines : No. of units × machine utilisation ratio.
(*v*) Depreciation : Same as (iv).
(*vi*) Labour amenities : on the basis of direct wages.
(*vii*) Works general : on the basis of direct wages.
(*viii*) Administration and selling Overhead : on the basis of works cost.

16. From the following particulars, calculate the Overheads allocable to production departments P & Q. There are also two service departments S_1 and S_2.

S_1 renders service worth Rs. 6,000 to S_2 and the balance to *P* and *Q* as 3 : 2. S_2 renders service to *P* and *Q* as 9 : 1.

	P	*Q*	S_1	S_2
Floor space (sq. ft.)	2,500	2,000	500	500
Assets (Rs. in lakhs)	5	2·5	1·5	0·5
H.P. of machines	500	250	200	50
No. of workers	100	50	50	25
Light and fan points	50	30	20	20

Expenses and charges :

	Rs.		Rs.
Depreciation	95,000	Rent, Rates and Taxes	18,000
Insurance	7,600	Power	10,000
Canteen expenses	5,400	Electricity	2,400

[C.U. B.Com.' (H)]

[Ans. P—Rs. 92,926; Q—Rs. 45,474]

17. A factory has three production departments A, B and C and also two service departments 'X' and 'Y'. The primary distribution of the estimated overheads in the factory has just been completed. These details and the quantum of service rendered by the service departments to the other departments are :

	DEPARTMENTS				
	A	*B*	*C*	*X*	*Y*
Primary distribution (Rs.)	2,40,000	2,10,000	2,50,000	1,40,000	96,000
Service rendered by					
Dept. 'X'	30%	20%	35%	—	15%
Dept. 'Y'	25%	40%	25%	10%	—

Prepare a statement showing the distribution of service dept. overheads to the production departments, by the simultaneous equation method. *[I.C.W.A. Dec. 2004]*

[Ans. A : Rs. 75,259; B : Rs. 77,889; C : Rs. 82,852]

18. A manufacturing company provides you with a summary of its production costs at three production levels :

Cost Item	*1,000 Units*	*2,000 Units*	*3,000 Units*
	Rs.	*Rs.*	*Rs.*
A	5,000	5,000	5,000
B	1,400	1,800	2,200
C	3,000	6,000	9,000

(i) Indicate the cost behaviour for the cost items.

(ii) What would be total costs if the company produces 2,500 units ? *[C.U. B.Com (H) 2001]*

[Ans. (*i*) *A* : Fixed; *B* : Semivariable; *C* : Variable

(*ii*) Total Costs for 2,500 units :		**Rs.**
***A* : Fixed**		**5,000**
***B* : Fixed**	**1,000**	
Variable @ Re. 0.40 per unit	**1,000**	**2,000**
***C* : Variable @ Re. 0.30 per unit**		**7,500**
		14,500]

19. From the following particulars, show distribution of overhead and calculate overhead rate per labour hour after redistribution of service department expenses :

	Production Departments			*Service Departments*		
Shop	*Shop 1*	*Shop 2*	*Shop 3*	*Toolroom*	*Stores*	*Factory Office*
Direct Material (Rs.)	1,80,000	1,20,000	1,00,000	—	—	—
Direct Wages (Rs.)	1,00,000	80,000	60,000	40,000	—	—
Indirect Labour (Rs.)	25,200	35,200	32,000	22,200	9,000	6,600
Indirect Materials (Rs.)	24,000	36,000	12,000	7,200	9,600	3,600
Value of Machine (Rs.)	1,50,000	2,70,000	60,000	9,000	15,000	15,000
Area (Sq. mt.)	2,000	1,500	3,000	1,000	1,500	1,000

Effective H.P.	180	180	40	—	—	—
Labour Hours	60,000	60,000	40,000	—	—	—
Machine Hours	32,000	24,000	12,000	—	—	—
No. of Employees	600	600	400	100	100	200

Other information regarding the production :
Insurance Rs. 12,000, Depreciation 10%, Factory rent Rs. 60,000, Light & Heat Rs. 24,000 and Power Rs. 54,000.
The expenses of service departments are to be apportioned to the shops as follows :
Toolroom; based on value of machines;
Stores : based on Direct labour hrs;
Factory office : based on Direct Wages. *[C.U. B.Com. (H) 2002]*

[Ans. Overheads (before redistribution). Shop 1 Rs. 1,13,923. Shop 2 Rs. 1,39,134. Shop 3 Rs. 79,041. Tool Room Rs. 78,908. Stores Rs. 33,047. Factory office Rs. 20,447.
Overheads (after redistribution)
Shop 1 Rs. 1,59,494. Shop 2 Rs. 2,02,729. Shop 3 Rs. 1,02,277.
Overhead rate per labour hour :
Shop 1 Rs. 26,582. Shop 2 Rs. 33,788. Shop 3 Rs. 25,569]

20. The following is the budget of a manufacturing concern for the year 1989 :

Factory Overhead	Rs. 1,24,000
Direct Labour costs	Rs. 1,96,000
Direct Labour Hours	Rs. 3,10,000
Machine Hours	Rs. 10,000

(1) From the above figures prepare the overhead application rates using the methods :
(*i*) Direct Labour Hours;
(*ii*) Direct Labour costs;
(*iii*) Machine Hour.
(2) Prepare a comparative statement of cost showing the result of application of each of the above rates of Job No. 551 from the undermentioned data :

Direct Materials	Rs. 90,000
Direct Labour Cost	Rs. 180
Direct Labour Hours	150
Machine Hours	60

(3) In this case which method do you think to be appropriate.
[B.U. B.Com. (Hons.), 1986]

[Ans. Direct Labour hour rate Rs. 40 (ii) Direct Labour Cost rate Rs. 63 (iii) Machine Hour rate Rs. 12.40; Work cost under (i) Rs. 330 (ii) Rs. 384 (iii) Rs. 1,128]

21. Calculate machine hour rate for recovery of overheads for a group of 4 machines from the following data :
Original cost of 4 machines Rs. 76,800
Depreciation under Straight Line method at 10% p.a.
Maintenance average cost Rs. 8 per day of 8 hours for the group of machines.
Power 25 paise per running hour per machine.
Supervision for the group of machines Rs. 640 per month.
Allocation of building depreciation for the four machines on floor area basis Rs. 80 per month.
Share of manufacturing overhead Rs. 240 per month for the group of machines.
Normal working days in a year 300.
Normal idle time 20%.
Normal running : 1 shift of 8 hours. *[M.Com. C.U.]*
[Ans. Rs. 3.06]

22. From the following information compute a comprehensive Machine Hour Rate :

Original cost of the machine	Rs. 1,25,000
Customs duty, insurance and freight paid	Rs. 15,000
Installation expenses	Rs. 16,500

Estimated scrap value after 12 years — 10% of the original cost.
The machine is expected to operate 8 hours per day of 280 working days in the year out of which 160 hours are required for normal setting and another 80 hours for routine maintenance.

	Rs.
Rent and rates of the shop p.a.	4,800
General lighting of the shop p.m.	200
Insurance premium for the machine per quarter	300
Estimated cost of repairs and maintenance for the entire life of the machine	6,600
Shop supervisor's salary p.m.	1,000
Wages, workmen's compensation insurance etc. of each of two operators (each operator is incharge of 2 machines) p.a.	9,600
Power consumption of machine per hour	10 units
Rate of power per 100 units	75
Consumable stores for the shop p.a.	1,250

Additional information ; (i) There are four identical machines in the shop. (ii) The supervisor is expected to devote his time equally to the machines. ***[C.U. B.Com. (Hons.)]***

[Ans. Rs. 19.33]

23. The following expenses have been incurred in respect of a shop having 5 identical machines :

	Rs.
(*a*) Rent & Rates	4,000
(*b*) Power consumed by the shop @ $6\frac{1}{4}$ Paise per unit	3,750
(*c*) Repairs and maintenance for the machines	1,000
(*d*) Lighting charges for the shop	500
(*e*) Attendant's Salary (Two attendants and each is paid @ Rs. 50 p.m.)	—
(*f*) Supervisor's Salary (He devotes 1/5th time for the machine, his salary Rs. 300 p.m.)	—
(*g*) Lubricants and cotton waste for the shop	100
(*h*) Hire-purchase instalment for the machines (including Rs. 300 for interest)	2,300
(*i*) Each machine consumes 10 units of power per hour	
(*j*) Depreciation on each machine	600 p.a.

[Ans. Machine Hour Rate = Rs. 2.87]

(**Hints.** The interest on hire-purchase instalment has not been included in calculations. However, machine hour rate can be calculated by adding this interest also. Then this interest will be considered as standing charges then the answer will be Rs. 2.92 hour rate)

24. The following particulars have been obtained for a machine installed in a factory. The number of effective hours is 174. The machine was purchased on the hire-purchase system and the work of the factory has been mostly carried on with the help of this machine :

Year of running	Second
Cash down price (Rs.)	22,259
Scrap value (Rs.)	9,259
Number of Instalments	5
Amount of each instalment (Rs.)	5,000
Rate of Interest per annum	4%
Life of machine (in effective working hours)	30,000 hrs
Other overhead charges (Rs.)	913.50

[M.Com. Allahabad]

[Ans. Rs. 9.85]

25. From the undernoted data calculate the Machine Hour Rate of a milling machine :

Cost of machine	Rs. 30,500
Scrap value	Rs. 2,500
Estimated life	12 years
Effective working days	200 days of 8 hours 100 days of 6 hours
Maintenance and Repairs	7.5% of Capital Cost
Stores consumed	Rs. 1,000
Supervision Expenses	Rs. 7,500
Power Consumption	Rs. 2 per operating hour
Insurance Premium	1% of Capital Cost
Idle time estimated	10%

[B.Com. C.U]

[Ans. Rs. 8.78]

26. Compute the machine hour rate to cover the overhead expenses indicated below :

		Per hour	*Per annum*
Electric Power		75 Paise	
Steam		10 Paise	
Water		2 Paise	
Repairs			Rs. 530
Rent			Rs. 270
Running hours			2,000
Original Cost	Rs. 12,500		
Book Value	Rs. 2,870		
Present Replacement Value	Rs. 11,500		
Depreciation	$7\frac{1}{2}$% per annum		

[B.Com. Andhra]
[Ans. Rs. 1.74]

27. Calculate the machine hour rate from the following :

	Rs.
(*i*) Cost of Machine	19,200
(*ii*) Estimated Scrap Value	1,200
(*iii*) Average repairs and maintenance charges per month	150
(*iv*) Standing charges allocated to machine per month	50
(*v*) Effective working life of machine	10,000 hours
(*vi*) Running time per month	166 hours

(*vii*) Power used by machine : 5 units per hour @ 19 paise per unit.

[B.Com. Punjab]
[Ans. Rs. 3.95]

28. Work out the machine hour rate for the following machine whose scrap value is nil :

Cost of machine	Rs. 90,000
Freight & Installation charges	Rs. 10,000
Working Life	10 years
Working hours	2,000 per year
Repair charges	50% of depreciation
Power—10 units per hour	@ 10 paise per unit
Lubricating oil	@ Rs. 2 per day of 8 hours
Consumable stores	@ Rs. 10 per day of 8 hours
Wages of an operator	@ 4 per day

[B.Com. Meerut]
[Ans. Rs. 10.50]

29. X Ltd. having fifteen types of automatic machines furnishes information for 1996-97 as under :

(*i*) Overhead expenses : Factory rent Rs. 96,000/- (Floor area 80,000 Sq.ft.). Heat and gas Rs. 45,000 and supervision Rs. 1,20,000.

(*ii*) Wages of the operator are Rs. 48 per day of 8 hours. He attends to one machine when it is under set-up and two machines while they are under operation.

In respect of machine B (one of the above machines), the following particulars are furnished :

(*i*) Cost of machine Rs. 45,000, Life of machine—10 years and scrap value at the end of its life Rs. 5,000.

(*ii*) Annual expenses on special equipment attached to the machine are estimated at Rs. 3,000.

(*iii*) Estimated operation time of the machine is 3,600 hours while setup time 400 hours per annum.

(*iv*) The machine occupies 5,000 Sq.ft. of floor area.

(*v*) Power costs Rs. 2 per hour while machine is in operation.

Find out the comprehensive machine hour rate of machine B. Also find out machine costs to be absorbed in respect of use of machine B on the following two work orders :

	Work order 31	Work order 32
Machine set-up time (Hours)	10	20
Machine operation time (Hours)	90	180

[C.A. Inter]

[Ans. M.H.R : Set-up rate/Hour Rs. 12 ; Operating rate/Hour Rs. 11. Work order 31 Rs. 1,110. work order 32. Rs. 2,220.]

30. A manufacturing unit has added a new machine to its fleet of five existing machines. The total cost of purchase and installation of the machine is Rs. 7,50,000. The machine has an estimated life of 15 years and is expected to realise Rs. 30,000 as scrap at the end of its working life.

Other relevant data are as follows :

(*i*) Budgeted working hours are 2,400 based on 8 hours per day for 300 days. This includes 400 hours for plant maintenance.

(*ii*) Electricity used by the machine is 15 units per hour at a cost of Rs. 2.00 per unit. No current is drawn during maintenance.

(*iii*) The machine required special oil for heating which is replaced once in every month at a cost of Rs. 2,500 on each occasion.

(*iv*) Estimated cost of maintenance of the machine is Rs. 500 per week of 6 working days.

(*v*) 3 Operators control the operations of the entire battery of six machines and the average wage per person amounts to Rs. 450 per week plus 40% fringe benefits.

(*vi*) Departmental and general works overheads allocated to the operation during the last year were Rs. 60,000. During the current year it is estimated that there will be an increase of 12·5% of this amount. No incremental overhead is envisaged for the installation of the new machine.

You are required to compute the machine-hour rate for recovery of the running cost of the machine.

[I.C.W.A. Inter]

[Ans. M.H.R. Rs. 95.00]

31. Calculate from the following data the machine hour rate for a Mercedes Printing machine :

Cost of machine	Rs. 21,000
Estimated Scrap value	Rs. 1,000
Effective working hours	40,000 hours
Running time for 4-weekly period	150 hours
4-weekly service charges for maintenance of machine	Rs. 20
Standing charges allocated to the machine for 4-weekly period	Rs. 100
Electric power used by the machine during 4-weekly period	Rs. 75

[C.A. (Inter)]

[Ans. Rs. 3.00]

32. Compute total machine hour rate from the following data :

(*i*) Total machine cost to be depreciated Rs. 2,30,000

(*ii*) Life 10 yrs.

(*iii*) Depreciation on Straight Line Method

(*iv*) Departmental overheads (annual)
Rent Rs. 50,000, Heat and Light Rs. 20,000, Supervision Rs. 1,30,000.

(*v*) Departmental Area 70,000 sq. ft.
Machines Area 2,500 sq. ft.

(*vi*) 26 machines in the department

(*vii*) Hours run on production 1,800

(*viii*) Hours for setting and adjusting 200

(*ix*) Power cost 50 paise per hour of running time

(*x*) Labour (*a*) When setting and adjusting full time attention.
(*b*) When machine is producing one man can look after 3 machines.

(*xi*) Labour Rates Rs. 6 per hr.

[C.A. Adopted]

[Ans. Machine Hour Rate Rs. 20.14]

33. A machine was purchased on January 1, 1990 for Rs. 5 lakhs. The total cost of all machinery inclusive of the new machine was Rs. 75 lakhs.
The following further particulars are available :
Expected life of the machine 10 years.
Scrap value at the end of 10 years Rs. 5,000. Repairs and maintenance for the machine during the year Rs. 2,000. Expected number of the woking hours of the machine per year 4,000 hours.
Insurance premium annually for all machines Rs. 4,500.
Electricity consumption for the machine per hour (@ 0.75 paise per unit) 25 units.
Area occupied by the machine — 100 sq. ft.
Area occupied by other machines 1,500 sq. ft.
Rent per month of the department Rs. 800
Lighting charges for 20 points for the whole department, out of which three points are for the machine Rs. 120 per month.
Compute the machine hour rate for the new machine on the basis of the data given above.

[C.A. (Inter)]

[Ans. Machine Hour Rate Rs. 31.90]

34. In a certain factory, three products are made from different materials by similar processes. For a typical period production costs are as under :

	Product A	*Product B*	*Product C*
Materials used	160	200	80
Direct Labour Cost	120	100	40
Overhead (actual)	80	65	35

Overhead is charged to cost of each product @ 25% Prime Cost.
Do you see something wrong in principle in this method of charging overheads ? If so, suggest a preferable method.

[Adopted I.C.W.A. Inter]

[Ans. A = 66.67%; B = 65%; C = $87\frac{1}{2}$%]

35. Gemini Enterprises undertakes three different Jobs A, B and C. All of them require the use of a special machine and also the use of a computer. The computer is hired and the hire charges works out to Rs. 4,20,000 p.a. The expenses regarding the machine are estimated as follows :

	Rs.
Rent per quarter	17,500
Depreciation per annum	2,00,000
Indirect charges per annum	1,50,000

During the first month of operation the following details were taken from the job register :

	A	*B*	*C*
Number of hours the machine was used :			
(*a*) Without the use of the computer	600	900	—
(*b*) With the use of the computer	400	600	1,000

You are required to compute the machine hour rate :
(*a*) For the firm as a whole for the month when the computer was used and when the computer was not used.
(*b*) For the individual job A, B and C.

[C.A. Inter]

[Ans. (*a*) Rs. 27.50 per hour and Rs. 10.00 per hour, respectively.
(*b*) Machine hour rate : A = Rs. 17; B = Rs. 17; C = Rs. 27.50]

36. A manufacturing unit has predetermined the overhead recovery rates as 400% on direct wages, 20% on works cost and 25% on cost of production for works expenses, management expenses and commercial expenses, respectively.
At the end of the year, it has been found that the works overhead stands under-absorbed to the extent of 30% of the total productive wages, management o/h show under-recovery of one-eighth of the absorbed amount, and the recovery of commercial expenses results in an over-absorption of the total amount absorbed.
If the prime costs of three jobs are as under, find the profit/loss on the respective selling prices (both on the basis of standard cost and on the basis of full absorption overheads).

	Job A	*Job B*	*Job C*
Direct materials	Rs. 45.50	Rs. 32.60	Rs. 26.80
Direct wages	Rs. 15.20	Rs. 8.60	Rs. 7.20
	Rs. 60.70	Rs. 41.20	Rs. 34.00
Selling price	Rs. 200.00	Rs. 130.00	Rs. 90.00

[I.C.W.A. Inter]

[Ans.

	A	**B**	**C**
Cost of Sales (at standard cost)	**182.25**	**113.40**	**94.20**
at full absorption.	**177.70**	**110.31**	**91.65]**

37. B & Co. has recorded the following data in the two most recent periods :

Total cost of production (Rs.)	Volume of production (UNITS)
14,600	800
19,400	1,200

What is the best estimate of the firm's fixed costs per period ? *[C.A. Inter, Nov—1995]*

[Ans. Fixed Cost : Rs. 5,000]

38. The standard departmental overhead rate is Rs. 15 per hour. Based on the following details provided to you, workout the activity level at which the overhead rate has been fixed :

Activity Level	**Overhead Allowance**
6,000 hours	Rs. 1,20,000
8,000 hours	Rs. 1,44,000
10,000 hours	Rs. 1,68,000

[I.C.W.A. Inter]

[Ans. Required Activity Level = 16,000 Hours.]

39. Segregation of variable and fixed overheads.

Meera Industries Ltd. Is a single product organisation having a manufacturing capacity of 6,000 units per week of 48 hours. The output data vis-a-vis different elements of cost of three consecutive weeks are given below :

Units produced	**Direct material**	**Direct Labour**	**Total Factory Overheads (Variable and Fixed)**
2,400	Rs. 4,800	Rs. 6,000	Rs. 37,200
2,800	" 5,600	" 7,000	" 38,400
3,600	" 7,200	" 9,000	" 40,800

As Cost Accountant, you are asked by the company management to work out the selling price assuming an activity level of 4,000 units per week and a profit of 20% on selling price.

[I.C.W.A. Inter]

[Ans. Total selling price Rs. 75,000
Selling Price Per unit. Rs. 18.75]

40. (*a*) What is a Composite Machine Hour Rate ?

(*b*) Three machines P, Q and R which are of different nature are used in a department of a factory. From the following information, compute machine hour rate of machine R :

(*i*) Total cost of machine P, Q and R is Rs. 50,000, out of which cost of machine R is Rs. 10,000. Its estimated scrap value and working life are Rs. 1,000 and 18,000 hours, respectively.
(*ii*) Rent (Total area 1,000 sq. ft and machine R occupies 250 sq. ft) Rs. 780 p.a.
(*iii*) Lighting (Total light points 12, out of which 2 points used for machine R) Rs. 288 p.a.
(*iv*) Insurance for all machines Rs. 45 per quarter
(*v*) Consumable stores for machine R Rs. 60 p.m.
(*vi*) Salary of supervisor (supervisor devotes 1/4th of his time for machine R) Rs. 6,000 p.a.
(*vii*) Repairs & maintenance for the entire life of machine R Rs. 1,800
(*viii*) Machine R consumes 5 units of power per hour at a cost of Rs. 16 per 100 units.

(*ix*) Machine R will work 2,000 hours p.a., out of which normal idle time estimated at 8% of total working hours and time for routine maintenance estimated at 40 hours p.a.

[C.U. B.Com. (H) 2001]

[Ans. (*b*) Rs. 2.788]

41. A production department of a manufacturing concern has three distinct machines—*A, B* and *C.* It is estimated that each machine will normally work for 50 weeks a year, 45 hours per week, and it is anticipated that the machines will remain idle 20% of the time due to normal repairs and maintenance.

The budgeted figures of the production department for the year ended 31st March 1996 are as follows :

	Rs.
Rent and rates	4,800
Lighting	900
Depreciation	10,500
Indirect wages	4,500
Canteen expenses	2,500
Repairs and maintenance	6,300
Sundries	3,000
Power	12,000

Other information :

	Machine A	*Machine B*	*Machine C*
Space occupied (sq. ft.)	100	150	150
Light points	5	5	8
Cost of machines (Rs.)	25,000	30,000	50,000
H.P. of machines	2	2.5	3
No. of workers	3	3	3
Direct wages (Rs.)	6,000	4,000	5,000

During the 4 weeks of February 1996, at 80% capacity utilisation, actual overheads incurred were : For Machine A—Rs. 1,200, for Machine B—Rs. 900 and for Machine C—Rs. 2,000.

You are required to calculate for each machine :

(*a*) Pre-determined overhead rate based on effective working hours;

(*b*) The amount of under/over-absorption of overhead; and

(*c*) The revised overhead application rate.

[C.U. B.Com.]

	A	*B*	*C*
	Rs.	*Rs.*	*Rs.*
[Ans. (*a*) Overhead rate	**6.89**	**7.00**	**10.28**
(*b*) Under-absorption	**506.00**	**94.00**	**816.00**
(*c*) Revised rate	**10.42**	**7.81**	**17.36]**

42. The particulars relating to four machines are as follows :

Machine Numbers	*I*	*II*	*III*	*IV*
Cost (Rs.)	50,000	40,000	30,000	20,000
Area occupied (sq. ft.)	500	450	300	250
Light points	10	8	6	4
No. of workers	20	15	8	7
Direct wages (Rs.)	1,500	1,200	1,000	500
Horse-power of machines	25	20	16	14
Consumable stores (Rs.)	100	80	75	50

The expenses incurred were as follows :

	Rs.
Rent and Taxes	600
Lighting	140
Depreciation	2,800
Repairs and maintenance	700
Power	375
Indirect wages	840
Consumable stores	305
Canteen expenses	100
General expenses	420

(*a*) Compute the comprehensive machine hour rate for a month of 25 working days with 8 working hours on an average.

(*b*) Calculate the cost of production of one unit of product *A*, if the material cost is Rs. 10, labour cost Rs. 20 and if processed for one hour in machine *I*, two hours in machine *II*, three hours in machine *III* and four hours in machine *IV*. *[C.U. B.Com. (H)]*

[Ans. (*a*) I—Rs. 18.575; II—Rs. 14·95; III—11.855; IV—Rs.7.02 (*b*) Rs. 122.12]

Notes : (1) A comprehensive machine hour rate includes direct wages.
(2) In computing (b) labour will not be separately considered as it is already included in comprehensive machine hour rate.

43. A machine shop has 6 identical machines manned by 5 operators. The machine cannot be worked without any operator wholly engaged on it. The original cost of all these 6 machines works out at Rs. 6 lakhs.

The following estimates are available for the year 1999 :

(*a*) Normal working hours per month	220 hours
(*b*) Absenteeism (without pay) per month	20 hours
(*c*) Leave with pay per month	20 hours
(*d*) Normal idle time (unavoidable)	20 hours
(*e*) Average rate of wages per day of 8 hours	Rs. 40
(*f*) Production bonus	15% of wages
(*g*) Cost of power for the period	Rs. 20,700
(*h*) Supervision and indirect labour cost for the year	Rs. 8,100
(*i*) Lighting and electricity per annum	Rs. 3,070
(*j*) Repairs and maintenance of machines2% of the value of the machines p.a.	
(*k*) Insurance charges	Rs. 30,000 p.a.
(*l*) General management expenses as allocated for the year	Rs. 84,000
(*m*) Depreciation under straight line method 15% on original cost of machines	

You are required to work out a comprehensive machine hour rate for the machine shop. *[C.U. B.Com. (H)]*

[Ans. Rs. 33.00]

44. Following are the particulars relating to 3 machines for a particular period of 320 hours :

	Machine A	*Machine B*	*Machine C*
Cost of machine	Rs. 20,000	Rs. 30,000	Rs. 40,000
Power	Rs. 90	Rs. 160	Rs. 300
Direct Wages	Rs. 600	Rs. 1,600	Rs. 2,400
Area Occupied	200 Sq. mts.	500 Sq. mts.	800 Sq. mts.
Number of workers	4	10	20
Light points	4	8	12

During the period following expenses were incurred :

	Rs.
Rent and Rates	900
Depreciation	2,700
Power	550
Canteen expenses	102
Lighting expenses	96
Indirect wages	920
Repairs	3,600
Sundries	600

Compute comprehensive machine hour rate for each of the above machines.

[C.U. B.Com. (H) 2004]

[Ans. A : 7.61; B : 14.85; C : 21.50]

45. In Moon Light Manufacturing Company, the output is produced through three machine departments *A, B* and *C*. The company follows pre-determined factory overhead absorption rates for the machine departments. Hourly rates fixed up for the year 2001 are Rs. 16.00 per hour for Dept. *A*, Rs. 18.80 per hour for Dept. *B* and Rs. 17.50 per hour for Dept. C.

The actual expenses of these machine departments for the year 2001 are as follows :

	Rs.		*Rs.*
Depreciation on Machinery	20,000	Repairs to Machinery	12,000
Rent of Factory Shed	18,000	Lighting	4,000
Indirect Materials	10,000	Canteen Expenses	15,000
Indirect Wages	12,000	Insurance of Machines	8,000
Power	16,000	Sundry Expenses	18,000

The particulars relating to the machine departments are given below :

Departments	*Machine A*	*Machine B*	*Machine C*
Area Occupied (Sq. Ft.)	800	600	400
Value of Machinery (Rs.)	80,000	60,000	60,000
Direct Wages (Rs.)	50,000	40,000	30,000
Direct Materials (Rs.)	60,000	80,000	60,000
No. of Light Points	9	5	6
Power of Machines (H.P.)	20	40	20
No. of Workers	12	8	10
Actual Working Hours	3,000	2,500	2,000

You are required to (*a*) calculate overhead absorption rate per working hour for the departments; (*b*) compute the price to be charged for a job which requires Materials of Rs. 1,500 and Wages of Rs. 1,000 assuming the office and administration overhead is charged @ 20% on works cost, selling and distribution overhead @ 20% on cost of production and profit @ 25% on sale (the job requires 15, 12 and 10 hours of time in machines *A*, *B* and *C*, respectively) and (*c*) determine over or under-absorption of factory overhead.

[C.U. B.Com. (H) 2002]

[Ans. (*a*) *A* Rs. 17.27; *B* Rs. 18.00; *C* Rs. 18.10
(*b*) Rs. 6,029.95
(*c*) *A* under-absorption (–) Rs. (3,800)
***B* Over-absorption (+) Rs. 1,250**
***C* Under-absorption (–) Rs. 1,200**
Total under-absorption (–) Rs. 3,750

46. Following expenses are incurred in respect of a factory having five identical machines :

	Rs.
(*i*) Rent & Rates	4,000
(*ii*) Power consumed by the factory @ $6^1/_4$ paise per unit	3,750
(*iii*) Repairs and maintenance for the machines	1,000
(*iv*) Lighting charges for the factory	500
(*v*) Attendant's salary (There are two attendants, each is paid, Rs. 50 per month)	Rs. 100
(*vi*) Supervisor's salary (devotes 1/5 time for the machine)	300 p.m.
(*vii*) Lubricants and Cotton wool for the factory	100
(*viii*) Hire-purchase instalment for the machines (including Rs. 300 for interest)	2,300
(*ix*) Each machine consumed 10 units of power per hour	—
(*x*) Depreciation of each machine	600

[Ans. Machine Hour Rate Rs. 2.87 excluding interest on hire-purchase instalment; Machine Hour Rate Rs. 2.92 (Including interest on hire-purchase instalment]

47. A manufacturing company has three production and three service departments namely X, Y, Z and P, Q, R, respectively. For a period the total overheads as per primary distribution are as under :

Production Departments			*Service Departments*		
A	*B*	*C*	*P*	*Q*	*R*
10,000	12,500	30,000	16,000	14,000	20,000

The service dept. cost should be apportioned as under :

	A	*B*	*C*	*Q*	*R*
P	20%	25%	25%	10%	20%
Q	30%	30%	20%	—	20%
R	40%	45%	15%		

Ascertain the total overheads of Departments A, B, C using step methods.

[Ans. A = Rs. 35,930; B = Rs. 36,165; C = Rs. 30,405]

48. Following data is available relating to a company for a certain month :

	Territory I	Territory II	Territory III
Selling expenses	Rs. 7,600	Rs. 4,200	Rs. 6,240
Distribution Costs	Rs. 4,000	Rs. 1,800	Rs. 2,000
No. of units Sold	16,000	6,900	10,000
Sales	Rs. 76,000	Rs. 28,000	Rs. 52,000

The company adopts sales basis and quantity basis for application of selling and distribution costs, respectively. Compute : (*a*) the territorywise overhead recovery rates separately for selling and distribution costs, and (*b*) the amounts of selling and distribution costs chargeable to consignment of 2,000 units of a product, sold in each territory at Rs. 4.50 per unit.

[I.C.W.A. Inter, Dec. 1986]

[Ans. (*a*) The territorywise overhead recovery rates separately for Selling and Distribution Costs are 10%, 15% and 12% of Sales of Territory I, II & III, respectively. (*b*) Total Selling & Distribution costs are Rs. 1,400, Rs. 1,950 and Rs. 1,480]

49. A factory is having three production departments A, B and C, and two service departments Boiler-house and Pump room. The boiler-house has to depend upon the pump-room for supply of water and pump room in its turn is dependent on the boiler-house for supply of steam power for driving the pump. The expenses incurred by the production departments during a period are : A—Rs. 8,00,000 ; B—Rs. 7,00,000 and C—Rs. 5,00,000. The expenses for boiler-house is Rs. 2,34,000 and the Pump-room Rs. 3,00,000.

The expenses of the boiler-house and pump-room are apportioned to the production departments on the following basis :

	A	*B*	*C*	*B.H.*	*P.R.*
Boiler house	20%	40%	30%	—	10%
Pump-room	40%	20%	20%	20%	—

Show clearly as to how the expenses of Boiler-house and Pump-room would be apportioned to A, B and C departments. Use algebraical equation. *[C.S. (Final), CS (inter)]*

[Ans. A = Rs. 9,92,000; B = Rs. 8,86,000; C = Rs. 6,56,000]

50. Following data is available relating to a company for a certain month :

	Territory I Rs.	Territory II Rs.	Territory III Rs.
Selling Expenses	7,600	4,200	6,240
Distribution Costs	4,000	1,800	2,000
No. of units sold	16,000 units	6,900 units	10,000 units
Sales	76,000	28,000	52,000

The company adopts sales basis and quantity basis for application of selling and distribution costs, respectively. Compute : (a) The territorywise overhead recovery rates separately for selling and distribution costs, and (b) The amounts of selling and distribution costs chargeable to a consignment of 2,000 units of a product, sold in each territory at Rs. 4.50 per unit.

[I.C.W.A. Inter]

[Ans. (*a*) (*i*) 0.25 per unit (*ii*) 0.30 per unit (*iii*) 0.20 per unit
(*b*) (*i*) Rs. 1,400 (*ii*) Rs. 1,950 (*iii*) Rs. 1,480]

51. (*a*) Explain how selling and distribution overheads are allocated to products.

(*b*) Marketing Division of a company wishes to discontinue the sale of one of the products in view of unprofitable operations.

Following details are available with regard to turnover costs and activity for the year ending 30 June 1994 :

	PRODUCTS *P*	*Q*	*R*	*S*
Sales Turnover	Rs. 6,00,000	Rs. 10,00,000	Rs. 5,00,000	Rs. 9,00,000
Cost of Sale	Rs. 3,50,000	Rs. 8,00,000	Rs. 3,70,000	Rs. 4,80,000
Storage Area (sq. ft.)	Rs. 40,000	Rs. 60,000	Rs. 70,000	Rs. 30,000
No. of cartons sold	Rs. 2,00,000	Rs. 3,00,000	Rs. 1,50,000	Rs. 3,50,000
No of Bills received	Rs. 1,00,000	Rs. 1,20,000	Rs. 80,000	Rs. 1,00,000

Overhead cost and basis of apportionment are :

Fixed Expenses	*Rs.*	*Basis of apportionment*
Administrative wages and salaries	1,00,000	Number of bills raised
Salesmen's Salaries & Expenses	1,20,000	Sales Turnover
Rent and Insurance	60,000	Storage area
Depreciation	20,000	No. of Cartons
Variable costs	4% of Sales	
Commission packing materials and wages	50 P per carton	
Stationery	20 P per Bill	

Based on the above data you are required to (*i*) prepare a statement showing summary of Selling and Distribution Costs to the products, and (*ii*) prepare a Profit & Loss statement showing contribution and Profit or Loss on sale of each of the products to enable the marketing department to take an appropriate decision on discontinuance of the sale of a product.

[I.C.W.A. (Int.)]

6 Specific Order Costing

Section I : Job Costing and Batch Costing

Authors' Comments and Suggestions :

1. ***Generally one question either from Job/Batch or from Contract Costing is being set from this chapter for all examinations.***
2. ***Distinction between Job/Batch/Contract is an important factor.***
3. ***Adjustment of opening and closing stock of raw material, W.I.P., and finished goods is vital in case of Job/Batch costing.***
4. ***The readers should be very careful in determining the profit of an incomplete contract.***
5. ***The students should know how to show the balance of W.I.P. in Balance Sheet.***
6. ***For Escalation clause both changed quantity and price should be considered.***

Definition—Difference between Job and Batch Costing—Features—Procedures—Advantages and Disadvantages—Specimen of Job Cost Sheet, Workedout Problems and Solutions—Exercises.

Introduction

There are two principal methods of accumulating and applying costs to products *viz.*, specific order costing and process costing. CIMA. terminology defines specific-order-costing as, "the basic costing method applicable where work consists of separate contracts, jobs or batches, each of which is authorized by a special order or contract". Hence, this method is generally used by the business concerns which carry on production against customers' specification or special requirements. Under this method costs are collected and accumulated separately in respect of each job, work order or contract.

Definition

(*a*) **Job Costing.** It is a particular form of specific-order-costing which applies where work is undertaken to customer's specific requirements and each order is of comparatively shorter duration than contract costing. Under the method costs are collected in respect of each job separately. The method is used in such industries as printing, foundry, repair shop, engineering, readymade garments, shoes etc.

(*b*) **Batch Costing.** It is a special type of job costing. Here a batch of similar products is treated as a job. This type of costing applies where similar articles are manufactured in batches either for sale or for use within the undertaking. Under this method costs are collected and analysed according to batch numbers allotted. The method is suitable for making component parts, pharmaceutical industries, spare parts, watches, radio-sets, cycles etc.

Features of Job Costing

Following are the main features of job costing :

(*i*) A separate job cost-sheet is to be prepared for calculating cost in respect of each job.

(*ii*) A separate work-in-progress ledger is to be maintained for each job, as W.I.P. differs from period to period depending on the number of jobs on hand.

(*iii*) Production is always against customer's orders.
(*iv*) Each job is of shorter duration (compared to contract costing).
(*v*) Each job has its own characteristics and needs separate treatment.
(*vi*) The distinction between direct and indirect cost is more urgent under the method.
(*vii*) There is no uniformity in the flow of production from one department to another in respect of jobs.
(*viii*) This method is labour intensive.

Advantages of Job Costing

Some specific advantages of job costing are listed below :

(*i*) Profitability can be analysed job-wise.
(*ii*) It helps the management in preparing estimates for like jobs for the purpose of submitting quotations.
(*iii*) It helps in producing detailed analysis of materials, labours and overheads, as the distinction between direct and indirect costs is more important here.
(*iv*) Spoilage and defective work is easily identified with each job or product and hence responsibility can be fixed on departments or persons.
(*v*) The management can fix selling price more easily for each job.
(*vi*) Job costing is particularly helpful for cost-plus contracts where contract price is determined directly on the basis of costs.
(*vii*) It helps in the introduction of budgetary control of overheads, since the overhead is applied on the basis of predetermined overhead rates.
(*viii*) It helps management to know the cost trends in respect of jobs and the efficiency of operation.

Disadvantages of Job Costing

The various disadvantages of Job-order-costing are :

(*i*) It requires more clerical work, hence is very much expensive.
(*ii*) It is essentially historical costing and possesses all the defects of historical costing.
(*iii*) Comparison between two periods becomes meaningless if there is some economic changes.
(*iv*) Chances of errors are increased because of increase in clerical work.

Job Cost Card/Job Cost Sheet

It is a document that records in details the cost incurred for direct material, direct labour, factory overhead, administration overheads etc. for a particular job. Separate job cost sheets/cards are maintained for each job. It accumulates the total cost assigned to the job. It also serves as the subsidiary ledger for work-in-progress inventory control account.

A specimen of Job Cost Card/Sheet is given below :

Job Cost Sheet/Card

Job No. .... Quantity ....
Job Description .... Date of Completion..............
Customer .... Date of Commencement........
Particulars of Job........

Material				*Labour*				*Overhead*			
Date	*Dept.*	*M.R. No.*	*Amt.*	*Date*	*Dept.*	*Time Ticket No.*	*Amt.*	*Date*	*Dept.*	*Rate*	*Amt.*
Total											

Summary

	Estimate Cost (Rs.)	*Actual Cost (Rs.)*	*Variance (+)/(–)*
Material			
Labour			
Overhead			
Total			

Explanation of Variance......... Prepared by............

Date.................................. Checked by............

Remarks............................

Batch Costing

According to CIMA London, "Batch Costing is a specific form of costing which applies where similar articles are produced in batches either for sales or for other purposes'.

Elements of Costs relating to Batch Costing

There are two types of cost generally found in Batch costing *viz.* *(i)* Set-up or preparation Cost *(ii)* Carrying Cost.

Set-up cost means the cost involved in setting up of the machines or tools for production which is fixed in nature and it should be computed after taking into consideration the time lost due to change-over from one batch to another, loss of speed due to change-over, material wastage etc.

Carrying cost means the costs which are related with the cost of manufacture, storage, interest on capital invested, depreciation etc.

Formulae used for Batch Costing

$$\text{Economic Batch Quantity } (EBQ) = \sqrt{\frac{2AS}{C}}$$

where

A = Annual consumption

S = Set-up cost per batch

C = Carrying cost per unit p.a.

Illustration 1. A manufacturing unit has predetermined the overhead rates as 400% on direct wages, 20% on works cost and 25% on cost of production for work expenses, management expenses and commercial expenses, respectively.

At the end of the year, it has been found that the works overhead stand under-absorbed to the extent of 30% of the total productive wages. Management overheads show under-recovery of 1/8th of the absorbed amount, and the recovery of the commercial expenses results in an over-absorption of 1/3rd of the total amount absorbed.

If the prime costs of three Jobs are as under, find the profit/loss on the respective selling prices (both on the basis of standard cost and on the basis of full absorption of overheads) :

	Job A	*Job B*	*Job C*
	Rs.	*Rs.*	*Rs.*
Direct Materials	45·50	32·60	26·80
Direct Wages	15·20	8·60	7·20
	60·70	41·20	34·00
Selling Price	200·00	130·00	90·00

[I.C.W.A. (Int.) Dec. 1995]

Solution

Under-absorption in works overheads is 30% on wages. Under-absorption in management overheads is 1/8th of the absorbed amount and over-absorption in commercial expenses is 1/3rd of the total amount absorbed.

	Job A Rs.	*Job B* Rs.	*Job C* Rs.
Direct Materials	45·50	32·60	26·80
Direct Wages	15·20	8·60	7·20
Work Overheads	60·80	34·40	28·80
Work Cost	121·50	75·60	62·80
Management Expenses (20% on works cost)	24·30	15·12	12·56
Cost of Production	145·80	90·72	75·36
Commercial Expenses (25% of cost of Product)	36·45	22·68	18·84
Cost of Sales (at standard recovery)	182·25	113·40	94·20
Add : Under-recovery of works overheads (30% on total Productive wages)	4·56	2·58	2·16
Add : Under-recovery of management expenses (1/8th of the absorbed amount)	3·04	1·89	1·57
	189·85	117·87	97·93
Less : Over-absorption of commercial expenses (1/3rd of the absorbed amount)	12·15	7·56	6·28
Cost of Sales (on full absorption of overheads)	177·70	110·31	91·65

Statement of Profit/Loss

	Job A Rs.	*Job B* Rs.	*Job C* Rs.
Selling Price (*i*)	200·00	130·00	90·00
Cost of Sales (*ii*)	182·25	113·40	94·20
Profit/Loss at Standard Cost (*i–ii*)	17·75	16·60	4·20

Section II : Contract Costing or Terminal Costing

Definition—Features—Some terminology and their treatment—Retention money—Certified work—Uncertified work; Escalation clauses—Work-in-progress—Cost Plus Contract—Guidelines for Profit and Loss—Transfer of incompleted contract, Specimen of Contract Account—Workedout Problems and Solutions—Exercises.

Introduction

The term contract costing is used by contractors, builders and engineers,who undertake definite contracts such as building construction, ship building, bridge construction and so on. A contract is usually undertaken for a fixed period and price (called contract price), which is payable either on the completion of the contract or by instalments according to the progress of work done.

Definition and Concept

According to CIMA terminology the term 'contract costing' refers to "the form of specific order costing which applies where work is undertaken to customer's special requirements and each order is of long duration (compared with those to which job costing applies). The work is usually constructional and in general the method is similar to job costing".

So it is a special type of job costing where the unit of cost is a single contract and separate distinguishing numbers are allotted for each contract to collect cost.

Features

The salient features of contract costing are :

(i) The work is generally carried out at a site and not in the factories.

(ii) Each contract is given a distinguishing number in respect of which cost is ascertained.

(iii) It is the contract between the contractor and contractee.

(iv) Many contracts require more than one accounting year.

(v) Most of the items of cost are directly chargeable to individual contract.

(vi) More often, one contract differs from others.

(vii) Part payments are made depending on the certificate issued by the architect, showing value of work completed and retention money.

(viii) An "escalation clause", under which the contractor is compensated for increase in costs on account of inflation, may be included in the contract.

(ix) In case of non-fulfilment of contract within the stipulated time, the contractor is required to pay penalty.

Some Terminology and their Treatment

(A) **Surveyor's Certificate and Retention Money**

In case of large contract which extends for more than a year it is normal practice to make payment against the portion of the contract completed on the basis of work certified by the contractee's surveyor. The certificate issued by the surveyor (or technical assessor) in this respect is known as *Surveyor's Certificate.* Generally, as per terms of the contract, full amount of the work certified is not paid to the contractor. A certain percentage (say 10% to 20%) of the amount is retained by the contractee and is paid some time after the completion of the contract. The sum of money thus retained is known as *Retention Money.* This is done to give protection to the contractee in case the contractor does not fulfil the terms and conditions of the contract.

(*B*) **Uncertified Work**

The work which has been done by the contractor but not certified by the architect on the date of accounting due to insufficient progress is known as *Uncertified Work.*

In case of incompleted contract for which profit is required to be calculated, the value of uncertified work should be taken into account and it is justifiable to evaluate such work at cost. Because, it is not logical to calculate profit on the work which is not complete. Thus the Contract A/c is credited with this cost of uncertified work and Work-in-progress is debited with the same. This entry is reversed at the beginning of the next year.

Escalation Clause

Increase in price due to inflation is a common feature of today. Generally, a contract takes longer duration to complete and during this period the price of material, labour, plant, may increase beyond a point. In such case the clause, which safeguards the interest of both the contractor and the contractee against unfavourable price change in future, is called *Escalation Clause.* By virtue of this clause, the contractee has to bear the additional cost arising out of such inflation. Such clause may also apply where material and labour utilization exceeds a particular limit. Often there might be a De-escalation or Reverse Clause, providing for reduction in the contract price and passing on the benefit to the contractee.

Work-in-Progress

Work-in-progress means incomplete contract which is in progress. The contractor may prepare a Work-in-progress A/c by debiting the account with the value of work certified and cost of uncertified work and by crediting the profit not transferred to Profit & Loss A/c (*i.e.* reserve profit). The difference between the two sides of the account less cash received is the work-in-progress, which is shown in the Balance Sheet.

Cost-Plus-Contract

It is the reverse of a fixed price contract. Here the contractor is paid the actual cost incurred plus a certain percentage of profit over the cost of production. Generally, it is provided in the agreement as to items of expenditure to be included in the actual cost and the percentage of profit to be added to the actual cost. This type of contract is suitable in those cases where probable cost of the contract cannot be estimated with a reasonable degree of accuracy in advance due to various reasons (such as longer duration, wide fluctuation in price etc.). Government contracts (such as dams, bridges, power house, aircraft etc.) are usually on cost-plus basis. The books and documents of the contract shall remain open for checking and verifying by its customers.

The cost-plus contracts have some advantages and disadvantages for both the parties to the contract.

On behalf of manufactures

Advantages

(*i*) There is no chance of loss due to price fluctuation.
(*ii*) The contractor can know well in advance the percentage of profit which he will earn.
(*iii*) It is particularly helpful where probable cost cannot be predicted in advance.
(*iv*) The possibility of incurring any loss is completely eliminated.

Disadvantages

(*i*) In case of favourable market, the contractor is deprived of earning extra profit.
(ii) There may arise some dispute in future as to ascertainment of cost.
(*iii*) The percentage of profit may be too inadequate to cover the overhead expenses.

On behalf of Contractee

Advantages

(*i*) The contractee feels satisfied as the price is not arbitrary.
(*ii*) The price is based on actual cost.
(*iii*) Purchase risk of the contractee are eliminated.

Disadvantages

(*i*) Total cost of the contract cannot be ascertained in advance.
(*ii*) As there are no incentive for cost reduction, the contractee has to bear the extra cost due to inefficiency of the contractor.

Profits on Incomplete Contract—Some Guidelines

The contract started and finished within the financial year poses no problem. But big contracts may extend over more than one accounting year and in that case it is very difficult to ascertain profit with precision until and unless they are completed. This method cannot be followed because this would lead to wide fluctuations in profits every year. Such a fluctuation is not desirable from the viewpoint of payment of dividends to the shareholders, payment of income-tax etc. So it is desirable to determine profit of incompleted contract carefully and cautiously so that a reasonable portion of the same should be credited to the Profit & Loss A/c every year. The "reasonable profit" may vary depending upon the practice and circumstances of the case.

The calculation of profit on imcomplete contracts is laid down in Statement of Standard Accounting Practices 9. The key points on the standard are :

"The overriding principle being that there can be no attributable profit until the outcome of a contract can reasonably be foreseen. Of the profit which in the light of all the circumstances can be foreseen with a reasonable degree of certainty to arise on completion of the contract there would be regarded as earned to date only that part which prudently reflects the amount of work performed to date. The method used for taking up such profits need to be consistently applied."

The standard continues by elaborating on the profit calculation as follows :

"In calculating the total estimated profit on the contract, it is necessary to take into account not only the total costs to date and total estimated further costs to completion (calculated by reference to the same principles as were applied to cost to date) but also the estimated future costs of rectification and guarantee work and any other future work to be undertaken under the terms of the contract. These are then compared to the total sales value of the contract. In considering future costs it is necessary to have regard to likely increases in wages and salaries to likely increases in the prices of raw materials and to rises in general overheads so far as these items are not recoverable from the customer under the terms of the contract."

The profit taken in any year is calculated on a cumulative basis having regard to profit taken in earlier years. The appropriate part of the standard is :

"The amount to be reflected in the year's profit and loss account will be the appropriate proportion of this total profit by reference to the work done to date less any profit already taken in previous year."

The profit calculation is as follows :

	Amount Rs.	*Amount Rs.*
Total Contract Value		....
Less : Costs incurred to date	....	
Estimated costs to completion	....	
Rectification and guarantee work	....	
Total estimated contract costs		....
Estimated contract profit or loss		....

If a loss is disclosed from the above calculation then this should be provided in full in the period's acccounts. If there is a projected profit disclosed this would be used in the following formula :

Profit to date = Cost of works completed ÷ Total estimated contract × Estimated contract profit.

The amount of profit to be recognized in the current period is calculated on cumulative principles as follows :

Profit to date Rs....................................	Rs....................................
Less : Profit recognized to end of previous period	Rs....................................
Profit recognized in current period	Rs....................................

(*a*) **When the contract has just started**

In such case no profit should be taken into account, as it is impossible to see the future position clearly. Generally, up to 1/4th completion of the contract, this principle is followed.

(*b*) **When the contract has sufficiently advanced** (*i.e.* more than 1/4th of the contract is completed)

A reasonable portion of the notional profit (difference between value of work certified and cost of work certified) should be credited to Profit & Loss A/c and the balance is carried forward in the same contract as a profit in suspense as adequate reserve for future losses and contingencies. The portion of notional profit to be taken will depend upon the progress of the work.

	Profit
(*i*) For completion less than 50% of contract	1/3 × Notional Profit
(*ii*) For completion 50% or more of contract	2/3 × Notional Profit

Where the cash received in respect of an incompleted contract is less than the value of the work certified, the above proportion (*i.e.* $^1/_3$ or $^2/_3$) of profit should also be reduced in accordance with the percentage of cash received to the value of work certified.

(*c*) **When the contract is almost complete**

If the contract is nearly completed and only a small portion of the work remains to be done, the cost of completing it should be estimated and added to the actual expenditure already incurred thereon. The total estimated cost will then be deducted from the contract price to calculate the estimated profit. Sometimes the estimated total cost includes a further provision for contingencies. Thus, like case (*b*), a portion of the estimated profit is to be credited to the Profit and Loss A/c, remaining a portion for guard against unforeseen circumstances.

The profit may be taken by adopting any one of the following formulae :

(*i*) $\text{Estimated Profit} \times \dfrac{\text{Value of Work Certified}}{\text{Contract Price}}$

(*ii*) $\text{Estimated Profit} \times \dfrac{\text{Value of Work Certified}}{\text{Contract Price}} \times \dfrac{\text{Cash Received}}{\text{Value of Work Certified}}$

$$= \text{Estimated Profit} \times \frac{\text{Cash Received}}{\text{Contract Price}}$$

(*iii*) $\text{Estimated Profit} \times \dfrac{\text{Cash of Work–to–date}}{\text{Estimated Total Cost}}$

(*iv*) $\text{Estimated Profit} \times \dfrac{\text{Cost of Work–to–date}}{\text{Estimated Total Cost}} \times \dfrac{\text{Cash Received}}{\text{Value of work Certified}}$

Loss of Incomplete Contract

If any contract suffers loss, that loss is to be charged to the Profit & Loss A/c. Again, if it is expected that there may arise a further loss before the completion of the contract, necessary provision should be made in the Profit & Loss A/c for such loss also.

Proforma for Contract Account

Contract A/c

Dr. (Rs.)				*Cr. (Rs.)*
To Material			By Material c/d	xx
Purchased	xx		By Bank Salvage Value	xx
Issued from stores	xx	xx	By P/L A/c (Loss on sale of material)	xx
To Direct Wages		xx	By Material transferred to other job	xx
To Outstanding Wages c/d		xx	By Plant transferred to other contract	xx
To Plant		xx	By Plant c/d	xx
To Plant hire charge		xx	By Cost c/d (balancing figure)	xx
To Subcontractor		xx		
To Direct Expenses		xx		
To Outstanding Expenses		xx		
To Share of General Overhead		xx		
To Sundry Expenses		xx		
To Profit & Loss A/c		xx		
Profit on Sale of Material		xx		
		xx		xx
To Cost b/d		xx	By Contractee A/c	
To Notional Profit c/d		xx	Value of certified Work	xx
(bal. figure)			By Uncertified Work c/d	xx
		xx		xxx
To Profit & Loss A/c		xx	By Notional Profit b/d	xx
To Profit Provision c/d		xx		
		xx		xx
To Material b/d		xx	By Profit Provision b/d	xx
To Plant b/d		xx	By Outstanding Wages b/d	xx
To Uncertified Work b/d		xx	By Outstanding Exp. b/d	xx

Illustration

From the following information prepare Contract A/c for the period ended 31.12.06 :
Cost incurred during the year :

	Rs.
Material Purchased	1,00,000
Material Returned	10,000
Material lost by the fire sold (Costing Rs. 5,000)	4,000
Material at Site on 31.12.06	15,000
Wages paid	28,000
Wages accrued	2,000
Direct expenditure paid	5,000

Share of General Overhead	2,500
Plant purchased	80,000
A piece of plant sold on 1.7.06 (costing Rs. 10,000)	11,000
Work certified	2,00,000
Cost of uncertified work	20,000
Value of contract	2,50,000
Rate of Depreciation	10%
Retention money	10%

Solution

Contract A/c for the period ended 31.12.06

Dr. (Rs.)			*Cr. (Rs.)*
To Material	1,00,000	By Material Returned	10,000
To Wages	28,000	By Bank Savage value	4,000
To Wages c/d	2,000	By Profit & Loss A/c	1,000
To Direct Expenditure	5,000	(Loss on material sold)	
To Share of general overhead	2,500	By Material c/d	15,000
To Plant	80,000	By Bank	11,000
To Profit & Loss A/c	1,500	Plant Sold	
Profit of plant sold		By Plant c/d	63,000
		By Cost c/d	1,15,000
	2,19,000		2,19,000
To cost b/d	1,15,000	By Contractee's A/c	2,00,000
		(Value of certified work)	
To Notional Profit c/d	1,05,000	By Uncertified work c/d	20,000
	2,20,000		2,20,000
To Profit & Loss A/c	63,000	By Notional Profit b/d	1,05,000
To Profit provision c/d	42,000		
	1,05,000		1,05,000
To Plant b/d	62,500	By Profit provision b/d	42,000
To Material b/d	15,000		
To Uncertified work c/d	20,000		

Workings :

(*i*) Calculation for closing balance of Plant

	Rs.
Cost of Plant	80,000
Less : Cost of Plant Sold	10,000
	70,000
Less : Dep. @ 10%	7,000
	63,000

(*ii*) Calculation for Profit on Sale of Plant

	Rs.
Cost of Plant Sold	10,000

Less :	Dep. from the date of sale (10% of Rs. 10,000 for 1/2 yr)	500
	W.D.V.	9,500
	Sale proceeds of Plant	11,000
Less :	W.D.V.	9,500
	Profit on Sale of Plant	1,500

(*iii*) Calculation for Profit to be charged to P/L

$$\frac{2}{3} \times 1{,}05{,}000 \times \frac{1{,}80{,}000}{2{,}00{,}000} = 63{,}000$$

WORKEDOUT PROBLEMS

Problem 1

A construction company undertook two contracts namely Contract No. 005 and Contract No. 052, on 1.1.06 and 1.7.06, respectively. On 31st December 2006, when the accounts were closed, the portion of the contracts were as follows :

	Contract No. 005	*Contract No. 052*
Contract Price	5,00,000	4,00,000
Material Purchased	1,50,000	90,000
Wages Paid	25,000	20,000
General Expenses	10,000	5,000
Material Transferred from 005 to 052	—	5,000
Plant Transferred at cost from 052 to 055 (on 31.12.06)	20,000	—
Wages accrued	5,000	—
Percentage of Cash received	90%	80%
Plant Purchased	1,00,000	1,00,000
Rate of Depreciation	10%	10%
Value of Material on hand	10,000	6,000
Cash received	2,25,000	1,60,000
Completed work not certified	12,000	6,000

The total establishment expenses incurred during the year amounted to Rs. 25,000. These are to be charged to the two contracts in proportion to wages.

Prepare the Contract A/cs.

Solution

Contract A/cs

Particulars	*Contract No. 005*	*Contract No. 052*	*Particulars*	*Contract No. 005*	*Contract No. 052*
To Material Purchased	1,50,000	90,000	By Contract 052		
To Wages	25,000	20,000	Material Transferred	5,000	—
To General Exp.	10,000	5,000	By Contract 005		
			Plant Transferred	—	20,000
To Contractor's Material			By Plant c/d	1,10,000	70,000
transferred	—	5,000	By Material c/d	10,000	6,000
To Contract 052			By Cost c/d	2,00,000	1,34,000

Plant Transferred	20,000				
To Wages c/d	5,000				
To Plant	1,00,000	1,00,000			
To Establishment Exp. (3 : 2)	15,000	10,000			
	3,25,000	2,30,000		3,25,000	2,30,000
To Cost b/d	2,00,000	1,34,000	By Contractee A/c	2,50,000	2,00,000
To Notional Profit c/d	62,000	72,000	Value of certified work		
			By Uncertified Work c/d	12,000	6,000
	2,62,000	2,06,000		2,62,000	2,06,000
To Profit & Loss A/c	37,200	38,400	By Notional Profit b/d	62,000	72,000
To Profit Provision c/d	24,800	33,600			
	62,000	72,000		62,000	72,000
To Plant b/d	1,10,000	70,000	By Wages b/d	5,000	—
To Material b/d	10,000	6,000	By Uncertified Work b/d	12,000	6,000
To Uncertified Work b/d	12,000	6,000			

Workings :

Calculation for Profit to be charged to P/L A/c.

(*a*) Contract No. 005 = $\frac{2}{3} \times \frac{2,25,000}{2,50,000} \times 62,000 = 37,200$

(*b*) Contract No. 052 = $\frac{2}{3} \times 72,000 \times \frac{1,60,000}{20,000} = 38,400$

Problem 2

M/s Pine Corporation undertook a contract for Rs. 2,40,000. You are requested to prepare the Contract A/c and Contractee's and Work-in-Progress A/c for the year ended 31st December 2006 from the following information :

Material purchased	30,000
Wages paid	50,000
Wages unpaid	10,000
Other charges	12,000
Plant purchased	20,000
Cash received	1,28,000
(Being 80% of work certified)	
Material lying at site on 31.12.06.	4,000
Plant at site on 31.12.06.	18,000

10% of value of material and 15% of wages may be considered as being incurred for the proportion of works completed but not certified. Other charges are charged as a proportion of direct wages.

Solution

M/S Pine Corporation Contract A/c for the year ended 31.12.06

Dr.			*Cr.*
	Rs.		*Rs.*
To Material	30,000	By Material c/d	4,000
To Wages	50,000	By Plant c/d	18,000
To Accrued Wages c/d	10,000	By Cost c/d	1,00,000
To other Charges	12,000		
To Plant	20,000		
	1,22,000		1,22,000
To Cost b/d	1,00,000	By Contractee's A/c Value of certified work $\left(1{,}28{,}000 \times \frac{100}{80}\right)$	1,60,000
To Notional Profit c/d	72,300	By Uncertified work c/d	12,300
	1,72,300		1,72,300
To Profit & Loss A/c	38,560	By Notional Profit b/d	72,300
To Profit provision c/d	33,740		
	72,300		72,300
To Material b/d	4,000	By Profit Provision b/d	33,740
To Plant b/d	18,000	By Accrued Wages b/d	10,000
To Uncertified work b/d	12,300		

Workings :

(*i*) Calculation for cost of uncertified work

	Rs.
Material (10% of Rs. 30,000)	3,000
Wages (15% of Rs. 50,000)	7,500
Other charges $\left(\frac{12{,}000}{50{,}000} \times 7{,}500\right)$	1,800
	12,300

(*ii*) Calculation for Profit to be charged to Profit & Loss A/c

$$\text{Profit to be charged} = \frac{2}{3} \times 72{,}300 \times \frac{1{,}28{,}000}{1{,}60{,}000} = 38{,}560$$

W.I.P A/c

Dr.			*Cr.*
To Contract A/c	*Rs*	By Contract A/c	*Rs.*
Value of Certified work	1,60,000	Profit provision	33,740
Cost of Uncertified work	12,300	By Bank/Cash	1,28,000
		By Balance c/d	10,560
	1,72,300		1,72,300

Problem 3

ABC Ltd. has undertaken to construct a building. The following particulars relate to the contract for the period ended 31st March 2007 :

	Rs.
Material Purchased	1,00,000
Material issued from stores	20,000
Wages paid	90,000
Plant	2,00,000
Direct expenses	7,000
Share of general overhead	4,000
Material lost by fire	1,000
Salvage value thereof	300
Outstanding wages	10,000
Outstanding expenses	1,000
Material at site on 31.3.07	2,000
Plant at site on 31.3.07	1,80,000
Value of certified work	3,18,000
Cost of uncertified work	9,000
Retention money	10%
Contract value	4,30,000

From the above information prepare the Contract Account, and the value of W.I.P., the Contractee A/c and show how the various items will appear in the Balance Sheet.

Solution

Contract A/c

Dr.			*Cr.*
To Material		By Bank (Salvage value)	300
Purchased	1,00,000		
Issued from stores	20,000	By Profit & Loss A/c (Loss on fire)	700
To Wages	90,000		
To Plant	2,00,000	By Material c/d	2,000
To Direct Expenses	7,000	By Plant c/d	1,80,000
To General Overhead	4,000	By Cost c/d (Bal. figure)	2,49,000
To Outstanding Wages c/d	10,000		
To Outstanding exp. c/d	1,000		
	4,32,000		4,32,000
To Cost b/d	2,49,000	By Contractee's A/c	3,18,000
To Notional Profit c/d	78,000	(Value of certified work)	
		By Uncertified Work c/d	9,000
	3,27,000		3,27,000
To Profit & Loss A/c	46,800	By Notional Profit c/d	78,000
To Profit Provision c/d	31,200		
	78,000		78,000
To Material c/d	2,000	By Profit Provision b/d	31,200
To Plant b/d	1,80,000	By Outstanding Wages b/d	10,000
To Uncertified Work b/d	9,000	By Outstanding Exp. b/d	1,000

Workings :

(*a*) Cash received = 3,18,000 – 10% of 3,18,000
= 3,18,000 – 31,800 = Rs. 2,86,200

(*b*) Profit Charged to Profit & Loss A/c

$$\frac{2}{3} \times \text{Notional Profit} \times \frac{\text{Cash received}}{\text{Work certified}}$$

$$\frac{2}{3} \times 78{,}000 \times \frac{2{,}86{,}200}{3{,}18{,}000} = \text{Rs. } 46{,}800$$

Statement showing Value of W.I.P.

	Rs.
Value of certified work	3,18,000
Add : Cost of uncertified work	9,000
	3,27,000
Less : Profit provision	31,200
	2,95,800
Less : Cash received	2,86,200
∴ Value of W.I.P.	9,600

Contractee's A/c

Dr.			*Cr.*
To Contract A/c	3,18,000	By Cash on Account	2,86,200
		By Balance c/d	31,800
	3,18,000		3,18,000

Balance Sheet (Extract form)
as at

Liabilities	*Rs.*	*Amount Rs.*	*Assets*	*Amount Rs.*
Profit & Loss A/c			Plant	1,80,000
Profit on contract	46,800		Material	2,000
Less : Loss on fire	700	46,100	W.I.P.	9,600
Outstanding Wages		10,000		
Outstanding Exp.		1,000		

Problem 4

Following is the trial balance of Basu & Das Co. :

Credit Balances	*Rs.*
Share Capital	7,20,000
Profit and Loss A/c	50,000
Provision for Dep. on Plant	1,20,000
Cash received on account of contract	25,60,000
Creditors	1,60,000
	36,10,000

Debit balances	*Rs.*
Building	1,56,000
Plant at cost	1,04,000
Bank balance	90,000
Material	12,00,000
Labour	16,60,000
Expenses	80,000
Plant for the contract	3,20,000
	36,10,000

The contract was started on 1.1.06. The contractee has paid Rs. 25,60,000 being 80% of work certified up to 31.12.06. The cost of work done but not certified is Rs. 32,000.

On 31.12.88 plant costing Rs. 64,000 were returned and material on site were Rs. 54,000. Depreciate all plants by $12\frac{1}{2}\%$ of cost and provide for outstanding wages Rs. 12,000.

You are required to prepare Contract A/c and Balance Sheet as at 31.12.06.

Solution

Contract A/c
for the year ended 31.12.06

Dr.			*Cr.*
To Material	12,00,000	By Material c/d	54,000
To Wages	16,60,000	By Plant returned $\left[64{,}000 \times \frac{25}{2} \times \frac{1}{100}\right]$	56,000
To Plant	3,20,000		
To Accrued Wages c/d	12,000	By Plant c/d working (i)	2,24,000
To Expenses	80,000	By Cost c/d	29,38,000
	32,72,000		32,72,000
To Cost b/d	29,38,000	By Contractee's A/c	32,00,000
To Notional Profit c/d	2,94,000	Value of certified work $\left[25{,}60{,}000 \times \frac{100}{80}\right]$	
		By Uncertified Work c/d	32,000
	32,32,000		32,32,000
To Profit & Loss A/c	1,56,800	By Notional Profit c/d	2,94,000
To Profit provision c/d	1,37,200		
	2,94,000		2,94,000
To Material c/d	54,000	By Profit Provision b/d	1,37,200
To Plant b/d	2,24,000	By Wages b/d	12,000
To Uncertified work b/d	32,000		

Workings :

(*i*) Calculation of Plant c/d

Plant Cost	3,20,000
Less : Return	64,000
	2,56,000
Less : Depreciation @ $12\frac{1}{2}\%$	32,000
	2,24,000

(*ii*) Calculation for Depreciation

	Rs.
Provision for Depreciation (Opening)	1,20,000
Add : Depreciation for Contract (32,000 × $12\frac{1}{2}$%)	40,000
Add : Depreciation for Other Plant	13,000
	1,73,000

(*iii*) Calculation for profit to be charged to Profit & Loss A/c

Profit to be charged to Profit & Loss A/c = $\frac{2}{3} \times 2{,}94{,}000 \times \frac{25{,}60{,}000}{32{,}00{,}000} = 1{,}56{,}800$

Calculation for value of W.I.P.

	Rs.
Value of Certified work	32,00,000
Cost of Uncertified work	32,000
	32,32,000
Less : Profit provision	1,37,200
	30,94,800
Less : Cash received	25,60,000
	5,34,800

Balance Sheet as on 31.12.06

Liabilities	*Amount*	*Assets*		*Amount*
Share Capital	7,20,000	Buildings		1,56,000
Reserves & Surplus :			Rs.	
Profit/Loss	1,93,800	Plant	1,04,000	
		Add : Addition	3,20,000	
			4,24,000	
		Less : Dep.	1,73,000	2,51,000
Current Liabilities :		**Current Assets :**		
Creditors	1,60,000	Materials		54,000
Outstanding Wages	12,000	W.I.P.		5,34,800
		Bank		90,000
	10,85,800			10,85,800

Calculation for Profit & Loss A/c

	Rs.
Balance as per trial balance	50,000
Add : Profit	1,56,800
	2,06,800
Less : Depreciation on Plant 1,04,000 @ $12\frac{1}{2}$%	13,000
	1,93,800

Calculation for Depreciation

	Rs.
Provision for Depreciation (Opening)	1,20,000
Depreciation for Contract 3,20,000 × $12\frac{1}{2}$%	40,000
Depreciation for other plant	13,000
	1,73,000

Problem 5

XYZ Construction Co. Ltd. supplied you the following information relating to a contract for Rs. 4,25,000 during the period ended 31.12.06 :

	Rs.
Opening material	10,000
Plant	1,20,000
Value of uncertified work	10,000
Expenses incurred during the period :	
Material purchased	1,40,000
Wages paid	30,000
Direct charges	20,000
General overhead	25,000
Material unused for the contract	6,000
Salvage value thereof	2,000
Sub-contract	10,000

Additional information :

(*i*) Accrued wages on 31.12.06	Rs. 800 expenses 1,000
(*ii*) Additional plant purchased	80,000
(*iii*) Rate of depreciation	15%
(*iv*) Value of works certified up to 15th December	3,00,000
(*v*) Retention money	10%
(*vi*) Material on site	2,000
(*vii*) Value of certified work includes profit & loss	25% on cost

Prepare a Contract A/c and find out the value of W.I.P.

Solution

Contract A/c
for the period ended 31.12.06

Dr.				*Cr.*
To Uncertified work b/d		10,000		
To Material b/d		10,000	By Bank	
To Material Purchased		1,40,000	(Salvage value)	2,000
To Wages paid		30,000	By Profit & Loss A/c	4,000
To Accrued wages c/d		800	(Loss on Material)	
To Direct Charges		20,000	By Material c/d	2,000
To Direct expenses c/d		1,000	By Plant c/d	1,70,000
To General overhead		25,000	(2,00,000 – 15% of 2,00,000)	
To Sub. Contract		10,000	By Cost c/d	2,58,800
	Rs.			
To Plant b/d	1,20,000			
Add : Additional Purchase	80,000			
		2,00,000		
		4,36,800		4,36,800
To Cost b/d		2,58,800	By Contractee A/c	
To Notional Profit c/d		60,000	Value of certified work	3,00,000
			Uncertified work c/d	18,800
		3,18,800		3,18,800

	Rs.		Rs.
To Profit & Loss A/c	36,000	By Notional Profit c/d	60,000
To Profit provision c/d	24,000		
	60,000		60,000
To Uncertified work b/d	18,800	By Profit provision b/d	24,000
To Plant b/d	1,70,000	By Accrued wages b/d	800
To Material b/d	2,000	By Direct expenses b/d	1,000

Workings :

(*i*) Calculation for cost of certified work

Profit of certified work = $\frac{1}{4}$ on cost = $\frac{1}{5}$ on contract value

∴ Profit on contract value on certified work = $\frac{1}{5} \times 3{,}00{,}000 = 60{,}000$

∴ Cost of certified work = (3,00,000 – 60,000) – 2,40,000.

	Rs.
Total cost up to date	2,58,800
Less : Cost of certified work	2,40,000
∴ Cost of uncertified work	18,800

(*ii*) Calculation for Cash received

Cash received = Value of certified work – 10% of value of certified work (as retention money is 10%).

= (3,00,000 – 10% of Rs. 3,00,000) = Rs. 2,70,000

(*iii*) Calculation for Profit to be charged to Profit & Loss A/c

Profit to be charged to P/L A/c = $\frac{2}{3}$ × Notional Profit × Cash received/Work certified

$= \frac{2}{3} \times 60{,}000 \times \frac{2{,}70{,}000}{3{,}00{,}000} = 36{,}000$

(*iv*) Calculation for value of W.I.P.

	Rs.	*Rs.*
Cost of uncertified work		18,800
Value of certified work		3,00,000
		3,18,800
Less : Profit provision	24,000	
Cash received	2,70,000	2,94,000
Value of W.I.P.		24,800

Problem 6

Sterling Construction obtained a contract for the building of an office for Rs. 3,00,000. Construction work commenced on 1st April 2006 and at the end of the financial year they received payment of Rs. 1,20,000 representing 80% of the amount of work certified.

The following information is available from the books of the contractors :

	Rs.
Materials issued	60,000
Materials on hand on 31.3.2007	2,500
Wages paid	80,000
Plant installed at site	60,000
Direct Expenses	11,000
Overheads allocated to this contract	5,500
Work finished but not yet certified at cost	5,000
Plant to be depreciated at 10%	

Prepare the contract account for the year ended 31.3.2007 and show your calculation of the amount adjusted to the credit of Profit & Loss Account. **[*B.Com., Madras*]**

Solution

Sterling Construction Contract Account
for the year ended 31st March 2007

Particulars	*Amount Rs.*	*Particulars*	*Amount Rs.*
To Materials	60,000	By Materials c/d	2,500
To Wages	80,000	By Cost of Contract c/d	1,60,000
To Direct Expenses	11,000		
To Depreciation on Plant (@ 10% of Rs. 60,000 *i.e.* Rs. $60,000 \times \frac{10}{100}$)	6,000		
To Overheads	5,500		
	1,62,500		1,62,500
To Cost of Contract b/d	1,60,000	By Contractee's A/c (Value of work certified)	1,50,000
		By Cost of work uncertified	5,000
		By Profit & Loss A/c (balancing figure)	5,000
	1,60,000		1,60,000
To Material b/d	2,500		

Note : As loss arises, there is no question of provision. The total loss should be transferred to Profit & Loss A/c.

Problem 7

The following figures are supplied to you by a contractor for the year ended on 31st Dec. 2006.

	Rs.
Contract Value	2,00,000
Work-in-Progress on 31.12.05	25,000
Wages	18,500
Material Purchased	16,000
Material issued from Stores	20,500
Working Expenses	11,500
Administrative exp.	12,500
(2,500 should be charged to Profit & Loss A/c)	
Plant	22,500
Material returned to suppliers	1,450
Material returned to stores	1,500
Cash received being 90% of certified work	99,000
Profit charged to Profit & Loss A/c	24,000
Material in hand on 31.12.06	10,000
Plant on hand on 31.12.06	12,500

Prepare a Contract A/c, Contractee A/c and extracted Balance Sheet.

Solution

Contract A/c

Dr.	*Rs.*		*Cr.* *Rs.*
To W.I.P. b/d	25,000	By Material returned to suppliers	1,450
To Material		By Material returned to stores	1,500
Rs.		By Plant c/d	12,500
Purchased 16,000		By Material c/d	10,000
Issued 20,500	36,500	By Cost c/d	98,550
To Wages	18,500		
To Working expenses	11,500		
To Administrative exp. (12,500 – 2,500)	10,000		
To Plant	22,500		
	1,24,000		1,24,000
To Cost b/d	98,550	By Contractee A/c Value of certified work $(99,000 \times \frac{10}{9})$	1,10,000
To Notional Profit c/d	40,000	By Uncertified work c/d (balancing figure)	28,550
	1,38,550		1,38,550
To Profit & Loss A/c	24,000	By Notional Profit b/d	40,000
To Profit Provision c/d	16,000		
	40,000		40,000
To Uncertified work b/d	28,550	By Profit Provision b/d	16,000
To Material b/d	10,000		
To Plant b/d	12,500		

Workings :

Calculation for Notional Profit

As contract value is Rs. 2,00,000 and value of certified work is Rs. 1,10,000 hence we can assume $\frac{2}{3}$ of Notional Profit in proportion of cash received to work certified should be charged to Profit & Loss A/c. Therefore we can write

$$24{,}000 = \frac{2}{3} \times \text{Notional Profit} \times \frac{99{,}000}{1{,}10{,}000}$$

$$\therefore \text{ Notional Profit} = \frac{24{,}000 \times 10}{6} = \text{Rs. } 40{,}000$$

Contractee A/c

To Contract	1,10,000	By Cash	99,000
		By Balance c/d	11,000
	1,10,000		1,10,000

Statement Showing Value of W.I.P.

		Rs.
Value of certified work		1,10,000
Cost of uncertified work		28,550
		1,38,550
Less : Profit Provision	Rs. 16,000	
Cash received	99,000	1,15,000
Value of W.I.P.		23,550

Balance Sheet (extracted) as at 31.12.06

Liabilities	*Amount* *Rs.*	*Assets*	*Amount* *Rs.*
Profit Provision	16,000	Plant	12,500
		Material	10,000
		W.I.P.	23,550

Problem 8

Petro Ltd. undertook a contract for Rs. 7,50,000 on 1st July 2006. On 30th June 2007 when the accounts were closed, the following information were available :

	Rs.
Materials Purchased	1,25,000
Wages paid	60,000
Overhead expenses paid	12,000
A part of Material (Costing Rs. 10,000) sold at	12,000
Plant Purchased	1,00,000
Plant transferred to another contract on 30th June 2007 (at a cost)	10,000
Cost of Plant damaged on 31st Dec. 2006	10,000
Damaged plant sold on 1.4.2007	7,500
Plant to be depreciated at	10%
All other expenses for Administration	12,000
Material on hand	10,000
Material sent to other contract	2,000
Sub-contractor	5,000
Value of works completed up to 22nd May when the architect's certificates had been issued	3,50,000
Works completed from 23rd May to 30th June	25,000
Cash received	80%

Prepare Contract A/c and find out the value of W.I.P.

Solution

Contract A/c
for the year ended on 30th June 2007.

Dr.	*Rs.*		*Cr.* *Rs.*
To Material	1,25,000	By Bank (Sale of Material)	12,000
To Wages	60,000	By Plant (Transferred to other contract)	10,000
To Overhead	12,000	By Bank (damaged plant sold)	7,500
To Administration & other Exp.	12,000	By Material c/d	10,000
To Sub-contractor	5,000	By Material sent to other contract	2,000
To P/L A/c (Profit on Sale on Material)	2,000	By P/L A/c (Loss on damaged plant)	2,000
To Plant	1,00,000	By Plant c/d	70,500
		By Cost c/d	2,02,000
	3,16,000		3,16,000
To Cost b/d	2,02,000	By Contractee's A/c (Value of certifite work)	3,50,000
To Notional Profit c/d	1,73,000	By Uncertified work c/d	25,000
	3,75,000		3,75,000
To Profit & Loss A/c	92,267	By Notional Profit b/d	1,73,000
To Profit provision c/d	80,733		
	1,73,000		1,73,000
To Material b/d		By Profit Provision b/d	80,733
To Plant b/d			
To Uncertified work b/d			

Workings :

(*i*) Calculation for Loss on sale of damaged plant

		Rs.
	Cost price of damaged plant	10,000
Less :	Depreciation @ 10% for 1/2 yr.	500
		9,500
Less :	Sale proceeds	7,500
		2,000

(*ii*) Calculation for closing balance of plant

		Rs.	*Rs.*
	Purchase price of Plant		1,00,000
Less :	Cost Price of Plant damaged	10,000	
	Plant Transferred	10,000	
Less :	Depreciation	9,500	
	(@ 10% on Rs. 90,000 for 1 yr. and Rs. 10,000 for 1/2 yr.)		29,500
			70,500

(*iii*) Calculation for profit to be charged to Profit & Loss A/c

$$\text{Profit to be charged} = \frac{2}{3} \times 1{,}73{,}000 \times \frac{2{,}80{,}000}{3{,}50{,}000}$$

$$= \text{Rs. } 92{,}267.$$

Problem 9

Calcutta Construction Ltd. undertook a contract for construction of a bridge on 1st July 1992. The contract price was Rs. 5,00,000. The company incurred the following expenses up to December 1992 :

	Rs.
Materials consumed	1,10,000
Wages	40,000
Direct expenses	20,000
Plant purchased on 1.1.92	1,00,000
Materials in hand	5,000
Depreciation 10% p.a. on plant.	

Charge other works expenses @20% of wages and office expenses @10% of works cost. The amount certified by the engineer was Rs. 3,00,000, retention money being 20% of the certified value.

Prepare the contract account showing therein the amount of profit that the company can reasonably take to its Profit and Loss Account. **[*C.U. B.Com. (Hons.)*]**

Solution

In the Books of
Calcutta Construction Ltd.
Contract Account
for the half-year ended 31.12.92

Dr. *Cr.*

Particulars	*Amount Rs.*	*Particulars*	*Amount Rs.*
To Materials Consumed	1,10,000	By Cost of Contract	2,01,300
To Wages	40,000		
To Direct Expenses	20,000		
To Works Expenses (20% of wages)	8,000		
To Depreciation on Plant (@ 10% p.a. for 6 months)	5,000		
Works Cost	1,83,000		
To Office Expenses (@ 10% of Works Cost)	18,300		
	2,01,300		2,01,300
To Cost of Contract	2,01,300	By Work-in-progress (value of work certified)	3,00,000
To Notional Profit c/d	98,700		
	3,00,000		3,00,000

To Profit & Loss A/c (Porportion of profit transferred)	52,640	By Notional Profit c/d	98,700
To Profit provision c/d	46,060		
	98,700	By Profit	98,700
To Materials b/d	5,000	Provision b/d	46,060
To Plant b/d (1,00,000 – 5,000)	95,000		

Workings :

(*i*) Depreciation on plant should be charged for six months as the contract started on 1st July 1992.

(*ii*) Calculation for profit to be charged to Profit & Loss A/c

Cash received = 80% of Rs. 3,00,000 = 2,40,000

$$\therefore \quad \text{Profit to be charged} = \frac{2}{3} \times 98{,}700 \times \frac{2{,}40{,}000}{3{,}00{,}000} = 52{,}640$$

Problem 10

From the following particulars in respect of a particular contract for the year ended 31st December 2006, prepare Contract Account :

	Rs.
Materials sent to site	1,90,000
Wages paid	1,20,000
Wages outstanding	5,500
Direct expenses	60,000
Establishment charges	52,000
Special Plant installed at cost	2,00,000
Cost of work not certified	25,000
Value of special plant on 31.12.06	1,70,000
Materials at site on 31.12.06	21,000
Total Contract Price	12,00,000
Cash received	5,94,000
Retention—10% of work certified	—
Sale of Scrap	2,000

General Plant costing Rs. 1,20,000 was used for 3 months, depreciation on that is to be provided at 15% p.a. [*C.U. B.Com. (Hons.) Adopted*]

Solution

Contract Account

for the year ended 31st December 2006

Dr. Particulars	Amount Rs.	Particulars	Cr. Amount Rs.
To Materials Sent to site	1,90,000	By Plant c/d	1,70,000
To Wages	1,20,000	By Materials c/d	21,000
To Outstanding wages c/d	5,500	By Bank—Sale of Scrap	2,000
To Direct Expenses	60,000	By Cost c/d	4,39,000
To Establishment charges	52,000		
To Special plant	2,00,000		
To Depreciation on general plant (@ 15% p.a. for 3 months)	4,500		
	6,32,000		6,32,000
To Cost b/d	4,39,000	By Contractee's A/c Work certified	6,60,000
To Notional Profit c/d	2,46,000	By Cost of work not certified c/d	25,000
	6,85,000		6,85,000
To Profit & Loss A/c	1,47,600	By Notional Profit b/d	2,46,000
To Profit provision c/d	98,400		
	2,46,000		2,46,000
To Plant b/d	1,70,000	By Profit provision b/d	98,400
To Material b/d	21,000	By Wages b/d	5,500
To Uncertified work b/d	25,000		

Problem 11

Mirik Construction Limited earned a contract to construct a building. The contract value is Rs. 6,50,000 to be realised in instalments on the basis of the value of work certified by the architect, subject to a retention of 10%. The work commenced on 1.4.88 but it remained incomplete on 31.12.88 when the final accounts are to be prepared.

The facts and figures of the contract are :

	Rs.
Plant charged to contract at the commencement	32,000
Materials charged to contract	1,80,000
Wages paid	87,000
Expenses incurred on the contract	38,750

Total establishment expenses amounted to Rs. 41,000 out of which 25% is attributable to this contract. Out of the materials issued to the contract, material costing Rs. 4,000 were sold for Rs. 5,000. A part of the plant (costing Rs. 2,000) was damaged on 1.10.88 and the scrap realised Rs. 300 only. Plant costing Rs. 3,000 was transferred to another contract site on 31.12.88.

Plant is to be depreciated @	10% p.a.
Materials in hand on 31.12.88	Rs. 17,500

Cash received from Contractee Rs. 3,06,000

Cost of work yet to be certified Rs. 30,000

Prepare Contract Account showing therein the amount of Profit or Loss to be transferred to Profit & Loss Account. **[*C.U. B.Com (Hons.) 1989*]**

Solution

In the Book of Mirik Construction Ltd.
Contract Account
for the year ended 31.12.88

Dr. *Cr.*

Particulars	*Amount* Rs.	*Particulars*	*Amount* Rs.
To Materials Charged	1,80,000	By Bank (materials sold)	5,000
To Wages	87,000	By Bank (Sale price of damaged Plant as Scrap)	300
To Expenses	38,750	By Plant (transferred to another contract)	2,775
To Establishment Expenses (25% of Rs. 41,000 *i.e.* $41{,}000 \times \frac{25}{100}$)	10,250	By Materials in hand c/d	17,500
To Profit & Loss A/c (Profit on materials sold *i.e.* Rs. 5,000 – Rs. 4,000)	1,000	By Plant c/d	24,975
To Plant charged to contract	32,000	By Cost of Contract c/d	2,98,450
	3,49,000		3,49,000
To Cost of contract b/d	2,98,450	By Contractee's (Work certified)	3,40,000
To Notional Profit c/d	71,550	By Cost of uncertified work c/d	30,000
	3,70,000		3,70,000
To Profit & Loss A/c	42,930	By Notional Profit b/d	71,550
To Profit provision c/d	28,620		
	71,550		71,550
To Material b/d	17,500	By Profit provision b/d	28,620
To Plant b/d	24,975		

Workings :

(*i*) Calculation for closing balance of Plant

	Rs.	Rs.
Plant purchased		32,000
Less : Cost of plant damaged	2,000	
Cost of plant transferred	3,000	5,000
		27,000
Less : Depreciation for 9 months $\left[27{,}000 \times \frac{10}{100} \times \frac{9}{12}\right]$		2,025
		24,975

(*ii*) Calculation for W.D.V. of plant transferred to another contract

	Rs.
Cost of Plant Transferred	3,000
Less : Depreciation for 9 months	225
	2,775

Problem 12

United Construction Company got a contract in January 1990 for construction of a Bridge. The contract price was Rs. 5,00,000. The Company incurred the following expenses up to 31.12.1990 :

	Rs.
Materials issued	1,10,000
Wages	40,000
Direct Expenses	20,000
Plant purchased on 30.6.90	1,00,000
Materials in hand	5,000
Cost of uncertified work	2,000

Depreciation to be charged on plant @ 10% per annum. Other works expenses to be charged @ 20% of wages and office expenses @ 10% of works cost.

The amount certified by the engineer up to 31.12.90 was Rs. 3,00,000, retention money being 20% of the certified value.

Prepare a Contract Account showing therein the amount of profit or loss to be transferred to Profit & Loss Account. **[*C.U. B.Com. (Hons.) 1991*]**

Solution

In the Books of United Construction Company
Contract A/c
for the year ended 31.12.90

Dr. *Cr.*

Particulars	*Amount* Rs.	*Particulars*	*Amount* Rs.
To Material	1,10,000	By Material c/d	5,000
To Wages	40,000	By Plant c/d [1,00,000—5,000]	95,000
To Direct expenses	20,000	By Cost c/d	1,95,800
To Plant	1,00,000		
To Other work expenses (20% of Rs. 40,000)	8,000		
To Office expenses (see Note)	17,800		
	2,95,800		2,95,800
To Cost b/d	1,95,800	By Contractee's A/c (Value of certified work)	3,00,000
To Notional Profit c/d	1,06,200	By Uncertified work c/d	2,000
	3,02,000		3,02,000

To Profit & Loss A/c	56,640	By Notional Profit b/d	1,06,200
To Profit Provision c/d	49,560		
	1,06,200		1,06,200
To Material b/d	5,000	By Profit Provision b/d	49,560
To Plant b/d	95,000		
To Uncertified work b/d	2,000		

Workings :

Calculation for office expenses :

		Rs.
	Material consumed (1,10,000 – 5,000)	1,05,000
	Wages	40,000
	Direct Expenses	20,000
	Prime Cost	1,65,000
Add :	Factory overhead :	
	Depreciation on plant	5,000
	Other work expenses	8,000
∴	Work Cost	1,78,000

∴ Office Expenses = 10% of Rs. 1,78,000
= Rs. 17,800

Problem 13

Mr. Sudhir undertook a contract for the construction of a building on 1st January 2006, the contract price being Rs. 7,50,000. The following details are available for the year 2006 :

	Rs.
Materials Purchased	1,20,000
Materials issued from stores	1,50,000
Labour employed on site	45,000
Plant installed on site	60,000
Direct expenses	30,000
Proportionate establishment charges	7,500
Cash received (80% of work certified)	3,00,000
Work uncertified	75,000
Materials returned to stores	7,500
Materials in hand at the end	3,000
Plant in hand at the end	45,000
Wages outstanding	9,000
Direct expenses accrued	12,000

Prepare the Contract Account and show the amount that would appear in the Balance Sheet.

[*B.Com. Andhra*]

Solution

Contract Account

Dr. Cr.

Particulars	Amount Rs.	Particulars	Amount Rs.
To Materials purchased	1,20,000	By Materials returned to stores	7,500
To Materials issued from stores	1,50,000	By Materials in hand at the end	3,000
To Labour	45,000	By Cost of Contract c/d	3,78,000
To Wages outstanding	9,000		
To Direct expenses	30,000		
To Direct expenses accrued	12,000		
To Depreciation on Plant (Rs. 60,000 – Rs. 45,000)	15,000		
To Establishment charges	7,500		
Total Cost	3,88,500		3,88,500
To Cost of Contract b/d	3,78,000	By Contractee's Account—value of work certified $\left[3,00,000 \times \frac{100}{80}\right]$	3,75,000
To Notional Profit c/d	72,000	By Cost of work uncertified c/d	75,000
	4,50,000		4,50,000
To Profit & Loss A/c	38,400	By Notional Profit b/d	72,000
To Profit Provision c/d	33,600		
	72,000		72,000
To Material b/d	3,000	By Profit provision b/d	33,600
To Plant b/d	45,000		

Balance Sheet as on 31.12.06

(*Extract*)

Liabilities	Amount Rs.	Amount Rs.	Assets	Amount Rs.	Amount Rs.
Wages outstanding		9,000	Materials in hand		3,000
Direct expenses accrued		12,000	Plant	60,000	
Profit & Loss A/c		38,400	*Less* : Depreciation	15,000	45,000
			Work-in-progress[2]		1,16,400

Workings :

(*i*) Profit to be charged to Profit & Loss A/c

$$\frac{2}{3} \times 72,000 \times \frac{3,00,000}{3,75,000} = \text{Rs. } 38,400.$$

(*ii*) Calculation for value of W.I.P.

	Rs.
Value of certified work	3,75,000

		Rs.
Add : Cost of uncertified work		75,000
		4,50,000
Less : Profit provision	33,600	
Cash received	3,00,000	3,33,600
Value of W.I.P.		1,16,400

Problem 14

Compute a conservative estimate of profit on a contract (which has been 80% complete) from the following particulars :

	Rs.
Total expenditure to date	8,50,000
Estimated further expenditure to complete the contract (including contingencies)	1,70,000
Contract Price	15,30,000
Works certified	10,00,000
Works not certified	85,000
Cash received	8,16,000

[*Adopted I.C.W.A.*]

Solution

		Rs.
Value of work certified		10,00,000
Work not certified		85,000
Total work done		10,85,000
Less : Total expenses		8,50,000
Notional Profit		2,35,000
Contract Price		15,30,000
Less : Uptodate expenses	Rs. 8,50,000	
Add : Further expenditure to complete the contract	Rs. 1,70,000	10,20,000
Estimated total profit		5,10,000

Problem 15

Rex Ltd. commenced a contract on 1.7.88, the total contract prices was Rs. 5,00,000, but Rex Ltd. accepted the same for Rs. 4,50,000. It was decided to estimate the total profit and to take to the credit of Profit & Loss A/c that portion of estimated profit on cash basis, which the work completed before to the total contract.

Actual expenditure till 31.12.88 and estimated expenditure in 1989 are :

Expenses	*Actual till 31.12.88* *Rs.*	*Estimated for 1989* *Rs.*
Material	75,000	1,30,000
Labour	55,000	60,000

Plant Purchased (Original Cost)	40,000	—
Misc. Expenses	20,000	35,500
Plant returned to stores on 31.12.88 at original cost	10,000	25,000 (as at 30.9.89)
Material at site	5,000	Nil
Work certified	2,00,000	Full
Work uncertified	7,500	Nil
Cash received	1,80,000	Full

The Plant is subject to annual depreciation @ 20% of original cost. The contract is likely to be completed on 30.9.89. It is the policy of the company to charge depreciation on time basis.

You are required to prepare the Contract A/c for the year ended 31.12.88.

[*C.A. (Inter) Nov. 1990*]

Solution

M/S Rex Ltd. Contract A/c
for the year ended 31.12.88

Dr. *Cr.*

Particulars	*Amount Rs.*	*Particulars*	*Amount Rs.*
To Material	75,000	By Plant Returned	10,000
To Labour	55,000	By Material c/d	5,000
To Plant	40,000	By Plant c/d (40,000 – 10,000 – 4,000)	26,000
To Misc. Expenses	20,000	By Cost c/d	1,49,000
	1,90,000		1,90,000
To Cost b/d	1,49,000	By Contractee's A/c	
		(Value of certified work)	2,00,000
To Notional Profit c/d	58,500	By Uncertified Bank c/d	7,500
	2,07,500		2,07,500
To Profit & Loss A/c	26,400	By Notional Profit b/d	58,500
To Profit Provision c/d	32,100		
	58,500		58,500

Workings :

(*i*) Calculation for Depreciation on plant

On Rs. 40,000 @ 20% for the period 1.7.88 to 31.12.88 *i.e.* for 1/2 yr.

$$= 40{,}000 \times \frac{20}{100} \times \frac{1}{2} = \text{Rs. } 4{,}000$$

On Rs. (40,000 – 10,000) @ 20% for 9 months *i.e.* 1.1.89 to 30.9.89

$$= 30{,}000 \times \frac{20}{100} \times \frac{9}{12} = \text{Rs. } 4{,}500$$

(*ii*) Calculation for Estimated Profit

	Rs.
Cost uptodate	1,49,000

		Rs.	
Add :	Estimated cost to complete the contract		
	Materials (5,000 + 1,30,000)	1,35,000	
	Misc. Exp.	35,500	
	Labours	60,000	
	Depreciation on plant	4,500	2,35,000
	Estimated Total Cost ....(1)		3,84,000
	Contract price ... (2)		4,50,000
∴	Estimated Profit (2 – 1)		66,000

(*iii*) Calculation for profit to be charged to Profit & Loss A/c

$$\text{Profit to be charged} = \text{Estimated profit} \times \frac{\text{Cash received}}{\text{Contract Price}}$$

$$= \frac{66{,}000 \times 1{,}80{,}000}{4{,}50{,}000} = \text{Rs. } 26{,}400.$$

Problem 16

M/s Manholes and Sewers Ltd. undertook a contract for erection of sewerage treatment plant for a municipality for a total value of Rs. 24 lakhs.

It was expected that the contract would be completed by 31st January 1989. You are required to prepare a Contract Account for the year ended 31st January 1988 from the following particulars :

(*i*) Wages Rs. 6,00,000
(*ii*) Special plant Rs. 2,00,000
(*iii*) Materials Rs. 3,00,000
(*iv*) Overheads Rs. 1,20,000
(*v*) Depreciation @ 10% to be provided on plant.
(*vi*) Materials lying at the site on 31.1.1988 Rs. 40,000.
(*vii*) Work certified was to the extent of Rs. 16,00,000 and 80% of the same was received in cash.
(*viii*) 5% of the value of material issued and 6% of wages may be taken to have been incurred for the portion of work completed but not yet certified.
(*ix*) Overheads are charged as a percentage of direct wages.
(*x*) Ignore depreciation on plant for use on uncertified portion of the work.
(*xi*) Ascertain the amount to be transferred to Profit & Loss Account on the basis of realised profit. **[*I.C.W.A. Inter*]**

Solution

In the books of M/s Manholes and Sewers Ltd.

Contract Account

Dr. *Cr.*

Particulars	*Amount* Rs.	*Particulars*	*Amount* Rs.
To Material	3,00,000	By Materials at site c/d	40,000
To Wages	6,00,000	By Plant at site	
		(Cost less depreciation @ 10%) c/d	1,80,000
To Special Plant	2,00,000	By Cost c/d	10,00,000
To Overheads	1,20,000		
	12,20,000		12,20,000

	Rs.		Rs.
To Cost b/d	10,00,000	By Contractee's A/c value of certified work	16,00,000
To Notional Profit c/d	6,58,200	By Uncertified work c/d	58,200
	16,58,200		16,58,200
To Profit & Loss A/c (Profit transferred)	3,51,040	By Notional Profit b/d	6,58,200
To Profit Provision c/d (balancing figure)	3,07,160		
	6,58,200		6,58,200
To Material b/d	40,000	By Profit provision b/d	3,07,160
To Plant b/d	1,80,000		
To Uncertified work b/d	58,200		

Workings :

(*i*) Calculation for cost of uncertified work

	Rs.
Materials (5% of Rs. 3,00,000)	15,000
Wages (6% of Rs. 6,00,000)	36,000
Overhead $\left(\frac{1,20,000}{6,00,000} \times 36,000\right)$	7,200
	58,200

(*ii*) Calculation for Profit to be charged to Profit & Loss A/c

$$\frac{2}{3} \times 6,58,200 \times \frac{12,80,000}{16,00,000} = \text{Rs. } 3,51,040$$

Problem 17

Workout the Contract Account from the following information. The terms of the contract are Rs. 20 per sq. ft. of the covered floor area built and certified as correct by the engineer of the contractee.

Building materials at start of the work Rs. 10,000.

Purchases of materials during the contract work :

(*a*) Cement 900 bags at Rs. 100 per bag.

(*b*) Bricks 10,000 at Rs. 1,000 per 1,000 bricks

(*c*) Sand 1,000 cft. at Rs. 200 per 10 cft.

(*d*) Woodwork 900 cft. Rs. 20 per cft.

The value of materials on hand on completion of work Rs. 20,000.

Labour :

100 masons at Rs. 7 each per day for 40 days.

500 coolies at Rs. 2 each per day for 40 days.

Tools and Plants :

Two new concrete mixers were purchased at the commencement of the work costing Rs. 10,000 each. The residual value of each of these after completion would be Rs. 3,500 each.

Supervision :

50% of the 4 engineers' pay at Rs. 500 per month each for two months.

50% of the 10 overseers' pay at Rs. 250 per month each for four months.

Administration Overheads :

20% of the head-office expenses for the period of the contract. The head office expenses were Rs. 5,000.

Quantity of work done :

15,000 sq. ft. of the covered floor area certified as correct by the contractee.

[*B.Com. Mysore*]

Solution

Contract A/c

Dr. Particulars	Amount Rs.	Particulars	*Cr.* Amount Rs.
To Material b/d (Cost of Material at the start of work)	10,000	By Material c/d	20,000
To Purchase of cement (900 × Rs. 100)	90,000	By Concrete Mixer c/d (3,500 × 2)	7,000
To Purchase of brick (10,000 × Re. 1)	10,000	By Cost c/d	2,17,000
To Purchase of sand (1,000 × Rs. 20)	20,000		
To Purchase of Wood (900 × Rs. 20)	18,000		
To Labour			
For Mansons (100 × 7 × 40)	28,000		
For Coolies (500 × 2 × 40)	40,000		
To Concrete mixure (2 × Rs. 10,000)	20,000		
To Supervision Exp.			
For Engineers $\left[\frac{1}{2}\times 4\times \text{Rs. } 500\times 2\right]$	2,000		
For Overseers $\left[\frac{1}{2}\times 10\times 250\times 4\right]$	5,000		
To Administration overhead (20% of Rs. 5,000)	1,000		
	2,44,000		2,44,000
To Cost b/d	2,17,000	By Contractee's A/c value of certified work $(15{,}000\times 20)$	3,00,000
To Notional Profit c/d	83,000		
	3,00,000		3,00,000
To Profit & Loss A/c $\left[\frac{2}{3}\times 83{,}000\right]$	55,333	By Notional Profit b/d	83,000
To Profit provision c/d	27,667		
	83,000		83,000
To Material b/d	20,000	By Profit provision b/d	27,667
To Plant b/d	7,000		

Note : (1) In absence of Cash received or retention money in the problem, 2/3rd of Notional Profit being charged to Profit & Loss A/c.

(2) It is assumed more than 50% of contract is completed.

Problem 18

Mr. Bhagwan Das undertook a contract for Rs. 15,00,000 on an arrangement that 80% of the value of the work done, as certified by the architect of the contractee, should be paid immediately and that the remaining 20% be retained until the contract was completed.

In 1990 the amounts expended were : Materials Rs. 1,80,000; Wages Rs. 1,70,000; Carriage Rs. 6,000; Cartage Rs. 1,000; Sundry Expenses Rs. 3,000; The work was certified for Rs. 3,75,000 and 80% of this was paid as agreed.

In 1991 the amounts expended were : Materials Rs. 2,20,000; Wages Rs. 2,30,000; Carriage Rs. 23,000; Cartage Rs. 2,000; Sundry Expenses Rs. 4,000. Three-fourths of the contract was certified as done by 31st December and 80% of this was received accordingly. The value of unused stock and work-in-progress uncertified was ascertained at Rs. 20,000.

In 1992 the amounts expended were : Materials Rs. 1,26,000; Wages Rs. 1,70,000; Cartage Rs. 6,000; Sundry Expenses Rs. 3,000 and on 30th June the whole contract was completed.

Show how the contract account and also contractee's account would appear, each of these years, in the books of the contractor assuming that the balance due to him was paid on completion of the contract. **[*M.Com. Raj. University—Adopted*]**

Solution

Contract A/c

Dr. *Cr.*

Particulars	*Amount* Rs.	*Particulars*	*Amount* Rs.
1990		1990	
To Materials	1,80,000	By Work-in-progress	3,75,000
To Wages	1,70,000	(value of work certified)	
To Carriage	6,000		
To Cartage	1,000		
To Sundry Expenses	3,000		
To Notional Profit c/d (balancing figure)	15,000		
	3,75,000		3,75,000
To Profit & Loss A/c	4,000	By Notional Profit b/d	15,000
To Profit Provision c/d	11,000		
	15,000		15,000
1991		1991	
To Work-in-progress		By Work-in-progress (value of	
(3,75,000—11,000)	3,64,000	work certified (3/4 × 15,00,000)	11,25,000
To Materials	2,20,000	By Cost of work uncertified c/d	20,000
To Wages	2,30,000		
To Carriage	23,000		
To Cartage	2,000		
To Sundry Expenses	4,000		
To Notional Profit c/d (balancing figure)	3,02,000		
	11,45,000		11,45,000

	Rs.		Rs.
To Profit & Loss A/c	1,61,067	By Notional Profit b/d	3,02,000
To Profit provision c/d	1,40,933		
	3,02,000		3,02,000
1992		1992	
To Work-in-progress (11,45,000 – 1,40,933)	10,04,067	By Contractee's A/c	15,00,000
To Materials	1,26,000		
To Wages	1,70,000		
To Cartage	6,000		
To Sundry Expenses	3,000		
To Profit & Loss A/c	1,90,933		
	15,00,000		15,00,000

Contractee's Account

	Rs.		Rs.
1990		1990	
To Balance c/d	3,00,000	By Bank A/c	3,00,000
1991		1991	
To Balance c/d	9,00,000	By Balance b/d	3,00,000
		By Bank A/c	6,00,000
	9,00,000		9,00,000
1992		1992	
To Contract A/c	15,00,000	By Balance b/d	9,00,000
		By Bank A/c	6,00,000
	15,00,000		15,00,000

Workings :

Calculation for profit to be charged to Profit & Loss A/c

1990 Profit to be charged to Profit & Loss A/c

$$= \frac{1}{3} \times 15,000 \times \frac{3,00,000}{3,75,000} = \text{Rs. } 4,000$$

1991 Profit to be charged to Profit & Loss A/c

$$= \frac{2}{3} \times 3,02,000 \times \frac{80}{100} = \text{Rs. } 1,61,067$$

1992 Profit to be charged to Profit & Loss A/c

= The whole amount as the contract was completed.

Problem 19

M/s J. Das, contractors, undertook a contract for Rs. 4 lakhs on 1st January 2005. The following expenses were incurred up to 31st December 2005 :

	Rs.
Materials issued from stores	35,000
Materials charged direct	5,000
Direct charges	2,000
Wages	20,000

The amount of work certified was Rs. 80,000 of which the contractors receive 75% in each.

The transactions for 2006 are :

Material issued from stores	90,000
Wages	40,000
Direct charges	4,000

The cost of plant issued on 1st January 2006 was Rs. 80,000. Further, work certified amounted to Rs. 2,20,000, 75% of which was received, work done and not certified valued at Rs. 15,000. Plant is to be depreciated 25% per annum on the original cost. Material on site valued at Rs. 10,000.

The contract was completed on 31st January 2007 up to which date the following expenses were incurred :

	Rs.
Material issued	40,000
Material charged direct	7,000
Wages	15,000
Direct charges	1,350

The General Reserve on cost each year to be taken at 5% of the amount of material consumed and wages paid during the year. The Plant on 31st January 1985 was valued at Rs. 50,000. The material at site were sold at Rs. 7,000 and those returned to store amounted to Rs. 13,000.

Prepare Contract Account and Contractee's Account showing the result of the transactions assuming that the balance due from the contractee was duly received.

Solution

Contract Account
for the year ending 31.12.2005

Dr. *Cr.*

Particulars	*Amount Rs.*	*Particulars*	*Amount Rs.*
To Materials issued from stores	35,000	By Cost of contract c/d	65,000
To Materials charged direct	5,000		
To Wages	20,000		
To Direct charges	2,000		
To General Reserve on cost (5% of material wages)	3,000		
	65,000		65,000
To Cost of contract b/d	65,000	By Contractee's A/c Value of work certified	80,000
To P & L A/c (Profit taken)	Nil		
To Profit Provision c/d	15,000		
	80,000		80,000

Note. As the contract is at initial stage it is wise not to charge any amount of Profit to Profit & Loss A/c. So the whole amount of Notional Profit is Transferred to Profit Provision A/c.

Solution

Contract Account
for the year ending 31.12.2006

Dr. Particulars		Amount Rs.	*Cr.* Particulars	Amount Rs.
To Materials		90,000	By Profit in suspense b/d	15,000
To Wages		40,000	By Materials on site	10,000
To Direct Charges		4,000	By Cost of Contract c/d	1,35,000
To Depreciation of Plant (25% on Rs. 80,000)		20,000		
To General Reserve (5% of Materials and Wages)				
i.e. 5% of Rs. 90,000	4,500			
Wages *i.e.* 5% of (40,000 – 10,000)	1,500	6,000		
		1,60,000		1,60,000
To Cost of Contract b/d		1,35,000	By Contractee's Account (Value of work certified)	2,20,000
To Profit & Loss Account (Profit taken)		50,000		
To Profit in suspense c/d		50,000	By Cost of work not certified	15,000
		2,35,000		2,35,000

Contractee's A/c

Dr. Particulars	Amount Rs.	*Cr.* Particulars	Amount Rs.
31.12.05		31.12.05	
To Contract A/c	80,000	By Bank	
		(Cash paid relating to certified work)	60,000
		By Balance c/d	20,000
	80,000		80,000
1.1.06		31.12.06	
To Balance b/d	20,000	By Bank	1,65,000
31.12.06		By Balance c/d	75,000
To Contract A/c	2,20,000		
	2,40,000		2,40,000
1.1.07		31.12.07	
To Balance b/d	75,000	By Bank	1,75,000
To Contract A/c	1,00,000		
	1,75,000		1,75,000

Contract A/c
for the year ended 31.12.06

Dr. Particulars	Amount Rs.	Particulars	*Cr.* Amount Rs.
To Cost of uncertified work b/d	15,000	By Profit provision b/d	50,000
To Material b/d	10,000	By Bank Material sold	7,000
To Material issued	40,000	By Material Returned	13,000
To Material directly charged	7,000	Plant c/d	50,000
To Wages	15,000	By Cost c/d	30,950
To Direct charges	1,350		
To General Reserve (5% on cost = 5% on Wages & Material = 5% on Rs. 57,000 + 15,000 – 7,000 – 13,000)	2,600		
To Plant b/d (80,000 – 20,000)	60,000		
	1,50,950		1,50,950
To Cost b/d	30,950	By Contractee's A/c (value of certified work)	1,00,000
To P/L A/c	69,050		
	1,00,000		1,00,000

Calculation of Value of certified work in the year ended 31.12.06

		Rs.	Rs.
	Total value of contract		4,00,000
Less :	Value of work certified in 2005	80,000	
	Value of work certified in 2006	2,20,000	3,00,000
	Value of W.I.P. for 1985		1,00,000

Problem 20

Das Gupta Engineering Co. Ltd. secured a contract on 1.1.05 for a sum of Rs. 7,50,000. The Contract should be completed within 31.3.07.

The following expenses were incurred up to 31.12.05.

	Rs.
Material issued from stores	75,000
Material transferred from other work	5,000
Wages	20,000
Direct Expenses	15,000
Plant Purchased	1,00,000
Material on hand on 31.12.05	5,000
Plant on hand on 31.12.05	90,000

The amount of work certified Rs. 1,25,000 and cash received @ 75% of work certified.

The transaction for the period ended 31.12.06 was as follows :

	Rs.
Material Purchased	2,90,000
Material lost by fire	1,000
Salvage value thereon	250
Wages paid	50,000
Direct Expenses	20,000

Subcontractor fees	1,00,000
Additional Plant Purchased on 1.1.06	30,000
Rate of depreciation	10%
Material on site on 31.12.06	10,000
Works completed and certified	5,80,000
Value of uncertified work	10,000
Retention money	20%

The company estimated that the following expenditure would be required to complete the contract. The expenditures are :

(*i*) The residual value of plant would be Rs. 80,000.
(*ii*) The wages and direct expenses would be Rs. 20,000 and 10,000, respectively.
(*iii*) 3% of the total cost of the contract should be provided for contingencies.
(*iv*) The cost of material that should be purchased Rs. 15,000.

Prepare Contract Account for the period ended 31.12.05 and 31.12.06.

Solution

Contract Account
for the year ended 31.12.05

Dr. *Cr.*

Particulars	*Amount Rs.*	*Particulars*	*Amount Rs.*
To Material		By Material c/d	5,000
Issued from stores	75,000	By Plant c/d	90,000
Transferred from other works	5,000	By Cost c/d	1,20,000
To Wages	20,000		
To Direct Expenses	15,000		
To Plant	1,00,000		
	2,15,000		2,15,000
To Cost b/d	1,20,000	By Contractee A/c	
To Notional Profit c/d	5,000	(Value of certified work)	1,25,000
	1,25,000		1,25,000
To Profit & Loss A/c	Nil	By Notional Profit b/d	5,000
To Profit Provision c/d	5,000		
	5,000		5,000

Note : As the amount of certified work is only Rs. 1,25,000 *i.e.,* less than 25% of the contract value of 7,50,000, no profit on certified work should be transfered to Profit & Loss A/c.

Contract A/c
for the year ended 31.12.06

Dr. *Cr.*

Particulars	*Amount Rs.*	*Particulars*	*Amount Rs.*
To Balance b/d		By Bank (Salvage value)	250
Material	5,000	By Profit & Loss A/c Loss on fire	750
Plant	90,000	By Plant c/d	
		(1,20,000 – 10% of 1,20,000)	1,08,000
To Material Purchased	2,90,000	By Material c/d	10,000
To Wages	50,000	By Cost c/d	4,66,000
To Direct Expenses	20,000		
To Additional Plant	30,000		
To Sub-contractor fees	1,00,00		
	5,85,000		5,85,000

	Rs.		Rs.
To Cost b/d	4,66,000	By Contractee A/c (value of certified work)	5,80,000
To Notional Profit c/d	1,24,000	By Uncertified work c/d	10,000
	5,90,000		5,90,000
To Profit & Loss A/c	68,891	By Notional Profit b/d	1,24,000
To Profit provision c/d	55,109		
	1,24,000		1,24,000
To Material b/d	10,000	By Profit provision b/d	54,933
To Plant b/d	1,08,000		

Workings :

(*i*) Calculation for Estimated Cost

			Rs.
	Cost up to date as per Contract A/c on 31.12.06.		4,66,000
Add :	Additional cost required :	*Rs.*	
	Material (10,000 + 15,000)	25,000	
	Plant (1,08,000 – 80,000)	28,000	
	Wages	20,000	
	Direct expenses	10,000	83,000
			5,49,000
Add :	Contingency (3% of Rs. 5,49,000)		16,470
	Estimated Cost		5,65,470

(*ii*) Calculation for Estimated Profit

	Contract Value	7,50,000
Less :	Estimated Cost	5,65,470
	Estimated Profit	1,84,530

(*iii*) Calculation for profit to be charged to Profit & Loss A/c

$$\text{Profit to be charged} = \text{Estimated Profit} \times \frac{\text{Cash received}}{\text{Contract value}}$$

$$= 1{,}84{,}530 \times \frac{2{,}80{,}000}{7{,}50{,}000} = \text{Rs. } 68{,}891$$

Problem 21

A contractor secured a contract for the sum of Rs. 1,50,000. An agreement was made with him regarding the contract, that he was to receive payment from time to time equal to 90% of the certified work.

He started the work on January 1, 1991 and incurred the following expenses during the year : Material—20,000, Plant and Tools—20,000, Wages—15,000, Sundry Charges—10,000, Establishment charges—5,000.

A part of plant costing Rs. 5,000 was unsuitable to the contract and was sold immediately at a profit of Rs. 1,000. The value of plant and machinery on 31.12.91 was Rs. 10,000 and material was Rs. 5,000; up to 31.12.91 he had received Rs. 90,000. The value of uncertified work was Rs. 10,000.

In order to calculate the profits made on the contract up to 31.12.91, the contractor estimated the further expenditure that would be incurred in completing the contract and profit to be charged to Profit & Loss A/c for the year ended in proportion of the estimated net profit.

He estimated :

(*a*) that the contract would be completed within next three months.

(*b*) that plant and tools would have a residual value of Rs. 1,000 upon the completion of the contract.

(*c*) that the wages and material for the next three months would be Rs. 3,000 and 5,000 respectively.

(*d*) The establishment expenses would be increased by 10% p.a..

(*e*) 5% of contract value should be considered as contingency.

Prepare the Contract A/c.

Solution

Contract A/c

Dr. *Cr.*

Particulars	*Amount* *Rs.*	*Particulars*	*Amount* *Rs.*
To Material	20,000	By Bank (sale of Plant)	6,000
To Plant & Tools	20,000	By Plant c/d	10,000
To Wages	15,000	By Material c/d	5,000
To Sundry Charges	10,000	By Cost c/d	50,000
To Establishment Charges	5,000		
To Profit & Loss A/c (Profit on sale of plant)	1,000		
	71,000		71,000
To Cost b/d	50,000	By Contractee A/c Value of certified work $\left(90,000 \times \frac{100}{90}\right)$	1,00,000
To Notional Profit c/d	60,000	By Uncertified work c/d	10,000
	1,10,000		1,10,000
To Profit & Loss A/c	41,475	By Notional Profit b/d	60,000
To Profit Provision c/d	18,525		
	60,000		60,000
To Plant b/d	10,000	By Profit Provision b/d	18,525
To Material b/d	5,000		
To Uncertified work b/d	10,000		

Workings :

(*i*) Calculation for Estimated Total cost

		Rs.
	Cost uptodate	50,000
Add :	Cost to be incurred to complete the contract	
	Plant & Tools (10,000 – 1,000)	9,000
	Material (5,000 + 5,000)	10,000
	Wages	3,000

	Establishment Expenses	
	$(5{,}000 + 10\%$ of $5{,}000) \times \frac{3}{2}$	1,375
	Contingency (5% of Rs. 1,50,000)	7,500
	Estimated Total Cost	80,875

(*ii*) Calculation for Estimated Profit

		Rs.
	Value of Contract	1,50,000
Less :	Estimated Cost	80,875
	Estimated Profit	69,125

(*iii*) Calculation for Profit to be charged to Profit & Loss

$$\text{Profit to be charged} = \text{Estimated Profit} \times \frac{\text{Cash received}}{\text{Contract value}}$$

$$= 69{,}125 \times \frac{90{,}000}{1{,}50{,}000} = \text{Rs. } 41{,}475$$

Problem 22

M/s Tom and Dick, obtained a contract to build quarters. The price being Rs. 1,00,000. Work was started on 1st April 1990 and the following expenditure was incurred :

	Rs.
Plant	5,000
Stores	18,000
Wages	16,250
Sundry Expenses	1,325
Establishment Charges	2,925

A part of the material was unsuitable and was sold for Rs. 3,625 (cost being Rs. 3,000). A portion of plant was scraped and disposed of for Rs. 575.

The value of plant on 31st March 1991 was Rs. 1,550 and of stores Rs. 850. Cash received on account was Rs. 35,000, representing 80% of the work certified. The work uncertified was valued at Rs. 5,475 and this was certified later for Rs. 6,250.

M/s Tom and Dick decided to estimate that further expenditure would be incurred in completing the contract to compute from this estimate and the expenditure already incurred, the total profit that would be made on the contract and to take to credit of Profit & Loss A/c for the year 1990-91, that portion of the total which corresponded to the work certified on 31.3.91.

Their estimate reveals that contract would be completed after 9 months, till then wages likely to be incurred Rs. 17,875. The cost of stores etc. required, in addition to those in stock on 31.3.91, would be Rs. 17,150, and that further contract expenses would amount to Rs. 1,500. A further investment of Rs. 6,250 would be required on Plant which would be valuing on 31.12.91 at Rs. 750. The establishment charges would be same on monthly bases, as in the preceding year. Lastly, $2\frac{1}{2}\%$ of the total cost of contract should be kept as reserve for contingencies.

Prepare Contract, Stores and Plant Accounts for the year ended 31st March 1991, and also show your calculation of the amount credited to Profit & Loss A/c for the year.

[*C.A. (Final) England, Adopted*]

Solution

Contract Account
for the year ended 31.3.91

Dr. *Cr.*

Particulars	*Amount* Rs.	*Particulars*	*Amount* Rs.
To Material—issued from Stores	18,000	By Material c/d	850
To Wages	16,250	By Bank, (Material sold)	3,625
To Plant	5,000	By Bank (Plant sold)	575
To Sundry Expenses	1,325	By Plant c/d	1,550
To Establishment Expenses	2,925	By Cost c/d	37,525
To Profit & Loss A/c (Profit on Sales of Material)	625		
	44,125		44,125
To Cost b/d	37,525	By Contractee's A/c (value of certified work) [35,000 × $\frac{100}{80}$]	43,750
To Notional Profit c/d	11,700	By Uncertified work c/d	5,475
	49,225		49,225
To Profit & Loss A/c	6,014	By Notional Profit b/d	11,700
To Profit Provision c/d	5,686		
	11,700		11,700
To Plant b/d	1,550	By Profit Provision b/d	5,683
To Material b/d	850		

Workings :

(*i*) Calculation for Estimated Cost

		Rs.	*Rs.*
	Cost uptodate		37,525
Add :	Further Cost required		
	Material (850 + 17,150)	18,000	
	Plant (1,550 + 6,250 – 750)	7,050	
	Wages	17,875	
	Contract Expenses	1,500	
	Establishment Expenses	2,194	46,619
		Total Cost	84,149
Add :	Contingency ($2\frac{1}{2}$%)		2,104
	Estimated Total Cost		86,253

(*ii*) Calculation for Estimated Profit

		Rs.
	Value of Contract	1,00,000
Less :	Estimated Cost	86,253
	Estimated Profit	13,747

(*iii*) Calculation for Profit to be charged to Profit & Loss A/c

$$\text{Estimated Profit} \times \frac{\text{Value of certified work}}{\text{Value of contract}}$$

$$= 13{,}747 \times \frac{43{,}750}{1{,}00{,}000} = \text{Rs. } 6{,}014 \text{ (Approx.)}$$

CONTRACT WITH ESCALATOR CLAUSE

Problem 23

XYZ Ltd. obtained a contract for Rs. 7,50,000 on 1.1.06. At the end of the year the following information were collected :

	Rs.
Material purchased	1,50,000
Wages paid	62,000
Wages due but not paid	5,500
General expenses	15,000
Plant purchased	70,000
Cost of Installation	5,000
Share of Head Office expenses	2,000
Material on hand (31.12.06)	35,000
Rate of depreciation	10%
Work certified	3,00,000
Works uncertified	22,500
Cash received	75% of work certified

The above contract contained an escalator clause :

"In the event of price of raw material and rates of wages increased more than 10%, the contract price would be increased accordingly by 25% of the rise in the cost of materials and wages beyond 10% in each case."

It was found that since the date of signing of the contract the price of material and rate of wages increased by 25%. The value of the work certified should not be considered in the effect of escalator clause.

Solution

Contract Account

Dr. *Cr.*

Particulars	*Amount Rs.*	*Particulars*	*Amount Rs.*
To Material	1,50,000	By Material c/d	35,000
To Wages paid	62,000	By Plant c/d (75,000 – 7,500)	67,500
To Accrued Wages c/d	5,500	By Cost c/d	2,07,000
To General Expenses	15,000		
To Share of Head Office Expense	2,000		
To Plant (70,000 + 5,000)	75,000		
	3,09,500		3,09,500

To Cost b/d	2,07,000	By Contractee's A/c (Value of certified work)	3,00,000
To Notional Profit c/d	1,24,200	By Uncertified work c/d	22,500
		By Escalation of Contract Price	8,700
	3,31,200		3,31,200
To Profit & Loss A/c	62,100	By Notional Profit b/d	1,24,200
To Profit provision c/d	62,100		
	1,24,200		1,24,200
To Material b/d	35,000	By Profit provision b/d	62,100
To Plant b/d	67,500		

Workings :

(*i*) Calculation for the amount of Contract Price increased due to Escalation Clause.

Name of Expenses	*Total* $\left(\frac{Actual \times 25}{125}\right)$	*Up to 10%* ($\frac{1}{5}$*th of total)*	*Beyond 10%* *(4/5 of total)*
Material	$\frac{1{,}50{,}000 \times 25}{125} = 30{,}000$	6,000	24,000
Wages (62,000 + 5,000)	$\frac{67{,}500 \times 25}{125} = 13{,}500$	2,700	10,800
Total	43,500	8,700	34,800

As the wages and material cost increased by Rs. 34,800 beyond escalation clause the contract price will be increased by 25% of Rs. 34,800 = 8,700.

(*ii*) Calculation for Profit to be charged to Profit & Loss A/c

$$= \frac{2}{3} \times 1{,}24{,}200 \times \frac{2{,}25{,}000}{3{,}00{,}000} = \frac{2}{3} \times 1{,}24{,}200 \times \frac{3}{4} = 62{,}100.$$

Problem 24

Modern Construction Co. with a paid up share capital of Rs. 50 lakhs undertook a contract to construct LIG houses. The contract work commenced on 1.1.95 and the contract price was Rs. 50 lakhs. Cash received on account of contract on 31.12.95 was Rs. 18 lakhs (90% of the work certified). Work completed but not certified was estimated at Rs. 1,00,000. As on 31.12.95, material at site was estimated at Rs. 30,000 and machinery at site costing to Rs. 2,00,000 was returned to stores. Plant and machinery at site is to be depreciated at 5%. Wages outstanding on 31.12.95 was Rs. 5,000.

The following were ledger balance (*Dr*) as per Trial Balance as on 31.12.95 :

Land and Building	Rs. 15,00,000
Plant and Machinery at cost (60% at site)	Rs. 25,00,000
Lorries and other vehicles	Rs. 8,00,000
Furniture	Rs. 50,000
Office Equipment	Rs. 10,000
Materials sent to site	Rs. 14,00,000
Fuel and Power	Rs. 1,25,000
Site Expenses	Rs. 5,000

Postage and Telegrams	Rs. 4,000
Office Expenses	Rs. 8,000
Rates and Taxes	Rs. 15,000
Cash at Bank	Rs. 1,33,000
Wages	Rs. 2,50,000

Prepare a Contract Account to ascertain the profit from the contract and show the W.I.P. in the balance sheet. *[I.C.W.A. (Inter)]*

Solution

In order to solve the problem, it is advisable to prepare a Trial Balance.

Trial Balance as on 31.12.95

Particulars	*Debit* *Rs.*	*Credit* *Rs.*
Paid up Share Capital		50,00,000
Cash received (90% of work certified)		18,00,000
Land and Buildings	15,00,000	
Machinery at cost	25,00,000	
Lorries and Vehicles	8,00,000	
Furniture	50,000	
Office Equipments	10,000	
Materials sent to site	14,00,000	
Fuel and Power	1,25,000	
Site Expenses	5,000	
Postage and Telegrams	4,000	
Office Expenses	8,000	
Rates and Taxes	15,000	
Cash at Bank	1,33,000	
Wages	2,50,000	
	68,00,000	68,00,000

Contract A/c for the year ended 31.12.95

Dr. *Cr.*

Particulars	*Rs.*	*Rs,*	*Particulars*	*Rs.*	*Rs.*
To Material	14,00,000		By Work-in-progress :		
Less Unused	30,000	13,70,000	Certified	20,00,000	
To Wages	2,50,000		Uncertified	1,00,000	21,00,000
Add : Outstanding	5,000	2,55,000			
To Site Expenses		5,000			
To Postage etc.		4,000			
To Fuel and Power		1,25,000			
To Office Expenses		8,000			
To Rates and Taxes		15,000			
To Depreciation on Plant and Machine $\left(\frac{60}{100} \times 25{,}00{,}000\right) \times 5\%$		75,000			

	Rs.		Rs.
To Profit c/d	2,43,000		
	21,00,000		21,00,000
		By Profit b/d	2,43,000
To Profit and Loss A/c transferred $\left(\frac{1}{3}\times\frac{90}{100}\times 2{,}43{,}000\right)$	72,900		
To Reserve—transferred to W.I.P.	1,70,000		
	2,43,000		2,43,000

Balance Sheet as at 31.12.95

Liabilities	*Rs.*	*Rs.*	*Assets*	*Rs.*	*Rs.*
Paid up Capital		50,00,000	Land and Buildings		15,00,000
Profit and Loss A/c		72,900	Plant and Machinery	25,00,000	
Outstanding Wages		5,000	*Less* : Depreciation	75,000	24,25,000
			Lorries and Vehicles		8,00,000
			Furniture		50,000
			Office Equipment		10,000
			Materials at site		30,000
			Work-in-progess		1,29,900
			Cash at Bank		1,33,000
		50,77,900			50,77,900

Working for Work in Progress :

	Rs.
Work in Progress (Total)	21,00,000
Less : Cash received	18,00,000
	3,00,000
Less : Profit transferred to W.I.P.	1,70,100
Transferred to Balance Sheet	1,29,900

Problem 25

The following particulars relate to a contract undertaken by a firm of engineers :

	Rs.
Material Consumed	65,000
Labour	24,000
Plant at cost	15,000
Direct Expenses	3,000
Establishment Charges	4,000
Materials Returned to Stores	500
Cash received (in respect of 80% of work certified)	1,00,000
Cost of work uncertified	4,500
Materials in hand (31st December)	1,800
Wages outstanding	2,500
Value of Plant (31st December)	10,000
The contract price was agreed at	2,00,000

Prepare Contract Account showing profit to be taken to the credit of Profit and Loss Account in the books of the contractor. **[*C.U. B.Com. (Hons.) 1994*]**

Solution

Contract A/c
for the period ended 31st Dec.

Dr. Particulars	Rs.	Particulars	*Cr.* Rs.
To Material Consumed	65,000	By Material return	500
To Labour	24,000	By Material c/d	1,800
To Plant at Cost	15,000	By Plant c/d	10,000
To Direct Expenses	3,000	By Cost c/d	1,01,200
To Establishment Charges	4,000		
To Wages outstanding c/d	2,500		
	1,13,500		1,13,500
To Cost b/d	1,01,200	By Contractee's A/c (Value of certified work) $\left[1,00,000 \times \frac{100}{80}\right]$	1,25,000
To Notional Profit c/d	28,300	By Uncertified work c/d	4,500
	1,29,500		1,29,500
To Profit and Loss A/c	15,093	By Notional Profit b/d	28,300
To Profit Provision c/d	13,207		
	28,300		28,300
To Material b/d	1,800	By Profit provision b/d	13,207
To Plant b/d	10,000	By Wages outstanding b/d	2,500
To Uncertified work	4,500		

Working :

Amount to be charged to Profit and Loss A/c

$$= \frac{2}{3} \times 28,300 \times \frac{1,00,000}{1,25,000} = \frac{45,280}{3} = \text{Rs. } 15,093.$$

Problem 26

One of the building contracts, currently engaged in by a construction company, commence[d] 15 months ago and remains unfinished. The following information relating to the work on the contrac[t] has been prepared for the year just ended :

	Rs. ('000)
Contract price	2,500
Value of work certified at the end of year	2,200
Cost of work certified at the end of year	40
Costs incurred :	
Opening balances	
Cost of work completed	300
Materials at site (Physical stock)	10
During the year :	
Materials delivered to site	610

Wages	580
Hire of Plant	110
Other expenses	90
Closing balance	
Materials at site (Physical stock)	20

As soon as materials are delivered to the site, they are charged to the contract account. A record is also kept of materials as they are actually used on the contract. Periodically a stock check is made and any discrepancy between book stock and physical stock is transferred to a general contract material discrepancy account. This is absorbed back to each contract, currently at the rate of 0·5% of material booked. The stock check at the year end revealed a stock shortage of Rs. 5,000.

In addition to the direct charges listed above, general overheads are charged to contract at 5% of the value of work certified. General overheads of Rs. 15,000 had been absorbed into the cost of work completed at the beginning of the year.

It has been estimated that further costs to complete the contract will be Rs. 2,20,000. This estimate includes the cost of materials on site at the end of the year just finished and also a provision for rectification.

Required :

(*a*) Determine the profitability of the above contract and recommend how much profit (to the nearest Rs. '000) should be taken for the year ended. (Provide a detailed schedule of costs).

(*b*) State how your recommendation in (a) would be affected if the contract price was Rs. 40,00,000 (rather than Rs. 25,00,000) and if no estimate has been made of costs to completion. (If required, suitable assumptions should be made). **(I.C.W.A. Inter, Nov. 1995)**

Solution

(*a*) **Schedule showing Cost and Profit to be taken to Profit and Loss A/c.**

Particulars	*Rs. '000*	*Rs. '000*
Cost of work already completed (Opening balance)		300
Material consumed :		
Opening balance	10	
Add : Material delivered during the year	610	
	620	
Less : Closing balance	20	
	600	
Less : Stock shortage	5	595
Wages		580
Hire of plant		110
Other expenses		90
Stock discrepancy (0·5% of 595)		3
General Overhead :		
5% of work certified	110	
Less : Overhead in Opening Balance	15	95
		1,773
Add : Further cost to complete the work		220
Estimated cost		1,993
Contract Price		2,500
Estimated Profit (2,500 – 1993)		507

Profit to be taken to costing P & L A/c.

= Estimated Profit × Cost of work to date/Estimated total cost.

= Rs. 5,07,000 × Rs. 17,73,000/Rs. 19,93,000 = Rs. 4,51,034.

(*b*) When the contract price happens to be Rs. 40,00,000 and the nature of work certified happens to be Rs. 22,00,000, it means that the stage of completion is only a little more than 50%. Supposing that cash received to work certified is 80%.

Notional Profit will be :

Value of work certified + cost of work not certified – Cost of contract to date

= Rs. 22,00,000 + 40,000 – 17,73,000 = Rs. 4,67,000.

Profit to be taken to Profit and Loss A/c :

$$= \frac{2}{3} \times \text{Notional Profit} \times (\text{Cost received/Work certified})$$

$$= \frac{2}{3} \times \text{Rs. } 4{,}67{,}000 \times \frac{80}{100} = \text{Rs. } 2{,}49{,}067 \text{ (or Rs. } 2{,}49{,}000.)$$

Problem 27

MNP Construction Ltd. commenced a contract on April 1, 1999. The total contract was for Rs. 17,50,000. It was decided to estimate the total profit and to take to the credit of P & L A/c. the proportion of estimated profit on cash basis, which work completed bore to the total contract. Actual expenditure in 1999-2000 and estimated expenditure in 2000-2001 :

	1999-2000 (Actual)	2000-2001 (Estimated)
	Rs.	*Rs.*
Materials issued	3,00,000	5,50,000
Labour : Paid	2,00,000	2,50,000
Outstanding at end	20,000	30,000
Plant purchased	1,50,000	—
Expenses : Paid	75,000	1,50,000
Prepaid at end	15,000	
Plant returned to store	50,000	1,00,000
(historical cost)		(on Dec. 31, 2000)
Material at site	20,000	50,000
Work certified	8,00,000	Full
Work uncertified	25,000	—
Cash received	6,00,000	Full

The Plant is subject to annual depreciation @ 25% of WDV cost. The contract is likely to be completed on December 31, 2000.

Prepare the Contract A/c. Determine the profit on the Contract for the year 1999-2000 on prudent basis, which has to be credited to P & L A/c.

[*C.A. Inter (h) May 2000*]

Solution

MNP Construction Ltd.
Contract Account (1 April 1999 to 31 March 2000)

Dr. *Cr.*

Particulars	*Rs.*	*Amount* *Rs.*	*Particulars*	*Amount* *Rs.*
To Materials issued		3,00,000	By Plant returned to stores (Note 1)	37,500
To Labour paid	2,00,000		By Materials at site	20,000
Add : Outstanding	20,000	2,20,000		
To Plant purchased		1,50,000	By Work certified	8,00,000
To Expenses paid			By Work uncertified	25,000
	75,000			
Less : Prepaid	15,000	60,000		
Notional Profit c/d		2,27,500	By Plant at site (Note 2)	75,000
		9,57,500		9,57,500
To Profit & Loss A/c (Note 4)		66,321	By Notional Profit c/d	2,27,500
To Work-in-Progress A/c		1,61,179		
		2,27,500		2,27,500

MNP Construction Ltd.
Contract Account
(For computing estimated profit)

Dr. *Cr.*

Particulars	*Amount* *Rs.*	*Particulars*	*Amount* *Rs.*
To Materials used (Rs. 3,00,000 + Rs. 5,50,000)	8,50,000·00	By Material at site	50,000·00
To Labour (Rs. 2,00,000 + 2,50,000 + 30,000)	4,80,000·00	By Plant returned to store on 31 March 99	37,500·00
By Plant purchased	1,50,000·00	By Plant returned to store on 31 Dec. 2000 (Note 3)	60,937·50
To Expenses (75,000 + 1,50,000)	2,25,000·00	By Contractor A/c.	17,50,000·00
To Estimated Profit	1,93,437·50		
	18,98,437·50		18,98,437·50

Workings :

(*i*) Value of Plant returned to store on 31 March 2000 :

	Rs.
Historical cost of plant returned	50,000
Less : Depreciation at 25% for 1 year	12,500
Value of Plant returned to store on 31 March 2000	37,500

(*ii*) Value of Plant at site

Historical cost	1,00,000
Less : Depreciation at 25% for 1 year	25,000
	75,000

(*iii*) Value of Plant returned to store on 31 December 2000

Value of Plant on 31 March 2000	75,000·00
Less : Depreciation at 25% for 9 months	14,062·50
(Rs. 75,000 × $(\frac{25}{100}) \times \frac{9}{12})$	
	60,937·50

(*iv*) Profit to be credited to P & L A/c on 31 March 2000 for the contract likely to be completed on 31 December 2000.

Estimated Profit × Cash received/Work certified × Work certified/Total Contract price = Rs. 1,93,437·50 × Rs. 6,00,000/Rs. 8,00,000 × Rs. 8,00,000/Rs. 17,50,000 = Rs. 66,321·43.

Problem 28

Rina, a contractor got a contract to supply 100 wooden dolls per day to M/s R. K. Mitra & Co. The cost of holding a doll is Rs. 2 p.a. and the set-up cost of production is Rs. 3. Assume there are 300 working days in a year.

What would be the optimum run size for unit manufacture ?

Solution

We know optimum run size

$$\text{or} \quad EBQ = \sqrt{\frac{2AS}{C}}$$

where A = Annual production units
= 100 × 300 = 30,000
S = Setting cost per unit = Rs. 3
C = Carrying cost per unit = Rs. 2

$$\therefore \quad EBQ = \sqrt{\frac{2 \times 30{,}000 \times 3}{2}} = 300 \text{ units}$$

Problem 29

Saha & Bose Ltd. has made a contract with Mitra & Das Ltd. to supply 4,800 T.V. sets per annum.

It is estimated that the carrying cost per T.V. per annum will be Rs. 10 and that the set-up cost per batch is Rs. 648. Find out :

(*a*) Economic Batch Quantity.

(*b*) The time interval between two consecutive optimum runs.

(*c*) The minimum inventory holding cost.

Solution

$$(a)\ EBQ = \sqrt{\frac{2AS}{C}} = \sqrt{\frac{2 \times 4{,}800 \times 648}{12}}$$

$$= \sqrt{2 \times 4{,}800 \times 54} = 720$$

(*b*) Time interval between two consecutive optimum runs

$$= \frac{365}{\text{No. of set-up per annum}}$$

Again, No. of set-up per annum $= \frac{\text{Annual Production}}{\text{EBQ}}$

$$= \frac{4{,}800}{720} = \frac{20}{3}$$

∴ Time interval between two consecutive optimum runs

$$= \frac{365}{\frac{20}{3}} = \frac{365 \times 3}{20}$$

$$= \frac{1{,}095}{20} = 54{\cdot}75 \text{ days} = 55 \text{ days}$$

(*c*) Minimum inventory holding cost per annum

$$\frac{720}{2} \times 12 = \text{Rs. } 4{,}320$$

EXERCISES

JOB, CONTRACT, BATCH COSTING

1. *State which of the following statements are correct or incorrect* :

(*i*) In contract costing credit is taken only for a part of the profit on incomplete contracts.
(*ii*) Escalation clause in a contract provides that the contract price is fixed.
(*iii*) Final contract price is to be paid is certain in cost plus contract.
(*iv*) In contract plus costing, the contract runs â risk of incurring loss.
(*v*) Most of the items of cost are direct in contract costing than in job costing.
(*vi*) Contract costing is a basic method of specific order costing.

Ans. Correct : (*i*), (*v*), (*vi*)
Incorrect : (*ii*), (*iii*), (*iv*).

2. *Which of the following is correct ?*

A. An essential of long-term costing is that :
(*i*) It has a duration in excess of twelve calendar months.
(*ii*) It is a progress at a financial year-end and has a significant effect on the activity of the contractor for the period under review.
(*iii*) Its completion will require a number of stages, each of which must be certified and valued for profit calculation purpose.
(*iv*) It has a duration in excess of six calendar months.

B. A debit balance on the contractee account should be incorporated in the balance sheet as :
(*i*) A current liability as 'contract balances outstanding'.
(*ii*) Set-off against contract stock valuation.
(*iii*) Excess payments on account not set off against contract stock value.
(*iv*) In debtors as 'amount recoverable on contract'.

C. Retention monies are best defined as :
(*i*) Cash withheld by the contractee in order to improve the cash flow of the contractor.
(*ii*) Payment to the contractor, where it is desired to secure his services for a future contract.
(*iii*) Cash return to the contractee if actual profits on a contract are 10% higher than an agreed figure.
(*iv*) Cash withheld by the contractee under the terms of the contract when payment of the value certified are being made.

D. A zero value of attributable profit should be assumed where :
(*i*) Any foreseeable loss is estimated for a later stage in the contract.
(*ii*) The interim estimated profit is less than 10% of value certified.
(*iii*) The profit outcome of the contract cannot be estimated with reasonable certainty.
(*iv*) The contract is less than 60% completed.

E. Which of the following is the most appropriate definition of turnover at intermediate stage in a contract ?

(*i*) The value of work done which leaves the agreed attributable profit when the cost of work certified is subtracted from it.

(*ii*) Cost of work certified to date plus estimated profit to the end of the contract.

(*iii*) The value of work certified less any foreseeable losses.

(*iv*) Cost of work to date minus the cost of work not certified plus estimated profit to date.

F. Foreseeable losses estimated for a contract should be treated in which of the following ways ?

(*i*) Ignore until they are known to be accurate with reasonable certainty.

(*ii*) Write off immediately that they are estimated.

(*iii*) Write off in the same proportion as any estimated profits are recognised.

(*iv*) Write-up only if the work to which they relate is 50% completed.

Ans. A (*i*), B (*iv*), C (*iv*), D (*iii*), E (*i*), F (*ii*).

THEORETICAL QUESTIONS

(*a*) Job and Batch Costing

1. Explain Job Costing and Batch Costing. **[*I.C.W.A (I) D, 1985*]**
2. What is Job Costing ? In which type of industries this systems would be suitable ? Give a specimen of cost sheet. **[*I.C.W.A (Int) J, 1986*]**
3. How do you distinguish Job Costing from Process Costing ? **[*C.U. B.Com. (H) 1987*]**

(*b*) Contract Costing

1. What are the basic types of contract jobs ? Explain them briefly.
2. What are the advantages and disadvantages of Cost-Plus-Profit Contract jobs ?
3. In what different ways the Plant & Machinery used for contract jobs are to be treated in Contract Accounts ?
4. Why profits on incomplete contract jobs need be taken into account ?
5. What are the general rules for the computation of 'Notional Profit' on an incomplete contract ?
6. Write short notes on : (*i*) Escalation Clause (*ii*) De-escalation Clause and (*iii*) Value of W.I.P. on an Incomplete Contract.
7. Discuss the treatment of "Profit On Incompleted Contracts" in Contract A/c.

[*I.C.W.A. (I) June 89; C.U. B.Com. (H) 1981*]

PROBLEMS

1. Saha & Roy Co. is a construction concern. It took a contract at an agreed value of Rs. 1,50,000. Following are the information relating to the period ended 31.3.92 :

	Rs.
Material issued from stores	20,000
Wages paid	40,000
Material lost by the fire (costing Rs. 5,000)—salvage value thereon	3,000
Plant & Machinery purchased	25,000
Overhead Expenses	2,000
Carriage & other charges	5,000
Share of general overhead	2,000
Cash received (80% of certified work)	64,000
Cost of uncertified work	10,000
Material at site on 31.3.92	5,000
Plant site on 31.3.92	20,000

Prepare (*i*) Contract A/c (*ii*) Contractee's A/c.

[Ans. Notional Profit = Rs. 26,000; Profit charged to Profit & Loss A/c = Rs. 13,867; Contractee's A/c Bal. = 16,000]

2. XYZ Ltd. undertook a contract for the construction of College building on 1.1.89 at a contract price of Rs. 4,00,000. Following information are gathered at the end of the year 1989 :

	Rs.
Materials Purchased	1,00,000
Material issued from stores	15,000
Material returned to suppliers	5,000
Wages paid	40,000
Wages due but not paid	5,000
Advance payment to subcontractors	5,000
Payment to subcontractor	25,000
Overhead expenses	5,000
Plant purchased	40,000
Depreciation on plant	10%
Material at site on 31.12.89	10,000
Value of certified work	2,00,000
Retention money	10%
Cost of uncertified work	25,000

Prepare Contract A/c for the year ended 31.12.89.

[Ans. Notional Profit = Rs. 51,000; Net profit charged to Profit & Loss = Rs. 30,600]

3. B. Ltd. made a contract with A. Ltd. to build an office building at Burdwan. The work commenced at the site on 1st Sept. 1991. During the period ended on 31st August 1992 the expenditure on the contract was as follows :

	Rs.
Material purchased on credit	1,40,350
Material issued from stores	47,055
Direct expenses	30,745
Wages paid	90,000
Accrued wages	2,465
Other expenses	10,780
Plant Purchase on 1.9.91	60,900
Material at site on 31.8.92	10,820
Outstanding direct expenses	2,075
Payment to creditors for material	80,000

B. Ltd. received Rs. 3,20,850 which represents the amount of certified work completed up to 20 July 1992. The work completed but not certified yet to the extent of Rs. 25,000.

The following relevant information are also available :

(*a*) The plant has an effective life of 5 years with no residual value.

(*b*) Retention money 10%.

You are required :

(*i*) to prepare a Contract A/c.

(*ii*) W.I.P. A/c.

[Ans. (*i*) Notional Profit = Rs. 56,670; Cost of contract = Rs. 3,24,830, Profit credit to Profit & Loss A/c = Rs. 34,002; (*ii*) Value of W.I.P. = Rs. 37,982]

4. Ram and Rahim made a joint venture for construction of a small bridge at a contract price of Rs. 5,00,000. They incurred the following expenses during the period ended 31.12.91 :

	Rs.
Materials Purchased	1,50,000
Labour payment	40,000
Mixer machine purchased	20,000

Transport expenses paid	20,000
Paid to Supervisor	12,000
Paid for Godown rent	8,000
Share of general overhead	2,000

Additional information relating to the contract for the above period :

	Rs.
Material on site at the end	20,000
Material sold (at a profit of Rs. 1,000)	6,000
Mixer machine at the end	15,000
Cost of works completed from the period 21st Nov. to 31st Dec. 1991	10,000
Works completed and certified up to 21st Nov. 1991	2,00,000
Cash received	1,80,000

Prepare Contract A/c and find out the value of W.I.P.

[Ans. Loss charged to Profit & Loss Rs. 2,000; Value of W.I.P. = Rs. 30,000]

5. On 1.1.89 M. Construction Co. Ltd. made a contract with P.Q. Ltd. for construction of a factory building. The contract price is Rs. 4,50,000. The work should be completed within 31.12.91. The following figures are collected at the end of 31.12.89 :

	Rs.
Materials Purchased	1,20,000
Materials lost in transit	20,000
Materials issued from stores	5,000
Wages paid	40,000
Wages paid in advance	5,000
Insurance premium due but not paid	2,500
Overhead paid	10,000
Sundry charges	5,000
Plant purchased	60,000
A piece of plant damaged on 1.7.89 (Costing Rs. 5,000) sold	1,250
A plant costing Rs. 6,000 transferred to other contract on 1.10.91	
Cash received being 80% of work certified	1,80,000
Cost of uncertified work	20,000
Rate of Depreciation	10%
Material at site	20,000

Prepare : (*i*) Contract A/c (*ii*) Plant A/c (*iii*) Contractee's A/c (*iv*) Extracted Balance Sheet.

[Ans. Profit charged to Profit & Loss A/c = Rs. 54,347; Plant A/c Bal= Rs.44,100]

6. A building contractor undertook to construct a building for which the following details are supplied :

Construction Started	1.1.90
Total Contract price	5,00,000
Raw material supplied	1,00,000
Direct Labour cost	60,000
Other Expenses	5,000
Plant installed at site (at cost)	80,000
Proportionate overhead expenses	20,000
Material in hand at end	2,000
Expenses incurred but not paid	1,000
Value of work certified	2,50,000
Work not yer certified	10,000
Cash received from contractee	2,00,000

Prepare Contract A/c for the year ending on 31.12.90 by transferring reasonable profit to Profit & Loss A/c after adjusting depreciation on plant @ 20% p.a. *[C.U. B.Com. (Hons.)]*

[Ans. Notional Profit = Rs. 60,000; Profit Transferred to Profit & Loss A/c = Rs. 32,000]

7. Calcutta Construction Ltd. undertook a contract for construction of a bridge on 1st July 1991. The contract price was Rs. 5,00,000. The company incurred the following expenses up to December 1991 :

	Rs.
Materials consumed	1,10,000
Wages	40,000
Direct expenses	20,000
Plant purchased on 1.1.91	1,00,000
Material on hand	5,000

Depreciation 10% p.a. on plant. Charge other works expenses @ 20% of wages and office expenses @ 10% on work cost.

The amount certified by the engineer was Rs. 3,00,000; retention money being 20% of the certified value.

Prepare the Contract A/c showing the amount of profit that the company can reasonably take to its Profit & Loss A/c. *[C.U. B.Com. (Hons.)]*

[Ans. Cost of Contract Rs. 2,01,300; Notional Profit = 98,700; Profit charged to Profit & Loss A/c = Rs. 52,640]

[**Hint.** As material consumed is given, hence there is no need for adjustment of closing stock of material.]

8. The following particulars relate to a contract undertaken by a firm of engineers :

	Rs.
Materials consumed	65,000
Labour	24,000
Plant at cost	15,000
Direct expenses	3,000
Establishment charges	4,000
Materials returned to Stores	500
Cash received (in respect of 80% of work certified)	1,00,000
Cost of work uncertified	4,500
Materials in hand (31st December)	1,800
Wages outstanding	2,500
Value of plant (31st December)	10,000

The contract price was agreed at Rs. 2,00,000.

Prepare Contract Account showing profit to be taken to the credit of Profit & Loss Account in the books of the contractor. *[C.U. B.Com. (H) 1994]*

[Ans. Accounting profit Rs. 26,000; Profit transferred to P/L A/c Rs. 13,867]

Note : Value of materials consumed Rs. 65,000 has been given in the problem which may be debited to the Contract A/c without requiring any further adjustment for materials in hand or returned to stores.

Alternatively, materials sent to contract Rs. 58,300 (Rs. 56,000 + Rs. 500 + Rs. 1,800) may be debited to the Contract A/c and materials returned to stores and materials in hand credited to the Contract A/c.

9. Deluxe Limited undertook a contract for Rs. 5,00,000 on 1st January 1997. The company furnishes the following details for the year ended 31st December 1997 :

	Rs.
Materials consumed	1,65,000
Direct expenses	5,000
Wages	30,000
Materials returned to stores	5,000
Materials stolen from site	10,000
Insurance claim admitted	6,000
Other works expenses @20% on wages	
Office expenses @ 10% on Works Cost	
Materials in hand on 31st December 1997	15,000
Cash received to the extent of 90% of works certified	2,70,000
Cost of work uncertified	11,000

Plant sent to site cost Rs. 60,000 with a scrap value of Rs. 10,000 and a useful life of 5 years. The plant was used in the contract for 146 days.

Prepare Contract Account showing therein the cost of materials issued to site and the amount of profit or loss to be transferred to the Profit & Loss Account.

Show the value of work-in-progress separately. [*C.U. B.Com. (H) (1998)*]

[Ans. Accounting Profit Rs. 80,000; Profit transferred to P/L A/c Rs. 48,000; Cost of materials issued to site Rs. 1,95,000; Office expenses Rs. 21,000; Depreciation on plant Rs. 4,000]

10. P. Ltd. has supplied the following information in respect of an incomplete contract as on 31.3.99 :

	Contract A	*Contract B*
	Rs.	Rs.
Contract price	2,40,000	1,50,000
Work certified	2,16,000	1,00,000
Estimated cost of completion of contract	2,10,000	1,20,000
Cash received	1,60,000	80,000
Uncertified work	10,000	7,000
Cost of contract (expenditure incurred up to 31.3.99)	1,80,000	95,000

Calculate the profit to be carried to P/L A/c for the year ended 31.3.99. [*C.U. B.Com. (H) (2000)*]

[Ans. Contract *A* Rs. 20,000; Contract *B* Rs. 16,000]

11. A firm of Building Contractors undertook a contract for Rs. 3,00,000. The following particulars are furnished for the year ended 31st March 2001 :

	Rs.
Materials :	
Direct Purchase	50,000
Issued from stores	10,000
Wages for labour	40,000
General Plant in use :	
Written-down value	90,000
Depreciation thereon	10,000
Direct expenses	2,500
Sub-contract charges	6,000
Share of general overhead	2,000
Materials in hand on 31.3.2001	2,000
Materials lost by fire	500
Salvage value thereof	150
Wages accrued on 31.3.2001	6,000
Direct expenses accrued on 31.3.2001	1,000
Cash received (90% of work certified)	1,62,000
Cost of uncertified work	5,000

Prepare Contract Account, value the work-in-progress and show how the various items would appear in the Balance Sheet. [*C.U. B.Com. (H) 2002*]

[Ans. Accounting Profit Rs. 59,850; Profit to P/L A/c Rs. 31,920; Value of work-in-progress Rs. 1,57,070]

Balance Sheet :

Liability side—Cash from contractee Rs. 1,62,000; Profit on contract Rs. 31,920; Abnormal loss Rs. 350; Outstanding expenses Rs. 7,000.

Asset side—WIP Rs. 1,57,070; Materials in hand Rs. 2,000; Plant Rs. 90,000.

Note : It has been assumed that materials in hand on 31.3.01 (Rs. 2,000) is after considering scrap value of materials lost by fire.

12. Modern Construction Ltd. has taken two contracts on 1st October 1985. The position of contract on 30th September 1986 is as follows :

	Contract I	*Contract II*
Contract price	27,00,000	60,00,000
Materials	5,80,000	10,80,000
Wages paid	11,24,000	16,50,000
Other expenses	28,000	60,000
Plant at site	1,60,000	3,00,000
Unused materials at site	40,000	60,000
Wages payable	36,000	54,000
Other expenses due	4,000	9,000
Work certified	16,00,000	30,00,000
Cash received	12,00,000	22,50,000
Work completed but not certified	80,000	90,000

The plant at site is to be depreciated at 10%.

Prepare the Contract Accounts in respect of each work showing the notional profit and also the profit to be transferred to Profit & Loss Account.

[*C.S. (Inter) Dec. 1987*]

[Ans. (*i*) Cost of Contract : Contract No 1 = Rs. 17,48,000; Contract No II = Rs. 28,23,000

(*ii*) Loss on Contract No. I = Rs. 68,000

Profit transferred to Profit & Loss A/c for Contract No II = Rs. 1,33,500]

13. Jain & Co. obtained a contract for the building of an office for Rs. 3,00,000. Building operations started on 1st April 1987 and at the end of the financial year, *i.e.* 31st March, 1988, they received from the party a sum of Rs. 1,20,000 being 80% of the amount of the surveyors certificate. The following additional information are available from the books of Jain & Co. :

	Rs.
Stores issued to Contract	60,000
Stores on hand as on 13.3.88	5,000
Wages paid	82,000
Plant purchased for the contract	10,000
Direct expenses	4,300
Plant to be depreciated at 10%	

You are required to prepare an account showing profit on contract up to 31.3.88. Also discuss whether Jain & Co. would be justified in taking the full amount of this profit to be credit of their Profit & Loss Account.

[*C.S. (Inter) June, 1990*]

[Ans. Profit on Contract up to 31.3.88 = Rs. 7,700; Jain & Co. would not be justified in taking the full amount of profit as the work has not yet been completed. 'Profit to be credited to Profit & Loss A/c = Rs. 4,107]

14. G.K. Basak carrying on business as contractor undertook a contract for Rs. 15,000 from 1st January 1991 and his expenditure during the calendar year was :

	Rs.
Plant purchased on the date of commencement	1,500
Machinery	1,000
Materials purchased	4,560
Wages	2,200
Direct Expenses	480
Charges for administration expenses	800

Part of machinery costing Rs. 400, being unsuitable for the work, was disposed of for Rs. 500.

It is better to charge 2% for contingencies on net estimated cost, not on Total Cost.

On 31st December 1991 there were wages accrued Rs. 200 and the values of machinery and materials in hand were Rs. 300 and Rs. 900, respectively. The plant had an effective life of three years.

G.K. Basak received the progress payment of Rs. 8,865 being 90% of the certified value of the work completed up to 31st December 1991.

To arrive at the figure of profit made on the contract for the first year, the contractor estimated the additional expenditure that would be required to complete the construction and took to the credit of the revenue for the year that portion of net estimated profit to be realised on the contract which the certified value of the work done bore to the contract price.

His estimates were

(*i*) the contract would take, in all, 18 months to complete ;

(*ii*) that additional machinery and materials to the value of Rs. 100 and Rs. 1,000 would be required to be purchased in the subsequent period; that direct expenses and wages would be Rs. 200 and Rs. 1,200, respectively;

(*iii*) charges for administration would continue to be the same every month;

(*iv*) provision for contingencies in the subsequent period to be made at 2% of the total cost of the contract. [*C.A. Final, Adopted*]

[Ans. Estimated Total Cost = Rs. 12,745; Estimated Total Profit = Rs. 2,255; Profit to be charged to Profit & Loss A/c = Rs. 1,333]

15. Deluxe Limited undertook a contract for Rs. 5,00,000 on 1st July 1986. On 30th June 1987 when the accounts were closed the following details about the contract were gathered :

	Rs.
Materials Purchased	1,00,000
Wages Paid	45,000
General Expenses	10,000
Plant Purchased	50,000
Materials on hand 30.6.87	25,000
Wages Accrued 30.6.87	5,000
Work certified	2,00,000
Cash received	1,50,000
Work uncertified	15,000
Depreciation on plant	5,000

The above contract contained an escalator clause which reads as follows :

"In the event of prices of materials and rates of wages increase by more than 5% the contract price would be increased accordingly by 25% of the rise in the cost of materials and wages beyond 5% in each Case."

It was found that since the date of signing the agreement the prices of materials and wage rates increased by 25%. The value of work certified does not take into account the effect of the above clause.

Prepare the Contract account. Working should form part of the answer.

[*I.C.W.A. (Inter) Dec. 1991; C.A. (Inter) Nov. 1987*]

[Ans. Notional Profit = Rs. 80,000; Profit credited to Profit & Loss A/c = Rs. 19,512; Cost of contract = Rs. 1,40,000]

16. M/s Excellent Erectors Ltd. took up a contract for the construction of a building at a contract price of Rs. 15,00,000. During the first year the following amounts were spent as against which a sum of Rs. 5,62,500, which represented 90% of the work, certified by the contractor :

	Rs.
Material	2,62,500
Wages	1,50,000
Overhead expenses	37,500

During the second year, the firm spent the following amounts :

	Rs.
Material	3,75,000
Labour Cost	3,00,000
Overhead	75,000

In the second year the contract was completed and a sum of Rs. 8,75,000 was received by the contractor. You are required to prepare the Contract Accounts and Contractee's Account for both the years and calculate the profit.

Note. Consider only 2/5th or 40% of the Notional profit to be taken to the credit of Profit & Loss A/c in the first year as the work done is less than 50%. *[I.C.W.A. (Inter)]*

[Ans. Profit to be charged to Profit & Loss A/c = Rs. 70,000]

Note. As the degree of completion is higher than 25% but below 50%, 40% of Notional Profit is charged to Profit & Loss A/c.

17. Write-up Contract No. 007 from the following information :
Direct Material Rs. 40,000, Wages Rs. 26,000, Special plant Rs. 17,600, Store issued Rs. 7,040, Loose Tools Rs. 3,300, Other expenses Rs. 8,360.
The contract was completed in 13 weeks at the end of which period plant was returned subject to depreciation of 15% of the original cost. The value of loose tools and stores returned were Rs. 2,200 and Rs. 890, respectively. The value of the tractor was Rs. 20,000 and depreciation charged @ 15% p.a. on the tractor. The administration expenses should be provided @ 10% on total cost. The contract price was Rs. 1,00,000. **[Ans. Profit = Rs. 6,500]**

18. The Overhead Contractor Ltd., having an authorised capital of Rs. 1,00,000, comprised of 5% Pref. Shares of Rs. 100 each and 5,000 Equity Shares of 10 each. Commenced operation of construction business from 1.1.90. During the year 1990 the company engaged on one contract of which the contract price was Rs. 4,00,000.
The trial balances extracted from their book on 31.12.90 were as follows :

	Rs.	Rs.
Share Capital		
5% Pref. Shares fully paid		40,000
Equity Shares of Rs. 8 paid		40,000
Sundry Creditors		8,000
Land & Building	34,000	
Cash at Bank	9,000	
Materials	75,000	
Plant	20,000	
Wages	1,05,000	
Expenses	5,000	
Cash received (8% of work certified)	—	1,60,000
	2,48,000	2,48,000

Of the plant and materials charged to the contract, plant costing Rs. 3,000 and material costing Rs. 2,400 were destroyed by fire. On 31.12.90, plant costing Rs. 4,000 were returned to store, the value of material at site was Rs. 3,000 and the cost of uncertified work was Rs. 2,000. Charge 10% Depreciation on plant.
Prepare the Contract A/c and the Balance Sheet as an 31.12.90.

[Ans. Profit charged to Profit & Loss A/c = Rs. 11,040; Value of W.I.P. = Rs. 32,340]

19. The following particulars relate to two houses which an engineering cooperative firm of builders had in course of construction under contract :

	House No. I	House No II
Work-in-progress on 1.1.87 (excluding Rs. 800 charged to Profit & Loss A/c in 1986)	14,000	—
Materials Purchased	23,000	16,600
Wages	20,000	14,000
Electric Service & Fittings	1,400	300
Road making expenses	8,000	—
Contract Price (including road making price)	60,000	40,000
Cash received up to 31-12-87	60,000	24,000
% of cash received to work certified	100%	$66\frac{2}{3}$%

Value of material in hand on 31.12.87	400	540
Work completed but not certified	—	2,500
Value of plant on site	12,000	6,000
Period of plant remained on sites during the year	10 months	8 months

The total establishment expenses incurred during the year 1987 amounted to Rs. 12,240. These are to be charged to the two houses in proportion to wages. Depreciation of plant is 10% p.a.

Prepare the Contract A/c and the sum which you consider appropriately transferable to the Profit & Loss A/c.

[Ans. Loss on house No. I = Rs. 15,000; Profit charged of Profit & Loss A/c for the house No. II = Rs. 1,200]

20. Mr. Abul Khair, a contractor, entered into two contracts namely contract A and contract B. Contract A commenced on 30th September 1989 and contract B commenced on 1st January 1990. Both contracts were incomplete at the end of the year 30th June 1990.

From the following information prepare the account for each contract and show the amount of Profit & Loss A/c for the year ended and also the balance sheet as at that date :

Necessary information

	Contract A *Rs.*	*Contract B* *Rs.*
Plant installed at commencement of contract	20,000	18,000
Material sent to sites	71,200	68,500
Labour paid	69,500	69,000
Direct Expenses	3,125	2,900
Establishment Exp.	3,775	3,550
Material returned	600	450
The value of certified work	1,80,000	1,40,000
Cost of uncertified work	5,000	3,000
Stock of material on hand	2,100	1,800
Wages due but not paid	2,000	1,900
Outstanding expenses	225	200
Value of contract	2,60,000	2,00,000
Cash received	1,60,000	1,10,000
Rate of depreciation on plant	20%	20%

[Ans. Profit of contract A = Rs. 33,875; Loss of contract B = Rs. 4,400; Profit charged to Profit & Loss A/c for A = Rs. 20,074]

21. Prakash Co. Ltd. undertook a contract for Rs. 3,00,000 on 1.1.90 and completed the same on 31st March 1992. You are given the following information for the contract :

1990—Material issued Rs. 40,000, Wages Rs. 20,000, Other expenses 2,000.

On 31.12.90—Material on site Rs. 4,000, Work certified Rs. 75,000.

1991—Material issued Rs. 70,000, Wages Rs. 50,000 ; Other charges 5,000; Special Plant Rs. 80,000.

On 31.12.91—Material on site Rs. 10,500, Works certified Rs. 1,50,000, Works completed but uncertified Rs. 25,000.

1992—Material issued Rs. 5,000, Wages Rs. 12,500 and other expenses Rs. 1,200

On 31.12.92—Material return Rs. 1,000. Plant was returned to store at W.D.V. rate of Depreciation 10% p.a.

80% of the certified work value was received in cash every year.

Prepare Contract A/c and Contractee's A/c and show how the W.I.P. would be shown in the Balance Sheet of each year.

[Ans. 1990—No profit should be charged to Profit & Loss A/c; Value of W.I.P. Rs. 2,000; Contractee's Balance = Rs. 60,000 1991—Profit charged to Profit & Loss A/c Rs. 34,933; Value of W.I.P. = 39,433 Contractees A/c Balance= Rs. 1,80,000; 1992 = Profit charged to Profit & Loss A/c = 50,367]

22. The following information are collected from the books of a contractor for the year ended 31.12.86 :

	Rs.	*Rs.*
W.I.P. on 31.12.85	1,70,000	
Less : Advances from Contractees on 31.12.85	1,10,000	60,000

Transactions during the year were :

Material supplied directly to the contract Rs. 12,000, material issued from stores 21,000, wages Rs. 15,000, working expenses Rs. 5,000, administration expenses (of which Rs. 2,000 were chargeable to general Profit & Loss A/c) 4,000. Plant issued Rs. 5,000, material returned to stores Rs. 1,100, material returned to suppliers Rs. 900. Contract finished Rs. 45,000, Profit taken on contracts Rs. 23,000. Advances from contractees Rs. 80,000.

Prepare the Contract A/c and the Contractee's A/c and value of W.I.P. which will appear in the Balance Sheet as on 31.12.86.

[Ans. Value of certified work = 2,06,000; Contractee's Balance = Rs. 1,45,000; Value of W.I.P. for Balance Sheet purpose = Rs. 61,000]

23. DS Ltd. started a contract on 1st June 2002 for construction of a Link Road for a contract price of Rs. 5,00,000 to be completed by 31st March 2004. The budgeted cost of the contract was Rs. 4,50,000. The following particulars are obtained for the year ended 31st March 2003 :

	Rs.
Materials issued from stores	48,000
Materials bought direct at site	40,000
Materials from other contract	24,500
Material at site (Closing)	6,000
Materials returned	2,000
Materials lost in accident	8,000
Insurance claim accepted	5,000
Wages paid	74,500
Plant issued to site at WDV	30,000
Hire charges of plant	38,500
Supervision expenses	13,500
Normal loss of materials	2,000
Uncertified work-in-progress	17,500
Share of other expenses	5,500
Paid to sub-contractors	25,000
Outstanding wages on 31.3.2003	1,500
Payment due to sub-contractor on 31.3.2003	2,000
Value of work certified	2,75,000
Advance from contractee (90% of work certified)	?
Sale of unused materials (Cost of Rs. 10,000)	8,000
Opening balance of a plant lost in accident	6,000
Depreciation on plant @ 20% p.a.	

Draw the Contract A/c and Contractee's A/c. Also compute the Value of Work-in-progress.

[*C.U. B.Com. (H) 2004*]

[Ans. Notional Profit : Rs. 40,500; Profit transferred to costing P/L A/c; Rs. 24,300]

24. An amount of Rs. 19,80,000 was incurred on a contract work up to 31.03.2004. Certificates have been received to date to the value of Rs. 24,00,000 against which Rs. 21,60,000 has been received in cash. The cost of work done but not certified amounted to Rs. 45,000. It is estimated that by spending an additional amount of Rs. 1,20,000 (including provision for contingencies) the work can be completed in all respects in another two months. The agreed contract price of the work is Rs. 25 lakhs.

Compute a conservative estimate of the profit to be taken to the Profit and Loss Account.

[*I.C.W.A. Inter, Dec. '04*]

25. From the following information, ascertain the profit in respect of the contract of construction of building undertaken by a firm. The term of the contract is Rs. 10 per. sq. feet of the covered floor area as accepted and certified by the engineer of the contractee.

During the year, the following expenses were made :

(*a*) *Materials.* Building material in stock at the beginning Rs. 10,000, purchase during the year—Cement 75 bags @ Rs. 60, bricks 12,500 @ Rs. 400 per thousand, sand 10,000 c.ft @, Rs. 10 per 100 c.f.t., Wood work 450 c.ft @ Rs. 20 per c.ft. Value of material in hand Rs. 10,000.

(*b*) *Labour.* 20 masons @ Rs. 20 per day for 25 days; 80 mazdoors @ Rs. 10 per day for 25 days.

(*c*) *Tools & Machinery.* Two concrete mixer machines were purchased at Rs. 12,000 and 8,000, respectively, and the residual value at the end of the contract was Rs. 5,000 and Rs. 2,000, respectively.

(*d*) *Supervision.* 25% of two engineers' pay, at Rs. 2,000 p.m. for each engineer, for two months. 25% of 5 overseers' pay, at Rs. 800 p.m. for each overseer, for four months.

(*e*) *Administrative Overhead.* 20% of Head office expenses for the period of the contract. The head office expenses for the period is Rs. 5,000.

(*f*) *Quantity of work done.* Works accepted and certified by the contracee's engineer—12,000 sq. ft. of covered floor area.

[Ans. Profit = Rs. 10,000]

26. The following figures are extracted from the book of Moonlight Construction Co. for the year ended 31.12.87 :

	Rs.	*Rs.*
W.I.P. on 31.12.86	8,50,000	
Cash received	5,50,000	14,00,000
Transaction during the year :		
Material supplied to contract directly		60,000
Material issued from stores		1,05,000
Wages		85,000
Working Expenses		15,000
Administration Expenses (of which Rs. 2,500 is chargeable of general Profit & Loss A/c)		12,500
Plant issued		25,000
Material returned to suppliers		4,500
Materials returned to stores		5,500
Contracts certified		2,25,000
Work certified		1,50,000
Profit taken from contract		1,15,000
Advances from contractees		4,00,000

Prepare the Contract A/c, Contractee's A/c and value of W.I.P. *[Adopted—Lucknow, B.Com.]*

[Ans. Contractee's A/c Bal = Rs. 7,25,000; W.I.P. A/c = Rs. 10,30,000 including Rs. 8,80,000 pertaining to work certified in earlier years, works uncertified for this year and for earlier years and the residual value of plant.]

27. A contractor secured a contract to supply and erect machinery for the sum of Rs. 7,50,000. He was to receive payments on account from time to time equal to 90% of the certified value of work done.

He started the work on 1.1.91 and incurred the following expenditure during the year :

	Rs.
Plant & Tools	70,000
Stores & Machinery	2,00,000
Wages	1,50,000
Sundry Expenses	30,000
Establishment Charges	40,000

A part of machinery costing Rs. 20,000 was unsuitable to the contract and was sold immediately at a profit of Rs. 5,000.

Value of Machinery and stores at end	40,000
Plant & Tools on 31.12.91	30,000

By 31.1.92 he had received on account of 90% of certified value of work done up to 31.12.91—Rs. 4,38,750.

In order to complete the undone work, the contractor estimated further expenditure as follows :

(*i*) That the contract would be completed within next six months.

(*ii*) That Plant & Tools would have a residual value of Rs. 10,000 upon the completion of the contract.

(*iii*) The cost of machinery and stores, in addition to those in stock on 31.12.91, would be Rs. 1,00,000 and Sundry expenses would be Rs. 20,000.

(*iv*) That the wages of the contract for next six months would be Rs. 80,000.

(*v*) That the establishment cost would be the same per month as in the previous period.

(*vi*) That $2\frac{1}{2}$% of the total cost of the contract should be provided for contingencies.

Prepare Contract A/c for the year ended 31.12.91 and show the calculations of the profit to be credited to Profit & Loss A/c for the year.

[Ans. Profit to be credited to Profit & Loss A/c = Rs. 34,450]

28. M/s Rahaman Construction Co. showed the following expenditure on account of a contract on 31.12.83 :

	Rs.
Materials	2,10,000
Plant	70,000
Wages	3,93,000
Sundry Expenses	15,000
Establishment charges	10,000

The contract was started on 1.1.83 and the contract value was settled at Rs. 10,00,000. Cash received to date was Rs. 4,80,000 representing 80% of work certified. The value of plant and material on 31.12.83 were Rs. 20,000 and 6,000, respectively. The cost of work completed after getting work certificate was Rs. 50,000.

Some of the materials costing Rs. 20,000 was sold at a loss of Rs. 4,000. A part of the plant costing Rs. 5,000 was sold at Rs. 6,000.

In order to calculate the profit made on the contract up to 31st Dec. 1983, the contractors estimated further expenditure that would be incurred in completing the contract and took to the Profit & Loss A/c in proportion of the estimated profit. The estimates were :

(*i*) That the contract would be completed by 30th June 1984.

(*ii*) That a further sum of Rs. 30,000 would have to be spent on plant and the residual value of the plant on the completion of the contract would be Rs. 12,000.

(*iii*) The material in additional to those on 31.12.88 would cost Rs. 1,00,000 and the further sundry expenses of Rs. 7,000 would be incurred.

(*iv*) That the wages on the contract for next six months would amount to Rs. 1,69,900.

(*v*) That the establishment charges would cost the same per month as in the previous year.

(*vi*) That Rs. 18,000 should be provided to meet the contingencies.

Prepare the Contract A/c for the year ended 31.12.83, and also show the amount of profit to be credited to Profit & Loss A/c.

[Ans. Profit to be credited to Profit and Loss A/c = Rs. 65,460]

29. The following Trial Balance was extracted on 31.12.92 from the books of Sunlight Constructions Ltd. which have an authorised capital of Rs. 3,50,000 divided into 35,000 equity share of Rs. 10 each :

Credit Balances

	Rs.
Share Capital :	
35,000 equity shares of Rs. 10 fully paid	3,50,000
Creditors	83,000
Profit & Loss A/c on 1.1.92	25,000
Provision for Depreciation	63,000
Cash received on account of contract	12,80,000
	18,01,000

Debit Balances

	Rs.
Land & Building	74,000
Special Plant Tools at cost	52,000
Bank	45,000
Material issued	6,00,000
Direct Labour	8,30,000
Expenses	40,000
Plant & Tools on site at cost	1,60,000
	18,01,000

The contract was begun on 1.1.92. The contract price is Rs. 24,00,000 and the contractee has so far paid Rs. 12,80,000 being 80% of the work certified. The cost of work done since certification is estimated at Rs. 16,000.

On 31.12.92, after the above trial balance was extracted, plant costing Rs. 32,000 was returned to stores and material then on site were valued at Rs. 27,000.

Provision is to be made for direct labour accrued but not paid Rs. 6,000 and for depreciation of all plant and tools @ $12\frac{1}{2}\%$ on cost.

You are requested to : (*a*) prepare Contract A/c, (*b*) show your computation of the profit to be charged to Profit & Loss A/c., (*c*) Prepare Balance sheet as on 31.12.92.

[Ans. Cost of Contract = Rs. 14,69,000; Notional Profit = Rs. 1,47,000; Profit charged to Profit & Loss A/c = Rs. 78,400; Value of W.I.P. = Rs. 2,67,400; Balance Sheet Total = 6,05,400]

30. Deluxe Ltd. undertook a contract for Rs. 5,00,000 on 1st July 1988. On 30th June 1989, when the accounts were closed, the following details about the contract gathered :

	Rs.
Material Purchased	1,00,000
Wages paid	45,000
General Expenses	10,000
Plant purchased	50,000
Material on hand (30.6.89)	25,000
Wages accrued	5,000
Work certified	2,00,000
Cash received	1,50,000
Works uncertified	15,000
Depreciation of Plant	5,000

The above contract contained an escalator clause which reads :

"In the event of price of materials and rates of wages increase by more than 5%, the contract price would be increased accordingly by 25% of the rise in the cost of materials and was beyond 5% in each case".

It was found that since the date of signing the agreement the price of materials and wage rate increased by 25%. The value of the work certified does not take into account the effect of the above clause. Prepare the Contract A/c. [*C.A. (Inter)*]

[Ans. Cost of Contract = 1,40,000; Increase in contract price = Rs. 5,000; Price to be charged to Profit & Loss—20,000]

31. The following information regarding Contract No. 608 were collected at the end of 31.12.92 :

	Rs.
Direct Wages	13,800
Direct Material	68,000
Stores issued	7,600
Materials returned	1,100
Subcontractors' fees	12,600
Plant	24,000

The work started on 1.1.92 and the total contract price is Rs. 1,20,000 upto 15th Dec, the engineers had certified the 4/5th of the work. Depreciation of plant December 15 is Rs. 9,600.

The summary set out above includes items relating to the period since December 15th as follows :

	Rs.
Wages	1,400
Material	3,240

The material on site on 31.12.92 was Rs. 10,000 and stores on site Rs. 800.

Establishment charges are 40% on direct wages. A fine of Rs. 2,000 is likely to be imposed for late completion.

You are required :

(*i*) to prepare Contract A/c

(*ii*) Profit/Loss to be charged to Profit & Loss A/c

(*iii*) Amount of profit or loss raised on work certified.

[Ans. Loss to be charged to Profit & Loss A/c Rs. 6,020 (including fine)]

32. Usha Ltd. undertakes to supply 10,000 p.a. table fans to M/s Electro Cooling. The fixed cost incurred for production per fan is Rs. 400 and the carrying cost per annum per fan is Rs. 2. Find out : (*a*) EBQ (*b*) Carrying cost for minimum inventory holding per annum.

[Ans. (*a*) EBQ = 2,000 units; (*b*) = Rs. 2,000]

33. From the following information find out : (*i*) EOQ, (*ii*) Time interval between two consecutive optimum runs, (*iii*) Minimum inventory holding cost.

S.A. Ltd. has to supply 1,000 garments per day to P.K. Ltd. The cost of holding per garment p.a. is Rs. 2 and the set up cost is Rs. 40 per batch.

[Ans. (*i*) 200 units; (*ii*) 73 days; (*iii*) Rs. 200]

7 Process Costing

Section I : Principles of Process Cost and Inter Process Profit

Authors' Comments and Suggestions :

1. ***At least one (sometimes two) question either from Normal/Abnormal Loss/Abnormal Gain, or from Inter-Process Profit, or from Equivalent Production or from Joint Product/By-product are expected from this chapter for all examinations.***
2. ***The various methods of valuation of work-in-progress, completed Production, Abnormal Loss/Gain should be understood carefully and Abnormal Loss or Abnormal Gain should be treated as good units.***
3. ***It should be remembered that the cost data relating to valuation of stock are required for decision making and performance reporting for controlling cost of various processes.***
4. ***Difference among Joint Product, By-product and Co-product should be clearly understood.***
5. ***A common mistake with reference to further processing is to inclusion of joint cost. Decision should be taken on the basis of incremental cost and incremental revenue (viz. Incremental Cost Benefit Approach). If incremental revenue is higher than that of cost, further processing should be recommended.***
   In short, Joint cost are not relevant to the decision to sell at split-off point or after further processing.
6. ***The students should not forget to carryout adjustment of scrap (whether normal or abnormal) at the time of preparation of ledger accounts.***

Introduction—Features—Application—Procedure—Treatment of Normal Loss—Abnormal Loss and Abnormal Gain—Inter Process Profit—Specimen of different Accounts—Workedout Problems and Solutions—Exercises.

Concept of Process Costing

Process costing is such a separate method of costing which refers to a costing of operations or process involved in converting raw material into finished goods or products. It is suitable for those types of business where continuous and mass production of homogeneous products are produced.

In process costing particular attention is given to : (*a*) cost relating to the process, (*b*) period for which cost for the process is collected, (*c*) complete and incomplete units produced during the period and (*d*) unit cost of the process for the period.

Features of Process Costing

(*i*) The products are produced in one or more process.

(*ii*) The products are of standardised and homogeneous nature.

(*iii*) When a product is produced through more than one process, then the output of each process will be input of the next process.

(*iv*) The cost of one process is transferred to next process.

(*v*) The total cost of each process after deducting Scrap value is divided by the total Production units to obtain Cost Per Unit in the process.

Difference between Job Costing and Process Costing

Job Costing	*Process Costing*
1. Production is done by specific orders.	1. Production is carried on in continuous flow.
2. Costs are determined by job.	2. Costs are calculated by dividing total Input Cost, Scrap Value to total input unit-Scrap unit.
3. Job costing is applied where the objective is to identify the cost with the job.	3. Process costing is applied where material is converted into Finished goods through different stages or process.
4. Costs are calculated after the completion of the job.	4. Costs are calculated at the end of each process.
5. There may or may not be any opening or closing W.I.P.	5. As the productions are carried on continuous basis, hence there is usually some opening or closing W.I.P.
6. Here jobs are not usually transferred from one to another.	6. Here products are moved from one process to another.
7. As production is not continuous more managerial attention is required for proper control.	7. Comparatively, control of process activities is easy.

Normal Loss, Abnormal Loss and Abnormal Gain

Normal Loss. Normal loss means that loss which is inherent in the processing operations. It can be expected or anticipated in advance *i.e.* at the time of estimation.

Accounting treatment. The cost of normal loss is considered as part of the cost of production in which it occurs. If normal loss units have any realisable scrap value, the process account is credited by that amount. If there is no abnormal gain, then there is no necessity to maintain a separate account for normal loss.

Journal Entry : (i) Normal Loss A/c ...Dr.
To Process A/c

(ii) Cost Ledger Control A/c ...Dr.
(Scrap value)
To Normal Loss

Abnormal Loss. Abnormal loss means that loss which is caused by unexpected or abnormal conditions such as accident, machine breakdown, substandard material etc. From accounting point of view we can say that Abnormal loss is that loss which occurred over and above normal loss. These losses are segregated from process costs and investigated to prevent their occurrence in future.

Process account is to be credited by abnormal loss account with cost of material, labour and overhead equivalent to good units and the loss due to abnormal is transferred to Costing Profit and Loss Account.

Journal Entries : (i) Abnormal Loss A/c ...Dr.
To Process A/c

(ii) Cost Ledger Control A/c ...Dr. (Scrap value)
Costing Profit & Loss A/c ...Dr.
To Abnormal Loss

Abnormal Gain. If the actual loss of a Process is less than that of expected loss then the difference between the two will be treated as abnormal gain. In another way we can define it as the difference between actual production and expected production.

Accounting Treatment. The value of abnormal gain is transferred to the debit side of the relevant process and ultimately closed by crediting it to the Costing Profit and Loss Account.

Journal Entries : (i) Process A/c ..Dr.
To Abnormal Gain
(ii) Abnormal Gain A/c ..Dr.
To Normal Loss
To Costing Profit & Loss A/c

Application of Process Costing

Process costing can be used in a large variety of industries. It is very suitable for such industries where the product is manufactured through a continuous sequence of operations.

Generally, the process costings are used in the following types of industries :

(*i*) Textile and Chemical Industries.
(*ii*) Manufacturing Industries like iron and steel, cement, paper mill, soap-making etc.
(*iii*) Mining Industries—coal, oil etc.
(*iv*) Public utility services—such as gas, electricity, water supply etc.

Basic Approach/Procedure

1. The industry should be divided into distinct process centre and an account should be maintained for each process centre.

2. All costs relating to each process are recorded at the end of the period.

3. Average cost per unit is found out by dividing total cost of each process by total production. In order to get average unit cost, normal loss in production and incomplete units at the beginning and at the end of the period are taken into consideration.

4. Cost of one process is transferred to the subsequent process so that total cost and unit cost of products are accumulated.

Advantages of Process Costing

1. Costs are computed at the end of a particular period.
2. Average costs are easily computed.
3. It involves less clerical work than job costing.
4. Cost data are available process or department-wise for exercising managerial control.
5. It helps the management in determining or fixing up price quotations.

Limitations of Process Costing

(*i*) The whole concept of Process Costing is based on average cost and therefore these are not of much use for effective control.

(*ii*) Computation of average cost becomes more complicated when more than one type of product is produced.

(*iii*) Process costing system presumes that production activity of a factory is divided according to processes or departments. A process or department is an organisational entity or section of a firm, in which specific and repetitive work is done. Thus process becomes a practical unit in a plant for purpose of supervision of production. Often process is an unsatisfactory unit for cost accounting purposes.

Following illustration will be helpful to understand the treatment of Normal Loss, Abnormal Loss and Abnormal Gain.

Illustration

The following are the details of Process X, Process Y and Process Z :

	Process X	*Process Y*	*Process Z*
Input units	2,000	1,840	1,740
Normal loss unit	10%	5%	10%
Direct Material	40,000	60,400	69,240
Wages	70,000	84,520	1,00,000
Overhead	30,000	40,000	50,000
Scrap value (per unit)	25	50	60

Output of Process Z is 1,600 units. Prepare the necessary Accounts.

Solution

Process X A/c

Dr. *Cr.*

Particulars	*Units*	*Rate*	*Amount Rs.*	*Particulars*	*Units*	*Rate*	*Amount Rs.*
To Direct Material	2,000	—	40,000	By Normal Loss	200	25	5,000
" Wages	—	—	70,000	" Processing	1,840	75	1,38,000
" Overhead	—	—	30,000				
	2,000	—	1,40,000				
To Abnormal Gain	40	75	3,000				
	2,040	—	1,43,000		2,040		1,43,000

$$\text{Cost Per unit} = \frac{1{,}40{,}000 - 5{,}000}{2{,}000 - 200} = \frac{1{,}35{,}000}{1{,}800}$$

Process Y A/c

Dr. *Cr.*

Particulars	*Units*	*Rate*	*Amount Rs.*	*Particulars*	*Units*	*Rate*	*Amount Rs.*
To Process X	1,840	75	1,38,000	By Normal Loss	72	50	3,600
" D/M	—	—	60,400	" Process 'Z'	1,740	180·61	3,14,263
" Wages	—	—	84,520	" Ab. Loss	28	180·61	5,057
" Overhead	—	—	40,000				
	1,840	—	3,22,920		1,840		3,22,920

Process Z A/c

Dr. *Cr.*

Particulars	*Units*	*Rate*	*Amount Rs.*	*Particulars*	*Units*	*Rate*	*Amount Rs.*
To Processing	1,740	180·61	3,14,263	By Normal Loss	174	60	10,440
" Material	—	—	69,240	" Finished stock	1,600	334	5,34,420
" Labour	—	—	1,00,000				
" Overhead	—	—	50,000				
	1,740	—	5,33,503				
To Abnormal Gain	34	334	11,357				
	1,774	—	5,44,860		1,774	—	5,44,860

Normal Loss

Dr. Cr.

Particulars	Units	Rate	Amount Rs.	Particulars	Units	Rate	Amount Rs.
To Process X	200	25	5,000	By C.L.C	160	25	4,000
" Process Y	72	50	3,600	" Abnormal gain	40	25	1,000
" Process Z	174	60	10,440	" C.L.C.	72	50	3,600
				" C.L.C.	140	60	8,400
				" Ab. Gain	34	60	2,040
	446	—	19,040		446	—	19,040

Abnormal Gain A/c

Dr. Cr.

Particulars	Units	Rate	Amount Rs.	Particulars	Units	Rate	Amount Rs.
To Normal Loss	40	25	1,000	By Process X	40	75	3,000
" Normal Loss	34	60	2,040	" Process Z	34	334	11,357
" Costing P/L	—	—	11,317				
	74	—	14,357		74	—	14,357

Abnormal Loss A/c

Dr. Cr.

Particulars	Units	Rate	Amount Rs.	Particulars	Units	Rate	Amount Rs.
To Processing	28	180·61	5,057	By C.L.C	28	50	1,400
				" Costing P/L A/c	—	—	3,657
	28	—	5,057		28	—	5,057

Inter Process Profit

In some cases the output of one process is transferred to the next process by adding certain percentage of profit and this profit is called the inter-process profit. The main logic behind this is to charge to the next process not at the cost of the transferor but at its market selling price. This helps to assess the profitability in respect of each product. On the other hand, the system creates unnecessary problem in respect of valuation of closing stock and unrealised profit on the same. The provision for unrealised profit on closing stock for each process can be calculated by using the simple formula :

$$\text{Value of Closing Stock} \times \frac{\text{Total Profit on the Process}}{\text{Total Cost to the Process}}$$

Illustration

The following illustration will be helpful to understand how to calculate the interprocess profit.

A product passes through three processes before it is transferred to Finished Stock. The following details for January 1992 are available :

Particulars	*I*	*II*	*III*	*Finished Stock*
Opening Stock	20,000	24,000	16,000	60,000
Direct Material	40,000	42,000	60,000	—
Direct Wages	30,000	30,000	32,000	—
Production Overheads	28,000	12,000	80,000	—
Closing Stock	10,000	12,000	8,000	30,000
Profit on Cost	$33\frac{1}{3}\%$	25%	25%	—
Sales	—	—	—	7,00,000
Inter-process Profit for Opening Stock	—	4,000	4,000	22,000

Stock in processes are valued at Prime Cost and Finished Stock at the price at which it is received from process III.

Find out the amount of provision to be made to offset the inter-process profits added.

Solution

Process I A/c

Dr. *Cr.*

Particulars	*Cost* Rs.	*Profit* Rs.	*Total* Rs.	*Particulars*	*Cost* Rs.	*Profit* Rs.	*Total* Rs.
To Opening Stock	20,000	—	20,000	By Process II A/c	1,08,000	36,000	1,44,000
To D/M	40,000	—	40,000				
To D/W	30,000	—	30,000				
	90,000	—	90,000				
Less : Closing Stock	10,000	—	10,000				
Prime Cost	80,000	—	80,000				
To Production Overhead	28,000	—	28,000				
Total Cost	1,08,000		1,08,000				
Profit $33\frac{1}{3}\%$ on cost	—	36,000	36,000				
	1,08,000	36,000	1,44,000		1,08,000	36,000	1,44,000

Process II A/c

Dr. *Cr.*

Particulars	*Cost* Rs.	*Profit* Rs.	*Total* Rs.	*Particulars*	*Cost* Rs.	*Profit* Rs.	*Total* Rs.
To Opening Stock	20,000	4,000	24,000	By Process III	2,02,000	98,000	3,00,000
To Process I	1,08,000	36,000	1,44,000				
To D/M	42,000	—	42,000				
To D/W	30,000	—	30,000				
	2,00,000	40,000	2,40,000				
Less : Closing Stock	10,000	2,000	12,000				
Prime Cost	1,90,000	38,000	2,28,000				
Production overhead	12,000	—	12,000				
Total Cost	2,02,000	38,000	2,40,000				
Profit		60,000	60,000				
	2,02,000	98,000	3,00,000		2,02,000	98,000	3,00,000

Note : Profit on Closing Stock : $\frac{40,000}{2,40,000} \times 12,000 = 2,000$

Process III A/c

Dr.							Cr.
Particulars	*Cost* Rs.	*Profit* Rs.	*Total* Rs.	*Particulars*	*Cost* Rs.	*Profit* Rs.	*Total* Rs.
To Opening Stock	12,000	4,000	16,000	By Finished Stock	3,80,000	2,20,000	6,00,000
To Process II	2,02,000	98,000	3,00,000				
To D/M	60,000	—	60,000				
To D/W	32,000	—	32,000				
	3,06,000	1,02,000	4,08,000				
Less : Closing stock	6,000	2,000	8,000				
Prime Cost	3,00,000	1,00,000	4,00,000				
Production Overhead	80,000	—	80,000				
Total Cost	3,80,000	1,00,000	4,80,000				
Profit (25% on Cost)	—	1,20,000	1,20,000				
	3,80,000	2,20,000	6,00,000		3,80,000	2,20,000	6,00,000

Finished Stock A/c

Dr.							Cr.
Particulars	*Cost* Rs.	*Profit* Rs.	*Total* Rs.	*Particulars*	*Cost* Rs.	*Profit* Rs.	*Total* Rs.
To Opening Stock	38,000	22,000	60,000	By Sales	3,99,000	3,01,000	7,00,000
" Process III	3,80,000	2,20,000	6,00,000				
	4,18,000	2,42,000	6,60,000				
Less : Closing Stock	19,000	11,000	30,000				
Total Cost	3,99,000	2,31,000	6,30,000				
Profit		70,000	70,000				
	3,99,000	3,01,000	7,00,000		3,99,000	3,01,000	7,00,000

Profit on Closing Stock $= \frac{2,42,000}{6,60,000} \times 30,000 =$ Rs. 11,000

Statement showing the amount of provision to be made to offset the inter-process profits added

Process	*Provision to be made*
I	Nil
II	2,000
III	2,000
Finished stock	11,000
	15,000

WORKEDOUT PROBLEMS

Problem 1

The product of a chemical factory passes through two processes namely Process A and Process B and then to Finished Stock. From the following particulars prepare the necessary Process A/c :

	Process A	*Process B*
Material	10,000	8,000
Labour	15,000	10,000
Overhead	5,000	4,000

The output produced in December 1989 is 3,000 units.

Solution

Process A A/c

Dr. *Cr.*

Particulars	*Units*	*Rate*	*Amount* Rs.	*Particulars*	*Units*	*Rate*	*Amount* Rs.
To Material	3,000	—	10,000	By Process B	3,000	10	30,000
" Labour	—	—	15,000				
" Overhead	—	—	5,000				
	3,000	—	30,000		3,000	—	30,000

Process B A/c

Dr. *Cr.*

Particulars	*Units*	*Rate*	*Amount* Rs.	*Particulars*	*Units*	*Rate*	*Amount* Rs.
To Process A	3,000	10	30,000	By Finished Stock A/c	3,000	17·333	52,000
" Material	—	—	8,000				
" Labour	—	—	10,000				
" Overhead	—	—	4,000				
	3,000	—	52,000		3,000	—	52,000

Problem 2

X. Ltd. produces a standard product through three processes namely Process A, B and C, respectively. From the following particulars prepare the necessary Process A/c :

Particulars	*Process A*	*Process B*	*Process C*
Material	40,000	20,000	—
Direct Wages	20,000	10,000	20,000
Direct Expenses	8,000	10,000	12,000

Total production overhead incurred during the month is 25,000. Production overhead is recovered on the basis of the percentage of direct wage.

1,000 units of Input put into Process A at the rate of Rs. 2 per unit.

Solution

Process A A/c

Dr. *Cr.*

Particulars	*Units*	*Rate*	*Amount Rs.*	*Particulars*	*Units*	*Rate*	*Amount Rs.*
To Input	1,000	2	2,000	By Process B A/c	1,000	80	80,000
" Material	—	—	40,000				
" D/W	—	—	20,000				
" D/Exp.	—	—	8,000				
" Production off (50% of D/W)	—	—	10,000				
	1,000	—	80,000		1,000	—	80,000

Process B A/c

Dr. *Cr.*

Particulars	*Units*	*Rate*	*Amount Rs.*	*Particulars*	*Units*	*Rate*	*Amount Rs.*
To Process A	1,000	80	80,000	By Process C A/c	1,000	115	1,15,000
" Material	—	—	20,000				
" D/Wages	—	—	10,000				
" Overhead	—	—	5,000				
	1,000	—	1,15,000		1,000	115	1,15,000

Process C A/c

Dr. *Cr.*

Particulars	*Units*	*Rate*	*Amount Rs.*	*Particulars*	*Units*	*Rate*	*Amount Rs.*
To Process B	1,000	115	1,15,000	By Finished Stock	1,000	157	1,57,000
" Direct Wages	—	—	20,000				
" Direct Exp.	—	—	12,000				
" Overhead	—	—	10,000				
	1,000	—	1,57,000		1,000	157	1,57,000

Note : *Calculation for % overhead :*

Total Direct Wages = Rs. 50,000

Total Production overhead = Rs. 25,000

$\therefore$ % Production Overhead on Direct Wages $= \frac{\text{Rs. } 25,000}{50,000} \times 100$

$= 50\%$

Problem 3

Product A passes through two processes I and II and then to Finished Stock. From the following data prepare the Process A/c's :

Particulars	*Process I*	*Process II*
Input	2,000	1,900
Material consumed	30,000	20,000
Wages	20,000	20,000
Overhead	7,200	6,170
Normal Loss	5%	10%
Scrap Value (per unit)	2	3

Solution

Process I A/c

Dr. *Cr.*

Particulars	*Units*	*Rate*	*Amount* Rs.	*Particulars*	*Units*	*Rate*	*Amount* Rs.
To Material	2,000		30,000	By Normal Loss	100	2	200
" D/Wages	—	—	20,000	" Process II A/c	1,900	30	57,000
" Overhead	—	—	7,200				
	2,000	—	57,200		2,000	—	57,200

$$\text{Cost per unit} = \frac{57{,}000 - 200}{2{,}000 - 100} = \frac{57{,}000}{1{,}900} = \text{Rs. } 30$$

Process II A/c

Dr. *Cr.*

Particulars	*Units*	*Rate*	*Amount* Rs.	*Particulars*	*Units*	*Rate*	*Amount* Rs.
To Process I A/c	1,900	30	57,000	By Normal Loss	190	3	570
" Material	—	—	20,000	" Finished Stock	1,710	60	1,02,600
" Wages	—	—	20,000				
" Overhead			6,170				
	1,900	—	1,03,170		1,900	—	1,03,170

$$\text{Cost per unit} = \frac{1{,}03{,}170 - 570}{1{,}900 - 190} = \frac{1{,}02{,}600}{1{,}710} = \text{Rs. } 60$$

Problem 4

Mukherjee & Co. produces an article through two processes X and Y which is then sent to the finished stock. The details of the processes are :

	Process X	*Process Y*
Material used	60,000	30,000
Wages	70,000	40,000
Overhead	20,000	40,000
Normal loss	5%	10%
Scrap value (Per 100 units)	80	100
Output (units)	9,500	8,500

10,000 units were brought into Process @ Rs. 10 per unit.

Prepare Process A/cs.

Solution

Process I A/c

Dr. *Cr.*

Particulars	Units	Rate	Amount Rs.	Particulars	Units	Rate	Amount Rs.
To Input	10,000	10	1,00,000	By Normal Loss	500	0·80	400
" Material	—	—	60,000	" Process II A/c	9,500	26·27	2,49,600
" Wages	—	—	70,000				
" Overhead	—	—	20,000				
	10,000		2,50,000		10,000		2,50,000

$$\text{Cost per unit} = \frac{2{,}49{,}600}{9{,}500} = \text{Rs. } 26{\cdot}27$$

Process II A/c

Dr. *Cr.*

Particulars	Units	Rate	Amount Rs.	Particulars	Units	Rate	Amount Rs.
To Process I	9,500	26·27	2,49,600	By Normal Loss	950	1·00	950
" Material	—	—	30,000	" Abnormal Loss	50	41·947	2,097
" Wages	—	—	40,000	" Finished Stock	8,500	41·947	3,56,553
" Overhead	—	—	40,000				
	9,500		3,59,600		9,500	—	3,59,600

$$\text{Cost per unit} = \frac{3{,}59{,}600 - 950}{9{,}500 - 950} = \frac{3{,}58{,}650}{8{,}550} = \text{Rs. } 41{\cdot}947$$

Problem 5

From the following informations prepare the Process A/cs.

	Process I	Process II	Process III
Wages	15,000	8,000	17,250
Material	15,400	4,000	12,000
Overhead	5,600	5,250	6,000
Units Produced	36,000	37,500	48,000
Opening Stock	—	4,000	16,500
Closing Stock	—	1,000	5,500

Solution

Process I A/c

Dr. *Cr.*

Particulars	Units	Rate Rs.	Amount Rs.	Particulars	Units	Rate Rs.	Amount Rs.
To Opening Stock	—	—	—	By Process II	36,000	1	36,000
" Wages	36,000	—	15,000				
" Material	—	—	15,400				
" Overhead	—	—	5,600				
	36,000	—	36,000		36,000	—	36,000

Process II A/c

Dr. Cr.

Particulars	Units	Rate	Amount Rs.	Particulars	Units	Rate	Amount Rs.
To Op. Stock	4,000	1	4,000	By Process III	37,500	1·5	56,250
" Process I	36,000	1	36,000	" Wastage	1,500	—	—
" Material	—	—	4,000	" Closing Stock	1,000	1·0	1,000
" Wages	—	—	8,000				
" Overhead	—	—	5,250				
	40,000	—	57,250		40,000	—	57,250

Process III A/c

Dr. Cr.

Particulars	Units	Rate Rs.	Amount Rs.	Particulars	Units	Rate Rs.	Amount Rs.
To Opening Stock	16,500	1·5	24,750	By Wastage	500	—	—
" Process A/c	37,500	—	56,250	" Closing Stock	5,500	1·5	8,250
" Wages	—	—	17,250	" Finished Stock	48,000	2·25	1,08,000
" Material	—	—	12,000				
" Overhead	—	—	6,000				
	54,000	—	1,16,250		54,000	—	1,16,250

Problem 6

A product passes through three processes for completion. During December 1990, 1,000 units were produced. The data relating to the process were :

Particulars	A	B	C
Material	30,000	15,000	10,000
Labour	25,000	20,000	15,000
Direct Expenses	5,000	21,600	9,050

The Indirect expenses for the period were Rs. 14,000. The Scrap of Process B and C were sold at Rs. 1,450 and Rs. 1,660, respectively. Prepare the Process A/cs and Cost of Production A/c.

Solution

Process A A/c

Dr. Cr.

Particulars	Units	Rate Rs.	Amount Rs.	Particulars	Units	Rate Rs.	Amount Rs.
To Material	1,000	—	30,000	By Process 'B' A/c	1,000	60	60,000
" Labour	—	—	25,000				
" D/Exp.	—	—	5,000				
	1,000	—	60,000		1,000	60	60,000

Process B A/c

Dr. *Cr.*

Particulars	*Units*	*Rate Rs.*	*Amount Rs.*	*Particulars*	*Units*	*Rate Rs.*	*Amount Rs.*
To Process A	1,000	60	60,000	By C.L. Scrap Value	—	—	1,450
" Material	—	—	15,000	" Process C	1,000	114·15	1,15,150
" Labour	—	—	20,000				
" D/Exp.	—	—	21,600				
	1,000	—	1,16,600		1,000	—	1,16,600

Solution

Process C A/c

Dr. *Cr.*

Particulars	*Units*	*Rate Rs.*	*Amount Rs.*	*Particulars*	*Units*	*Rate Rs.*	*Amount Rs.*
To Process 'B'	1,000	114·15	1,15,150	By C.L.	—	—	1,660
" Material	—	—	10,000	" Finished stock	1,000	147·54	1,47,540
" Labour	—	—	15,000				
" Direct Exp.	—	—	9,050				
	1,000	—	1,49,200		1,000	—	1,49,200

Finished Stock A/c

Dr. *Cr.*

Particulars	*Units*	*Rate Rs.*	*Amount Rs.*	*Particulars*	*Units*	*Rate Rs.*	*Amount Rs.*
To Process 'C' A/c	1,000	146·54	1,47,540	By Balance c/d	1,000	—	1,61,540
" Indirect Expenses	—	—	14,000				
	1,000	—	1,61,540		1,000	—	1,61,540

Problem 7

Banerjee Enterprises produces an article through three successive processes. The following data relate to 31st March 1991. Prepare Process Accounts showing unit Cost at each process.

The output produced in March 1991 is 200 units.

	Process I	*II*	*III*
	Rs.	*Rs.*	*Rs.*
Materials Consumed	20,000	8,000	3,000
Wages booked	16,000	28,000	18,000
Direct charges	4,000	10,000	5,000

Overhead amounts to Rs. 15,500 for the period. Overhead is recovered on the basis of direct wages.

[*B.Com. (Pass) C.U. 1991*]

Solution

Process I Account

Dr. *Cr.*

Particulars	*Units*	*Rate Per unit Rs.*	*Amount*	*Particulars*	*Units*	*Rate Per unit Rs.*	*Amount Rs.*
To Materials	200	100	20,000	By Process II A/c			
" Wages	—	80	16,000	(Transfer)	200	220	44,000
" Direct charges	—	20	4,000				
" Overheads	—	20	4,000				
	200	220	44,000		200	220	44,000

Process II Account

Dr. *Cr.*

Particulars	*Units*	*Rate Per unit Rs.*	*Amount Rs.*	*Particulars*	*Units*	*Rate Per unit Rs.*	*Amount Rs.*
To Process I A/c				By Process III A/c			
(Transfer)	200	220	44,000	(Transfer)	200	485	97,000
" Materials		40	8,000				
" Wages		140	28,000				
" Direct Charges		50	10,000				
" Overhead		35	7,000				
	200	485	97,000		200	485	97,000

Process III Account

Dr. *Cr.*

Particulars	*Units*	*Rate Per unit Rs.*	*Amount Rs.*	*Particulars*	*Units*	*Rate Per unit Rs.*	*Amount Rs.*
To Process II A/c				By Finished Stock A/c	200	637·50	1,27,500
(Transfer)	200	485	97,000				
" Materials		15	3,000				
" Wages		90	18,000				
" Direct Charges		25	5,000				
" Overhead		22·50	4,500				
	200	637·50	1,27,500		200	637·50	1,27,500

Problem 8

The product of a manufacturing concern passes through two processes A and B and then to finished stock. It is ascertained that in each process normally 5% of the total weight is lost and 10% is scrap which realises Rs. 80 per tonne and Rs. 200 per tonne from processes A and B, respectively.

The following are the figures relating to both the processes :

	Process A	*Process B*
Materials	1,000 tonnes	70 tonnes
Cost of materials per tonne	Rs. 125	Rs. 200
Wages	Rs. 28,000	Rs. 10,000

Manufacturing expenses	Rs. 8,000	Rs. 5,250
Output	830 tonnes	780 tonnes

Prepare Process Accounts showing cost per tonne of each process. There was no stock of work-in-progress in any process. **[*C.U. B.Com. (Pass)*]**

Solution

Process A Account

Dr. *Cr.*

Date	*Particulars*	*Units Tonne*	*Rate Rs.*	*Amount Rs.*	*Date*	*Particulars*	*Units Tonne*	*Rate Rs.*	*Amount Rs.*
	To Materials	1,000	125	1,25,000		By Normal Loss A/c [5% of 1,000]	50	—	—
	" Wages			28,000		" Normal Scrap. [10% of 1,000, @ Rs. 80]	100	80	8,000
	" Manufacturing Expenses			8,000		" Abnormal Loss A/c @ Rs. 180	20	180	3,600
						" Process B A/c output (Transfered)	830	180	1,49,400
		1,000		1,61,000			1,000		1,61,000

Process B Account

Dr. *Cr.*

Date	*Particulars*	*Units Tonne*	*Rate Rs.*	*Amount Rs.*	*Date*	*Particulars*	*Units Tonne*	*Rate Rs.*	*Amount Rs.*
	To Process A A/c Input	830	180	1,49,400		By Normal Loss A/c [5% of (830 + 70)	45	—	—
	" Materials	70		14,000		" Normal Scrap A/c [10% of (830 + 70) @ Rs. 200]	90	200	18,000
	" Wages			10,000		" Finished Goods A/c (Transferred to Finished Stock A/c)	780	210	1,63,800
	" Manufacturing Expenses			5,250					
	" Abnormal Gain A/c	15	210	3,150					
		915		1,81,800			915		1,81,800

Workings :

(i) In Process 'A'

Valuation of Cost of Production and Abnormal Loss per unit

$$= \frac{\text{Rs. } (1,25,000 + 28,000 + 8,000 - 8,000)}{1,000 - 50 - 100} = \text{Rs. } 180$$

(ii) In Process 'B'

Valuation of Cost of Production and Abnormal gain per unit

$$= \frac{\text{Rs. } (1,49,400 + 14,000 + 10,000 + 5,250 - 18,000)}{830 + 70 - 90 - 45}$$

$$= \text{Rs. } 210$$

Problem 9

The manufacture of product 'Fanta' requires three distinct processes. On completion, the product is passed from Process B to finished stock. During the month of December 2006, the following information was obtained :

Elements of Costs	*Total*	*Process I*	*Process II*	*Process III*
	Rs.	*Rs.*	*Rs.*	*Rs.*
Direct Material	26,000	15,000	11,000	—
Direct Labour	26,500	12,500	6,000	8,000
Direct Expenses	8,000	3,000	—	5,000
Production overhead	79,500	—	—	—

Production overhead is absorbed by process at a percentage of direct wages. Production during the period was 1,000 kg. There was no stock of raw materials or work-in-progress at the beginning or at the end of the month.

Show the Process Accounts and Finished Stock Account.

[*C.U. B.Com. (Hons.) Adopted*]

Solution

Process I Account

Dr. *Cr.*

Particulars	*Units*	*Rate Rs.*	*Amount Rs.*	*Particulars*	*Units*	*Rate Rs.*	*Amount Rs.*
To Direct Material	1,000	—	15,000	By Process II	1,000	68	68,000
" Direct Labour	—	—	12,500				
" Direct Expenses	—	—	3,000				
" Production Overhead (300% of D/Labour)	—	—	37,500				
	1,000		68,000		1,000		68,000

Process II Account

Dr. *Cr.*

Particulars	*Units*	*Rate Rs.*	*Amount Rs.*	*Particulars*	*Units*	*Rate Rs.*	*Amount Rs.*
To Process	1,000	68	68,000	By Process III	1,000	103	1,03,000
" Direct Material	—	—	11,000				
" Direct Labour	—	—	6,000				
" Production Overhead (300% of D/Labour)	—	—	18,000				
	1,000		1,03,000		1,000		1,03,000

Process III Account

Dr. Cr.

Particulars	Units	Rate Rs.	Amount Rs.	Particulars	Units	Rate Rs.	Amount Rs.
To Process II	1,000	103	1,03,000	By Finished Stock	1,000	140	1,40,000
" Direct Labour	—	—	8,000				
" Direct Exp.	—	—	5,000				
" Production overhead (300% of D/Labour)			24,000				
	1,000		1,40,000		1,000		1,40,000

Finished Stock A/c

Dr. Cr.

Particulars	Units	Rate Rs.	Amount Rs.	Particulars	Units	Rate Rs.	Amount Rs.
To Process III	1,000	140	1,40,000	By Balance c/d	1,000	140	1,40,000

Problem 10

A product is finally obtained after it passes through three distinct processes. The following information is available from the cost records :

	Process I Rs.	Process II Rs.	Process III Rs.	Total Rs.
Materials	2,600	2,000	1,025	5,625
Direct Wages	2,250	3,680	1,400	7,330
Production Overheads				7,330

500 units @ Rs. 4 per unit were introduced in Process I. Production overheads are absorbed as a percentage of direct wages.

The actual output and normal loss of the respective processes are :

	Output (Units)	Normal Loss as % of input	Value of Scrap (per unit) Rs.
Process I	450	10%	2·00
Process II	340	20%	4·00
Process III	270	25%	5·00

Prepare the process accounts and the abnormal Gain/Loss accounts.

[I.C.W.A. (Inter)]

Solution

Process I A/c

Dr. Cr.

Particulars	Units	Rate Rs.	Amount Rs.	Particulars	Units	Rate Rs.	Amount Rs.
To Input	500	4	2,000	By Normal Loss A/c	50	2	100
" Materials			2,600	" Process II A/c (Transferred)	450	20	9,000
" Direct Wages			2,250				
" Production overhead			2,250				
	500		9,100		500		9,100

Process II Account

Dr. *Cr.*

Particulars	Units	Rate Rs.	Amount Rs.	Particulars	Units	Rate Rs.	Amount Rs.
To Process I A/c (Transferred)	450		9,000	By Normal Loss A/c	90	4	360
" Materials			2,000	" Abnormal Loss A/c	40	50	2,000
" Direct Wages			3,680	" Process III A/c (Transferred)	320	50	16,000
" Production overheads			3,680				
	450		18,360		450		18,360

Process III Account

Dr. *Cr.*

Particulars	Units	Rate Rs.	Amount Rs.	Particulars	Units	Rate Rs.	Amount Rs.
To Process II A/c (Transferred)	320		16,000	By Normal Loss A/c	80	5	400
" Materials			1,025	" Finished Stock A/c	270	80·93	21,853
" Direct Wages			1,400				
" Production Overhead			1,400				
" Abnormal Gain A/c	30	80·93	2,428				
	350		22,253		350		22,253

Problem 11

A product passes through processes A, B and C. The normal wastage of each process is :
Process A = 5% Process B = 6% and Process C = 10%

Wastage of Process A was sold at Rs. 2 per unit, that of Process B at Rs. 5 per unit and that of Process C at Rs. 10 per unit.

1,000 units were issued to Process A in the beginning of April, 2007, at a loss of Rs. 2 per unit. The other expenses were :

	Process A	Process B	Process C
	Rs.	Rs.	Rs.
Materials	2,000	3,000	1,000
Labour	5,000	8,000	6,000
Direct Expenses	1,550	2,946	3,738
Actual Output (units)	950	910	810

Prepare Process Accounts assuming that there were no opening or closing stocks.

Solution

Process A Account

Dr. Cr.

Particulars	Units	Rate Rs.	Amount Rs.	Particulars	Units	Rate Rs.	Amount Rs.
To Units issued	1,000	2	2,000	By Normal Loss A/c	50	2	100
" Materials			2,000	(5% on 1,000)			
" Labour			5,000	" Process B A/c	950	11	10,450
" Direct Expenses			1,550	Transferred			
	1,000		10,550		1,000		10,550

Process B Account

Dr. Cr.

Particulars	Units	Rate Rs.	Amount Rs.	Particulars	Units	Rate Rs.	Amount Rs.
To Process A A/c transferred	950	11	10,450	By Normal Loss A/c	57	5	285
" Materials			3,000	(6% on 950)			
" Labour			8,000	By Process C A/c			
" Direct Expenses			2,946	Transferred	910	27	24,570
" Abnormal Gain A/c	17	27	479				
	967		24,855		967		24,855

Process C Account

Dr. Cr.

Particulars	Units	Rate Rs.	Amount Rs.	Particulars	Units	Rate Rs.	Amount Rs.
To Process B				By Normal Loss A/c	91	10	910
A/c Transferred	910	27	24,570	Transferred			
" Materials			1,000	" Abnormal Loss A/c	9	42	378
" Labour			6,000				
" Direct Expenses			3,738	" Finished Stock A/c	810	42	34,020
	910		35,308		910		35,308

Problem 12

From the following particulars relating to two processes—Process A and Process—B, prepare necessary accounts for a period :

	Process A	*Process B*
Input (units)	5,000	4,600
Normal Loss	16%	5%
Cost incurred :	Rs.	Rs.
Materials	8,000	1,500
Direct Labour	3,000	4,000
Overhead	2,750	2,150
Realisable scrap value per unit	Re. 0·50	Rs. 2

The output of Process A is transferred to Process B and that of Process B to finished goods. The output of Process B was 4,300. Assume that there was no closing work-in-progress and finished goods.

[*C.U. M.Com.*]

Solution

Process A Account

Dr. Particulars	Units	Rate Rs.	Amount Rs.	Cr. Particulars	Units	Rate Rs.	Amount Rs.
To Material	5,000	1·60	8,000	By Normal Loss A/c	800	0·50	400
" Direct Labour			3,000	" Process 'B' A/c (Transferred)	4,600	3·18	14,622
" Overhead			2,750				
	5,000		13,750				
" Abnormal Gain A/c	400	3·18	1,272				
	5,400		15,022		5,400		15,022

Process B Account

Dr. Particulars	Units	Rate Rs.	Amount Rs.	Cr. Particulars	Units	Rate Rs.	Amount Rs.
To Process 'A' A/c	4,600	3·18	14,622	By Normal Loss A/c	230	2·00	460
" Materials			1,500	" Abnormal Loss A/c	70	4·99	349
" Direct Labour			4,000	" Finished Goods A/c	4,300	4·99	21,463
" Overhead			2,150				
	4,600		22,272		4,600		22,272

Normal Loss Account

Dr. Particulars	Units	Rate Rs.	Amount Rs.	Cr. Particulars	Units	Rate Rs.	Amount Rs.
To Process 'A' A/c	800	0·50	400	By *Cash A/c	400	0·50	200
" Process B A/c	230	2·00	460	" Abnormal Gain A/c	400	0·50	200
				" Cash A/c	230	2·00	460
	1,030		860		1,030		860

Abnormal Loss Account

Dr. Particulars	Units	Rate Rs.	Amount Rs.	Cr. Particulars	Units	Rate Rs.	Amount Rs.
To Process B A/c	70	4·99	349	By *Cash A/c	70	2·00	140
				" Profit & Loss A/c (Transferred)			209
	70		349		70		349

Abnormal Gain Account

Dr. Particulars	Units	Rate Rs.	Amount Rs.	Cr. Particulars	Units	Rate Rs.	Amount Rs.
To Normal Loss A/c	400	0·50	200	By Process 'A' A/c	400	3·18	1,272
" Profit & Loss A/c (Transferred)			1,072				
	400		1,272		400		1,272

Finished Goods Account

Dr.							*Cr.*
Particulars	*Units*	*Rate* *Rs.*	*Amount* *Rs.*	*Particulars*	*Units*	*Rate* *Rs.*	*Amount* *Rs.*
To Process B A/c	4,300	4·99	21,463	By Balance c/d	4,300	4·99	21,463
	4,300		21,463		4,300		21,463
To Balance b/d	4,300		21,463				

***Note :** Here Cash A/c can also be called C.L.C. A/c

Workings :

(i) In Process A

Valuation of Cost of Production and Abnormal Gain per unit

$$= \frac{\text{Rs. } (13{,}750 - 400)}{5{,}000 - 800} = \text{Rs. } 3{\cdot}18 \text{ (approx.)}$$

(ii) In Process B

Valuation of Cost of Production and Abnormal Loss per unit

$$= \frac{\text{Rs. } (22{,}272 - 460)}{4{,}600 - 230} = \text{Rs. } 4{\cdot}99$$

Problem 13

Product B is obtained after it passes through three distinct processes. The following information is obtained from the accounts for the week ending May 30, 2007 :

		Process		
	Total	*I*	*II*	*III*
	Rs.	*Rs.*	*Rs.*	*Rs.*
Direct Material	7,542	2,600	1,980	2,962
Direct Wages	9,000	2,000	3,000	4,000
Production Overhead	9,000			

1,000 units at Rs. 3 each were introduced to Process I. There was no stock of materials or work-in-progress at the beginning or end of the period. The output of each process passes direct to the next process and finally to finished stores.

Production overhead is recovered on 100% of direct wages.

The following additional data are obtained :

Process	*Output during the week*	*Percentage of normal loss to input*	*Value of scrap per unit* *Rs.*
I	950	5%	2
II	840	10%	4
III	750	15%	5

Prepare process cost accounts and abnormal loss or gain account.

[*C.S. (Inter) Adopted*]

Solution

Process I Account

Dr. *Cr.*

Particulars	Units	Rate Rs.	Amount Rs.	Particulars	Units	Rate Rs.	Amount Rs.
To Input	1,000	3	3,000	By Normal Loss (5%)	50	2	100
" Material	—	—	2,600	" Process II	950	10	9,500
" Wages	—	—	2,000				
" Production Overhead (100% of wages)	—	—	2,000				
	1,000	—	9,600		1,000	—	9,600

$$\text{Cost per unit} = \frac{9{,}600-100}{1{,}000-50} = \frac{9{,}500}{950} = \text{Rs. } 10$$

Process II Account

Dr. *Cr.*

Particulars	Units	Rate Rs.	Amount Rs.	Particulars	Units	Rate Rs.	Amount Rs.
To Process I	950	10	9,500	By Normal Loss (10%)	95	4	380
" D/Material	—	—	1,980	" Abnormal Loss	15	20	300
" Wages	—	—	3,000	" Process III	840	20	16,800
" Overhead (100% of D/W)	—	—	3,000				
	950	—	17,480		950	—	17,480

$$\text{Cost per unit} = \frac{17{,}480-380}{950-95} = \frac{17{,}100}{855} = \text{Rs. } 20$$

Process III Account

Dr. *Cr.*

Particulars	Units	Rate Rs.	Amount Rs.	Particulars	Units	Rate Rs.	Amount Rs.
To Process II	840	20	16,800	By Normal Loss (15%)	126	5	630
" Material	—	—	2,962	" Finished Stock	750	38	28,500
" Direct Wages	—	—	4,000				
" Overhead (100%)	—	—	4,000				
	840		27,762				
To Abnormal Gain	36	38	1,368				
	876		29,130		876		29,130

$$\text{Cost per unit} = \frac{27{,}762-630}{840-126} = \text{Rs. } \frac{27{,}132}{712} = \text{Rs. } 38$$

Normal Loss Account

Dr. Cr.

Particulars	Units	Rate Rs.	Amount Rs.	Particulars	Units	Rate Rs.	Amount Rs.
To Process I	50	2	100	By C.L.C.	50	2	100
" Process II	95	4	380	" C.L.C.	95	4	380
" Process III	126	5	630	" Abnormal Gain	36	5	180
				" C.L.C.	90	5	450
	271		1,110		271		1,110

Abnormal Gain Account

Dr. Cr.

Particulars	Units	Rate Rs.	Amount Rs.	Particulars	Units	Rate Rs.	Amount Rs.
To Normal Loss	36	5	180	By Process III	36	38	1,368
" Costing P/L A/c	—	—	1,188				
	36	—	1,368		36	—	1,368

Abnormal Loss Account

Dr. Cr.

Particulars	Units	Rate Rs.	Amount Rs.	Particulars	Units	Rate Rs.	Amount Rs.
To Process II	15	20	300	By C.L.C.	15	4	60
				" Costing P/L A/c	—	—	240
	15	—	300		15	—	300

Problem 14

The following are the details in respect of Process X and Process Y of a processing factory:

	Process X Rs.	*Process Y* Rs.
Materials	10,000	—
Labour	10,000	14,000
Overheads	4,000	10,000

The output of Process X is transferred to Process Y at a price calculated to give a profit of 20% on the transfer price and the output of Process Y is charged to Finished Stock at a profit of 25% on the transfer price. The Finishing department realised Rs. 1,00,000 for the finished goods received from Process Y.

You are asked to show Process Accounts and total profits assuming that there was no opening and no closing work-in-progress. **[*C.A. Inter*]**

Solution

Process X Account

Dr. Cr.

Particulars	Amount Rs.	Particulars	Amount Rs.
To Material	10,000	By Transfer to Process A/c	30,000
" Labour	10,000		
" Overheads	4,000		
" Profit 20% of Transfer Price (*i.e.* 25% of cost price)	6,000		
	30,000		30,000

Process Y Account

Dr. *Cr.*

Particulars	*Amount* Rs.	*Particulars*	*Amount* Rs.
To Transfer from Process X A/c	30,000	By Transfer to Finished Stock A/c	72,000
" Labour	14,000		
" Overheads	10,000		
" Profit (25%) of the transfer price (*i.e.* $33\frac{1}{3}$% of cost price)	18,000		
	72,000		72,000

Profit & Loss Account

Dr. *Cr.*

Particulars	*Amount* Rs.	*Particulars*	*Amount* Rs.
To Cost of Sale	72,000	By Sales	1,00,000
To Profit c/d	28,000		
	1,00,000		1,00,000
To Total Costing Profit	52,000	By Profit on Process X	6,000
		" Profit on Process Y	18,000
		" Profit on Sales	28,000
	52,000		52,000

Problem 15

A product which uses 100 tonnes as input per month passes through two processes. The details of cost in Process I for April 2007 are :

Process I	*Cost per tonne (Rupees)*
Direct Material Cost	26,100
Direct Labour Cost	7,800
Overhead	13,500

The total loss in process I is 2% of input, and the scrap is 8% of input with a value of Rs. 12,000 per tonne.

The material is transferred to Process II at cost. The process Direct Labour Cost at Process II is Rs. 9,000 per tonne of input. The overhead is 60% of Direct Labour Cost. The scrap at Process II is at 20% of input with a value of Rs. 12,000 per tonne.

Draw up a Cost Sheet to present the manufacturing cost of the product showing clearly the cost of scrap and waste at each stage of manufacture.

[*C.S. (Inter) Adopted*]

Solution

Process I Account

Dr. *Cr.*

Particulars	*Units*	*Rate* Rs.	*Amount* Rs.	*Particulars*	*Units*	*Rate* Rs.	*Amount* Rs.
To Direct Material	100	26,100	26,10,000	By Normal Loss (2%)	2	—	—
" Direct Labour	—	7,800	7,80,000	" Scrap (8%)	8	1,200	96,000
" Overhead	—	13,500	13,50,000	" Process II	90	51,600	46,44,000
	100	—	47,40,000		100	—	47,40,000

$$\text{Cost per unit} = \frac{47{,}40{,}000 - 96{,}000}{100 - 10} = \text{Rs. } 51{,}600$$

Process II Account

Dr. Particulars	Units	Rate Rs.	Amount Rs.	Particulars	Units	Rate Rs.	Amount Rs. Cr.
To Process I	90	51,600	46,44,000	By Scrap (20%)	18	12,000	2,16,000
" Direct Labour	—	9,000	8,10,000	" Finished Stock	72	79,500	57,24,000
" Overhead (60% of Direct Labour)	—	—	4,86,000				
	90	—	59,40,000		90	—	59,40,000

$$\text{Cost per unit} = \frac{59,40,000 - 2,16,000}{90 - 18}$$

$$= \frac{57,24,000}{72} = \text{Rs. } 79,500$$

$\therefore$ Manufacturing cost of Final Product $= \text{Rs. } 79,500 \times 72$
$= \text{Rs. } 57,24,000$

Problem 16

From the following particulars relating to two processes : Process X and Process Y prepare the necessary accounts for a period from the following data :

	Process X	*Process Y*
Input (units)	50,000	46,000
Normal Loss	10%	?
Cost incurred :	*Rs.*	*Rs.*
Materials	80,000	15,000
Direct Labour	30,000	40,000
Overhead	27,500	30,100
Realisable Scrap value per unit	Re. 0·50	Rs. 2

The output of Process X is transferred to Process Y. The output of Process Y was 43,000 units. They were sold at Rs. 6 per unit showing a profit of 20% on cost. Assume that there was no closing work-in-progress and finished goods. **[*M.Com. C.U., Adopted*]**

Solution

Process X Account

Dr. Particulars	Units	Rate Rs.	Amount Rs.	Particulars	Units	Rate Rs.	Amount Rs. Cr.
To Material	50,000	—	80,000	By Normal Loss A/c [10% on 50,000 units]	5,000	0·50	2,500
" Direct Labour	—	—	30,000	" Process Y A/c [Transferred]	46,000	3	1,38,000
" Overhead	—	—	27,500				
	50,000		1,37,500				
To Abnormal Gain A/c	1,000	3	3,000				
	51,000		1,40,500		51,000		1,40,500

Valuation of cost of Production and Abnormal gain per unit

$$= \frac{1,37,500 - 2,500}{50,000 - 5,000} = \frac{1,35,000}{45,000} = \text{Rs. } 3$$

Process Y Account

Dr. Cr.

Particulars	Units	Rate Rs.	Amount Rs.	Particulars	Units	Rate Rs.	Amount Rs.
To Process X A/c	46,000	3	1,38,000	By Normal Loss A/c[1]	2,300	2	4,600
" Materials	—	—	15,000	" Abnormal Loss A/c	700	5	3,500
" Labour	—	—	40,000	" Finished goods	43,000	5	2,15,000
" Overhead	—	—	30,100				
	46,000		2,23,100		46,000		2,23,100

Workings :

1. Sales Price = Rs. 6

Profit = 20% on Cost *i.e.* $\frac{1}{5}$th of Cost

= $\frac{1}{6}$th of Sales

∴ Profit = Rs. $6 \times \frac{1}{6}$ = Re. 1

∴ Cost per unit = Rs. (6 − 1) = Rs. 5.

Let, Normal Loss = x unit.

∴ We know cost per unit = $\dfrac{\text{Total value of Input} - \text{Scrap value}}{\text{Unit} - \text{Normal Loss}}$

or, $5 = \dfrac{\text{Rs. } 2{,}23{,}100 - 2x}{46{,}000 \text{ units} - x}$

or, $2{,}30{,}000 - 5x = 2{,}23{,}100 - 2x$

or, $3x = 6{,}900$

∴ $x = \dfrac{6{,}900}{3} = 2{,}300$ units.

Problem 17

A product passes through three processes—A, B and C. 10,000 units at a cost of Rs. 1·10 were issued to process A. The other direct expenses were :

	Process A Rs.	Process B Rs.	Process C Rs.
Sundry Materials	1,500	1,500	1,500
Direct Labour	4,500	8,000	6,500
Direct Expenses	1,000	1,000	1,503

The wastage of Process A was 5% and in process B 4%. The wastage of Process A was sold at Rs. 0·25 per unit and that of B at Re. 0·50 per unit and that of C at Re. 1·00 per unit.

The overhead charges were 160% of direct labour. The final product was sold at Rs. 10 per unit fetching profit of 20% on Sales.

Find out the percentage of wastage in process C.

[*I.C.W.A. (Final)*]

Solution

Process A Account

Dr. Particulars	Units	Rate Rs.	Amount Rs.	Particulars	Units	Rate Rs.	Cr. Amount Rs.
To Input	10,000	1·10	11,000	By Normal Loss (5%)	500	0·25	125
" Material	—	—	1,500	" Process 'B'	9,500	2·64	25,075
" Labour	—	—	4,500				
" Direct Expenses	—	—	1,000				
" Overhead (160% of Direct Labour)	—	—	7,200				
	10,000	—	25,200		10,000		25,200

$$\text{Cost per unit} = \frac{25{,}200 - 125}{10{,}000 - 500} = \frac{25{,}075}{9{,}500}$$

$$= \text{Rs. } 2{\cdot}64 \text{ (approx.)}$$

Process B Account

Dr. Particulars	Units	Rate Rs.	Amount Rs.	Particulars	Units	Rate Rs.	Cr. Amount Rs.
To Process A	9,500	2·64	25,075	By Normal Loss (4%)	380	0·50	190
" Material	—	—	1,500	" Process C	9,120	5·283	48,185
" Labour	—	—	8,000				
" Direct Expenses	—	—	1,000				
" Overhead	—	—	12,800				
	9,500	—	48,375		9,500	—	48,375

$$\text{Cost Per Unit} = \frac{48{,}375 - 190}{9{,}500 - 380} = \frac{48{,}185}{9{,}100} = \text{Rs. } 5{\cdot}283$$

Process C Account

Dr. Particulars	Units	Rate Rs.	Amount Rs.	Particulars	Units	Rate Rs.	Cr. Amount Rs.
To Process B	9,120	5·283	48,185	By Normal Loss	696	1·00	696
" Material	—	—	1,500	" Finished Stock	8,424	8	67,392
" Labour	—	—	6,500				
" Direct Expenses	—	—	1,503				
" Overhead	—	—	10,400				
	9,120	—	68,088		9,120	—	68,088

Workings :

$$\text{Profit} = 20\% \text{ on Sale} = \frac{1}{5} \text{ on Sale}$$

$$\therefore \text{Profit per unit} = \frac{1}{5} \times \text{Rs. } 10 = 2$$

$\therefore$ Cost per unit = (10 − 2) = 8

Let Normal Loss = x unit.

Now we can write $8 = \dfrac{\text{Total Value of Input – Scrap Value}}{\text{Input Units – Normal Loss Units}}$

$\therefore 8 = \dfrac{68{,}088 - 1 \times \mathbf{x}}{9{,}120 - \mathbf{x}}$

$\therefore 72{,}960 - 8x = 68{,}088 - x$

$\therefore 72{,}960 - 68{,}088 = 7x$

$\dfrac{4{,}872}{7} = x \quad \therefore x = 696$

$\therefore$ Normal Loss = 696 units.

Problem 18

Product ZENU is made by three sequential Processes I, II and III. In Process III a by-product arises and after further processing in Process XY, at a cost of Rs. 2 per unit, by-product XYZ is produced. Selling price Rs. 9 per unit, distribution expenses Re. 1 per unit.

	Process I	*Process II*	*Process III*
Standard Provided for :			
Normal Loss in Process of input	10%	5%	10%
Loss in process, having a scrap value per unit, of	Re. 1	Rs. 3	Rs. 5

For the month of April 1990 the following data are given :

	Process I	*Process II*	*Process III*	*Process XY*
Output in units	8,800	8,400	7,000 of ZENU	420 of XYZ
Cost	*Rs.*	*Rs.*	*Rs.*	Total *Rs.*
Direct Materials introduced (10,000 units)	20,000			20,000
Direct Materials added	6,000	12,640	23,200	41,840
Direct Wages	5,000	6,000	10,000	21,000
Direct Expenses	4,000	6,200	4,080	14,280

Budgeted production overhead for the month was Rs. 84,000. Absorption is based on a percentage of direct wages. There are no stocks at the beginning or end of the month.

You are required, using the information given, to prepare accounts for :

(*i*) Each Process—I, II and III, (*ii*) Process XY. ***[I.C.W.A. (Inter) Dec. 1990]***

Solution

Process I Account

Dr. *Cr.*

Particulars	*Units*	*Rate Rs.*	*Amount Rs.*	*Particulars*	*Units*	*Rate Rs.*	*Amount Rs.*
To Direct Material (20,000 + 6,000)	10,000	—	26,000	By Normal Loss (10%)	1,000	1	1,000
" Direct Wages	—	—	5,000	" Abnormal Loss	200	6	1,200
" Prod. OH (400% of D/W)	—	—	20,000	" Process II A/c	8,800	6	52,800
" Direct Expenses	—	—	4,000				
	10,000	—	55,000		10,000	—	55,000

$$\text{Cost per unit} = \frac{\text{Total Value of Input} - \text{Scrap Value}}{\text{Input Units} - \text{Normal Loss Units}}$$

$$= \frac{55{,}000 - 1{,}000}{10{,}000 - 1{,}000} = \frac{54{,}000}{9{,}000} = \text{Rs. } 6$$

Process II Account

Dr. Particulars	Units	Rate Rs.	Amount Rs.	Particulars	Units	Rate Rs.	Amount Rs. *Cr.*
To Process I	8,800	6	52,800	By Normal Loss (5%)	440	3	1,330
" Direct Mat.	—	—	12,640	" Process III	8,400	12	1,00,800
" Direct Wages	—	—	6,000				
" Direct Expenses	—	—	6,200				
" Prod. Overhead	—	—	24,000				
	8,800	—	1,01,640				
To Abnormal Gain	40	12	480				
	8,840	—	1,02,120		8,840	—	1,02,120

$$\text{Cost per Unit} = \frac{1{,}02{,}640 - 1{,}330}{8{,}400 - 440} = \text{Rs. } \frac{1{,}00{,}320}{8{,}360} = \text{Rs. } 12$$

Process III Account

Dr. Particulars	Units	Rate Rs.	Amount Rs.	Particulars	Units	Rate Rs.	Amount Rs. *Cr.*
To Process II	8,400	12	1,00,800	By Normal Loss (10%)	840	5	4,200
" Direct Material	—	—	23,200	" Abnormal Loss	140	24	3,360
" Direct Wages	—	—	10,000	" Product XY	420	6	2,520
" Prod. Overhead	—	—	40,000	" Zenu—Finished Stock	7,000	24	1,68,000
" Direct Expenses	—	—	4,080				
	8,400	—	1,78,080		8,400	—	1,78,080

Workings :

1. Calculation for value per unit of Product XY

	Rs.	Rs.
Sales price of by product = 420 × 9		3,780
Less : Further Processing Cost (420 × 2)	840	
Distribution Exp. (420 × 1)	420	1,260
∴ Net realisable amount from by—product		2,520

$$\therefore \text{Per Unit Realisable Value} = \frac{2{,}500}{420} = \text{Rs. } 6$$

2. Calculation for Cost Per Unit of ZENU

$$\text{Cost Per Unit} = \frac{\text{Total Value of Input} - \text{Scrap Value} - \text{By Product realisable value}}{\text{Input units} - \text{Normal Loss Units} - \text{By Product Units}}$$

$$= \frac{1{,}78{,}080 - 4{,}200 - 2{,}520}{8{,}400 - 840 - 420} = \frac{1{,}71{,}360}{7{,}140}$$

$$= \text{Rs. } 24$$

3. Calculation for Absorption Rate of Production Overhead on Direct Wages
   Total Direct Wages for the process = 21,000
   Total Production overhead = Rs. 84,000
   $\therefore$ % of Prod. Overhead on Direct Wages = $\frac{84,000}{21,000} \times 100 = 400\%$

Process XY Account

Dr. *Cr.*

Particulars	*Units*	*Rate Rs.*	*Amount Rs.*	*Particulars*	*Units*	*Rate Rs.*	*Amount Rs.*
To Process III	420	6	2,520	By XYZ	420	8	3,360
" Further processing		2	840				
	420	—	3,360		420	—	3,360

Problem 19

The product of a manufacturing unit passes through two distinct processes. From past experience the incidence of wastage is ascertained as :

Process A	2%
Process B	10%

In each case the percentage of wastage is computed on the number of units entering the process concerned. The sales realisation of wastage in Processes A and B are Rs. 25 per 100 units and Rs. 50 per 100 units, respectively.

The following information is obtained for the month of April 2007 : 40,000 units of crude material were introduced in Process A at a cost of Rs. 16,000.

	Process A	*Process B*
	Rs.	*Rs.*
Other Material	16,000	5,000
Direct Labour	9,000	8,000
Direct Expenses	8,200	1,500
	Units	*Units*
Output	39,000	36,500
Finished Product Stock :		
April 1	6,000	5,000
April 30	5,000	8,000
Value of Stock per unit on	*Rs.*	*Rs.*
April 1	1·20	1·60

Stocks are valued and transferred to subsequent process at weighted average costs. Prepare respective Process Accounts and Stock Accounts.

[*I.C.W.A. Inter Adopted*]

Process A Account

Dr. Cr.

Particulars	Units	Rate Rs.	Amount Rs.	Particulars	Units	Rate Rs.	Amount Rs.
To Units introduced	40,000	0·40	16,000	By Normal Loss [2% of 40,000]	800	0·25	200
" Material	—	—	16,000	" Abnormal Loss	200	1·25*	250
" Labour	—	—	9,000	" Finished Stock	39,000	1·25	48,750
" Direct Expenses	—	—	8,200				
	40,000		49,200		40,000		49,200

*Cost per unit for output and abnormal loss

$$= \frac{(\text{Rs. } 49{,}200 - \text{Rs. } 200)}{(40{,}000 - 800)} = \frac{49{,}000}{39{,}200} = \text{Rs. } 1·25$$

Process A Stock Account

Dr. Cr.

Particulars	Units Rs.	Rate Rs.	Amount	Particulars	Units Rs.	Rate Rs.	Amount
To Opening Stock	6,000	1·20	7,200	By Process B A/c	40,000	1·2433*	49,733
" Process A	39,000	1·25	48,750	" Balance (Closing Stock)	5,000	1·2433*	6,217
	45,000		55,950		45,000		55,950

* Weighted Average Cost per unit = Rs. 55,950 – 45,000 units = Rs. 1·2433

Process B Account

Dr. Cr.

Particulars	Units	Rate Rs.	Amount Rs.	Particulars	Units	Rate Rs.	Amount Rs.
To Process A Stock A/c	40,000	1·2433	49,733	By Normal Loss [10% of 40,000]	4,000	0·50	2,000
" Material	—	—	5,000				
" Labour	—	—	8,000	By Process B Stock A/c	36,500	1·7287*	63,097
" Direct Expenses	—	—	1,500				
" Abnormal Gain A/c	500	1·7287*	864				
	40,500		65,097		40,500		65,097

*Cost per unit for output and abnormal gain :

= (Rs. 64,233 – Rs. 2,000) ÷ (40,000 – 4,000)
= Rs. 62,233 ÷ 36,000 units
= Rs. 1·7287

Process B Stock Account

Dr. Cr.

Particulars	Units	Rate Rs.	Amount Rs.	Particulars	Units	Rate Rs.	Amount Rs.
To Opening Stock	5,000	1·60	8,000	By Finished Stock A/c	33,500	1·7132*	57,392
" Process B	36,500	1·7287	63,097	" Closing Stock	8,000	1·7132*	13,705
	41,500		71,097		41,500		71,097

* Weighted Average Cost per unit = Rs. 71,097 ÷ 41,500 units = Rs. 1·7132

Problem 20

A product is produced through two distinct processes—Process I and Process II. On completion, it is transferred to finished stock.

From the following particulars during the month of December 1994, prepare Process Accounts and Finished Stock Account :

	Process I	Process II
Units Introduced	10,000	9,000
Transfer to next process/Finished goods	9,000	8,250
Normal loss (on inputs)	10%	5%
Realisable Value of normal loss (Per unit)	Rs. 2	Rs. 4
Cost incurred :	Rs.	Rs.
Direct Materials	40,000	—
Direct Labour	20,000	20,000
Direct Expenses	12,000	10,050
Production overhead (100% of Direct Labour)		

Assume that there was no opening or closing stock of raw materials and work-in-progress.

[C.U. B.Com. (Hons.) 1995]

Solution

Process I A/c

Dr. Cr.

Particulars	Units	Rate Rs.	Amount Rs.	Particulars	Units	Rate Rs.	Amount Rs.
To Material	10,000	—	40,000	By Normal Loss [10% of input]	1,000	2	2,000
" Labour	—	—	20,000	" Process II	9,000	10	90,000
" Expenses	—	—	12,000				
" Production Overhead (100% of D/L)	—	—	20,000				
	10,000		92,000		10,000		92,000

Process II A/c

Dr. Cr.

Particulars	Units	Rate Rs.	Amount Rs.	Particulars	Units	Rate Rs.	Amount Rs.
To Process I	9,000	10	90,000	By Normal Loss 5%	450	4	1,800
" Labour	—	—	20,000	" Finished Stock	8,250	16·17	1,33,400
" Expenses	—	—	10,050	" Abnormal Loss	300	16·17	4,850
" Production Overhead (100% of D/L)	—	—	20,000				
	9,000		1,40,050		9,000		1,40,050

$$\text{Cost per unit} = \frac{\text{Total value of Input} - \text{Scrap Value}}{\text{Input units} - \text{Normal loss units}}$$

$$= \frac{1,40,050 - 1,800}{9,000 - 450} = \frac{\text{Rs. } 1,38,250}{8,550} = \text{Rs. } 16{\cdot}17$$

Finished Stock A/c

Dr. *Cr.*

Particulars	*Units*	*Rate Rs.*	*Amount Rs.*	*Particulars*	*Units*	*Rate Rs.*	*Amount Rs.*
To Process II	8,250	16·17	1,33,400	By Cost of goods	8,250	16·17	1,33,400

Problem 21

A Ltd. produces a product which passes through two processes before it is completed and transferred to finished stock. The following data relate to September 1990 :

Particulars	*Process I*	*Process II*	*Finished Stock*
	Rs.	*Rs.*	*Rs.*
Opening Stock	3,000	3,600	9,000
Direct Materials	6,000	6,300	
Direct Wages	4,480	4,500	
Factory Overheads	4,200	1,800	
Closing Stock	1,480	1,800	4,500
Interprocess profit included in Op. Stock		600	3,300

Output of Process I is transferred to Process II at 25% profit on the transfer price and output of Process II is transferred to finished stock at 20% profit on the transfer price. Stocks in process are valued at prime cost. Finished stock is valued at the price at which it is received from Process II. Sales during the period were Rs. 56,000.

Required. Prepare Process Cost A/c and Finished Stock A/c showing the profit element at each stage. **[*C.A. Nov. (Int.) 1981 and Nov. 1990*]**

Solution

Process I Account

Dr. *Cr.*

Particulars	*Cost*	*Profit*	*Total*	*Particulars*	*Cost*	*Profit*	*Total*
To Opening Stock	3,000	—	3,000	By Process II	16,200	5,400	21,600
" Direct Material	6,000	—	6,000	A/c (transfer)			
" Direct Wages	4,480	—	4,480				
	13,480	—	13,480				
Less : Closing Stock	1,480	—	1,480				
Prime Cost	12,000	—	12,000				
To Factory Overhead	4,200	—	4,200				
To Cost	16,200	—	16,200				
" Profit		5,400	5,400				
(25% Transferred *i.e.* $\frac{1}{3}$rd on cost)							
	16,200	5,400	21,600		16,200	5,400	21,600

Process II Account

Dr. Particulars	Cost	Profit	Total	Particulars	Cost	Profit	Cr. Total
To Opening Stock	3,000	600	3,600	By Finished	30,300	14,700	45,000
" Process I (A/c transfer)	16,200	5,400	21,600	Stock (transfer)			
" Direct Material	6,300	—	6,300				
" Direct Wages	4,500	—	4,500				
	30,000	6,000	36,000				
Less : Closing Stock	1,500	300*	1,800				
Prime Cost	28,500	5,700	34,200				
To Factory Overhead	1,800	—	1,800				
Total Cost	30,300	5,700	36,000				
" Profit (20% on T.P. *i.e.* 25% on cost)		9,000	9,000				
	30,300	14,700	45,000		30,300	14,700	45,000

$$* \text{[Closing Stock} \times \frac{\text{Profit}}{\text{Total cost}} = 1{,}800 \times \frac{6{,}000}{36{,}000} = 300]$$

Finished Stock A/c

Dr. Particulars	Cost	Profit	Total	Particulars	Cost	Profit	Cr. Total
To Opening Stock	5,700	3,300	9,000	By Sales A/c	33,000	23,000	56,000
" Process II A/c transfer	30,300	14,700	45,000				
	36,000	18,000	54,000				
Less : Closing Stock	3,000	1,500*	4,500				
Total Cost	33,000	16·500	49,500				
" Profit		6,500	6,500				
	33,000	23,000	56,000		33,000	23,000	56,000

$$*\text{[Closing Stock} \times \frac{\text{Profit}}{\text{Total Cost}} = 4{,}500 \times \frac{18{,}000}{54{,}000} = \text{Rs. } 1{,}500]$$

EXERCISES

OBJECTIVE TYPE

1. *Indicate whether following statements are true or false :*

(*a*) Normal Loss does not increase the cost per unit of Usual Production.
(*b*) Abnormal Loss is spread on good units of production.
(*c*) Abnormal gain should reduce the normal loss and the balance is transferred to costing Profit & Loss A/c.
(*d*) Process costing is applied in garment industry.
(*e*) Process costing is used in chemical works.
(*f*) Inclusion of inter-profit in accounts will not require any adjustment in stocks.

[Ans. True : (c) (e)
False : (a) (b) (d) (f)]

2. *An abnormal gain in a process occurs in which of the following situations ?*
   (*a*) When the process output is greater than planned.
   (*b*) When actual losses are less than the normal level.
   (*c*) When actual losses are greater than the normal loss Level.
   (*d*) When costs are reduced through increased machine speed.

[Ans. (*b*)]

3. *Where process scrape is re-cycled for use in conjunction with new material as well as being sold externally, which of the following is most likely to be the value at which it is debited to the process ?*
   (*a*) At the same price as it is sold externally.
   (*b*) At the cost of normal losses.
   (*c*) At the cost attached to abnormal losses.
   (*d*) NIL value.

[Ans. (*a*)]

4. *Purchased materials are added in the second department of a three department process; this will increase the number of units produced in the second department and would always :*
   (*a*) Change the direct labour cost percentage in the ending work in process inventory.
   (*b*) Cause no adjustment to the unit cost transferred in from the first department.
   (*c*) Increase in total unit costs.
   (*d*) Decrease total ending work-in-process inventory.

[Ans. (b)]

5. *In process cost computation, the cost of ending work-in-progress inventory is calculated on the*
   (*a*) Quantities Schedule.
   (*b*) Computation of equivalent production.
   (*c*) Total costs to Account for schedule.
   (*d*) Total costs Accounted for schedule.

[Ans. (b)]

THEORETICAL QUESTIONS
PRINCIPLES OF PROCESS COST AND INTER PROCESS PROFIT

1. Distinguish between Job Costing and Process Costing.

   [*I.C.W.A. (Inter) June 1990; C.U. B.Com. (H) 1981, 1987.*]

2. (*a*) In what type of industries process costing is generally accepted ?
   (*b*) Discuss with figures the method of treatment of process loss and wastage under a process costing method. [*I.C.W.A. (Inter).*]
3. Define normal and abnormal process losses explaining with possible causes. [*I.C.W.A. (Inter).*]
4. State the special features of process costing.
5. State the advantages and disadvantages of process costing.
6. Write short notes on : Abnormal Gain in process costing. [*C.A. Inter (May) 1995*]
7. Explain normal loss, abnormal loss and abnormal gain and state how they should be dealt within process cost accounts. [*C.A. Inter Nov. 98*]

PROBLEMS

1. A product passes through two processes namely 'Process X' and 'Process Y'. The following data relate to March 1991. Prepare the Process A/cs.

	Process X	*Process Y*
Input (Units)	4,000	3,600
Normal Loss	10%	5%
Scrap Value Per Unit	Re. 1	Rs. 3
Material Consumed	20,000	1,540
Wages	12,400	2,000
Overhead	4,000	2,000

The output of Process Y transferred to Finished stock.

[Ans. Cost Per Unit : Process X = Rs. 10 ; Process Y= Rs. 11,988]

2. Bengal Chemical Ltd. produces a new chemical product which passes through three processes before completion and transferred to finished stock.

During the year ended 31.12.90, data relating to the product were :

	Process I Rs.	*Process II* Rs.	*Process III* Rs.
Input Units (10,000)	10,000	—	—
Direct Material	18,000	12,000	—
Direct Wages	12,400	4,500	6,000
Direct Expenses	2,680	3,200	4,000
Normal Loss	10%	10%	5%
Scrap Value	1	1·50	2·00
Output	9,000	8,200	7,700

Prepare the necessary A/cs.

[Ans. Cost per unit Process I = Rs. 4·675; Cost per unit Process II = Rs. 7·4605; Cost per unit Process III = Rs. 17·8946; Abnormal Gain = Rs. 596; Abnormal Loss = Rs. 1,430]

3. An article passes through three processes of manufacture. From the following details, show the cost of each of the three processes and the cost per article produced during the month of January 1993 :

	Process I Rs.	*Process II* Rs.	*Process III* Rs.
Materials used	75,000	27,000	9,000
Labour	45,000	90,000	30,000
Direct Expenses	12,000	36,000	12,600

The indirect expenses amounted to Rs. 42,900 and may be apportioned on the basis of wages. No account need be taken to stocks in hand and work-in-progress at the beginning and at the end of the month. The number of articles produced during the month was 1,200. **[*C.U. B.Com. (Pass)*]**

[Ans. (*i*) Value of goods of Process I—Rs. 1,43,700; Process II—Rs. 3,20,100; Process—III Rs. 3,79,500; (ii) Cost per unit—Process I—Rs. 119·75; Process II—Rs. 266·75; Process III—Rs. 316·25]

[**Hints.** Indirect expenses are to be apportioned in the ratio 3 : 6 : 2.]

4. Prepare necessary accounts from the following details :

	Process A	*Process B*
1. Materials	30,000	3,000
2. Labour	10,000	12,000
3. Overheads	7,000	8,600
4. Input	20,000	17,500
5. Normal Loss	10%	4%
6. Sales Value of wastes per unit	1	2

There was no Opening Stock or Closing Stock or work-in-progress. Final output from Process B was 17,000 units. **[*M.Com. Bombay*]**

[Ans.	***Process A***	***Process B***
Abnormal Loss	**Rs. 1,250**	**—**
Abnormal Gain	**—**	**Rs. 785**
Value of finished goods		**Rs. 66,735.]**

5. A product is produced after passing it through three processes *A*, *B* and *C*.

From the following particulars prepare Process *B* Account for the year 2001 :

Output of Process *A* transferred—3,000 units @ Rs. 5 each;

Process Materials added—Rs, 1,000;

Direct Wages—Rs. 10,000;

Direct Expenses—Rs. 4,000;

Production Overhead—20% of wages;

Output of Process *B*—2,750 units;

Normal loss—10%;

Scrap value of lost units—Rs. 2 per unit. **[*C.U. B.Com. (H) 2002*]**

[Ans. Transfer to Process C : Rs. 31,981; Abnormal Gain (50 units) Rs. 581]

6. In the Process Q, 300 units of a product were transformed from Process P at a cost of Rs. 5,240. The additional expenses incurred for the Process Q were Rs. 760 and overhead was charged @ 10% of expenses incurred, 20% of the inputs are normally lost and sold at Rs. 8 per unit. 220 units were produced in the Process Q.
Prepare Process Q Account and Abnormal Loss or Abnormal Gain Account.

[*C.U. B.Com. (H) 2003*]

[Ans. Transfer to next process/finished goods Rs. 5,130 (220 units @ Rs. 23,31,667). Abnormal Loss (20 units) Rs. 466; transfer to costing Profit & Loss A/c Rs. 306]

7. The Bharat Manufacturing Company's product passes through two distinct processes, X and Y, and then to the finished stock. It is known from the past experience that wastage occurs in the process as under:
In process X, 5% of the units entering the process.
In process Y, 10% of the units entering the process.
The scrap value of the wastages in Process X is Rs. 8 per 100 units and in Process Y is Rs. 10 per 100 units.

	Process X Rs.	*Process Y* Rs.
Materials Consumed	6,000	3,000
Wages	7,000	4,000
Manufacturing expenses	2,000	2,000

10,000 units were brought into Process *X*, Costing Rs. 5,000. The outputs were :

Process X	9,500 units
Process Y	8,500 units

Prepare Process Cost Accounts showing the cost of the output. [*B.Com. Chennai*]

[Ans. Process X, Cost Rs. 2·101; Output 9,500 units; Cost Rs. 19,960. Process Y, Abnormal Loss 50 units; Cost Rs. 3·772; Output 8,500 units; Cost Rs. 28,696]

8. A product passed through three processes X, Y and Z. The normal wastage of each process is :

Proces X	3%
Process Y	5%
Process Z	8%

Wastage of Process X was sold at Rs. 2·50 per unit and that of Y at Rs. 5·00 per unit and that of Z at Rs. 8·00 per unit.
1,00,000 units were issued to Process X in the beginning of July 1990 at a Cost of Rs. 10 per unit.

	Process X	*Process Y*	*Process Z*
Sundry materials	10,000	15,000	5,000
Labour	50,000	80,000	65,000
Direct expenses	10,450	15,995	20,090

Actual Output was :
Process X 95,000; Process Y 97,000; Process Z 81,000
Prepare Process Accounts assuming that there was no opening or closing stocks. Also give abnormal wastage and abnormal gain accounts, if any. [*B.Com. Madurai University (Adopted)*]

[Ans. Cost per unit of Process X = Rs. 10·958; Cost per unit of Process Y = Rs. 12·744; Cost per unit of Process Z = Rs. 13·2026]

9. A product of a chemical enterprise passes through two processes A and B, and then to finished stock. The normal wastage of each process is :
Process A : 3 per cent. ; Process B : 5 per cent.
Wastage of Process A was sold @ Rs. 2·50 per unit and that of Process B @ Rs. 5·00 per unit. 10,000 units were issued to Process A in the beginning of April, 1977 at a cost of Rs. 10 per unit.
The other expenses were :

	Process A Rs.	*Process B* Rs.
Sundry Materials	10,000	15,000
Wages	50,000	80,000
Manufacturing Expenses	10,500	11,800

Actual output of Process A was 9,500 units and that of Process B was 9,100 units. There were no opening or closing stocks.
Prepare the Process Accounts and determine the cost per unit of finished product. Briefly explain the treatment of wastage in process accounts. [*M.Com. Nagarjuna University*]

[Ans. Process A—Rs. 17·58; Process B—Rs. 30·39]

10. The finished goods of a factory pass through three processes known as A, B and C; the production of each process being passed on to the next process. From the following figures, show the cost of each process.

	Process A	Process B	Process C
	Rs.	*Rs.*	*Rs.*
Wages & Materials	19,200	36,000	87,750
Works on Cost	16,800	15,750	18,000
General on Cost	9,000	10,000	12,000

Production for July 1984 :

A = 36,000 units; B = 37,500 units; C = 48,000 units

Stock on 1st July 1984 :

B = 4,000 units; C = 16,500 units

Stock on 31st July 1984 :

B = 1,000 units; C = 5,500 units **[*B.Com. Kanpur University*]**

[Ans. Cost of Production : Process A = Rs. 45,000; B = Rs. 1,10,500; C = Rs. 2,60,663]

11. A particular brand of chemical oil passed through three important processes. During the period ended on 31st December 1989, 600 gallons of oil is produced. The cost book shows the following information :

	Process A	Process B	Process C
	Rs.	*Rs.*	*Rs.*
Materials	40,000	20,000	15,000
Labour	30,000	25,000	23,000
Direct Expenses	6,000	2,000	5,000
Cost of Containers	—	20,300	3,250

The Indirect expenses for the period were Rs. 16,000. The by-product of 'Process B' is sold for Rs. 2,400 and that of 'Process C' sold at Rs. 1,255. Make assumption where necessary.

Prepare the Process A/cs.

[Ans. Cost per gallon—Process A = Rs. 136·90; Process B = Rs. 256·60; Process C = Rs. 336·50]

N.B. : Indirect expenses have been distributed according to Labour Cost Ratio.

12. A product passes through two processes I and II and the normal loss is estimated at 2% for Process I and 5% for Process II of the respective inputs. The loss in each process is sold as scrap as :

Process I Rs. 10 per 100 units.

Process II Rs. 20 per 100 units.

40,000 units of crude materials were introduced in Process I at a cost Rs. 16,000.

From the information supplied prepare the process accounts :

	Process I	Process II
	Rs.	*Rs.*
Materials Consumed	8,000	2,800
Labour	12,200	14,000
Expenses	3,080	1,000
	Units	*Units*
Finished output	39,000	38,500
Stock on 1st January	4,000	6,000
Stock on 31st December	3,000	8,000
Stock Valuation on 1st January	90 Paise per unit	1·47 Paise per unit

Stock on 31st December is to be valued at the costs shown by the year's Process A/c.

[*M.Com. 1988, Madras University*]

[Ans. (i) Cost per unit Process 1 = Re. 1·00; Process II = Rs. 1·45

(ii) Abnormal Loss = Rs. 180; Abnormal Gain = Rs. 640]

13. The product of a soap factory passes through three stages before the article comes out in finished form. The processes are known as A, B and C. The wastage in each process is :

Process A = 2%, Process B = 5% and Process C = 10%

In each case, the percentage of wastage is computed on the number of units entering the process concerned. The wastage of each process is sold at Rs. 5 per hundred units in case of processes A and B and at Rs. 20 per 100 units in case of process C. The output of each process passes immediately to the next process and the finished units are passed from process C into stock.

The following additional information is available :

	Processes		
	A	*B*	*C*
	Rs.	*Rs.*	*Rs.*
Materials Consumed	8,000	4,000	2,000
Direct Labour	12,000	8,000	6,000
Manufacturing Expenses	2,000	2,000	3,000

40,000 units have been issued to Process A at a cost of Rs. 16,000. The output of each process has been as under :

Process A—39,000; Process B—37,600 and Process C—32,000.

There is no stock or work-in-progress in any process.

Prepare process cost accounts showing per unit cost of product at each stage and the total cost per unit.

[*B.Com. Bhopal*]

[Ans.	***Process***		***Cost Rs.***	***Output units***	***Cost Rs.***
A	***Abnormal wastage units***	**200**	**194**	**32,000**	**37,766**
B	***Abnormal effective units***	**550**	**767**	**37,600**	**52,435**
C	***Abnormal wastage units***	**1,840**	**3,408**	**32,000**	**59,275]**

14. A product is produced through two distinct processes—Process *I* and Process *II*. On completion, it is transferred to finished stock.

From the following particulars during the month of December 1994, prepare Process Accounts and Finished *Stock Account* :

	Process I	*Process II*
Units introduced	10,000	9,000
Transfer to next process/finished goods	9,000	8,250
Normal loss (on inputs)	10%	5%
Realisable value of loss (per unit)	Rs. 2	Rs. 4
Cost incurred :	Rs.	Rs.
Direct materials	40,000	
Direct labour	20,000	20,000
Direct expenses	12,000	10,050

Production overhead (100% of direct labour).

Assume that there was no opening or closing stock of raw materials and work-in-progress.

[*C.U. B.Com. (H) 1995*]

[Ans. Transfer to next process/finished goods from :
Process *I* — Rs. 90,000; Process *II* — Rs. 1,33,399
Abnormal Loss — Process *II* — Rs. 4,851 (300 units @ 16·17)]

15. XYZ Ltd. manufactures a product which passes through two processes—Process A and Process B and then it is transferred to Finished Stock A/c.

From the following particulars prepare Process Accounts :

	Process A	Process B
Input (Units)	30,000	26,000
Materials (Rs.)	60,000	8,000
Labour (Rs.)	36,000	30,550
Overhead (Rs.)	18,000	21,900
Normal Loss	10%	?
Scrap Value per unit (Rs.)	2	3

There was no opening or closing work-in-progress. The final output from Process B transferred to Finished Stock was 25,000 units. These finished goods are sold at Rs. 7·50 per unit with a profit of Re. 1 per unit.

What was normal loss rate in Process B ? **[*C.U. B.Com. (H) 2004*]**

[Ans. Process A : Abnormal Loss—1,000 Units; Tr. to Pr. B : 26,000 Units; Rs. 1,04,000 Process B : Rate of Normal Loss : 5%; Tr. to finished Stock : Rs. 1,62,500]

16. In a factory, a product is produced through two distinct processes : Process *A* and Process *B*. On completion, the product is transferred to finished stock.

During the month of December 1996, the following information was obtained :

	Process A	*Process B*
Units introduced	2,000	—
Units transferred to next process	1,800	—
Units transferred to finished stock		1,750
Value of units introduced	Rs. 11,000	—
Materials	—	Rs. 1,000
Labour	Rs. 7,300	Rs. 4,500
Overhead	Rs. 2,800	Rs. 2,240

The normal loss in each process is 5% and it was sold at Rs. 2 per unit. There was no stock of raw materials or work-in-progress at the beginning or at the end of the month.

Prepare the Process Accounts and Finished Stock Account.

[*C.U. B.Com. (H) (1997)*]

[Ans. Transfer to next process/finished goods from : *Process A*—Rs. 19,800; *Process B*—Rs. 28,000; Abnormal Loss : *Process A* — (100 units) Rs. 1,100; Abnormal Gain : *Process B* — (40 units) Rs. 640]

17. X Ltd. produces product 'Z' through two distinct processes—*Process A* and *Process B*. On completion, it is transferred to finished stock.

From the following information relating to the year 1997-98, prepare Process Accounts and Finished Stock Account :

Particulars	*Process A*	*Process B*
(i) Raw materials used	1,000 units	
(ii) Cost per unit	Rs. 200	
(iii) Transfer to next process/finished stock	940 untis	870 units
(iv) Normal loss (on inputs)	5%	10%
(v) Direct wages	Rs. 15,600	Rs. 13,200
(vi) Direct expenses	75% of direct wages	75% of direct wages
(vii) Sundry expenses	—	Rs. 2,954
(viii) Realisable value of scrap per unit	Rs. 4·50	Rs. 5·75

800 units of finished goods were sold at a profit of 20% on cost. Assume that there was no opening or closing stock of work-in-progress. **[*C.U. B.Com. (H) (1999)*]**

[Ans. Transfer to next process/finished goods from : *Process A*—Rs. 2,24,685; *Process B*—Rs. 2,57,295; Abnormal Loss : *Process A*—Rs. 2,390 (10 units @ Rs. 239·03); Abnormal Gain : *Process B*—Rs. 7,098 (24 units @ Rs. 295·74); Balance of Finished Stock A/c Rs. 20,702 (70 units @ Rs. 295·74; Transfer to costing P/L A/c from Finished Stock A/c Rs. 47,319]

18. Z Ltd. produced product X through three processes—P_1, P_2 and P_3. On January 1, raw materials 1,000 units were introduced in Process P_1 at Rs. 50 per unit.

The details of expenses incurred on the three processes during the year 2000 were :

		P_1		P_2		P_3
Sundry other materials	Rs.	1,600		Rs. 3,315		Rs. 3,220
Labour	Rs.	2,600		Rs. 8,000		Rs. 6,392
Normal loss (% of input)		5%		10%		5%
Scrap Value per unit	Re.	1	Rs.	3	Rs.	6
Actual output (units)		940		846		410
Sales price of output per unit	Rs.	70	Rs.	100	Rs.	200

Entire output of P_1 was passed to the next process while $\frac{1}{2}$ of the output of P_2 was passed to the next process and the balance was sold. The entire output of P_3 was sold. Management expenses and selling expenses were Rs. 6,000 and Rs. 9,000, respectively. These are not allocable to the process.

You are required to prepare—(a) Process A/cs, and (b) Statement of Profit. **[*C.U. B.Com. (H) 2001*]**

[Ans. Process P_1 : Transfer to Process P_2 940 units @ Rs. 57 = Rs. 53,540

Process P_2 : Transfer to Finished Stock 423 units @ Rs. 76·375 = Rs. 32,307 and to Process P_3 423 units Rs. 32,307

Process P_3 : Transfer to Finished Stock 410 @ Rs. 103·960 = Rs. 42,624

Abnormal Loss : From Process P_1 10 units Rs. 570; Transfer to Costing P/L A/c Rs. 560

Abnormal Gain : From Process P_3 8 units Rs. 832; Transfer to Costing P/L A/c Rs. 784

Profit as per cost accounts Rs. 34,589]

19. A product passes through two distinct processes A and B and thereafter it is transferred to finished stock. From the following information you are required to prepare process accounts :

	Process A	*Process B*
	Rs.	*Rs.*
Material Consumed	12,000	6,000
Direct Labour	14,000	8,000
Manufacturing Expenses	4,000	4,000
Input in Process A (units)	10,000	
Input in Process A (value)	10,000	
Output (units)	9,400	8,300
Normal wastage percentage of input	5%	10%
Value of normal wastage (per 100 units)	8	10

[*I.C.W.A. Inter*]

[Ans.

Process	*Abnormal Loss* *Units*	*Costs*	*Output transferred* *Units*	*Cost (Rs.)*
A	**100**	**421**	**9,400**	**39,539**
B	**160**	**1,086**	**8,300**	**56,359]**

20. A company operates a process plant to produce a single product from one process. At the month end, work-in-progress consisting of 1,700 units of product completed but not passed to stores was valued as :

	Rs.	
Direct Material	12,750	
Direct Wages	5,100	
Overhead	5,100	(100% of direct wages)

During the next month 18,500 further units were put into further process, the cost figures being Rs. 1,38,750 for direct materials, Rs. 55,500 for direct wages, and using 100% direct wages. Rs. 55,500 for overhead. 18,000 units were completed and transferred to the finished stock and 2,200 remained at the month-end as work-in-progress, complete as to material and half complete as to wages and overhead.

The average method of valuing the work-in-progress is used.

Compile a process cost and production sheet to show the total and the unit process costs for each element, effective units of output, and the apportionment of the production cost as between the completed product and the closing work-in-progress for the month.

[*I.C.W.A. Inter*]

[Ans. Effective units : Materials Rs. 20,000; Labour and Overhead Rs. 19,100 each; Cost per unit Rs. 7·50 and Rs. 3·173 each]

21. A product passes through three processes A, B and C. 10,000 units at a cost of Rs. 1·10 were issued to Process A. The other direct expenses were :

	Process A	*Process B*	*Process C*
	Rs.	*Rs.*	*Rs.*
Sundry Materials	1,500	1,500	1,500
Direct Labour	4,500	8,000	6,500
Direct Expenses	1,000	1,000	1,503

The wastage of Process 'A' was 5% and in Process 'B' 4%. The wastage of Process 'A' was sold at Re. 0·25 per unit and that of 'B' at Re. 0·50 per unit and that of C at Re. 1·00 per unit.
The overhead charges were 160% of direct labour. The final product was sold at Rs. 10 per unit fetching a profit of 20% on Sales.
Find out the percentage of wastage in Process 'C'.

[*I.C.W.A. Final*]

[Ans. Loss 7·63%]

22. Product A passes through three processes. In January 1978 the following information is obtained in respect of Process II : opening stock : 2,200 units valued at Rs. 1,200 made up of Rs. 700 for materials, Rs. 150 for labour and Rs. 350 for overhead. Degree of completion : Material 60% ; Labour 40% ; Overhead 40%. Transferred from Process I ; 14,000 units @ Re. 0·20 each. Transferred to Process III : 12,000 units.

Direct Materials added in Process II	Rs. 1,560
Direct Labour amounted	Rs. 2,000
Production Overhead	Rs. 4,400

Units scraped : 2,000 on completion of Process II. Closing stock : 2,800 units ; Degree of completion : Materials 80%, Labour 60%, Overhead 60%.
10% Loss during production is considered normal loss. Units scraped recovered Re. 0·40 each.
Prepare statement of cost of Process II and show the unit cost of units transferred to Process II.

[*C.I.M.A. Final*]

[Ans. Re. 0·78 per unit]

23. A company manufactures its sole product by passing the raw material through three distinct processes in its factory. During the months of April 2004, the company purchased 96,000 kg of raw material at Rs. 5 per kg and introduced the same in Process I.
Further particulars of manufacture for the month are :

	Process I	*Process II*	*Process III*
Materials consumed	Rs. 33,472	Rs. 27,483	Rs. 47,166
Direct labour	80,000	72,000	56,000
Overheads	1,20,000	1,08,000	84,000
Normal waste in process as % of input	3%	1%	1%
Sale value of waste (Rs./kg)	2	3	5
Actual output during the month (kg)	93,000	92,200	91,500

Prepare the three process accounts and accounts relating to Abnormal Loss/Gain, if any.

[*I.C.W.A. (Inter) Dec. 04*]

[Ans.	**Transfer Price**	**Abnormal (Loss)/Gain**
	Process I Rs. 7·60 p.u.	**(120 Unit) @ 7·60**
	Process II Rs. 9·90 p.u.	**130 Unit @ 9·90**
	Process III Rs. 12·00 p.u.	**222 Unit @ 12·00]**

24. A manufacturing company produces two types of articles P and Q in which materials used are identical in all respects. Each type of article undergoes two processes ; (*i*) Factory, and (*ii*) Finishing. The direct labour cost is recorded separately. The material is allocated in the ratio of the output and the general expenses are treated similarly. Factory and Finishing overhead charges are apportioned on the basis of the direct labour ratio of each process.

Prepare process accounts from the following particulars showing the total and the cost per unit of each product.

Also show the percentage of profit, assuming that selling prices of the articles per unit are : P, Rs. 400 and Q, Rs. 450.

			Rs.
Opening Stock :			
Factory Materials			10,600
Finishing Materials			5,000
Purchases :			
Factory			3,17,400
Finishing			1,35,000
Closing Stock :			
Factory			82,000
Finishing			44,000
Factory Wages (direct)	P		1,60,000
	Q		1,20,000
Finishing Wages (direct)	P		90,000
	Q		30,000
Factory Overheads			63,000
Finishing Overheads			24,000
General Expenses			1,44,000
	P	2,000	
	Q	1,000	

[*C.A. Inter*]

[Ans. Cost per unit : P = Rs. 314; Q = Rs. 345]

25. The ABC Co. Ltd. produced three chemicals, during the months of March 1993, by three consecutive processes. In each process, 2% of the total weight of input is lost and 10% is scrap, which from Process X and Process Y realises Rs. 100 per ton and from Process Z Rs. 20 per ton.

The product of three processes are dealt with as :

	Process X	*Process Y*	*Process Z*
Passed to next process	75%	50%	
Stock kept for sale	25%	50%	100%

Expenses incurred during the period ended :

	Process X		*Process Y*		*Process Z*	
	Rs.	Tons	Rs.	Tons	Rs.	Tons
Raw material	1,20,000	1,000	28,000	140	1,07,840	1,348
Wages	20,500	—	18,520	—	15,000	—
Overhead	10,300	—	7,240	—	3,100	—

Prepare Process A/cs. showing the cost per ton of each process.

[Ans.	**Process X**	**Process Y**	**Process Z**
Cost Per ton :	**Rs. 160**	**Rs. 215**	**Rs. 132·5]**

26. In a chemical industry a product has to pass through three distinct processes to completion viz. Process I, Process II and Process III.

It is estimated that the normal loss of each process will be :

Process I—2%, Process II—5%, Process III—10%

The wastage of each process is sold as follows :

Process I—Rs. 5 per 100 units

Process II—Rs. 5 per 100 units

Process III—Rs. 20 per 100 units

The following information is obtained :

	Process I	*Process II*	*Process III*
Output	19,500	18,800	16,000
Material	6,000	4,000	2,000
Direct Labour	8,000	6,000	3,000
Manufacturing Exp.	1,000	1,000	1,500

20,000 units have been introduced to Process I at a cost of Rs. 10,000. There is no work-in-progress in any process.

Prepare Process A/cs, Normal Loss A/c, Abnormal Loss A/c, and Abnormal Gain A/c.

[Ans.

	Process I	**Process II**	**Process III**
Cost per unit	**1·274**	**1·933**	**2·509**

Abnormal Loss charged to Profit & Loss A/c = Rs. 122;
Abnormal Gain charged to Profit & Loss A/c = Rs. 261·25]

27. A product passes through three processes A, B and C for completion. 5,000 units at a cost of Rs. 10 each were issued to Process A on 1.1.91. The other expenses were :

	Process A	*Process B*	*Process C*
Material	3,000	3,000	6,000
Labour	10,000	6,000	4,000
Direct Expenses	2,000	2,000	2,500

The normal wastage of the 'Process A' was 10% 'Process B' was 2%. The scrap value were : Process A = Rs. 3·50; Process B = Rs. 5 per unit; Process C = Rs. 8 per unit

The overhead charges were 2 times of Labour. The final product was sold at Rs. 41·24 per unit at a profit of 25% on sales. There is no Abnormal Loss or Gain in Processes A and B. The output of Process C was 3,800 units.

Prepare Process A/cs, Normal Loss A/c and Abnormal Loss A/c.

[Ans. Cost Per unit : Process A = Rs. 18·50; Process B = Rs. 24·00; Process C = Rs. 30·93;
Abnormal loss units = 169; Normal loss units = 441]

28. The output of different processes is partially sold and partially transferred to next process. Robust Ltd. processes a patent material. The material is produced in three consecutive grades—soft, medium and hard.

	Process I	*Process II*	*Process III*
Raw Material used	1,000 tonnes		
Cost per tonne	Rs. 200		
Manufacturing wages and expenses	Rs. 87,500	Rs. 34,500	Rs. 10,710
Weight Lost (% of the input of process)	5%	10%	20%
Scrap (Sale price Rs. 50 per tonne)	50 tonnes	30 tonnes	51 tonnes
Sale price of output per tonne	Rs. 350	Rs. 500	Rs. 800

Management expenses were Rs. 17,500 and selling expenses Rs. 10,000.

Two-thirds of the output of Process I and one-half of the output of Process II are passed on the next process and the balances are sold. The entire output of Process III is sold.

Prepare the three Process Accounts and a Statement of Profit.

Make approximations where necessary.

[B.Com. Andhra]

[Ans.

	Process **I**	**II**	**III**
Cost of production	**2,85,000**	**2,23,000**	**1,19,660**
Total net profit	**1,260**	**—**	**—**]

29. A company manufactures a product which involves two processes *viz.*, pressing and polishing. For 1990 the following information is available :

	Pressing	*Polishing*
Opening Stock	—	—
Input of units in process	1,200	1,000
Units completed	1,000	500

Units under process	200	500
Cost of material	Rs. 9,600	Rs. 8,800
Conversion costs	Rs. 2,28,000	Rs. 52,000

For incomplete units in process charge material cost at 100% and conversion costs at 60% in the pressing process and at 50% in the polishing process.

Prepare a statement of cost and calculate the selling price per unit which will result in 25% profit on sale price.

[*C.A. Inter*]

[Ans. Cost price per unit = Rs. 415·38; Selling price per unit = Rs. 553·71]

30. A product is finished in three stages I, II and III. At the first stage a quantity of 72,000 kg was delivered at a cost of Rs. 2·50 per kg. The entire material was consumed.

The production particulars along with the allocated expenses were as indicated in the table below :

Stage	*Input*	*Output*	*Direct Wages*	*Fixed Overhead*	*Varying Overhead*
	kg.	*kg.*	*Rs.*	%	%
I	72,000	67,680	7,500	150	200
II	65,000	60,125	12,000	125	150
III	55,600	50,000	14,500	200	250

(On direct wages)

The producer, as was his usual practice, assessed his cost at Rs. 6·77 per kg, based on his input expenditure and the finished output. With a selling price of Rs. 7·50 per kg he estimated his profit at Rs. 36,500. If you do not approve of his assessment of the end results of the operation, convince him of the real end results in a tabular form.

You should assume the normal wastages as only 5% on input at each stage and any excess wastages should not be allowed to inflate the cost of the end product.

[*I.C.W.A. (Inter) Dec. 1989*]

[Ans. Process I = Cost Per Unit Rs. 3·125; Process II Cost Per Unit = 4·018; Process III Cost Per Unit = 5·7395, Abnormal Loss; Process I = Rs. 2,250; Process II = Rs. 6,536; Process III = Rs. 16,186]

31. A product passes through three processes *viz.,* Process I, Process II and Process III.

The normal wastage of each process is :

Process I : 3%; Process II : 6% and Process III : 10%

The percentage of normal wastage in each case is computed on the basis of the number of units entering the process concerned. The wastage of Process I is sold @ 25 paise per unit, that of Process II is sold @ 50 paise per unit and that of Process III is sold @ Re. 1 per unit. 15,000 units of crude material were introduced in Process I @ Re. 1 per unit. The other expenses are :

	Process I	*Process II*	*Process III*
	Rs.	*Rs.*	*Rs.*
Material Consumed	1,500	2,250	750
Direct Labour	7,500	12,000	9,750
Manufacturing Expenses	1,575	1,425	3,015

The output of each process has been :

Process I : Rs. 14,250 ; Process II : Rs. 13,650 ; Process III : Rs. 12,012

Prepare Process Cost Accounts and abnormal wastage and abnormal effective accounts.

[*A.C.S. (Inter) Dec. 1987 (New Syllabus)*]

[Ans. Process I : Cost per unit = Rs. 1·75; Abnormal Loss = 300 units Process II : Cost per unit = Rs. 3·00; Process III : Cost per unit = Rs. 4·322 Abnormal Loss charged to Profit & Loss = Rs. 1,357; Abnormal Gain = Rs. 637·50]

32. The product of a manufacturing concern passes through two processes A and B and then to finished stock. It is ascertained that in each process normally 5% of the total weight is lost and 10% is scrap which from processes A and B realizes Rs. 80 per ton and Rs. 200 per ton, respectively.

The following are the figures relating to both the processes :

	Process A	*Process B*
Materials in tons	1,000	70
Cost of materials in rupees per ton	125	200
Wages in rupees	28,000	10,000

Manufacturing Expenses rupees	8,000	5,250
Output in tons	830	780

Prepare Process Cost Accounts showing cost per ton of each process. There was no stock or work-in-progress in any process. *[B.Com. (Hons.) Delhi]*

[Ans. Process A : Abnormal Loss 20 units; Cost Rs. 180; Output 830 units; Cost Rs. 1,49,400, Process B : Cost Rs. 210; Output 780 units; Cost Rs. 1,63,800]

33. A product passes through Process A, Process B and Process C to completion. From experience it is estimated that the normal loss in each process will be :

Process	*Normal Loss*	*Sale price per unit of scrap*
A	4%	0·50
B	8%	1·00
C	5%	1·20

The expenses incurred during the period were :

	Process A	*Process B*	*Process C*
Input (8,000 Units @ Rs. 2)	16,000	—	—
Material	20,000	14,000	12,000
Direct Labour	34,000	16,800	15,800
Factory Overhead	6,000	6,416	6,582
Office & Administrative	2,160	3,600	4,200
Overhead output	7,700	7,200	7,000

Prepare Process A/cs and also work out the selling price per unit of finished stock which will fetch a profit @ 25% on selling price.

[Ans. Process A—Cost Per Unit = Rs. 10·156; Process B Cost Per Unit = Rs. 16·685; Process C—Cost Per Unit = 22·858; Selling Price = 30·477]

34. A producer produces a product which requires two processes, the product of 1st process being passed to the next process and so on to finished stock.

During the year ended the finished product was 2,000 kg and the following was the expenditure :

	Process I	*Process II*	*Total*
Raw Material	6,000	4,000	10,000
Direct Labour	3,000	6,000	9,000
Direct Expenses	1,000	4,000	5,000

Total overhead expenses being Rs. 36,000. These are to be absorbed as a percentage of Direct Labour. (*i*) Show the relevant A/cs. (*ii*) If 10% of the output is estimated to be lost in the course of selling, what should be the selling price per unit so as to provide a gross profit of 25% on selling Process ?

[Ans. Process I : Cost per kg = Rs. 11; Process II : Cost per kg = Rs. 30; Selling Price = Rs. 44·444]

35. A product produced through two distinct processes I and II. The by-product of each process is sold directly. Prepare Process A/cs and their respective By-product A/cs showing the amount of profit made by each by-product.

The following information are collected from cost book :

	Process I	*Process II*
Material consumed	60,000	—
Wages Paid @ 5 per hour.	7,000 hr.	5,000 hr.
Manufacturing overhead @ Rs. 2·50 per hour	7,000 hr.	5,000 hr.
Normal wastages	100 units	60 units
By product sales	140 units	120 units
Selling price	Cost plus 20%	Cost plus 25%

[Ans. Cost per unit : Process I = Rs. 80·357; Process II = Rs. 115·625. Profit on sale of by-product : Process I = Rs. 2,250; Process II = Rs. 3,469]

36. M. Ltd. processes a patent material used in building. The material is produced in three consecutive grades—namely soft, medium and hard.

Figures relating to production for the year 1993 are :

	Process I	*Process II*	*Process III*
Raw materials used	1,000 tonnes	—	—
Cost per ton (Rs.)	200	—	—
Manufacturing Wages and Expenses (Rs.)	72,500	40,800	10,710

Weight lost	5%	10%	20%
Scrap sold at Rs. 50 per tonne	50 tonnes	30 tonnes	51 tonnes
Sale price per tonne (Rs.)	350	500	800

Management expenses were Rs. 17,500; Selling expenses Rs. 10,000 and interest on borrowed capital Rs. 4,000.

Two-thirds of Process I and one-half of Process 2 are passed on to the next process and the balance are sold.

You are required to prepare process cost accounts in a form suitable for presentation to the directors at their next meeting when the production policy of the company will be discussed.

[*M.Com. C.U.*]

[Ans. Cost per tonne : Process I = Rs. 300; Process II = Rs. 430; Process III = Rs. 770; Net Profit = Rs. 37,440]

37. A product passes through two consecutive processes having relative standard output of 80% and 90% of inputs. In addition, standard yield is obtained by giving scrap allowances of 10% and 5% of outputs of Processes I and II, respectively. Scraps of each process are sold at Rs. 1,000 per tonne. There was no W.I.P. at any stage. All materials, as follows, are issued in Process I only and all scrap arising from processes were sold excepting closing stock of 10 tonnes (Opening stock was Nil).

Material issued :

'A' 100 tonnes @ Rs. 2,000 per tonne
'B' 400 tonnes @ Rs. 1,500 per tonne
'C' 500 tonnes @ Rs. 1,200 per tonne

The actual outputs and scraps were 85% and 8% in Process I and 80% and 10% in Process II. Assume that there was no price variance.

You are required to find out the Standard Cost and Actual Cost per tonne of a product.

[I.C.W.A]

[Ans. Process I Standard yield = 720 tonnes, valued at Rs. 13,20,000, Actual yield 782 tonnes, valued at Rs. 13,32,000, Process II 615·6 tonnes, valued at Rs. 12,87,600, Actual yield 563·04 tonnes, valued at Rs. 12,69,440]

38. Product B passes through two processes before it is completed and transferred to finished stock. The following data are available for the month of March 1992 :

Particulars	*Process I*	*Proces II*
Opening Stock (At Prime Cost)	5,000	8,000
Direct Materials	40,000	12,000
Direct Labour	35,000	40,000
Production Overheads	20,000	24,000
Closing Stock (At Prime Cost)	10,000	4,000

Output of Processes are transferred to the next ones at the following transfer prices :

Process I—@ 25% on the Transfer price to Process II.
Process II—@ 20% on the Transfer price to Finished Stock.

Finished stocks are valued at price at which they are received from Process II, and are :

	Rs.
Opening Stock	20,000
Closing Stock	30,000
Sales for the month amounted to	3,00,000

Provisions for internal process profit as on 1st March 1992 :

	Rs.
Included in W.I.P. of Process II	1,500
Included in Finished Stock	6,500
	8,000

Calculate : (*a*) Process Cost; (*b*) Gross Profit; (*c*) Write-up the provision for inter-process profit.

[Ans. Provision for inter-process profit :

			I	**II**
Process II = Rs. 700		**Process Cost**	**90,000**	**1,69,200**
Finished Stock = 9,700		**Gross Profit**	**30,000**	**80,800]**

Section II : Equivalent Production

Definition—Procedure of Evaluation—Different methods of Calculation—Illustrations—Worked out Problems—Exercise

Introduction

In process industries, there are most likely the problem of work-in-progress in respect of each process. Further, the degree of completion in respect of each elements of cost also varies. In such circumstances it is very difficult to find out the related cost of each unit of incomplete product. So incomplete units require to be converted into completed units.

Definition

The term "equivalent units" defines by C.I.M.A. as : "notional whole units representing completed work". The term 'equivalent production' represents a technique through which incomplete units are expressed as completed units. As the incompleted units do not bear the same cost as completed units, it requires to be converted into their equivalent completed units for finding out the cost of process—both finished and unfinished units. For example, if out of 3,000 units of closing stock, 1,000 units are of 100% completion stage and the remaining 2,000 units are of 50% completion stage, the total closing stock should be calculated as :

Input (units)	*Output*	*Units*	*Degree of completion*	*Equivalent Production (units)*
(1)	*(2)*	*(3)*	*(4)*	*(5) = (3) × (4)*
3,000	Completely Processed	1,000	100%	1,000
	Incompleted units (*i.e.* W.I.P.)	2,000	50%	1,000
3,000	Total	3,000		2,000

Thus, though there are 3,000 incompleted units of closing stock, it should be treated as 2,000 equivalent completed units for the purpose of evaluation. So it represents the production of a process in terms of completed units.

Procedure of Evaluation

For transferring the number of units and its related cost the following steps are necessary :

Step I. Ascertain the number of units introduced and finished.

Step II. Convert the production into equivalent units after taking into consideration the process losses, opening/closing work-in-progress with their degree of completion.

Step III. Find out the total cost of material, labour and overhead.

Step IV. Determine the cost per unit of equivalent production separately elementwise, by dividing each element of cost by its respective equivalent units.

Step V. Finally, ascertain the cost of production including the cost of work-in-progress.

Thus, for solving the practical problem, three statements are required to be prepared :

(1) Statement of equivalent production.
(2) Statement of Cost, and
(3) Statement of Evaluation.

Methods of Calculation

There are two basic methods of calculation for finding out the cost of opening stock and their related equivalent units of production :

(*i*) Average Cost Method.
(*ii*) First-in-First-Out Method (FIFO), and
(*iii*) Last-in-First-Out Method (LIFO).

(*i*) **Average Cost Method.** Under this method, the opening inventory costs are combined with the current periods costs, and the work done in prior periods is completely ignored. The aim of this method is to treat all units finished during the period as if they were started and finished within the same period. The cost of closing work-in-progress in the previous period is added to the cost of the current period and an average rate is obtained; when price is fluctuating this method is used.

(*ii*) **First-in-First-Out Method** (FIFO). Under this method, the work started first, have to be completed first. So this method assumes that the opening work-in-progress completed and transferred first and then the current year's production is completed. Cost of the opening stock carried over from the previous period and the cost of the units started and completed in the current period are calculated separately. Thus, it distinguishes between work done in the current as well as previous periods. Closing stock of work-in-progress, if any, shall include within the current year's product only. So, to obtain the total as well as unit costs for the carried over units at the beginning, the additional cost incurred to complete these units should be added to the cost of the opening stock.

Difference between FIFO and Average Cost Method

(*i*) FIFO method separates the cost composition of opening work-in-progress units and the costs related to work done in the current period, as cost of opening inventory includes previous year's cost also. Whereas, the average cost method is based on averaging the work done to date as contained in work-in-process beginning inventory with the work done in the current period.

(*ii*) The main difference between the two methods concern the assignment of costs to the work-in-progress.

The following illustration will help us to understand the distinction between the two methods.

Illustration

From the following information prepare : (*i*) statement of equivalent production. (*ii*) statement of cost and (*iii*) find out the value of output transferred and closing W.I.P. under (A) Average Cost Method, and (B) FIFO Method of valuation of process stock.

Opening W.I.P. (2,000 units) :

Materials (100% complete)	Rs. 7,000
Wages (60% complete)	Rs. 3,000
Overheads (70% complete)	Rs. 1,000
	11,000

There are 2,000 units in process and the stage of completion is estimated to be :

Materials	100%
Wages	50%
Overheads	50%

8,000 units are transferred to the next process. The process costs for the period are :

Materials	Rs. 1,00,000
Wages	Rs. 78,000
Overheads	Rs. 44,000

Solution

(A) Under Average Cost Method

(i) Statement of Equivalent Production

Input		Output		Equivalent Productions			
				Materials		Wages & Overheads	
Items	Units	Items	Units	% Completion	Eqv. Units	% Completion	Eqv. Units
Opening W.I.P.	2,000	Finished & Transferred (including opening W.I.P.)	8,000	100	8,000	100	8,000
Units introduced	8,000						
		Closing W.I.P.	2,000	100	2,000	50	1,000
Total	10,000		10,000		10,000		9,000

(ii) Statement of Cost

	Materials Rs.	Wages Rs.	Overhead Rs.	Total Rs.
Cost of opening W.I.P.	7,000	3,000	1,000	11,000
Add : Cost incurred during the period	1,00,000	78,000	44,000	2,22,000
Total Cost (*a*)	1,07,000	81,000	45,000	2,33,000
Equivalent Units (*b*)	10,000	9,000	9,000	
Cost per unit (*a*) ÷ (*b*)	10·70	9·00	5·00	24·70

(*iii*) (*a*) Value of output transferred :
8,000 units @ Rs. 24·70 — 1,97,600

(*b*) Value of Closing W.I.P. :

Materials 2,000 units @ Rs. 10·70	21,400	
Wages 1,000 units @ Rs. 9·00	9,000	
Overhead 1,000 units @ Rs. 5·00	5,000	
		35,400
		2,33,000

(B) Under FIFO Method

(i) Statement of Equivalent Production

Input		Output		Equivalent Productions					
				Materials		Wages		Overheads	
Items	Units	Items	Units	% Compl.	Eqv. Units	% of Compl.	Eqv. Unit	% Compl.	Eqv. Unit
Opening W.I.P.	2,000	Opening W.I.P	2,000	—	—	40	800	30	600
Units introduced	8,000	Completely processed during the year (8,000 – 2,000)	6,000	100	6,000	100	6,000	100	6,000
		Closing W.I.P.	2,000	100	2,000	50	1,000	50	1,000
Total	10,000		10,000		8,000		7,800		7,600

(ii) Statement of Cost

	Materials Rs.	Wages Rs.	Overhead Rs.	Total Rs.
Cost of opening W.I.P. (Not Considered)				
Cost incurred during the year (a)	1,00,000	78,000	44,000	2,22,000
Equivalent units (b)	8,000	7,800	7,600	
Cost per unit (a) ÷ (b)	12·50	10·00	5·79	28·29

(iii) (a) *Value of output transferred* :
(8,000 units)

		Rs.	
* For opening 2,000 units of W.I.P. Opening Balance :			
Add : Related cost during the year		11,000	
Material			
Wages 800 units @ Rs. 10·00	= Rs. 8,000		
Overhead 600 units @ Rs. 5·79	= Rs. 3,470		
		11,470	
			22,470
For units completely processed during the year 6,000 units @ Rs. 28·29			1,69,740
		Total	1,92,210

(b) *Value of Closing W.I.P.* :

Materials 2,000 units @ Rs. 12·50	= 25,000	
Wages 1,000 units @ Rs. 10·00	= 10,000	
Overhead 1,000 units @ Rs. 5·79	= 5,790	
		40,790
	Total	2,33,000

Comparison Table and Comments

	Charged for 8,000 units	Closing Stock Value
Average Cost	Rs. 1,97,600	Rs. 35,400
FIFO	Rs. 1,92,210 **Lower*	Rs. 40,790 **Higher*

(iii) **Last-in-First-Out Method (LIFO).** This method is based on the principle that products are charged at their latest price. Under the method cost incurred is used :

(i) first to complete the newly introduced units, and

(ii) then, to finish the opening work-in-progress, if any.

Hence, the opening W.I.P. remains within the closing W.I.P., if not completed within the period. So when the closing inventory is greater than the opening inventory, it is presumed that all the opening units remain in closing stock at the end of the period.

When LIFO method is followed, the closing inventory value will consist of one or both of the two following points :

(i) proportional value of opening W.I.P., and

(ii) Value of newly introduced units lying in closing stock.

Difference between FIFO and LIFO

The main difference between the two methods of valuation is in the valuation of closing work-in-progress. Under FIFO method all the closing units are valued at current price, whereas, under LIFO method the closing stocks are valued at mixing of the two costs (*i.e.* value of opening W.I.P. and the proportional cost incurred during the period), provided closing work-in-progress is higher than the opening work-in-progress.

The following illustration will help us to understand the LIFO method clearly.

Illustration

The following information is available regarding process X during the year ended 31.3.95.

Production Records

Units in process as on 1.4.94		10,000
Degree of completion :	Material 100%	
	Labour and Overhead 50%	20,000
Net units started in process		30,000

Production report shows following results for the period :

Units completed	15,000
Units in process on 31.3.95	15,000

(all materials used, 50% completed regarding labour & overhead)

Cost Record

Work-in-process as on 1.4.94 :
Material Rs. 25,500 Labour Rs. 15,000
Overhead Rs. 12,000
Cost for the year 94-95
Material Rs. 60,000, Labour Rs. 35,000, Overhead Rs. 17,500

Prepare the (*a*) Statement of Equivalent Production
(*b*) Statement of Cost for each element
(*c*) Statement of Evaluation.

Solution

(*a*) Statement of Equivalent Production

Input		*Output*		*Equivalent Productions*			
				Materials		*Labour & Overheads*	
Items	*Units*	*Items*	*Units*	*% Completion*	*Eqv. Units*	*% Completion*	*Eqv. Units*
Opening W.I.P.	10,000	Units Completed	15,000	100	15,000	100	15,000
Units introduced	20,000	Closing inventory					
		(*i*) Opng. W.I.P.	10,000*	—	—	—	—
		(*ii*) New units	5,000	100	5,000	50	2,500
	30,000		30,000		20,000		17,500

*No work has been done on units which represented opening W.I.P.

(*b*) Statement of Cost of each Element

Elements of cost	*Cost in Process Rs.*	*Equivalent Production (Units)*	*Cost per unit (Rs.)*
Material	60,000	20,000	3·00
Labour	35,000	17,500	2·00
Overhead	17,500	17,500	1·00
		Total	6·00

(c) Statement of Evaluation

(A) Value of output transferred :			90,000
15,000 units @ Rs. 6·00			
(B) Value of Closing Inventory :			
Cost of Op. W.I.P.			
(25,500 + 15,000 + 12,000)		52,500	
Cost of New units :			
Material 5,000 @ Rs. 3·00 =	15,000		
Labour 2,500 @ Rs. 2·00 =	5,000		
Overhead 2,500 @ Re. 1·00 =	2,500		
		22,500	
			75,000
			Rs. 1,65,000

Introduction of material at different stages of operation

Materials may be introduced in processes : (*a*) at the beginning of operation, (*b*) at the end of operation, (*c*) at a particular stage, and (*d*) continuously through the process.

(*a*) When materials are introduced at the beginning of the operation, opening stock of W.I.P. will not bear the cost of material, but the closing stock of W.I.P. as well as units introduced and completed will share the material cost for the period.

(*b*) When materials are introduced at the end of the process and FIFO method of valuation is followed, the closing stock of W.I.P. will not bear any cost of material introduced.

(*c*) When materials are introduced at a particular stage of operation, the opening and closing stock of W.I.P. will share the cost of material introduced depending on their stage of completion.

(*d*) When materials are continuously introduced, cost of material is distributed like labour and overhead on the basis of stage of completion (*i.e.* the materials required to finish the work).

The following illustration will clarify the problem from different angles.

Illustration

The following information is available relating to a process X, during the year ended 31.3.95 :

Units in process (at the beginning, 1.4.94)	10,000
(Degree of completion 50%)	
Units introduced	20,000
	30,000

Production report shows the following :

Units completed	25,000
Units in Process on 31.3.95	5,000
(Degree of completion 80%)	
Process Loss	Nil
	30,000

Cost Record :

Work-in-progress as on 1.4.94.	
Material	36,000
Labour	50,000
Overhead	28,000
	1,14,000

Cost during the year 94-95 :

Materials	72,000
Direct Labour	1,60,000
Overhead	1,52,000
	3,84,000

Company adopts FIFO Method of valuation.

Prepare (*a*) Statement of Equivalent Production.

(*b*) Statement of Cost, and

(*c*) Satement of Evaluation, when materials is

(*i*) introduced at the beginning of process,

(*ii*) introduced at the end of the process,

(*iii*) introduced at 40% stage of completion, and

(*iv*) introduced continuously throughout the year.

Solution

(*i*) When material is introduced at the beginning of the Process (FIFO Method)

(*a*) Statement of Equivalent Production

Input		*Output*		*Equivalent Productions*					
				Materials		*Wages*		*Overheads*	
Items	*Units*	*Items*	*Units*	*% of Compl.*	*Eqv. Units*	*% of Compl.*	*Eqv. Unit*	*% of Compl.*	*Eqv. Unit*
Opening W.I.P.	10,000	Opening W.I.P	10,000	—	—	50	5,000	50	5,000
Introduced	20,000	Completely processed during the year (25,000 – 10,000)	15,000	100	15,000	100	15,000	100	15,000
		Closing W.I.P.	5,000	100	5,000	80	4,000	80	4,000
Total	30,000		30,000		20,000		24,000		24,000

(*b*) Statement of Cost

Element of Cost	*Cost in Process (Rs.)*	*Equivalent Production (Units)*	*Cost per unit (Rs.)*
Material	72,000	20,000	3·60
Labour	1,60,000	24,000	6·67
Overhead	1,52,000	24,000	6·33
	3,84,000	68,000	16·60

(*c*) Statement of Evaluation

(A) *Value of output transferred* (25,000 units) :

*For opening 10,000 units of W.I.P. :		
Opening Balance :	Rs. 1,14,000	
Add : Related cost during the year :		
Material	—	
Labour 5,000 unit @ Rs. 6·67	33,350	
Overhead 5,000 units @ Rs. 6·33	31,650	
		1,79,000
*For units completely processed during the year 15,000 units @ Rs. 16·60		2,49,000
C/F		4,28,000
(*B*) *Value of Closing W.I.P.* :		
Materials 5,000 units @ Rs. 3·60 =	18,000	
Labour 4,000 units @ Rs. 6·67 =	26,680	
Overhead 4,000 units @ Rs. 6·33 =	25,320	
		70,000
Total		4,98,000

(*ii*) When material is introduced at the end of the Process (FIFO Method)

(*a*) Statement of Equivalent Production

Input		*Output*		*Equivalent Productions*					
				Materials		*Wages*		*Overheads*	
Items	*Units*	*Items*	*Units*	*% of Compl.*	*Eqv. Units*	*% of Compl.*	*Eqv. Unit*	*% of Compl.*	*Eqv. Unit*
Opening W.I.P.	10,000	Opening W.I.P	10,000	100	10,000	50	5,000	50	5,000
Introduced	20,000	Completely Processed during the year	15,000	100	15,000	100	15,000	100	15,000
		Closing W.I.P.	5,000	—	—	80	4,000	80	4,000
	30,000		30,000	—	25,000	—	24,000	—	24,000

(*b*) Statement of Cost

Elements of Cost	*Cost in Process (Rs.)*	*Equivalent Production (Units)*	*Cost per unit (Rs.)*
Materials	72,000	25,000	2·88
Labour	1,60,000	24,000	6·67
Overhead	1,52,000	24,000	6·33
	3,84,000		15·88

(*c*) Statement of Evaluation

	Rs.	*Rs.*
(*A*) *Value of output transferred* (25,000 units) :		
*For opening 10,000 units of W.I.P. :		
Opening Balance :	Rs. 1,14,000	
Add : Related cost during the year :		
Material 10,000 units @ Rs. 2·88	28,800	
Wages 5,000 units @ Rs. 6·67	33,350	
Overhead 5,000 units @ Rs. 6·33	31,650	
		2,07,800
*For units completely processed during the year 15,000 units @ Rs. 15·88		2,38,200
		4,46,000
(*B*) *Value of Closing W.I.P.* :		
Material	—	—
Labour 4,000 units @ Rs. 6·67 =	26,680	
Overhead 4,000 units @ Rs. 6·33 =	25,320	
		52,000
	Total	4,98,000

(*iii*) When material is introduced at 40% stage of completion (FIFO Method)

(*a*) Statement of Equivalent Production

Input		*Output*		*Equivalent Productions*					
				Materials		*Wages*		*Overheads*	
Items	*Units*	*Items*	*Units*	*% of Compl.*	*Eqv. Units*	*% of Compl.*	*Eqv. Unit*	*% of Compl.*	*Eqv. Unit*
Opening W.I.P.	10,000	Opening W.I.P	10,000	—	—	50	5,000	50	5,000
Introduced	20,000	Completely Processed during the year	15,000	100	15,000	100	15,000	100	15,000
		Closing W.I.P.	5,000	100	5,000	80	4,000	80	4,000
	30,000		30,000	—	20,000	—	24,000	—	24,000

(*b*) Statement of Cost

Elements of Cost	*Cost in Process (Rs.)*	*Equivalent Production (Units)*	*Cost per unit (Rs.)*
Materials	72,000	20,000	3·60
Labour	1,60,000	24,000	6·67
Overhead	1,52,000	24,000	6·33
	3,84,000		16·60

(*c*) Statement of Evaluation

(*A*) *Value of output transferred* (25,000 units) :

		Rs.
*For opening 10,000 units of W.I.P. :		
Opening Balance :		1,14,000
Add : Related cost during the year :		
Material		
Wages 5,000 units @ Rs. 6·67 =	33,350	
Overhead 5,000 units @ Rs. 6·33 =	31,650	65,000
		1,79,000
*For units completely processed during the year (15,000 units @ Rs. 16·60)		2,49,000
		4,28,000

(*B*) *Value of Closing W.I.P.* :

Materials	5,000 units @ Rs. 3·60 = 18,000	
Labour	4,000 units @ Rs. 6·67 = 26,680	
Overhed	4,000 units @ Rs. 6·33 = 25·320	
		70,000
	Total	4,98,000

Note : Since both the opening and closing stocks of W.I.P. are at more than 40% stage of completion, the solution and valuation of (*iii*) remain same as (*i*).

(*iv*) When material is introduced continuously throughout the year. (FIFO Method)

(*a*) Statement of Equivalent Production

Input		*Output*		*Equivalent Productions*					
				Materials		*Wages*		*Overheads*	
Items	*Units*	*Items*	*Units*	*% of Compl.*	*Eqv. Units*	*% of Compl.*	*Eqv. Unit*	*% of Compl.*	*Eqv. Unit*
Opening W.I.P.	10,000	Opening W.I.P	10,000	50	5,000	50	5,000	50	5,000
Introduced	20,000	Completely Processed during the year (25,000 – 10,000)	15,000	100	15,000	100	15,000	100	15,000
		Closing W.I.P.	5,000	80	4,000	80	4,000	80	4,000
Total	30,000		30,000		24,000		24,000		24,000

(*b*) Statement of Cost

Elements of Cost	*Cost in Process (Rs.)*	*Equivalent Production (Units)*	*Cost per unit (Rs.)*
Materials	72,000	24,000	3·00
Labour	1,60,000	24,000	6·67
Overhead	1,52,000	24,000	6·33
	3,84,000		16·00

(*c*) Statement of Evaluation (25,000 units)

		Rs.
(*A*) *Value of output transferred*		
For opening 10,000 units		
Opening Balance	1,14,000	
Add : Related Cost during the year (5,000 @ Rs. 16·00)	80,000	
		1,94,000
For units completely processed during the year (15,000 units @ Rs. 16·00)		2,40,000
		4,34,000
(*B*) *Value of closing W.I.P.*		
4,000 units @ Rs. 16·00		64,000
Total		4,98,000

Introduction of Material in Each of the Processes

(*With Normal Loss, Abnormal Loss and Abnormal Gain*)

In most cases, in addition to transferred material from its previous process, new material is introduced by the process itself. In such case the two types of materials should be denoted (or marked) separately for valuing its opening as well as closing W.I.P. As the material just introduced in the process and the material introduced in its previous process behave in different manner with the opening and closing work-in-progress. In respect of normal loss, equivalent units should be treated as nil but the realisable value, if any, should be deducted from material. In respect of abnormal loss, equivalent units should be calculated depending on the degree of completion. But in case of abnormal gain, equivalent units should be treated as 100% complete. The following illustration will clarify the problems.

Illustration

Product Zero requires three distinct processes and after the third process the product is transferred to the finished stock. From the following information relating to product Zero, prepare Process II and Process III A/c (when the cost of transfer from Process I is Rs. 11 per unit).

	Process II	*Process III*
Transferred from Previous Process	8,000 units	8,800 units
Transferred to the Next Process or Finished Stock	8,800	10,000
Estimated Normal Loss (%) on production	10	10
Opening Stock of W.I.P.		
Units	3,000	2,200
Value (Rs.)	45,000	66,000
Degree of Completion (%) :		
Material	80	—
Labour	70	80
Overhead	70	80
Closing Stock of W.I.P. :		
Units	1,000	Nil
Degree of Completion (%) :		
Material	80	—
Labour	60	—
Overhead	60	—
Units scrapped	1,200	1,000
Degree of completion (%) :		
Material	100	—
Labour	75	75
Overhead	75	75
Cost incurred during the period (Rs.)		
Material	37,000	—
Labour	44,700	56,980
Overhead	22,350	28,490
Realisable value of Scrap (per unit Rs.)	0·50	3·00

Solution

For the purpose of differentiating between materials introduced in different processes, the material transfer from Process I is denoted as Material A, the material added to Process II is termed as Material B. Again, material transfer from Process II to Process III is denoted as Material C and the material added to Process III is termed as Material D.

Calculation for Process II

Opening W.I.P. + Input – Cl. W.I.P. = Production

3,000 + 8,000 – 1,000 = 10,000

So Normal Loss 10% of 10,000 = 1,000 units

Abnormal Loss = Total Loss – Normal Loss

= 1,200 – 1,000 = 200 units

(a) Statement of Equivalent Production

Input		Output		Equivalent Productions					
				Material A		Material B		Labour and Overheads	
Items	*Units*	*Items*	*Units*	*% of Compl.*	*Eqv. Units*	*% of Compl.*	*Eqv. Unit*	*% of Compl.*	*Eqv. Unit*
Opening W.I.P.	3,000	Opening W.I.P.	3,000	—	—	20	600	30	900
Introduced (Transferred from Process I)	8,000	Normal Loss	1,000	—	—	—	—	—	—
		Abnromal Loss	200	100	200	100	200	75	150
		Completely processed during the period	5,800	100	5,800	100	5,800	100	5,800
		Closing W.I.P.	1,000	100	1,000	80	800	60	600
Total	11,000		11,000		7,000		7,400		7,450

(b) Statement of Cost

Element of Cost	*Cost in Process (Rs.)*	*Equivalent Production (Units)*	*Cost per unit (Rs.)*
Materials A (8,000 @ Rs. 11)	88,000		
Less : Scrap Value of Normal Loss (@ 0·50 × 1,000)	500		
	87,500	7,000	12·50
Add : Material B (as introduced in the process further)	37,000	7,400	5·00
Labour	44,700	7,450	6·00
Overhead	22,350	7,450	3·00
	1,91,550		26·50

(c) Statement of Evaluation

			Rs.	
(A)	*For opening W.I.P. (3,000 Units)*			
		Opening Balance		45,000
	Add :	Material A	= Nil	
		Material B 600 units @ Rs. 5·00	= 3,000	
		Labour 900 units @ Rs. 6·00	= 5,400	
		Overhead 900 units @ Rs. 3·00	= 2,700	
				11,100
(B)	*For Units completely Processed*			
		5,800 units @ Rs. 26·50		1,53,700
		Value of Stock Transferred (8,800 units)		2,09,800
(C)	*For Closing W.I.P.*			
		Materials A 1,000 units @ Rs. 12·50	= 12,500	
		Materials B 800 units @ Rs. 5·00	= 4,000	
		Labour 600 units @ Rs. 6·00	= 3,600	
		Overhead 600 units @ Rs. 3·00	= 1,800	
				21,900

(*D*) *For Value of Abnormal Loss*

Material A 200 units @ Rs. 12·50 =	2,500	
Material B 200 units @ Rs. 5·00 =	1,000	
Labour 150 units @ Rs. 6·00 =	900	
Overheads 150 units @ Rs. 3·00 =	450	
		4,850
Total		2,36,550

Process II A/c

Particulars	*Units*	*Amount (Rs.)*	*Particulars*	*Units*	*Amount (Rs.)*
To Balance b/d	3,000	45,000	By Normal Loss	1,000	500
" Process I A/c	8,000	88,000	" Abnormal Loss	200	4,850
" Materials		37,000	" Process III A/c transfer	8,800	2,09,800
" Labour		44,700	" Balance c/d	1,000	21,900
" Overhead		22,350			
	11,000	2,37,050		11,000	2,37,050

Calculations for Process III

As no material is added to Process III, hence there is no function of Material D here.

Production = Opening W.I.P. + Input – Closing W.I.P.
= 2,200 + 8,800 – 0 = 11,000

Expected Normal Loss 10% of 11,000 = 1,100

Abnormal Gain = Normal Loss – Actual Loss
= 1,100 – 1,000 = 100 Units.

(*a*) Statement of Equivalent Production

Input		*Output*		*Equivalent Production*			
			Units	*Material C*		*Labour & Overhead*	
Items	*Units*	*Items*	*Units*	*% of Comp.*	*Unit*	*% of Comp.*	*Unit*
Opening W.I.P.	2,200	Opening W.I.P.	2,200	—	—	20	440
Introduced (Transferred from Process II)	8,800	Normal Loss	1,100	—	—	—	—
		Completely Processed	7,800	100	7,800	100	7,800
		Total	11,100		7,800		8,240
		Less : Abnormal Gain	100	100	100	100	100
Total	11,000		11,000		7,700		8,140

(*b*) Statement of Cost

Element of Cost	*Cost in Process (Rs.)*	*Equivalent Production (Units)*	*Cost per unit (Rs.)*
Material C (Transferred from Process II)	2,09,800		
Lees : Scrap Value of Normal Loss (1,100 × 3)	3,300		
	2,06,500	7,700	26·8182
Labour	56,980	8,140	7·0000
Overhead	28,490	8,140	3·5000
	2,91,970		37·3182

(c) Statement of Evaluation

			Rs.	Rs.
(A)	*For opening W.I.P. (2,200 units)*			
	Opening Balance		66,000	
Add :	Related Cost during the period :			
	Material C	Nil		
	Labour 440 units @ Rs. 7·00	3,080		
	Overheads 440 units @ Rs. 3·50	1,540		
			4,620	
			70,620	
(B)	*For Units Completely Processed*			
	7,800 units @ Rs. 37·3182		2,91,082	
	Value of Finished Stock transferred (10,000 units)			3,61,702
(C)	*For Value of Abnormal Gain*			
	100 units @ Rs. 37·3182			(–) 3,732
			Total	3,57,970

Process III A/c

Particulars	*Units*	*Amount (Rs.)*	*Particulars*	*Units*	*Amount (Rs.)*
To Balance b/d	2,200	66,000	By Normal Loss	1,100	3,300
" Process II	8,800	2,09,800	" Finished Stock A/c (transfer)	10,000	3,61,702
" Labour		56,980			
" Overhead		28,490			
	11,000	3,61,270			
" Abnormal Gain	100	3,732			
	11,100	3,65,002		11,100	3,65,002

WORKEDOUT PROBLEMS

Problem 1

The following data are available in respect of Process I for Feb. 2007.

1. Opening stock of W.I.P. : 800 units at a total cost of Rs. 4,000.
2. Degree of completion of opening W.I.P. :
   Materials 100%
   Labour 60%
   Overheads 60%
3. Input of materials at a total cost of Rs. 36,800 for 9,200 units
4. Direct wages incurred Rs. 16,740
5. Production overhead Rs. 8,370
6. Units scrapped 1,200 units. The stage of completion of these units was :
   Materials 100%
   Labour 80%
   Overheads 80%
7. Closing W.I.P. : 900 units. The stage of completion of these units was :
   Materials 100%
   Labour 70%.
   Overheads 70%

8. 7,900 units were completed and transferred to the next process.
9. Normal loss is 10% of the total input (opening W.I.P. plus units put in)
10. Scrap value is Rs. 4 per unit.

You are required to :

(*a*) Compute equivalent production

(*b*) Calculate the cost per equivalent unit for each element

(c) Calculate the cost of abnormal loss (or gain), closing work in process and the units transferred to the next process using the FIFO method.

(*d*) Show the Process Account for February 2007.

[C.A. (Inter) Adopted]

Solution

(*a*) Statement of Equivalent Production (FIFO method)

Input		*Output*	Equivalent Production				
			Units	*Materials*		*Labour & Overhead*	
Items	*Units*	*Items*	*Units*	*% of Comp.*	*Unit*	*% of Comp.*	*Unit*
Op. Stock of W.I.P.	800	Op. W.I.P.	800	—	—	40	320
Introduced	9,200	Normal Loss	800	—			
		Abnormal Loss	400	100	400	80	320
		Completely processed	7,100	100	7,100	100	7,100
		Closing W.I.P.	900	100	900	70	630
	10,000		10,000		8,400		8,370

(*b*) Statement of Cost per equivalent units for each elements

Element of Cost		*Cost (Rs.)*	*Eqv. Units*	*Cost per unit (Rs.)*
Materials	36,800			
Less : Scrap value of Normal Loss (800 × Rs. 4)	3,200	33,600	8,400	4·00
Labour		16,740	8,370	2·00
Overheads		8,370	8,370	1·00
		58,710		7·00

(c) Statement showing cost of abnormal loss, Closing W.I.P. and units transferred to the next process

Abnormal Loss

	Rs.
Materials 400 units @ Rs. 4	1,600
Labour 320 units @ Rs. 2	640
Overheads 320 units @ Re. 1	320
	2,560

Closing W.I.P.

Materials 900 units @ Rs. 4	3,600
Labour 630 units @ Rs. 2	1,260
Overheads 630 units @ Re. 1	630
	5,490

For 7,900 units transferred to Next Process

		Rs.
(a) Cost of Op. W.I.P. (800 units)		4,000
(b) Cost for Op. W.I.P. (additional)		
Labour 320 units @ Rs. 2	640	
Overhead 320 units @ Re. 1	320	
		960
(c) Cost for units completely processed during the year : (7,100 units)		
7,100 units @ Rs. 7		49,700
Total		54,660

Problem 2

A company manufactures a product which involves two consecutive processes, viz., Processing and Polishing. For the month of October 1994, the following information is available :

	Processing	*Polishing*
Opening stock	—	—
Input of units in process	1,200	1,000
Units completed	1,000	500
Units under process	200	500
Materials cost	Rs. 96,000	8,000
Conversion cost	Rs. 3,36,000	54,000

For incomplete units in process, share materials cost at 100% and conversion cost at 60% in the Pressing Process and 50% Polishing Process.

Prepare statement of cost and calculate selling price per unit which will result in 25% profits on sale price. **[C.A. (Inter)]**

Solution

For solving this problem, separate calculations and statements are necessary for the two differen processes.

For Pressing Process

Statement of Equivalent Production

Input		*Output*		*Equivalent Productions*			
				Materials		*Labour & Overhead*	
Items	*Units*	*Items*	*Units*	*% of Comp.*	*Unit*	*% of Comp.*	*Unit*
Introduced	1,200	Introduced and Completely processed	1,000	100	1,000	100	1,000
		Closing W.I.P.	200	100	200	60	120
	1,200		1,200		1,200		1,120

Statement of Cost

Element of Cost	*Cost (Rs.)*	*Equivalent Production (Units)*	*Cost per unit (Rs.)*
Materials	96,000	1,200	80·00
Conversion Costs	3,36,000	1,120	300·00
	4,32,000		380·00

Statement of Evaluation

(*a*) *For units completely processed and transferred*

		Rs.
1,000 units @ 380		3,80,000
(*b*) *For Closing W.I.P.*		
Materials 200 units @ Rs. 80	16,000	
Conversion Cost 120 units @ Rs. 300	36,000	
		52,000
Total		4,32,000

For Polishing Process

Statement of Equivalent Production

Input		*Output*		*Equivalent Production*			
				Materials		*Labour & Overhead*	
Items	*Units*	*Items*	*Units*	*% of Comp.*	*Unit*	*% of Comp.*	*Unit*
Transfer from Pressing Process	1,000	Introduced & Completed	500	100	500	100	500
		Closing W.I.P.	500	100	500	50	250
	1,000		1,000		1,000		750

Statement of Cost

Element of Cost	*Cost*	*Equ. Units*	*Cost per unit*
Cost of Inputs	3,80,000		
Add : Further cost of materials	8,000		
	3,88,000	1,000	388
Add : Conversion costs	54,000	750	72
Total	4,42,000		460

Statement of Evaluation

(a) For units completely processed and transferred to finished stock

		Rs.
500 units @ Rs. 460 per units		2,30,000
(b) For Closing W.I.P.		
Materials 500 units @ Rs. 388	1,94,000	
Conversion Cost 250 units @ Rs. 72	18,000	
		2,12,000
		4,42,000

Statement Showing Selling Price per Unit

	Rs.
Cost	460·00
Add : Profit @ 25% on Sales *i.e.* 1/3 on cost	153·33
Total	613·33

Problem 3. (*Under Average Cost Method*)

There was a process inventory in Process No. 2 at the beginning of a period and was valued at Rs. 2,950 made up of Rs. 1,400 towards materials, Rs. 1,000 towards labour and Rs. 550 towards overheads for 100 units. The value added during the period was Rs. 53,600 towards an introduction of 4,100 units from the previous process besides Rs. 40,800 towards labour and Rs. 19,400 towards overheads. Out of 3,600 units completed, 3,300 units were transferred to the next process leaving the balance in stock, 400 units were held back in the next process leaving the balance in stock. 400 units were held back in process with half completion towards labour and overheads while 200 units were lost in processing considered normal and hence should be borne by the inventory.

Prepare a cost of production statement using average cost basis.

[*I.C.W.A. (Int.) June 1990*]

Solution

(A) Statement of Equivalent Production
(Average Cost method)

Input		*Output*		*Equivalent Production*			
				Materials		*Labour & Overhead*	
Items	*Units*	*Items*	*Units*	*% of Comp.*	*Unit*	*% of Comp.*	*Unit*
Opening W.I.P.	100	Finished & transferred	3,300	100	3,300	100	3,300
Introduced	4,100	Finished & not transferred (i.e. Cl. Stock of Goods)	300	100	300	100	300
		Normal Loss	200	—	—	—	—
		Cl. Stock of W.I.P.	400	100	400	50	200
	4,200		4,200		4,000		3,800

(*B*) Statement of Cost

	Materials	*Labour*	*Overhead*	*Total*
Cost of Opening W.I.P.	1,400	1,000	550	2,950
Add : Cost incurred during the processing	53,600	40,800	19,400	1,13,800
Total Cost (*a*)	55,000	41,800	19,950	1,16,750
Equivalent Units (*b*)	4,000	3,800	3,800	
Cost per unit (*a*) ÷ (*b*)	13·75	11·00	5·25	30·00

(*C*) Statement of Evaluation

			Rs.
(a)	Value of units completed and transferred 3,300 units @ Rs. 30		99,000
(b)	Value of units completed and not transferred 300 units @ Rs. 30		9,000
(c)	Value of Closing Stock (W.I.P)		
	Material 400 units @ Rs. 13·75	5,500	
	Labour 200 units @ Rs. 11·00	2,200	
	Overhead 200 units @ Rs. 5·25	1,050	
			8,750
	Total		1,16,750

EXERCISES

EQUIVALENT PRODUCTION

1. *State which of the following statements are correct or incorrect.*

(*i*) Equivalent production represents the production in the terms of completed units.

(*ii*) The two of the special problems that arise in process costing are valuation of work-in-progress and process losses.

(*iii*) Inclusion of inter-process profits in account will not require any adjustment in stocks.

(*iv*) Abnormal gain should reduce the normal loss and balance is transferred to costing profit and loss account.

(*v*) Abnormal loss is spread on goods unit of usual production.

(*vi*) Process costing is used in chemical workers.

(*vii*) Process costing is applied in garment industry.

[Ans. Correct : (*i*), (*ii*), (*iv*), (*vi*)
Incorrect : (*iii*), (*v*), (*vii*).]

2. *Which of the following is correct ?*

A. The monetary value attributed to normal losses in a process should be :

(*i*) A share of the process cost according to the stage of completion of the losses.

(*ii*) A nil value with no other monetary adjustment under any circumstances.

(*iii*) A full share of process cost on the same as good output.

(*iv*) A nil share of process costs which have been reduced by the scrap value of the normal loss.

B. Details for the past month of a continuous process are :

(*i*)	Opening W.I.P.	400 units	60% complete
(*ii*)	Closing W.I.P.	600 units	20% complete
(*iii*)	Unit started	1,000	
(*iv*)	Unit finished	800	

Three quarters of the materials are added at the start of the process and the remaining quarter added when the process is 50% complete.

C. An abnormal gain in a process occurs in which of the following situations ?

(*i*) When actual losses are greater than the normal loss level.

(*ii*) When costs are reduced through increased machine speed.

(*iii*) When actual losses are less than the normal level.

(*iv*) When the process output is greater than planned.

D. Where process scrap is re-cycled for use in conjunction with new material as well as being sold externally, which of the following is most likely to be the value at which is debited to the process ?

(*i*) At the same price as it sold externally.

(*ii*) At the cost of normal losses.

(*iii*) At the cost attached to abnormal losses.

(*iv*) Nil value.

E. Which of the following is the best explanation of the relevance of equivalent production units in process costing ?

(*i*) A means of equalising production charged into stock each period.

(*ii*) The conversion partly completed units into an equivalent number of completed units in order that costs may be shared on an equitable basis.

(*iii*) The expression of losses in terms of an equivalent number of units of good production in order that their value may be calculated.

(*iv*) A means by which the output achieved may be compared with the equivalent quantity budgeted for the period under review.

F. Purchased materials are added in the second department of a three department process, this order does not increase the number of units produced in the second department and would—

(*i*) Not change the amount transferred to the next department.
(*ii*) Decrease total work in process inventory.
(*iii*) Increase the factory overhead portion of the ending work-in-process inventory.
(*iv*) Increase total unit cost.

G. The physical flow of units into and out of departments is shown on the

(*i*) Quantities schedule.
(*ii*) Equivalent production schedule.
(*iii*) Cost of account for schedule.
(*iv*) Cost of Accounted for schedule.

H. Purchased materials are added in the second department of a three department process; this increases the number of units produced in the second department and would always—

(*i*) Change the direct labour cost percentage in the ending work-in-process inventory.
(*ii*) Cause no adjustment to the unit cost transferred in from the first department.
(*iii*) Increase total units costs.
(*iv*) Decrease total ending work-in-process inventory.

I. An equivalent unit of material or conversion cost is equal to

(*i*) The amount of material conversion cost necessary to complete one unit of production.
(*ii*) A unit of work-in-process inventory.
(*iii*) The amount of material or conversion cost necessary to start a unit of production into work in process inventory.
(*iv*) Fifty percent of material or conversion cost of a unit to finished goods inventory (assuming a linear production pattern).

[Ans. A (*iv*) ; B (*ii*) ; C (*iii*) ; D (*i*) ; E (*ii*) ; F (*iv*) ; G (*ii*) ; H (*ii*) ; I (*i*).]

PROBLEMS

1. Product 'X' passes through three processes. In December 1994, the following information is obtained in respect of Process II :

Opening Stock : 3,000 units, valuing
Materials Rs. 1,000
Labour Rs. 500
Transfer from Process I : 10,000 units at Rs. 3 per unit.
Transfer to Process III : 11,000 units.

Closing work-in-process 1,000 units.
Normal loss : 10% of production
Degree of completion :

	Opening Stock	*Closing Stock*
Materials	60%	70%
Labour	50%	60%
Overheads	40%	50%

Costs incurred in the current process :

Materials	Rs. 10,000
Wages	Rs. 10,000

It is the practice of the firm to recover overheads as 50% of wages. It is estimated that the units scrapped will realise Rs. 2 per unit.

Prepare equivalent production statement and statement of cost. Also show the value of closing work-in-progress. Use Average Method. ***[M.B.M. C.U. Adopted]***

[Ans. Cost per unit Rs. 4·7421; Closing W.I.P. Rs. 3,134 (Approx.)]

2. Value Ltd. produces article 'X' from a material which passes 'A' and 'B', whose details are given below :

	A	*B*
Materials introduced (units)	10,000	
Transferred to next process (units)	9,000	

Work-in-process :

At the beginning of the month (units)	—	600
At the end of the month (units)	1,000	400
Expenses :	Rs.	Rs.
W.I.P. at the beginning of the month		9,400
Materials introduced at the beginning of the process	1,20,000	
Labour and Overheads	27,600	18,200

Stage of completion of W.I.P. :

Process A : Closing W.I.P. — 20% complete in respect of labour and overheads.

Process B : Opening W.I.P. — $33\frac{1}{3}$% complete in respect of labour and overheads.

Closing W.I.P. — 25% complete in respect of labour and overheads.

The finished output 'X' emerging out of Process B is sold at Rs. 20 per unit. The management is considering an alternative by which the finished output 'X' could be further treated by installing a new machine at a capital cost of Rs. 8,00,000. In that event, the final product, known as article 'Y', produced by this operation, could be sold at Rs. 25 per unit. The operating expenses of the aforesaid further treatment are estimated at Rs. 23,000. The company desires a return on investment of 25%.

(*a*) Prepare Process Cost A/cs for Process A and B (showing the workings of equivalent units and cost per equivalent units in each process).

(*b*) Prepare a statement of profitability of Product 'X' as it emerges from Process 'B'.

(*c*) Advise the management whether further treatment of Product 'X' by installing the new machine should be taken up or not. ***[I.C.W.A. (Final)]***

[Ans. (*a*) 'A' : value of transfer Rs. 1,35,000, Closing W.I.P. = Rs. 12,600 Cost per unit of equivalent production = Rs. 15; 'B' : (a) Value of transfer Rs. 1,56,400, Closing W.I.P. = Rs. 6,200; Cost per unit = Rs. 17. (*b*) Rs. 27,600 or 15% on sales. (*c*) Expected additional return from additional processing = Rs. 2,875. The proposal does not appear to be profitable.]

3. SM. Ltd. furnishes you the following information relating to Process B for the month of October 1990 :

(*i*)	Opening W.I.P.	Nil
(*ii*)	Units introduced	10,000 units @ Rs. 3 per unit
(*iii*)	Expenses debited to the process :	
	Direct materials	Rs. 14,650
	Labour	Rs. 21,148
	Overheads	Rs. 42,000
(*iv*)	Normal loss in process	1% of Input
(*v*)	Closing W.I.P.	350 units
	Degree of completion :	
	Material	100%
	Labour and overheads	50%
(*vi*)	Finished output	9,500 units
(*vii*)	Degree of completion of abnormal loss :	
	Material	100%
	Labour & overhead	80%.
(*viii*)	Units scrapped as normal loss were sold at Re. 1 per unit.	

(*ix*) All the units of abnormal loss were sold at Rs. 2·50 per unit.

Prepare : (*a*) Statement of Equivalent Production, (*b*) Statement of cost.
(*c*) Process B account, (*d*) Abnormal loss account. [*C.A. Inter*]

[Ans. (*a*) Material = 9,900; Labour & Overhead = 9,715; (*b*) Cost per unit of Eq. Prod. = Rs. 11·00 (*c*) Abnormal Loss = Rs. 485, Closing W.I.P. = Rs. 1,07,698; Transferred to Finished Stock = Rs. 1,04,500]

4. AB Ltd. is engaged in Process Engineering Industry. During the month of April 1990, 2,000 units were introduced in a process. The normal loss was estimated at 5% of input. At the end of the month 1,400 units had been produced and transferred to next process 460 units incomplete and 140 units after passing through fully the entire process, had to be scrapped.

The incomplete units had reached the following stage of completion :

Material	75% completed
Labour	50% completed
Overhead	50% completed

Following are the further information on the Process 'X' :

	Rs.
Cost of the 2,000 units	58,000
Additional Direct Materials	14,400
Direct Labour	33,400
Direct Overheads	16,700

Units scrapped realised Rs. 10 each.

Prepare Statement of Equivalent Production, Statement of Cost, Statement of Evaluation and the Process 'X' A/c. [*I.C.W.A. Inter*]

[Ans. Equivalent Production units; Material = 1,785; Labour & Overhead = 1,670 Cost per unit = Rs. 70; Abnormal Loss = Rs. 2,800; Value of W.I.P. = Rs. 20,700; Transferred to Next Process = Rs. 98,000]

5. From the following information for the month of January 1994, prepare Process—II Account :

		Units	*Rs.*
Opening Stock in Process II		800	6,400
Transfer from Process I		25,000	1,71,130
Added in Process II :	Direct Material		71,130
	Direct wages		23,860
	Overheads		47,720
Units scrapped during the Period		1,200	
Transfer to Process III		23,600	
Closing Stock		1,000	

	Opening Stock	*Closing Stock*
Material	75%	80%
Labour	50%	75%
Overhead	50%	75%

Normal loss is 5% of the total input and the realisable value of scrap is Rs. 4 per unit.

6. A manufacturing company makes a product by two processes and the data below relate to the second process for the month of April. A work-in-process balance of 1,200 units brought forward from March was valued at cost as follows :

	Rs.		*Rs.*
Direct materials, complete	10,800	Direct Wages 60% complete	6,840

Production overhead 60% complete Rs. 7,200

During April 4,000 units were transferred from the first process to the second process at a cost of Rs. 7·50 each. This input being treated as direct material within the second process.

Other costs incurred by the second process were :

	Rs.		*Rs.*
Additional direct material	4,830	Direct Wages	32,965
Production overhead	35,538		

3,200 completed units were transferred to finished goods store. A loss of 520 units, being normal, occurred during the Process. The average method of pricing is used work-in-progress at the end of April consisted of 500 completed units awaiting transfer to the finished goods store and a balance of unfinished units which were completed as ragards direct material and 50% complete as regards direct wages and production overhead.

You are required : (*a*) To prepare for the month of April the account for the second process (*b*) To present a statement for management selling out the : (*i*) cost per unit of the finished product by element of cost and total; (*ii*) cost of production transferred to finished goods; (*iii*) cost of production of completed units awaiting transfer to finished goods; (*iv*) cost of incompleted units in closing W.I.P., by element of cost and in total. **[*C.A. (Inter) Adopted*]**

7. The following details are supplied in respect of Process A for the month of April 1994 :

	Units	*Rs.*
Opening work-in-progress	1,000	
Material		4,000
Labour		750
Overheads		2,250
Materials introduced	19,000	74,000
Direct Wages		17,950
Overheads		53,850
Units scrapped	1,500	
Degree of completion		
Material 100%		
Labour & overheads 80%		
Closing work-in-progress	1,000	
Units completed and transferred to next Process B	17,500	

Normal process loss is 5% of the total input and scrap value is Rs. 2 per unit.

You are required to : (1) compute the equivalent production, (2) compute the cost per equivalent unit for each element and the cost of completed units transferred to next process, abnormal loss and value of closing W.I.P., (3) Prepare Process Accounts.

8. The following data are available in respect of Process I for February 1990 :

1. Opening stock of work-in-process : 800 units at a total cost of Rs. 4,000.
2. Degree of completion of opening work-in-process :
   Material 100% ; Labour 60% ; Overhead 60%
3. Input of materials at a total cost of Rs. 36,800 for 9,200 units.
4. Direct wages incurred Rs. 16,740
5. Production overhead Rs. 8,370
6. Units scrapped 1,200 ; The stages of completion of these units were :
   Materials 100% ; Labour 80% Overhead 80%
7. Closing work-in-process : 900 units. The stages of completion of these units were :
   Materials 100% ; Labour 70% Overhead 70%
8. 7,900 units were completed and transferred to the next process
9. Normal loss is 80% of the total input (opening stock + units put in)
10. Scrap value is Rs. 4 per unit.

You are required to : (*a*) compute equivalent production, (*b*) calculate the cost per equivalent unit for each element, (*c*) calculate the cost of abnormal loss (or gain), closing work-in-process and the units transferred to the next process using the FIFO method, (*d*) show the process account for February 1990. **[*C.A. (Inter) May 1990*]**

9. The following details are supplied in respect of Process A for the month of April 1994 :

	Units	Rs.
Opening work-in-progress	1,000	3,000
Degree of Completion :		
Material	100%	
Labour and overheads	75%	
Materials introduced	19,000	74,000
Direct Wages		17,950
Overheads		53,850
Units scrapped	1,500	
Degree of Completion :		
Materials	100%	
Labour and overheads	80%	
Closing work-in-progress	1,000	
Units completed and transferred to next Process B	17,500	

Normal process loss is 5% of the total input and the scrap value is Rs. 2 per unit.

You are required to : (1) compute the equivalent production, (2) compute the cost per equivalent unit for each element and the cost of completed units transferred to next process, abnormal loss and value of closing work-in-progress, and (3) Prepare Process accounts. **[*C.A. (Inter) Adopted*]**

10. A processing company produces a single product passing through two Processes X and Y. The following figures pertain to a month's operation :

	Rs.		Rs.
Opening stock	Nil	Direct materials Purchased	1,50,000
Wages Paid	90,000	Overheads incurred	51,000
Cost Process X			
Direct material	1,08,000	Direct Labour	55,000
Overheads	30,000		
Cost Process Y			
Direct material	30,000	Direct Labour	35,000
Overheads	21,000		

	Units
Output Process X :	
Completed and passed on to Process Y	28,000
Lying-in-process awaiting inspection	4,000
Work-in-process complete as to direct materials 50% complete for Labour & overhead	4,000
Process Y :	
Completed & transferred to finished stock	22,000
Work-in-process : 50% complete for direct materials, Labour and overheads	4,000

Work out the process accounts and find out the value of closing stock. **[*I.C.W.A. (Inter)*]**

11. In a certain department of a processing factory, production is continuous and at any point of time the work-in-progress is regarded as half done. The raw material is charged at the start of the process and that is all.

At the commencement of a Period, 70 tonnes were in process and this was valued at :

Material	Rs. 300 per tonne
Labour	Rs. 200 per tonne
Overhead	Rs. 200 per tonne

During the period 560 tonnes of materials at a cost of Rs. 1,71,000 were put into process. Labour cost for the period were Rs. 1,19,500 and overheads amounted to Rs. 1,15,000. Output in terms of finished product was 500 tonne and 100 tonnes remained as work-in-progress. The unreconciled balance between input and output units is to be treated as process loss.

(*a*) Prepare a Process account assuming that the "weighted average price" method of valuation was used.

(*b*) Also prepare a Production cost statement to show how you have calculated the costs.

[*Adopted from C.I.M.A. London*]

Section III : Joint Products, By-Products and Co-Products

Definition—Distinction—Accounting Methods—Illustrations—Workedout Problems.

Introduction

There are some industries where two or more products come out of a single raw material which is equally important. These are referred to as joint products.

C.I.M.A. defines joint product as 'Two or more products separated in the course of processing, each having a sufficiently high saleable value to merit recognition as a main product'.

According to T. Lang, Joint products means "Two or more products separated in the course of the same processing operation, usually requiring further processing, each product being in such proportion that no single product can be designated as major product".

In short, we can say, when two or more products of equal importance are simultaneously produced, then they are known as joint products.

Example. In oil industry kerosene, gasoline, fuel oil, lubricants etc. are all produced from the same product, crude petroleum. They are of equal important, hence they are called joint products.

By-Products. Terminologically, a by-product is defined as "a product which is recovered incidentally from the material used in the manufacture of recognised main products, such a by-product having either a net realisable value or a usable value which is relatively low in comparison with the saleable value of the main products. By-product may be further processed to increase their realisable value."

Example. (*a*) In soap-making industry—in the process of mixing and boiling ingredients many rejections take place. These rejections are collected for recovery as by-product.

(*b*) In coke ovens—gas and tar are treated as by-products.

Distinctions between Joint products and By-products

The following are points of distinctions :

(*i*) Joint products are of equal importance while by-products are of not equal importance as compared to that of the main products.

(*ii*) Joint products are produced simultaneously while by-products are produced incidentally.

(*iii*) Joint products are of more or less equal sales value while by products are of insignificant sales value.

Co-products. Co-products are such products which are produced simultaneously with the main product but not necessarily from the same raw material.

Example. In lumbering operations, it is possible to obtain oak, pine and walnut boards at the same time but from different trees.

The concept of joint product, by-product and co-product can be clarified by the following diagram :

Diagram I

Concept of Joint and By-Product

M = Material

P_1 & P_2 = Process I and Process II

S = Split-off point.

Diagram II

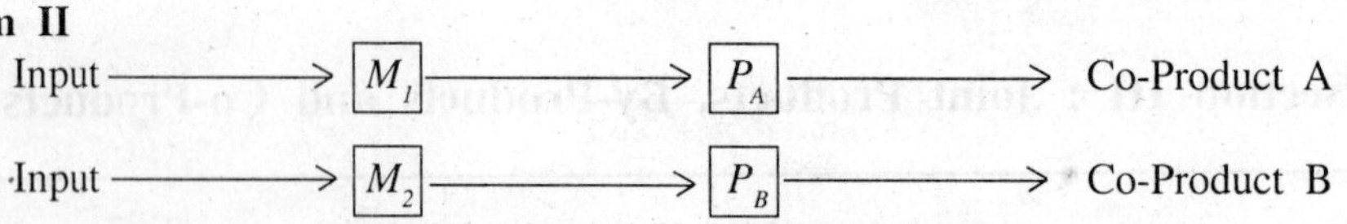

Concept of Co-product

M_1 = Material required for co-product A
M_2 = Material required for co-product B
P_A & P_B = Process operation for Products A and B, respectively.

Accounting for Joint Products

The terminology defines joint cost : 'The cost of providing two or more products or services whose production could not, for physical reasons, be segregated". In short, joint cost means all costs incurred prior to the point of separation. The apportionment of joint cost is very important for finding out the total cost of each joint product. The basis of allocation must be rational and reasonable. Unless the joint costs are properly and reasonably apportioned to different joint products produced, the costs of joint products will vary considerably and this will affect—

(*i*) Valuation of closing inventory.
(*ii*) Pricing of products.
(*iii*) Profit or Loss on sale of different products.

Although there are no scientific methods of apportionment of joint costs, the *following methods* are generally used in apportioning total process costs :

(*i*) Average unit cost method,
(*ii*) Physical units methods,
(*iii*) Survey method,
(*iv*) Standard cost method,
(*v*) Contributory margin method,
(*vi*) Market value method :
 (*a*) At point of separation.
 (*b*) After further processing.
 (*c*) Net realisable value.

Average Unit Cost Method. Under this method total process cost (up to the point of separation) are divided by total units produced to get average cost per unit of production.

$$\text{Average cost per unit} = \frac{\text{Total Joint cost up to the point of separation}}{\text{Total units produced}}$$

According to this method no effort is made to calculate separate costs for each of the joint products. This method is simple and can be applied where processes are common and homogeneous in nature. But if the end products are heterogeneous in nature and cannot be expressed in some common units, in this case this method cannot be applicable.

Illustration

From the following information find out the cost of joint products X, Y and Z :

(*a*) Pre-separation cost Rs. 60,000
(*b*) Units produced—

X	2,000
Y	800
Z	1,200

Solution

$$\text{Average cost per unit} = \frac{\text{Total Joint cost}}{\text{Total units produced}}$$

$$= \frac{60{,}000}{2{,}000 + 800 + 1{,}200} = \frac{60{,}000}{4{,}000} = \text{Rs. } 15$$

Joint cost apportioned to three products would be :

Products	*Units*	*Cost per unit*	*Amount of apportionment*
X	2,000	15	30,000
Y	800	15	12,000
Z	1,200	15	18,000
	4,000		60,000

Physical Units Method. Under this method joint cost is apportioned to different products on the basis of some physical units like raw materials, weight, labour hours etc. Though this method is technically sound, but this method is not applicable in many cases such as when products are expressed in different units.

Illustration

Following data have been extracted from the books of Coal India Limited :

Joint Products	*Production per tonne of coal*
Coke	600 kg
Coal tar	100 kg
Gas	140 kg
Benzol	160 kg
	1,000 kg

The price of coal is Rs. 200 per tonne. Direct labour and overhead costs of point of split-off are Rs. 75 and Rs. 25.

Solution

	Per tonne
Cost of Coal	200
Labour	75
Overhead	25
	300

Joint Products	*Production per tonne*	*% of total*	*Apportionment Cost*
Coke	600	60%	180
Coal tar	100	10%	30
Gas	140	14%	42
Benzol	160	16%	48
	1,000		300

Survey Method. In this method joint costs are apportioned to joint products after considering the important factors like volume, selling price, technical side etc. Accordingly, percentage or points value are assigned to individual products to consider their relative importance. This method is, to some extent, more equitable than Average Cost and Physical units method. Here the combined factors relating to production and marketing are given due consideration.

Illustration

Total pre-separation cost Rs. 40,000
Production :

Product A	1,000
Product B	2,000
Product C	3,000

Apportion the joint costs to the products if the value assigned for A, B and C are Rs. 4, 5 and 2 per unit, respectively.

Solution

Apportionment of Joint Cost.

Product	*Units*	*Value assigned per unit*	*Total value*	*Apportionment cost*
A	1,000	4	4,000	8,000
B	2,000	5	10,000	20,000
C	3,000	2	6,000	12,000
			20,000	40,000

Working Notes :

Total joint cost = Rs. 40,000
Apportionment of Joint cost

Product A = $\frac{4,000}{20,000} \times 40,000$ = Rs. 8,000

Product B = $\frac{10,000}{20,000} \times 40,000$ = Rs. 20,000

Product C = $\frac{6,000}{20,000} \times 40,000$ = Rs. 12,000

Standard Cost Method. Under this method, the by-products are valued at a standard rate which is pre-determined. It may be based on technical assessment and scientific analysis. Here the standard cost of main product would reflect changes, but that of by-product is credited to the process account of the main product. By this method, cost control of main product can be exercised effectively.

Contributory Margin Method. This method uses the technique of marginal costing for the apportionment of joint cost. Under this method at first the total joint costs are segregated into two parts—variable and fixed. The variable parts are apportioned on the basis of average cost or physical units method, and fixed part is apportioned on the basis of total contribution made by various products.

Illustration.

XYZ Ltd. obtains three joint products A, B and C from a process of manufacture. From the following information apportion the joint costs A, B and C under contributory margin method :

Products	*Units Produced*	*Selling Price per unit*	*Per unit post separation (Variable Cost)*
A	500	20	8
B	300	15	4
C	200	14	5

Pre-separation costs :

	Rs.
D/M	2,000
D/L	3,000
V/OH	2,000
Fixed overhead	8,200
	15,200

Solution

Total variable costs = 2,000 + 3,000 + 2,000
= Rs. 7,000

Total output = 1,000

$\therefore$ Per unit pre-separation variable cost = $\frac{\text{Rs. } 7{,}000}{1{,}000}$ = Rs. 7

Product	*Per unit presep. variable cost*	*Per unit post-sep. variable cost*	*Total variable cost*	*Selling Price*	*Contribution per unit*	*Total contribution*
A	7	8	15	20	5	5 × 500 = 2,500
B	7	4	11	15	4	4 × 300 = 1,200
C	7	5	12	14	2	2 × 200 = 400
						4,100

Now fixed cost of Rs. 8,200 should be apportioned to joint products A, B and C on the basis of total contribution by the following way :

$$A = \frac{2{,}500}{4{,}100} \times 8{,}200 = \text{Rs. } 5{,}000$$

$$B = \frac{1{,}200}{4{,}100} \times 8{,}200 = \text{Rs. } 2{,}400$$

$$C = \frac{400}{4{,}100} \times 8{,}200 = \text{Rs. } 800$$

Total 8,200

Market Value Method

Under the market value method each type of joint product is charged for 'what the traffic can bear'. According to this method, the number of units of each product manufactured is multiplied by the product's selling price to obtain the sales value of production. Joint costs are apportioned in the ratio of sales value of individual products. There are some limitations of this method. These limitations are :

(*i*) In the determination of relative selling price a number of problems come up.

(*ii*) Selling price of joint product may not be an accurate indicator of cost incurred up to their point of separation.

(*iii*) If the price of some products are stable and other products are changeable, then this method will give different costs of joint product for different periods. Therefore the share of joint cost will change without the change of cost structure.

Market value may mean any of the following :

(*a*) Market value at separation point.

(*b*) Market value after further processing.

(*c*) Net realisable value.

(*a*) Market value at separation point. Under this method market value of the joint product at the point of separation is ascertained and joint cost is apportioned in the ratio of sales value. This method is effective where further processing of products incurs disproportionate costs.

Illustration

Joint cost = Rs. 12,000

Products	*Production Units*	*Selling Price*
A	500	20
B	300	30
C	200	25

Solution

Products	*Production Units*	*Selling Price*	*Sales Value*	*Apportioned joint cost (Ratio 10 : 9 : 5)*
A	500	20	10,000	5,000
B	300	30	9,000	4,500
C	200	25	5,000	2,500
	1,000		24,000	12,000

Satement of Cost

Product	*Joint Cost*	*Units*	*Cost per unit*
A	5,000	500	10·00
B	4,500	300	15·00
C	2,500	200	12·50

(*b*) **Market Value after further Processing.** This method is easy to operate because selling price of the various joint products (after further processing) will be readily available. Pre-separation costs are apportioned on the basis of Market value after further processing. This method is, however, unfair where further processing costs of production are disproportionate.

Illustration

Joint cost Rs. 12,000

Product	*Production units*	*Selling price*	*Further processing cost*
A	500	20	2,000
B	300	30	1,000
C	200	25	1,000

Solution

Statement showing Apportionment of Joint Costs

Product	*Units Produced*	*Selling Price*	*Sales Value*	*Further Processing Cost*	*Sales Value less further Processing Cost*	*Ratio*	*Share of Joint Cost*
A	500	20	10,000	2,000	8,000	$\frac{2}{5}$	$\frac{2}{5} \times 12,000 = 4,800$
B	300	30	9,000	1,000	8,000	$\frac{2}{5}$	$\frac{2}{5} \times 12,000 = 4,800$
C	200	25	5,000	4,000	4,000	$\frac{1}{5}$	$\frac{1}{5} \times 12,000 = 2,400$
Total					20,000		12,000

Working Notes :

$$\text{Ratio } A = \frac{8,000}{20,000} = \frac{2}{5}; \text{ Ratio } B = \frac{8,000}{20,000} = \frac{2}{5}; \text{ Ratio } C = \frac{4,000}{20,000} = \frac{1}{5}$$

(*c*) **Net Realisable value or Reverse Cost Method.** Under this method, from the sales value of joint products : (*a*) the estimated profit, (*b*) selling and distribution cost, and (*c*) post-separation costs are deducted.

The resultant figure is net realisable value of joint products and joint costs are apportioned in the ratio of net realisable values.

Illustration

A factory produces three products X, Y and Z, which produces from a joint process.
Joint cost Rs. 12,000
Further Processing Cost :

	X	*Y*	*Z*
Material	1,500	2,500	3,000
Labour	1,000	500	1,500
Overhead	1,500	1,000	2,500
	4,000	4,000	7,000
Sales Value	40,000	40,000	50,000
Estimated Profit	30%	25%	20%
Selling & Distribution Exp.	4,000	6,000	3,000

Solution

Statement showing Apportionment of Joint Costs

Particulars	*A* Rs.	*B* Rs.	*C* Rs.
Sales	40,000	40,000	50,000
Less : Estimated Profit	12,000	10,000	10,000
	28,000	30,000	40,000
Less : Selling & Distribution Overhead	4,000	6,000	3,000
	24,000	24,000	37,000
Less : Further Processing Cost	4,000	4,000	7,000
Basis of Apportionment	20,000	20,000	30,000

Joint Cost should be borned by

$$\text{Product } A = \frac{20,000}{70,000} \times 12,000 = 3,429$$

$$\text{Product } B = \frac{20,000}{70,000} \times 12,000 = 3,429$$

$$\text{Product } C = \frac{30,000}{70,000} \times 12,000 = 5,142$$

WORKEDOUT PROBLEMS

Problem 1

In the process line of XY Company three joint products are produced for the month of May 1990. The following data were available :

Products	L	M	N
Sale price per kg	5	10	20
Post-separation cost	10,000	5,000	15,000
Output in kgs	2,500	1,000	1,500

Pre-separation point costs amounted to Rs. 20,000. The joint products are manufactured in one common process; after which they are separated and may undergo further individual processing. The pre-separation point costs are apportioned to joint products according to weight.

You are required to prepare a statement showing the estimated profit or loss for each product and in total.

Solution

Statement showing Apportionment of Joint Cost (on the basis of weight)

Product	*Weight*	*Share of Joint cost*
L	2,500	$\frac{2,500}{5,000} \times 20,000$ = Rs. 10,000
M	1,000	$\frac{1,000}{5,000} \times 20,000$ = Rs. 4,000
N	1,500	$\frac{1,500}{5,000} \times 20,000$ = Rs. 6,000
Total	5,000	20,000

Statement showing Estimated Profit/Loss

Particulars	*L*	*M*	*N*	*Total*
Sales Value (weight × Price) (A)	12,500	10,000	30,000	52,500
Less : Total Cost				
Pre-separation Cost	10,000	4,000	6,000	20,000
Post-separation Cost	10,000	5,000	15,000	30,000
Total Cost (B)	20,000	9,000	21,000	50,000
∴ Profit/Loss (A – B)	– 7,500	1,000	9,000	2,500

Problem 2

From the following information, find the profit made by each product apportioning joint cost on sales value basis :

		Rs.
Joint costs :		
Direct materials		1,26,000
Power		25,000
Petrol, Oil, Lubricants		5,000
Labour		7,500
Other charges		4,100
	Product X	*Product Y*
Selling cost	20,000	80,000
Sales	1,52,000	1,68,000

[I.C.W.A. (Inter)]

Solution

Statement showing Apportionment of Joint Cost

Particulars	*Total*	*Product A* Rs.	*Product B* Rs.
Sales Value	3,20,000	1,52,000	1,68,000
Less : Selling Cost	1,00,000	20,000	80,000
Basis of Apportionment of Joint Cost	2,20,000	1,32,000	88,000

Total Joint Cost

	Rs.
Direct Material	1,26,000
Power	25,000
Petrol, Oil, Lubricants	5,000
Labour	7,500
Other charges	4,100
	1,67,600

∴ Joint Cost should be borned by :

$$\text{Product A} = \frac{1,32,000}{2,20,000} \times 1,67,600 = 1,00,560$$

$$\text{Product B} = \frac{88,000}{2,20,000} \times 1,67,600 = 67,040$$

Statement showing Profit of each Product.

Particulars	*Product X (Rs.)*	*Product Y (Rs.)*
Sales Value (A)	1,52,000	1,68,000
Share of Joint Cost	1,00,560	67,040
Selling Expenses	20,000	80,000
Total Cost (B)	1,20,560	1,47,040
Profit (A – B)	31,440	20,960

Problem 3

In manufacturing the main product A, a company processes the resulting waste materials into two by-products M_1 and M_2. Use the method of working back from sales value to an estimated cost.

You are required to prepare a comparative profit and loss statement of the products from the following data :

(*i*) Total cost up to separation point was Rs. 1,36,000

	A	M_1	M_2
(*ii*) Sales (all production) Rs.	3,28,000	32,000	48,000
(*iii*) Cost after separation	—	9,600	14,400
(*iv*) Estimated net profit percentage to sales value	—	20%	30%
(*v*) Estimated selling expenses as percentage of sales value	20%	20%	20%

[*I.C.W.A. Inter*]

Solution

Statement showing the Share Pre-separation Cost under Reverse Cost Method

Particulars	*By-Product* M_1	*By-Product* M_2
Sales Value	32,000	48,000
Less : Estimated Profit	6,400	14,400
	25,600	33,600
Less : Estimated Selling Exp.	6,400	14,400
	19,200	19,200
Less : Cost after separation	9,600	14,400
Cost up to separation	9,600	4,800
∴ Total cost up to separation for main product :	Rs.	
Total Joint Cost to By-Product	1,36,000	
Less : Cost up to separation		
M_1 9,600		
M_2 4,800	14,400	
	1,21,600	

Statement showing Comparative Profit & Loss

Particulars	*Total*	*Main Product*	*By-Product*	
	Rs.	*A*	M_1	M_2
Sales Value (A)	4,08,000	3,28,000	32,000	48,000
Pre-separation Cost	1,36,000	1,16,800	9,600	4,800
Cost after separation	24,000	—	9,600	14,400
Total cost (B)	1,55,200	1,16,800	19,200	19,200
Gross Profit (A – B)	2,52,800	2,11,200	12,800	28,800
Less : Selling Expenses	81,600	65,600	6,400	9,600
Net Profit	1,71,200	1,45,600	6,400	19,200

Problem 4

The following information have been extracted from the books of a processing company :

Joint Products	*Yield (in kg) per tonne of coal*
Coke	585
Coal tar	72
Benzol	18
Ammonia sulphate	27
Gas	198
	900

The price of Coal is Rs. 200 per tonne. Direct labour and overheads to the point of separation are Rs. 150 and Rs. 200, respectively, per tonne of coal.

Calculate the cost of each product on the basis of weight. **[*I.C.W.A. Final*]**

Solution

(*i*) Total Joint cost per tonne of coal

	Rs.
Price of coal	200
Direct Labour	150
Overhead	200
	550

(*ii*) **% of weight per tonne of coal of each Joint Product**

Product	*Per tonne of coal*	*% of Relative weight per tonne of coal*
Coke	585	$\frac{585}{900} \times 100 = 65\%$
Coal tar	72	$\frac{72}{900} \times 100 = 8\%$
Benzol	18	$\frac{18}{900} \times 100 = 2\%$
Ammonia Sulphate	27	$\frac{27}{900} \times 100 = 3\%$
Gas	198	$\frac{198}{900} \times 100 = 22\%$
	900	100%

Statement showing Apportionment of Joint Cost

Product	*% of Relative weight per tonne*	*Joint cost per tonne*	*Share of Joint cost*
Coke	65%	550	357·50
Coal Tar	8%	550	44·00
Benzol	2%	550	11·00
Ammonia Sulphate	3%	550	16·50
Gas	22%	550	121·00
	100%	—	550·00

Problem 5

In the month of January, 180 tonnes of Product A and 120 tonnes of Product B were manufactured jointly and the following costs were incurred :

Direct Material Rs. 30,000, Direct Labour Rs. 20,000

Variable Overhead Rs. 8,000, Factory Overhead Rs. 12,000

Selling Price : A = Rs. 350 per tonne, B = Rs. 250 per tonne.

Apportion the joint cost to Products A and B, using the following methods :

(*a*) On the basis of weight,

(*b*) On the basis of weight for variable cost and contribution of fixed cost, and

(*c*) On the basis of sales value.

Solution

Cost :

	Rs.
Direct Material	30,000
Direct Labour	20,000
Variable Overhead	8,000
Marginal Cost	58,000
Fixed Cost	12,000
Total Cost	70,000

(*a*) **Apportionment of Joint Cost on the basis of Weight** (*i.e.* output)

A.	180 tonnes	*i.e.*	60%
B.	120 tonnes	*i.e.*	40%
	300 tonnes		100%

Cost of A = $70{,}000 \times \frac{60}{100}$ = 42,000 and Cost of B = $70{,}000 \times \frac{40}{100}$ = 28,000

(*b*) **Apportionment of Joint Cost on the basis of Weight and Contribution**

Marginal (or Variable) Cost of A is 60% of Rs. 58,000 = 34,800

Marginal (or Variable) Cost of B is 40% of Rs. 58,000 = 23,200

58,000

Contribution :

	A (Rs.)	*B (Rs.)*
Sales @	350	250
Sales Value	63,000	30,000
Less : Marginal Cost	34,800	23,200
Contribution	28,200	6,800
Fixed Cost Rs. 12,000 apportioned in ratio 282 : 68		
Share of Fixed Cost	9,670	2,330
Share of Marginal Cost	34,800	23,200
Total Cost	44,470	25,530

(c) Apportionment of Joint Cost on the basis of Sales Value

A 180 tonnes @ 350 per tonne	Rs. 63,000	i.e.	67·7%
B 120 tonnes @ 250 per tonne	Rs. 30,000	i.e.	32·3%
Total	93,000		100·00

Cost apportionment :

A 67·7% of Rs. 70,000 = 47,390

B 32·3% of Rs. 70,000 = 22,610

70,000

Summary of Cost Apportionment

	A (Rs.)	B (Rs.)	Total (Rs.)
(a)	42,000	28,000	70,000
(b)	44,470	25,530	70,000
(c)	47,390	22,610	70,000

Using Differential/Incremental Cost Approach

Problem 6

A chemical factory produces four products from a single raw material. The cost of raw material for a year is Rs. 67,000 and the initial processing costs amounted to Rs. 1,28,200. All the four products *viz.,* A, B, C and D are produced simultaneously at a single split off point. Product C is sold immediately without further processing. A, B and D are processed further.

The output, sales and further processing costs are :

Products	*Output (in units)*	*Sales (Rs.)*	*Further Processing cost (Rs,)*
A	4,00,000	1,92,000	40,000
B	89,725	58,000	32,000
C	5,000	8,000	—
D	9,000	60,000	1,000

If these products were sold out at the split-off point, the prices attained per unit would be A = Rs. 0·32, B = Rs. 0·40, C = Rs. 1·60 and D = Rs. 5·00.

(*A*) Find out the profitability under present condition, as well as if products are sold at split-off stage and comment on the results.

(*B*) Using the concepts of relevancy of costs and differential costs, advise your management whether further processing should be undertaken or not.

[*I.C.W.A. (Final)*]

Solution

(*A*) Workings :

Apportionment of Joint Cost

Total Common Cost	Rs. 67,000
Initial Processing Cost	Rs. 1,28,200
	1,95,200

	A	*B*	*C*	*D*
Output	4,00,000	89,725	5,000	9,000
Sales Price (Rs.)	0·32	0·40	1·60	5·00
Sales Value (Rs.)	1,28,000	35,890	8,000	45,000
Ratio	12,800	3,589	800	4,500

A's Share of Common Cost = $1{,}95{,}200 \times \dfrac{12{,}800}{21{,}689} = 1{,}15{,}200$

B'S Share of Common Cost = 1,95,200 × $\frac{3,589}{21,689}$ = 32,300

C's Share of Common Cost = 1,95,200 × $\frac{800}{21,689}$ = 7,200

D's Share of Common Cost = 1,95,200 × $\frac{4,500}{21,689}$ = 40,500

1,95,200

Profitability Under Present Condition

	A	*B*	*C*	*D*	*Total*
1. Sales	1,92,000	58,000	8,000	60,000	3,18,000
2. Cost of Production					
(*a*) Apportionment of Common Cost (see workings)	1,15,200	32,300	7,200	40,500	1,95,200
(*b*) Additional Processing Cost	40,000	32,000	—	1,000	73,000
(*a*) + (*b*)	1,55,200	64,300	7,200	41,500	2,68,200
3. Profit/(Loss) (1 – 2)	36,800	(6,300)	800	18,500	49,800

Profitability if sold at Split-off Stage

	A	*B*	*C*	*D*	*Total*
Sales	1,28,000	35,890	8,000	45,000	2,16,890
Less : Common Cost	1,15,200	32,300	7,200	40,500	1,95,200
	12,800	3,590	800	4,500	21,690

Comment. Profit under present condition is highter than the profit if it is sold at split-off stage.

(*B*) The decision with regard to furhter processing should be based on whether the incremental revenue as a result of further processing exceeds additional cost of further processing. The additional charges which are relevant to decisions are, therefore, relevant cost.

	A	*B*	*D*	*Total* (*Rs.*)
Sales Value after further processing	1,92,000	58,000	60,000	3,10,000
Sales Value at split-off	1,28,000	35,890	45,000	2,08,890
Additional Revenue (Differential Revenue)	64,000	22,110	15,000	1,01,110
Differential Cost (*i.e.* further Processing Cost)	40,000	32,000	1,000	73,000
Additional Profit/Loss	24,000	(9,890)	14,000	28,110

Therefore, it is evident that products A and D should continue to be further processed after point of separation, while product B should be sold at split-off stage.

Problem 7

Bright Chemicals Ltd. electrolyses common salt to obtain three Joint Products—caustic soda, chlorine and hydrogen. During a costing period the expenditure relating to the inputs for the common process amounted to Rs. 3,50,000. After separation, expenses amounting to Rs. 1,60,000, Rs. 75,000 and Rs. 10,000 were incurred for caustic soda, chlorine and hydrogen, respectively. The entire production was sold off, Rs. 3,75,000, Rs. 2,50,000 and Rs. 60,000 were realised for caustic soda, chlorine and hydrogen, respectively. The selling expenses were estimated at 5% of realisation from sales. The management expected profit @ 15%, 10% and 5%, respectively of realisation from sales of caustic soda, chlorine and hydrogen.

Draw a columnar statement showing the apportionment of Joint Costs and profitability of each product. **[I.C.W.A. *Inter, December 1991*]**

Solution

Statement showing the Apportionment of Joint Costs to the three Joint Products and their Profitability

Particulars	Caustic Soda Rs.	Chlorine Rs.	Hydrogen Rs.	Total Rs.
Realisation from salts	3,75,000	2,50,000	60,000	6,85,000
Less : Expected profit (15%, 10%, 5% on realisation)	56,250	25,000	3,000	84,250
Less : Selling expenses (5% on realisation)	18,750	12,500	3,000	34,250
Estimated Cost of Production	3,00,000	2,12,500	54,000	5,66,500
Less : After Separation Cost	1,60,000	75,000	10,000	2,45,000
	1,40,000	1,37,500	44,000	3,21,500
Estimated Joint Cost and their percentage	43·5%	42·8%	13·7%	100%
Actual Joint Cost Apportionment	1,52,250	1,49,800	47,950	3,50,000
Add : After separation cost	1,60,000	75,000	10,000	2,45,000
Actual Cost of Production	3,12,250	2,24,800	57,950	5,95,000
Add : Selling Expenses	18,750	12,500	3,000	34,250
Profit realised	44,000	12,700	(950)	55,750
	3,75,000	2,50,000	60,000	6,85,000

Apportionment of Joint Cost

Problem 8

If the Products are truly Joint Products, the cost of the process can be applied to these Products :

(*i*) on the basis of weight or other physical quantity of each Product;

(*ii*) in respect of marginal costs of the process on the basis of physical quantities of various products and in respect of fixed costs of the Process on the basis of contribution made by the various Products;

(*iii*) on the basis of sales value of different Products.

Illustrate the above statement by using the following figures in respect of joint production of A & B for a month.

		Rs.
Total Cost :	Direct Materials	5,000
	Direct Labour	3,000
	Variable Overheads	2,000
	Fixed Overheads	2,000
Sales :	A = 100 quintals @ Rs. 80 per quintal	
	B = 150 quintals @ Rs. 40 per quintal	

Also compute the profit and loss per product under each of these methods.

[*I.C.W.A. Inter, June 1993*]

Solution

Sales :	A = 100 × 80	=	Rs. 8,000
	B = 150 × 40	=	Rs. 6,000
			14,000
Marginal Cost (5,000 + 3,000 + 2,000)			10,000
Contribution			4,000
Less : Fixed Cost			2,000
Profit			2,000

Total Joint Cost for A and B = Marginal Cost + Fixed Cost

= Rs. 10,000 + Rs. 2,000 = Rs. 12,000

(*i*) Apportionment of Joint Costs on the basis of weight

Product	*Quantity (quintals)*	*Jt. Cost apportioned on the basis of weight*	*Sales Value*	*Profit/(Loss)*
		Rs.		
A	100	4,800	8,000	3,200
B	150	7,200	6,000	(1,200)
		12,000	14,000	2,000

Note. Joint Cost Apportioned in the Ratio 100 : 150

(*ii*) Apportionment of Marginal Costs on the basis of physical quantity and Fixed Cost on the basis of contribution.

Product	*Quantity (in quintals)*	*Sales value*	*Marginal Cost apportioned on the basis of weight*	*Contribution Rs.*	*Fixed Cost on the basis of contribution*	*Profit/ (Loss)*
(1)	(2)	(3)	(4)	(5)	(6)	(7)
A	100	8,000	4,000	4,000	2,000	2,000
B	150	6,000	6,000	—	—	Nil
		14,000	10,000	4,000	2,000	2,000

(*iii*) Apportionment on the basis of sales value.

Product	*Sales Value Rs.*	*Joint Cost apportioned on the basis of Sales Value*	*Profit*
A	8,000	6,857	1,143
B	6,000	5,143	857
	14,000	12,000	2,000

Note : Joint Cost apportioned in the Ratio 8,000 : 6,000.

Problem 9

In a manufacturing concern, Production of A yields by-products B and C. The joint expenses of manufacturing are :

	Rs.
Materials	8,500
Labour	9,000
Overhead	7,500

Subsequent expenses are :

	Materials	*Labour*	*Overhead*
A	2,500	1,900	1,500
B	1,200	1,600	900
C	1,400	2,000	1,050

Selling Price A Rs. 30,000
B Rs. 20,000
C Rs. 15,000

Profit on selling price A 40%, B 30%, C 25%.

Show how you would apportion Joint expenses and ascertain profit on each product.

[*B.Com. Osmania, March 1992*]

Solution

Statement of Cost and Profit

	A	*B*	*C*	*Total*
Selling Price (Rs.)	30,000	20,000	15,000	65,000
Less : Profit on Selling Price (Rs.) A 40%, B 30%, C 25%	12,000	6,000	3,750	21,750
Cost of Sales	18,000	14,000	11,250	43,250
Less : Selling & Distribution Exp. (See Note)	1,938	1,293	969	4,200
Cost of Production	16,062	12,707	10,281	39,050
Less : Subsequent expenses	5,900	3,700	4,450	14,050
Joint Cost	10,162	9,007	5,831	25,000

Joint Cost may be apportioned in the ratio 10,162 : 9,007 : 5,831.

	A	B	C	Total
Joint Cost	10,162	9,007	5,831	25,000
Subsequent Expenses	5,900	3,700	4,450	14,050
Cost of Production	16,062	12,707	10,281	39,050
Selling and Dist. Expenses	1,938	1,293	969	4,200
	18,000	14,000	11,250	43,250
Profit	12,000	6,000	3,750	21,750
	30,000	20,000	15,000	65,000

Note : Total joint cost of Rs. 25,000 and subsequent expenses of Rs. 14,050 comes to Rs. 39,050. While cost of sales comes to Rs. 43,250. The difference of (43,250 – 39,050) Rs. 4,200 is assumed to be selling and distribution expenses.

Problem 10

Apportionment of joint cost on sales value basis and selling at split-off point.

Tee Pee Ltd. in the course of refining crude oil obtains four Joint Products A, B, C and D. The total cost till the split-off point was Rs. 97,600.

The output and sales in the year 1990 were :

Product	*Output (Gallons)*	*Sales (Rs.)*	*Separate Cost (Rs.)*
A	5,00,000	1,15,000	30,000
B	10,000	10,000	6,000
C	5,000	4,000	—
D	9,000	30,000	1,000

You are required to :

(*i*) Calculate the net income of the company from each product if the Joint Costs are apportioned on the basis of sales value of the different products.

(*ii*) What would be the net income of the company from each product if it decides to sell the products at the split-off point itself @ A 15 paise, B 50 Paise; C 80 paise and D Rs. 3 per gallon?

(*iii*) In case the company expects to operate at the same level of production and sales in the year 1991, could the company increase the net income by altering its processing decisions ? If so, what would be the expected overall net income ? Which product should be processed further and which would be sold at split-off point ?

Assume that all costs incurred after the split-off are variable. [*C.S. Inter, December 1991*]

Solution

(i) Net Income when Joint Cost apportioned on Sales Value basis

Product	*Sales value*	*Separate cost*	*S.V. at split off point*	*Apportioned Joint Cost.*	*Net income*
	Rs.	*Rs.*	*Rs.*	*Rs.*	*Rs.*
1	2	3	4 = (2 – 3)	5	6 = (4 – 5)
A	1,15,000	30,000	85,000	68,000*	17,000
B	10,000	6,000	4,000	3,200	800
C	4,000	—	4,000	3,200	800
D	30,000	1,000	29,000	23,200	5,800
	1,59,000	37,000	1,22,000	97,600	24,400

*Rs. 97,600 × 85,000/1,22,000 = 68,000 and so on.

(ii) Net income of each product if sold at split of point

Product	*Output*	*S.P. per unit*	*Sales value at split-off point*	*Allocated J.C.*	*Net income*
A	5,00,000	Re. 0·15	Rs. 75,000	65,946**	9,054
B	10,000	0·50	5,000	4,397	603
C	5,000	0·80	4,000	3,517	483
D	9,000	Rs. 3·00	27,000	23,740	3,260
			1,11,000	97,600	13,400

**Rs. 97,600 × 75,000/1,11,000 = Rs. 65,946 and so on.

(iii) Determination of additional net income by altering the processing decisions

Product	*Sales value after further processing*	*Sales value at split-off point*	*Incremental sales value*	*Separate Cost*	*Incremental Gain/Loss*
	Rs.	*Rs.*	*Rs.*	*Rs.*	*Rs.*
A	1,15,000	75,000	40,000	30,000	10,000
B	10,000	5,000	5,000	6,000	(1,000)
C	4,000	4,000	—	—	—
D	30,000	27,000	3,000	1,000	2,000
	1,59,000	1,11,000	48,000	37,000	11,000

Note : Products A and D should be sold after further processing. However products B and C should be sold at split off point.

Problem 11

A chemical company carries on production operation in two processes. Materials first pass through process I where a compound is produced. A loss in weight takes place at the start of processing. The following data, which can be assumed to be representative, relates to the month just ended :

Quantities (kg) :

Materials input	2,00,000
Opening work-in-process (half processed)	40,000
Work completed	1,60,000
Closing work-in-process (2/3 processed)	30,000

Cost : Materials		Rs. 75,000
	Processing Cost	96,000
Opening work-in-process :		
	Materials	20,000
	Processing cost	12,000

Any quantity of the compound can be sold for Rs. 1·60 per kg. Alternatively, it can be transferred to Process II for further processing and packing to be sold as starcomp for Rs. 2·00 per kg. Further materials are added in Process II such that for every kg of compound used, 2 kg of starcomp result.

Of the 1,60,000 kg per month of work completed in Process I, 40,000 kg are sold as a compound and 1,20,000 kg are passed through process II for sale as starcomp. Process II has facilities to handle up to 1,60,000 kg of compound per month if required. The monthly cost incurred in Process II (other than the cost of the compound) are :

	1,20,000 kg of compound input	1,60,000 kg of compound input
Materials	Rs. 1,20,000	Rs. 1,60,000
Processing Costs	Rs. 1,20,000	Rs. 1,40,000

Required :

(*a*) Determine, using the average method, the cost per kg in Process I and the value of both work completed and closing work-in-process for the month just ended.

(*b*) Demonstrate that it is worthwhile further processing 1,20,000 kg of compound.

(*c*) Calculate the minimum acceptable selling price per kg, if a potential buyer could be found for the additional output of starcomp that could be produced with the remaining compound.

[*C.I.M.A. (F)*]

Solution

	kg.
(*a*) Opening WIP	40,000
Add : Input	2,00,000
	2,40,000
Less : Cl. WIP	30,000
	2,10,000
Output	1,60,000
Normal Loss	50,000

Statement of Equivalent Production

Input		Output		Equivalent Production			
				Material		*Processing Cost*	
Items	*Units*	*Items*	*Units*	*% of Comp.*	*Units*	*% of Comp.*	*Units*
Op. WIP	40,000	Normal Loss	50,000	—	—	—	—
Introduced	2,00,000	Units finished and completed	1,60,000	100	1,60,000	100	1,60,000
		Closing WIP	30,000	100	30,000	$66\frac{2}{3}$	20,000
	2,40,000		2,40,000		1,90,000		1,80,000

Statement of Cost

	Material Cost	*Processing Cost*	*Total*
Opening WIP (Rs.)	20,000	12,000	32,000
Introduced (Rs.)	75,000	96,000	1,71,000
Total (*a*)	95,000	1,08,000	2,03,000
(*b*) Eqv. Units	1,90,000	1,80,000	
(*c*) Cost per unit (a ÷ b)	0·50	0·60	1·10

Statement of Evaluation

Value of completely processed 1,60,000 kg. @ Rs. 1·10		1,76,000
Value of Closing W.I.P. :		
Materials 30,000 kg @ Rs. 0·50	= 15,000	
Processing Cost 20,000 kg @ Rs. 0·60	= 12,000	
		27,000
	Total	2,03,000

(*b*) The decision with regard to further processing of 1,20,000 kg should be based on whether incremental revenue as a result of further processing exceeds additional cost.

Sale value of starcomp after further processing [(1,20,000 × 2)kg @ Rs. 2]	Rs. 4,80,000	
Less : Sales value before further processing (1,20,000 × Rs. 1·60)	Rs. 1,92,000	
		2,88,000
Less : Further processing cost (*i.e.* incremental cost)		
Material	1,20,000	
Processing	1,20,000	2,40,000
Additional Profit		48,000

Therefore, it is worthwhile further processing 1,20,000 kg of compound.

(*c*) The minimum acceptable selling price for additional output of (40,000 × 2 kg) of Starcomp, which can be produced with the remaining compound, should cover the additional cost of further processing and the loss of sales revenue, if it is sold without further processing.

Additional Material cost (Rs. 1,60,000—Rs. 1,20,000)	= Rs. 40,000
Additional Processing cost (Rs. 1,40,000 —Rs. 1,20,000)	= Rs. 20,000
Add : Loss of sales revenue before further processing (40,000 × Rs. 1·60)	Rs. 64,000
	1,24,000

Hence, the minimum acceptable selling price $= \dfrac{\text{Rs. } 1{,}24{,}000}{40{,}000 \times 2} = \text{Rs. } 1{\cdot}55$

Problem 12

A food processing company produces four products from a single raw material. These four products are obtained simultaneously at the point of separation. The product R does not require further processing before being taken to the market. The other three products P, Q and S require further processing before being sold. The company follows the net market value method for allocating common costs to products.

The cost of the raw material used for the year just ended was Rs. 18,000. The initial processing costs were Rs. 30,000 for the same period. The output, sales and further processing costs for the last year were :

Product	*P*	*Q*	*R*	*S*
Output (in units)	4,000	3,500	2,500	1,200
Sales (in Rs.)	36,000	14,000	20,000	12,000
Further Processing Cost (Rs.)	5,000	1,750	—	3,250

You are required to

(*a*) Prepare a comparative Profit and Loss statement showing the Profit/Loss made on each of the four products ;

(*b*) Assess the change in the Profit/Loss given in answer to : (*a*) above, if the proposal (stated below) made by the top management is accepted.

Proposal : To sell all the products directly to other processors just after separation without any further processing. The expected price per unit for the products are :

P—Rs. 7, Q—Rs. 3·50, R—Rs. 8 and S—Rs. 9.

[*I.C.W.A. (Inter), Dec. 1995*]

Solution

(*a*) Comparative Profit and Loss Statement

Product	*Sales*	*Further Processing Cost (Rs.)*	*Net Sales (Rs.)*	*Apportioned Common Cost (Rs.)*	*Profit (Rs.)*
P	36,000	5,000	31,000	20,667	10,333
Q	14,000	1,750	12,250	8,167	4,083
R	20,000	—	20,000	13,333	6,667
S	12,000	3,250	8,750	5,833	2,917
Total :	82,000	10,000	72,000	48,000	24,000

Apportion of Common Costs :

Common Costs = Rs. 48,000

Net Sales = Rs. 72,000

Product	*Apportioned Rs.*
P	$31{,}000 \times \dfrac{48{,}000}{72{,}000} = 20{,}667$
Q	$12{,}250 \times \dfrac{48{,}000}{72{,}000} = 8{,}167$
R	$20{,}000 \times \dfrac{48{,}000}{72{,}000} = 13{,}333$
S	$8{,}750 \times \dfrac{48{,}000}{72{,}000} = 5{,}833$

(*b*) Statement of change in Profit/Loss if the Products are sold just after separation

Product	*Output (in units)*	*Expected sale price at the point of separation (Rs.)*	*Expected sale value at the point of separation (Rs.)*	*Apportioned Common Cost (Rs.)*	*Profit (Rs.)*
P	4,000	7·00	28,000	20,667	7,333
Q	3,500	3·50	12,250	8,167	4,083
R	2,500	8·00	20,000	13,333	6,667
S	1,200	9·00	10,800	5,833	4,967
Total			71,050	48,000	23,050

If all the products are sold directly to the other processors just after separation, the overall net profit will come down from Rs. 24,000 to Rs. 23,050. Therefore the proposal of the top management would not be accepted.

EXERCISES

OBJECTIVE TYPE QUESTIONS

1. *State whether the following statements are true or false.*

(*a*) The allocation of Joint costs to Joint and by-product affects the total Profit or Loss.

(*b*) By-products may be sold in their original form, *i.e.* without further processing.

(*c*) The product has generally no control over the relative quantities of by-products and the main products.

(*d*) The sales value method apportions the Joint Costs on the basis of principles of what the traffic will bear.

(*e*) Joint products and by-products are the samé.

(*f*) There is a clear-cut distinction between main product and by-products.

[Ans. True : (b) (c) (d) (f)
False : (a) (e)]

2. *Which of the following is a by-product ?*

(*a*) Metal trimmings sold to a scrap metal dealer.

(*b*) Glue made from residual fluids in a chemical process.

(*c*) Sawdust sold by a timber company.

(*d*) Fabric off cuts sold by a cloth manufacturer as industrial rags.

[Ans. (b)]

3. *The use of physical units basis for the apportionment of process costs to Joint products will give an unacceptable stock value for one of the Joint products*

(*a*) Where the stock value is greater than sales value at separation point.

(*b*) Because the profit percentage is lower than that of other Joint products.

(*c*) Where the Joint product in question requires no further processing.

(*d*) Where the amount of further processing varies from one product to another.

[Ans. (a)]

4. *In the reversal cost method, the manufacturing cost of the main product is reduced by*

(*a*) The estimated replacement costs of the by-products.

(*b*) The actual revenues received from the by-products.

(*c*) The estimated market value of the by-products.

(*d*) None of the above.

[Ans. (c)]

5. *Which of the following components of production are allocable as Joint costs when a single manufacturing process produces several saleable products ?*

(*a*) Direct materials, direct labour, factory overhead.

(*b*) Direct Labour and factory overhead only.

(*c*) Direct materials and direct labour only.

(*d*) Factory overhead and direct materials only.

[Ans. (*a*)]

6. *Which method of accounting for by-products allocates a portion of Joint costs to the by-products ?*

(*a*) Net realisable method.

(*b*) Reversal cost method.

(*c*) Both (a) and (b).

(*d*) None of the above.

THEORETICAL QUESTIONS

1. Explain the treatement of by-products in a process costing. **[*C.S. Inter, June 1994*]**
2. Discuss, in brief, the problems faced in accounting for Joint products costs. Suggest methods of equitable allocation. **[*M.Com. C.U. 1987*]**
3. Explain the distinction between co-products, by-products and waste. **[*I.C.W.A. Inter June 1985*]**
4. Distinguish between Joint products and By-products and explain various methods of accounting for them. **[*C.A. Inter May, 1989 ; I.C.W.A. Inter*, 1985 ; C.S. Inter, June 1987]**

PROBLEMS

1. In a concern engaged in process industry, four products emerge from a particular process of operation. The total cost of input for the period ended 30th September 1995 is Rs. 2,53,500.

The details of output, additional cost, after "split-off point" and sales value of the products are :

Products	*Output* (*kg.*)	*Additional Processing cost after split-off* (*Rs.*)	*Sales value* (*Rs.*)
A	8,000	60,000	1,68,000
B	5,000	10,000	1,10,000
C	3,000	—	60,000
D	4,000	20,000	90,000

If the products are sold at "the split-off point" without further processing, the sales value would have been

	Rs.
A	1,15,000
B	90,000
C	55,000
D	80,000

You are required to prepare a Statement of Profitability based on the products being sold. (*i*) after further processing, and (*ii*) at the split-off point. **[*I.C.W.A. (Inter) Dec. 1989*]**

[Ans. (*i*) Profit = Rs. 84,500; (*ii*) Profit = Rs. 86,500]

2. In a manufacturing company 10,000 kilolitres of 'A' is processed to produce 6,000 kilolitres of 'B' and 4,000 kilolitres of 'C'. The joint cost before separation point came to an amount of Rs. 24,000. From the following particulars, calculate the apportionment of the joint cost and the profit of each product under : (*a*) physical measurement, (*b*) market value at separation point, and (*c*) market value after further processing :

	B (Rs.)	*C (Rs.)*
Unit selling price at separation point	5·00	3·75
Unit selling prices after further processing	7·00	7·50
Further processing costs after separation	5,000	7,500

[*I.C.W.A. (Inter) June1992*]

[Ans.	***B(Rs.)***	***C(Rs.)***
(*a*) Cost	**14,400**	**9,600**
Profit	**15,600**	**5,400**
(*b*) Cost	**16,000**	**8,000**
Profit	**14,000**	**7,000**
(*c*) Cost	**14,000**	**10,000**
Profit	**23,000**	**12,500]**

3. In manufacturing the main product, a company processes the incidental waste into two products, A and B.

From the following data relating to the products, you are required to prepare a comparative profit and loss statement showing individual costs and other details. The total costs up to the separation point were Rs. 3,10,400.

	Main Product	*By Products*	
		A	*B*
Sales	Rs. 8,00,000	Rs. 64,000	Rs. 96,000
Cost after separation	80,000	12,800	14,400
Estimated net profit (% on sales)	20%	15%	—
Estimated selling ex. (% on sales)	20%	10%	15%

[*C.A. (Inter)*]

[Ans. Allocated to by-products Rs. 80,000; Profit Rs. 3,29,000; Rs. 12,800; Rs. 19,200]

[**Hints.** Reverse cost method to be followed for separation of joint costs.]

4. A company produces three products A, B and C from a joint process. Relevant costs and other data are :

	Joint Product	*Products*		
	(Rs.)	*A (Rs.)*	*B (Rs.)*	*C (Rs.)*
Materials	20,000	1,500	3,500	2,000
Labour	8,000	1,000	1,000	1,500
Expenses	4,000	500	1,000	500
	32,000	3,000	5,500	4,000
Sales Value		10,000	25,000	15,000
Selling & Distribution Exp. (as % Sales Value)		20%	20%	20%
Estimated Net profit (as % of Sales Value)		20%	10%	20%

Prepare a statement showing the apportionment of joint costs over the different products stating clearly the reasons for the basis adopted. **[*M.Com. C.U.*]**

[Ans. A = Rs. 7,467; B = Rs. 13,867; C = 10,666]

[**Hints.** Net value method to be followed for separation of Joint Cost]

5. Three joint products A, B and C along with by-product D are obtained from material. They require further processing at a cost of Re. 1·00 for A, Re. 0·80 for B and Re. 0·50 for C per unit before sale. The selling price per unit for the three joint products and the by-product, assuming they should yield an estimated profit of 25% on cost, are Rs. 2·75, Rs. 1·75 and Rs. 1·50, respectively, for the joint products and Re. 0·20 for the by-product.

During the period, the joint input cost was Rs. 18,160 and the respective outputs were :

A	8,000 units	C	4,000 units
B	6,000 units	D	1,000 units.

Net realisation from the sale of by-product should be credited to joint cost before its allocation to joint products.

Calculate joint cost per unit of A, B and C, taking into account the output of each of the joint products. **[*M.Com. C.U.*]**

[Ans. A = Rs. 1·35; B = Rs. 0·675; C = Rs. 0·7875]

6. A factory produces joint products of two varieties. The following data are extracted from the books :

	Total (Rs.)
Sales of products X and Y	7,50,000
Direct Materials	2,25,000
Direct Labour	1,10,000
Variable Overhead (150% of labour)	
Fixed Overhead	2,00,000

The analysis of sales reveals that the percentages of sales of product X is $66\frac{2}{3}$%.

Management contemplates to process further the joint products so that they could be sold at higher rates. Facilities for this are available. The additional information relating to further processing are :

	Products		*Total*
	X(Rs.)	*Y(Rs.)*	*(Rs.)*
Sales after further processing	6,00,000	3,00,000	9,00,000
Additional Material	50,000	20,000	70,000
Additional Direct Labour	20,000	8,000	28,000

Make recommendations presenting the effect of the proposal.

[Ans. Additional Profit for Product Y Rs. 10,000; should be processed further.]

7. The costs of manufacturing Co. for the year 1994 are :

	Rs.
Direct Materials	1,20,000
Direct Wages	80,000
Production Overheads (Variable)	60,000
Production Overheads (Fixed)	40,000
Selling & Distribution Overheads (Variable)	20,000
Selling & Distribution Overheads (Fixed)	40,000
During the period, sales were :	
Main Product	3,40,000
By-product A (8,000 units)	40,000
By-product B (5,000 units)	20,000

It is discovered that a further process combining 5,000 units of by-product B with 4,000 units of by-product A and adding further material, costing Rs. 60,000 will yield another product C with a sales value of Rs. 1,80,000. An additional direct wages of Rs. 30,000 will have to be incurred in this connection together with an additional fixed overhead of Rs. 12,000.

Plant worth Rs. 35,000 with a life of 10 years and a scrap value of Rs. 2,000 will be required to be installed at a cost of Rs. 5,000, for manufacturing C.

Will you recommend the manufacture of product C ? **[*C.U. M.Com.*]**

[Ans. Manufacture of product C is recommended, beacause of its more profitability]

8. XY company buys crude vegetable oil. The refining of this oil results in four products A, B, C and D. The cost of oil refined in 1994 was Rs. 2,76,000 and the refining department had total processing cost of Rs. 7,00,000. The output and sales for the four products in 1994 were :

Products	*Outputs*	*Sales (Rs.)*	*Additional Processing Cost a fter split-off (Rs.)*
A	5,00,000 gallons	11,50,000	3,00,000
B	10,000 gallons	1,00,000	60,000
C	5,000 gallons	40,000	—
D	9,000 gallons	3,00,000	10,000

Required :

(*i*) Assume that the net realisable value at split-off is used for allocating joint costs. What is the net income for products A, B, C and D ? Joint costs Rs. 9,76,000.

(*ii*) The company had been tempted to sell out at split-off directly to other processors. If that alternative had been selected, sales per gallon would have been A Rs. 150, B Rs. 5·00, C Rs. 8·00 and D Rs. 30·00. What would the net income have been for each product under this alternative ?

(*iii*) The company expects to operate at the same level of production and sales in the forthcoming year. Could the company increase net income by altering its processing decisions ? If so, what would be the expected overall net income ? Which products should be processed further and which should be sold at split-off ? Assume that all costs incurred after split-off are variable.

[*I.C.W.A. (Inter)*]

[Ans.	***A***	***B***	***C***	***D***
	Net Income		**(Rs. in lakhs)**	
(*i*)	**1·70**	**0·08**	**0·08**	**0·58**
(*ii*)	**0·70**	**0·18**	**0·08**	**0·38**
(*iii*)	**1·70**	**0·18**	**0·08**	**0·58]**

9. If the products are truly joint products, the cost of the process can be applied to these products :

(*i*) On the basis of the weight or other physical quantity of each product.

(*ii*) In respect of marginal cost of the process on the basis of physical quantities, and in respect of the fixed costs of the process on the basis of the contribution made by the various products.

(*iii*) On the basis of selling value of the different products.

[*A Report on Marginal Costing (Appendix II), (I.C.M.A.)*]

Discuss the above statement, using, for purposes of illustration, the following figures in respect of the joint production of A and B for a month :

Total Costs :	*Rs.*
Direct Materials	2,600
Direct Labour	1,000
Variable Overheads	800
Fixed Overheads	2,200

Sales A 100 tonnes Rs. 60 per tonne.
Sales B 120 tonnes Rs. 20 per tonne.

[*I.C.W.A. (Final)*]

[**Ans.** (*i*)

	Prorated cost (total)	***Profit (Rs.)***
A	**3,000**	**3,000**
B	**3,600**	**(–) 1,200**
	6,600	**1,800**

(*ii*)

	Prorated Marginal cost	***Profit***
A	**2,000**	**1,800**
B	**2,400**	**Nil**
	4,400	**1,800**

(*iii*)

	Prorated Cost (total)	***Profit***
A	**4,714**	**1,286**
B	**1,886**	**514**
	6,600	**1,800**

]

10. J.B. Ltd. produces four joint products A, B, C and D. All of which emerge from the processing of one raw material. The following are the relevant data :

Joint Products	*Production for the period Number of units*	*Selling Price per unit Rs.*
A	500	18·00
B	900	8·00
C	400	4·00
D	200	11·00

The company budgets for a profit of 10% of sales value. The other estimated costs are :

Carriage	Rs. 1,000
Direct wages	Rs. 3,000
Manufacturing overhead	Rs. 2,000
Administration overhead	10% of sales value

You are required to :

(*a*) calculate the maximum price that may be paid for the raw material.

(*b*) prepare a comprehensive cost statement for each of the products allocating the materials and other costs based upon :

(*i*) Number of units (*ii*) Sales value. [*C.A. (Inter)*]

[**Ans.** (*a*) **Rs. 10,000, (*b*) (*i*) A = Rs. 4,500; B = 8,100; C = 3,600; D = 1,800 (*b*) (*ii*) A = Rs. 8,100; B = Rs. 6,480; C = 1,440; D = Rs. 1,980**]

11. The following information have been extracted from the books of a processing company :

Joint Products	*Yield (in kg) per tonne of coal*
Coke	585
Coal tar	72
Benzol	18
Ammonia Sulphate	27
Gas	198
	900

The Price of coal is Rs. 200 per tonne. Direct labour and overheads to the point of separation are Rs. 150 and Rs. 200, respectively, per tonne of coal.

Calculate the cost of each product on the basis of weight. [*Adopted from I.C.W.A.I. (Final)*]

[**Ans. Coke Rs. 357·50; Coal Tar Rs. 44; Benzol Rs. 11; Ammonia Rs. 16·50; Gas Rs. 121**]

12. A factory is engaged in the production of a chemical BOMEX and in the course of its manufacture, a by-product BRUCIL is produced which after further processing has a commercial value. For the month of April 1990, the following are the summarised data :

	Joint Expenses	*Separate Expenses*	
	Rs.	*Bomex* *Rs.*	*Brucil* *Rs.*
Material	1,00,000	6,000	4,000
Labour	50,000	20,000	18,000
Overheads	30,000	10,000	6,000
Selling Price Per unit		98	34
Estimated Profit per unit on sale BRUCIL	—	—	4
No. of units Produced		2,000 units	2,000 units

The factory uses reverse cost method of accounting for by-products whereby the sales value of by-products after deduction of estimated profit, Post-separation cost and selling and distribution expenses relating to the by-products is credited to the joint process cost account.

You are required to prepare statements showing

(*i*) The joint cost allocable to BOMEX.

(*ii*) The product-wise and overall profitabilities of the factory for April 1990.

[*C.A. (Inter) May 1990*]

[Ans. (*i*) Rs. 1,48,000 (*ii*) BOMEX = Rs. 12,000; BRUCIL = Rs. 8,000]

13. In manufacturing the main product—A a company processes the resulting waste materials into two by-products M_1 and M_2. Using the method of working back from sales value to an estimated cost, you are required to prepare a comparative Profit and Loss Statement of the three products from the following data :

(*i*) Total cost up to separation point was Rs. 1,36,000

	A	M_1	M_2
(*ii*) Sale (all production), Rs.	3,28,000	32,000	48,000
(*iii*) Cost after separation	—	9,600	14,400
(*iv*) Estimate net profit percentage of sales value	—	20%	30%
(*v*) Estimated selling expenses as percentage of sales value	20%	20%	20%

[*I.C.W.A.I. Inter*]

14. In a process line of XY Company three joint products are produced for the month of May 1990; the following data were available :

Products	*L*	*M*	*N*
	Rs.	*Rs.*	*Rs.*
Sale price per kg	5	10	20
Post separation point costs	10,000	5,000	15,000
Output in kg	2,500	1,000	1,500

Pre-separation point cost estimated to Rs. 20,000. The joint products are manufactured in one common process, after which they are separated and may undergo further individual processing. The pre-separation point costs are apportioned to Joint Products according to weight.

You are required to prepare a statement showing the estimated profit and loss for each product and in total.

[*I.C.W.A. (Inter) June, 1990*]

[Ans. L = Rs. 7,500; M = Rs. 1,000; N = Rs. 900]

15. In a chemical processing factory 1,000 kg of a raw material X are used per batch of production. After processing, five joint products are recovered one of which is a gas and the rest solid. Production and sale prices are estimated as :

Product	*Production per 1,000 kg of X*	*Sale Price*
C — 01	50 kg	Rs. 30 per kg.
C — 02	200 kg	Rs. 25 per kg.
C — 03	100 kg	Rs. 40 per kg.
C — 04	300 kg	Rs. 15 per kg.
A — 01	2,500 litres	Rs. 2 per litre

Processing cost (labour and factory overhead) is estimated at Rs. 6,410 per batch, material handling charges at Rs. 680 per 1,000 kg. of raw material and selling and distribution overhead at 10% of sales. The factory expects a return of 10% on the turnover.

One per cent of the raw material is retrieved at the end of the process at original cost (without handling charges) and is used for the next batch of production. The balance of raw material, unacccounted for, is invisible waste.

(*a*) State what should be the purchase price per kg of X in order to achieve the above result.

(*b*) Compute the unit cost of sales of each of the Joint Products on the basis of this sales value.

[*I.C.W.A.I. Final*]

[Ans. (*a*) Rs. 9 per kg (*b*) Rs. 27; Rs. 22·50; Rs. 36; Rs. 13·50; Rs. 1·80]

16. Calculate the estimated cost of production of by-products *X* and *Y* at the point of separation from the main product :

	By Product X	*By Product Y*
	Rs.	*Rs.*
Selling price per unit	12	24
Cost per unit after separation from the main product	3	5
Unit Produced	500 units	200 units

Selling expenses amount to 25% of total works cost, *i.e.* including both Pre-separation and Post-separation works cost. Selling processes are arrived at by adding 20% of total cost *i.e.* the sum of works cost and selling expenses. [*C.A. Final Adopted*]

[Ans. X—Rs. 5·00 per unit, Y—Rs. 11·00 per unit, Total X—Rs. 2,500, Y—Rs. 2,200.]

17. In the course of manufacture of the main product 'P', by-product A an B also emerge; joint expenses of manufacture amount to Rs. 1,19,550. All the three products are processed further. After separation they are sold as per details given :

	Main Product	*By Product*	
	P	*A*	*B*
Sales (Rs.)	90,000	60,000	40,000
Costs incurred after separation (Rs.)	6,000	5,000	4,000
Profit as percentage on sales	25	20	15

Total fixed selling expenses are 10% of the total cost of sales, which are apportioned to the three products in the ratio of 20 : 40 : 40.

(*i*) Prepare a statement showing the apportionment of joint costs to the main product and the two by-products.

(*ii*) If the by-product '*A*' is not subject to further processing and is sold at the point of separation for which there is a market at Rs. 58,500 without incurring any selling expenses. Would you advise its disposal at this stage ? Show the workings.

[*C.A. Inter, adopted*]

[Ans. (*i*) P = Rs. 58,510; A = Rs. 37,020; B = Rs. 24,020
(*ii*) P and B = Rs. 22,520; A = Rs. 21,480.]

18. Three joint products are produced by passing chemicals through two consecutive processes. Output from Process—I is transferred to Process—II, from the which three joint products are produced and immediately sold. The data regarding the Processes for April 1990 :

	Process I	*Process II*
	Rs.	*Rs.*
Direct materials : 2,500 kilos @ Rs. 4 per kilo	10,000	—
Direct Labour	6,250	6,900
Overheads	4,500	6,900
Normal Loss	10% of input	—
Scrap value of loss	Rs. 2 per kilo	—
Output	2,300 kilos	Joint Product A : 900 kilos B : 800 kilos C : 600 kilos

There were no opening or closing stocks in either process and the selling prices of the output from Process II were :

Joint Product A	Rs. 24 per kilo
Joint Product B	Rs. 18 per kilo
Joint Product C	Rs. 12 per kilo

Required :

(*a*) Prepare an account for Process I together with any loss or gain. Account your consideration necessary to record the month's activities.

(*b*) Calculate the profit attributable to each of the Joint Products by apportioning the total costs from Process II

(*i*) According to weight of output

(*ii*) By the market value of production.

[*C.A. Inter, May 1991*]

[Ans. (*a*) Units transferred to Process II 2,300 kg at Rs. 20,700 (*b*) (*i*) A—Rs. 13,500; B—Rs. 12,000; C—Rs. 9,000 (*ii*) A — Rs. 17,250; B—Rs. 11,500; C—Rs. 5,750]

19. The standard input and output in a chemical process are :

Input (Standard)

Raw materials 2,000 kg at Rs. 2 per kg.

Labour and overhead Re 1 of each per kg.

Output standard :

Three Joint Products : A 1,000 kg at Rs. 3 per kg. sale price Rs. 4 per kg.
B 800 kgs at Rs. 5 per kg, sale price Rs. 6·5 per kg.
C 100 litre at Rs. 10 per litre, sale Price Rs. 12 per litre.

A can be processed further into another Product X, after incurring an additional expenditure of Re. 1 per kg on labour and Re. 0·50 per kg on overhead. No loss in the process is anticipated. B can also be processed further into another Product Y, for which Process, labour and overhead at Re. 1 per kg. each are to be incurred. There will be a process loss of 2% which is to be taken as normal. X & Y have ready market and the prices which they are likely to fetch are Rs. 4·50 and Rs. 10 per kg., respectively.

You are required to :

(*i*) Analyse and present the data in a suitable form with a view to evaluating the depth-in-processing of X & Y;

(*ii*) Give your interpretation of the situation for the benefit of top management stating what other information (which is not revealed in the analysis) you would seek before making your recommendation. **[*I.C.W.A.I. Final*]**

[Ans. Before Further Processing — (*i*) A = Rs. 924; B = Rs. 1,200; C = Rs. 276
After Further Processing — A = Rs. 76; Y = Rs. 2,240
(*ii*) Interpretation :
Profit on alternative decision — A = Rs. 924; B = Rs. 2,240; C = Rs. 276]

8 Operating Costing / Service Costing

Authors' Comments and Suggestions :

1. ***This is an important chapter related to undergraduate and post-graduate, including professional examination.***
2. ***Calculation of composite unit is very much relevant for solving these problems.***
3. ***Here total cost is divided in two parts—running maintenance and standing charges. The costs charged on period basis will be covered under Standing Charges.***
4. ***Generally it is used by Transport companies, Hospital/Nursing-home, Lodges, Electricity companies, Schools/Colleges, Cinema Hall etc.***

Introduction; Definition; Objectives; Features; Transport costing—clasification and collection of transportation cost—Fixed or Standing charges, Maintenance charges, Operating and running charges; Selection of units; Proforma; Operating cost and Management decision; Boiler House costing—Proforma; Canteen House Costing; Hospital costing; Cost statement; Workedout problems; Exercise—Objective questions, Theoretical questions—Problems.

Introduction

Service costing is usually applied to transport services, utility services and distribution services. It is generally adopted by such types of industries as render services instead of producing goods. Services may be classified into two parts—internal and external. The services which can be performed on an inter-departmental basis in factory itself, *i.e.,* supplying electricity from own power house to other departments. Services are termed as external when they have to be rendered to outside parties, such as, services rendered by State Transport Corporations, Hospitals, Gas Companies etc. In both cases service costing are required. It is just a variant of unit of output costing.

Definition

The term 'Operating Costing' has now been replaced by 'Service/Function Costing' as per latest CIMA Terminology. It is defined as — The cost of providing a service or function. The cost of rendering the services for a particular period is related to quantum of services rendered during the period to arrive at cost per unit of service rendered.

Objectives

The following are the objectives of operating/service costing :

(*i*) It is used for computing the related operating cost.

(*ii*) To collect actual cost under different heads.

(*iii*) To fix up the rate to be charged for providing service to customers.

(*iv*) To decide the definite policy either to use own source or hire from outside for providing services especially in case of transport costing.

(*v*) To help the concern to take appropriate decision for reducing the service cost.

Features/Characteristics

The method of operating costing has some specific features by which we can distinguish it from other methods of costing. These features are :

(*a*) This method is applied to those organisations which provide services to the outsiders.

(*b*) In this method costs are classified into three heads, viz., Standing Charges (*i.e.,* Fixed Cost), Running Charges (*i.e.,* Variable Cost) and Maintenance Cost.

(*c*) Here costs are usually computed on periodic basis.

(*d*) Single or composite units like per tonne, per passenger km are generally used for computing servicing cost.

Transport Costing

Costing in a transport undertaking consists of determining the operating cost of each vehicle and applying this cost to find out the cost per unit of service rendered by a vehicle. The cost unit is selected by taking into account factors like weight, bulk of goods carried and distance covered etc. In most cases composite units are chosen. The example of composite units are per-tonne-kilometre, passenger-km etc.

Classification and Collection of Transportation Cost

The operating costs of a transport company are classified and accumulated under the following three heads—(*a*) Fixed or Standing Charges (*b*) Maintenance Charges (*c*) Operating and Running Charges.

(*a*) *Fixed or Standing Charges*

The expenses or charges which are incurred whether vehicles are operating or not are known as fixed or standing charges. These expenses include :

Salary of operating manager, supervisor, insurance, tax, licence fees, garage rent, interest on capital, etc.

(b) Maintenance Charges

These are semi-variable in nature. These include :

Tyres and tubes, repairs and overhauls, paintings, garaging, etc.

(c) Operating and Running Charges

These are variable costs, the extent of which is almost directly proportional to the distance covered. Such costs include—cost of fuel, lubricating oil, wages of driver, conductor, attendant etc. (if payment is related to time and distance of trip), commission of takings etc.

After determining the unit cost to which the total expenditure should be allocated, the cost relating to the service rendered should be collected. The cost thus collected is presented under the heads for control purposes.

Selection of Units

In transport costing a composite unit is generally used. The composite unit is nothing but the two types of units considered simultaneously, such as, when time and kilometre are both considered simultaneously, then the composite unit would be tonne-km. The following are some expamples of composite units :

Service	*Cost Units*
1. Passenger Transport	Per-passenger-k.m.
2. Goods Transport	Per-tonne (or per quintal) k.m
3. Hospital/Nursing Home	Per bed-per day
4. Lodge	Per Border-per day
5. Electricity Companies	Per kilowatt-per hour
6. Professional Firm	Per client-hour
7. Cinema	Per seat-per show
8. School/College	Per student-hour
9. Swimming Pool	Per attendant-per hour

In case of services of non-specific nature, like service of accountants or auditors, or managers, it is very difficult to measure per unit cost.

Proforma for Operating Costing/Service Costing of a Transport Co.

Statement of Operating Cost : Tonne-mile......

Particulars	*Total*	*Per Unit*
Operating and Running Cost		
Petrol Oil	××	××
Depreciation	××	××
Oil and Grease	××	××
Wages of conductor, attendent etc.	××	××
Repairs and Maintenance		
Repairs	××	
Overhaul	××	
Tyre	××	
Garage charge	××	××
Fixed/Standing Charge		
Salary of operating manager, supervisor etc.	××	
Insurance	××	
Motor vehicle's tax, licence	××	
Garage rent	××	
General supervision	××	
Interest on capital	××	
Road tax	××	××
Cost per unit		×××

Proforma for Calculation of Composite Unit

Composite units = No. of trips × Distance × Days × Capacity

Operating Cost and Management Decision

Sometimes service costs are used for decisional purpose. In such a case, the decision has to be taken on the basis of unit service cost, when the total units remain constant under different alternatives, but if units are subject to fluctuation from alternative to alternative, decision will be on the basis of total service cost, *i.e.,* total cost under each of the alternatives should be considered and the alternative having lowest cost should be the profitable one.

But there are certain circumstances, where comparative cost may not be the only decisive factor, in such case, other non-cost factors like necessity, public service, customer's satisfaction etc. may influence a particular decision irrespective of its costs.

Boiler House Costing

The main purpose of boiler-house costing is to ascertain the cost per unit of steam produced in the boiler-house. The fundamental principles remain the same. A proforma for boiler-house costing is given next :

Boiler-House Costing Sheet

Steam produced in 1,000 lbs.		××
Less : Boiler-house use	××	
Less : Mains loss	××	××
Total consumption		××

Items	*Total cost*		*Cost per 1,000 lbs*		
	Current period	*Previous period*	*Current*	*Previous*	*Remarks*
1. **Fuel and labour**					
Coal or fuel oil					
Coal handlers					
Stockers					
Ash removers					
Electric power					
Fuel handling etc.					
2. **Water**					
Purchase					
Softening					
3. **Miscellaneous expenses**					
Supervision					
Sweeper, cleaners					
General labour					
Small tools					
Service materials etc.					
Boiler cleaning					
4. **Maintenance**					
Fixed plant					
Boilers					
Meters rent					
Furnace					
5. **Fixed overheads**					
Rent & rates					
Depreciation of plant, building					
Interest on capital					
Proportion of G. Factory overhead					

Canteen House Costing

Nowadays many organisations provide the facilities of canteen to its employees. The principle of service costing may also be extended to this field. The following is the proforma of canteen cost sheet.

CANTEEN OPERATING COST SHEET

Particulars	*Total Cost*	*Cost Per meal*
Provisions :		
Rice		
Bread		
Vegetable		
Meat		
Milk		
Ice-cream		
Cold drinks		
Wages and Salaries :		
Wages for cooks		
Wages for kitchen assistants		
Wages for porters and bearers		
Salary of supervisors		
Services :		
Power and lighting		
Gas and Electricity		
Water		
Stores :		
Crockery and glassware		
Cleaning materials		
Miscellaneous :		
Rent		
Insurance		
Depreciation		
Total Cost		
Profit		
Sales		

Hospital Costing

Nowadays many organizations maintain hospitals to provide effective and timely medical facilities to their workers. Thus arises the need of hospital costing.

The hospitals are generally departmentalised into the following activities :

(*a*) Out-patient department
(*b*) Wards
(*c*) Medical service departments
(*d*) General service departments
(*e*) Other service departments

Cost of departments (*a*) to (*d*) can be determined separately on the basis of cost procedure which is used for cost accumulation of service, while the cost of departments mentioned in (*e*) will have to be apportioned to other departments on suitable basis.

Generally following units are used for hospital costing :

Purpose	*Units*
Out-patient	Per out-patient attendance
Wards	Per case
Pathology	Per 100 requests
Radiotherapy	Per course of treatment per day
Diagonostic X-ray	Per 100 units

Cost Statement

The expenses of a hospital are generally divided into two broad categories, viz., capital expenditure and maintenance expenses.

All items of cost are allocated appropriately in the above categories in order to ascertain the cost per unit of a specific hospital service.

WORKEDOUT PROBLEMS

Problem 1

The following details are available in respect of a 8-ton truck maintained by a transport Co. :

Cost of the truck	Rs. 1,20,000
Estimated life	10 years
Petrol, oil, grease etc.	Rs. 28 per trip
Driver's wages	Rs. 300 p.m.
Assistant's wages	Rs. 175 p.m.
Repairs and maintenance	Rs. 250 p.m.
Insurance	Rs. 3,600 p.a.
Tax	Rs. 1,200 p.a.
General Supervision Charges	Rs. 2,400 p.a.

The truck carries goods to and from a town covers a distance of 50 miles. On the return journey, freight is available only up to 25% of capacity. Assuming that the truck runs, on an average, 25 days a month, find out :

(*a*) Operating cost per ton-mile, and

(*b*) Rate per ton per journey that the Co. should charge if it wants to make a profit of 20% on freightage. *[Adopted]*

Solution

Capacity utilisation :

Outward journey	8 tons
Inward journey (25% of 8 tons)	2 tons
	10 tons

Ton-mile, per month : 10 tons × 50 miles × 25 days = 12,500.

(a) Statement of Operating Cost

Ton-miles (per month) : 12,500		*Rs.*	*Per month Rs.*	*Cost per ton mile Rs.*
1. Operating and Running Costs :				
Petrol, oil, etc. (28 × 2 × 25)		1,400		
Depreciation		1,000	2,400	0.192
2. Repair & Maintenance Cost :			250	0.020
3. Fixed Costs :				
Insurance		300		
Tax		100		
Supervision		200		
Wages :				
Driver	300			
Assistant	175	475	1,075	0.086
		Total	3,725	0.298

(b) Gross Profit : 20% on freightage

Cost per ton mile	Profit	Freight
80	20	100
0.298		$\frac{100}{80} \times 0.298 = 0.3725$

Freight per ton per journey = 0.3725 × 50 = 18.625

Problem 2

The Kangaroo Transport Limited operates a fleet of lorries. The records for lorry L14 reveal the following information for July 2007 :

Days maintained 30 ; Days operated 25 ; Days idle 5 ; Total hours operated 300 ; Total kms. covered 2,500 ; Total tonnage carried 200 (4 tonne load per trip, return journey empty).

The following further information is made available :

(A) Operating cost for the month : Petrol Rs. 400 ; Oil Rs. 170 ; Grease Rs. 90 ; Wages to drivers Rs. 550 ; Wages to khalasis Rs. 350.

(B) Maintenance cost for the month : Repairs Rs. 170 ; Overhaul Rs. 60 ; Tyres Rs. 150 ; Garage charges Rs. 100.

(C) Fixed cost for the month based on the estimates of the year : Insurance Rs. 50 ; Licence tax etc. Rs. 80 ; Interest Rs. 40 ; Other Overhead Rs. 190.

(D) Capital cost : Cost of acquisition : Rs. 54,000 ; Residual value at the end of the 5 years life is Rs. 36,000.

Prepare a cost sheet and Performance Statement showing : (*a*) cost per day maintained (*b*) cost per day operated (*c*) cost per kilometre (*d*) cost per hour (*e*) cost per commercial ton-km.

[I.C.W.A. Inter, Adopted]

Solution

In the books of Kangaroo Transport Limited
Operating Cost Sheet for the month of July 2007

Description	*Amount*	*Amount*
(A) Operating Cost :	*Rs.*	*Rs.*
Petrol	400	
Oil	170	
Grease	90	
Drivers' wages	550	
Khalasis' wages	350	
Total (A)		1,560
(B) Maintenance Cost :		
Repairs	170	
Overhauls	60	
Tyres	150	
Garage charges	100	
Total (B)		480
(C) Fixed Cost :		
Insurance	50	
Licence, Tax, etc.	80	
Interest	40	
Other overheads	190	
Depreciation	300	
Total (C)		660
(D) Total operating cost of the month (A + B + C)		2,700

Note : Depreciation calculated on fixed instalment basis is Rs. 300 as per calculation given below :

$$\frac{\text{Cost of acquisition} - \text{Residual value}}{\text{Life of Asset in year} \times 12} = \frac{\text{Rs. } (54{,}000 - 36{,}000)}{5 \times 12} = \text{Rs. } 300$$

Performance Statement

(*a*) Cost per day maintained $= \frac{\text{Total operating cost}}{\text{No. of days maintained}} = \frac{\text{Rs. } 2{,}700}{30 \text{ days}} = \text{Rs. } 90$

(*b*) Cost per kilometre $= \frac{\text{Total operating cost}}{\text{Total kilometres covered}} = \frac{\text{Rs. } 2{,}700}{2{,}500 \text{ km}} = \text{Rs. } 108$

(*c*) Cost per day operated $= \frac{\text{Total operating cost}}{\text{No. of days operated}} = \frac{\text{Rs. } 2{,}700}{25 \text{ days}} = \text{Rs. } 108$

(*d*) Cost per hour $= \frac{\text{Total operating cost}}{\text{Total hours operated}} = \frac{\text{Rs. } 2{,}700}{300 \text{ hours}} = \text{Rs. } 9$

(*e*) Cost per commercial ton-km. $= \frac{\text{Total operating cost}}{\text{Total commercial ton-km}} = \frac{\text{Rs. } 2{,}700}{5000 \text{ km}} = \text{Re. } 0.54$

Note : Calculation of commercial ton-km in July 2007

= Total ton-km covered per trip × Total carried per trip × Days operated

= 50 km × 4 ton × 25 Days = 5,000 ton-km

No. of trips (one trip includes return journey)

= Total ton/ton per trip = 200 ton/4 ton = 50 trips

Therefore, km covered per trip = Total km/No. of trip

= 2,500 km/50 trips = 50 km per trip

Problem 3

The Trade Transport Company has been given a twenty km long route to ply a bus. The bus costs the company Rs. 1,00,000. It has been insured at 3% per annum. Annual road tax amounts to Rs. 2,000. Garage rent is Rs. 400 per month. Annual repair is estimated to cost Rs. 2,360 and the bus is likely to last for 5 years.

The salary of the driver and the conductor is Rs. 600 and Rs. 200 per month, respectively, in addition to 10% of the takings as commission to be shared equally by them. The managers's salary is Rs. 1,400 per month and stationery will cost Rs. 100 per month. Petrol and oil will cost Rs. 50 per 100 km. The bus will make three round trips per day carrying on an average 40 passengers in each trip.

Assuming 15% profit on the taking and the bus will ply on an average 25 days in a month. Prepare Operating Cost Statement on full year basis and also calculate the bus fare to be charged to each passenger per kilometre.

Solution

(*a*) Total no. of days the bus to ply in a year = 25 days × 12 months = 300 days.

(*b*) The bus is plying on an average three round trips. Each round trip will cover 20 km for outgoing and 20 km for return journey. So, the total km travelled in a year will be 300 days × 3 trips × 2 (for outgoing and return journey) × 20 km = 3,600 km per annum.

In the Books of Trade Transport Company
Operating Cost Statement Per Annum

Particulars	*Amount*	*Amount*
Standing charges :	*Rs.*	*Rs.*
Depreciation (Rs. 1,00,000/5 years)	20,000	
Insurance @ 3% p.a. (Rs. 1,00,000 × 0.03)	3,000	
Road tax	2,000	
Garage rent @ 400 p.m. (400 × 12)	4,800	
Salary of driver @ 600 p.m. (600 × 12)	7,200	
Salary of conductor @ 200 p.m. (200 × 12)	2,400	
Manager's salary @ 1,400 p.m. (1,400 × 12)	16,800	
Stationery @ Rs. 100 p.m. (100 × 12)	1,200	
Total standing charge		57,400
Maintenance charges :		
Annual repairs		2,360
Running cost :		
Petrol and oil @ Rs. 50 per 100 km (36,000 km × 50/100)		18,000
Total operating cost excluding driver and conductor's commission		77,760
Add : Driver and conductor's commission @ 10% on taking [Note (a)]		10,368
Total operating cost of a year		88,128
Add : Profit @ 10% on taking [Note (*a*)]		15,552
Total bus fare to be recovered from passengers in a year		1,03,680
Total passenger-km run in a year [Note (*b*)]		14,40,000
Fare per passenger kilometre (Rs. 1,03,680/14,40,000 passenger-km)		0.072

Note : (*a*) Commission @ 10% of driver and conductor and profit @ 15% on takings will mean the calculations will be made on total proceedings from transportation. The calculations are shown below :

Takings	*Commission*	*Profit*	*Taking (net of commission & profit)*
100	10	15	75
	X	Y	77,760

X = (77,760 × 10)/75 = Rs. 10,368
Y = (77,760 × 15)/75 = Rs. 15,552

Note : (*b*) Total passenger km run
= 40 passengers × 20 km × 3 trips × 2 times × 300 days = 14,40,000

Problem 4

Shankar has been promised a contract to run a tourist car on a 20 km long route for the chief executive of a multinational firm. He buys a car costing Rs. 1,50,000. The annual cost of Insurance and taxes are Rs. 4,500 and Rs. 900, respectively. He has to pay Rs. 500 per month for a garage where he keeps the car when it is not in use. The annual repair cost is estimated at Rs. 4,000. The car is estimated to have a life of 10 years, at the end of which scrap value is likely to be Rs. 50,000. He hires a driver who is to be paid Rs. 300 per month plus 10% of taking as commission. Other incidental expenses are estimated at Rs. 200 per month.

Petrol and oil will cost Rs. 100 per 100 kms. The car will make four round trips each day. Assuming that a profit of 15% on takings is desired and that the car will be on the road for 25 days on an average per month, what should he charge per round trip ?

[C.A. Inter; I.C.W.A. Inter]

Solution

Statement showing Operating Cost of the Tourist car owned by Shankar per month

	Amount	
	Rs.	*Rs.*
(A) Variable expenses:		
Petrol and oil cost @ Rs. 100 per 100 kms. $\left(\frac{\text{Rs. } 100}{100 \text{ kms}} \times 4000 \text{ kms}\right)$		4,000
(B) Standing charges :		
Insurance $\left(\frac{\text{Rs. } 4{,}500}{12 \text{ months}}\right)$	375	
Taxes $\left(\frac{\text{Rs. } 900}{12 \text{ months}}\right)$	75	
Garage rent	500	
Repair cost $\left(\frac{\text{Rs. } 4{,}000}{12 \text{ months}}\right)$	334	
Depreciation (Working-b)	833	
Driver fixed salary	300	
Incidental expenses	200	
Total standing charge of the month .		2,617
(C) Total operating cost excluding driver's commission		6,617
Add : Driver commission @ 10% of the taking (Working-c)		882
(D) Total operating cost of the tourist car		7,499
Add : Profit of Shankar @ 15% on taking (Working-c)		1,324
(E) Total taking of the month		8,823
(F) Total no. of round trips in a month (4 round trips each day) 4 × 25 days		100
(G) Charge per trip (E/F)		88.23

Workings : (*a*) Total km run = 20 km × 2 times × 4 trips × 25 days = 4000 km.

(*b*) Depreciation of the car per month

$$= \frac{(\text{Cost price} - \text{Scrap value})}{\text{Life of the car}} = \frac{\text{Rs. } 1{,}50{,}000 - 50{,}000}{10 \text{ years} \times 12} = \text{Rs. } 833$$

1. (*c*) Calculation of drivers' commission and profit are made in the following manner:

Gross taking	Commission	Profit	Net taking
Rs. 100	Rs. 10	Rs. 15	Rs. 75
	Rs. X	Rs. Y	Rs. 6,617

$$X = \frac{(6{,}617 \times 10)}{75} = \text{Rs. } 882 \quad Y = \frac{6{,}617 \times 15}{75} = \text{Rs. } 1{,}323$$

Problem 5

A chemical factory runs its boiler on furnace oil obtained from Indian Oil and Bharat Petroleum, whose depots are situated at a distance of 12 km and 8 km from the factory site. Transportation of furnace oil is made only on full load and the lorries return empty. The filling-in-time takes an average 40 minutes for Indian Oil and 30 minutes for Bharat Petroleum. But the emptying time in the factory is only 40 minutes for all. From the records available, it is seen that the average speed of the company's lorries works out to 24 km per hour. The varying operating charges average 60 paise per km covered and fixed charges give an incidence of Rs. 7.50 per hour operation.

Calculate the cost per tonne-km from each source. ***[C.A. Inter]***

Solution

In the Books of Chemical Factory

Statement showing calculation of Total Time taken for carrying final per trip

Particulars	*Indian Oil*	*Bharat Petroleum*
(1) Distance of the depot from chemical factory	12 kms	8 kms
(2) Total distance to be covered in each trip (onward and return journeys of 12 kms each for Indian Oil and 8 kms each for Bharat Petroleum)	24 kms	16 kms
(3) Average speed of the lorries per hour	24 kms	24 kms
(4) Therefore, time required in each trip $\left(\frac{2}{3} \times 60 \text{ minute}\right)$	60 minutes	40 minutes
(5) Filling-in-time per trip	40 minutes	30 minutes
(6) Empty time per trip	40 minutes	40 minutes
(7) Therefore, total time taken for carrying fuel per trip [(4) + (5) + (6)]	140 minutes	110 minutes

Operating Cost Statement of Carrying Furnace Oil from Depots

Particulars	*Indian Oil*	*Bharat Petroleum*
Variable operating charges @ 60 paise per km (*i.e.,* 60 × 24 kms for Indian oil and 60 × 16 kms for Bharat Petroleum)	Rs. 14.40	Rs. 9.60
Fixed charges @ 7.50 per hour (*i.e.,* the rate is applicable on 140 minutes for Indian Oil and 110 minutes for Bharat Petroleum)	Rs. 17.50	Rs. 13.75
Total operating cost per trip (varible cost + fixed cost)	Rs. 31.90	Rs. 23.35
Material carried per trip	5 tons	5 ton
Total kms run with loaded truck	12 kms	8 kms
Total ton-km for each trip (5 tons × 12 kms for Indian Oil and 5 tons × 8 kms for Bharat Petroleum)	60 ton kms	40 ton kms
Therefore, operating cost per ton-km	$\frac{\text{Rs. } 31.90}{60}$ = Rs. 0.53	$\frac{\text{Rs. } 23.35}{40}$ = Rs. 0.58

Problem 6

In view of increasing cost of operating own fleet of cars, your company is presently considering two proposals, viz.

(*i*) To hire cars with drivers from agency @ Rs. 800 per month. The company will bear the cost of petrol, oil and tyres.

(*ii*) The executive will be given Rs. 25,000 interest free loan repayable in 5 years to buy his own car. The company will, however, provide him free petrol and Rs. 500 per month for maintenance and drivers' wages.

If the present cost of car is Rs. 50,000 and monthly average running is 2,000 kilometres, find out the most economic way with the help of the following data :

Petrol 65 paise per km, oil 8 paise per km, tyre 7 paise per km, repair 10 paise per km, tax and insurance Rs. 560 per year. Drivers' wages and bonus Rs. 720 per month. Life of a car 5 years, Resale value at the end of 5th year is Rs. 10,000. Assume interest @ 18% per annum.

[I.C.W.A. Final]

Solution

In order to arrive at a decision, a statement showing operating cost under different alternatives should be prepared and alternative having minimum operating cost should be accepted.

Cost statement providing transport facilities to executives under different alternatives

Particulars of costs	*Hired car* *Rs.*	*Car loan* *Rs.*	*Owned car* *Rs.*
Cost of Hiring car with driver from agency	800.00		
Cost of Petrol @ 65 paise per km (2,000 km × 65 paise)	1,300.00	1,300.00	1,300.00
Cost of Oil @ 8 paise per km (2,000 km × 8 paise)	160.00		160.00
Cost of Tyre @ 7 paise per km (2,000 km × 7 paise)	140.00		140.00
Cost of providing 25,000 interest free loan to executive interest rate 18%) (Note 1)		187.50	
Cost of repairing @ 10 paise per km (2,000 km × 10 paise)			200.00
Tax and insurance @ Rs. 560 per year			46.67
Drivers' wages & Bonus @ Rs. 720 p.m.			720.00
Depreciation (Note 2)			666.66
Allowance for maintenance and drivers' wages		500.00	
Total cost under different alternatives	2,400.00	1,987.50	3,233.33
Cost per km (total km run 2,000 p.m.)	Rs. 1.20	Rs. 0.99	Rs. 1.62

Remarks : Most economic way for the company is to give interest-free loan of Rs. 25,000 (repayable in 5 years) along with free petrol and Rs. 500 monthly allowance for maintenance and drivers' wages.

In this alternatives, cost of transportation is minimum of Rs. 0.99 per km as per table shown above.

Notes : 1. Interest-free loan of Rs. 25,000 is refundable in 5 equal yearly instalments. Due to this reason it is prudent to calculate 18% interest on the average loan balance. Average loan balance is the sum of initial loan balance (*i.e.,* Rs. 25,000) and the loan balance after repayment (*i.e.,* zero) divided by two. Therefore, average loan balance is Rs. 12,500 and will be calculated interest burden @ 18% per annum of this balance. Thus, monthly interest burden will be Rs. 12,500 × 0.18/12 months = Rs. 187.50.

2. Depreciation on owned car is calculated on straight line basis in the following manner :

$$\frac{\text{Cost of car} - \text{Resale value at the end of life}}{\text{Life of the car}} = \frac{\text{Rs. } 50{,}000 - \text{Rs. } 10{,}000}{5 \text{ years}} = \text{Rs. } 8{,}000.$$

Problem 7

Mr. Harry is a travelling inspector for the environment protection agency. He uses his own car and the agency reimbureses him at Rs. 1.80 per kilometre. Mr. Harry claims he needs Rs. 2.20 per kilometre just to break-even. A scrutiny of his expenses by the agency reveals the following:

	Rs.
Oil charge for every 4,800 kms	120
Maintenance (other than oil) for every 9,600 kms	1,800
Yearly insurance (comprehensive with accident benefits)	4,000
Cost of car, with an average residual value of Rs. 60,000 and with a useful life of 3 years	1,08,000

Petrol is Rs. 5 a litre and Harry gets 8 kms per litre in his car. When Harry is on the road, he averages 192 kilometres a day. He works 5 days a week, has 10 days vacation in a year besides 6 holidays and spends 15 working days a month in the office. You are required to determine :

(*a*) An equitable rate of reimbursement on the basis of the schedule he presently follows and

(*b*) The number of kilometres a year he would have to travel, to break-even at the current rate of reimbursement. ***[I.C.W.A. Inter]***

Solution

(*a*) (1) **Calculation of total km run by Mr. Harry**

Average run per day when Mr. Harry is on the road		192 kms
Total working days in a week of 52 when average per week is 5 days (52 × 5)		260 days
Less : Total days of vacation in a year	10 days	
Less : Total holidays in a year	6 days	
Less : Total days spend in office (15 days × 12 months)	180 days	196 days
Actual No. of days the car is used for official purpose in a year		64 days

Therefore, total km run for official purposes in the year (64 days × 192 kms) = 12,288 kms.

(2) **Statement of operating cost of car used for official purpose**

Cost of oil @ Rs. 120 for 4,800 kms $\left(\frac{\text{Rs. } 120 \times 12{,}288 \text{ kms}}{4{,}800 \text{ kms}}\right)$	307·20
Maintenance @ Rs. 1,800 for every 9,600 kms $\left(\frac{\text{Rs. } 1800 \times 12{,}288 \text{ kms}}{9{,}600 \text{ kms}}\right)$	2,304.00
Yearly insurance	4,000.00
Depreciation $\left(\frac{\text{Rs. } 1{,}08{,}000 - \text{Rs. } 60{,}000}{3 \text{ years}}\right)$	16,000.00
Petrol @ 8 kms per litre when petrol cost is Rs. 5 a litre $\left(\frac{\text{Rs. } 5 \times 12{,}288 \text{ kms}}{8 \text{ kms}}\right)$	7,680.00
Total operating cost of car used for official purpose	30,291.20

Therefore, operating cost per km to break-even = Total operating cost of car used for the official purpose/total kms run for official purpose = $\frac{30{,}291{\cdot}20}{12{,}288}$ = Rs. 2·46.

(*b*) Break-even is a point where Mr. Harry will neither gain nor loose. In other words he will be reimbursed the exact amount he spends.

For calculating break-even kms when reimbursement is Rs. 1.80 per km, firstly we will calculate contribution per km. Here contribution is the amount left after paying variable cost of running the car per km. Variable cost consists of oil charges, maintenance and cost of petrol consumption. So, contribution per km will be arrived at by deducting variable cost per km from Rs. 1.80.

Contribution for km will be used for recovering annual fixed operating cost. Therefore, next step is to ascertain annual fixed operating cost. Here fixed cost will include insurance and depreciation.

Finally, total operating fixed cost will be divided by the variable operating cost per km to get the break-even km. The details of calculation are as below :

(1) Calculation of variable cost per km :

	Rs.
Oil charge (Rs. 120/4,800 kms)	0.0250
Maintenance (Rs. 1,800/9,600 kms)	0.1875
Petrol (Rs. 5 per litre/8 kms)	0.6250
Variable operating cost per km	0.8375

(2) Contribution per km considering reimbursement of Rs. 1.80 per km

= 1.80 – 0.8375 = Re. 0.9625

(3) Total annual fixed cost = Depreciation + Insurance = Rs. (16,000 + 4,000) = Rs. 20,000

Therefore, number of kms to break-even = Total annual fixed cost/contribution per km

= Rs. 20,000/Re. 0.9625 = 20,779.22 kms

Note : The above problem has been solved on the assumption of 52 weeks in a year. Therefore, considering five days week, gross working days will be 52 × 5 = 260 days. Instead of this we may consider a year of 365 days. Then we have to deduct 2 days per week (i.e., 52 × 2 = 104 days) from 365 days and the result will be 261 gross working days. Automatically, cost per km to break-even will change. It will be Rs. 2.44 per km instead of Rs. 2·46 as shown in our solution. Students are advised to solve it under this alternative.

Problem 8

A bus and coach company has decided to introduce an express service between a railway station and a nearby town. The distance between the railway station and the bus stand is 40 kms. The company purchased a old bus by Rs. 1,00,000. It has been insured at 6% p.a. and the half yearly tax will amount to Rs. 1,000. Garage rent is Rs. 2,400 p.a. Annual repairing charge will be Rs. 2,000 and the bus will be likely to last for 5 years. The driver's salary will be Rs. 2,000 p.m., conductors' salary will be Rs. 1,500 p.m. in addition to 10% takings as commission (to be shared as per their salary ratio). Diesel and oil will be Rs. 10 per litre. The bus can run 10 km per litre diesel.

The bus will make 3 round trips per day. The capacity of the bus to carry the passenger is 50. On an average 80% of its capacity is utilised. Assuming profit is 15% on takings.

Calculate the bus fare to be charged from each passenger.

The bus will run on an average 25 days in a month.

Solution

$$\text{Passenger km} = 40 \times 3 \times 2 \times \frac{80}{100} \times 50 \times 25$$

$$= 40 \times 6 \times 40 \times 25 = 2{,}40{,}000$$

Statement showing the fare to be charged for a passenger km

Particulars	*Per annum*	*Per month*
	Rs.	*Rs.*
Standing charges		
Insurance	6,000	
Tax	2,000	
Garage rent	2,400	
Driver's salary	24,000	
Conductor's salary	18,000	
	52,400	4,366.67
Running charges		
Depreciation (1,00,000 ÷ 5)	20,000	1,666.67
Repairs	2,000	166.66
Diesel & oil (Re. 1 × 40 × 3 × 2 × 25)		6,000.00
Total cost without commission		12,200.00
Commission 10%		1,626.66
Profit 15%		2,440.00
Total takings		16,266.66

∴ Fare per passenger-km = Re. 0.067

Workings : Late total takings = x

$$\therefore \text{ Commission } = 10\% \text{ of } x = \frac{x}{10}$$

$$\text{Profit } = 15\% \text{ of } x = \frac{3x}{20}$$

$$\text{Now we can write } x = 12{,}200 + \frac{x}{10} + \frac{3x}{20}$$

$$\therefore \quad x = \frac{2{,}44{,}000 + 2x + 3x}{20}$$

$$\therefore \quad x = 16{,}266.66$$

$$\therefore \; 15x = 2{,}44{,}000$$

Problem 9

Holiday Hotel has 40 bedrooms with a maximum capacity of 490 sleeper nights per week. Average occupancy is 60% throughout the year. Meals provided to guest have been costed and the average food cost per person per day is as follows :

Breakfast Rs. 3.60 ; Lunch Rs. 11.00 ; Dinner Rs. 13.40 ; Direct wages and staff meals are as under :

Restaurant and kitchen Rs. 3,430 ; House-keeping Rs. 1,952 ; General Rs. 1,760 ; Direct expenses per annum are Rs. 45,760 for House-keeping and Rs. 52,000 for the Restaurant.

Indirect expenses amount to Rs. 3,41,120 which should be apportioned on the basis of floor area. The floor area are : Bedrooms 3,600 sq metres ; Restaurant 1,200 sq metres ; Services area 600 sq metres.

A net profit of 10% each must be made on the Restaurant takings and accommodation takings.

You are required to calculate what inclusive terms per person should be charged per day. Show the split between meals and accommodation charges. ***[I.C.W.A. Final]***

Solution

Since there are 490 sleeper-nights per week and average occupancy is 60% throughout the year, the actual occupancy will be 490 × 0·60 = 294 sleeper-night per week.

Statement Showing Operating Cost per Week of the Holiday Hotel

		Cost of		Total
		Meal	*Accommodation*	*Cost*
Food expenses : (Actual occupancy × rate)				
Breakfast (294 sleeper-nights × Rs. 3.60)	= 1,058.40			
Lunch (294 sleeper-night × Rs. 11.00)	= 3,234.00			
Dinner (294 sleeper-night × Rs. 13.40)	= 3,939.60	8,232.00		8,232.00
Direct wages and staff meal (Allocated directly)		3,430.00	1,952.00	5,382.00
Direct wages and staff meal of common nature is allocated in the ratio of direct wages		1,121.66	638.34	1,760.00
Direct expenses :				
Restaurant Rs. 52,000 p.a./52 weeks		1,000.00		1,000.00
House keeping Rs. 45,760 p.a./52 weeks			880.00	880.00
Indirect expenses apportioned on the basis of floor area (see Note 1)		2,186.67	4,373.33	6,560.00
Total cost (A)		15,970.33	7,843.67	23,814.00
Add : 10% profit of takings (*i.e.*, 1/9th of cost)		1,774.48	871.52	2,646.00
Total revenue to be earned per week (B)		17,744.86	8,715.14	26,460.00
Therefore, daily rate per person (B/294 sleeper-nights)		60.35	29.65	90.00

Therefore, owner should charges Rs. 90 per day from each customer which consists of Rs. 60.35 for food and Rs. 29.65 for accommodation.

Note : As per information given in the problem, indirect expenses are to be allocated on the basis of floor area, where floor area is 3,600 sq. metre for bedroom, 1200 sq. metre for restaurant and 600 sq. metre of service area and restaurant area are used for meal purpose. So, indirect expenditure related to the 1,200 + 600 = 1,800 sq. metre area is to be charged against meal and the rest will be charged against room accommodation.

EXERCISES

OBJECTIVE TYPE QUESTIONS

1. Indicate whether the following statements are true or false :

(*a*) Service costing is one of the basic methods of operating costing.
(*b*) Operating cost statement is prepared to calculate the cost in case of service costing.
(*c*) There is no difference between service costing and process costing.
(*d*) Service costing is applicable in canteens.
(*e*) Motor cost for passengers is ascertained with reference to per passenger per kilometer.

[Ans. True : (*a*), (*b*), (*d*), (*e*) False : (*c*)]

2. *Indicate whether the following statements are true or false.*

(*a*) Scrap is a residue which arises in a manufacturing process, but has no recoverable value.
(*b*) Cost sheet is the same as statement of cost and profit.
(*c*) Statement of cost and profit—when presented in 'T' form then it is Production Account.
(*d*) Operating costing is applied in those industries where different products are produced simultaneously.
(*e*) In the cement industries the unit at cost is per tonne.

[Ans. True : (*c*) (*e*) False : (*a*), (*b*), (*d*)]

3. As capacity utilisation of a service increases, the average total cost per unit of service will
(*a*) Fluctuate on a random basis.
(*b*) Remain constant unless price levels change.
(*c*) Increase since additional costs are incurred.
(*d*) Fall as the impact of fixed costs per cost unit is reduced.

[Ans. True : (*d*)]

4. The under-absorption of the actual cost of a maintenance department where the charge to users of the service is at a planned rate per hour will be due to :
(*a*) Demand for maintenance work being in excess of that planned.
(*b*) A rise in both expenditure levels and capacity utilisation of the service.
(*c*) An increase in expenditure levels which has been only partly offset by increased capacity utilisation.
(*d*) A reduction in capacity utilisation which has been more than offset by reduced expenditure levels.

[Ans. True : (*c*)]

THEORETICAL QUESTIONS

1. What is operating cost ? To what industries is this method of costing applicable ?
2. Distinguish between operating costing and output costing.
3. What do you understand by composite unit in service costing ?
4. Distinguish between operation costing and operating costing. ***[I.C.W.A. Inter, C.A. Inter]***
5. What is operating cost ? Draw a statement with imaginary figures for working out the running cost per kilometre of taxi. ***[I.C.W.A. Inter, June '85]***
6. "The more kilometres you travel with your own vehicle, the cheaper it becomes"—comment briefly on this statement. ***[C.A. Inter, Nov. 1995]***
7. What is "Composite Unit' ? Give three examples. ***[I.C.W.A. Inter, Dec. 1995]***

PROBLEMS

1. From the following data calculate cost per mile of a vehicle :
Value of the vehicle Rs. 15,000, Road licence of the year Rs. 500, Insurance charge per year Rs. 100, Garage rent per year Rs. 600, Drivers wages per month Rs. 200, COst of petrol per litre Rs. 0.80, Miles per litre 8, proportional charge for tyre and maintenance per mile Re. 0.20. Estimated life 1,50,000 miles. Estimated annual mileage 6,000 miles. ***[I.C.W.A. Inter]***

[Ans. Running cost per mile Re. 1.00]

2. Prakash Transport Company has been given a route 20 km long to run a bus. The bus costs the company a sum of Rs. 50,000. It has been insured at 3% p.a. and the annual tax will amount to Rs. 1,000. Garage rent is at Rs. 100 p.m. Annual repairs will be Rs. 1,000 and the bus is likely to last for 5 years.
The driver's salary will be Rs. 150 p.m. and the conductor's salary will be 100 p.m. in addition to 10% taking as commission (to be shared by driver and the conductor equally); cost of stationery will be Rs. 50 p.m. Manager-cum-Accountant's salary is Rs. 350 p.m. petrol and oil will be Rs. 25 per 100 km. The bus will make 3 round trips carrying on an average 40 passengers on each trip. Assuming 15% profit on takings, calculate the bus fare to be charged from each passenger. The bus will run on an average 25 days in a month. ***[I.C.W.A. Inter]***

[Ans. Fare per passenger km .03]

3. Raju, the owner of a taxi, supplies the following information : Cost of taxi — Rs. 1,50,000 with total life of 2,50,000 km., Driver's salary—Rs. 700 p.m., Cleaner's salary—Rs. 300 p.m., Repairs—Rs. 3,600 p.a., Garage rent—Rs. 2,400 p.a., Diesel consumption 8 km. per litre, Diesel cost Rs. 8 per litre, Oil and other sundries Rs. 20 per 125 km.
The taxi runs 100 km. per day for an average of 25 days in a month. 20% of the distance has been run without any passenger.
Calculate the cost of running the taxi per km. ***[C.U. B.Com. (H) 2000]***

[Ans. Operating cost per km Rs. 3.85]

Notes : (1) Effective running during a month = $25 \times 100 \text{ km} \times \frac{80}{100} = 2{,}000$ km

(2) Diesel cost per km = $\frac{2{,}500 \times \text{Rs. } \frac{8}{8}}{2{,}000} = 1.25$

(3) Oil and other sundries per km = $\frac{\text{Rs. } 20}{125} \times \frac{2{,}500}{2{,}000}$ = Re. 0.20

4. A truck starts with a load of 10 tonnes of goods from station D. It unloads 3 tonnes at station E and rest of goods at station F. It reaches back directly to station D after getting reloaded with 8 tonnes of goods at station F. The distance from D to E, E to F and then from F to D are 80 kms, 120 kms, and 160 kms, respectively.

Compute tonne-kms for the truck service.

[C.U. (H) 2001]

[Ans. 2,920 tonne-kms]

5. West Road Co. runs 10 buses between two places covering a distance of 25 kms. Seating capacity of each bus is 30 passengers. The expenses for the month of April, 2003 were as under :

Salaries of drivers and conductors	90,000
Salaries of mechanical staff	9,000
Diesel, oil and lubricants	60,000
Taxes, Insurances etc	7,800
Repairs and maintenance	12,000
Depreciation	48,000

60% of seating capacity was utilised in each case. All buses ran 25 days a month, each making four round trips daily.

(*a*) Find out cost per passenger-kilometre.

(*b*) What would have been the cost per round trip per passenger, if seating capacity utilisation were to go up to 80% ?

[C.U. (H) 2003]

[Ans. (*a*) Cost per passenger-km Re. 0.252
(*b*) Cost per round trip per passenger Rs. 9.45]

6. (*a*) What is a composite unit ?

(*b*) A truck carried 45 tons during a six-day week and travelled a total distance of 135 miles as given below :

Day	*Distance travelled (miles)*	*Tons carried*
Monday	10	5
Tuesday	20	10
Wednesday	30	5
Thursday	40	10
Friday	25	10
Saturday	10	5
	135	45

Calculate ton-miles for the week.

[C.U. (H) 2002]

[Ans. 1,100 ton-miles]

7. There are two warehouses for storing finished goods in a factory. Warehouse A is at a distance of 10 km and warehouse B at a distance of 15 km from the factory. A fleet of 5 tonne lorries is engaged in transporting the finished goods from the factory. The records show that the lorries average a speed of 30 kms per hour when running and regularly takes 40 minutes to load at the factory. At warehouse 'A' unloading takes 30 minutes per load while at warehouse 'B' it takes 20 minutes per load.

Drivers' wages, depreciation, insurance and takes amount to Rs. 18 per hour operated. Fuel oil, tyres and maintenance cost Rs. 2.40 per km.

You are required to draw up a statement showing the cost per tonne-kilometre for carrying the finished goods to the two warehouses.

[I.C.W.A. Inter]

[Ans. Warehouse A : Rs. 1.62 tonne-km, Warehouse B : Rs. 1.44 tonne-km]

8. From the following data calculate cost per mile of a vehicle :

Value of the vehicle Rs. 15,000, Road licence of the year Rs. 500, Insurance charge per year Rs. 100, Garage rent per year Rs. 600, Drivers' wages per month Rs. 200, Cost of petrol per litre Rs. 0.80, Miles per litre 8, Proportional charge for tyre and maintenance per mile Re. 0.20. Estimated life 1,50,000 miles; Estimated annual mileage 6,000 miles; Ignore interest on capital.

[I.C.W.A. Inter]

[Ans. Running cost per mile Re. 1.00]

9. A Transport Company which keeps a fleet of lorries shows the following information :

Mileage run for April 1999 Rs. 30,000; Wages for April Rs. 2,000; Petrol, oil etc. for April 4,000; Original cost of vehicle 1,00,000; Depreciation to be allowed @ 25% p.a. on original cost; Repairs for the month of April Rs. 6,000; Garage rent etc. for April 1,000; Licence, Insurance etc. for the year 6,000.

Prepare a statement for April 1999 showing the fixed and variable cost per running mile.

[I.C.W.A. Inter]

[Ans. Operating cost per running mile is Re. 0.519]

10. A company having a fleet of trucks undertakes to carry waste materials. They have the following capacity vehicles :

No. of vehicles	*Capacity*
40	5 tons
20	4 tons
50	3 tons

On an average each lorry makes 5 trips a day and in each trip covers an average distance of 5 km each. The truck carries only 75% of its capacity. 20% of the lorries are laid up for repairs everyday. Following charges incurred during the month :

Salary of the Supervisor Rs. 2,000 ; Salary of Foreman 3 nos. Rs. 600 each ; Wages of Drivers Rs. 200 each for 110 drivers ; Wages of Cleaners Rs. 100 each for 220 cleaners ; Consumable stores Rs. 16,000 ; Petrol Rs. 60,000 ; Lubricants Rs. 14,000 ; Replacement of tyre Rs. 6,000 ; Garage Rent Rs. 3,000 ; Electricity charge Rs. 1,000 ; Other expenses Rs. 12,000.

During the month old tubes and tyres are auctioned for Rs. 3,000.

Assuming that a month consists of 30 days calculate the cost per ton-km for conveying wastage.

[Mangalore University, B.Com.]

[Ans. Total cost Rs. 1,59,800, Net cost Rs. 1,56,800, Cost per ton-km Re. 0.81]

11. A Transport Service Company is running 4 buses between two towns which are 50 kms apart. Seating capacity of each bus is 40 passengers. The following particulars are obtained from the records for the month of April 1999 :

Wages of drivers, conductors and cleaners Rs. 2,000 ; Salaries of office and supervisory staff Rs. 1,000; Diesel and other oil Rs. 4,000; Repairs and maintenance Rs. 800; Taxes, insurance etc. Rs. 1,600; Depreciation Rs. 2,600; Interest and other charges Rs. 2,000; Total Rs. 14,400.

The seating capacity utilised was 75%. All the four buses ran on all days of the month. Each bus had made one round trip daily.

You are required to find out the cost per passenger-km. *[I.C.W.A. Inter]*

[Ans. Total passenger-kms 3,60,000, Cost per passenger-km Re. 0.04]

12. Rider Transport Co. owns a fleet of 10 luxury buses whose details of expenses are as follows : (*i*) Cost of each bus Rs. 1,50,000 (*ii*) Salary of office staff Rs. 4,000 per month (*iii*) Salary of garage staff Rs. 3,000 per month (*iv*) Rent of garage Rs. 2,000 per month (*v*) Drivers' salary (per bus) Rs. 800 per month (*vi*) Road Tax and repairs (per bus) Rs. 4,320 per annum. Salary of office and garage staff and garage rent were equally shared by all the buses. Insurance premium was 4% of cost per annum. The life of a bus was 3,00,000 km at the end of which it can be sold at Rs. 10,000. A bus runs on an average 3,200 km per month. Diesel consumption is 9 kms per litre costing Rs. 3.15 per litre. Mobile expenses amount to Rs. 10 per km.

(*a*) Calculate cost of running a bus per kilometre.

(*b*) If each bus has a capacity of 60 seats with 75% capacity utilisation and fare charged is Rs. 1.80 per kilometre, what is the annual profit made by the company from its fleet of buses.

[M.Com. CU]

[Ans. (1) Cost per km Rs. 1,162; (2) Cost per passenger km Re. 0.258; (3) Profit per passenger km Rs. 1.54; (4) Annual profit Rs. 2,66,11,200]

13. Victory Transport Co. runs a passenger bus on a 40 kms long route from Kolkata to Barasat. The bus costs Rs. 1,00,000 and has been insured for a premium of 3% per annum and has an expected life of 5 years.

Annual taxes amount to Rs. 4,000 and garage rent is Rs. 200 per month. The driver and conductor get a commission of 10% on collection to be shared equally between them. In addition the driver gets Rs. 500 per month while the conductor gets a salary of Rs. 300 per month. Helper's salary and allowance amount to Rs. 80 per month. Cost of stationery is Rs. 600 per annum. The cost of diesel and mobile is Rs. 25 per 100 kms. The bus makes three round trips per day carrying on an average 40 passengers on each trip and runs for 25 days in a month.

Assuming 20% profit on collection, calculate the bus fare to be charged from each passenger travelling from Kolkata to Barasat.

[M.Com. CU]

[Ans. (*a*) Total passenger-km 2,40,000; (*b*) Total profit Rs. 1,394; Collection Rs. 6,971; (*c*) Fare from Calcutta to Barasat per passenger Rs. 1.16]

14. National Transport Operator has obtained licence to run a passenger bus in a route covering 50 kms. The cost of acquisition of the bus is Rs. 4 lakhs and is being financed by a nationalised bank. Two drivers, two conductors, one helper and one cleaner are appointed at a monthly salary of Rs. 900, Rs. 350, and Rs. 250, respectively. Drivers and conductors are further entitled to 5% of the sale proceeds of the tickets. It is estimated that the annual charges for the bus will be : Road tax Rs. 2,500; Insurance premium Rs. 5,000; Repairs and maintenance Rs. 10,000; Replacement to tyres and tubes Rs. 8,000; and Garage Rent Rs. 3,000; Office and other administrative expenses are expected to be Rs. 12,000 per annum. Petrol, oil etc. will cost @ Rs. 100 per km. The effective life of the bus estimated to be 5 years and the expected scrap value of the bus at the end of such period will be Rs. 20,000. The passenger capacity of the bus is 50. The bus will run 2 two-way trips per day for 25 days in a month.

National Transport Operator requests you to prepare a passenger fare structure, after making an allowance of 25% profit on sales. The interest on bank loan will be approximately Rs. 10,000 per annum. Calculate passenger fare. *[M.Com. CU]*

[Ans. Total kms run per month 5,000; Total passenger kms 2,50,000; Total operating cost p.m. Rs. 5,15,958; Total collection Rs. 7,37,083, Passenger fare per km Rs. 2.94]

15. In view of increasing cost of operating own fleet of cars, your company is presently considering two proposals :

(*a*) To hire cars with drivers from agency @ Rs. 800 p.m. The company will bear the cost of petrol, oil and tyres.

(*b*) The executive will be given Rs. 25,000 interest-free loan repayable in 5 years to buy his own car. The company will, however, provide him free petrol and Rs. 500 p.m. for maintenance and drivers' wages.

If the present cost of car is Rs. 50,000 and monthly average running is 2,000 km, find out the most economic way with the help of the following data :

Petrol 65 per km, Oil 8 paise per km, Tyre 7 paise per km. Repair 10 paise per km. Tax and insurance Rs. 560 p.a., Drivers' wages and bonus Rs. 720 p.m. Life of a car 5 years. Resale value at the end of 5th year is Rs. 10,000. Assume interest @ 18% p.a. *[I.C.W.A. Final]*

[Ans. Hired car, Car loan, owned car cost per km Rs. 1·20, Rs. 0.99, Rs. 1.62]

16. S. K. Roy has been promised a contract to run a tourist car on a 20 km long route for the chief executive of a multinational firm. He buys a car costing Rs. 1,50,000. The annual cost of insurance and taxes are Rs. 4,500 and Rs. 900, respectively. He has to pay Rs. 500 per month for a garage where he keeps the car when it is not in use. The annual repair costs are estimated at Rs. 4,000. The car is estimated to have a life of 10 years at the end of which the scrap value is likely to be Rs. 50,000. He hires a driver who is to be paid Rs. 300 p.m. plus 10% of the takings as commission. Other incidental expenses are estimated at Rs. 200 p.m.

Petrol and oil will cost Rs. 100 per 100 km. The car will make 4 round trips each day. Assuming that a profit of 15% on takings is desired and that the car will be on the road for 25 days on an average per metre, what should be charge per round trip ?

[C.A. Inter]

[Ans. Charge per round trip = Rs. 88.22]

17. A practising Chartered Accountant spends Rs. 1.80 per km taxi fare. He is considering two other alternatives—the purchasing a new small car or an old big car.

The estimated cost figures for these two alternatives are as follows :

	New Small Car	*Old Big Car*
	Rs.	*Rs.*
Purchase price	70,000	40,000
Sale price after 10 years	30,000	20,000
Servicing and other fixed expenses p.a.	1,500	2,400
Tax & insurance p.a.	3,500	1,000
Km run per litre	10	7

Petrol price per litre is Rs. 7. His estimated annual requiremnt to travel is 10,000 km. Which of the three options will be most economical for him ? In case his annual travelling requirement is 20,000 km, what should be his decision ?

[Ans. Operating cost per km—New small car : Rs. 1.15, Old big car : Rs. 1.29, New small car is preferable]

18. A person owns a bus which runs between Krishnagar to Kolkata and back, for 10 days in a month. The distance from Krighnagar to Kolkata is 150 km. The bus completes the trip from Krishnagar to Kolkata and back in the same day. The bus goes another 10 days in a month towards Karimpur, the distance being 100 km. The trip is also completed in the same day. For the rest 4 days of its operation in a month it runs in the local city. Daily distance covered in local city is 40 km. Calculate the rate the person should charge from passengers when he wants to earn the profit of $33^1/_3$% on his takings. The other information are given below :

	Rs.
Cost of the Bus	60,000
Depreciation (20% p.a.)	350 p.m.
Salary of Driver	350 p.m.
Salary of Conductor	160 p.m.
Salary of part-time Accountant	1,680 p.a.
Insurance	Re. 1.00 per litre
Diesel consumption 4 km per litre costing	Rs. 600 p.a.
Tool tax and Lubricant oil	Rs. 10 per 100 km
Repairs and Maintenance	500 p.m.
Permit fee	284 p.m.
Normal capacity	50 passengers

The bus is generally occupied 90% of the capacity when it goes to Kolkata and 80% when it goes to Karimpur. It is always full when it runs within the city. Passenger tax is 20% of his net takings.

[Ans. Total passenger km = 2,39,000, Rate per passenger km = 3.6 paise]

19. Mr. S. K. Singh owns a fleet of taxis and the following information is available from the records maintained by him :

Number of taxis	10
Cost of each taxi	Rs. 20,000
Salary of manager	Rs. 600 p.m.
Salary of accountant	Rs. 500 p.m.

Salary of cleaner	Rs. 200 p.m.
Salary of mechanic	Rs. 400 p.m.
Garage rent	Rs. 600 p.m.
Insurance premium	5% per annum
Annual tax	Rs. 600 per taxi
Driver's salary	Rs. 200 p.m. per taxi
Annual repair	Rs. 1,000 per taxi

Total life of a taxi is about 2,00,000 km. A taxi runs in all 3,000 km in a month of which 30% it runs empty. Petrol consumption is one litre for 10 km, Rs. 1.80 per litre. Oil and other Sundrie's are Rs. 5.00 per 100 km.

Calculate the cost of running a taxi per km. *[B. Com. (Hons.), Delhi]*

[Ans. Cost per km per taxi = 0.78]

20. A transport company has been given a 20 km long route to run a bus. The bus costs Rs. 50,000 and has been insured @ 6% p.a. while annual taxes amount to Rs. 2,000. Garage rent is Rs. 100 p.m. yearly repairs will be Rs. 2,000 and the bus is likely to last for 5 years.

The driver's salary will be Rs. 3,000 p.a. and that of conductor's Rs. 1,800 p.a. in addition to 10% of the takings as commission (to be shared by the driver and the conductor equally). Cost of stationery will be Rs. 600 p.a. Manager's salary is Rs. 400 p.m. who also looks after accounts. Petrol and oil will be Rs. 25 per 100 km. The bus will make 3 round trips carrying on the average 40 passengers on each trip. Assume 25% profit on takings.

Calculate the bus fare to be charged from each passenger. The bus runs on an average 25 days in a month. *[Adopted]*

[Ans. Fare per passenger km = 3.8 paise or 4 paise (approx.)]

21. A truck carries goods covering a distance of 60 km. each way. On upward journey, freight is available for its full capacity but on downward journey only 25% of its capacity is filled up. The truck runs on an average 20 days a month.

Compute Ton-km per month for the truck if the capacity of the truck is 10 tons.

[C.U. B.Com (H) 2004]

[Ans. 15,000 Ton-kms]

22. Calculate the cost per running kilometre for a motor van from the following particulars :

Kilometrage run (annual)—15,000 ; Cost of motor van—Rs. 60,000.

Annual expenses—

	Rs.
Road licence	1,200
Insurance	800
Garage rent	600
Supervision expenses	2,800
Driver's monthly wage	800
Cost of petrol per litre	4
Repairs and maintenance per kilometre	1.80
Tyre cost (average) per kilometre	Re. 0.80
Kilometres run per litre of petrol	20
Estimated life of motor van	60,000 km.

[Ans. Operating cost per km. Rs. 4.80]

23. A 20 H.P. Unit is required to drive a pump for watering in an agricultural farm. Two plants A & B for supplying power are under consideration. The particulars of the plants are as follows :

	Plant A	*Plant B*
Purchase & Installation cost (Rs.)	10,000	4,000
Life (yrs.)	4	4
Salvage value (Rs.)	1,000	—
Interest on capital	10%	10%

Maintenance per year	3,000	—
Operating per hour	0.20	0
Power per hour	1.00	—
Fuel and oil per hour	—	2.00

Assuming about 3 million litres of water is to be pumped in a year and the pump will give out about 1,000 litres in an hour find out the cost per 1,000 litre of water under both the plants and find out the number of hours for which the operating costs of both the machines will be even. *[I.C.W.A.]*

[Ans. For less than 2,553 hours Plant B will be cheaper. For more than 2,553 hours Plant A will be cheaper]

24. SMC is a Public School having five buses each plying in different directions for the transport of its school students. In view of a large number of students availing of the bus service, the buses work two shifts—both in the morning and in the afternoon. The buses are garaged in the school. The work-load of the students has been so arranged that in the morning the first trip picks up senior students and the second trip plying an hour later picks up the junior students. Similarly in the afternoon the first trip drops the junior students and an hour later the second trip takes the senior students home.

The distance travelled by each bus one way is 8 kms. The school works 25 days in a month and remains closed for vacation in May, June and Dec. Bus fee, however, is payable by the students for all the 12 months in a year. The details of exps. for a year are as under :

	Rs.
Driver's salary	450 p.m. per driver
Cleaner's salary	350 p.m. per cleaner
(Salary payable for all 12 months)	
One cleaner employed for all the 5 buses)	
Licence fee, taxes etc.	860 per bus per annum
Insurance	1,000 per bus p.a.
Repairs & maintenance	3,500 per bus p.a.
Life 12 yrs.	
Purchase price of the bus	Rs. 1,50,000 each
Scrap value	30,000
Diesel cost	2.00 per litre

Each bus runs on an average mileage of 4 km per litre of diesel. Seating capacity of each bus 50 students.

The seating capacity is fully occupied during the whole year. Students picked up and dropped within a range of 4 kms of distance from the school are charged half fare and 50% of the students travelling in each trip are in this category. Ignore interest. The charges are to be based on average cost.

You are required to :

(*i*) Prepare a statement showing expenses of operating a single bus and the fleet of 5 buses for a year.

(*ii*) Work out the average cost per student p.m. in respect of :

(*a*) Students coming from a distance of up to 4 kms from the school, and

(*b*) Students coming from a distance beyond 4 kms from the school. *[C.A. Inter]*

[Ans. (*i*) Total operating expenses—Single bus Rs. 28,800, Fleet of 5 buses Rs. 1,44,000 (*ii*) (*a*) Cost per student p.m. (half fare) Rs. 16.00 (*b*) Cost per student p.m. (full fare) Rs. 32.00]

9 Cost Book-Keeping Cost Ledger Control Accounts

Authors' Comments and Suggestions :

1. ***Cost Accounting follows the fundamental principles of double entry book-keeping.***
2. ***Students need to have a clear idea about the integrated system and non-integrated system of accounts.***
3. ***In the Cost Ledger Accounting System, Cost Ledger Control Account—which is often referred to as General Ledger Adjustment Account—is kept to record all financial transactions.***
4. ***Cost Ledger Control Account is prepared to make the Cost Ledger self-balancing.***
5. ***Financial transactions relating to payments, such as those on account of material purchases, miscellaneous expenses, wages and salaries of workers etc are credited to Cost Ledger Control Account by Contra debit to the various Control Accounts.***
6. ***Purely Cost Accounting transactions, relating to non-financial items, do not pass through Cost Ledger Control Account.***
7. ***Intra-batch transfer will not affect the Control Accounts.***
8. ***Questions are generally set for journalisation of transactions for direct recording in the Ledger Accounts.***
9. ***This chapter is very important for CA, ICWA and for degree course students.***

Introduction; Interlocking Accounts; Integral Accounts; Advantages and Limitations of interlocking system; Importance of Cost Ledger; Principal Ledger Accounts—Cost Ledger/General Ledger, Stores Ledger Control Account, W.I.P. Control Account, F.G. Ledger Control Account, Wages Clearance Account, Factory Overhead Account, Administrative O/H, Selling & Distribution O/H Account, Cost of Sales Account, Costing P/L Account; Journal entries; Illustrations; Worked-out Problems; Exercises—Objective Questions—Theory Questions—Problems.

Introduction

The main purpose of financial accounting is to ascertain the financial position of enterprise at the end of the accounting period, whereas the purpose of cost accounting is to ascertain the cost of a product and record the transactions related to costs only. Under financial system no records relating to stock movement, cost apportionment, absorption of cost, wastages are available but under cost accounting system it is possible to know the movement of different stocks through W.I.P. Control A/c, Finished Goods Cost A/c and Cost of Sales A/c. Similarly, cost related to different departments as well as product units will be available separately when cost accounts are maintained properly. Under cost book-keeping system to link with financial accounts there are two types of cost accounts.

(*a*) Interlocking Accounts;

(*b*) Integral Accounts.

Interlocking Accounts

It is a system in which cost accounts are distinct from the financial accounts and are kept separately. It may be termed non-integral system also.

Integral Accounts

It is a single set of accounts, which provides both financial and cost accounting information required for management information system.

Advantages and Limitations of Interlocking System

Advantages

In order to plan an accounting system we consider first whether the system should be interlocking or integral. Now we may consider the advantages and limitations of the interlocking system :

(*i*) The object of maintaining the cost and financial books are quite different. The purpose of cost accounting is controlling of expenditures and ascertainment of costs, while the purpose of financial accounting are controlling of personal accounts of debtors, creditors and financiers etc. and ascertainment of profit by differentiating capital and revenue expenditures. Hence, interlocking system is necessary to fulfil two different objectives of financial and costing system separately.

(*ii*) While Cost Accountant is responsible for recording cost ledgers, Financial Accountant is responsible for financial ledgers only, hence no integration is possible.

(*iii*) The main objectives of the two types of accounting are different. The main purpose of financial accounting is to serve external people, but the objective of cost accounting is related to internal, management only.

(*iv*) Financial accounting is mostly based on historical cost that arise after happening of the event, but cost accounting does not restrict itself only to expose costs. The cost accounting includes both retrospective and anticipatory calculations, so it is to be kept separately.

(*v*) The main aim of financial accounts is to record the daily transactions without attaching any importance to control. But cost accounts through its detailed study assures control of materials, labour and overhead costs.

(*vi*) The financial accounts are to be kept according to the provisions of Companies Act and Income Tax Act. But cost accounts are kept voluntarily as per requirements of management and sometimes under Cost Accounting Record Rules.

(*vii*) Financial accounting provides information about the enterprise in a general way to all the interested people through its common financial statements. But under cost accounting separate reports are prepared for different levels and different decision-making areas of management. Hence no integration can perform a better result.

(*viii*) In big enterprises financial books are already overcrowded with hundreds of personal accounts, purchases, sales, revenue expenses, capital expenses etc. Costing books are also voluminous for handling transactions like consumption of material in work-in-progress or in overhead, wages in work-in-progress or in overhead, analysis of normal and abnormal items. Integration of two sets of books will be unwise.

Disadvantages

(*i*) Maintenance of two separate sets of books cause duplication of records of certain items—once in financial books and again in cost books.

(*ii*) Two sets of books cause two different profits due to existence of non-identical items under non integrated accounting system. Reconciliation of cost and financial accounts become necessary.

(*iii*) Maintenance of two sets of books enhances cost.

(*iv*) When transactions are not large maintenance of two sets of accounts separately is an unnecessary voluminous task.

Advantages/Importance of Cost ledger

If Cost Accounts are kept independently in addition to financial accounts prejudice reconciliation is necessary. The cost accounting as a separate branch of accounting has some added advantages than financial accounting. The importance/necessacity of maintaining cost ledger are :

(1) As the cost ledger summarises the detailed information regarding costs in subsidiary records, it is an invaluable tool of management in formulation of policies for decision-making.

(2) It provides information relating to unprofitable situation with their causes. Thus the system controls waste of material, labour and overhead costs, thereby reducing the cost of production.

(3) Under this system all the expenses are classified according to functions, elements and variability. These types of classifications will reveal the controllable and non-controllable portion of overhead.

(4) It assists by providing the basis for analysis of costs and preparation of accounts for each cost center or cost units for ascertainment and control of cost.

(5) Through the use of cost ledger purchases and issues of material and supplies may be properly controlled. Wages and overheads may also be analysed for the purpose of control. Overheads may be analysed according to function, elements and variability.

(6) This helps to reveal operating efficiency or inefficiency in order to take right action at the right time which helps in proper profit planning and price-fixing.

(7) For measuring and improving efficiency standards may be set as a guide. Thus cost ledger may furnish necessary variance accounts for submission to management for control purposes.

(8) Maintenance of cost ledger helps in preparation of financial statements as cost of inventories including W.I.P. can be easily obtained from cost records.

(9) It provides data to government for price fixation, price control, fixation of wages, payment of dividends, tariffs protection and settlement of disputes.

(10) It helps to prepare financial statement in more details. Cost and responsibility centers may be fixed in order to locate the responsible persons of the center.

Principal Ledger and Accounts

The cost accounting deptt. generally maintain the following principal ledgers :

(1) Cost Ledger—This is the main ledger which records the impersonal accounts i.e. accounts relating to income and expenditure. It is maintained under self-balancing system.

(2) Stores Ledger—This ledger contains stores accounts only.

(3) Work-in-Progress Ledger—This ledger records the details of each job undertaken and cost incurred therein.

(4) Finished Goods/Stock Ledger—This ledger records the details of completely finished goods or jobs.

Again, following are the accounts that are maintained in the cost ledger, which is the principal ledger in the cost department :

Cost Control Accounts—These accounts are prepared for exercising control over the three subsidiary ledgers viz. Store Ledger, W.I.P. Ledger and finished goods ledger and also to complete double entry in cost accounts. The important cost control accounts are :

1. General Ledger Adjustment/Cost Ledger Control A/c.—This account is prepared to complete double entry in cost ledger. Hence all such accounts which is related to fixed assets or cash or outsiders are posted to this accounts. All the expenditures are to be shown in the credit side of this account and the results or benefits of such expenditures in the form of sale is shown in the debit side of this account. Thus the balance represents the value of stores, work-in-progress and finished stock in hand.

2. Store Ledger Control Accounts—This account is debited with all purchases of materials for the stores and credited with all issues of materials from stores.

3. Work-in-progress Control Account—This account represents the total work in progress of different jobs at any time. This account is debited with the items relating to cost of production and production overhead recovered and credited with the value of finished goods completed.

4. Finished Goods Ledger Control Account—This account represents the total value of finished goods in a stock when goods are sold, the cost of such goods is credited to this account and debited to Cost of Sales A/c.

Other Accounts—These are the other impersonal accounts i.e. real as well as nominal which effects cost viz. wagers clearance account, factory overhead account, administration overhead account, selling and distribution overhead account, cost of sales, costing profit & loss account.

(*1*) **Wages Clearance Account**—Total wages whether direct or indirect are debited to this account. Direct wages are transferred to W.I.P. control account and indirect wages to respective overhead account.

(*2*) **Factory Overhead Account**—All indirect manufacturing expenses are to be debited to this account and credit is to be given to the amount of overhead recovered. The difference of this account is to be treated as under/over absorbed overehead.

(*3*) **Administration Overhead and Selling and Distribution Overhead**—All indirect administrative overhead and sales & distribution overhead incurred are to be debited and credited with the overhead recorded to this account. The difference of this account is to be treated as under/over absorbed overhead.

(*4*) **Cost of Sales**—This account is debited with the cost of finished goods transferred from finished goods control account and credited as well as with the amount of selling and distribution overhead recovered and credited to sales or costing Profit & Loss A/c.

(*5*) **Costing Profit & Loss A/c**—This account is debited with cost of goods sold, under absorbed overhead and abnormal losses. This account is again credited with the value of sales, over-absorbed overhead and abnormal gain. The net profit or loss is transferred to cost ledger control account.

Journal Entries

1. For purchase of materials
   (*a*) For Stores :
   Stores Ledger Control A/c ... Dr.
   To Cost Ledger Control A/c
   (*b*) For special jobs :
   Work-in-Progress Ledger Control A/c ... Dr.
   To Cost Ledger Control A/c
2. For materials issued for production :
   (*a*) As Direct Materials :
   Work-in-Progress Ledger Control A/c ... Dr.
   To Stores Ledger Control A/c
   (*b*) As Indirect Materials :
   Production/Administration/Selling & Distribution Overhead A/c ... Dr.
   To Store Ledger Control A/c ...
3. Material returns to suppliers :
   Cost Ledger Control A/c ... Dr.
   To Stores Ledger Control A/c

4. Material return from workshop :
   Store Ledger Control A/c ... Dr.
   To Work-in-Progress A/c
5. Material transferred from one job to another job :
   In the Work-in-Progress Ledger
   Transferee job A/c ... Dr.
   To Transferer Job A/c
6. (*a*) For normal shortage of stock :
   Factory Overhead A/c ... Dr.
   To Store Ledger Control A/c

Note : If there is any normal surplus of stock reverse entry will be passed.

   (*b*) For Abnormal shortage of stock :
   Costing P/L A/c ... Dr.
   To Store Ledger Control A/c
7. For payment of wages/salary :
   Wages Control A/c. ... Dr.
   To Cost Ledger Control A/c
8. For allocation of wages/salary :
   Work-in-Progress Control A/c ... Dr.
   (For direct wages)
   Production/Administration/Selling & Distribution Overhead A/c ... Dr.
   (For indirect wages)
   To Wages Control A/c
9. (*a*) For normal idle time wages :
   Production Overhead A/c. ... Dr.
   To Wages Control A/c.
   (*b*) For abnormal idle time.
   Costing Profit & Loss A/c ... Dr.
   To Wages Control A/c.
10. For Direct Expenses :
    Work-in-Progress Ledger Control A/c ... Dr.
    To Cost Ledger Control A/c
11. Payment of indirect expenses for Works, Office and Selling and Distribution Divn.
    Production/Administration/Selling and distribution A/c ... Dr.
    To Cost Ledger Control A/c
12. Recovery/absorption of overhead :
    (*a*) Production Overhead :
    Work-in-Progress Control A/c ... Dr.
    To Production Overhead A/c
    (*b*) Administrative Overhead :
    Finished Goods Control A/c ... Dr.
    To Administration Overhead A/c
    (*c*) For Selling & Distribution Overhead :
    Cost of Sales A/c ... Dr.
    To Selling & Distribution A/c
13. Cost of Production Transferred to finished stock :
    Finished Stock Ledger Control A/c ... Dr.
    To WIP Ledger Control A/c

14. Transfer of finished stock to cost of sales :
Cost of Sales A/c. ... Dr.
To Finished Stock Ledger Control A/c
15. For transfer of cost of sales to costing P/L A/c :
Costing Profit & Loss A/c ... Dr.
To Cost of Sales A/c
16. For Sale :
Cost Ledger Control A/c ... Dr.
To Costing P/L A/c
17. For sales return :
Costing P/L A/c. ... Dr.
To Cost Ledger Control A/c
18. For under-absorption :
Costing P/L A/c ... Dr.
To Production/Admn./Selling & Distribution O/H A/c.
(Note : For over absorption reverse entry will be passed)
19. For Profit :
Costing P/L A/c ... Dr.
To Cost Ledger Control A/c
(Note : For loss, reverse entry will be passed)

Illustration

The following balances are shown in the cost ledger of Vinak Ltd. As on 1st July 2006 :

	Dr. Rs.	Cr. Rs.
Work in progress account	7,056	
Factory overhead suspenses account	360	
Finished stock account	5,274	
Stores ledger control account	9,450	
Administration overhead suspense account	180	
General Ledger adjustment account		22,320

Transaction for the year ended 30th June 2007 were :

Stores issued to production	45,370
Stores purchased	52,400
Materials purchased for direct issue to production	1,135
Wages paid (including indirect labour Rs. 2,520)	57,600
Finished goods sold	1,18,800
Selling expenses	6,000
Administration expenses	5,400
Factory overheads	15,600
Stores issued for capital work-in-progress	1,500
Finished goods transferred to warehouse	1,08,000
Factory overheads applied to production	2,000
Factory overheads applied to production	16,830
Administration overheads charged to production	4,580
Factory overhead applicable to unfinished work	3,080
Selling overheads allocated to sales	5,500
Stores lost due to fire in stores (not insured)	150
Administration expenses on unfinished work	850
Finished goods stock on 30.6.07	14,274

You are required to record the entries in the cost ledger for the year ending 30th June 2007 and prepare a trial balance as on that date. ***[C.A. Inter, Adopted]***

Solution

Cost Ledger

General Ledger Adjustment Account

Dr.	*Rs.*	*Cr.*	*Rs.*
To Cost of Sales A/c	1,18,000	By Balance b/d	22,320
To Balance c/d	54,585	By Stores Ledger Control A/c	52,400
		By W.I.P. Control A/c	1,135
		By Wages Control A/c	57,600
		By Factory Overhead Control A/c	15,600
		By Administration Overhead Control A/c	5,400
		By Selling Overhead Control A/c	6,000
		By Costing Profit and Loss A/c	12,930
	1,73,385		1,73,385

Stores Ledger Control Account

	Rs.		*Rs.*
To Balance b/d	9,450	By WIP Control A/c.	45,370
To WIP Control A/c	52,400	By Capital WIP A/c.	1,500
		By Factory Overhead Control A/c.	2,000
		By Costing P & L A/c.	150
		By Balance c/d	12,830
	61,850		61,850

Finished Goods Control Account

	Rs.		*Rs.*
To Balance b/d	5,274	By Cost of Sales A/c.	99,000
To WIP Control A/c	1,08,000		
		By Balance c/d	14,274
	1,13,274		1,13,274

Work-in-Progress Control Account

	Rs.		*Rs.*
To Balance b/d	7,056	By Finished Goods Control A/c.	1,08,000
To General Ledger Adjustment A/c	1,135		
To Stores Ledger Control A/c.	45,370		
To Wages Control A/c.	55,080		
To Factory Overhead Control A/c	16,830	By Balance c/d	22,051
To Administrative Overhead Control A/c	4,580		
	1,30,051		1,30,051

Wages Control Account

	Rs.		Rs.
To General Adjustment A/c.	57,600	By WIP Control A/c.	55,080
		By Factory Overhead Control A/c.	2,520
	57,600		57,600

Factory Overhead Control Account

	Rs.		Rs.
To Factory Overhead Suspense A/c.	360	By WIP Control A/c.	16,830
To General Adjustment A/c.	15,600	By Factory Overhead Suspense A/c.	3,080
To Stores Control A/c.	2,000	By Costing Profit & Loss A/c.	570
To Factory Overhead Control A/c.	2,520		
	20,480		20,480

Administrative Overhead Control Account

	Rs.		Rs.
To Admn. Overhead Suspense A/c.	180	By WIP Control A/c.	4,580
To General Adjustment A/c.	5,400	By Admn. Overhead Suspense A/c.	850
		By Costing Profit & Loss A/c.	150
	5,580		5,580

Cost of Sales Account

	Rs.		Rs.
To Finished Control A/c.	99,000	By Costing Profit & Loss A/c.	1,04,500
To Selling Overhead Control A/c	5,500		
	1,04,500		1,04,500

Factory overhead Suspense Account

	Rs.		Rs.
To Balance b/d A/c.	360	By Factory Overhead Control A/c	360
To Factory Overhead Control A/c.	3,080	By Balance c/d	3,080
	3,440		3,440

Administrative Overhead Suspense Account

	Rs.		Rs.
To Balance b/d.	180	By Admn. Overhead Control A/c.	180
To Admn. Overhead Control A/c.	850	By Balance c/d	850
	1,030		1,030

Selling Overhead Control Account

	Rs.		Rs.
To Balance b/d	6,000	By Cost of Sales A/c.	5,500
		By Costing Profit & Loss A/c.	500
	6,000		6,000

Capital Work-in-Progress Account

	Rs.		Rs.
To Stores Ledger Control A/c.	1,500	By Balance c/d	1,500
	1,500		1,500

Costing Profit & Loss Account

	Rs.		Rs.
To Cost of sales A/c.	1,04,500	By General Ledger Adj. A/c.	1,18,800
To Stores Ledger Control A/c.	150		
To Factory Overhead Control A/c.	570		
To Selling Overhead Control A/c.	500		
To Admn. Overhead Control A/c.	150		
To Gen. Ledger Adj. A/c. (Profit)	12,930		
	1,18,800		1,18,800

Trial Balance

	Dr. Rs.	Cr. Rs.
Work-in-Progress A/c.	22,051	
Stores Ledger Control A/c.	12,830	
Finished Goods Control A/c.	14,274	
Factory Overhead Suspense A/c.	3,080	
Admn. Overhead Suspense a/c.	850	
Capital Work-in-progress A/c	1,500	
General Ledger Adjustment Account		54,585
	54,585	54,585

Journal entries illustrating the difference in accounting entries in Financial Accounts and Cost Accounts in the one hand and Integrated Accounts, on the other.

Materials Purchased 10,000 Kgs. @ Rs. 5/- per Kg. On credit

			Rs.	Rs.
(a)	**Financial Accounts :**			
	Purchase A/c	... Dr.	50,000	
	To Creditors A/c			50,000
(b)	**Cost Accounts :**			
	Stores Ledger Control A/c	... Dr.	50,000	
	To Cost Ledger Control A/c			50,000
	(Omitting Material Control A/c)			
(c)	**Integrated Accounts :**			
	Stores Ledger Control A/c	... Dr.	50,000	
	To Creditors A/c			50,000

Wages : Production wages : Rs. 10,000/-

			Rs.	*Rs.*
(*a*)	**Financial Accounts :**			
	Wages A/c	... Dr.	10,000	
	To Cash A/c			10,000
(*b*)	**Cost Accounts :**			
	Wages Clearance A/c	... Dr.	10,000	
	To Cost Ledger Control A/c			10,000
(*c*)	**Integrated Accounts :**			
	Wages Clearance A/c	... Dr.	10,000	
	To Cash A/c			10,000

Overhead : Production Overhead incurred : Rs. 5,000/-

			Rs.	*Rs.*
(*a*)	**Financial Accounts :**			
	Production Expenses A/c	... Dr.	5,000	
	To Cash A/c			5,000
(*b*)	**Cost Accounts :**			
	Production overhead A/c	... Dr.	5,000	
	To Cost Ledger Control A/c			5,000
(*c*)	**Integrated Accounts :**			
	Production Overhead A/c	... Dr.	5,000	
	To Cash A/c			5,000

Sales : Sales (on credit) : Rs. 1,00,000/-

			Rs.	*Rs.*
(*a*)	**Financial Accounts :**			
	Debtors A/c	... Dr.	1,00,000	
	To Sales A/c			1,00,000
(*b*)	**Cost Accounts :**			
	Cost Ledger Control A/c	... Dr.	1,00,000	
	To Sales A/c			1,00,000
(*c*)	**Integrated Accounts :**			
	Debtors A/c	... Dr.	1,00,000	
	To Sales A/c			1,00,000

Note : It may be observed that the Cost Ledger Control A/c has been eliminated in the integrated accounting system. In short this system records the essential points of both cost and financial accounting viz. Store and Creditors, Wages and Cash, Overhead and Cash, and Debtors and Sales have been recorded in Integrated Accounts.

WORKEDOUT PROBLEMS

Problem 1

Pass Journal entries in the cost books, maintained on non-integrated system for the following :

(*i*) Issue of materials	Direct Rs. 5,50,000, Indirect Rs. 1,50,000
(*ii*) Allocation of wages	Direct Rs. 2,00,000, Indirect Rs. 40,000
(*iii*) Under/Over absorbed overheads	Factory (Over) Rs. 20,000
	Administrative (Under) Rs. 10,000

[I.C.W.A. Inter, 2000]

Solution

Journal entries in Cost Books maintained on non-integrated system

				Rs.	*Rs.*
I.	Work in Progress Ledger Control A/c	...	Dr.	5,50,000	
	Factory Overhead Control A/c	...	Dr.	1,50,000	
	To Stores Ledger Control A/c.				7,00,000
	(Being the entry for issue of materials)				
II.	Work in progress Ledger Control A/c	...	Dr.	2,00,000	
	Factory Overhead Control A/c	...	Dr.	40,000	
	To Wages Control A/c.				2,40,000
	(Being the entry for allocation of wages and salaries)				
III.	Factory overhead control A/c	...	Dr.	20,000	
	To Costing Profit & Loss A/c				20,000
IV.	Costing Profit & Loss A/c	...	Dr.	10,000	
	To Administrative Overhead Control A/c.				10,000
	(Being transfer of under absorbed overhead)				

- Over-absorbed means it was credited more and now it is to be debited.
- Under-absorbed means debit side was more than credit side. Now administrative overhead control account should be credited.

Problem 2

Dutta Enterprises operates an integral system of accounting. You are required to pass the journal entries for the following transactions that took place for the year ended 30.06.2007 :

(Narrations are not required)

Raw material purchased (50% on credit)	6,00,000
Materials issued to production	4,00,000
Wages paid (15% direct)	2,00,000
Wages charged to production	1,00,000
Factory overhead incurred	80,000
Factory overhead charged to production	1,00,000
Selling & distribution overheads incurred	40,000
Finished goods at cost	5,00,000
Sales (50% credit)	7,50,000
Closing stock	—
Received from debtors	2,00,000
Payment to creditors	2,00,000

[C.A. Inter, Adopted]

Solution

Journal Entries—Integral System of Accounting

			Rs.	*Rs.*
Stores Ledger Control A/c.	...	Dr.	6,00,000	
To Sundry Creditors A/c.				3,00,000
To Cash or Bank A/c.				3,00,000
Work-in-Progress Control A/c.	...	Dr.	4,00,000	
To Store Ledger Control A/c.				4,00,000
Wages Control A/c	...	Dr.	2,00,000	
To Cash				2,00,000

(Contd.)

Work-in-Progress Control A/c.	... Dr.	1,00,000	
Factory Overhead Control A/c.	... Dr.	1,00,000	
To Wages Control A/c.			2,00,000
Factory Overhead Control A/c.	... Dr.	80,000	
To Cash or Bank A/c.			80,000
Work-in-Progress Control A/c.	... Dr.	1,00,000	
To Factory Overhead Control A/c.			1,00,000
Selling & Distribution Overhead Control A/c.	... Dr.	40,000	
To Cash or Bank A/c.			40,000
Finished Goods Ledger Control A/c.	... Dr.	5,00,000	
To Work-in-progress Control A/c.			5,00,000
Cost of Sales A/c	... Dr.	5,40,000	
To Finished Goods Ledger Control A/c.			5,00,000
To Selling & Distribution Overhead Control A/c.			40,000
Sundry Debtors A/c.	... Dr.	3,75,000	
Cash or Bank A/c.	... Dr.	3,75,000	
To Sales A/c.			7,50,000
Cash or Bank A/c.	... Dr.	2,00,000	
To Sundry Debtors A/c.			2,00,000
Sundry Creditors A/c.	... Dr.	2,00,000	
To Cash or Bank A/c.			2,00,000

Problem 3

The following balances are obtained from the books of XYZ Co. Ltd. on 1st January 2006 :

	Dr.	*Cr.*
Store Ledger Control A/c	5,000	
Work-in-Progress Ledger Control A/c	2,000	
Finished Goods Ledger Control A/c	1,000	
General Ledger Adj. A/c		8,000
	8,000	8,000

The following information is received at the end of the year		
Purchase for stores		29,500
Purchase for special job		1,800
Return to suppliers from stores		200
Direct wages	20,500	
Indirect factory wages	4,500	
Salaries to admn. Staff	3,400	
Salaries to S & D Staff	2,400	
Abnormal idle time	300	31,100
Direct expenses		2,200
Production expenses		5,100
Admn. Expenses		4,100

S&D expenses	2,600
Stores issued to production	3,500
Materials lost from stores by theft	400
Stores issued to maintenance a/c	1,300
Production overhead applied to production (20% of prime cost)	
Admn. Overhead applied to finished goods	7,200
S & D overhead applied to cost of sales (6% on sales value)	
Finished goods produced during the year	66,000
Goods sold during the period—at sales value	80,000
Goods sold during the period—cost	69,500

You are required to record the entries in the cost ledger for the year and prepare a trial balance.

Solution

COST LEDGER

General Adjustment A/c

		Rs.			Rs.
Dec. 31	To Stores Ledger Control A/c (Returns)	200	Jan. 1	By Balance b/d	8,000
	To Profit & Loss A/c. (Sales)	80,000	Dec. 31	By Stores Ledger Control A/c (Purchase)	29,500
	To Balance c/d	8,800		By W.I.P. Led. Control A/c (Spl. purchase)	1,800
				By Wages Control A/c	31,100
				By WIP Led. Control. A/c (direct expenses)	2,200
				By Production overhead A/c	5,100
				By Admn. Overhead A/c	4,100
				By Selling and distn. Overhead A/c	2,600
				By Costing P & L A/c. (Profit)	4,600
		89,000			89,000
			Jan. 1	By Balance b/d	8,800

Store Ledger Control A/c

		Rs.			Rs.
Jan. 1	To Balance b/d	5,000	Dec. 31	By WIP Ledger Control A/c	30,500
Dec. 31	To General Ledger Adj. A/c (Purchase)	29,500	Dec. 31	By Production Overhead A/c	1,300
				By General Adj. A/c (Return)	200
				By Abnormal Loss A/c (Loss by theft)	400
				By Balance c/d	2,100
		34,500			34,500
Jan. 1	To Balance b/d	2,100			

Wages Control A/c

		Rs.			Rs.
Dec. 31	To General Adj. A/c	31,100	Dec. 31	By WIP Ledger Control A/c	20,500
				By Production Overhead A/c	4,500
				By Admn. Overhead A/c	3,400
				By Selling & Distbn. Overhead A/c	2,400
				By Abnormal Loss A/c. (Idle time)	300
		31,100			31,100

Production Overhead A/c

		Rs.			Rs.
Dec. 31	To Stores Ledger A/c	1,300	Dec. 31	By WIP Ledger Control A/c	11,000
	To General Ledger Adj. A/c	5,100			
	To Wages Control A/c	4,500			
	To Overhead Adj. A/c	100			
		11,000			11,000

Administrative Overhead A/c

		Rs.			Rs.
Dec. 31	To General Ledger Adj. A/c	4,100	Dec. 31	By Finished Goods Ledger Control A/c	7,200
	To Wages Control A/c	3,400		By Overhead Adjustment A/c	300
		7,500			7,500

Selling & Distribution Overhead A/c

		Rs.			Rs.
Dec. 31	To General Ledger Adj. A/c	2,600	Dec. 31	By Cost of Sales A/c	4,800
	To Wages Control A/c	2,400		By Overhead Adjustment A/c	200
		5,000			5,000

Work-in-Progress Ledger Control A/c

		Rs.			Rs.
Jan. 1	To Balance b/d	2,000	Dec. 31	By Finished goods ledger control A/c	66,000
Dec. 31	To General Led. Adj. A/c Spl Purchase	1,800		By Balance c/d	2,000
	To Stores Ledger Control A/c	30,500			
	To Wages Control A/c	20,500			
	To General Led. Adj. A/c Direct expenses	2,200			
	To Production overhead A/c	11,000			
		68,000			68,000
Jan. 1	To Balance b/d	2,000			

Finished Goods Ledger Control A/c

		Rs.			Rs.
Jan. 1	To Balance b/d	1,000	Dec. 31	By Cost of Sales A/c	69,500
Dec. 31	To WIP Led. Control A/c	66,000			
	To Admn. Overhead A/c	7,200		By Balance c/d	4,700
		74,200			74,200
Jan. 1	To Balance b/d	4,700			

Cost of Sales A/c

		Rs.			Rs.
Dec. 31	To Finished goods ledger control A/c	69,500	Dec. 31	By Costing P & L A/c	74,300
	To S & D Overhead A/c	4,800			
		74,300			74,300

Abnormal Loss A/c

		Rs.			Rs.
Dec. 31	To Stores Ledger Control A/c – Loss by theft	400	Dec. 31	By Costing P & L A/c	700
	To Wages Control A/c (Idle time)	300			
		700			700

Overhead Adjustment A/c

		Rs.			Rs.
Dec. 31	To Admn. Overhead A/c	300	Dec. 31	By Production overhead A/c	100
	To S & D overhead A/c	200		By Costing P & L A/c	400
		500			500

Costing Profit & Loss A/c
(for the year ending 31st Dec., 2006)

	Rs.		Rs.
To Cost of sales A/c	74,300	By General Ledger Adj. A/c (Sales)	80,000
To Abnormal A/c	700		
To Overhead Adj. A/c	400		
To General Ledger adj. A/c. (Profit for the year)	4,600		
	80,000		80,000

Trial Balance
(As on 31st December 2006)

Particulars	*Amount*	*Amount*
Stores Ledger Control A/c	2,100	
Work-in-Progress Control A/c	2,000	
Finished goods ledger control A/c	4,700	
General ledger adjustment A/c		8,800
	8,800	8,800

Note : (1) Production overhead : Prime cost charged to work-in-progress during the year is Rs. 55,000/-. So production overhead is 20% of 55,000/- i.e. Rs. 11,000/-.

(2) Balances on Overhead A/c. have been transferred to overhead adjustment A/c.

Problem 4

ABC Ltd. operates an integrated accounting system and the following details are given for the year ended 31st March 2007 :

Trial Balance as on 31st March 2007

	Debit (Rs.)	*Credit (Rs.)*
Share Capital		20,00,000
Reserves		2,00,000
Creditors for purchase		1,50,000
Expense Creditors		20,000
Freehold buildings, at cost	5,00,000	
Plant & Machinery, at cost	13,00,000	
Provision for depreciation on Plant & Machinery		1,00,000
Stock of Raw Materials	2,20,000	
Work-in-Progress	40,000	
Finished goods	60,000	
Debtors	2,00,000	
Bank	1,50,000	
	24,70,000	24,70,000

The following data for the month of April 2007 are given :

	Rs.
Raw material purchased on credit	9,90,000
Raw materials returned to suppliers	40,000
Material issued to production	8,50,000
Material returned from shop floor	20,000
Factory wages paid :	
Productive	2,50,000
Non-productive	50,000
Salaries Paid :	
Administration	1,00,000
Selling & Distribution	75,000
Overhead expenses incurred but not paid :	
Productive	3,00,000
Administration	50,000
Selling & Distribution	1,00,000
Depreciation for the month on Plant & Machinery	50,000
Sales on credit	20,00,000
Cash received from Debtors	19,50,000
Paid the following by cheque :	
Creditors for purchases	10,00,000
Creditors for expenses	4,30,000
Production overhead applied to production	3,90,000
Administrative overhead applied to finished goods	1,45,000
Selling and distribution overhead applied to cost of sales	1,80,000
Closing Stock :	
Work-in-Progress	2,10,000
Finished goods	2,15,000

Required :

(*a*) Show the appropriate ledger accounts.
(*b*) Prepare the income statement for April 2007.
(*c*) Prepare the Balance Sheet as at 30th April 2007. **[CA Final]**

Solution

(A) Creditors for Purchase A/c

	Rs.		*Rs.*
To Raw Material A/c. (Returns)	40,000	By Balance b/d	1,50,000
To Bank A/c.	10,00,000	By Raw Materials A/c	9,90,000
To Balance c/d	1,00,000		
	11,40,000		11,40,000
		By Balance b/d	1,00,000

Expense Creditors A/c

	Rs.		*Rs.*
To Bank A/c	4,30,000	By Balance b/d	20,000
To Balance.c/d	40,000	By POH A/c	3,00,000
		By AOH A/c	50,000
		By S & D OH A/c	1,00,000
	4,70,000		4,70,000
		By Balance b/d	40,000

Provision for Dep. On P & M A/c

	Rs.		*Rs.*
To Balance c/d	1,50,000	By Balance b/d	1,00,000
		By POH A/c	50,000
	1,50,000		1,50,000
		By Balance b/d	1,50,000

Raw Materials A/c

	Rs.		*Rs.*
To Balance c/d	2,20,000	By Creditors for Purchases	40,000
To Creditors for Purchases	9,90,000	By WIP A/c	8,50,000
To WIP A/c	20,000	By Balance c/d	3,40,000
	12,30,000		12,30,000
To Balance c/d	3,40,000		

W.I.P. A/c

	Rs.		*Rs.*
To Balance b/d	40,000	By Raw Materials A/c	20,000
To Raw Materials A/c	8,50,000	By Finished goods A/c	13,00,000
To Wages Control A/c	2,50,000	By Balance c/d	2,10,000
To P.O.H A/c	3,90,000	(balancing figure)	
	15,30,000		15,30,000
To Balance b/d	2,10,000		

Finished Goods A/c

	Rs.		Rs.
To Balance b/d	60,000	By COS A/c. (balance figure)	12,90,000
To AOH A/c.	1,45,000	By Balance c/d.	2,15,000
To WIP A/c	13,00,000		
	15,05,000		15,05,000
To Balance b/d	2,15,000		

Debtors A/c

	Rs.		Rs.
To Balance b/d	2,00,000	By Bank A/c.	19,50,000
To Sales A/c.	20,00,000	By Balance c/d	2,50,000
	22,00,000		22,00,000
To Balance b/d	2,50,000		

Bank A/c

	Rs.		Rs.
To Balance b/d	1,50,000	By Wages Control A/c.	4,75,000
To Debtors A/c.	19,50,000	By Creditors for Purchases	10,00,000
		By Expense Creditors A/c.	4,30,000
		By Balance c/d	1,95,000
	21,00,000		21,00,000
To Balance b/d	1,95,000		

Wages Control A/c

	Rs.		Rs.
To Bank (Salaries & Wages) A/c	4,75,000	By WIP A/c.	2,50,000
		By POH A/c.	50,000
		By AOH A/c.	1,00,000
		By S & D OH A/c.	75,000
	4,75,000		4,75,000

Production Overhead A/c

	Rs.		Rs.
To Wages Control A/c	50,000	By WIP A/c	3,90,000
To Exp. Creditors A/c	3,00,000	By Income Statement	10,000
To Provision for Depreciation	50,000		
	4,00,000		4,00,000

Admn. Overhead A/c

	Rs.		Rs.
To Wages Control A/c	1,00,000	By Finished Goods A/c.	1,45,000
To Exp. Creditors A/c.	50,000	By Income Satement	5,000
	1,50,000		1,50,000

S & D Overhead A/c

	Rs.		Rs.
To Wages Control A/c.	75,000	By COS A/c.	1,80,000
To Exp. Creditors A/c.	1,00,000		
To Income Statement	5,000		
	1,80,000		1,80,000

Cost of Sales A/c

	Rs.		Rs.
To S & D Overhead A/c.	1,80,000	By Income Statement	14,70,000
To Finished goods A/c.	12,90,000		
	14,70,000		14,70,000

Sales A/c

	Rs.		Rs.
To Income Statement	20,00,000	By Debtors A/c	20,00,000

(B) Income Statement, For the month of April 2007

	Rs.
Sales	20,00,000
Less : Cost of sales	14,70,000
Gross Profit	5,30,000
Add : Over-absorption of S & D overhead	5,000
	5,35,000
Less : Under-absorption of POH and AOH	15,000
Net Profit	5,20,000

(C) Balance Sheet of ABC Ltd. as at 30.4.2007

Liabilities	Rs.	Rs.	Assets	Rs.	
Share Capital		20,00,000	Fixed Assets :		
Reserves		2,00,000	Freehold Buildings at Cost		5,00,000
Net Profit (for month)		5,20,000	Plant & Machinery	13,00,000	
Creditors for Purchase		1,00,000	*Less* : Prov. For Dept.	1,50,000	
Expenses Creditors		40,000			11,50,000
			Current Assets :		
			Stock of Raw Materials		3,40,000
			WIP		2,10,000
			Finished Goods		2,15,000
			Debtors		2,50,000
			Bank		1,95,000
		28,60,000			28,60,000

Problem 5

Dutta Enterprises operates an integral system of accounting. You are required to pass the Journal Entries for the following transactions that took place for the year ended 30.6.2007 :

(Narrations are not required).

Raw materials purchased (50% on credit)	6,00,000
Materials issued to production	4,00,000
Wages paid (50% direct)	2,00,000
Wages charged to production	1,00,000
Factory overheads incurred	80,000
Factory overheads charged to production	1,00,000
Selling and Distribution overheads incurred	40,000
Finished goods at cost	5,00,000
Sales (50% credit)	7,50,000
Closing stock	NIL
Receipts from Debtors	2,00,000
Payment to creditors	2,00,000

[C.A. Inter, Adopted]

Solution

Journal Entries

			Dr. (Rs.)	*Cr. (Rs.)*
1.	(*a*) Stores Ledger Control a/c.	... Dr.	6,00,000	
	To Sundry Creditors a/c.			3,00,000
	To Cash or Bank a/c.			3,00,000
	(*b*) Work-in-Progress Control a/c.	... Dr.	4,00,000	
	To Store Ledger Control a/c.			4,00,000
2.	(*a*) Wages Control a/c	... Dr.	2,00,000	
	To Cash or Bank a/c.			2,00,000
	(*b*) Work-in-Progress Control a/c.	... Dr.	1,00,000	
	Factory Overhead Control a/c.	... Dr.	1,00,000	
	To Wages Control a/c.			2,00,000
3.	(*a*) Factory Overhead Control a/c.	... Dr.	80,000	
	To Cash or Bank a/c.			80,000
	(*b*) Work-in-Progress control a/c.	... Dr.	1,00,000	
	To Factory Overhead Control a/c.			1,00,000
4.	Selling & Distribution Overhead Control A/c.	... Dr.	40,000	
	To Cash or Bank a/c.			40,000
5.	(*a*) Finished goods control a/c.	... Dr.	5,00,000	
	To Work-in-progress control a/c.			5,00,000
	(*b*) Cost of sales a/c	... Dr.	5,40,000	
	To Finished goods control a/c.			5,00,000
	To Selling & Distribution overhead control a/c.			40,000
6.	(*a*) Sundry Debtors a/c.	... Dr.	3,75,000	
	Cash or Bank a/c.	... Dr.	3,75,000	
	To Sales a/c.			7,50,000
7.	Cash or Bank a/c.	... Dr.	2,00,000	
	To Sundry Debtors a/c.			2,00,000
8.	Sundry Creditors a/c.	... Dr.	2,00,000	
	To Cash or Bank a/c.			2,00,000

Problem 6

M/s Essbee Ltd. maintains Integrated Account of Cost and Financial Accounts. From the following details write control accounts in the general ledger of the factory and prepare a trial balance :

	Rs.
Share Capital	3,00,000
Reserve	2,00,000
Sundry Creditors	5,00,000
Plant and Machinery	5,75,000
Sundry Debtors	2,00,000
Closing Stock	1,50,000
Bank and Cash Balance	75,000
Transactions during the year were :	
Stores Purchased	10,00,000
Stores issued to production	10,50,000
Stores in hand	95,000
Direct wages incurred	6,50,000
Direct wages charged to production	6,00,000
Manufacturing expenses incurred	3,00,000
Manufacturing expenses charged to production	2,75,000
Selling and distribution expenses	1,00,000
Finished stock production (at cost)	18,00,000
Sales at selling price	22,00,000
Closing stock	95,000
Payment to creditors	11,00,000
Receipt from Debtors	21,00,000

[I.C.W.A. Inter]

Solution

S & D A/c

	Rs.		Rs.
		By Balance b/d	3,00,000

Reserve A/c

	Rs.		Rs.
To Balance b/d	5,15,000	By Balance b/d	2,00,000
		By Costing P & L A/c	3,15,000
	5,15,000		5,15,000
		By Balance b/d	5,15,000

Sundry Creditors A/c

	Rs.		Rs.
To Bank A/c	11,00,000	By Balance b/d	5,00,000
To Balance c/d	4,00,000	By Stock Control A/c.	10,00,000
	15,00,000		15,00,000
		By Balance b/d	4,00,000

Plant & Machinery A/c

	Rs.		*Rs.*
To Balance b/d	5,75,000		

Sundry Debtors A/c

	Rs.		*Rs.*
To Balance b/d	2,00,000	By Bank a/c	21,00,000
To Sales	22,00,000	By Balance c/d	3,00,000
	24,00,000		24,00,000
To Balance b/d	3,00,000		

Stock Control A/c

	Rs.		*Rs.*
To Balance b/d	1,50,000	By WIP a/c.	10,50,000
To Sundry Creditors	10,00,000	By Mfg. Overhead control a/c.	5,000
		By Balance c/d	95,000
	11,50,000		11,50,000
To Balance b/d	95,000		

Bank A/c

	Rs.		*Rs.*
To Balance b/d	75,000	By Wages Control a/c	6,50,000
To Sundry Debtors	21,00,000	By Production overhead control	3,00,000
		By Selling Expenses	1,00,000
		By Sundry Creditors	11,00,000
		By Balance c/d	25,000
	21,75,000		21,75,000
To Balance b/d	25,000		

W.I.P A/c

	Rs.		*Rs.*
To Stores control a/c	10,50,000	By Finished stock a/c.	18,00,000
To Wages control a/c	6,00,000	By Balance c/d	1,25,000
To Production overhead control a/c	2,75,000		
	19,25,000		19,25,000
To Balance b/d	1,25,000		

Wages Control A/c

	Rs.		*Rs.*
To Bank a/c	6,50,000	By WIP a/c.	6,00,000
		By Production overhead	50,000
	6,50,000		6,50,000

Production Overhead Control A/c

	Rs.		Rs.
To Stores Control a/c	5,000	By WIP a/c.	2,75,000
To Bank a/c	3,00,000	By P & L a/c (Underabsorption)	80,000
To Wages Control a/c	50,000		
	3,55,000		3,55,000

Selling and Distribution Overhead Control A/c

	Rs.		Rs.
To Bank a/c	1,00,000	By Cost of sales a/c.	1,00,000

Cost of Sales A/c

	Rs.		Rs.
To Finished Stock Control a/c	17,05,000	By Costing P & L a/c.	18,05,000
To S & D Overhead Control a/c	1,00,000		
	18,05,000		18,05,000

Finished Stock Control A/c

	Rs.		Rs.
To WIP a/c	18,00,000	By Cost of Sales a/c.	17,05,000
		By Balance c/d	95,000
	18.00.000		18,00,000
To Balance b/d	95,000		

Sales A/c

	Rs.		Rs.
To Costing P & L a/c	22,00,000	By S. Debtors	22,00,000

Costing P & L A/c

	Rs.		Rs.
To Cost of Sales a/c	18,05,000	By Sales a/c	22,00,000
To Prod. Overhead Control a/c (Under absorption)	80,000		
To Net Profit a/c (transferred to Reserve)	3,15,000		
	22,00,000		22,00,000

Trial Balance

	Dr. Rs.	Cr. Rs.
Share Capital		3,00,000
Reserve		5,15,000
Sundry Creditors		4,00,000
Plant & Machinery	5,75,000	
Sundry Debtors	3,00,000	
Stock in hand	95,000	
Stock of Finished goods	95,000	
Bank a/c	25,000	
WIP a/c	1,25,000	
	12,15,000	12,15,000

EXERCISES

OBJECTIVE TYPE QUESTIONS

1. Indicate whether the follwing statements are true or false :

(*a*) General Ledger Adjustment Account represents the personal accounts shown in financial books.

(*b*) There is no need of reconciliation of cost and financial accounts in Cost Ledger accounting.

(*c*) Control Accounts are the total accounts maintained in the cost ledger.

(*d*) In Cost Ledger Accounting, transactions are recorded on the basis of double entry.

(*e*) Cost Ledger Accounting is a system of integrating cost and financial accounts.

(*f*) The balance of stores ledger control account represents the total balance of stock of each item of material.

(*g*) Selling and distribution expenses are debited to selling and distribution overhead control account.

(*h*) Debit balance of production overhead control account represents over-absorption of production overheads.

(*i*) The purpose of cost control accounts is to control the cost of production.

(*j*) Postings in wages control account are made from wage analysis sheet.

(*k*) Credit balance of selling and distribution overheads represents under-absorption of these expenses.

[Ans. True : (*a*), (*c*), (*d*), (*f*), (*g*) (*j*) False : (*b*), (*e*), (*h*), (*i*), (*k*)]

2. Which of the suggested solutions is the correct one ?

(*a*) A main use of the financial ledger control account in the cost ledger is

(*i*) It makes the cost ledger self-balancing.

(*ii*) It summarises the financial ledger entries.

(*iii*) It records the financial profit for the period.

(*iv*) Its balance is the profit reported in the cost ledger.

[Ans. (*i*)]

(*b*) Production overhead absorbed will be recorded in the cost ledger as :

(*i*) Debit-Work-in-Progress A/c ; Credit-Production Overhead A/c.

(*ii*) Debit-Production Overhead A/c ; Credit-Financial Ledger Control A/c.

(*iii*) Debit-Profit and Loss A/c ; Credit-Production Overhead A/c.

(*iv*) Debit-Finished Goods A/c ; Credit-Production Overhead A/c

[Ans. (*iii*)]

(*c*) In an integrated Ledger system the entry for gross direct wages earned is :

(*i*) Debit-Work-in-Progress ; Credit-Wages-Control A/c.

(*ii*) Debit-Bank A/c ; Credit-Wages-Control A/c.

(*iii*) Debit-Work-in-Progress ; Credit-Bank A/c.

(*iv*) Debit-Wages Control A/c ; Credit-Bank A/c

[Ans. (*i*)]

THEORETICAL QUESTIONS

1. Write short notes on 'Cost Ledger control A/c' *[C.A. Inter]*

2. Define Control Accounts. What is their function in relation to the reconciliation of financial and cost accounts ? *[I.C.W.A. June 1984]*

3. State the essential pre-requisites of 'Integrated Accounting System'. *[C.A. Inter, May 1996]*

4. Describe briefly what do you understand by the term "Integrated Cost Accounts." Mention the advantages of integrated cost accounts. *[C.A. Inter Nov '91; I.C.W.A. Inter, 1995]*

5. Write short notes on

(*i*) Integrated Accounting.

(*ii*) Cost Ledger Control Account

(*iii*) Advantages of Integrated Accounts.

6. State the pre-requisites of integrated Accounting System. *[C.A. Inter, Nov. 1996]*

PROBLEMS

1. Cost Control Accounts : In the absence of the Chief Accountant, you have been asked to prepare a month's cost accounts for a company which operates a batch costing system fully integrated with the financial accounts. The following relevant information is provided to you :

	Rs.	Rs.
Balance of the beginning of the month :		
Stores Ledger Control a/c		25,000
Work-in-Progress control a/c		20,000
Finished goods control a/c		35,000
Prepaid prod. Overhead brought forward from previous month		3,000
Transaction during the month :		
Material purchased		75,000
Material Issued :		
To Production	30,000	
To Factory maintenance	4,000	34,000
Material transferred between batches		5,000
Total wages paid :		
To Direct workers	25,000	
To Indirect workers	5,000	30,000
Direct wages charged to batches		20,000
Recorded non-production time of direct workers		5,000
Selling and distribution overheads incurred		6,000
Other production overheads incurred		12,000
Sales		1,00,000
Cost of finished goods sold		80,000
Cost of goods completed and transferred into finished goods during the month		65,000
Physical value of Work-in-Progress at the end of the month		40,000

The production overhead absorption rate is 150% of direct wages charged to work-in-Progress.
Prepare the following accounts for the month :
(*a*) Stores Ledger Control A/c. (*b*) Work-In-Progress Control A/c. (*c*) Finished Goods Control A/c. (*d*) Production Overhead Control A/c. and (*e*) Profit and Loss A/c. ***[C.A. Inter]***

[Ans. Store Ledger A/c, Closing Balance 66,000; Finished Goods A/c 20,000; Profit as per Costing P/L A/c 20,000]

2. From the following information, you are required to pass Journal entries and prepare the necessary accounts under the integral system of accounts :

	Rs.
Material purchased on credit	29,600
Wages paid	33,600
Wages productive	29,600
Wages unproductive	4,000
Material issued to production	25,600
Works expenses incurred	13,000
Works expenses charged to production	17,200
Administration expenses charged to production	8,700
Administration expenses paid	8,800
Selling overheads charged to sales	9,000
Sales—Cash	78,000
Finished goods at cost	60,000

[M.Com. Bangalore, May 1992]

3. A fire destroyed some accounting records of a company. You have been able to collect the following from the spoilt papers/records and as a result of consultation with accounting staff in respect of January 1997 :

(*i*) Incomplete Ledger Entries :

Raw Materials A/c

Beginning Inventory	Rs. 32,000/-		

W.I.P A/c

Beginning Inventory	Rs. 9,200/-	Finished Stock	Rs. 1,51,000/-

Creditors A/c

Closing Balance	Rs. 19,200/-	Opening Balance	Rs. 16,400/-

Manufacturing Overhead A/c

Amount spent	Rs. 29,600/-		

Finished Goods A/c

Opening Inventory	Rs. 24,000/-	Closing Inventory	Rs. 30,000/-

(*ii*) Additional Information :

(1) The Cash book showed that Rs. 89,200 have been paid to creditors for raw materials.

(2) Ending inventory of WIP included material Rs. 5,000 on which 300 direct labour hours have been booked against wages and overheads.

(3) The job card showed that workers have worked for 7,000 hours. The wage rate is Rs. 10 per labour hour.

(4) Overhead recovery rate was Rs. 4 per direct labour hour.

You are required to complete the above accounts in the cost ledger of the Company.

[C.A. Inter May, 1997]

4. The following are the balances in the Cost Ledger of a manufacturing company on 1st January 2006 :

	Dr. *Rs.*	*Cr.* *Rs.*
Store Ledger	9,000	
Work-in-Progress Ledger	8,000	
Finished goods Ledger	10,000	
Financial Ledger		27,000
	27,000	27,000

Summary of the transactions during the year 2006 :

	Rs.
Material Purchased	15,000
Materials issued to jobs	16,000
Materials issued for repairs in factory	2,000
Direct wages paid	10,000
Indirect wages paid	2,000
Factory expenses paid	8,000
Administrative Expenses paid	9,000
Selling Expenses paid	5,000
Cost of finished goods produced	40,000
Cost of finished goods sold	55,000
Sales	90,000

Prepare control accounts and costing Profit & Loss account in the Cost Ledger assuming that the overheads recovered and incurred are the same and that administration overheads are charged to finished goods. *[B.U. B.Com (H) Adopted]*

[Ans. Store Ledger (Dr) : 6,000; Financial Ledger Control (Cr) Rs. 16,000; W.I.P. Led. Cont (Dr) Rs. 6,000; F.G.Led. cont. (Dr) 4,000; Cost of Sales : Rs. 60,000; Net profit Rs. 30,000.]

5. The following balances appeared in the books of M.K.Ltd. as on 1st January :

	Dr. *Rs.*	*Cr.* *Rs.*
General Ledger Adjustment A/c		15,200
Store Ledger Control A/c	8,750	
Work-in-Progress Control A/c	4,280	
Finished Goods Ledger Control A/c	2,170	
	15,200	15,200

On 31st December the following information was supplied :

	Rs.
Purchase of stores	60,640
Purchase of special Jobs	1,950
Direct Wages	38,627
Indirect Factory Wages	9,543
Administrative salary	6,731
Selling and Distribution	4,252
Production Expenses	10,432
Administrative expenses	9,556
Selling and Distribution expenses	6,430
Stores issued to production	56,501
Stores issued to maintenance A/c	2,586
Returns to suppliers	312
Production overhead absorbed by production	23,410
Administrative overhead absorbed by finished goods	15,150
Selling overhead recovered on sales	9,515
Production finished during the year	1,18,517
Finished goods sold at cost	1,33,382
Sales	1,55,000

You are required to record the entries in Cost Ledger for the year and prepare a Trial Balance. *[C.A. Inter]*

[Ans. T.B. Rs. 18,697]

6. Akash Ganga Co. Ltd. operates cost accounting and financial accounting system. The following is the list of opening balances as on 1.4.2001 in the Cost Ledger :

	Dr. *Rs.*	*Cr.* *Rs.*
Stores Ledger Control A/c	53,375	
W.I.P. Control A/c	1,04,595	
Finished Goods Control A/c	30,780	
General Ledger Adjustment A/c		1,88,750
	1,88,750	1,88,750

Transactions for the quarter ended 30.6.2001 are :

	Rs.
(*i*) Materials Purchased	26,700
(*ii*) Materials issued to production	40,000
(*iii*) Materials issued for factory repairs	900
(*iv*) Factory wages paid (including indirect wages Rs. 23,000)	77,500
(*v*) Production overhead incurred	95,200
(*vi*) Production overhead under absorbed	3,200
(*vii*) Sales	2,56,000

The company's gross profit is 25% on Factory Cost. At the end of the quarter, WIP stock increased by Rs. 7,500.

Prepare the relevant Control Accounts, Costing P/L A/c and General Ledger Adjustment A/c to record the above transactions for the year ended 31.3.2002. *[C.A. Inter Nov. 2001]*

[Ans. G.L.Adj A/c : (Cr) 1,80,150; S.L.Control : Dr. 39,175; W.I.P. Cont. A/c : Dr. 1,12,095; Costing P/L : Profit 48,000; T.B. = Rs. 1,80,150]

7. The following figures have been extracted from the cost records of Dastur Co. Ltd. :

Stores :

	Rs.
Opening balance	30,000
Purchases	1,60,000
Transfer from W.I.P.	80,000
Issues to W.I.P.	1,60,000
Issues to repairs and maintenance	20,000
Defficiencies found in stock-taking	6,000
Work-in-Progress :	
Opening balance	60,000
Direct wages applied	60,000
Overheads applied	2,40,000
Closing balance	40,000

Finished products : Entire output is sold at a profit of 10% on actual cost from work-in-progress.

Others : Wages incurred Rs. 70,000 ; overhead incurred Rs. 2,50,000.

Items not included in cost records : Income from investment Rs. 10,000 ; Loss on sale of capital Assets Rs. 20,000.

Draw-up Stores Control Account, Work-in-Progress Control A/c, Costing Profit and Loss Account, Profit & Loss A/c (financial) and Reconciliation Statement. *[I.C.W.A. (Inter)]*

[Ans. S.L.C. : Rs. 84,000; W/P : Rs. 40,000; Net Profit : Rs. 40,000 (Costing P/L); Loss as per Financial A/c Rs. 16,000]

8. On 31.3.2004, the following balances were extracted from the books of the Supreme Manufacturing Company :

	Dr. *Rs.*	*Cr.* *Rs.*
Stores Ledger Control A/c	35,000	—
W.I.P. Control A/c	38,000	
Finished Goods Control A/c	25,000	
Cost Ledger Control A/c	—	98,000
	98,000	98,000

The following transactions took place in April 2004 :

	Rs.
Raw Materials :	
Purchased	95,000
Returned to suppliers	3,000
Issued to Production	98,000
Returned to store	3,000
Productive wages	40,000
Indirect wages	25,000
Factory overhead expenses incurred	50,000
Selling and administration expenses	40,000
Cost of finished goods transferred to warehouse	2,13,000
Cost of goods sold	2,10,000
Sales	3,00,000

Factory overheads are applied to production at 150% of direct wages and under- or over-absorbed overheads being carried forward for adjustment in the subsequent months. All administrative and selling expenses are treated as period cost and charged-off to the Profit and Loss A/c of the month in which they are incurred.

Show the following accounts :

(a) Cost Ledger Control A/c (b) Stores Ledger Control Ac (c) W.I.P. Control A/c (d) Finished Stock Control A/c. (e) Factory Overhead Control A/c. (f) Costing Profit & Loss A/c. (g) Trial Balance as on 30.4.2004. *[C.A. Inter]*

[Ans. Total cost Rs. 2,50,000; Profit earned as per Cost Accounts Rs. 50,000; Total of Trial Balance Rs. 95,000]

9. Eutopia Manufacturing Co. Ltd. opens the costing records, with the balances as on 1st July as :

	Dr. Rs.	*Cr.* Rs.
Material Control A/c	1,24,000	
Work-in-Progress A/c	62,500	
Finished Goods A/c	1,24,000	
Production Overhead A/c	8,400	
Administration Overhead		12,000
Selling and Distribution Overhead A/c	6,250	
General Ledger Control A/c		3,13,150
	3,25,150	3,25,150

The following are the transactions for the quarter ending 30th September :

	Rs.
Materials Purchased	4,80,100
Materials issued to Jobs	4,77,400
Materials to Works maintenance	41,200
Materials to administration office	3,400
Materials to selling department	7,200
Direct Wages	1,49,300
Indirect Wages	65,000
Transportation for incoming materials	8,400
Production overhead	2,42,250
Absorbed overheads production	3,59,100
Administration Overheads	74,000
Administration allocation to production	52,900
Administration allocation to Sales	14,800
Sales Overhead	64,200
Sales Overheads absorbed	82,000
Finished goods produced	9,58,400
Finished goods sold	9,77,300
Sales Realisation	14,43,000

Make-up the various accounts as you envisage in the Cost Ledger and prepare a Trial Balance as at 31.7.2002. *[C.A. Final, May 2002]*

[Ans. Material Control A/c : Rs. 74,900 (Dr.) General Ledger Control A/c : Rs. 3,22,300 (Cr.). Profit : Rs. 3,68,900. Trial Balance total : Rs. 3,28,950.]

10 Reconciliation of Cost Accounts with Financial Accounts

Authors' Comments and Suggestions :

1. ***This chapter is important for degree course C.A. (Inter) and I.C.W.A. (Inter) students.***
2. ***Transactions exclusively relevant to Cost Accounts and Financial Accounts are to be identified and to be considered in the reconciliation statement.***
3. ***The amount of difference in items of costs or incomes appearing in both sets are to be identified and to be considered while prepairing reconciliation statement.***
4. ***Sometimes profit as per Cost Accounts and Financial Accounts are to be workedout first and thereafter reconciliation statement is to be prepared.***
5. ***In the method of absorption of overhead at pre-determined rates, there arises difference between the actual expenses and the pre-determined amount charged to cost accounts.***
6. ***If the profit shown in the Cost Ledger is taken as starting point and the amounts that give rise to differences are added or subtracted from it, the resultant figure should agree with the profit as shown in the Financial Ledger.***

Why reconciliation is needed ? Reasons for variation in profit—under or over absorption, Adoption of different methods of valuation, Items purely of financial nature, Items purely of cost accounts, Appropriations of profit not dealt with in the cost accounts; Steps for reconciliation; Advantages of reconciliation; Illustrations; Worked out problems; Exercise—Objective questions—Theory questions—Problems.

Reconciliation of Financial Accounts and Cost Accounts

Why Reconciliation is needed ?

In an enterprise which maintains two sets of accounts, viz. Financial Accounts and Cost Accounts, they will not generally agree with each other's profit figure. Because of that reason reconciliation is necessary in order to match these two profit figures. Besides, management is also interested to know the causes of differences in order to check the arithmetical accuracy of both sets of accounts. Thus this will facilitate internal control by highlighting the variations causing increase or decrease in profits. Such reconciliation is to be made at regular intervals. The figures of profit either as per cost ledger or as per financial ledger is taken as the starting points for reconciliation. For instance if profit shown in the cost ledger is taken first and the amount that gives rise to differences are added or deducted from it, the resultant figure should agree with the profit shown in financial ledgers.

Reasons for variation in Profit

(*a*) Under or over absorption of overhead
(*b*) Adoption of different methods of valuation of stock.
(*c*) Items purely of financial accounts.

(*d*) Items purely of cost accounts.
(*e*) Appropriation of profit not dealt with in the cost accounts.
(*f*) Others.

(a) Under or over absorption :

In cost accounts in order to ascertain unit cost of a product predetermined rates are charged in respects of overhead. The basis normally used are percentage on prime cost, rate per unit, percentage of direct wages, rate per labour of machine hour. When overhead is recovered on predetermined rates it may not exactly agree with overheads actually incurred during a period. The difference between overhead 'incurred' and the overhead 'recovered' is known as over/under absorption of overhead. In case of under absorption the costing profit will be higher than financial profit and in case of over absorption costing profit will be lower than the financial profit. Now in order to reconcile costing profit with financial profit two adjustments are necessary with financial profit :

(*i*) In case of under absorption of overhead, the amount of under absorption overhead will have to be added back to financial profit and
(*ii*) In case over absorption of overhead, the amount of over absorption overhead will have to be deducted from financial profit.

(b) Adoption of different methods of valuation of Stock :

In financial accounts the stock is valued based on the principal of "Cost or Market Value, whichever is lower". But in cost accounts the stock of raw materials are valued on the basis of FIFO, LIFO or other methods of pricing issues, WIP may be valued at prime cost or prime cost plus variable cost or prime cost plus variable and fixed overhead. Thus the stock valuation under two sets of accounts will be different and, as such, reconciliation is necessary. This reconciliation will be easier if the following principles are followed :

(*i*) The lower the opening stock the higher will be the profit, and
(*ii*) The higher the closing stock the higher is the profit, and vise versa.

For instance if the opening stock figures are more in financial accounts, profit as per financial accounts are to be increased to arrive at the profit as per cost accounts, and vise versa.

(c) Items purely of financial nature :

There are some items which are of purely financial nature having no counterpart in cost accounting. This will lead to difference in profit. The common financial expenses are :

(1) Lapses on sale of fixed assets.
(2) Interest on bank loan, debentures, mortgage etc.
(3) Remuneration paid to proprietor in excess at fair reward for services rendered.
(4) Damages payable at Law.
(5) Penalties payable.
(6) Preliminary expenses or goodwill written-off.
(7) Cost for issue of shares, debentures and bonds.
(8) Discount on issue of bonds, debentures etc.

On the other hand, the common financial incomes are :

(1) Profit on sale of Fixed assets.
(2) Interest received on bank deposits.
(3) Interest, dividends etc. received on investments.
(4) Rent received.
(5) Fees or commission received on issue of shares, debentures etc.
(6) Transfer fees received.

(d) Items purely of cost accounts :

The items which appear only in cost accounts generally are :

(1) Interest on capital supplied by the proprietor.

(2) Rent on own premises.

(3) Depreciation on fully depreciated assets.

(e) Appropriations of profit not dealt with in the cost accounts :

(1) Transfer to Reserve or other funds.

(2) Corporate tax.

(3) Dividend paid.

(4) Additional provisions for depreciation, bad debts etc.

(5) Appropriation to sinking funds for the purpose of providing for repayment of loans or debentures.

(f) Others :

There are some other items which may lead to difference in profits in two sets of accounts. For example, the rates and methods of charging depreciation may vary in two sets of accounts. Someone may adopt the method of charging direct wages to cost of products at predetermined rates. This will result in a difference between the predetermined amount charged to cost accounts and the actual wages booked in the financial accounts.

Steps for Reconciliation

Step 1

Start with a profit as base as per any set of books (either cost or financial).

Step 2

Items of expenditures already deducted to calculate the above base profit, but not considered for profit shown by other set should be added back.

Step 3

Items of income already added to calculate the above base profit but not considered for profit shown by other set should be deducted.

Step 4

Similarly, the expenditures not taken into account in calculating the base profit should be deducted.

Step 5

The incomes not taken into accounts in calculating the base profit should be added back.

Step 6

The expenditures under-charged for calculating base profit should be deducted.

Step 7

The amount of income under-stated in calculating base profit should be added.

Step 8

The expenditures over-stated in calculating base profit should be added.

Step 9

The income over-stated in calculating base profit should be deducted.

Step 10

The resultant figures will be the profit as per the other set of books.

Advantages of Reconciliation

Although in a interlocking system both cost and financial accounts are to be maintained separately, it is preferred to integrated system, because of the following advantages :

(1) As the two profits are ascertained independentiy, arithmetical inaccuracies, if any, are detected quickly.

(2) From the magnitude of variations validity of cost account can be judged. As for example, a high under-absorption of overhead indicates that products are under cost.

(3) Further variation may also indicate inefficiency which required controlling measures.

(4) Frauds may also be detected if there is any wide difference in value of physical stock and the stock as per books of accounts.

(5) Independency of cost book is preferred as these are not relevant to preparing profit and loss account and so not subject to statutory audit.

Illustration

The following is available from the financial books of a company having a normal production capacity of 60,000 units for the year ended 31st March 1995 :

(*i*) Sales Rs. 10,00,000 (50,000 units)

(*ii*) There was no opening and closing stock of finished units.

(*iii*) Direct material and direct wages cost were Rs. 5,00,000 and Rs. 2,50,000, respectively.

(*iv*) Actual factory expenses were Rs. 15,00,000 of which 60% are fixed.

(*v*) Actual administrative expenses were Rs. 45,000 which are completely fixed.

(*vi*) Actual selling and distribution expenses were Rs. 30,000 of which 40% are fixed.

(*vii*) Interest and dividends received Rs. 15,000.

You are required to :

(*a*) Find out profit as per financial books for the year ended 31st March 1995.

(*b*) Prepare the cost sheet and ascertain the profit as per cost accounts for the year ended 31st March 1995 assuming that the indirect expenses are absorbed on the basis of normal production capacity, and

(*c*) Prepare a statement reconciling profits shown by financial and cost books.

[C.A. Inter, May 1995]

Solution

As per Financial Books
Profit & Loss A/c
(for the year ended 31st March 1995)

	Rs.		*Rs.*
To Direct Material	5,00,000	By Sales (50,000 units)	10,00,000
To Direct wages	2,50,000	By Interest & Dividend	15,000
To Factory Expenses (Actual)	1,50,000		
To Administrative Expenses	45,000		
To S & D expenses	30,000		
Profit	40,000		
	10,15,000		10,15,000

Cost Sheet

For the year ended 31st March 1995

Normal Production capacity (units)		60,000
Sales/Production units		50,000
	Rs.	*Rs.*
Direct materials		5,00,000
Direct wages		2,50,000
Prime cost		7,50,000
Factory overhead (variable)	60,000	
Fixed Rs. 90,000 × 5/6	75,000	1,35,000
Work cost		8,85,000
Administrative expenses Rs. 45,000 × 5/6		37,500
Total cost of production		9,22,500
Selling & Distribution expenses		
Variable	18,000	
Fixed Rs. 12,000 × 5/6	10,000	28,000
Cost of sales		9,50,500
Profit (balance)		49,500
Sales		10,00,000

Reconciliation Statement

Profit as per cost account	49,500	
Add : Income from dividend (Not considered in cost A/c)	15,000	64,500
Less : Expenses under-charged in cost A/c		
(*i*) Factory expenses (1,50,000 – 1,35,000)	15,000	
(*ii*) Admn. Expenses (45,000 – 37,500)	7,500	
(*iii*) Selling & distribution (30,000 – 28,000)	2,000	24,500
Profit as per financial accounts		40,000

Illustration

From the following figures prepare a statement reconciling the profits as per the cost accounts and the profits as per the financial accounts :

	Rs.
Net Profit as per the financial accounts	1,28,755
Net Profit as per the cost accounts	1,72,400
Works overhead under-recovered	3,120
Admn. Overheads over-recovered	1,700
Depreciation charged in the financial accounts	11,200
Depreciation charged in the cost accounts	12,500
Interest received but not included in the cost accounts	8,000
Loss due to obsolescence charged in the financial accounts	5,700
Income-tax provided in the financial accounts	40,300
Stores adjustment credited in the financial accounts	475
Depreciation of stock charged in the financial accounts	6,750
Bank interest credited in the financial accounts	750

[I.C.W.A. Inter]

Solution

Reconciliation Statement

	Rs.	Rs.
Net Profit as per the cost Accounts		1,72,400
Less : Works overheads under-recovered	3,120	
Loss due to obsolescence charged in the financial accounts	5,700	
Income-tax provided in the financial accounts	40,300	
Depreciations of stock charged in the financial accounts	6,750	55,870
		1,16,530
Add : Admn. Overhead over-recovered	1,700	
Excess depreciation charged in the cost a/c. 12,500 – 11,200	1,300	
Interest received but not included in the cost accounts	8,000	
Stores adjustment credited in the financial accounts	475	
Bank interest credited in the financial accounts	750	12,225
Net Profit as per the financial accounts		1,28,755

WORKEDOUT PROBLEMS

Problem 1

Given below is the Trading and Profit and Loss A/c of a company for the year ended 31st March 1998 :

	Rs.			Rs.
To Materials	27,40,000	By Sales (60,000 units)		60,00,000
To Wages	15,10,000	By Stock (2000 units)		1,60,000
To Factory expenses	8,30,000	By WIP :		
To Admn. Expenses	3,82,400	Materials	64,000	
To Selling expenses	4,50,000	Wages	36,000	
To Preliminary expenses	60,000	Factory expenses	20,000	1,20,000
Net Profit	3,25,600	By Dividend received		18,000
	62,98,000			62,98,000

The company manufactures standard units. In the Cost Account

(*a*) Factory expenses have been allocated to production at 20% of Prime Cost.

(*b*) Admn. Expenses at Rs. 6 per unit produced, and

(*c*) Selling expenses at Rs. 8 per unit sold.

Prepare the costing Profit and Loss Accounts of the Company and reconcile the same with the profit disclosed by the Financial Accounts.

[C.A. Inter, May 1993, May 1992, I.C.W.A. Inter, June 1993]

Solution

To Materials (Note a)	26,76,000	By Sales	60,00,000
To Wages (Note b)	14,74,000	By Closing Stock (Note f)	1,72,646
To Factory expenses (Note c)	8,30,000		
To Admn. Expenses (Note d)	3,72,000		
To Selling expenses (Note e)	4,80,000		
To Net Profit	3,40,646		
	61,72,646		61,72,646

Reconciliation Statement

Particulars	*Rs.*	*Rs.*
Profit as per Cost Accounts		3,40,646
Add :		
(*i*) Dividend not included in Cost Accounts	18,000	
(*ii*) Factory expenses over-absorbed in Cost Accounts (Rs. 8,30,000 – 8,10,000)	20,000	
(*iii*) Selling overhead over-absorbed in Cost Accounts (Rs. 4,80,000 – 4,50,000)	30,000	68,000
		4,08,646
Less :		
(*i*) Preliminary expenses not included in Cost Accounts.	60,000	
(*ii*) Admn. Overhead under-absorbed (Rs. 3,82,400 – 3,72,000)	10,400	
(*iii*) Closing Stock under-valued in Cost Accounts. (Rs. 1,72,646 – 1,60,000)	12,646	83,046
Profit as per Financial Accounts		3,25,600

Working Notes :

(*a*) Material = Rs. 27,40,000 – Rs. 64,000 = Rs. 26,76,000

(*b*) Wages = Rs. 15,10,000 – Rs. 36,000 = Rs. 14,74,000

(*c*) Factory expenses = 20% of Prime Cost = (Rs. 26,76,000 + 14,74,000) × 20% = Rs. 8,30,000

(*d*) Admn. Expenses = 62,000 units × Rs. 6 = Rs. 3,72,000

(*e*) Selling expenses = 60,000 units × Rs. 8 = Rs. 4,80,000

(*f*) Closing stock : [(26,76,000 + 14,74,000 + 8,30,000 + 3,72,000) ÷ 62,000] × 2,000 = Rs. 1,72,646.

Problem 2

The financial records of Modern Manufactures Ltd. reveals the following for the year ended 30.6.2004 :

(Rs. In thousands)

	Rs.	*Rs.*
Sales (20,000 units)		4,000
Materials		1,600
Wage		800
Factory overheads		720
Office and administrative overhead		416
Selling and Distribution overheads		288
Finished goods (1,230 units)		240
Work-in-Progress :		
Materials	48	
Labour	32	
Overheads (Factory)	32	112
Goodwill written-off		320
Interest on Capital		32

In the costing records, factory overhead is charged at 100% wages, administration overhead 10% of factory cost and selling and distribution overhead at the rate of Rs. 16 per unit sold.

Prepare a statement reconciling the profit as per cost records with the profit as per financial records of the company. ***[C.A. Inter, Nov. 1996]***

Solution

First of all it is necessary to find out profit as per financial accounts and as per cost accounts.

Profit & Loss A/c. of Modern Manufactures Ltd.
For the year ended 30th June 2004

	Rs.		Rs.
To Materials	1,600	By Sales (20,000)	4,000
To Wages	800	By Closing Stock :	
To Factory Overhead	720	Finished stock (1,230 units)	240
To Office & Admn. Overheads	416	WIP	112
To Selling & Distribution overhead	288		
To Goodwill written-off	320		
To Interest on capital	32		
To Net profit	176		
	4,352		4,352

Profit as per Cost Accounts

	Rs. '000
Materials	1,600·00
Wages	800·00
Prime Cost	2,400·00
Factory Overheads (100% of wages)	800·00
Factory Cost (Gross)	3,200.00
Less : Closing WIP	112·00
Factory Cost (21,230 units)	3,088.00
Office and admn. Overheads (10% of factory cost)	308.80
Total cost of production	3,396.80
Less : Closing Stock (finished goods) Note-1.	196·80
Cost of production of 20,000 units	3,200.00
Selling & distribution overheads Rs. 16 per units.	320·00
Cost of sales	3,520.00
Sales realisation for 20,000 units	4,000·00
Profit	480·00

Note 1 : Total cost of production (Rs. 33,96,800) ÷ Total number of units produced (21230 units) = Rs. 160 per unit. Cost of 1230 units = 1,230 × 160 = Rs. 1,96,800.

Statement reconciling the Profit as per Cost Accounts and Profit as per Financial Accounts

	Rs. '000	Rs. '000
Profit as per Cost Accounts		480.00
Add : Over-absorbed overheads :		
Factory overheads (800 – 720)	80.00	
Selling & distribution overheads (320 – 288)	32.00	
Over-valued closing stock in financial accounts (240 – 196.80)	43.20	155.20
		635.20
Less : Under-absorbed office & administration overhead (416.00 – 308.80)	107.20	
Goodwill debited in financial accounts only	320.00	
Interest of capital charged in financial accounts	32.00	459.20
Profit as per Financial Accounts		176.00

Problem 3

The following is the summarised Trading and Profit and Loss Account of T. Ltd. for the year ended 31st December 2004 :

	Rs.		*Rs.*	*Rs.*
Materials consumed	7,08,000	Sales		15,00,000
Direct wages	3,71,000	Finished stock (1,000 units)		40,000
Works overheads	2,13,000	Work in progress :		
Admn. Overheads	95,000	Materials	17,000	
Selling and Distribution OH	1,13,500	Wages	8,000	
Net Profit for the year	69,000	Works OH	5,000	30,000
	15,70,000			15,70,000

The company's cost records show that in course of manufacturing a standard unit (i) works overheads have been charged @ 20% on prime cost, (ii) Administration overheads have been recovered at Rs. 3 per finished unit, and (iii) selling and distribution overheads have been recovered at Rs. 4 per unit sold. The under absorbed overheads have not been adjusted in the Costing Profit and Loss A/c.

You are required to prepare (i) the Costing Profit and Loss Account indicating the net profit (ii) a statement reconciling the profit as disclosed by the cost accounts and that shown in the financial accounts. *[C.A. Inter, I.C.W.A. Inter]*

Solution

(i) Closing Profit & Loss A/c for the year ended 31st December 2004

	Rs.		*Rs.*
Material consumed	7,08,000	Sales (30,000 units)	15,00,000
Direct wages	3,71,000		
Prime cost	10,79,000		
Works overhead (20% of prime cost)	2,15,800		
	12,94,800		
Less : Work-in progress	30,000		
Factory cost	12,64,800		
Admn. Overheads @ Rs. 3 per unit	93,000		
Cost of production of goods produced	13,57,800		
Less : Finished stock	40,000		
Cost of production of goods sold	13,17,800		
Selling and distribution overheads @ Rs. 4 per unit sold	1,20,000		
Cost of sales	14,37,800		
Net Profit (balancing figure)	62,200		
	15,00,000		15,00,000

(ii) Statement reconciling the profit as per Costing Profit and Loss Account with the profit as per Financial Account

	Rs.	*Rs.*
Profit as per cost records		62,200
Add : Over-absorbed overheads :		
Works (2,15,800 – 2,13,000)	2,800	
Selling and Distribution (1,20,000 – 1,13,500)	6,500	9,300
		71,500
Less : Under absorbed admn. overheads (95,500 – 93,000)		2,500
Profit as per financial accounts		69,000

● Units produced = Number of units sold + finished stock = 30,000 + 1,000 = 31,000.

Problem 4

Gain More Ltd. showed a net loss of Rs. 6,30,000 as per the financial accounts for the year ended 31st March 2007. The cost accounts however disclosed a loss of Rs. 5,00,000 for the same period. On scrutiny of the two accounts the following are available :

Factory overheads under-recovered	70,000
Administrative overheads over-recovered	30,000
Depreciation charged to financial accounts	1,50,000
Depreciation charged in cost accounts	1,20,000
Interest on investment not included in cost accounts	30,000
Income tax provided in financial accounts	1,00,000
Stores adjustments (credit in financial accounts)	10,000

Prepare a Memorandum Reconciliation Accounts. *[I.C.W.A. Adopted]*

Solution

Gain More Ltd.

Memorandum Reconciliation Accounts for the year ended 31st March 2007

Particulars	*Rs.*	*Particulars*	*Rs.*
To Loss as per Financial Accounts	6,30,000	By Factory overhead under-recovered	70,000
To Admn. Overheads over-recovered	30,000	By Deprn. undercharged in cost Accounts (1,50,000 – 1,20,000)	30,000
To Interest on investment not included in Cost Accounts	30,000	By Provision for income tax not taken in Cost Accounts	1,00,000
To Store adjustments credited in financial accounts	10,000	By Balance c/d (net loss as per Cost accounts)	5,00,000
	7,00,000		7,00,000

Problem 5

The following figures have been extracted from the Financial Accounts of a manufacturing firm for the first year of its operation :

	Rs.
Direct Materials consumption	50,00,000
Direct Wages	30,00,000
Factory overheads	16,00,000
Administrative overheads	7,00,000
Selling and Distribution overheads	9,60,000
Bad Debt	80,000
Preliminery expenses written-off	40,000
Legal Charges	10,000
Dividend Received	1,00,000
Interest received on Deposits	20,000
Sales (1,20,000 units)	1,20,00,000
Closing Stock (4,000 units)	3,20,000
Work-in-Progress	2,40,000

The Cost Accounts for the same period revealed that the direct material consumption was Rs. 56,00,000. Factory overhead is recovered at 20% on prime cost. Administration overhead is recovered at Rs. 6 per unit of production. Selling and distribution overheads are recovered at Rs. 8 per unit sold.

Prepare the Profit & Loss Account both as per Financial records and as per Cost records. *[C.A. Inter]*

Solution

Dr. **Financial Profit & Loss A/c** *Cr.*

Particulars	*Rs.*	*Particulars*	*Rs.*
To Direct Materials	50,00,000	By Sales (1,20,000 units @ Rs. 100 each)	1,20,00,000
" Direct Wages	30,00,000	" Closing Stock :	
" Factory overheads	16,00,000	Work-in-Progress	2,40,000
" Gross Profit c/d	29,60,000	Finished Goods (4,000 units @ Rs. 80)	3,20,000
	1,25,60,000		1,25,60,000
To Administration overheads	7,00,000	By Gross Profit b/d	29,60,000
" Selling and Distribution overheads	9,60,000	" Dividend received	1,00,000
" Bad Debts	80,000	" Interest on Deposits	20,000
" Preliminery Expenses written-off	40,000		
" Legal Charges	10,000		
" Net Profit	12,90,000		
	30,80,000		30,80,000

Dr. **Costing Profit & Loss A/c** *Cr.*

Particulars	*Rs.*	*Particulars*	*Rs.*
To Direct Materials Consumed	56,00,000	By Prime Cost C/d	86,00,000
" Direct wages	30,00,000		
	86,00,000		86,00,000
To Prime Cost B/d	86,00,000	By Closing W.I.P.	2,40,000
" Factory Overhead (20% on Prime cost of Rs. 86,00,000)	17,20,000	" Works cost c/d (1,24,000 units produced)	1,00,80,000
	1,03,20,000		1,03,20,000
To Works Cost b/d	1,00,80,000	By Closing Finished Goods	
" Administration Overhead	7,44,000	$(1,08,24,000 \times \frac{4,000}{1,24,000})$	3,49,161
(Rs. 6 per unit for 1,24,000 units produced)		By Cost of Goods sold c/d	1,04,74,839
	1,08,24,000		1,08,24,000
To Cost of Goods sold b/d	1,04,74,839	By Sales	1,20,00,000
" S/D overhead	9,60,000	(1,20,000 Units @ Rs. 100 each)	
To Profit	5,65,161		
	1,20,00,000		1,20,00,000

Reconciliation Statement

Particulars	*Rs.*	*Rs.*
Profit as per Cost Accounts		5,65,161
Add : (*a*) Excess Materials consumed as per Cost Accounts (56,00,000 – 50,00,000)	6,00,000	
(*b*) Excess Factory overheads in Cost Accounts (17,20,000 – 16,00,000)	1,20,000	
(*c*) Excess Administration Overheads in Cost Accounts (7,44,000 – 7,00,000)	44,000	
(*d*) Dividend credited to Financial A/c	1,00,000	
(*e*) Interest credited to financial A/c	20,000	8,84,000
		14,49,161
Less : (*a*) Bad Debts charged in Financial A/c	80,000	
(*b*) Preliminery Expenses charged in Financial A/c	40,000	
(*c*) Legal charges debited in Financial A/c	10,000	
(*d*) Closing Stock of Finished goods overvalued in Cost Accounts (3,49,161 – 3,20,000)	29,161	1,59,161
Profit as per Financial Accounts		12,90,000

EXERCISES

OBJECTIVE TYPE QUESTIONS

1. *Indicate whether the following statements are true or false :*

(*a*) Costing profit and loss account includes all items of financial nature which are not included in cost ascertainment.

(*b*) Dividend received but not included in cost accounts is to be added back to costing profit in reconciling profit with financial profit.

(*c*) Cost and financial accounts are reconciled under non-integral accounting.

(*d*) Rent on owned building is not included in cost accounts.

(*e*) Income Tax is provided in cost accounts only.

(*f*) Over-absorption of production overheads in cost accounts is decided is costing profit to reconcile it with profit as per financial book.

[Ans. True : (*b*), (*c*) False : (*a*), (*d*), (*e*), (*f*)]

2. *Indicate whether the following statements are true or false :*

(*a*) The need of reconciliation arises only under integrated accounting system.

(*b*) There is only one figure of profit under integral accounting system.

(*c*) No accounts for debtors and creditors are opened in integrated accounts.

(*d*) Integrated accounts eliminate the necessity of operating General Ledger Control Accounts.

(*e*) Loss on the sale of capital assets is not included in accounts under integral system.

[Ans. True : (*b*), (*d*) False. (*a*), (*c*), (*e*)]

THEORETICAL QUESTIONS

1. Why is it necessary to reconcile the profits as shown by the cost and financial accounts ? Summarise the various causes for such differences. *[C.S. Inter, Dec. 1990]*
2. Enumerate the items which are generally excluded from Cost Accounts. *[B.Com. Delhi 1988]*
3. Why is it important that Cost Accounts and Financial Accounts should be capable of reconciliation one with the other ? *[I.C.W.A. Inter, June 1983]*
4. State the reasons for the difference between the profits shown in the cost accounts and those shown in the financial accounts of an industrial organisation. *[I.C.W.A. Inter, June 1991]*
5. There is generally a divergence between 'Financial Profit' and 'Cost Profit'. Explain this statement and give reasons for such divergence. *[C.S. Inter, June 1997]*
6. "Reconciliation of cost and financial accounts in the modern computer age is redundant." Comment. *[C.A. Inter, May 1998]*

PROBLEMS

1. M/s Rana Traders have furnished the following information from financial books for the year ended 30th June 1988 :

Trading and Profit & Loss A/c for the year ended 30th June 2004

Particulars	*Rs.*	*Particulars*	*Rs.*
To Opening Stock (500 units at Rs. 35 each)	17,500	By Sales (10,250 units)	7,17,500
To Raw material consumed	2,60,000	By Closing stock (250 units at Rs. 50 each)	12,500
Wages	1,50,000		
Gross Profit	3,02,500		
	7,30,000		7,30,000
To Factory overheads	94,700		
To Office overheads	1,06,000		
To Selling expenses	55,000		
To Bad debts	4,000	By Gross profit	3,02,500
To Goodwill written-off	5,000	By Interest	250
To Net Profit	48,050	By Rent	10,000
	3,12,750		3,12,750

The cost sheet shows the following :

(*a*) Cost of materials at Rs. 26 per unit and labour cost Rs. 15 per unit produced.
(*b*) Factory overheads are absorbed at 60% of labour cost.
(*c*) Office overheads are absorbed at 20% of factory cost.
(*d*) Selling expenses are charged at Rs. 6 per unit.
(*e*) Opening stock of finished goods is valued at Rs. 45 per unit and closing stock as in financial books.

You are required to prepare

(*i*) a statement showing cost and profit as per cost accounts for the year ended 30th June 2004, and
(*ii*) statement showing the reconciliation of profit disclosed in cost accounts with the profit shown in financial accounts.

[Ans. (i) Cost and profit as per Cost Accounts : Rs. 6,71,500; 46,000]

[C.S. Inter]

2. During the year ended 31st January 2004 the profit of a company as per Financial Profit and Loss A/c was Rs. 33,248 as given below. Prepare a reconciliation statement and arrive at the profit as per Cost Accounts using the additional information given :

Profit and Loss A/c for the year ended 31st January 2004

Particulars	*Rs.*	*Particulars*	*Rs.*
To Opening Stock	4,94,358	By Sales	6,93,000
To Purchases	1,64,308	By Sundry Income	632
	6,58,666		
Less : Closing Stock	1,50,242		
Material Consumed	5,08,424		
To Direct wages	46,266		
To Factory overhead	41,652		
To Admn. Expenses	19,690		
To Selling expenses	44,352		
To Net Profit	33,248		
	6,93,632		6,93,632

The Costing Records show :

(i) Closing Stock Rs. 1,56,394

(ii) Direct Wages absorbed Rs. 49,734

(iii) Factory overhead absorbed Rs. 39,428

(iv) Admn. Expenses calculated at 3% of sales

(v) Selling expenses absorbed @ 5% of sales *[I.C.W.A. Inter]*

[Ans. Profit as per Cost Accounts : Rs. 46,126]

3. The following figures have been extracted from the Financial Accounts of a Manufacturing Firm the first year of its operation :

Particulars		Rs.
Direct material consumption		50,00,000
Direct Wages		30,00,000
Factory overheads		16,00,000
Administrative Overheads		7,00,000
Selling and Distribution overheads		9,60,000
Bad debts		80,000
Preliminary expenses written-off		40,000
Legal charges		10,000
Dividends received		1,00,000
Interest received on deposits		20,000
Sales (1,20,000 units)		1,20,000
Closing stock :		
Finished goods (4,000 units)		3,20,000
Work-in-Progress		2,40,000

The cost accounts for the same period reveal that the direct material consumption was Rs. 56,00,000. Factory overhead is recovered at 20% on prime cost. Administration overhead is recovered at Rs. 6 per unit of production. Selling and distribution overheads are recovered at Rs. 8 per unit sold.

Prepare the Profit and Loss Accounts both as per financial records and as per cost records. Reconcile the Profit as per the two records. *[C.A. Inter May, 1990]*

[Ans. Profit as per Financial Accounts : Rs. 12,90,000 & as per Cost Accounts : Rs. 5,65,160]

4. A company profit as per the costing system was Rs. 46,126 whereas the audited financial accounts showed a profit of Rs. 33,248. From the following additional information you are required to prepare a reconciliation statement, showing clearly the reasons for the difference between the two figures :

	Rs.	Rs.		Rs.
Opening stock	4,94,358		Sales	6,93,000
Purchase	1,64,308			
	6,58,666			
Closing stock	1,50,242	5,08,424		
Direct wages		46,266		
Factory overheads		41,652		
Gross profit c/d		96,658		
		6,93,000		6,93,000
Admn. Expenses		19,690	Gross profit	96,658
Selling expenses		44,352	Sundry Income	632
Net Profit		33,248		
		97,290		97,290

The cost records show :

(i) Closing stock balance of Rs. 1,56,394.

(ii) Direct wages absorbed during the year Rs. 49,734.

(iii) Factory overhead absorbed Rs. 39,428.

(*iv*) Administration expenses charged @ 3% on sales.
(*v*) Selling expenses charged @ 5% of value of sales.
(*vi*) No mention of Sundry income. ***[C.S. Inter, June 1995]***

[Ans. Add Rs. 632.00, Rs. 3,468.00 & Rs. 1,100.00 to the profit as per Cost A/c. and deduct Rs. 6,152.00, Rs. 2,224.00 & Rs. 9,702.00]

5. The following is a summary of the Trading and Profit and Loss Account of a manufacturing company for the year ended 31st March 1988 :

Particulars	*Rs. '000*	*Particulars*	*Rs. '000*
To Material consumed	2,740	By Sales (1,20,000 units)	6,000
Wages	1,510	Finished stock (4,000 units)	160
Factory expenses	830	Work in progress :	
		Materials Rs. 64.00	
		Wages Rs. 36.00	
		Factory expenses Rs. 20.00	120
Administration expenses	382		
Selling and distribution expenses	450		
Preliminary expenses	40		
Goodwill written-off	20	Dividend received	18
Net Profit	326		
	6,298		6,298

In the cost accounts, the following allocations have been made :

(*a*) Factory expenses at 20% on prime cost.
(*b*) Administration expenses at Rs. 3 per unit of production.
(*c*) Selling and Distribution expenses at Rs. 4 per unit of sales.

You are required to prepare a costing profit and loss account of the company and to reconcile the profit disclosed with that shown in the financial account. ***[C.S. Inter, June 1990]***

[Ans. Profit as per cost accounts Rs. 3,41,000]

6. From the accounts of XYZ Ltd. the following Manufacturing, Trading and Profit and Loss Account for the year ended 31st December 2004 is extracted :

Particulars	*Rs.*	*Particulars*	*Rs.*
To Raw Materials :		By Raw Materials :	
Opening Stock	59,000	" Closing Stock	64,000
" R.M. Purchases	3,73,000	" W.I.P.	
" Wages paid	5,62,000	Materials	8,000
" Wages Accrued	34,000	Wages	11,000
" Factory Expenses	3,81,500	Factory Expenses	6,600
		" Cost of goods (18,000 units) Manufactured	13,19,900
	14,09,500		14,09,500
To Cost of Goods Manufactured	13,19,900	By Sales	18,24,000
" Administration Expenses	2,45,000	(15,200 units)	
" S/D Expenses	3,28,000	" Finished Stock	
" Preliminery Exp. (Written-off)	20,000	(2,800 units)	2,35,200
" Goodwill Written-off	15,000	" Interest on Investments	2,600
" Net profit transferred to Appropriation A/c	1,44,900	" Dividend earned	11,000
	20,72,800		20,72,800

The following procedure is adopted in connection with the costing of the product :

(a) Factory Expenses are allocated to production at 60% of direct labour cost.

(b) Administration expenses are applied at Rs. 12 per unit over the units produced.

(c) Selling and distribution expenses are charged so as to work out 20% of selling price.

Prepare costing Profit & Loss Account and the statement of reconciliation between the Profit or Loss as per the two accounts. *[C.A. (Final) Adopted]*

[Ans. Profit as per Cost Accounts : Rs. 1,82,400]

7. M/s. S. V. Ltd. has furnished you the following information from the financial books for the year ended 30th June 1980 :

Profit & Loss A/c

For the year ended 30th June 1980

Particulars	*Rs.*	*Particulars*	*Rs.*
Opening Stock (500 units at Rs. 35 each)	17,500	Sales : (10,259 units)	7,17,500
Materials consumed	2,60,000	Closing Stock : (250 units at Rs. 50 each)	12,500
Wages	1,50,000		
Gross profit c/d	3,02,500		
	7,30,000		7,30,000
Factory overheads	94,750	Gross Profit b/d	3,02,500
Administration overheads	1,06,000	Interest	250
Selling expenses	55,000	Rent received	10,000
Bad debts	4,000		
Preliminary expenses	5,000		
Net Profit	48,000		
	3,12,750		3,12,750

The cost sheet shows the cost of materials as Rs. 26 per unit and the labour cost Rs. 15 per unit, the factory overheads are absorbed at 60% of labour cost and administration overheads at 20% of factory cost.

Selling expenses are charged at Rs. 6 per unit, the opening stock of finished goods is valued at Rs. 45 per unit.

You are required to prepare :

(a) A statement showing profit as per cost accounts for the year ended 30th June 1980.

(b) A statement showing the reconciliation of profit disclosed in cost accounts with the profit shown in financial accounts. *[C.A. (Inter)]*

[Ans. Profit as per cost accounts Rs. 48,500]

8. The following is the Trading and Profit & Loss A/c of Time and Tide Ltd for the year ended on 31st December 2003 :

Dr. *Cr.*

Particulars	*Rs.*	*Particulars*	*Rs.*	*Rs.*
To Materials Consumed	7,08,000	By Sales (30,000 units)		15,00,000
" Direct Wages	3,71,000	" Finished Stock (1,000 units)		40,000
" Works overhead	2,13,000	" Work-in-Progress :		
" Administration overheads	95,500	Material	17,000	
" Selling and Distribution overheads	1,13,500	Wages	8,000	
" Net Profit for the year	69,000	Works overhead	5,000	30,000
	15,70,000			15,70,000

Manufacturing a standard unit, the company's cost record shows that :

(*i*) Works overheads have been charged to Work-in-Progress at 20% on Prime Cost;

(*ii*) Administration overheads have been recovered at Rs. 3 per finished unit;

(*iii*) Selling and Distribution overheads have been recovered at Rs. 4 per unit sold;

(*iv*) The under-absorbed or overabsorbed overheads have not been adjusted into costing Profit & Loss A/c.

Prepare (*a*) Costing Profit & Loss Account indicating net profit and (*b*) a statement reconciling the profit as disclosed by Cost Accounts and that shown in Financial Accounts.

[Delhi Univ. B.Com. (H)]

[Ans. Total cost Rs. 14,34,000; Value of closing Finished goods Rs. 43,800; Profit as per Cost Accounts Rs. 66,000. (Assume opening stock of finished goods and Work-in-Progress are all nil; (b) Quantity of production = 30,000 + 1,000 = 31,000 units. So cost of production per unit = 13,57,800 ÷ 31,000 = Rs. 43.80]

9. M/s Sellwell Ltd has furnished you the following information from the financial books for the year ended 31st December 1993 :

Dr. **Profit & Loss Account** *Cr.*

Particulars	*Rs.*	*Particulars*	*Rs.*
To Opening Stock of finished goods		By Sales (10,250 units)	3,58,750
(500 units @ 17·50)	8,750	" Closing stock of finished goods	6,250
" Materials consumed	1,30,000	(250 units @ Rs. 25 each)	
" Wages	75,000		
" Gross Profit c/d	1,51,250		
	3,65,000		3,65,000
To Factory overheads	47,375	By Gross profit c/d	1,51,250
" Admn. overheads	53,000	" Interest	125
" Selling expenses	27,500	" Rent received	5,000
" Bad Debts	2,000		
" Preliminery expenses	2,500		
" Net profit	24,000		
	1,56,375		1,56,375

The cost sheet shows :

(*i*) The cost of materials at Rs. 13 per unit.

(*ii*) The labour cost at Rs. 7·50 per unit.

(*iii*) The factory overheads are absorbed at 60% of labour cost.

(*iv*) Selling expenses are charged at Rs. 3 per unit.

(*v*) The opening stock of finished goods is valued at Rs. 22·50 per unit.

You are required to prepare :

(*i*) The cost sheet showing the number of units produced and the cost of production.

(*ii*) The statement of profit or loss as per cost accounts for the year ended 31st Dec. 1993.

(*iii*) Statement of Reconciliation. *[C.A. Inter, May 1994]*

[Ans. (*i*) Cost of production : Rs. 3,00,000; Rs. 30·00 per unit. (*ii*) Profit as per cost : Rs. 24,250; (*iii*) Profit as per Finance : 24,000]

10. The following is a summary of the Trading and Profit and Loss Account of ABC Ltd. for the year ended 31st Dec. :

Particulars	*Rs.*	*Particulars*	*Rs.*	*Rs.*
Direct Materials	69,800	Sales (60,000 units)		1,50,000
Direct Wages	38,100	Finished Stock (2,000 units)		4,000
Production overhead	21,300	Work-in-Progress :		
Administration overhead	9,550	Materials	1,600	
Selling and Dist. Overhead	11,350	Wages	900	
Preliminery Expenses written-off	1,000	Production overead	500	3,000
Goodwill written-off	2,350	Dividend Received		13,500
Dividend (Net)	2,500			
Taxation	5,000			
Net Profit	9,550			
	1,70,550			1,70,550

In the cost accounts, production overhead has been absorbed by production at 20% of prime cost, administration overhead at Re. 0·15 per unit, and selling and distribution overhead at Re. 0.20 per unit. The net profit shown by the cost accounts was Rs. 6,600.

Prepare :

(*a*) Control Accounts for production overhead, administration overhead and selling and distribution overhead;

(*b*) A statement reconciling the profit disclosed by the cost records with that shown in the financial accounts.

[Ans. Production O/H overabsorbed : Rs. 280.
Administration O/H underabsorbed : Rs. 250
Selling and Distribution O/H overabsorbed : Rs. 650
Profit as per Financial Accounts : 9,550]

11. The following figures are available from the Financial Accounts of M/s XYZ Ltd for the year ended 31st March 1996 :

	Rs.
Direct materials consumption	2,50,000
Direct Wages	1,00,000
Factory Overheads	3,80,000
Administration Overheads	2,50,000
Selling and Distribution overheads	4,80,000
Bad Debts	20,000
Legal charges	5,000
Preliminery expenses (Written-off)	10,000
Dividends received	50,000
Interest on deposits received	10,000
Sales (1,20,000 units)	7,00,000
Closing Stock :	
Finished Stock—40,000 units	1,20,000
Work-in-Progress	80,000

The Cost Accounts Reveal :

(*i*) Direct Material Consumption Rs. 2,80,000.

(*ii*) Factory Overhead Recovered @ 20% of Prime cost.

(*iii*) Administration overhead at Rs. 3 per unit of production.

(*iv*) Selling and distribution overheads Rs. 4 per unit sold.

Prepare : (*i*) Costing P/L A/c (*ii*) Profit & Loss A/c ; (*iii*) Reconciliation statement.

[C.A. Inter]

[Ans. (*i*) Costing Loss Rs. 5,16,000; (*ii*) Profit as per Profit & Loss A/c Rs. 5,35,000]

11 Budget and Budgetary Control

Authors' Comments and Suggestions :

1. ***Almost every year a question is set in the examinations of degree courses/I.C.W.A. (Inter)/C.A. (Int.).***
2. ***Students should first learn how to prepare functional budgets like Cash budget, Sales budget, Purchase budget, Production budget, Expenditure budget etc.***
3. ***Master Budget is to be prepared by considering the results of functional budgets.***
4. ***Flexible budgets are prepared to show the expenditure appropriate to various levels of output in the same period.***

Introduction—Budget—Budgetary Control—Different aspects of budgetary control—Different Types of Cost Budget—Master budget—Flexible budget—Illustration—Worked-out Problems—Exercises.

BUDGET

Introduction

The main objectives of cost accounting are to provide necessary information relating to the business to the management for planning and control. Budgetary control and standard costing are the two different tools used widely for assisting management in planning and control. In practice budget is used in various fields viz. in our private life, in business and also in the government departments. To begin with it will be very much useful to consider the following definitions given by the CIMA terminology :

Budget

"A plan expressed in money. It is prepared and approved prior to the budget period and may show income, expenditure and the capital to be employed. May be drawn up showing incremental effects on formal budgeted or actual figures or be complied by zero-based budgeting."

Budgetary Control

It is designed to assist management in carrying out its functions by allocating responsibility and authority, to aid in making plans and estimates for the future and to assist in the analysis of variation between the actual and estimates in order to develop the bases for measurement with the standard for the purpose of measuring efficiency of operations. Thus budgetary control is a system of planning and controlling cost through continuous comparison of actual with budgeted results. The CIMA terminology defines Budgetary Control as—"It is the establishment of budgets relating to responsibilities of executives to the requirement of a policy and the continuous comparison of actual with budgeted results either to secure by individual action the objective of the policy or to provide a basis for revision".

The following steps are required in a good budgetary control system :

1. Dividing the organisation according to function, known as budget centre.
2. Preparation of separate budget for each center.
3. Coordination between the centers for establishing the responsibilities.
4. Measurement of actual performance.
5. Comparison of actual performance with the budget in order to develop the deviations or variances.
6. Analysis of variances into its possible causes for motivating the right people to take right action at right time.
7. Taking a remedial action or to readjust the budgeted estimates.

Advantages/Objectives of Budgetary control

1. A budget forces a manager to plan ahead.
2. It smoothen seasonal variations in production and sales.
3. The Budget assists to coordinate the activities of various divisions according to the policies of the organization.
4. It establishes the divisional/departmental responsibilities.
5. It forces early consideration of basic policies.
6. It demands the most economical use of resources.
7. It facilitates periodic comparison of the activities of the organization.
8. It provides a method of measurement of operational efficiency.
9. The budgetary system centralizes control and decentralizes operational responsibilities.
10. It acts as an aid for better use of infrastructual facilities.
11. It reveals the variations of actual performance from budgetary performance through a process of "management by exception."

Different aspects of budgetary control

Budget Centre : Budget centre is an area/section of an organization for which control may be exercised and budget is prepared. A budget, which refers to a budget centre, is a departmental budget. A budget centre may consist of number of cost centres.

Budget Committee : A budget committee is a committee to formulate a general programmed for preparing budget and to exercise overall control. As budgeting aims at coordination of activities, the main functions of the budget committee is to reconcile divergent views, to coordinate and finally to submit proposals for approval of the top executives.

Budget Period : The budget period is defined as the period for which a budget is prepared and used for controlling actual performances. In fact there is no fixed period and the budget period varies according to requirements of the organisation.

Budget Manual : A budget manual is a schedule or document setting out the responsibilities of the persons engaged in, the routine of, and the forms and records required for budgetary control. It serves as a guide for departmental heads.

Organisation Chart : For an effective budgetary control proper coordination among the various executives of functional departments is necessary. The work of coordination goes through an organization chart for budgetary control. The chart establishes the responsibilities of each functional executive in fulfilling the target of the organization prepared beforehand in consultation on the suggestion and proposals sent by them. The Chief Executive is the head of the budgetary control system and generally designated as the Budget Controller. The functional managers shall be responsible for the preparation of functional budgets and to follow the directions and to fulfill the target as listed against them.

Budget Factor : Budget factor is the factor whose influence must first be assessed in order to ensure that functional budgets are reasonably capable of fulfillment. Often sales is the budget factor, but the other factors such as men, materials, machines, capital etc. may also act as budget factor. It may be termed as limiting or governing or key factor. It represents some influential factors which so dominates business operations as to present obstacles in the achievements of the ambitions contained in the functional budget. It is, therefore, necessary to assess the impact of this factor to begin with estimates for preparation of various budgets.

ORGANISATION CHART

CHIEF EXECUTIVE
or MANAGING DIRECTOR
↓
Budget Officer

↓	↓	↓	↓	↓
Personnel Manager	Purchase Manager	Production Manager	Sales Manager	Accounts Departement
↓	↓	↓	↓	↓
Labour Budget	Purchase Budget	Production Budget	Sales Budget	Other Expenditure Bud-gets/Flexible Budget, Master Budget

Functional Budget : A functional budget is a budget of income and expenditure relates to any of the functions of an enterprise. There are various types of functional budgets depending on the size and policy of the organization. The functions are like production, sales, administration, research and development etc. The budgets which are prepared frequently are :

1. Sales Budget.
2. Selling and Distribution Cost Budget.
3. Production Budget.
4. Production Cost Budget.
5. Purchase Budget.
6. Personnel Budget/Labour Budget.
7. Plant Utilisations Budget.
8. Capital Expenditure Budget.
9. Maintenance Cost Budget.
10. Administration Cost Budget.
11. Research and Development Cost Budget.

Sales Budget : Sales Budget is a quantitative statement of future sales of an organization expressed in monetary terms. It is the most important functional budget. As sales are the key factor, it is to be prepared first and all the other functional budgets are the follower of this budget. Sales budget are prepared showing sales under the headings (*a*) Product, (*b*) Territory, (*c*) Type of Customers, such as National/International, (*d*) Salesmens, and (*e*) Period—such as week, month, quarter, year etc.

Production Budget : It is a forecast for the quantities to be produced in a period for achieving the sales target. It may be prepared in terms of unit or standard hours. This type of budget is prepared by the production manager on the basis of sales budget, plant capacity, estimated stock to be maintained, the inherent loss in production, policy of the Govenment and prevailing law in the country.

Capital Expenditure Budget : Capital expenditure is a plan for the proposed outlay on fixed assets during the budget period. The capital expenditure budget is first prepared on long term basis keeping in view the potential demand for product, existing capacity of production and long-term business policy. The long term capital expenditure budget, say for 5 or 7 years, is broken down into short-term capital expenditure budgets according to budget period like other budgets, so that budget summaries can be prepared easily. The objects of capital expenditure budget are :

(*i*) To provide fund for capital expenditure during the budget period.
(*ii*) To restrict the capital expenditures within the limit.
(*iii*) To establish a system of priorities in expenditure.
(*iv*) To execute the long term scheme of extension.
(*v*) To make the under-utilized functional departments to its optimum capacity by putting little expenditures on fixed assets.

Personnel Budget : This budget is prepared to show the planned outlay on direct and indirect labour cost during the budget period as well as to show the number of skilled, semi-skilled and unskilled man power required to fulfill the production target or sales target of an organization. Manpower requirement is first expressed in convenient units like man-hours or man-days etc. and then converted into its cost. The objectives of this budget are to utilize the available manpower properly to estimated additional manpower required or reduction in manpower to fulfill the target of the organization and the cost to be incurred on them. This budget helps in reduction of labour turnover. Thus it shows clearly the total outlay segregating direct and indirect labour cost with a provision for shift and overtime work, implementation of programmes for training and revision of present wage system.

Purchase Budget : Purchase budget is prepared to show the materials to be bought during the budget period. This budget helps the organization in setting out the money required to purchase direct and indirect materials required for production or to purchase finished goods for trading operations. It is prepared showing quantity to be bought and its value. For preparing this budget the waitage is to be given on the factors like storage capacity, availability of finance, seasonal discount, storage space, stock levels to be maintained, EOQ etc. The Purchase Manager who is in the charge of preparation of Purchase Budget should have sound knowledge of different markets and of different products.

Selling & Distribution Cost Budget : The selling & distribution cost budget is prepared to show the estimated overhead expenses in selling and distribution of the goods to be sold during the budget period. It is prepared on the basis of sales budget, as it shows the cost of quantities on sales budget. Generally this budget is prepared by the Sales Manager in consultation with Zonal Sales Manager, Advertising Manager, Distribution Manager. After the product is brought in a saleable condition, a lot of cost is incurred on selling and distribution before it finally reaches the customers. The selling cost includes the cost of creation of demand in the market and the cost for securing orders. Advertising expenses, market research expenses, seminar expenses in developing customer-consciousness are included in selling expenses.

Distribution expenses include the cost for handling the order, after sales service expenditures, storage, outward freight, credit collection expenses, packing, export duty, insurance etc. After consolidation of all these estimates the final Selling & Distribution Cost Budget is to be presented to the Budget Committee for its approval.

Production Cost Budget : Production cost budget is the forecast of the estimated cost of production based on production budget. It is actually the summary of material budget, labour budget, factory overhead budget and may be expressed by analyzing into its departments and/or products. While preparing the production cost budget the factors like increase or decrease in the price of materials, increases or decreases in the rates of payment etc. are to be considered.

Plant Utilisation Budget : Plant Utilisation Budget is the budget closely connected with the production budget, which will show the estimated plant facilities required to meet the budgeted production. This enables one to estimate the number of machines required to be installed for production and at what time and for which production. The budget can be expressed in terms of working hours or in any other suitable units. This budget mainly represents the budgeted machine load for any department, overloading or underloading of some departments and the necessary adjustments required.

Administration Cost Budget : Administration Cost Budget is the budget showing the estimated cost of formulating the policies, directing the organization and controlling the operations of an undertaking. Administrative costs are mainly fixed in nature for a given period of time and, therefore, preparation of this budget is easier than the other functional budgets. The administrative cost budget contains expenses like director's remuneration, legal charges, audit fees, rent, salaries, office expenses, interest, postage, property taxes etc.

Research and Development Cost Budget : The Research and Development Cost Budget is the most important tool for planning and controlling the Research and Development Cost. It compels the management to think in advance about the fairness of the expenses related to various research programmes. A Research and Development Cost Budget is planned outlay on research and development for a given period. It helps in coordination with other plans and programmes of an organization. As there is no definite output for research and development division, it is very difficult to estimate the budgeted research and development cost accurately. Hence, the amount of research and development cost is mainly depending on the policy of the management.

This budget will show the permissible limit within which the activities are to be pursued. These costs are expensive in terms of money which are to be appropriated in different projects on some rational basis.

Cash Budget : Cash Budget is the forecast of cash receipts and payments for a given period. This budget is prepared after the preparation of all functional budgets. For efficient running of a business the anticipated cash requirements should be known well in advance. Failure to meet the said requirements will lead to irreparable loss to company's reputation. In most cases monthly or quarterly cash forecast for the budget period are made but it can also be prepared for a week or a day according to its business requirements. The business executives should appreciate the importance of cash budget as profit making may depend on the availability of cash.

The cash budget can be prepared by any of the following methods :

1. Receipts and payments method.
2. Adjusted profit and loss method.
3. The Balance Sheet method.

Ths cash budget is prepared for performing the following important functions :

(*a*) Cash budget ensures sufficient availability of cash as and when required by the organization.

(*b*) It assits for revealing any expected shortage of cash, so that action may be taken in time.

(*c*) It provides funds for normal growth of the organization.

(*d*) If facilitates in temporary investment of cash whenever and to whatever extent, found in excess.

(*e*) It also shows when and how much additional cash is needed to be borrowed.

(*f*) It helps in securing optimum working capital requirement for smooth operation of the business.

Master Budget : It is a budget which summarises all the functional budgets of an organization. A master budget normally includes :

(*a*) A budgeted profit & loss account.

(*b*) Budgeted profit & loss appropriation account.

(*c*) Budgeted Balance Sheet.

(*d*) A budgeted cash flow statement.

After preparation of Master Budget it has to be submitted by the budget committee to the top management for their approval. Budgeted costs are classified and summarized by types of expenses as well as by departments. The functional budgets are generally prepared for a small segment of a business enterprise. However, to achieve the business objectives it is necessary to have coordination among different budgets reflecting diverse activities of a business firm. It is the master budget through which the top management can be able to know the revenue position, expenses, net income and the financial position at a time.

Flexible Budget : A flexible budget has been defined as a budget which is designed to change in accordance with the activities attained. Practically it is a series of fixed budgets for different levels of activities. Here costs are analyzed behaviourwise, viz. variable, fixed and semi-variable.

Flexible budget will show the impact of various expenses on the operational and budgetary position of the organization. The main characteristics of the budget are to show the expenditures appropriate to various levels of output. The underlying principles of flexible budget are that every business is dynamic, ever-changing and continuous. It has the following advantages :

1. It is easy to change with variation in production level.
2. It shows the cost and profit in various levels of activities.
3. It facilitates measurement and evaluation of performance of an undertaking.
4. It helps profit planning.
5. It provides a very dynamic basis of comparison.

Illustration :

Based on the following information, prepare a Cash Budget for ABC Ltd. :

	1st Quarter Rs.	2nd Quarter Rs.	3rd Quarter Rs.	4th Quarter Rs.
Opening Cash balance	10,000			
Collection from customers	1,25,000	1,50,000	1,60,000	2,21,000
Payments :				
Purchase of materials	20,000	35,000	35,000	54,200
Other expenses	25,000	20,000	20,000	17,000
Salary & Wages	90,000	95,000	95,000	1,09,200
Income tax	5,000			
Purchase of machinery				20,000

The Company desires to maintain a cash balance of Rs. 15,000 at the end of each quarter. Cash can be borrowed or repaid in multiples of Rs. 500 at an interest of 10% per annum. Management does not want to borrow cash more than what is necessary and wants to repay as early as possible. In any event, loans cannot be extended beyond 4 quarters. Interest is computed and paid when the principal is repaid. Assume that borrowings taken place at the beginning and repayments are made at the end of the quarter. ***[I.C.W.A. Inter Adopted]***

Solution

Cash Budget for ABC Ltd.

	1st Quarter Rs.	2nd Quarter Rs.	3rd Quarter Rs.	4th Quarter Rs.
Opening Cash balance	10,000	15,000	15,000	15,325
Collection from customers	1,25,000	1,50,000	1,60,000	2,21,000
(A) Total receipts	1,35,000	1,65,000	1,75,000	2,36,325
Payments :				
Purchase of materials	20,000	35,000	35,000	54,200
Other expenses	25,000	20,000	20,000	17,000
Salary & Wages	90,000	95,000	95,000	1,09,200
Income tax	5,000			
Purchase of Machinery				20,000
(B) Total payments	1,40,000	1,50,000	1,50,000	2,00,400
Minimum Cash Balance	15,000	15,000	15,000	15,000
Total Cash required	1,55,000	1,65,000	1,65,000	2,15,400
Excess/(Deficit)	(20,000)	Nil	10,000	20,925

(c) Borrowing	20,000			
Repayment			9,000	11,000
Interest payment (Note : 1)			675	1,100
(D) Total			9,675	12,100
Closing Cash Balance : (A + B + C – D)	15,000	15,000	15,325	23,825

Note : As given in the question, interest is computed and paid when the principal is repaid. Borrrowing is at the beginning of the quarter and repayment made at the end of the quarter as given in the question.

Rs. 20,000 borrowed at the beginning of the first quarter.

Rs. 9,000 repayment made at the end of third quarter.

Interest is computed and paid when the principal is repaid.

Hence the interest on 9,000 for 3 quarters at 10% is calculated as :

$$9{,}000 \times \frac{9}{12} \times \frac{10}{100} = \text{Rs. } 675$$

Rs. 11,000 repaid at the end of 4th quarter. Hence interest on Rs. 11,000 for 4 quarters i.e. for one year at 10% will be Rs. 1,100.

Illustration :

Soloproducts Ltd. manufactures and sells a single product and has estimated a sales revenue of Rs. 126 lakhs this year based on a 20 per cent profit on selling price. Each unit of the product requires 3 lb. of material P and $1\frac{1}{2}$lbs. of material Q for manufacture as well as a processing time of 7 hours in the machine shop and $2\frac{1}{2}$ hours in the Assembly Section.

Overheads are absorbed at a blanket rate of $33\frac{1}{3}$% on direct labour. The factory works 5 days of 8 hours a week in normal 52 weeks a year. On an average statutory holidays, leave and absenteeism and idle time amount to 96 hours, 80 hours and 64 hours, respectively, in a year.

The other details are :

Purchase price	Material P		6 per lb.
	Material Q		4 per lb.
Comprehensive Labour Rate	Machine shop		4 per hour
	Assembly		3·20 per hour
No. of employees	Machine shop		600
	Assembly		180
	Finished goods	**Material P**	**Material Q**
Opening stock	20,000 units	54,000 lbs	33,000 lbs.
Closing stock (estimated)	25,000 units	30,000 lbs.	66,000 lbs.

You are required to calculate :

(*a*) The number of untis of the product proposed to be sold.

(*b*) Purchases to be made of Materials P and Q during the year in Rupees.

(*c*) Capacity utilization of Machine shop and Assembly Section, along with your comments.

(C.A. Inter)

Solution

A. Statement of Cost and Selling Price per unit

			Rs.
Consumption of materials	P 3 lbs. at Rs. 6	18·00	
	Q $1\frac{1}{2}$ lbs. at Rs. 4	6·00	24·00
Direct labour	Machine shop 7 hours at Rs. 4	28·00	
	Assembly Section $2\frac{1}{2}$ hours at Rs. 3·20	8·00	36·00
Direct expenses			Nil
Prime Cost			60·00
Overheads at $33\frac{1}{3}$% on Direct labour			12·00
Total Cost			72·00
Add : Profit at 20% on selling price i.e. 25% on total cost			18·00
Selling price per unit			90·00
			Units
No. of units to the sold=1,26,00,000/90			1,40,000
Opening stock of finished goods			(–) 20,000
Closing stock of finished goods (estimated)			(+) 25,000
No. of units to be purchased			1,45,000

B. Purchase Cost

Particulars	Material P lbs.	Material Q lbs.	Total lbs.
Consumption 1,45,000 × 3 =	4,35,000	2,17,500	6,52,500
Add : Closing stock	30,000	66,000	96,000
	4,65,000	2,83,500	7,48,500
Less : Opening stock	54,000	33,000	87,000
	4,11,000	2,50,500	6,61,500
	Rs.	**Rs.**	**Rs.**
Purchase per lb.	6·00	4·00	
Purchase cost	24,66,000	10,02,000	34,68,000

(C)	*Machine Shop*	*Assembly Shop*
Maximum hours	8×5×52×600 = 12,48,000	8×5×52×180= 3,74,400
Less : Holidays, leave etc. 96+80+64 = 240×600	1,44,000	(240 × 180) = 43,200
Hours available	11,04,000	3,31,200
Hours utilized for a production of 1,45,000 units at 7 hours in Machine Shop	10,15,000	3,62,500
Utilized hours	89,000	
Shortage of time		31,300

Capacity utilization ratio = No. of working hours/Maximum hours in a budget period = 10,15,000/12,48,000 × 100 = 81·33% = 3,62,500/3,74,400 × 100 = 96·82%

Comments :

There will be under-utilization of labour in Machine Shop. A portion of it can be utilized in Assembly Section provided the labourers can perform the duties in Assembly Section. Otherwise the shortage of time in Assembly Section is to be met by working overtime.

WORKEDOUT PROBLEMS

Problem 1

Prapare a Cash Budget for the three months ending 30th June 1986 from the information given below :

(A) Month	Sales	Materials	Wages	Overheads
February	14,000	9,600	3,000	1,700
March	15,000	9,000	3,000	1,900
April	16,000	9,200	3,200	2,000
May	17,000	10,000	3,600	2,200
June	18,000	10,400	4,000	2,300

(B) Credit terms are :

Sales/Debtors—10% sales are on cash, 50% of the credit sales are collected next month and the balance in the following month.

Creditors—Materials 2 months, Wages $\frac{1}{4}$ month, Overheads $\frac{1}{2}$ month.

(C) Cash and Bank Balance on 1st April , 1986 is expected to be Rs. 6,000.

(D) Other relevant information are :

(*i*) Plant and Machinery will be installed in February 1986 at a cost of Rs. 96,000. The monthly instalments of Rs. 2,000 is payable from April onwards.

(*ii*) Dividend @5% on Preference Share Capital of Rs. 2,00,000 will be paid on 1st June.

(*iii*) Advance to be received for sale of vehicles Rs. 9,000 in June.

(*iv*) Dividends from investments amounting to Rs. 1,000 are expected to be received in June.

(*v*) Income tax (advance) to be paid in June is Rs. 2,000.

(I.C.W.A. Inter, June 1986)

Solution

Sales Realization

Month	*Credit Sales*	*Realization from Debtors*	*Rs.*
Feb.	14,000 × 90% =	12,600 × 50%	6,300
March	15,000 × 90% =	13,500 × 50%	6,750
			13,050 in April 1986
March	15,000 × 90% =	13,500 × 50%	6,750
April	16,000 × 90% =	14,400 × 50%	7,200
			13,950 in May 1986
April	16,000 × 90% =	14,400 × 50%	7,200
May	17,000 × 90% =	15,300 × 50%	7,650
			14,850 in June 1986

Cash Budget

Particulars	*April '86*	*May '86*	*June '86*
A. Opening Balance	6,000	3,950	3,000
B. Receipts from :			
Cash sales	1,600	1,700	1,800
Debtors	13,050	13,950	14,850
Advance			9,000
Dividends from Investments			1,000
Total "B"	14,650	15,650	26,650
Total A + B	20,650	19,600	29,650
C. Payments :			
Creditors	9,600	9,000	9,200
Wages	750	800	900
	2,400	2,700	3,000
	950	1,000	11,100
Overheads	1,000	1,100	1,150
Plant & Machinery :			
Instalments	2,000	2,000	2,000
Preference dividend			10,000
Advance Income Tax			2,000
Total C	16,700	16,600	29,350
D. Closing Balance (A + B − C)	3,950	3,000	300

Problem 2

From the following information of Moon Ltd. prepare a cash budget for three months commencing on 1st June 2004, when the Bank Balance was 10,000 :

Month	*Sales*	*Purchases*	*Wages*	*Selling Expenses*	*Overhead*
	Rs.	*Rs.*	*Rs.*	*Rs.*	*Rs.*
April	1,00,000	70,000	8,500	3,500	4,000
May	1,20,000	80,000	9,500	3,500	4,500
June	1,40,000	90,000	9,500	3,500	6,000
July	1,60,000	1,00,000	12,000	3,500	6,500
August	1,80,000	1,10,000	14,000	3,500	7,000

A Sale commission of 5% on sales due 2 months after sales is payable in addition to the above selling expenses. Credit terms of sale are—payment by the end of the month following the month of supply. On average one half of sales is paid on the due date while the other half is paid during the next month. Creditors are paid during the month following the month of supply. Plant purchased in June Rs. 78,000 is payable on delivery Rs. 48,000 and balance in two equal monthly instalments in July and in August. A dividend of Rs. 30,000 will be paid in September. Wages are paid $\frac{3}{4}$th on due date while $\frac{1}{4}$th during the next month. Lag in payment of selling expenses and overheads is one month. **[*C.U. B.Com. (H)*]**

Solution

Moon Ltd.

Cash Budget for the period 01.06.2004 to 31.08.2004

Particulars	*June 2004*	*July 2004*	*August 2004*
Opening Balance	10,000	(30,500)	(32,375)
Receipts :			
Collection from Debtors (Note D)	1,10,000	1,30,000	1,50,000
Total A	1,20,000	99,500	1,17,625
Payments			
Payment to creditors (Note 2)	80,000	90,000	1,00,000
Wages (Note 3)	9,500	11,375	13,500
Selling Expenses (Note 4)	3,500	3,500	3,500
Overheads (Note 4)	4,500	6,000	6,500
Selling commission (Note 5)	5,000	6,000	7,000
Plant Purchased	48,000	15,000	15,000
Total B	1,50,500	1,31,875	1,45,500
Closing Balance (A – B)	(30,500)	(32,375)	(27,875)

Working 1

Collection from Debtors

June 2004 = $\frac{1}{2}$ of Sale April + $\frac{1}{2}$ of Sale of May = 1,10,000

July 2004 = $\frac{1}{2}$ of Sale of May + $\frac{1}{2}$ of Sale of June = 1,30,000

August 2004 = $\frac{1}{2}$ of Sale of June + $\frac{1}{2}$ of Sale of July = 1,50,000

Working 2

Payment of creditors = Purchase figure of the previous month.

Working 3

Wages : $\frac{3}{4}$th of current month's expenses + $\frac{1}{4}$th of previous month's expenses.

Working 4

Selling Expenses and overheads = Expenses of the previous month.

Working 5

Selling Commission = 2% of Sales made 2 months ago.

Problem 3

From the following particulars prepare monthly cash budget of the Sunclear Ltd. for October, November and December of 1996 :

Months	*Purchases* Rs.	*Sales* Rs.	*Wages* Rs.	*Expenses* Rs.
July '96	40,000	60,000	8,000	10,000
August '96	60,000	80,000	10,500	12,000
September '96	50,000	70,000	17,500	12,500
October '96	70,000	90,000	17,100	11,600
November '96	80,000	1,00,000	12,000	11,800
December '96	60,000	1,20,000	12,000	12,300

It is expected that 50% of sales will be in cash and 25% of the purchases can be made on credit.

Debtors are allowed 2 months' credit but will receive 5% each discount if they will pay-off their dues within the month next to the month of sale. 80% of the debtors normally clear their dues at the end of that period to avail the cash discount. Rest 20% of the debtors pay on the due date.

$\frac{4}{5}$th of the credit purchase is paid after 1 month of that purchase and next to that month the balance $\frac{1}{5}$th is paid.

Wages are paid within 5th of the following month.

Expenses include selling distribution expenses which are 10% of the sales.

Any deficiency in cash at the end of a month will be met by taking short term loan for two months from bank.

At the end of September 1996 the Sunclear Ltd. had Rs. 40,000 cash in hand.

[C.U. B.Com. (H) 1997]

Solution

Sunclear Ltd.

Cash Budget for three months ending 31st December 1996

Particulars	*October*	*November*	*December*
	Rs.	*Rs.*	*Rs.*
Opening Cash Balance	40,000	25,000	10,800
Receipts.			
Cash Sales (Working 1)	45,000	50,000	60,000
Collection from Debtors (Working 2)	34,600	41,200	47,000
Total	1,19,600	1,16,200	1,17,800
Payments			
Cash Purchase (Working 3)	52,500	60,000	45,000
Payment to Creditors (Working 4)	13,000	16,500	19,500
Wages (Working 5)	17,500	17,100	12,000
Expenses.	11,600	11,800	12,300
Total	94,600	1,05,400	88,800
Closing cash balance	25,000	10,800	29,000

Working 1

Cash Sales :

October = 50% of 90,000 = Rs. 45,000
November = 50% of 1,00,000 = Rs. 50,000
December = 50% of 1,20,000 = Rs. 60,000

Working 2

(*i*) *Collection from Debtors in October* :

Out of Credit sale of each month, 80% of them have cleared their dues in the next month to avail 5% discount offer and remaining 20% of the debtors pay their dues after 2 months.

∴ Collection from Debtors in October :	Rs.
20% of Credit sale in August.	8,000
80% of Credit sale in September	
Less : 5% discount.	26,600
	34,600

(ii) Collection from Debtors in December :

20% of credit sales in September	7,000
80% of credit sales in October. *Less*—5% Discount	34,200
	41,200

(iii) Collection from Debtors in December :

	Rs.
20% of Credit sales in October	9,000
80% of Credit sales in Nov. *Less*—5% discount	38,000
	47,000

Working 3

Cash Purchase of goods :

September = 75% of 70,000 = 52,500
October = 75% of 80,000 = 60,000
November = 75% of 60,000 = 45,000

Working 4

Payment to Creditors :

October	= $\frac{1}{5}$th Credit Purchase of Aug.	=	3,000
	$\frac{4}{5}$th " " " Sept.	=	10,000
			13,000
November	= $\frac{1}{5}$th " " " Sept.	=	2,500
	$\frac{4}{5}$th " " " Oct.		14,000
			16,500
December	= $\frac{1}{5}$th " " " Oct.		3,500
	$\frac{4}{5}$th " " " Nov.		16,000
			19,500

Working 5

Wages of each month is paid in the next month.

Payment in October = Wages for Sept. Rs. 17,500
" " November = " " Oct. Rs. 17,100
" " December = " " Nov. Rs. 12,000

Problem 4

Prepare a Cash Budget for three months ending on 30 September 2004 from the following information :

A.

Months	Sales Rs.	Materials Rs.	Wages Rs.	Overhead Rs.
May	56,000	19,200	6,000	3,400
June	60,000	18,000	6,000	3,800
July	64,000	18,400	6,400	4,000
August	68,000	20,000	7,200	4,400
September	72,000	20,800	8,000	4,600

B. Credit terms are :

Sales/Debtors—10% sales are on cash, 50% of the credit sales are collected in the next month and the balance in the following month.

Creditors—Raw materials 1 month, Wages $\frac{1}{2}$month, Overhead $\frac{1}{4}$month.

C. *Other relevant information :*

(*a*) Rent from a godown let out 1.1.2003 at yearly contract of Rs. 2,25,000 with a condition of 12% increase in each year is receivable in equal instalments in each month.

(*b*) Interest @ 15% p.a. on an amount of Rs. 2,00,000 borrowed on 01.1.2002 is to be paid in each month starting from 01.3.2004. Interest for the period from 01.1.2002 to 29.2.2004 is to be paid in 10 equal monthly instalments starting from 1.7.2004. Interest for the month of April 2004 remaining unpaid. This unpaid amount is to be paid in the month of September 2004 with a penal interest of Rs. 100.

(*c*) An advance of Rs. 50,000 will be paid to a contractor for the construction of a building in September 2004.

(*d*) Adequate overdraft facility may be arranged for, if needed.

Solution

Cash Budget for three months ending 30.09.2004

Particulars		*July 2004*	*August 2004*	*September 2004*
Opening Balance		NIL	42,450	87,550
Receipts :				
Cash Sales (Working 1)		6,400	6,800	7,200
Collection from Debtors (Working 2)		52,200	55,800	59,400
Rent (Working 3)		21,000	21,000	21,000
	Total	79,600	1,26,050	1,75,150
Payments :				
Payment to creditors (Working 4)		18,000	18,400	20,000
Wages (Working 5)		6,200	6,800	7,600
Overheads (Working 6)		3,950	4,300	4,550
Interest (Working 7)		9,000	9,000	11,600
Advance to contractor for Construction.		—	—	50,000
	Total	37,150	38,500	93,750
Closing balance		42,450	87,550	81,400

Working Notes :

1. Cash Sales = 10% of current month's sales.
2. Collection from Debtors = 50% of Credit sales of one month ago + 50% of Credit sales 2 months ago.
   Collection of July = 50% of credit sale of June + 50% of Credit sale of May.
   i.e. 50% of 54,000 + 50% of 50,400 = 52,200.
   Collection in August and September have been computed similarly.
3. Rent per annum in 2004 = 2,25,000 × 112% = 2,52,000
   Rent p.m. in 2004 = $\frac{2,52,000}{12}$ = 21,000.
4. Payment to creditors of Raw Materials = Amount of previous month's purchase.
5. Wages : Payment in a month = $\frac{1}{2}$ of current month's expenses + $\frac{1}{2}$ of previous month's expenses.
6. Overheads : Payment in a month = $\frac{3}{4}$th of Current month's expenses + $\frac{1}{4}$th of previous month's expense.
7. Interest :
   $$\text{Interest P.M.} = \frac{\text{Rs. } 2,00,000 \times 15\%}{12} = \text{Rs. } 2,500$$
   This interest of Rs. 2,500 is to be paid every month from 1.3.2004.

Interest for the period from 1.1.2002 to 29.2.2004 is to be paid in 10 equal monthly instalments starting from 1.7.2004.

$\therefore$ Amount of instalment per month from 1.7.2004 = Rs. $2{,}00{,}000 \times 15\% \times \frac{26}{12} \times \frac{1}{10}$ = 6,500

Amount to be paid in July and August
= Rs. 2,500 + Rs. 6,500
= Rs. 9,000 (each).

Amount to be paid in September
= 9,000 + 100 = 9,100.

Problem 5

A new company commences business on 1st July 2000 and deposits Rs. 10,000 in the bank. This amount will be inadequate to finance its operations over a period of six months and you are asked to prepare a Cash Budget up to 31st Dec. 2000 to determine the monthly overdraft units to seek from the company's bankers.

The data furnished to you are :

(*i*) Minimum cash balance to be maintained Rs. 500.

(*ii*) Plant purchases are made on net thirty days' terms and cheques are paid to creditors on the last day of the month due.

(*iii*) Budget figures are :

	July	Aug.	Sept.	Oct.	Nov.	Dec.
	Rs.	*Rs.*	*Rs.*	*Rs.*	*Rs.*	*Rs.*
Purchases	5,000	4,000	3,000	4,000	4,000	5,000
Wages	4,000	5,000	4,000	4,000	5,000	4,000
Cash Expenses	400	500	400	400	500	400
Sales	6,000	7,000	8,000	8,000	9,000	12,000

Interpret the results as shown by the preparation of Cash Budget. **[*M.Com. Delhi*]**

Solution

Cash Budget
For the months from July to December 2000

Particulars	*July*	*Aug.*	*Sept.*	*Oct.*	*Nov.*	*Dec.*
	Rs.	*Rs.*	*Rs.*	*Rs.*	*Rs.*	*Rs.*
Opening Cash Balance	10,000	600	500	500	500	500
Receipts.						
Collection against Sales.......	—	—	5,820	6,790	7,760	7,760
Total A	10,000	600	6,320	7,290	8,260	8,260
Payments :						
Payments to creditors against						
Purchase	—	5,000	4,000	3,000	4,000	4,000
Wages	4,000	5,000	4,000	4,000	5,000	4,000
Expenses	400	500	400	400	500	400
Plant	5,000					
Total Payments B	9,400	10,500	8,400	7,400	9,500	8,400
A – B = C	600	(9,900)	(2,080)	(110)	(1,240)	(140)
Overdraft to be taken :						
D = C + Rs. 500	Nil	10,400	2,580	610	1,740	640
Closing Balance (D – C)	600	500	500	500	500	500

Problem 6

The projected sales and purchases of ABC Ltd. for the months of July to Nov. 2000 are as follows :

Months	Sales	Purchase
July 2000	6,20,000	3,80,000
Aug. 2000	6,40,000	3,33,000
Sept. 2000	5,80,000	3,50,000
Oct. 2000	5,60,000	3,90,000
Nov. 2000	6,00,000	3,40,000

The Wages are expected to be Rs. 1,00,000 per month. The management is expected to pay two months' wages as bonus during October 2000.

The company is expected to pay an advance tax for income tax Rs. 90,000 before 15th September 2000. The company has ordered in June 2000 for a machine costing Rs. 16,00,000. IDBI has agreed to finance the purchase of machine which is expected to be delivered in January 2001. The company has made advance payment of 5% in June 2000 with order, and they have agreed to pay another 10% advance after 3 months. The company extends 2 months' credit for the customers and the company enjoys one month's credit from the suppliers. The general expenses for the company are Rs. 60,000 per month payable at the end of each month. The company anticipates to receive interim dividend of 10% for the investment of 90,000 shares of Rs. 10 each during October 2000. The company anticipates to have an overdraft of Rs. 40,000 on 1st September 2000 (limit sanctioned is Rs. 55,000).

Draw a cash budget for September to November 2000 for approaching your bankers for a short term further credit.

[C.S. Final]

Solution

A. B. C. Ltd.

Cash Budget for September to November 2000

Particulars	*September Rs.*	*October Rs.*	*November Rs.*
Receipts :			
Opening Cash Balance	—	—	—
Collection from Debtor	6,20,000	6,40,000	5,80,000
Interim Dividend on Investment	—	90,000	—
Total Cash available before current financing (A)	6,20,000	7,30,000	5,80,000
Payments :			
Payment to Creditors for purchases	3,33,000	3,50,000	3,90,000
Wages	1,00,000	1,00,000	1,00,000
Bonus to Workers	—	2,00,000	—
Advance Tax for Income Tax	90,000	—	—
Advance for purchase of machine	1,60,000	—	—
General Expenses	60,000	60,000	60,000
Total payments (B)	7,43,000	7,10,000	5,50,000
Surplus (Deficit) A – B.	(1,23,000)	20,000	30,000
Financing required :			
Borrowings.	1,23,000	—	—
Repayments	—	(20,000)	30,000
Effect of financing (C)	1,23,000	(20,000)	(30,000)
Closing Cash balance : A + C – B	—	—	—

The company is expected to make up deficit by raising Rs. 40,000 as bank overdraft and will have unutilized bank overdraft limit of Rs, 15,000. It would be appropriate for it to approach the banker for a further short term credit to cover the requirement of Rs. 1,23,000 in Sept. 2000.

Problem 7

Lookahed Ltd. produces and sells a single product. Sales budget calendar year 1987 by quarter is as under :

Quarter	No. of units to be sold
I	12,000
II	15,000
III	16,500
IV	18,000

In the year 1987 it is expected to open with an inventory of 4,000 units of finished product and close with an inventory of 6,500 units.

Production is customarily scheduled to provide for two-thirds of the current quarter's sales demand plus one-third of the following quarter's demand. Thus production anticipates sales volume by about one month.

The standard cost details for one unit of the product is :

Direct materials 10 lbs. @ 50 paise per lb.

Direct labour 1 hour 30 minutes @ Rs. 4 per hour.

Variable overheads 1 hour 30 minutes @ Rs. 2 per hour based on a budgeted production volume of 90,000 direct labour for the year.

(*i*) Prepare a Production Budget for 1987 by quarters showing the number of units to be produced and the total costs of direct material, direct labour, variable overheads and fixed overheads.

(*ii*) If the budgeted selling price per unit is Rs. 17, what would be the budgeted profit for the year as a whole ?

(*iii*) In which quater of the year is the Company expected to break even ?

[*C.A. Inter*]

Solution

(A) Production Budget for 1987 and total cost thereof

Particulars	*I*	*II*	*III*	*IV*	*Total*
2/3 of current qurt. Sales demand	8,000	10,000	11,000	12,000	41,000
1/3 of following qurt. Sales demand	5,000	5,500	6,000	6,500	23,000
	Rs.	*Rs.*	*Rs.*	*Rs.*	*Rs.*
Production budget for 1987 (units)	13,000	15,500	17,000	18,500	64,000
Direct Material Cost $10 \times 0{\cdot}50 = 5 \times 13{,}000 =$	65,000	77,500	85,000	92,500	3,20,000
Direct labour cost $1\frac{1}{2} \times 4 = 6 \times 13{,}000$	78,000	93,000	1,02,000	1,11,000	3,84,000
Variable Overheads $1\frac{1}{2}\times 1 = 1{\cdot}50\times 13{,}000$	19,500	23,250	25,500	27,750	96,000
Fixed Overhead 90,000 DLH × 2 = 1,80,000 i.e. each Qrt. 45,000	45,000	45,000	45,000	45,000	1,80,000
Total Cost	2,07,500	2,38,750	2,57,500	2,76,250	9,80,000

(*ii*) Sales Value 61,500 units at Rs. 17 per unit	10,45,500
Less : Variable cost 61,500 × 12·50 = (5·00 + 6·00 + 1·50)	7,68,750
Contribution : 17·00(–) 12·50 = Rs. 4·5 per unit on 61,500 units	2,76,750
Less : Fixed Overheads	1,80,000
Budgeted Profit for 1987	96,750

(*iii*) BEP (Units) = F/C per unit = 1,80,000/4·50 = 40,000 units

Quarter No. I	12,000 Units sold
Quarter No. II	15,000 Units sold
Quarter No. III	16,500 Units sold
	43,500

In the third quarter, the company will break-even.

Problem 8

A company is drawing its production plan for the year 1997-98 in respect of two of its products 'Gamma' and 'Delta'. The company's policy is not to carry any closing WIP at the end of any month. However, its policy is to hold a closing stock of finished goods at 50% of the anticipated quantity of sales of succeeding month. For the year 1997-98 the company's budgeted production is 20,000 units of "Gamma" and 25,000 units of "Delta".

The following is the estimated cost data :

	Gamma	*Delta*
Direct material per unit	Rs. 50	Rs. 80
Direct labour per unit	20	30
Other manufacturing expenses approtionable to each type of product based on production	2,00,000	3,75,000

The estimated units to be sold in the first 7 months of the year 1997-98 are :

	April	May	June	July	August	Sept.	Oct.
Gamma	900	1,100	1,400	1,800	2,200	2,200	1,800
Delta	2,900	2,900	2,500	2,100	1,700	1,700	1,900

You are required to :

(*a*) Prepare a production budget showing month-wise number of units to be manufactured.

(*b*) Present a summarized production cost budget for the half year ending 30.9.97.

[*I.C.W.A. Inter, June 1996*]

Solution

(a) Production Budget for the half year ending 30th Sept. 1997
(Month-wise in units)

Details	*April*	*May*	*June*	*July*	*Aug.*	*Sept.*	*Oct.*
Product—Gamma							
Budgeted sales	900	1,100	1,400	1,800	2,200	2,200	9,600
Add : C/stock to be built (Refer to Note 1)	550	700	900	1,100	1,100	900	900
	1,450	1,800	2,300	2,900	3,300	3,100	10,500
Less : Opening stock (Refer to Note 2)	450	550	700	900	1,100	1,100	450
Budgeted Production	1,000	1,250	1,600	2,000	2,200	2,000	10,050
Products—Delta							
Budgeted sales	2,900	2,900	2,500	2,100	1,700	1,700	13,800
Add : Stock to be built	1,450	1,250	1,050	850	850	950	950
	4,350	4,150	3,550	2,950	2,550	2,650	14,750
Less : Opening stock*	1,450	1,450	1,250	1,050	850	850	1,450
	2,900	2,700	2,300	1,900	1,700	1,800	13,300

* Equal to closing stock of previous month of 50% of sale of same month in this situation.

(b) Production Budget for the half year ending 30th Sept. 1997
(Month-wise in units)

Products	***Gamma***		***Delta***	
Production (in units)	10,050		13,300	
Details	*Per unit Rs.*	*Total Rs.*	*Per unit Rs.*	*Total Rs.*
Direct material	50	5,02,500	80	10,64,000
Direct labour	20	2,01,000	30	3,99,000
Other manufacturing overhead	10	1,00,500	15	1,99,500
Note :: 3	80	8,04,000	125	16,62,500

Note 1 Closing stock is equal to 50% of the anticipated quantity of sales of the succeeding month.

Note 2 Opening stock is the closing stock of previous month or opening stock is equal to 50% of the stock of the same month in this situation.

Note 3 Other manufacturing expenses are apportioned on the basis of production and details for the same are as under :

	Gamma	Delta
Units to be produced in 1997-98	20,000	25,000
Other manufacturing expenses (Rs.)	2,00,000	3,75,000
∴ Rate per unit (Rs.)	10	15

Problem 9

The following information relating to the third and last quarter of 2003-04 are furnished by a company which manufactures and sells a single product :

		Third quarter (Actual)	Last Quarter (Estimate)
Sales		Rs. 6,24,000	Rs. 6,60,000
Inventory of raw materials and finished goods :	Opening balance	Closing balance	Closing balance
Raw material "A" (Kg.)	25,000	23,500	25,000
Raw material "B" (Kg.)	12,650	13,400	15,000
Finished goods (units)	670	700	1,000

Unit cost data :

Raw material "A"	10 Kg. @ Rs. 3	= Rs. 30
Raw material "B"	5 Kg. @ Rs. 2	= Rs. 10
Direct Labour (machine time 5 hrs. @ Rs. 4)	Machine shop	= Rs. 20
Assembly 2 hrs. @ Rs. 5 (labour time)		= Rs. 10

Production Overheads :
Machine Shop @ 12 per machine hour.
Assembly @ Rs. 10 per labour hour.
Selling and Administration OH : 20% of production cost.
Profit margin : 10% on selling price.
Production and sales occur evenly during the budget period.
You are required to prepare for the last quarter of the year :

(a) Statement of Cost of Production and Selling price per unit.
(b) Production budget (in units)
(c) Purchase budget (quantity and value)
(d) Production cost budget. **[*I.C.W.A. June 2004*]**

Solution

(a) Cost of Production and Selling Price per Unit

Particulars	*Rs.*	*Rs.*
Direct Materials		
"A" = 10 Kgs. @ Rs. 3	30·00	
"B" = 5 Kgs. @ Rs. 2	10·00	40·00
Direct Labour :		
Machine shop = 5 hours @ Rs. 4	20·00	
Assembly = 2 hours @ Rs. 5	10·00	30·00
Production overheads :		
Machine shop = 5 hours @ Rs. 12	60·00	
Assembly = 2 hours @ Rs. 10	20·00	80·00
Production cost		150·00
Selling and administration overheads @ 20%		30·00
Cost of sales		80·00
Profit Margin 10% on S.P. (or 10/90 on cost)		20·00
Selling Price		200·00

(b) Production Budget for last quarter of 2003-04

	Units
Sales in last quarter (4th quarter) 660,000/200	3,300
Add : Closing balance at end of 1st quarter	1,000
Less : Opening balance	(700)
Production for last quarter	3,600

(c) Purchase Budget for last quarter of 2003-04

	Material A	Material B	Total Value (Rs.)
Consumption	36,000	18,000	
(Production × Qty/unit)			
A = 3,600 × 10 kgs.			
B = 3,600 × 5 kgs.			
Add : Closing Balance	25,000	15,000	
Less : Opening Balance	(23,500)	(13,400)	
Purchase to be made	37,500	19,600	
Price per kg.	3	2	
Total Value	1,12,500	39,200	1,51,700

(d) Production Cost Budget for last quarter of 2003-04

Particulars	*Cost (Rs.)*	*Total (Rs.)*
Direct Materials		
A : 36,000 @ Rs. 3	1,08,000	
B : 18,000 @ Rs. 2	36,000	1,44,000
Direct Labour :		
Machine Shop : 18,000 hrs. @ Rs. 4	72,000	
Assembly : 7,200 @ Rs. 5	36,000	1,08,000
Production overheads :		
Machine Shop : 18,000 hrs. @ Rs. 12	2,16,000	
Assembly Shop : 7,200 hrs. @ Rs. 10	72,000	2,88,000
		5,40,000

Problem 10

The following are the estimated sales of a company for eight months ending 30.11.1998 :

Months	***Estimated Sales (units)***
April '98	12,000
May '98	13,000
June '98	9,000
July '98	8,000
August '98	10,000
September '98	12,000
October '98	14,000
November '98	12,000

As a matter of policy, the company maintains the closing balance of finished goods and raw materials as follows :

Stock items	**Closing balance of a month**
Finished goods	50% of the estimated sales for the next month
Raw materials	Estimated consumption for the next month

Every unit of production required 2 Kg. of raw material costing Rs. 5 per Kg.

Prepare Production Budget (in units) and Raw Material Purchase Budget (in units and cost) of the company for the half year ending 30 Sept. 1998. ***[I.C.W.A. Inter, June 1999]***

Solution

(i) Production budget (in units) for half year ending 30th Sept. 1998

Months	**Sales (In units)**	**Closing balance 50% of the estimated sales for the next month**	**Opening balance (for the month)**	**Production**
April '98	12,000	6,500	6,000	12,500
May	13,000	4,500	6,500	11,000
June	9,000	4,000	4,500	8,500
July	8,000	5,000	4,000	9,000
Aug.	1,000	6,000	5,000	11,000
Sept.	12,000	7,000	6,000	13,000
	64,000			65,000

(ii) Purchase Budget (in costs and units) for the half year period ending 30.9.1998

Consumption @ 2 Kg. Per unit (Kgs.)	Closing Balance	Opening Balance	Purchase (in Kg.) = 3+2+1	Rate (Rs.)	Amount (Rs.)
25,000	22,000	25,000	22,000	5	1,10,000
22,000	17,000	22,000	17,000	5	85,000
17,000	18,000	17,000	18,000	5	90,000
18,000	22,000	18,000	22,000	5	1,10,000
22,000	26,000	22,000	26,000	5	1,30,000
26,000	26,000	26,000	26,000	5	1,30,000
1,30,000					6,55,000

Note 1. It should be kept in view that consumption and purchase of raw materials are two different aspects. Raw materials, as per policy of the company, are purchased one month before for the whole consumption of the next month but is consumed subsequently to meet the sales target.

Note 2. Closing balance of raw material is kept relating to consumption for the next month in April, consumption is 12,500 × 2 = 25,000 Kgs. As per table given above for this reason, it is presumed that closing balance of raw materials relating to March 1999 is Rs. 25,000 Kgs.

Note 3. In April, production will include :

(*a*) Completing the finished goods, which is already 50% complete.

(*b*) Getting the finished goods ready for closing stock equal to 50% of the estimated sales for the next months.

Flexible budget

Problem 11

The monthly budgets for manufacturing overhead of a concern for two levels of activity were as follows :

Capacity	60%	100%
Budget production (units)	600	1,000
	Rs.	Rs.
Wages	1,200	2,000
Consumable stores	900	1,500
Maintenance	1,100	1,500
Power & Fuel	1,600	2,000
Depreciation	4,000	4,000
Insurance	1,000	1,000
	9,800	12,000

You are required to :

(*i*) Indicate which of the items are fixed, variable and semi-variable.

(*ii*) Prepare a budget for 80% capacity; and

(*iii*) Find the total cost, both fixed and variable, per units of output at 60%, 80% and 100% capacity.

[*C.S. Inter, Dec. 1990*]

Solution

(*i*) Fixed Costs : Depreciation Rs. 4,000
Insurance Rs. 1,000

Variable Costs : Wages = Rs. 1,200 ÷ 600 units or Rs. 2,000 ÷ 1,000 units = Rs. 2·00 per units.

Consumable Stores = Rs. 900 ÷ 600 units or Rs. 1,500 ÷ 1,000 units = Rs. 1·50 per unit.

Semi-variable Costs :

Maintenance =	1,000 units	Rs. 1,500
	600 units	Rs. 1,100
Difference	400 units	Rs. 400

Variable = Rs. 400 ÷ 400 units = Re. 1·00 per unit.

Fixed = Total amount (–) variable
= 1,500 – (1000 × 1·00) = Rs. 500 Fixed

Power & Fuel :	1,000 units	Rs. 2,000
	600 units	Rs. 1,600
Difference	400 units	Rs. 400

Variable = Rs. 400 ÷ 400 units = Re. 1·00 per unit.

Fixed = Total amount (–) variable.
= 1,600 – (600 × 1) = Rs. 1,000 fixed.

(*ii*) Budget for 80% capacity. Output 800 units.

Wages : 800 × 2·00	Rs. 1,600
Consumable stores 800 × 1·50	Rs. 1,200
Maintenance = 500 + (800 × 1)	Rs. 1,300
Power & Fuel = 1,000 + (800 × 1)	Rs. 1,800
Depreciation : Fixed	Rs. 4,000
Insurance : Fixed	Rs. 1,000
Total Cost	Rs. 10,900

(iii) Statement of Total Cost

Capacity	60%	80%	100%
Units	600	800	1,000
	Rs.	**Rs.**	**Rs.**
A. Fixed cost	4,000	4,000	4,000
Depreciation	1,000	1,000	1,000
Insurance	500	500	500
Maintenance			
Power & Fuel	1,000	1,000	1,000
Total "A"	6,500	6,500	6,500
B. Variable Cost			
Wages at Rs. 2·00 per unit	1,200	1,600	2,000
Consumable stores at Rs. 1·50 per unit	900	1,200	1,500
Maintenance at Re. 1·00 per unit	600	800	1,000
Power & Fuel at Re. 1·00 per unit	600	800	1,000
Total "B"	3,300	4,400	5,500
C. Total Cost (A + B)	9,800	10,900	12,000
Fixed Cost per unit	10·833	8·125	6·50
Variable cost per unit	5·50	5·50	5·50
Total cost per unit	16·333	13·625	12·00

Problem 12

Viveka Elementary School has a total of 150 students consisting of 5 sections with 30 students per section. The school plans for a picnic around the city during the weekend to places such as the zoo, the amusement park, the planetarium etc. A private transport operator has come forward to lease out the buses for taking the students. Each bus will have a maximum capacity of 50 (excluding 2 seats reserved for the teachers accompanying the students). The school will employ two teachers for each bus, paying them an allowance of Rs. 50 per teacher. It will also lease out the required number of buses. The following are the other cost estimates :

	Cost per student
Breakfast	5
Lunch	10
Tea	3
Entrance fee at Zoo	2

Rent Rs. 650 per bus
Special permit fee Rs. 50 per bus.
Block Entrance fee at the planetarium Rs. 250.
Prizes to students for games Rs. 250.

No Costs are incurred in respect of the accompanying teachers (except the allowance of Rs. 50 per teacher).

You are required to prepare :

(*a*) A fexible budget estimating the total cost for the levels of 30, 60, 90, 120 and 150 students. Each item of cost is to be indicated separately.

(*b*) Compare the average cost per student at these levels.

(*c*) What will be your conclusions regarding the break-even level of students if the school proposes to collect Rs. 45 per student ?

[C.A. Inter]

Solution

(*a*) Flexible Budget :

Level of Students.	30	60	90	120	150
Variable Cost (Rs.)					
Breakfast at Rs. 5	150	30	450	600	750
Lunch at Rs. 10	300	600	900	1,200	1,500
Tea at Rs. 3	90	180	270	360	450
Entrance fee at Zoo at Rs. 2	60	120	180	240	300
Variable cost at Rs. 20	600	1,200	1,800	2,400	3,000
Semi-variable Costs :					
Rent of Bus	650	1,300	1,300	1,950	1,950
Special permit fee	50	100	100	150	150
Allowance to teachers	100	200	200	300	300
	800	1,600	1,600	2,400	2,400
Fixed Costs :					
Block entrance fee	250	250	250	250	250
Prizes to students for games	250	250	250	250	250
	500	500	500	500	500
Total Cost	1,900	3,300	3,900	5,300	5,900

(b) Average cost per student	1,900 ÷ 30	3,300 ÷ 60	3,900 ÷ 90	5,300 ÷ 120	5,900 ÷ 150
	63·33	55	43·33	44·17	39·33

(c) Break-even level.

First let us work out semi-fixed cost for levels of 50, 100 and 150 students.

Level of students	50	100	150
Semi-fixed costs	800	1,600	2,400
Fixed cost	500	500	500
	1,300	2,100	2,900

Collection per student	: 45
Variable cost per student	: 20
Contribution per student	: 25

Fixed Cost	1,300	2,100	2,900
Contribution per student	25	25	25
Break-even Point	52	84	116

There are two break-even levels i.e. 84 students and 116 students.

Note : 52 is outside the level of 50.

Problem 13

A newly established manufacturing company has an installed capacity to produce 1,00,000 units of a consumer product annually. However, its practical capacity is only 90%. The actual capacity utilization may be substantially lower, as the firm is new to the market and demand is uncertain. The following budget has been prepared for 90% capacity utilisation :

	Cost per Unit (Rs.)	
Direct materials	12	
Direct labour	8	
Direct expenses	5	
Production overheads	10	(40% variable)
Administration overheads	5	(100% fixed)
Selling and Distribution	6	(50% variable)

You are required to prepare budgets at 60%, 70% and 80% levels of capacity utilisation giving clearly the unit variable cost, the unit fixed cost and the total costs under various heads at all the above levels.

[*I.C.W.A. Dec. 2003*]

Solution

(1) Variable overheads :

Production overhead : 40% of Rs. 10 = Rs. 4·00

Selling & Distribution overhead : 50% of Rs. 6 = Rs. 3·00

(2) Fixed Overheads :

Practical capacity is 90% i.e. 90% of 1,00,000 = 90,000 units.

Production overhead : (60% of Rs. 10 = Rs. 6) = 90,000 × Rs. 6 = Rs. 5,40,000.

Administration overhead : (100% of Rs. 5 = 5) 90,000 × 5 = Rs. 4,50,000.

Selling and Distribution overhead (50% of Rs. 6 =3) : 90,000 × 3 = Rs. 2,70,000.

Flexible Budget of a consumer product

Capacity	60%		70%		80%	
Production (units)	60,000		70,000		80,000	
	Total Cost (Rs. in lakhs)	Cost per unit (Rs.)	Total cost (Rs. in lakhs)	Cost per unit (Rs.)	Total cost (Rs. in lakhs)	Cost per unit (Rs.)
Direct costs :						
Direct materials	7·20	12·00	8·40	12·00	9·60	12·00
Direct labour	4·80	8·00	5·60	8·00	6·40	8·00
Direct expenses	3·00	5·00	3·50	5·00	4·00	5·00
Variable Overheads :						
Production overhead	2·40	4·00	2·80	4·00	3·20	4·00
S & D Overhead (Ref. W.N. 2)	1·80	3·00	2·10	3·00	2·40	3·00
Total variable Cost (A)	19·20	32·00	22·40	32·00	25·60	32·00
Fixed Overheads :						
Production overheads	5·40	9·00	5·40	7·71	5·40	6·75
Administration overhead	4·50	7·50	4·50	6·43	4·50	5·62
S&D Overhead (Ref. W.N. 2)	2·70	4·50	2·70	3·86	2·70	3·38
Total Fixed cost (B)	12·60	21·00	12·60	18·00	12·60	15·75
Total cost (A + B)	31·80		35·00		38·20	
Cost per Unit (Rs.)		53·00		50·00		47·75

Problem 14

MASTER BUDGET

Carryon Ltd. manufactures two products, B and T. It is going to prepare its budget for the year ending 31st December 1988. Expectations for 1988 include :

	Rs.	Rs.	Rs.
(A) Opening Balance :			
Fixed Assets :			
Land		20,000	
Building and Plant		1,50,000	
Cumulative depreciation		(60,000)	1,10,000
Current Assets :			
Stock : Raw Materials (P & Q)		3,000	
B		3,400	
T		7,200	
		13,600	
Debtors		45,000	
Cash/Bank		10,000	
		68,600	
Less : Current Liabilities :			
Creditors	29,000		
Taxation	28,000	57,000	11,600
			1,21,600
Represented by :			
Share capital		71,600	
Retentions		50,000	1,21,600

(B) Finished Products	**B**	**T**
Budgeted sales (Units)	5,000	1,000
Budgeted selling price (per unit)	Rs. 30	Rs. 50
Opening stock of finished goods (in units)	200	300
Budgeted closing stock (in units)	1,200	200
(*c*) Production Details		
(*i*) Direct Materials	P	Q
Raw materials per unit of Production		
B	5 Kg.	3 Kg.
T	2 Kg.	4 Kg.
Opening Stock of Raw materials	2,000 Kg.	2,000 Kg.
Budgeted closing stock	2,500 Kg.	1,500 Kg.
Cost per Kg. of material purchased	Rs. 0·50	Rs. 1·00

(*ii*) Direct Labour :

Labour is paid at the rate of Rs. 2 per hour, 3 direct labour hours are required to produce one unit of B and 5 labour hours are required for one unit of T.

(*iii*) Factory Overheads :

It has been estimated that factory overheads will be Rs. 33,750 including Rs. 11,750 for depreciation. Factory overheads are absorbed on a direct labour hour basis.

(*iv*) Work-in-Progress

This is negligible and can be ignored (i.e. no opening or closing stocks).

(*d*) Administrative Overheads :

These are estimated to be Rs. 11,625. They are charged to goods leaving work in progress and entering finished goods stocks and are absorbed as a percentage of factory cost.

(*e*) Selling and Distribution Overheads :

These are estimated to be Rs. 20,000. They are charged to the cost of sales on the basis of percentage of selling price.

(*f*) Stock Pricing :

Goods are priced on FIFO basis. Opening stocks of raw materials are 2,000 Kgs. of P at Rs. 0·50 (Rs. 1,000) and 2,000 Kg. of Q at Rs. 1 (Rs. 2,000).

(*g*) Taxation on 1988 profit is estimated at Rs. 30,000. Overdraft Interest in 1988 is expected to be Rs. 595, Rs. 500 of which will be paid during third quarter of the year.

You are required to prepare the following budgets for 1988 for Carryon Ltd. using absorption costing methods :

(*a*) Sales budget
(*b*) Production budget (quantities only)
(*c*) Direct Materials budget (usage and purchases)
(*d*) Direct Labour budget
(*e*) Overhead absorption rate
(*f*) Closing stock budget
(*g*) Cost of goods sold budget
(*h*) Budgeted Profit & Loss A/c. **[*I.C.W.A. (Final)*]**

Solution

(a) Sales Budget

Product	Quantity	Selling Price	Sales (Rs.)
B	5,000	Rs. 30	1,50,000
T	1,000	Rs. 50	50,000
			2,00,000

(b) Production Budget (Quantities)

	B (Units)	T (Units)
Budgets sales	5,000	1,000
Add : Closing stock	1,200	200
	6,200	1,200
Less : Opening stock	200	300
Production Budget	6,000	900

(c) Direct Materials Budget

	P (Kg.)	Q (Kg.)
To Produce :		
B 6,000 × 5 =	30,000	6,000 × 3 = 18,000
T 900 × 2 =	1,800	900 × 4 = 3,600
Direct Materials Usage	31,800	21,600
Add : Closing stock	2,500	1,500
	34,300	23,100
Less : Opening stock	2,000	2,000
Direct Materials purchase	32,300	21,100
Cost per Kg.	Re. 0·50	Re. 1·00
Cost of purchase Rs. 37,250	Rs. 16,150	Rs. 21,100

(d) Direct Labour Budget :

B 6,000 units at 3 hours = 18,000 hrs. at Rs. 2 = Rs. 36,000.

T 900 units at 5 hours = 4,500 hrs. at Rs. 2 = Rs. 9,000

(e) Overhead absorption rates :

(i) Budgeted factory overhead Rs. 33,750

Budgeted direct labour hours 22,500

Budgeted Fixed Overhead absorption rate 33,750 ÷ 22,500 = Rs. 1·50 per DLH

(f) Closing Stock Budget

Raw Materials	*P*		*Q*	
	Kg.	*Rs.*	*Kg.*	*Rs.*
Opening Stock	2,000	1,000	2,000	2,000
Purchase	32,300	16,150	21,100	21,100
	34,300	17,150	23,100	23,100
Less : Consumption	31,800	15,900	21,600	21,600
Closing stock =	2,500	1,250	1,500	1,500

(g) Cost of Goods Sold Budget (Rs.)

Particulars	*B*	*T*
Direct Materials consumed		
P 30,000 × 0·50	15,000	1,800 × 0·50 = 900
Q 18,000 × 1·00	18,000	3,600 × 1·00 = 3,600
Direct materials	36,000	9,000
Prime cost	69,000	13,500

Factory Overheads 18,000 × 1·50	27,000	4,500 × 1·50 = 6,750
Factory cost of goods produced	96,000	20,250
Admn. Overheads at 10% of Factory cost	9,600	2,025
Cost of Production	1,05,600	22,275
Cost of Production Per Unit	17·60	22,275 ÷ 900 = 24·75
1,05,600 ÷ 6,000		
Cost of production	1,05,600	22,275
Add : Opening stock of Finished Goods 200 units	3,400	300 units 7,200
Finished Goods 200 units	1,09,000	29,475
Less : Closing stock of finished goods (FIFO basis) 1,200 × 17·60 =	21,120	200 × 24·75 = 4,950
Cost of Goods Sold	87,880	24,525
Add : S&D overheads Rs. 20,000 at 10% on sales	15,000	5,000
Cost of sales	1,02,880	29,525

(h) Budgeted Profit & Loss A/c.

	B (Rs.)	T (Rs.)	Total (Rs.)
Sales	1,50,000	50,000	2,00,000
Less : Cost of sales	1,02,880	29,525	1,32,405
Profit before interest	47,120	20,475	67,595
Overhead interest			595
Profit before tax			67,000
Tax			30,000
Profit after tax			37,000

Note : Factory cost =	B	96,000
	T	20,250
		1,16,250
Admn. Overheads		11,625 i.e. 10% on Factory Cost.

Problem 15

Manufacturers Ltd. produces three products from three basic raw materials in three departments. The company operates a budgetary control system and values its stock of finished goods on a total cost basis. From the following data, you are required to produce for the month of July 1986 the following budgets :

(*a*) Production

(*b*) Material usage

(*c*) Purchase

(*d*) Profit and Loss A/c for each product and in total.

Budgeted data for July 1986.

	Products		
	A (Rs.)	*B (Rs.)*	*C (Rs.)*
Sales	15,00,000	10,80,000	16,80,000
Stock of finished products at July 1, 1986 (units)	3,000	2,000	2,500

	Departments		
	I	II	III
Production overhead (Rs.)	2,39,000	2,01,300	3,91,200
Direct Labour hours	47,800	67,100	65,200
Direct Materials	M1	M2	M3
Stock at July 1, 1986 in units	24,500	20,500	17,500

The company is introducing a new system of inventory control which should reduce stock. The forecast is that stocks as at 31st July 1986 will be reduced as follows: Raw Material by 10% and finished products by 20%.

Fixed production overhead is absorbed on a direct labour hour basis. It is expected that there will be no work-in-progress at the beginning or end of the month.

Administration cost is absorbed by products at a rate of 20% of production cost and selling and distribution cost is absorbed by products at a rate of 40% of production cost.

Profit is budgeted as a percentage of total cost as :

Product A 25%, Product B $12\frac{1}{2}$% and Product C $16\frac{2}{3}$%.

Standard cost data per unit of product :

	Price per unit	A	B	C
Direct Materials :	Rs.	Unit	Unit	Unit
M1	2·00	5		12
M2	4·00		10	9
M3	1·00	5	5	
Direct Wages :	Rate per Hour (Rs.)	Hour	Hour	Hour
Depart. I	2·50	4	2	2
Deptt. II	2·00	6	2	3
Deptt. III	1·50	2	4	6
		Rs.	Rs.	Rs.
Other variable costs		10	20	15

[*C.A. Final*]

Solution

In the question, budgeted sales value has been given but not the budgeted selling price and sales in units. First let us find out the budgeted selling price :

Budgeted Selling Price (all data per unit)

	Products		
	A (Rs.)	B (Rs.)	C (Rs.)
A. Direct Materials :			
M1	10		24
M2		40	36
M3	5	5	
	15	45	60
B. Direct Wages ::			
Dept. I	10	5	5
Deptt. II	12	4	6
Deptt. III	3	6	9
	25	15	20

	A	B	C
C. Other variables costs	10	20	15
D. Marginal Cost (A + B + C)	50	80	95
E. Fixed Production Overheads :			
Deptt. I 2,39,000 ÷ 47,800 = Rs. 5 p/hour	20	10	10
Deptt. II 2,01,300 ÷ 67,100 = Rs. 3 p/hour	18	6	9
Deptt. III 3,91,200 ÷ 65,200 = Rs. 6 p/hour	12	24	36
Total E	50	40	55
F. Production Cost (D + E)	100	120	150
Admn. Cost 20%	20	24	30
S & D cost 40%	40	48	60
Total Cost	160	192	240
Profit	40	24	40
Selling Price (budgeted)	200	216	280
Sales value	15,00,000	10,80,000	16,80,000
Sales in unit 15,00,000 ÷ 200	7,500	5,000	6,000

(a) Production Budget (units)

	A	*B*	*C*
Sales	7,500	5,000	6,000
Add : Closing stock 3,000 – 20% =	2,400	1,600	2,000
Total requirement	9,900	6,600	8,000
Less : Opening stock	3,000	2,000	2,500
Production Budget	6,900	4,600	5,500

(b) Materials usage budget (unit)

Product	*M1*	*M2*	*M3*
A	6,900 × 5 = 34,500		6,900 × 5 = 34,500
B		4,600 × 10 = 46,000	4,600 × 5 = 23,000
C	5,500 × 12 = 66,000	5,500 × 9 = 49,500	
Materials usage (unit)	1,00,500	95,500	57,500

(c) Materials purchase budget

	M1	*M2*	*M3*
Usage (units)	1,00,500	95,500	57,500
Add : Closing stock 24,500—10%	22,050	18,450	15,750
Less : Opening stock	24,500	20,500	17,500
Materials purchase budget	98,050	93,450	55,750
Price per unit (Rs.)	2·00	4·00	1·00
Purchase cost (Rs.)	1,96,100	3,73,800	55,750

Total Purchase Cost for July 1986 is Rs. 6,25,650

(D) Budgeted P & L A/c for July 1986 (Rs. in lakhs)

	Products.			
	A	*B*	*C*	*Total*
Total cost of production 6,900 × 160	11·04	8·832	13·20	33·072
Add : Opening stock 3000 × 100	4·80	3·84	6·00	14·64
	15·84	12·672	19·20	47·712
Less : Closing stock : 2,400 × 160	3·84	3·072	4·80	11·712
Cost of sales	12·00	9·60	14·40	36·00
Sales	15·00	10·80	16·80	42·60
Profit	3·00	1·20	2·40	6·60

Note : Stock of finished goods has been valued on total cost basis as given in the question.

EXERCISES

OBJECTIVE TYPE QUESTIONS

1. *Which of the following statements are true or false.*

(*i*) Limiting factor is a major constraint on all operational activities of the organisation.
(*ii*) The budget relating to the key factor should be prepared last.
(*iii*) For control purpose, long term budgets should be prepared.
(*iv*) Sales estimate given in the budget is a mere guess.
(*v*) Sales budget is the most important and forms the basis on which all other budgets are built up.
(*vi*) Zero-base budgeting overcomes the weakness of functional budgets.
(*vii*) A fixed budget is useful only when the actual level of activity corresponds to the budgeted level of activity.

[Ans. True—(*i*), (*v*), (*vii*) False—(*ii*), (*iii*), (*iv*), (*vi*)]

2. *Which of the following is a correct definition of the principal budget factor ?*

(*a*) The factor which limits the activities of the undertaking.
(*b*) That factor which maximises sales.
(*c*) The factor which most members of management feel is important.
(*d*) The amount of cash available during the budget period.

[Ans. (*a*)]

3. *The direct material usage budget and direct material purchase budget differ because of which of the following ?*

(*a*) The level of Material scrape forecast occur.
(*b*) The level of efficiency of men or machines.
(*c*) A change in the level of finished goods stock.
(*d*) A planned change in the level of material stock.

[Ans. (*d*)]

4. *What type of budget is designed to take into account forcast changes in costs, prices etc.*

(*a*) Rolling budget.
(*b*) Functional budget.
(*c*) Flexible budget.
(*d*) Master budget.

[Ans. (*a*)]

5. The question of raw material in the purchase budget may be higher than the quantity of raw material in the production budget because :

(*a*) Stock levels are being reduced.
(*b*) Raw material prices are falling.
(*c*) The company obtains discount for bulk purchases.
(*d*) Units sold will be higher than units made.

[Ans. (*c*)]

THEORETICAL QUESTIONS

1. What is budget ? What is meant by budgetary control ? How do you distinguish between the two ? What is the importance of Budgetary Control ? ***[C.U. B.Com. (Hons.)]***
2. What factors should be considered at the time of preparation of budget. ***[C.U. B.Com. (Hons.) 1995]***
3. Define budget and budgetary control. State the advantages of budgetary control in an organisation.
4. What is budgetary control ? How would you distinguish it from standard costing ? ***[B.Com. Delhi, 1994]***
5. Distinguish clearly between any two of the following :
   (*a*) Budgetary control and standard costing.
   (*b*) Cost control and cost reduction.
   (*c*) Differential cost and marginal cost. ***[I.C.W.A. Inter, B.Com. Delhi]***
6. Comment on the following :
   (*a*) In applying budgetary control why are we to treat a group of costs a fixed cost when we know that in the long run all costs are truly variable.
   (*b*) Budgets and standards can be set on different basis of achievement.
   (*c*) State the importance of 'budget key factor' in budgeting.
7. What is Zero base budgeting ? How does it differ from traditional budgeting ? Discuss its advantages and disadvantages. ***[C.U. B.Com (Hons)]***
8. What do you understand by the term flexible budget ? How is it drawn up and what difficulties would you expect to face in its computation ? Is flexible budget useful to the management ? ***[I.C.W.A. Inter. C.S. Inter]***
9. Distinguish between fixed and flexible budget. State the circumstances in which flexible budgets are used. ***[C.A. (Inter), Nov. 1989]***
10. What is meant by "Flexible budgeting" ? How is it prepared ? Give any two applications. ***[I.C.W.A. Inter, Dec. 2002]***
11. Write short-notes on :
    (*a*) Differential Cost Analysis.
    (*b*) Flexible budget. ***[I.C.W.A. Inter-2004]***
12. Explain briefly the salient features of sales budget, production budget and cash budget.
13. What do you mean by Master Budget ? ***[B.Com. Madurai, 1992]***
14. (*a*) What is Production Budget ?
    (*b*) What are the steps involved in preparation of production budget ?***[I.C.W.A. Inter, Dec. '93]***

PROBLEMS

1. From the following information, prepare a cash budget for the quarter ending on 30.06.2000 :

Months	*Sales* Rs.	*Purchases* Rs.	*Wages* Rs.	*Misc. Exp.* Rs.
February	1,20,000	84,000	10,000	7,000
March	1.30,000	1,00,000	12,000	8,000
April	80,000	1,04,000	8,000	6,000
May	1,16,000	1,06,000	10,000	12,000
June	88,000	80,000	8,000	6,000

Additional information :

(*i*) Cash on hand on 1.4.2000 Rs. 5,000.
(*ii*) Sales—20% realised in the month of Sale, Discount allowed 2%; balance realised after two months.
(*iii*) Purchases are paid one month after.
(*iv*) Wages—25% in arrears paid in the following month.
(*v*) Other expenses are paid at a lag of one month.
(vi) Income Tax Rs. 25,000 due on or before 30.6.2000. ***[C.U. B.Com. (H)]***

[Ans. Cash balance at the end of April, May & June Rs. (–) 320; Rs. 6,916, Rs. (–) 63,336]

2. From the following information supplied by Bright Ltd. prepare a cash budget for the period from 21st September 1989 to 31st December 1989 :

Months	Credit Purchases	Credit Sales	Wages	Selling Expenses	Overhead
	Rs.	Rs.	Rs.	Rs.	Rs.
July	85,000	1,60,000	32,000	8,000	10,000
August	92,000	1,85,000	37,000	9,500	11,500
September	1,00,000	2,10,000	42,000	10,500	13,000
October	1,20,000	2,45,000	49,000	12,500	14,500
November	90,000	1,78,000	35,500	8,900	10,500
December	98,000	1,92,000	36,000	9,000	11,000

Additional Information :

(*a*) Expected Cash Balance on 1st September—Rs. 10,500

(*b*) Period of Credit allowed to Debtors—2 months.

(*c*) Period of credit allowed by Creditors—1 month.

(*d*) Lag in payment for Wage, Selling Expenses and overhead—1 month.

(*e*) Selling commission @ 2% on sales is payable one month after sales.

(*f*) Expenditure of Machinery worth Rs. 50,000 is payable in October.

(*g*) Expected cash sales per month Rs. 15,000. No Commission is payable on cash sales.

[*C.U. B.Com. (H) 1989*]

[Ans. Closing Cash at the end of Sept. Rs. 31,800; Oct. Rs. 12,100; Nov. Rs. 36,200 and Dec. Rs. 1,47,740]

3. On 30th Sept. 1996, the balance sheet of M. Ltd. (retailer) was as under :

	Rs.		*Rs.*
Equity shares of 10 each fully paid	20,000	Equipment (at cost)	20,000
Reserves	10,000	*Less* : Depreciation	5,000
Trade creditors	40,000		15,000
Proposed dividend	15,000	Stock	20,000
		Trade debtors	15,000
		Balance at Bank	35,000
	85,000		85,000

The company is dveloping a system of forward planning and on 1st October 1996 it supplies the following information :

	Sales (Rs.)		*Purchase (Rs.)*
	Credit	*Cash*	*Credit*
September 1996 (actual)	15,000	14,000	40,000
October 1996 (budget)	18,000	5,000	23,000
November 1996 (budget)	20,000	6,000	27,000
December 1996 (budget)	25,000	8,000	26,000

All trade debtors are allowed one month's credit and are expected to settle promptly.

All trade creditors are paid in the months following delivery.

On 1st October 1996 all equipments were replaced at a cost of Rs. 30,000. Rs. 14,000 was allowed in exchange for the old equipment and a net payment of Rs. 16,000 was made.

The proposed dividend will be paid in December 1996.

The following expenses will be paid :

Wages Rs. 3,000 per month, Administration Rs. 1,500 per month and Rent Rs. 3,600 for the year up to 30th September 1997 (to be paid in October 1996).

You are required to prepare a Cash Budget for the months of October, November and December, 1996.

[Ans. Closing overdraft at the end of October, Rs. 9,100; November., Rs. 12,600 and December Rs. 31,100]

4. You are requested to prepare a Sales Overhead Budget from the estimates given below :

	Rs.
Advertisement	2,500
Salaries of the Sales department	5,000
Expenses of sales department	1,500
Counter-salesman's salaries and Dearness allowances	6,000

Commission to counter-salesman at 1% on their sales.

Travelling salesmen's commission at 10% on their sales and expenses at 5% on their sales.

The sales during the period were estimated as follows :

Counter Sales *Rs.*	Travelling Salesmens' Commission *Rs.*
80,000	10,000
1,20,000	15,000
1,40,000	20,000

[*C.A. Inter*]

[Ans. Rs. 17,300; 18,450; 19,400]

5. Bright Ltd. have prepared the budget for the production of 1,00,000 units of a product for a costing period as under :

	Per Unit *Rs.*
Raw materials	10·08
Direct Labour	3·00
Direct Expenses	·40
Works overhead (60% fixed)	10·00
Administration overhead (80% fixed)	1·60
Sales overhead	0·80

Actual production in the period was only 60,000 units.

Prepare budgets for the original and revised levels of output. **[*B.Com. Madurai*]**

[Ans. Original : 25·88, Per unit. Total : Rs. 25,88,000
Revised : 31·00, Per unit. Total : Rs. 18,60,000]

6. From the following information, prepare a Cash Budget for the three months ending 31.3.05 :

Months	*Sales* *Rs.*	*Purchases* *Rs.*	*Other Expenses* *Rs.*
December	1,00,000	60,000	10,000
January	1,20,000	80,000	12,000
February	1,50,000	90,000	15,000
March	1,40,000	1,00,000	18,000

Additional information :

1. 10% of sales are in cash and the remaining customers are allowed one month's credit.
2. Lag in payment of other expenses is one month.
3. Suppliers allow credit for one month.
4. Income tax Rs. 20,000 is to be paid in March 2005.
5. Expected Cash balance on 1.1.2005 is Rs. 20,000.

[*C.U. B.Com. 2004*]

7. A company making for stock in first quarter of the year is assisted by its bankers with overdraft accommodation. The following are the relevant figures :

Months	*Sales*	*Purchases*	*Wages & Expenses*
	Rs.	*Rs.*	*Rs.*
November	1,20,000	83,000	10,000
December	1,28,000	96,000	10,000
January	72,000	1,62,000	11,000
February	1,16,000	1,64,000	10,000
March	84,000	40,000	12,000

Given the following further information, you are required to prepare a cash budget for the quarter January to March showing the budgeted amount of bank facilities required, if any, at each month end :

(*a*) Budgeted cash at bank on 1st January Rs. 20,000.

(*b*) Credit terms of sales are—payment by the end of the month following the month of supply, on average one-half of sales are paid on the due date, while the other half are paid during the next month. Creditors are paid during the months following the month of supply.

(*c*) Wages and Expenses are paid twice in a month on 1st and 16th, respectively.

[*C.U. M.Com*]

[Ans. January : Bank balance Rs. 37,500
February : Overdraft Rs. 35,000
March : Overdraft Rs. 81,000]

8. Prepare a cash Budget of Modern Garments Ltd. for the six months ending september 2000, on the basis of the following information :

(*i*) **Sales Forecast**

January	Rs. 2,40,000	June	Rs. 1,80,000
February	Rs. 2,00,000	July	Rs. 2,10,000
March	Rs. 2,60,000	August	Rs. 2,00,000
April	Rs. 1,40,000	September	Rs. 2,00,000
May	Rs. 1,60,000	October	Rs. 1,60,000

(*ii*) Cash sales represent 20% of total sales, 60% of the credit sales are collected in 30 days, 30% in 60 days and balance in 90 days.

(*iii*) Gross profit margin is maintained at 20% of selling price.

(*iv*) Anticipated sales of each month is purchased and paid in cash in the preceding month.

(*v*) Administration and selling distribution expenses are budgeted as follows :

April	Rs. 11,000	July	Rs. 14,500
May	Rs. 12,000	August	Rs. 14,500
June	Rs. 13,500	September	Rs. 15,000

(*vi*) Payment for installation of a machine costing Rs. 80,000 is due on 1st May 2000.

(*vii*) Interest on Fixed Deposit of Rs. 2 Lakhs @ 12% p.a. is payable quarterly in April and July.

(*viii*) Advance Tax of Rs. 24,000 is payable on 14th June 20,000.

(*ix*) Interest on investment amounting to Rs. 10,000 per quarter is receivable in June and Sept.

(*x*) 25% of the value of an asset sold for Rs. 1 Lakh is due in August 2000.

(*xi*) The company has a cash balance of Rs. 57,500 on 31st March 2000. If at any time cash balance reduces below Rs. 50,000 level, short-term Loan @ Rs. 10,000 at a time is arranged @ 18% p.a. interest payable on monthly basis.

[*I.C.W.A. Inter, Adopted*]

[Ans. Closing cash balance : April : Rs. 1,32,500; May : 74,100; June : Rs. 55,800; July : Rs. 53,150; August Rs. 90,450; September : Rs. 1,58,250]

Note : (1) In June borrowing are to be made for Rs. 10,000, otherwise the closing cash balance will reach below Rs. 50,000.

(2) Short term loan will be repaid in August.

9. The monthly budgets for manufacturing overhead of a concern for two levels of activity were as follows :

Capacity	60%	100%
Budgeted production (units)	600	1,000
	Rs.	*Rs.*
Wages	1,200	2,000
Consumable stores	900	1,500
Maintenance	1,100	1,500
Power & Fuel	1,600	2,000
Depreciation	4,000	4,000
Insurance	1,000	1,000
	9,800	12,000

You are required to :

(*i*) Indicate which of the items are fixed, variable and semi-variable.

(ii) Prepare a budget for 80% capacity, and

(iii) Find the total cost, both fixed and variable, per unit of output at 60%, 80% and 100% capacity.

[C.S. Inter, Dec. 1990]

[Ans. Depreciation and insurance fixed, wages and consumable stores variable and maintenance and power semi-variable at 80% capacity Rs. 10,900 per unit variable Rs. 5·50 at each level, and fixed Rs. 10·83; Rs. 8·13 and Rs. 6·50]

10. Workout a flexible budget for overhead expenses on the basis of the following data available from the cash records and determine the overhead rates at 70%, 80% and 90% plant capacity levels.

Variable overheads :At 80% capacity level	
Indirect Material	Rs. 1,44,000
Indirect Labour	Rs. 64,000
Semi variable overheads :	
Power (70% variable)	Rs. 2,00,000
Repair and Maintenance (60% fixed)	Rs. 50,000
Fixed Overheads :	
Depreciation	Rs. 36,000
Insurance	Rs. 16,000
Others	Rs. 1,08,000

Estimated direct Labour hours : 2,40,000 Hours.

[I.C.W.A. Inter, Dec. 2001]

[Ans.

	70%	**80%**	**90%**
Total overheads.	**5,72,000**	**6,18,000**	**6,64,000**
Direct Labour-Hours.	**2,10,000**	**2,40,000**	**2,70,000**
O/H rate per Labour Hour	**2·724**	**2·575**	**2·459]**

11. The budgeted cost of ABC Ltd., a factory specialising in the production of a single product at the optimum capacity of 6,400 units, per annum amounts to Rs. 1,76,048 as detailed below :

	Rs.	*Rs*
Fixed Costs		20,688
Variable Costs :		
Power	1,440	
Repair etc.	1,700	
Miscellaneous	540	
Direct Material	49,280	
Direct Labour	1,02,400	1,55,360
		1,76,048

Taking note of the possible impact on sales turnover by market trends, the company decides to have a flexible budget with a production target of 3,200 and 4,800 units (the actual quantity proposed to be produced being left to a later date before commencement of the budget period.)

Prepare a flexible budget for production levels at 50% and 75%.

Assuming selling price per unit is maintained at Rs. 40 as at present, indicate the effect on net profit. Administration, selling and distribution expenses continue at Rs. 3,600.

[*C.A. Final. Adopted*]

[Ans.

	50%	**75%**	**100%**
Total costs :	**1,01,968**	**1,40,808**	**1,79,648**
Profit :	**26,032**	**51,192**	**76,352]**

12. A company incurs the following expenses to produce 1,000 units of an article :

	Rs.
Direct Materials	30,000
Direct Labour	15,000
Power (20% fixed)	10,000
Repairs and Maintenance (15% fixed)	8,000
Depreciation (40% variable)	6,000
Administration Expenses (100% fixed)	12,000

Prepare a Flexible Budget showing individual expenses of production level at 1,500 units and 2,000 units.

[*C.U. B.Com. (H) 1998*]

[Ans. Budget for 1,500 units; Marginal Cost per unit Rs. 62·20 and Total Rs. 93,300; Cost Per unit Rs. 74·73 and Total Rs. 1,12,100; Budget for 2,000 units; M.C. per unit 2·20 and Total Rs. 1,24,400; T.C. per unit Rs. 71·60 and Total Rs. 1,43,200]

13. A factory is currently running at 50% capacity and produces 5,000 units at a cost of Rs. 90 per unit as per details below :

	Rs.	
Material	50	
Labour	15	
Factory Overheads	15	(Rs. 6 fixed)
Administrative Overhead	10	(Rs. 5 fixed)

The current selling price is Rs. 100 per unit. At 60% working material cost per unit increases by 2% and selling price per unit falls by 2%.

Estimate profits of the factory at 60% working. [*C.U. B.Com.*]

[Ans. Production and sales at 60% capacity = 6,000 units; selling price per unit Rs. 98; material cost per unit Rs. 51; Gross Profit Rs. 1,08,000; Net Profit Rs. 53,000 (per unit) Rs. 8·83]

14. The cost of an article at a capacity level of 5,000 units is given in the table below under column A. For a variation of 25% in capacity above or below this level, the individual expenses vary, as indicated in column B :

	A (Rs.)	B (Rs.)
Material cost	25,000	100% variable
Labour cost	15,000	100% variable
Power	1,250	80% semi-variable
Repairs and maintanance	2,000	75% semi-variable
Stores	1,000	100% variable
Inspection	500	20% semi-variable
Administration overheads	5,000	25% semi-variable
Selling overheads	3,000	50% semi-variable
Depreciation	10,000	100% fixed
Total	62,750	
Cost per unit	12·55	

You are required to prepare the production Cost Budget (flexible) at 4,000 units and 6,000 units.

[I.C.W.A. Dec. 2004]

15. From the following particulars prepare flexible budget for the three months ending 30th September, showing the estimated sales, costs and profit for 60%, 80% and 100% activity.

Assume that all items produced are sold.

Fixed Expenses	*Rs.*
Management Salaries	4,20,000
Rent and Rates	2,80,000
Depreciation of Machinery	3,50,000
Sundry Office Cost	4,45,000
	14,95,000
Semi-variable Expenses at 50% activity :	
Plant Maintenance	1,25,000
Indirect Labour	4,95,000
Salesmen's Salaries & Expenses	1,45,000
Sundry Expenses	1,30,000
	8,95,000
Variable Expenses at 50% activity :	
Materials	12,00,000
Labour	12,80,000
Salesmen's Commission	1,90,000
	26,70,000

Semi-variable expenese remain constant between 40% and 70% activity, Increase by 10% of the above figures between 70% and 80% acitivity and increase by 15% of the above figures between 80% and 100% activity; Fixed expenses remain constant whatever be the level of activity. Sales at 60% activity are Rs. 51,00,000; at 80% activity are Rs. 68,00,000 and at 100% activity are Rs. 85,00,000.

C.U. B.Com. (H) 2003]

[Ans. A_1 = Assuming the gross figures are related to a period of 3 months A_2 = Assuming the gross figures are annual figure At 50% Level (Loss) : A_1 = Rs. 8,10,000, A_2= 2,02,500.
At 60% Level loss A_1 : Rs. 4,94,000; A_2 : Rs. 1,23,500.; At 80% Level Profit A_1: Rs. 48,500; A_2 :12,125 At 100% Level Profit A_1 = Rs. 6,35,750; A_2 = Rs. 1,58,938]

16. A company manufactures two products X and Y. A forecast of unit to be sold in the first 4 months of the year is given below :

Months	*Product X*	*Product Y*
January	1,000	2,800
February	1,200	2,800
March	1,600	2,400
April	2,000	2,000
May	2,400	1,600

Other information are as follows :

Cost per unit (Rs.)	*Product X*	*Product Y*
Direct Material	12·50	19·00
Direct Labour	4·50	7·00
Factory overhead/unit	3·00	4·00

There will be no opening and closing work-in-progress (WIP) at the end of any month and finished product (in units) is equal to half of the budgeted sale of the next month should be in stock at the end of each month (including previous year December).

You are required to prepare :

(*i*) Production Budget for the period January to April, and

(*ii*) Summarised Production Cost Budget.

[*I.C.W.A. Dec. 04*]

17. From the particulars of Arab Ltd. given below, prepare a forecast on Profit & Loss Account for the year ended on 31st December 1998 and a projected Cash Account for the year ended on that date.

(*a*) Extract from Profit & Loss Account for the year ended 31st December 1997 :

	Rs.
Material consumed	24,000
Wages	20,000
Overhead (50% variable)	40,000
Sales (All production)	
1,000 Units @ 100 per Unit.	1,00,000

(*b*) **Balance Sheet, as on 31.12.97.**

Share capital	70,000	Fixed Assets	60,000
Reserve & Surplus	24,000	(Costless Dep.)	
S/Creditors	4,000	Stock (Materials)	8,000
Proposed Dividend	7,000	Debtors	25,000
		Cash & Bank	12,000
	1,05,000		1,05,000

(*c*) Other relevant information :

(*i*) Arab Ltd. contemplates an increase in the sales volume by 20%. This would necessitate @ 5% reduction in selling price.

(*ii*) Estimated increase in costs. Material 2%; Wages 3%; Variable overhead 2%; and Fixed overhead 1%.

(*iii*) Terms of payment : Debtors 3 months, creditors 2 months, wages and expenses within the month in which they are due.

(*iv*) Stock (Materials) carrying policy 4 months production requirements. Materials are issued on FIFO basis.

(*v*) Income Tax at 30% should be paid in advance. A dividend @ 10% may be proposed to pay in the subsequent year.

(*vi*) Fixed costs include depreciation which is a fixed instalment of Rs. 10,000 p.a. charged in full to overheads.

Assume that there will not be any closing Work-in-Progress and Production and Sales will coincide.

[*C.U. M.Com. Adopted*]

[Ans. Purchase : 31,168; Wages : 24,720; Sales : 1,14,000; G.P. 59,904; Net Profit : 8,324; Cash : 23,730]

12 Marginal Costing

Authors' Comments and Suggestions :

1. ***It is the most important chapter and not less than one question is set from this chapter in C.A., I.C.W.A. and degree course examination.***
2. ***Students should first learn the actual implication of different marginal cost equations and the effect on those equations due to change in cost.***
3. ***Break-even Analysis is the most important area of this chapter. Hence a thorough knowledge of Fixed and Variable cost and its implication in product cost is necessary.***
4. ***Students should have clear understanding on the meaning and use of contribution which is the key to different problems.***
5. ***Effect on Profit-Volume-ratio is an important part of this chapter. Students should go through these problems very carefully as P/V ratio helps to eliminate the unprofitable lines which are having either a lower P/V ratio or low volume.***
6. ***Students should also know in details about the margin of safety and Angle of incidence.***

Section I : Marginal Costing and Break-even-Analysis.

Introduction—Marginal costing and Marginal cost—Absorption costing—Contribution—Marginal Cost equation—Break-even point—Break-even chart—Advantages and Disadvantages of Break-even chart. Profit-volume Ratio—Margin of Safety—Angle of incidence—Formula used in Marginal costing—Illustrations—Workedout Problems.

Introduction

It is a common knowledge that profit is the difference between sales revenue and cost. But this concept is not sufficient for a manager who wishes to discharge the functions of planning, controlling and decision making. Because all costs are not of the same nature. Costs are divided according to their behavior mainly into two parts, namely, fixed cost and variable cost. Based on these changes in behavior of costs an effective cost accounting technique emerges. It is known as marginal costing. Marginal costing is concerned basically with the determination of product costs, which consist of total cost less the fixed cost. It is said to have begun around the turn of the 19th century when the idea of estimating overhead in advance and predetermined overhead rate was developed.

Marginal Costing and Marginal Cost

The term marginal costing is generally used in Great Britain while it is referred to as 'direct costing' in the U.S.A. Indeed, both marginal costing and direct costing mean the same thing.

Marginal costing has been used mainly for internal reporting with a view to enabling the management to effectively plan and control the operations. It is a management technique of ascertaining marginal costs and of the effect on profit of changes in volume or type of output by differentiating the total cost into fixed and variable.

CIMA defines marginal costing as 'the accounting system in which variable costs are charged to the cost units and fixed costs of the period are written-off in full against the aggregate contribution. Its special value is in decision-making'.

The salient features of marginal costing are :

(*a*) The usefulness of the marginal cost system largely depends upon a correct appreciation of the behaviors of costs with change of output.

(*b*) Only the variable or marginal costs are taken into consideration for determining product costs.

(*c*) Fixed costs are written-off during the period in which they are incurred, hence it has no impact on the valuation of finished or semi-finished stocks. They are valued only on the basis of variable cost.

(*d*) Prices are based on marginal cost and contribution.

(*e*) Profitability of departments or products is determined in terms of the contribution.

Marginal Cost

According to economists, marginal costs are the additional cost of an additional unit. But the accountants define this as the aggregate of variable costs i.e. prime cost plus variable overhead. Actually it is the added costs. These are out of pocket outlay, which would not be incurred if a particular product or product line was eliminated.

According to CIMA marginal cost is "The cost of one unit of product or service which would be avoided if that unit was not produced or provided".

Example : Suppose per unit variable cost is Rs. 2/-, Fixed cost for a particular period is Rs. 1000/-, Present activity level = 100 units. Then present total cost (2 × 100 + 1,000) = Rs. 1,200/-. Now if the activity level is changed to 101 units then the total cost will be (2 × 101 + 1,000) = Rs. 1,202/-. Hence the change in cost is (Rs. 1,202 – 1,200) = Rs. 2.

Change in units = (101 – 100) = 1 unit.

From the above example it is clear that for an additional unit of production, the additional cost is Rs. 2/- which is equal to variable cost. Therefore, we can say marginal cost is nothing but the total of variable cost.

Absorption Costing

It is a technique, which considers the accumulation of all costs i.e. both fixed and variable cost. Here all manufacturing expenses are charged to product cost. It is also known as total costing or conventional costing.

The differences between marginal and absorption costing.

Marginal costing	Absorption costing
(*i*) Under this system only variable cost is taken into consideration for valuation of both finished and semifinished stock.	(*i*) Under this system both fixed and variable costs are taken into consideration for valuation of finished and semi-finished stock.
(*ii*) It shows a constant profit figure because the changes of inventory level cannot affect the profit.	(*ii*) It shows a fluctuating profit figure because with the changes of inventory level the profit changes.
(*iii*) Here fixed cost is considered as period cost.	(*iii*) Here a reasonable portion of fixed cost is charged to each product as product cost.
(*iv*) Profits are determined through contribution technique i.e. Sales – variable cost = contribution and profit = contribution – fixed cost.	(*iv*) Profits are determined through conventional method i.e. Sales – Total cost = Profit.

Some Important Terminology Relating To Marginal Costing

Contribution

The difference between sales and variable costs or marginal costs is known as contribution. It is also called as contribution margin, marginal income, marginal balance etc. It is vital in marginal costing. It is the margin, not the profit.

Marginal cost equation

This equation is developed through the concept of contribution. The contribution is the difference between sales and variable cost or may be said to be equal to fixed cost and profit (or loss).

From the above we can write :

Total Cost = Variable Cost (V) + Fixed Cost (F)

Profit (P) = Sales (S) – Total Cost (V + F)

As, Contribution (C) = Sales – Variable Cost.

Hence we can write :

$S = V + F + P$ (if any)

$\therefore S - V = F + P$ (if any)

$\therefore C = F + P$

in case of loss $C = F - L$

Break-even point

Break-even point is a point where there is neither profit nor loss. Here the contribution is equal to fixed cost. It is the level of output which breaks even the costs and revenues and hence is called BEP. In graphical representation of cost volume profit relationship break-even point is the point at which the total cost line and the total sales line intersect each other.

J. Wayne Kellen defines BEP as the level of sales income, which equals the sum of its variable costs and fixed expenses.

The BEP can be calculated as :

(*i*) BEP (unit) = Fixed Cost ÷ unit contribution.

(*ii*) BEP (Sales value) :

(*a*) Fixed Cost/unit contribution × unit selling price

(*b*) Total Fixed costs/Total contribution × total sales

(*c*) Total Fixed costs/P/V Ratio = $F \times S \div C$.

Break-even Chart

The Break-even Chart is a graphical representation of marginal costing. It can be defined as a chart which shows the profitability or otherwise of an undertaking at various levels of activity and as a result indicates the point at which neither profit nor loss is made.

The B.E. Chart can express the following information at various level of activity :

(1) Variable Cost, Fixed Cost and Total Costs.
(2) Total sales and Break-even point or B.E. Sales
(3) Profit or loss
(4) Margin of safety
(5) Angle of incidence.

Assumption for B.E. Chart

(1) Fixed cost remains constant throughout the period under consideration.
(2) Per unit variable cost will remain unchanged.
(3) Semi-variable cost can easily be segregated.
(4) The method of production, product specification and selling procedure will not be changed.
(5) There will not be any change in pricing policy due to competition, change in volume etc.
(6) Product mix will not be changed.

The following chart shows the B.E. Point in Units as well as value, Margin of safety, Angle of incidence, Profit/Loss area, and the total revenue and cost lines :

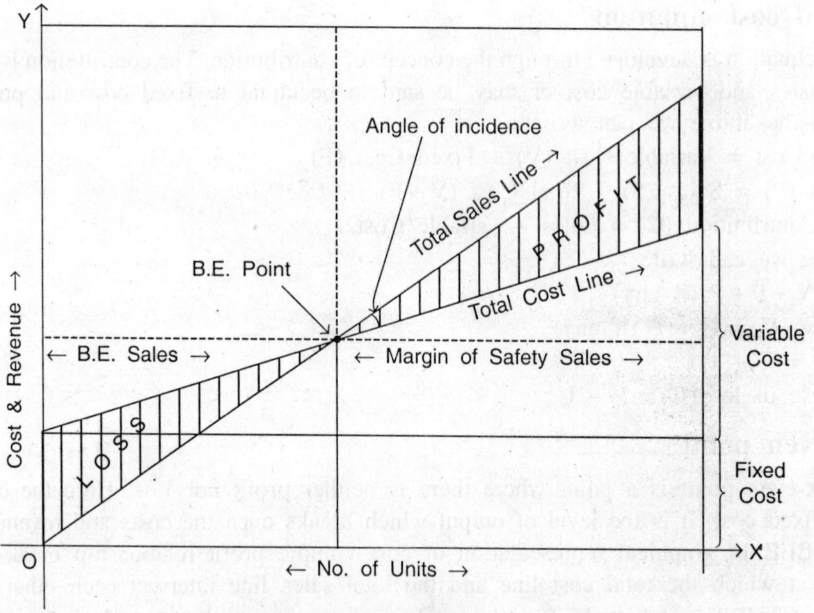

Break-even Chart

Multi product Break-even Chart

Sometimes a company may produce more than one product of varying profitability. In such case it is very difficult to find out the appropriate break-even point. Generally, in that case, BEP is considered to be the point where the average contribution line cuts the fixed cost line, assuming that the proportion of sales-mix remains unchanged.

The procedure for drawing up a multi-product break-even chart can be explained as follows :

(*i*) Firstly, calculate P/V ratio for each product and arrange them on the basis of P/V Ratio in descending order.
(*ii*) The horizontal axis would represent sales and the vertical axis would represent contribution.
(iii) Draw the total fixed cost line.
(*iv*) Choose the product having the height P/V ratio and plot its contribution against sales. Then take the second heights P/V ratio and plot cumulative contribution against cumulative sales. This process continues till the plotting of the lowest P/V ratio.
(*v*) Obtain the average contribution slope by joining the origin to the end of the last line plotted. The BEP is the point of interesection of average contribution line and fixed cost line.

The following illustration will make it clear about the multi-product break-even chart :

Illustration

Product	Sales (Rs.)	Variable Cost (Rs.)	Contribution	Fixed Cost (Rs.)
B	2,500	1,500	1,000	
A	4,000	2,000	2,000	
C	3,500	2,800	700	
Total	10,000	6,300		1,850

Therefore, the P/V Ratio for the Products :

$$B \rightarrow \frac{(2{,}500 - 1{,}500)}{2{,}500} \times 100 = 40\%,\ A \rightarrow \frac{(4{,}000 - 2{,}000)}{4{,}000} \times 100 = 50\%,\ C \rightarrow \frac{(3{,}500 - 2{,}800)}{3{,}500} \times 100 = 20\%$$

Now, choosing the product having highest P/V ratio, the following table can be formed :

	A	B	C
P/V Ratio	50%	40%	20%
Cum. Sales	4,000	6,500	10,000
Cum contribution	2,000	3,000	3,700

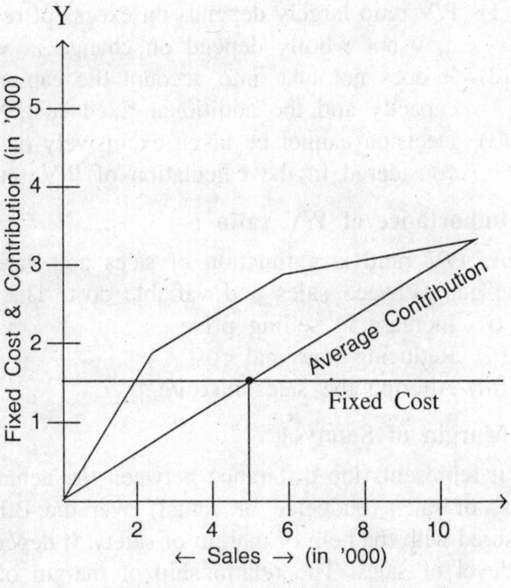

Multiproduct Break-even Chart

Advantage and Disadvantage of a Break-even Chart

Advantages :

(1) It is very easy to understand.
(2) It is an important tool to the Management in taking various decisions like price fixation, target of production and sales etc.
(3) The profit-earning capacity and the prospect of the business can be ascertained through this chart.
(4) The chart can also show the effect of alternative product mixes on contribution.

Disadvantages :

(1) This chart is informative as long as the 'no change' assumptions hold. But completion, efficiency in production, unit variable cost etc. will change during a particular period because they are controlled by outside factors.
Hence, in actual practice, a break-even chart is quite unlikely to look like a straight-line graph. A typical break-even chart may show a number of break-even points.
(2) The effect of various product mixes on profits cannot be studied from a single break-even chart.
(3) Capital employed which is also an important factor for decision-making is not considered in break-even chart.

Profit Volume (P/V) Ratio :

It is the ratio of contribution to sale. Generally it is expressed in percentage form. It can be symbolically expressed as P/V Ratio = C ÷ S × 100 or S – V ÷ S × 100

Where C = Contribution, S = Sales, V = Variable cost.

It can also be expressed as a ratio of change in contribution to change in sales i.e.

P/V Ratio = Changes in contribution ÷ change in sales.

Or, Changes in Profit ÷ Changes in sales (in case of Profit).

It remains constant at different levels of operations, in spite of changing its fixed cost, as P/V ratio is the relationship between contribution and sales.

Suppose : Selling price = Rs. 100/-

Per unit variable cost = Rs. 75/-

∴ Per unit contribution = Rs. 100 – Rs. 75 = Rs. 25/-

∴ P/V ratio = 25/100 × 100 = 25%

Advantages of P/V ratio :

(1) It helps to eliminate the unprofitable lines which are having either a lower P/V ratio or low volume.
(2) It helps in determining the profit at various levels of sales.
(3) It helps to find out the B.E.P. (Sales).
(4) It helps to estimate the sales required to earn the desired profit.
(5) It helps to assess the relative profitability of various products, processes or departments.
(6) It helps to fix up the selling price required to earn desired profit.

Disadvantages :

(1) P/V ratio largely depends on excess of revenue over variable cost. Hence change in profit may not wholly depend on change in volume of sales.
(2) It does not take into account the capital outlays required by the additional productive capacity and the additional fixed cost.
(3) Decision cannot be taken exclusively on the basis of P/V ratio because all costs are not considered in the calculation of P/V ratio.

Importance of P/V ratio :

As P/V ratio is a function of sales and variable cost, its improvement implies an increase in the gap between sales and variable cost. This can be done in the following ways :

(*i*) Increase in selling price
(*ii*) Reducing marginal cost
(*iii*) Altering the sales mixture.

Margin of Safety :

It represents the difference between the actual sales and B.E. sales. In other words, it is the excess of sales (budgeted or actual) over the B.E. sales. The soundness of the business can be measured with the help of margin of safety. It depends on the level of fixed cost, rate of contribution and level of sales. The relationship of margin of safety with sales can be expressed as :

(*i*) Margin of safety = Sales – Break-even Sales.
(*ii*) Margin of Safety = Profit ÷ P.V. Ratio.

Improvement of Margin of safety :

The margin of safety can be improved by adopting the following steps :

(1) Increase in sales volume or selling price.
(2) Decrease in Fixed cost.
(3) Increasing contribution by reducing variable cost.
(4) Change in product mix for improving contribution.

Angle of incidence :

It is the angle formed between the sales line and the total cost line. It indicates the rate at which profits are earned. It also indicates the profit-earning capacity of a business. When the angle of incidence is large, it indicates a high margin of profit. On the other hand, a low angle of incidence means a low rate of profit. The soundness and weakness of a business can also be indicated with the help of the angle of incidence and the margin of safety.

Different formulas used while solving the problems relating to this chapter :

1. Sales = Cost + Profit
2. Sales = Fixed Cost + Variable Cost + Profit.
3. Sales – Variable Cost = Fixed Cost + Profit. or S – V = F + P.
4. Sales – Variable cost = Contribution, or S – V = C.

   ∴ Contribution = Fixed Cost + Profit, or C = F + P.
5. P/V ratio = $\frac{\text{Contribution}}{\text{Sales}} \times 100$
6. P/V ratio = $\frac{\text{Change in Profit}}{\text{Change in Sales}}$

   or $\frac{\text{Change in Contribution}}{\text{Change in Sales}}$
7. P/V ratio = $\frac{\text{Fixed Cost}}{\text{Breakeven Sales}} \times 100$

   or $\frac{\text{Profit}}{\text{Margin of Safety}} \times 100$
8. Sales = $\frac{\text{Contribution}}{\text{P/V ratio}}$

   ∴ Sales × P/V ratio = Contribution
9. Total Sales = Break-even Sales + Margin of safety.

   ∴ Break-even sales × P/V ratio = Fixed cost;

   Margin of Safety × P.V. ratio = Profit.

   Margin of safety = Total Sales – B.E.Sales.
10. M/S ratio = $\frac{\text{Total Sales} - \text{B.E.Sales}}{\text{Total Sales}} \times 100$
11. Break-even Sales = $\frac{\text{Fixed Cost}}{\text{P/V ratio}}$

    or $\frac{\text{Fixed Cost}}{\text{Contribution}} \times \text{Sales}$
12. B.E.P. (in units) = $\frac{\text{Fixed Cost}}{\text{Contribution per unit}}$
13. Sales to earn a desired profit = $\frac{\text{Fixed Cost} + \text{Profit}}{\text{P/V ratio}}$
14. Sales in units to earn a desired profit = $\frac{\text{Fixed Cost} + \text{Profit}}{\text{Contribution per unit}}$

Illustration

U.P.S. Ltd. makes toys only. An analysis of cost records gives the following information :

	Amount
Sales (12,000 units)	2,40,000
Direct material	48,000
Direct Labour	36,000
Variable production O/H	24,000
Fixed Expenses	1,05,600

You are required to calculate :

(*a*) Contribution per unit
(*b*) P/V ratio
(*c*) Break-even point
(*d*) Margin of safety
(*e*) If the fixed expenses is increased by Rs. 20,020, then
 (*i*) What will be the new break-even point ?
 (*ii*) If variable production O/H is increased by Rs. 6,000, what will be the new P/V ratio and B.E.P. in this revised situation ?
(*f*) Sales required to earn a profit of Rs. 49,500.

Answer

(*a*) Contribution = Sales – Variable Cost

		Rs.	Total *Rs.*
	Sales		2,40,000
Less :	Variable cost		
	Direct material	48,000	
	Direct Labour	36,000	
	Variable production O/H	24,000	1,08,000
			1,32,000

Contribution per unit = Rs. $\dfrac{\text{Rs. } 1,32,000}{12,000 \text{ unit}}$ = Rs. 11.00

Alternatively : Sales price per unit – Variable cost per unit = Contribution per unit.

Sales price per unit = $\dfrac{2,40,000}{12,000}$ =	Rs. 20.00
Variable cost per unit = $\dfrac{1,08,000}{12,000}$ =	Rs. 9.00
Contribution per unit (S – V)	Rs. 11.00

(*b*) P.V. ratio (or contribution Sales ratio) :

$$\frac{\text{Contribution}}{\text{Sales}} \times 100$$

$$\frac{1,32,000}{2,40,000} \times 100 = 55\%$$

(*c*) Break-even point (units) :

$$\frac{\text{Fixed cost}}{\text{Contribution P.V.}}$$

$$\frac{\text{Rs. } 1,05,600}{\text{Rs. } 11} = 9,600 \text{ units}$$

B.E.P (in sales value) : 9,600 units × Rs. 20 P.V = Rs. 1,92,000

Alternatively : $\dfrac{\text{Fixed Cost}}{\text{P.V. ratio}}$

$$\frac{\text{Rs. } 1,05,600}{55} \times 100 = \text{Rs. } 1,92,000$$

(*d*) Margin of Safety :
Actual Sales – B.E.P. Sales
2,40,000 – 1,92,000 = Rs. 48,000

Alternatively : $\frac{\text{Profit}}{\text{P.V. ratio}}$

Contribution		Rs. 1,32,000
Less : Fixed Cost		Rs. 1,05,600
	Profit	26,400

$\therefore \frac{26,400}{55} \times 100 = \text{Rs. } 48,000$

(*e*) (*i*) New Break-even point if the fixed cost is increased by Rs. 20,000 :
If Fixed cost is increased the contribution per unit remain unchanged.

$$\text{B.E.P.} = \frac{\text{Rs. } 1,05,600 + \text{Rs. } 20,020}{\text{Rs. } 11} = \frac{1,25,620}{11} = 11,420 \text{ unit}$$

Alternatively :
Due to change in fixed cost the P.V. remain, unchanged.

$$\text{B.E.P.} = \frac{\text{Fixed Cost}}{\text{P/V ratio}}$$

$$\therefore \frac{1,25,620}{55} \times 100 = 2,28,400$$

$$\text{unit} = \frac{2,28,400}{20} = 11,420 \text{ unit}$$

(*ii*) If variable cost changes contribution per unit, P.V.ratio and B.E.P. will also change.
Contribution : S – V

Sales = 12,000 unit × 20 =	2,40,000
Less : Variable Cost (1,08,000 + 6,000)	1,14,000
Contribution	1,26,000

$$\text{Contribution per unit} = \text{Rs. } \frac{1,26,000}{1,200 \text{ unit}} = 10.50 \text{ per unit}$$

$$\text{Revised P.V. ratio} : \frac{\text{Contribution}}{\text{Sales}} \times 100$$

$$\frac{1,26,000}{2,40,000} \times 100 = 52{\cdot}5\%$$

$$\text{Revised B.E.P.} = \frac{\text{Revised Fixed Cost}}{\text{Revised P.V. ratio}} \times 100$$

$$\frac{1,25,620}{52{\cdot}5} \times 100 = 2,39,276$$

$$\text{Alternatively : B.E.P (units)} = \frac{\text{Fixed Cost}}{\text{Contribution per unit}} = \frac{1,25,620}{10{\cdot}50} = 11,963{\cdot}809 \text{ units}$$

Sales value = 11,963·809 units × Rs. 20 per unit
= Rs. 2,39,276

(*f*) Sales required to earn a profit of Rs. 49,500

$$\text{Requires sales} = \frac{\text{Required Contribution}}{\text{P.V.Ratio}}$$

Required Contribution = Fixed cost + Profit i.e. 1,05,600 + 49,500 = 1,55,100

$$\text{Required Sales} = \frac{1,55,100}{55} \times 100 = \text{Rs. } 2,82,000$$

$$\text{Unit} = \frac{2,82,000}{20} = 14,100 \text{ units}$$

Check : Total contribution from 14,100 units =

14,100 units × Rs. 11 per unit =	1,55,100
Less : Fixed cost =	1,05,600
Profit	49,500

Alternatively :

Required sales = BEP + M.S.

$$\text{M.S.} = \frac{\text{Profit}}{\text{P.V. ratio}} \text{ i.e. } \frac{49,500}{55} \times 100 = 90,000$$

BEP + MS = 1,92,000 + 90,000 = 2,82,000.

Illustration

S.D. Ltd. furnishes the following information :

	Rs.
Fixed cost	18,000
BEP	45,000
Profit	8,000

You are required to find out :

(*a*) P.V. Ratio
(*b*) Sales
(*c*) Sales required to earn same profit when there is a decrease in fixed cost by Rs. 2,000.

Answer

(*a*) P.V. Ratio :

We know : $\frac{\text{Fixed Cost}}{\text{P.V. Ratio}} = \text{B.E.P.}$

$$\therefore \frac{18,000}{\text{P.V. Ratio}} = 45,000$$

∴ P.V. Ratio = 40%

Alternatively, we know in the B.E.P :

Fixed cost = Contribution

$$\therefore \text{P.V. Ratio} = \frac{\text{Contribution}}{\text{Sales}} \times 100$$

$$\therefore \frac{18,000}{45,000} \times 100 = 40\%$$

(*b*) $\text{Sales} = \frac{\text{Contribution}}{\text{P.V. Ratio}}$

Contribution = Fixed cost + Profit = 18,000 + 8,000 = 26,000

$$\text{Sales} = \frac{26,000}{40} \times 100 = 65,000$$

Alternatively (by using margin of safety)

$$\text{M.S.} = \frac{\text{Profit}}{\text{P.V. Ratio}}$$

$$\frac{8,000}{40} \times 100 = 20,000$$

Sales = B.E.P. + M.S

= 45,000 + 20,000 = 65,000

(*c*) If fixed cost changes the required contribution will also change :
Contribution = 16,000 + 8,000 = 24,000

$$\text{Sales} = \frac{24{,}000}{40} \times 100 = 60{,}000$$

WORKEDOUT PROBLEMS

Problem 1

The Asian Industries specializes in the manufacture of small capacity motors. The cost structure of a motor is as under :

Material	Rs. 50/-
Labour	Rs. 80/-
Variable overheads	70% of labour cost

Fixed overheads of the company amount to Rs. 2.40 lakhs per annum. The sale price of the motor is Rs. 230 each.

(*a*) Determine the number of motors that have to be manufactured and sold in a year in order to break-even.

(*b*) How many motors have to be made and sold to make a profit of Rs. 1 lakh per year ?

(*c*) If the sale price is reduced by Rs. 15 each, how many motors have to be sold to break even ? ***[I.C.W.A. Inter]***

Solution

(*a*) Sale price per motor		230
Less : Marginal cost per motor		
Material	Rs. 50	
Labour	Rs. 80	
Variable overheads 75% of Rs. 80/-	Rs. 60	190
Contribution per unit		Rs. 40
Fixed Overheads per year =	Rs. 2,40,000	
B.E.P. (units) =	F/C. per unit = 2,40,000/40 = 6,000 Motors	
Sales (Units) =	F + P/C. Per unit = 2,40,000 + 1,00,000/40 = 8,500 Motors	
Revised Selling Price	230 − 15 = 215	
Marginal Cost	190	
Revised Contribution per motor.	25	

B.E.P. (Units) = 2,40,000/25 = 9,600 Motors.

Reconciliation :

Sales 9,600 × 215	Rs. 20,64,000
Less : Marginal cost 9,600 × 190	Rs. 18,24,000
Contribution 9,600 × 25	Rs. 2,40,000
Less : Fixed Overheads	Rs. 2,40,000
Profit	NIL

Problem 2

S. Ltd. furnishes you the following information relating to the half year ending 30th June 1980 :

Fixed expenses	Rs. 50,000
Sales value	Rs. 2,00,000
Profit	Rs. 50,000

During the second half of the same year the company has projected a loss of Rs. 10,000. You are required to workout :

(*i*) The P/V ratio, break-even point and margin of safety for six months ending 30th June, 1980.

(*ii*) Expected sales volume for second half of the year assuming that selling price and fixed expenses remain unchanged in the second half year also.

(*iii*) The break even point and margin of safety for the whole year 1980.

[I.C.W.A. Inter]

Solution

(*i*) Contribution = F + P = 50,000 + 50,000 = Rs. 1,00,000

P/V Ratio = C/S × 100 = 1,00,000/2,00,000 × 100 = 50%

BEP = F/P/V ratio = 50,000/50% = Rs. 1,00,000

Margin of Safety = Sales – BEP = 2,00,000 – 1,00,000 = 1,00,000

(*ii*) Contribution = F + P or F – Loss = 50,000 – 10,000 = Rs. 40,000.

C = S × P/V ratio

40,000 = S × 50%

S = 40,000/50% = Rs. 80,000 for second half year.

(*iii*) For Full year 1980 :

Sales 2,00,000 + 80,000	= Rs. 2,80,000
Fixed expenses 50,000 + 50,000	= 1,00,000
P/V ratio	= 50% (Same because no change in selling price)
BEP 1,00,000/50%	= Rs. 2,00,000
Profit (50,000 – 10,000)	= Rs. 40,000

Margin of Safety 2,80,000 – 2,00,000 = Rs. 80,000 OR

Margin of Safery = P/P.V ratio + 40,000/50% = Rs. 80,000.

Problem 3

The following figures relating to the performance of a company of the years I and II are available. Assuming that (*i*) the ratio of variable costs to sales and (*ii*) the fixed costs are the same for both the years, ascertain :

(*a*) the profit-volume ratio

(*b*) the amount of the fixed costs

(*c*) the break even point and

(*d*) the budgeted profit for the year III, if the budgeted sales for that year are Rs. 1 Crore.

	Total sale (Rs. In '000)	Total Cost (Rs. In '000)
Year I	7,000	5,800
Year II	9,000	6,600

[I.C.W.A. Inter]

Solution

Year	Sales	Total cost	Profit
I	9,000	6,600	2,400
II	7,000	5,800	1,200
Differences	2,000	800	1,200

(*a*) P/V ratio = Change in Profit/Change in Sales = 1,200/2000 × 100 = 60%

(*b*) Profit = (S × P/V ratio) – F or F = (S × P/V ratio) – P = (90,00,000 × 60%) – 24,00,000 = 54,00,000 – 24,00,000 = Rs. 30,00,000 fixed costs.

(*c*) BEP = F/P.V ratio = 30,00,000/60% = Rs. 50,00,000

(*d*) Budgeted Profit for the year III

Profit = (S × P/V ratio) – F = (1,00,00,000 × 60%) – 30,00,000 = 60,00,000 – 30,00,000 = Rs. 30,00,000.

Problem 4

The following figures are available from the records of Venus Enterprises as at 31st March :

	1988 (Rs. In lakhs)	1989 (Rs. In lakhs)
Sales	150	200
Profit	30	50

Calculate :

(*a*) The P/V ratio and total fixed expenses.

(*b*) The break-even level of sales.

(*c*) Sales required to earn a profit of Rs. 90 lakhs.

(*d*) Profit or loss that would arise if the sales were Rs. 280 lakhs.

[C.A. Inter]

Solution

Year	Sales	Profit
1989	200 lakhs	50 lakhs
1988	150 lakhs	30 lakhs
Change	50 lakhs	20 lakhs

(*a*) P/V ratio = Change in Profit/Change in Sales × 100 = 20 lakhs/50 lakhs × 100 = 40%

P = (S × P/V ratio) – F

F = (S × P/V ratio) – P = (200 lakhs × 40%) – 50 lakhs = 80 lakhs – 50 lakhs = Rs. 30 lakhs (in 1989)

F = (150 × 40%) – 30 = 60 – 30 = Rs. 30 lakhs (in 1988)

(*b*) B.E.P. = F/P.V. ratio = 30 Lakhs/40% = Rs. 75 lakhs.

(*c*) Sales = F + P/P.V. ratio = 30 lakhs + 90 lakhs/40% = 120 lakhs/40% = Rs. 300 lakhs sales required to earn a Profit of Rs. 90 lakhs.

(*d*) Desired Profit = (S × P/V ratio) – F

(280 lakhs × 40%) – 30 lakhs = 112 lakhs – 30 lakhs = Rs. 82 lakhs.

Problem 5

The profit volume (P/V) ratio of BB & Co. dealing in precision instruments is 50% and the margin of safety is 40%.

You are required to work out the break-even point and the net profit if the sale volume is Rs. 50 lakhs. ***[C.S. Inter June, 1991]***

Solution

(*a*) B.E.P.	Rs. In lakhs
Sales	50
Margin of safety 40%	20
B.E.P.	30

(*b*) Net Profit if the sales volume is Rs. 50 lakhs;

P = (Sales × P/V ratio) – F

The amount of fixed overheads is not given in the question. This is ascertained as follows :

Contribution at B.E.P.	
Sales at B.E.P. × P/V ratio	
30 × 50%	= Rs. 15 lakhs
Sales at B.E.P.	= 30
Less : Contribution at BEP	= 15
Fixed Overheads	= Rs. 15 lakhs.

Net Profit if the sales volume is Rs. 50 lakhs.

P = (Sales × P/V ratio) – F

= (50 × 50%) – 15

= 25 – 15 = Rs. 10 lakhs profit.

Problem 6

Find the profit from the following data :

Sales	Rs. 80,000
Marginal cost	60,000
Break-even point	60,000 sales.

Solution

P/V ratio = S – V/S × 100 = 80,000 – 60,000/80,000 × 100 = 25%
BEP = F/P.V. ratio
60,000 = F/25%
F = 60,000 × 25% = Rs. 15,000 Fixed Cost.
Profit = (S × P.V. ratio) – F
= (80,000 × 25%) – 15,000
= 20,000 – 15,000 = Rs. 5,000.

Problem 7

A company manufactures a product, currently utilizing 80% capacity with a turnover of Rs. 8,00,000 at Rs. 25 per unit. The cost data are as under :

Materials cost	Rs. 7.50 per unit
Labour cost	Rs. 6.25 per unit
Semi-variable cost (Including variable cost of Rs. 3.75/per unit)	Rs. 1,80,000
Fixed cost	Rs. 90,000

(upto 80% level of output, beyond this an additional Rs. 20,000 will be incurred)

Calculate :

(*a*) Activity level at Break-even Point.
(*b*) Number of units to be sold to earn a net income of 8% of sales.
(*c*) Activity level needed to earn a profit of Rs. 95,000 and
(*d*) What should be the selling price per unit, if break-even point is to be brought down to 40% activity level ?

[C.A. Inter Nov., 2000]

Solution

Working Notes :

(1) Selling Price — Rs. 25.00
Variable cost (7.50 + 6.25 + 3.75) — 17.50
Contribution per unit — 7.50

(2) Number of units sold at 80% capacity = Rs. 8,00,000 ÷ 25 = 32,000 units and Maximum capacity = (32,000 ÷ 0.80) × 100 = 40,000 units.

(3) Fixed cost element in semi-variable cost
Semi-variable cost — Rs. 1,80,000
Less : Variable cost 32,000 × Rs. 3.75 — 1,20,000
Fixed Cost — 60,000

(4) Total fixed cost of 80% capacity = Rs. 90,000 + Rs. 60,000 = Rs. 1,50,000.

(5) P/V Ratio = (Rs. 7·50 ÷ 25) × 100 = 30%

(*a*) Activity level of break-even point.

We know that :

Sales BEP × P/V ratio = Fixed

Or Sales at BEP = Fixed ÷ P/V ratio

Or Activity level of break-even point
= (Fixed cost ÷ P/V ratio) ÷ Selling Price
= {(Rs. 1,50,000 ÷ (7.50/25)} ÷ 25
= 20,000 units
= (20,000 ÷ 40,000) × 100 = 50%

(*b*) Let *x* be the number of units sold to earn a net income of 8% of sales.
Or Rs. 25x – 17·50x = Rs. 1,50,000 + 8% (Rs. 25x)
Or Rs. 25x – 17·50x = Rs. 1,50,000 + 2x
Or x = 27273 units.

(*c*) Activity level needed to earn a profit of Rs. 95,000 :
Sales required to earn a profit of Rs. 95,000 = Fixed Cost + Desired Profit ÷ Contribution per unit.
Required sales = (Rs. 1,50,000 + 20,000 + 9,500) ÷ 7.50 = 35,333 units.
Activity level to earn profit of Rs. 95,000 = (35333/40,000) × 100 = 88.33%

(*d*) Selling price per unit if break even point is to be brought down to 40% (or 16,000 units)
Suppose selling price = x
Activity level at BEP = 16,000 units.
16,000 units = (Fixed cost ÷ P/V ratio) ÷ Selling Price
16,000 units = Rs. 1,50,000 × x ÷ (x – 1750) ÷ x
or 16,000x – Rs. 2,80,000 = Rs. 1,50,000
or x = (2,80,000 + 1,50,000) ÷ 16,000 = Rs. 26·88.

Problem 8

A company sells its product at Rs. 15 per unit. In a period if it produces and sells 8,000 units, it incurs a loss of Rs. 5 per unit. If the volume is raised to 20,000 units, it earns a profit of Rs. 4 per unit.

Calculate break-even point—both in terms of rupees as well as in units.

[C.A. Inter, Adopted]

Solution

We know that S – V = F + P
∴ Suppose Variable cost = x
Fixed cost = y

In the first situation :
15 × 8 + 8,000 x = Y – 40,000
In second situation :
15 × 20,000 + 20,000x = Y + 80,000
or 1,20,000 – 8,000 x = Y – 40,000
3,00,000 – 20,000 x = Y + 80,000

From 3 and 4 we get x = Rs. 5
Variable cost per unit = Rs. 5
Putting this value in 3rd equation :
1,20,000 – (8,000 × 5) = y – 40,000
or y = Rs. 1,20,000
Fixed cost = Rs. 1,20,000
P/V ratio = S – V ÷ S = 15 – 5 ÷ 15 × 100 = 200 ÷ 3 = $66\frac{2}{3}$%

Suppose break-even sales = x
15x – 5x = 1,20,000 (at BEP, contribution will be equal to fixed cost)
x = 12,000 units.
Or Break-even sales in units = 12,000
Break-even sales in rupees = 12,000 × 15 = Rs. 1,80,000.

Problem 9

A company had incurred fixed expenses of Rs. 4,50,000 with sales of Rs. 15,00,000 and earned a profit of Rs. 3,00,000 during the first half year. In the second half it suffered a loss of Rs. 1,50,000.

Calculate :

(*a*) The profit volume ratio, break-even point and margin of safety for the first half year.

(*b*) Expected sales volume for the second half year assuming that selling price and fixed expenses remained unchanged during the second half year.

(*c*) The break-even point and margin of safety for the whole year.

[C.A. Inter, May 1996 Adopted]

Solution

(*a*) P/V Ratio = (S – V)/S

Contribution = F.C. + Profit

= Rs. 4,50,000 + 3,00,000

= 7,50,000

S – V = Contribution

S – C = Variable cost

= Rs. 15,00,000 – 7,50,000 = 7,50,000

P/V ratio = {(15,00,000 – 7,50,000)/15,00,000} × 100 = 50%

B.E. Point = Fixed Cost ÷ P/V ratio = Rs. 4,50,000 ÷ 50% = Rs. 9,00,000

Margin of Safety = Sales – B.E.Sales = Rs. 15,00,000 – 9,00,000 = Rs. 6,00,000

(*b*) Contribution during the 2nd half = Rs. 4,50,000 + (–1,50,000) = Rs. 3,00,000

Expected volume = Contribution ÷ P/V ratio = Rs. 3,00,000 ÷ 50% = Rs. 6,00,000

(*c*) B.E. point for the whole year = Fixed Cost for the whole year ÷ P/V ratio

= Rs. 9,00,000 ÷ 50% = Rs. 18,00,000

Margin of safety = Rs. 1,50,000 ÷ 50% = Rs. 3,00,000

Or

= Sales – B.E. Sales

= Rs. 21,00,000 – 18,00,000 = Rs. 3,00,000

Problem 10

A company producing a single product sells it at Rs. 50 per unit. Unit variable cost is Rs. 35 and fixed cost amounts to Rs. 12 lakhs per annum. With this data you are required to calculate the following, treating each independent of the other :

(*a*) P/V ratio and Break-even Point.

(*b*) New Break-even sales if variable cost increases by Rs. 3 per unit, without increase in selling price.

(*c*) Increase in sales required if profits are to be increased by Rs. 2.4 lakhs.

(*d*) Percentage increase/decrease in sales volume units to off-set :

(*i*) an increase of Rs. 3 in the variable cost per unit.

(*ii*) A 10% increase in selling price without affecting existing profits quantum.

(*e*) Quantum of advertisement expenditure permissible to increase sales by Rs. 1.2 lakhs, without affecting existing profits.

[I.C.W.A. Inter, June 1995]

Solution

(*a*) P/V Ratio = $\frac{\text{Sales} - \text{Variable cost}}{\text{Sales}} \times 100$

i.e., $\frac{\text{Rs. } 50 - 35}{\text{Rs. } 50} \times 100 = 30\%$

Break-even sales × P.V. ratio = Fixed cost.

B.E. sales × 30% = 12 lakhs.

∴ B.E.Sales = $\frac{12 \text{ lakhs}}{30} \times 100 = 40$ lakhs.

(*b*) Sales price = Rs. 50 ; New variable cost = Rs. 35 + 3 = Rs. 38

Contribution per unit = Rs. 50 – Rs. 38 = Rs. 12.

B.E.S × P/V ratio = 12 lakhs (Fixed cost)

or B.E.S. × $\frac{12}{50}$ = 12 lakhs

∴ Revised B.E.S = 12 lakhs × $\frac{50}{12}$ = 50 lakhs.

(*c*) Additional sales required = x

Additional profit = Additional contribution

Additional contribution required = 2·4 lakhs.

∴ x × 30% = 2·4 lakhs.

∴ x = 2·4 lakhs × $\frac{100}{30}$ = 8 lakhs.

(*d*) (*i*) New variable cost = Rs. 38 per unit.

New contribution = 12 per unit.

Reduction in contribution = 15 – 12 = Rs. 3

Sales required to earn a contribution of Rs. 3 = Rs. 3 × $\frac{50}{12}$ = Rs. 12·5 or $\frac{12{\cdot}5}{50}$ × 100 = 25% ; i.e. 25% increase in sales volume will offset increase of Rs. 3 in variable cost per unit.

(*ii*) New selling price = Rs. 55

New contribution = Rs. 55 – Rs. 35 = Rs. 20.

Increase in contribution = Rs. 20 – Rs. 15 = Rs. 5

Sales required to earn a contribution of Rs. 5

= Sales required × P/V ratio = Rs. 5

or Sales required × $\frac{\text{Rs. } 20}{\text{Rs. } 55}$ = 5

or Sales required = $\frac{\text{Rs. } 5 \times 55}{20}$ = 13·75

or $\frac{13{\cdot}75}{55}$ × 100 = 25% decrease in sales volume.

(*e*) Contribution increase by additional sales by Rs. 1·2 lakhs = 1,20,000 × $\frac{30}{100}$ = 36,000

∴ Rs. 36,000 should be the maximum permissible advertisement expenditure to set-off an increase of Rs. 1·2 lakhs without affecting existing profit.

Problem 11

A company has three factories situated in North, East and South with its Head office in Mumbai. The management has received the following report on the operations of each factory for a period :

Rs. '000

	Actual Sales	*Over/(Under) Budgeted sales*	*Actual Profit*	*Over/(Under) Budgeted Profit*
North	1,100	(400)	135	(180)
East	1,450	150	210	90
South	1,200	(200)	330	(110)

Calculate for each factory and for the company as a whole for the period :

(*i*) The fixed costs

(*ii*) Break-even sales. ***[C.A. Inter, Nov. 1996, Adopted]***

Solution

(*i*) We are to solve this problem by applying following formula : P/V ratio = $\frac{\text{Change in Profit}}{\text{Change in Sales}}$

	North.	*East*	*South*
		Rs. '000	
Actual Sales	1,100	1,450	1,200
Less : Change in Sale (a)	(400)	150	(200)
Budgeted sales	1,500	1,300	1,400
Actual profit	135	210	330
Less : Change in profit (b)	(180)	90	110
Budgeted Profit	315	120	440
P/V ratio ($\frac{b}{a}$ × 100)	45%	60%	55%

We know that Sales × P/V ratio = Contribution and Contribution – Profit = Fixed cost.

	Actual Sales	*P/V ratio*	*A Contribution*	*B Profit*	*Fixed Cost (A – B)*
North	1,100	45%	495·00	135	360
East	1,450	60%	870.00	210	660
South	1,200	55%	660.00	330	330
Total	3,750			675	1,350

(*ii*) Break-even sales

We know : BES × P.V. ratio = Fixed cost

$\therefore$ BES = $\frac{\text{Fixed cost}}{\text{P/V ratio}}$

North = $\frac{360}{45}$ × 100 = 800

East = $\frac{660}{60}$ × 100 = 1,100

South = $\frac{330}{55}$ × 100 = 600

Now we are to work out Break-even sales for company :

We know sales × P/V ratio = Fixed cost + Profit

$\therefore$ 3,750 × P/V ratio = 1,350 + 675

$\therefore$ P/V ratio = $\frac{2,025}{3,750}$ × 100 = 54%

B.E.Sales (company) = $\frac{\text{Fixed cost}}{\text{P/V ratio}}$ – i.e. $\frac{1,350}{54}$ × 100 = Rs. 2,500

Problem 12

The variable cost structure of a product manufactured by a company during the current year is as under :

Material	Rs. 120 per unit
Labour	Rs. 30 per unit
Overhead	Rs. 12 per unit

The selling price per unit is Rs. 270 and the fixed cost and sales during the current year are Rs. 14 lakhs and Rs. 40.5 lakhs, respectively.

During the forthcoming year the direct workers will be entitled to a wage increase of 10% from the begining of the year and the material cost, variable overhead and fixed overhead are expected to increase by 7·5%, 5% and 3%, respectively.

You are required to compute :

(*a*) New sale price in the forthcoming year if the current P/V ratio is to be maintained.

(*b*) Number of units that would require to be sold during the forthcoming year so as to yield the same amount of profit in the current year, assuming that selling price per unit will not be increased. ***[I.C.W.A. Inter, June 1997; C.A. Inter, May 1985]***

Solution

No. of units sold = $\frac{\text{Total Sales}}{\text{Selling price per unit}}$

i.e. Rs. $\frac{40,50,000}{270}$ = 15,000 units.

Contribution per unit = Sales – Variable cost,

i.e. Rs. 270 – (120 + 30 + 12) = 108 per unit

Total contribution = 15,000 units × 108	= Rs. 16,20,000
Less : Fixed cost	Rs. 14,00,000
Total Profit	Rs. 2,20,000

P/V ratio = $\frac{\text{Contribution per unit}}{\text{Sales per unit}} \times 100$

i.e. $\frac{108}{270} \times 100 = 40\%$

(*a*) Statement showing the new selling price for the forthcoming year by maintaining the current year's P/V ratio.

Revised variable cost/unit

Material = $120 \times \frac{107\cdot5}{100}$ =	129·00
Labour = $30 \times \frac{110}{100}$ =	33·00
Variable O/H = $12 \times \frac{105}{100}$ =	12·60
	Rs. 174·60

P/V ratio = $\frac{S - V}{S}$

$\therefore 40\% = \frac{S - 174\cdot60}{S}$ $\therefore S = 291\cdot00$

Revised selling price = 291·00

(*b*) Revised contribution per unit = Sales – Variable cost

= Rs. 270 – Rs. 174·60 = 95·40 p. per unit.

Desired contribution = Fixed cost + Desired Profit

Fixed cost = $14,00,000 \times \frac{103}{100}$ =	14,42,000
Add : Desired profit	2,20,000
Total contribution	16,62,000

Total number of units to be sold = $\frac{\text{Total Contribution}}{\text{Contribution/Unit}}$

$= \frac{16,62,000}{95\cdot40}$ = 17,422 units.

Problem 13

W.F. Limited makes and sales a range of plastic garden furniture. These items are sold in sets of one table with four chairs for Rs. 80 per set.

The variable cost per set are Rs. 20 for manufacturing and Rs. 10 for variable selling and distribution expenses.

Total fixed costs of manufacturing, including depreciation of the plastic-moulding machinery, are Rs. 8,00,000 per annum. Budgeted profit for the forthcoming year is Rs. 4,00,000.

Increased competition has resulted in the management of W.F. Limited engaging market research consultants. The consultants have recommended three possible strategies, as follows :

	Reducing Selling Price per set by	Expected increase in sales (sets)
Strategy 1	5·0%	10%
Strategy 2	7·5%	20%
Strategy 3	10·0%	25%

You are required to assess the effect on profits of each of the three strategies and to recommend which strategy, if any, ought to be adopted. *[CIMA, London, Nov. 1994]*

Solution

Statement showing profit from each strategy

	Per Set
Sales	Rs. 80
Variable costs (Rs. 20 + 10)	Rs. 30
Contribution	Rs. 50

Fixed cost per annum Rs. 8,00,000
Budgeted production : 24,000 Sets.
(Rs. 8,00,000 + Rs. 4,00,000 or Rs. 12,00,000 ÷ Rs. 50)

Strategy	Units*	Contribution Per unit** Rs.	Total Cost Rs.	Fixed Rs.	Profit Rs.
1	26,400	46	12,14,400	8,00,000	4,14,400
2	28,800	44	12,67,200	8,00,000	4,67,200
3	30,000	42	12,60,000	8,00,000	4,60,000

The second strategy should be implemented as the profit is maximum from this strategy.

Working—

	Units*	Contribution Per Unit** Rs.
Strategy 1	$24{,}000 \times \frac{110}{100} = 24{,}400$	50 − 4 = 46
Strategy 2	$24{,}000 \times \frac{120}{100} = 28{,}800$	50 − 6 = 44
Strategy 3	$24{,}000 \times \frac{125}{100} = 30{,}000$	50 − 8 = 42

Problem 14

Two manufacturing companies, which have the following operating details, decide to merge :

	Company 1	Company 2
Capacity utilisation	90%	60%
Sales (Rs. in lakhs)	540	300
Variable costs (Rs in lakhs)	396	225
Fixed costs (Rs. in lakhs)	80	50

Assuming that the proposal is implemented, calculate :

(*i*) Break-even sales of the merged plant and the capacity utilization at that stage.

(*ii*) Profitability of the merged plant at 80% capacity utilization.

(*iii*) Sales turnover of the merged plant to earn a profit of Rs. 75 lakhs.

(*iv*) When the merged plant is working at a capacity to earn a profit of Rs. 75 Lakhs, what % increase in selling is required to sustain an increase of 5% in fixed overheads.

[I.C.W.A. Final 1992]

Solution

(Rs. in lakhs)

(*i*)	Company 1	Company 2	Merged Plant
Capacity Utilisation	100%	100%	100%
Sales	600	500	1,100
Variable costs	440	375	815
Contribution	160	125	285
Fixed cost	80	50	130
Profit	80	75	155

$\therefore$ P/V ratio (Merged Plant) $= \frac{\text{Contribution}}{\text{Sales}} \times 100$

$= \frac{285}{1{,}100} \times 100 = 25{\cdot}91\%$

B.E.P. of the Merged Plant $= \frac{\text{Fixed Cost}}{\text{P/V ratio}}$

$= \frac{130}{25{\cdot}91} \times 100 = 501{\cdot}74$

Capacity utilisation at B.E.P $= \frac{501{\cdot}74}{1{,}100} \times 100 = 45{\cdot}61\%$

(*ii*) Profitability of the merged plant at 80% capacity.

Sales (1,100 × 80%)	Rs. 880
Variable cost	Rs. 652
Contribution	Rs. 228
Less : Fixed cost	Rs. 130
Profit	Rs. 98

i.e. 11·14% on sales

(*iii*) Sales turnover to earn a profit of 75 Lakhs.

Contribution required = Fixed cost + Desired Profit

= 130 Lakhs + 75 Lakhs = 205 Lakhs.

Required Sales $= \frac{\text{Required contribution}}{\text{P/V ratio}}$

$= \frac{\text{Rs. 205 Lakhs}}{25{\cdot}91} \times 100 = 791{\cdot}20$ Lakhs

(*iv*) Percentage increase in selling price to set off 5% increase in fixed cost.

Revised Fixed cost $= 130 \times \frac{105}{100} = 136{\cdot}50$

Sale price to be increased $= \frac{6{\cdot}50}{791{\cdot}20} \times 100 = 0{\cdot}8215\%$

Section II : Cost Volume Profit Analysis and Decision Making

Introduction—Uses of Cost volume profit analysis—Application of Marginal costing—Fixation of Selling Price—Selling at or below marginal cost—Level of activity planning—Evaluation of Profitability—Sales Mix—Key/Limiting Factor—Make or Buy—Illustrations; Workedout problems—Exercise.

Introduction

Profit is always the final goal to the businessman as well as to the management. The expression cost-volume-profit relationship is thus important to the management. Profit is actually the result of interplay of cost-volume and selling price. The effectiveness of a manager largely depends upon his ability to make correct prediction about future profits. The knowledge of cost-volume profit relationship helps the management to find out the right path to solve the various problems that it faces in the course of its actions.

Use of cost volume Profit analysis

The uses of cost-volume-profit analysis are as follows :

(1) It helps the management to estimate or predict profit over a wide range of volumes.

(2) It helps the management in taking many crucial decisions viz. whether capacity or volume of sales should be increased or not, how can the profit be increased by utilizing the existing capacity etc.

(3) With the help of this relationship the profit performance of a concern can be easily evaluated.

(4) It helps in profit planning.

(5) It helps the management in product pricing.

Assumptions of cost Volume Profit analysis

The following assumptions are made in cost volume profit analysis :

(1) Selling prices are constant.

(2) All costs can be divided into fixed and variable components.

(3) Total variable costs are directly proportional to volume; hence variable cost per unit remains constant.

(4) Prices of factors of production are constant.

(5) Efficiency and productivity are constant.

(6) Total fixed cost remains constant.

(7) Revenue and cost are being compared on per unit basis.

The production volume and sales will be equal at all points of time i.e. changes in beginning and ending inventory levels are zero.

This analysis presumes that the influence of managerial policies, technological methods, efficiency etc. will remain constant.

The analysis either covers a single product or presumes that product mix will not change.

Application of Marginal Costing

(1) Fixation of Selling Price

The following are some of the important areas where marginal costing can be applied to serve the day-to-day needs of management in taking many strategic decisions.

Price fixation is one of the principal functions of the management. Product pricing is necessary under different circumstances such as—

(*a*) Under normal situations;

(*b*) In times of competitions or trade depressions;

(*c*) At the time of accepting additional order for utilizing idle capacity, exporting etc.

(2) Selling at or below Marginal Cost

In most of the cases the prices are equal to marginal cost plus a certain mark-up. The amount to be added will vary depending upon various factors, like demand and supply, competition, variety of products etc. But pricing at or below marginal cost may be necessary in some cases for the following reasons :

(*i*) Expansion and establishment of the product in the foreign market.

(*ii*) Introduction of new product in the market.

(*iii*) Driving out the weaker competitor(s).

(*iv*) To retain the existing market in near future.

(*v*) To dispose off the perishable goods.

(*vi*) To prevent loss of trade.

(*vii*) To push up the sales of joint products.

(*viii*) To keep the employees occupied.

(*ix*) To keep the machine ready for full production.

(3) Level of Activity Planning

The technique of marginal costing helps the management to decide the optimum level of activity. In deciding the optimum level of activity the management must calculate the contribution per unit at different levels of activity. Where contribution is maximum that will be the optimum level of activity.

(4) Evaluation of Profitability

The decision whether a department should continue or not depends to a large extent on their comparative profitability. Marginal costing technique helps the management in taking such decision. As long as a concern makes a contribution towards fixed cost, closing down or suspending activity would not be profitable.

(5) Selection of Profitable Sales-mix

The technique of marginal costing can be applied in determination of most profitable product or sales-mix. Especially, when a concern produces or sells more than one product. The best product mix is that which yields the maximum contribution. So long as fixed cost remains constant, the most profitable sales-mix is determined on the basis of contribution only.

(6) Key/Limiting Factor

The key factor is that which puts a limit on production or sales. There are various things which can be considered as key factors such as shortage of materials, labour, plant capacity, capital, demand of the product etc. Ordinarily, when there is no limiting factor, the choice of the product should be based on P.V. ratio, but when there are some limiting factors, selection of the product should be based on contribution per units of limiting factors. When two or more limiting factors operate simultaneously, it is not possible to determine real ranking of product, without using linear programming.

(7) Make or Buy

A concern may have some idle capacity, which can be utilized for making components or parts instead of buying them from outside. In arriving at such a make or buy decision the market price should be compared with the marginal cost of producing component parts. If the marginal cost is lower than the price quoted by outside vendors, it will be more profitable to manufacture the component in the factory instead of purchasing from outside. Fixed costs are not taken into consideration on the assumption that they have been already incurred. So only variable cost is considered. It is also important to note that, buying may be preferable than making, in spite of lower variable cost where the additional fixed cost for making the product cannot be recovered by the producing units.

On the other hand, when there are no idle capacities, making or buying decision should be taken on the basis of loss of contribution. Loss of contribution means the contribution forgone by the company from the displaced work. If the contribution from making component instead of buying is higher than the loss of contribution, making is more profitable than buying.

Illustration.

From the following figures find the break even volume :

Selling Price per tonne	Rs. 69.50
Variable cost per tonne	Rs. 35.50
Fixed Expenses	Rs. 18.02 lakhs.

If this volume represents 40% capacity, what is the additional profit for an added production of 40% capacity, the selling price of which is 10% lower for 20% capacity production and 15% lower, than the existing price, for the other 20% capacity. *[I.C.W.A. Inter June, 1988]*

Answer

Contribution per tonne = 69.50 – 35.50 = Rs. 34

BEP (volume) = F/C. per unit = 18,02,000/34 = 53,000 tonnes.

BEP (volume) of 53,000 tonnes represents 40% capacity.

Selling price lower by 10% = 69.50 – 10% = 62.55

Contribution per tonne = 62.55 – 35.50 = Rs. 27.05

Selling price lower by 20% = 69.50 – 15% = Rs. 59·075

Contribution per tonne = 59·075 – 35.50 = Rs. 23·575.

	Rs.
20% capacity 26,500 tonnes : Contribution at Rs. 27.05	7,16,825
Another 20% capacity 26,500 tonnes : Contribution at 23·575	6,24,738
Added production of 53,000 tonnes contribution	13,41,563

i.e. Contribution after BEP is the additional profit for an added production of 40% capacity = Rs. 13,41,563.00

Illustration

From the following particulars, find the most profitable product mix and prepare a statement of profitability of that product mix :

	Product A	Product B	Product C
Unit budgeted to be produced and sold	1,800	3,000	1,200
Selling price per unit (Rs.)	60	55	50
Direct Materials	5 Kg.	3 Kg.	4 Kg.
Direct Labour	4 hrs.	3 hrs.	2 hrs.
Variable Overheads	Rs. 7	Rs. 13	Rs. 8
Fixed Overheads	Rs. 10	Rs. 10	Rs. 10
Cost of direct materials per Kg.	Rs. 4	Rs. 4	Rs. 4

Direct labour hour rate	Rs. 2	Rs. 2	Rs. 2
Maximum possible units of sales	4,000	5,000	1,500

All the three products are produced from the same direct materials using the same type of machines and labour. Direct labour, which is the key factor, is limited to 18,600 hours.

[C.A. Inter, May 1990]

Answer

Statement of Contribution per Direct Labour Hour

Product	A	B	C
Direct Materials @ Rs. 4/Kg	20	12	16
Direce Wages @ Rs. 2/Hour	8	6	4
Variable cost	7	13	8
Marginal cost	35	31	28
Selling Price	60	55	50
Contribution per unit	25	24	22
Contribution per DLH	25/4 = 6.25	24/3 = 8	22/2 = 11
Priority	III	II	I

Statement of Profitability on the basis of Budget

Product	No. of units	DLH	Cont. per unit	Total Amount (Rs.)
A	1,800	7,200	25	45,000
B	3,000	9,000	24	72,000
C	1,200	2,400	22	26,400
Total		18,600		1,43,400
Less : Fixed Overheads :				
A 1,800 × 10 = 18,000				
B 3,000 × 10 = 30,000				
C 1,200 × 10 = 12,000				60,000
Profit				83,400

Statement of most profitable product mix and profitability of that product mix

Product mix	Priority	No. of Units	DLH
C	I	1,500 (Maximum)	3,000
B	II	5,000 (Maximum)	15,000
A	III	150 (600 ÷ 4) (Balance)	600
			18,600

Profitability :

Products	No. of units	Cont. per unit	Total Amount (Rs.)
C	1,500	22	33,000
B	5,000	24	1,20,000
A	150	25	3,750
Total Contribution			1,56,750
Less : Fixed Overheads			60,000
Profit			96,750

WORKEDOUT PROBLEMS

Problem 1

Two companies, ABC Ltd. and XYZ Ltd., sell the same type of products. Their budgeted Profit and Loss A/c. for the year shows the following :

	ABC Ltd. ('000)	XYZ Ltd. (Rs. '000)
Sales	150	150
Total Cost	135	135
ABC Ltd. = (V.C. 120 + F.C.15 = 135)		
XYZ Ltd. = (V.C. 100 + F.C.35 = 135)		
Budgeted profit	15	15

You are required to calculate the break-even point of each company. Also state which company is likely to earn greater profit if there is (i) High demand, and (ii) Low demand for its products.

[C.S. Inter, Dec. 1990]

Solution

Statement of Break-even Point

	ABC Ltd. (Rs. '000)	XYZ Ltd. (Rs. '000)
Sales	150	150
Variable cost	120	100
Contribution	30	50
Fixed Cost	15	35
Budgeted Profit	15	15
P.V. Ratio = C ÷ S × 100	30 ÷ 150 × 100 = 20%	50 ÷ 150 × 100 = $33^1/_3$%
BEP = F ÷ P/V ratio	15,000 ÷ 20% = 75,000	35,000 ÷ $33^1/_3$% = 1,05,000
Margin of Safety = Sales – BEP	1,50,000 – 75,000 – 75,000	1,50,000 – 1,05,000 = 45,000

(*i*) In the condition of high demand, XYZ Ltd. is more profitable as its P/V ratio is higher at $33\frac{1}{3}$%. After meeting its fixed cost of Rs. 35,000, the profit in XYZ will be $33\frac{1}{3}$% of sales, whereas it will be 20% of sales only in case of ABC Ltd., after meeting its fixed cost of Rs. 15,000.

(*ii*) In the conditions of low demand, ABC Ltd is more profitable as its fixed cost and B.E.P. are very low. After meeting its fixed cost of Rs. 15,000 it will earn profit. Margin of safety is also higher in case of ABC Ltd. Even if the sales is required to 50% due to low demand, it will touch BEP and it will not incur any loss.

Problem 2

Mr. X has Rs. 2,00,000 investment in his business firm. He wants a 15 per cent return on his money. From an analysis of recent cost figures, he finds that his variable cost of operating is 60 per cent of sales, his fixed costs are Rs. 80,000 per year.

Show computations to answer the following questions :

(*a*) What sales volume must be obtained to break-even ?

(*b*) What sales volume must be obtained to get 15 per cent return on investment ?

(*c*) Mr. X estimates that even if he closed the doors of his business, he would incur Rs. 25,000 as expenses per year. At what sales would he be better-off by locking his business up ?

Solution

Working Notes :

Return at 15% on investment of Rs. 2,00,000 = Rs. 30,000

Variable cost is 60% of sales i.e. P/V ratio is 40%.

(*i*) B.E.P. = F/P.V. ratio = 80,000/40% = Rs. 2,00,000

(*ii*) Sales = F + P/P.V. Ratio = 80,000 + 30,000/40% = Rs. 2,75,000.

(*iii*) 25,000/40% = Rs. 62,500

At sales of Rs. 62,500 it would be better-off by locking his business.

Problem 3

P & Q Ltd. has been offered a choice to buy a machine between A and B. You are required to compute :

(*a*) Break-even point for each of the machine.

(*b*) Level of sales at which both machines earn equal profits.

(*c*) Range of sales at which one is more profitable than the other.

Relevant data are given below :

	Machines	
	A	B
Annual output in units	10,000	10,000
Fixed cost Rs.	30,000	16,000
Profit at the above level of production	Rs. 30,000	Rs. 24,000

Market Price of the product is expected to be Rs. 10/- per unit.

[C.S. Inter & I.C.W.A. Inter]

Solution

	A	B
Annual output in units	10,000	10,000
Fixed cost	Rs. 30,000	Rs. 16,000
Profit	Rs. 30,000	Rs. 24,000
Contribution	Rs. 60,000	Rs. 40,000
Contribution per unit	Rs. 60,000/10,000 = 6	Rs. 40,000/10,000 = 4
Break Even Point F. Cost/Cont. per unit.	30,000/6 = 5,000	16,000/4 = 4,000

(*b*) Level of sales at which both machines earn equal profits.

= Difference in fixed cost/Difference in contribution per unit = 30,000 – 16,000/6 – 4 =14,000/2 = 7,000 per unit.

	A (Rs.)		B (Rs.)
Contribution 7,000 × 6	42,000	7,000 × 4	28,000
Less : Fixed Cost	30,000		16,000
Profit	12,000		12,000

(*c*) B.E.P. of machine B is lower. Contribution per unit from Machine A is higher. Hence at range of sales from 4,000 to 7,000 units, B is more profitable.

At the sale of 7,000 units, both profits are equal. Above the sale of 7,000 units, A is more profitable as the contribution per unit is higher.

Reconciliation

Sales Level Units	4,000		5,000		6,000		7,000		8,000	
	A	B	A	B	A	B	A	B	A	B
Contribution	24,000	16,000	30,000	20,000	36,000	24,000	42,000	28,000	48,000	32,000
Fixed Cost	30,000	16,000	30,000	16,000	30,000	16,000	30,000	16,000	30,000	16,000
Profit/Loss (–)	(–)6,000	Nil	Nil	4,000	6,000	8,000	12,000	12,000	18,000	16,000
Result	Lower	BEP	BEP	Higher	Lower	Higher	Equal	Equal	Higher	Lower

Problem 4

Hero Cycles Ltd. purchases 20,000 bells per annum from an outside supplier at Rs. 5 each. The management feels that these be manufactured and not purchased. A machine costing Rs. 50,000 will be required to manufacture the items within the factory. The machine has an annual capacity of 30,000 units and life of 5 years. The following additional information are available :

Material cost per bell will be	Rs. 2.00
Labour cost	Re. 1.00
Variable overheads	100% of labour cost.

You are required to advise whether :

(*i*) The company should continue to purchase the bells from outside suppliers or should make them in the factory, and

(*ii*) The company should accept an order to supply 5,000 bells to the market at a selling price of Rs. 4.50 per bell ?

Solution

		Rs.
(*a*)	Manufacturing cost of one unit of bell	
	Materials cost	2.00
	Labour cost	1.00
	Variable overhads 100% of labour cost	1.00
	Variable cost	4.00
	Add : Depreciation : Rs. 50,000 ÷ 5 yrs. = Rs. 10,000 per annum	
	= Rs. 10,000 ÷ 20,000 bells =	0.50
	Cost of Manufacture	4.50
	Purchase cost	5.00
	Saving if manufactured	0.50
	Saving per annum, if manufactured 0.50 × 20,000. Hence the company should manufacture the same in the factory.	10,000
(*b*)	Depreciation has been recovered on 20,000 bells. Hence variable cost of Rs. 4.00 per unit is to be considered for decision making. Further, machine has additional capacity of 10,000 units per annum (30,000 – 20,000).	
	Selling price (per unit in Rs.)	4.50
	Variable cost (per unit in Rs.)	4.00
	Profit	0.50
	Profit on 5,000 units at Rs. 0.50 = Rs. 2,500.	
	Hence the company should accept an order to supply 5,000 bells at a selling price of Rs. 4.50 per unit.	

Problem 5

A company has prepared the following budget of Sales :

Product	Sales	P/V ratio
A	6,00,000	40%
B	9,00,000	30%
C	10,00,000	25%

The fixed costs amount to Rs. 8,00,000.

You are required to revise the sales mix to ensure a profit of Rs. 10,000 in such a way that not more than Rs. 8,00,000 of sales of product A is possible and that the present total value of sales should not be altered. *[C.A. Inter, Nov. 2001]*

Solution

Present contribution

$$A = 6,00,000 \times \frac{40}{100} = 2,40,000$$

$$B = 9,00,000 \times \frac{30}{100} = 2,70,000$$

$$C = 10,00,000 \times \frac{25}{100} = 2,50,000$$

Total Contribution	7,60,000
Less : Fixed cost	8,00,000
Loss	40,000

Contribution required to earn a profit of Rs. 10,000. Current Loss + require profit = additional contribution i.e. 40,000 + 10,000 = 50,000.

Total contribution required = 50,000 + 7,60,000 = 8,10,000

Ranking of the three profits will be according to ranking of P.V. ratio i.e. A.B.C.

As per problem not more than Rs. 8,00,000 of sales of product A is possible and the total value of sales should not be altered.

Then contribution from product A = $8,00,000 \times \frac{40}{100} = 3,20,000$

Remaining contribution 8,10,000 – 3,20,000 = 4,90,000 to be earned from B & C.

But the total sales of B and C must be Rs. 17,00,000 (Total sale : 25,00,000 – Sale of A : 8,00,000). To do that, sale of B required to be increased. Because if sale of B is not increased then the contribution from B and C will be less than 4,90,000 (Then it will be, B : $9,00,000 \times \frac{30}{100}$ + C : $8,00,000 \times \frac{25}{100} = 4,70,000$).

Let x be the additional sales amount product B.

$$\text{Then } 4,90,000 = (9,00,000 + x)\frac{30}{100} + (8,00,000 - x)\frac{25}{100}$$

$$2,70,000 + 0{\cdot}3x + 20,000 - 0.25x = 4,90,000$$

$$\therefore 0.05x = 20,000 \text{ or } x = 4,00,000$$

Revised Sales & Contribution

		Sale	*Contribution*
A =		8,00,000	$8,00,000 \times \frac{40}{100}$ = 3,20,000
B =	9,00,000		
	4,00,000	13,00,000	$13,00,000 \times \frac{30}{100}$ = 3,90,000
C =	17,00,000		
	(13,00,000)	4,00,000	$4,00,000 \times \frac{25}{100}$ = 1,00,000
		25,00,000	8,10,000

Profit = C – F i.e. 8,10,000 – 8,00,000 = Rs. 10,000

Problem 6

A company manufactures three products. The budgeted quantity, selling prices and unit costs are as follows :

	A	*B*	*C*
	Rs.	*Rs.*	*Rs.*
Raw materials (Rs. 20 per kg)	80	40	20
Direct wages (Rs. 5 per hour)	5	15	10
Variable overheads	10	30	20
Fixed overhead	9	22	18
Budgeted production in units	6,400	3,200	2,400
Selling price per unit	140	120	90

You are required to :

(*i*) Present a statement of budgeted profit.

(*ii*) Set optimal product-mix and determine the profit, if the supply of raw materials is restricted to 8,400 kgs.

(*iii*) A supplier comes forward to supply 20,000 kgs of raw material at a premium of Rs. 15 per kg. This supply is over and above the stocks of 18,400 kgs available with the company. State whether the company should accept the entire quantity or any part of it. If not, what lowest price should be negotiated ? ***[C.A. Inter, Nov. 2001]***

Solution

(i) Statement of Budgeted Profit :

	A	B	C
Sales price/unit (a)	140	120	90
Less, variable cost/unit (b)			
Raw materials	80	40	20
Direct wages	5	15	10
Variable overhead	10	30	20
	95	85	50
Contribution/unit (a – b)	45	35	40
Budgeted Production (units)	6,400	3,200	2,400
Contribution	2,88,000	1,12,000	96,000

Total contribution : A + B + C		Rs. 4,96,000
Less : Fixed costs :	A 6,400 × 9 = 57,600	
	B 3,200 × 22 = 70,400	
	C 2,400 × 18 = 43,200	Rs. 1,71,200
	Profit	Rs. 3,24,800

(ii) Statement of optimal product-mix when Raw Material is the key factor :

	A	*B*	*C*
Contribution/unit	45	35	40
Raw material/unit (kg)	4	2	1
Contribution/kg	11.25	17.50	40
Ranking	3	2	1

i.e. CBA	*C*	*B*	*A*
units * $\frac{(18{,}400 - 2{,}400 \times 1 - 3{,}200 \times 2)}{4\text{kg/unit.}}$	2,400	3,200	*2,400
R.M/kg	1	2	4
Raw material Required (kg)	2,400	6,400	9,600
Contribution/unit	40	35	45
Contribution	96,000	1,12,000	1,08,000

Total contribution : A + B + C	= Rs. 3,16,000
Less : Fixed overhead	Rs. 1,71,200
Profit	Rs. 1,44,800

(*iii*) Product A can be produced 6,400 – 2,400 = 4,000 units more if raw material is available.
Raw material required = 4,000 units × 4 kg = 16,000 kg

Variable cost/unit of A	Rs. 95
Add : Additional cost/unit due premium on Raw material for additional units 4 kg × 15	Rs. 60
Revised variable cost/unit. Rs.	155

Loss per unit = S – V : 140 – 155 = 15/unit.

∴ Offer to supply additional raw materials at a premium of Rs. 15 is not viable.

Loss of Rs. 15 per unit can be covered if the raw material cost is reduced by (15 per unit ÷ 4 kg per unit) Rs. 3·75 per kg i.e. 15 – 3·75 = 11·25 per kg or less.

Lowest price for 16,000 kg can be negotiated at a premium of less than 11·25 per kg. i.e. at a cost of less than (20 + 11·25) Rs. 31·25.

Problem 7

	Strategy 1	Strategy 2	Strategy 3
Reduction in selling price per set by	5%	7·5%	10%
Expected increase in sales volume	10%	20%	25%

You are required to assess the effect on profits of each of the three strategies, and to recommend which strategy, if any, ought to be adopted. ***[C.I.M.A. London Nov. 94 Adopted]***

Solution

Contribution per unit = Sales/unit – Variable cost/unit = Rs. 80 – Rs. 30 = Rs. 50.

Fixed cost per annum Rs. 8,00,000

Budgeted production : 24,000 sets i.e. $\frac{\text{Rs. } 8{,}00{,}000 + \text{Rs. } 4{,}00{,}000}{\text{Rs. } 50}$

	Strategy 1	*Strategy 2*	*Strategy 3*
(*a*) Sales (units)	26,400	28,800	30,000
(*b*) Revised selling price per unit	76	74	72
(*c*) Variable cost/unit	30	30	30
(*d*) Contribution/unit (b – c)	46	44	42
(*e*) Total Contribution (a × d)	12,14,400	12,67,200	12,60,000
(*f*) Fixed cost	8,00,000	8,00,000	8,00,000
(*g*) Profit (e – f)	4,14,400	4,67,200	4,60,000

Recomendation : Strategy 2 should be implemented.

Problem 8

XYZ Ltd. is selling three brands of its product in the brand names X, Y and Z. The details regarding unit costs and selling prices are as under :

(figures in Rs.)

	X	*Y*	*Z*
Direct materials	6	12	16
Direct labour	8	8	20
Variable Overhead	6	20	14
Selling Price	36	50	96

The monthly fixed expenditure is Rs. 5,40,000/-. Sales volume for the months of July and August of 1989 are as follows :

	X	*Y*	*Z*
July	20,000/-	20,000/-	20,000/-
August	40,000/-	26,000/-	10,000/-

Find out the monthly profits and if your computation brings out that higher profit was earned in the month having lower sales volume, kindly justify the finding with reasons.

[I.C.W.A. Inter, Dec. 1989]

Solution

Statement of contribution per unit and P/V Ratio

Products	*X*	*Y*	*Z*
Direct Materials	6	12	16
Direct Labour	8	8	20
Variable Overhead	6	20	14
Marginal Cost	20	40	50
Selling Price	36	50	96
Contribution per Unit	16	10	46
P/V Ratio = C/S × 100	16/36 × 100 = 44.44%	10/50 × 100 = 20%	46/96 × 100 = 47.92%

Statement of Monthly Profits

	Contribution from :	*Rs.*	*Rs.*
July 1989	X 20,000 × 16	3,20,000	
	Y 20,000 × 10	2,00,000	
	Z 20,000 × 46	9,20,000	
Total	60,000	14,40,000	
Fixed Expenses		5,40,000	
Profit			9,00,000/-
August 1989	X 40,000 × 16	6,40,000	
	Y 26,000 × 10	2,60,000	
	Z 10,000 × 46	4,60,000	
Total	76,000	13,60,000	
Fixed Expenses		5,40,000	
Profit			8,20,000

Higher profit was earned in July 1989 having lower sales volume of 60,000 units compared to 76,000 units in August 1989.

Reasons : Though the overall sales volume was lower in July 1989, the sales volume of Z was higher. The contribution per unit and P/V ratio are highest in respect of Z. Hence the profit of Z was higher by Rs. 4,60,000 (9,20,000 – 4,60,000).

This has contributed to the overall increase in Profit in July 1989.

Problem 9

Taurus Ltd. produces three products A, B and C from the same manufacturing facilities. The cost and other details of the three products are as follows :

	A	B	C
Selling price/unit (Rs.)	200	160	100
Variable cost/unit (Rs.)	120	120	40
Fixed expenses/month (Rs.)			2,76,000
Maximum production per month (units)	5,000	8,000	6,000
Total hours available for the month			200
Maximum demand per month (units)	2,000	4,000	2,400

The processing hours cannot be increased beyond 200 hours per month.

You are required to :

(a) Compute the most profitable product mix.

(b) Compute the overall break-even sales of the company for the month based on the mix calculated in (a) above. *[C.A. Inter, May 1988]*

Solution

(a) Statement of Contribution and Priority

		A	B	C
(a)	Maximum Production per month (units)	5,000	8,000	6,000
(b)	Maximum production per Hour (units) (A ÷ 200 Hrs)	25	40	30
(c)	Hours required for maximum demand	$\frac{2,000 \text{ units}}{25 \text{ units}}$ = 80 Hrs.	$\frac{4,000}{40}$ = 100 Hrs.	$\frac{2,400}{30}$ = 80 Hrs.
		Rs.	*Rs.*	*Rs.*
(d)	Selling price per unit	200	160	100
(e)	Variable cost per unit	120	120	40
(f)	Contribution per unit (d – e)	80	40	60
(g)	Contribution per hour (f × b)	2,000	1,600	1,800
(h)	Ranking	1	3	2

Statement of Profitable Product Mix

	Hrs.
A = 2,000 units, Hours required = $\frac{2,000 \text{ units}}{25 \text{ units per Hr}}$ =	80
C = 2,400 units, " " = $\frac{2,400}{30}$ =	80
B = *1,600 units, " " = $\frac{1,600}{40}$ =	40
Total	200

* Hours available for B was 200 – 80 – 80 = 40 hrs. By utilising 40 hrs B can be produced 1,600 units.
(40 Hrs × 40 units per hour as per "B" above)

		A	B	C
	Units	2,000	1,600	2,400
		Rs.	*Rs.*	*Rs.*
	Sales price per unit	200	160	100
	Sales value	4,00,000	2,56,000	2,40,000
Less :	Variable cost	2,40,000	1,92,000	96,000
	Contribution	1,60,000	64,000	1,44,000

	Total contribution = A + B + C =	Rs. 3,68,000
Less :	Fixed Expenses	Rs. 2,76,000
	Profit per month	92,000

(*b*) P/V ratio = $\frac{\text{Contribution}}{\text{Sales}} \times 100$

i.e. $\frac{3,68,000}{8,96,000} \times 100 = 41{\cdot}07\%$

Overall break-even sales = $\frac{\text{Fixed Cost}}{\text{P/V ratio}}$ i.e. $\frac{2,76,000}{41{\cdot}07} \times 100 = 6,72,000$

EXERCISES

OBJECTIVE TYPE QUESTIONS

1. *Indicate whether the following statements are true or false* :

(*a*) Variable cost per unit varies with the increase in the volume of output.
(*b*) Conversion cost is equal to direct wages plus factory overhead.
(*c*) All costs are controllable.
(*d*) Depreciation is an out-of-pocket cost.
(*e*) An item of cost that is direct for one business may be indirect for another.
(*f*) Fixed cost per unit remains constant.

[Ans. True : (*b*), (*e*) False : (*a*), (*c*), (*d*), (*f*)]

2. *Indicate whether the following statements are true or false* :

(*a*) Profit = Contribution – Fixed cost.
(*b*) P/V ratio = Profit/sales.
(*c*) Marginal costing and direct costing are the same.
(*d*) Marginal costing is based on the distinction between fixed and variable costs.
(*e*) Profit = P/v ratio × margin of safety.
(*f*) For decision-making, absorption costing is more suitable than marginal costing.
(*g*) In Marginal costing, under- and over-absorption of fixed overheads is bound to arise.
(*h*) Marginal costing cannot be applied in Job costing.
(*i*) Margin of safety = Contribution/P.V. ratio.
(*j*) Marginal costing can be used with process costing.
(*k*) In marginal costing, valuation of stock is done on total cost basis.
(*l*) Profit = Sales – Contribution.
(*m*) Variable + Profit = Sales

[Ans. True : (*a*), (*d*), (*e*), (*j*) False. (*b*), (*c*), (*f*), (*g*), (*h*), (*i*), (*k*), (*l*), (*m*)]

3. (*a*) *Which of the following is true at break even point* :

(*i*) Profit = Fixed Cost + Variable Cost
(*ii*) Contribution = Fixed cost.
(*iii*) Sales Revenue = Total cost – variable cost.
(*iv*) Sales Revenue = Variable cost.

[Ans. (*ii*)]

(*b*) *The margin of safety may be defined as* :

(*i*) The point at which break even point sales are achieved.
(*ii*) The difference between planned sales and break-even point sales.
(*iii*) The extent to which sales revenue exceeds fixed costs.
(*iv*) The excess of planned sales over the current actual sales.

[Ans. (*ii*)]

(*c*) *Increase in fixed cost will result in which of the following* :

(*i*) A decrease in the contribution : Sales ratio.
(*ii*) A decrease in the contribution per unit.
(*iii*) An increase in the break-even-point sales level.
(*iv*) An increase in the margin of safety.

[Ans. (*iii*)]

(*d*) *Existing sales are Rs. 1,00,000 (500 units) variable costs are Rs. 60,000. Fixed costs are Rs. 24,000. If selling price is reduced by 10% which of the following is the break-even sales quantity ?*

(*i*) 334 units.
(*ii*) 400 units.
(*iii*) 500 units.
(*iv*) 450 units.

[Ans. (*ii*)]

(*e*) *An increase in variable costs where selling price and fixed cost remain constant will result in which of the following ?*

(*i*) An increase in the margin of safety.
(*ii*) A fall in the sales level at which break even point will occur.
(*iii*) A rise in the sales level at which break even point will occur.
(*iv*) No change in the sales level at which break even point will occur.

[Ans. (*iii*)]

THEORETICAL QUESTIONS

1. What do you understand by cost volume profit analysis ? ***[C.U. B.Com. (Hons.) 1999]***

2. What information is expressed by margin of safety and angle of incidence ? ***[C.U. B.Com. (Hons.) 2003]***

3. "The technique of marginal costing can be a valuable aid to management"—Discuss.

4. "While variable costs are controllable, fixed costs are not"—Comment. ***[C.S. Inter, Dec. 1997]***

5. "One of the main objection to the contribution approach to costing is that it ignores fixed cost."—Discuss and explain the advantages of the contribution approach. ***[I.C.W.A. Inter, Dec. 1983]***

6. What are the important areas of management decisions opened up by the application of marginal costing technique ? ***[I.C.W.A. Inter, June 1988]***

7. "Under some circumstances, it may be advisable to sell at prices equal to or below the marginal cost ignoring fixed cost"—you are required to enumerate the circumstances. ***[C.S. Inter, Dec. 1996]***

8. Discuss the influence of fixed cost, variable cost and selling price on P/V ratio, BEP and profit. ***[C.S. Inter, Dec. 1994]***

9. Write short notes on :

(*i*) Break-even analysis.
(*ii*) Break-even point.
(*iii*) Contribution.
(*iv*) Importance of break-even point ***[C.S. Dec. 1996]***

10. Explain cost-volume-profit analysis and discuss briefly the limitations of a profit volume graph.

11. The choice between using absorption costing and marginal costing is determined by certain factors. What are they ?
What are advantages and disadvantages of using marginal costing ?

12. "Absorption costing observes the total amount of fixed costs whereas variable costing highlights it".—Discuss.

13. Explain the technique of 'Marginal costing' and state its importance in decision making.

14. What factors have to be considered in taking decisions for "Buy or make" or 'Lease or buy' ?

15. Describe the various costs used in decision making and explain their characteristics.

16. What is differential costing ?

17. What factors to be considered in a "make or buy" decision ? ***[C.S. Inter, June 1990]***

PROBLEMS

1. A. Sen manufactures a single product with a sale price of Rs. 16 per unit and a variable cost Rs. 10 per unit. Fixed costs are Rs. 48,000 p.a.
Calculate :

(*i*) P/V ratio.
(*ii*) Number of units to be sold to break even.
(*iii*) Number of units to be sold to achieve a profit of Rs. 30,000 p.a. ***[C.U. B.Com (H) 1994]***

[Ans. (*i*) P/V Ratio 37.5%; (*ii*) Break-even (units) 8,000 units; (*iii*) Required sales 13,000 units.]

2. X Ltd. made sales during a certain period for Rs. 1,00,000. The net profit for the same period was Rs. 10,000 and the fixed overheads were Rs. 15,000. Find out :
   (*i*) Profit Volume (P/V) Ratio,
   (*ii*) Break Even Point (BEP) Sales,
   (*iii*) Number of units to be sold to earn a profit of Rs. 15,000 and,
   (*iv*) Net Profit from the Sales of Rs. 1,50,000. *[C.U. B.Com. 1995]*

   [Ans. (*i*) P/V Ratio 25% ; (*ii*) Break-even Sales Rs. 60,000; (*iii*) Required Sales 1,20,000; (*iv*) Required Profit Rs. 22,000]

3. A business produces 200 units of a product by making following expenditure :
   (*i*) Materials—Rs. 30,000; (*ii*) Labour—Rs. 20,000; (*iii*) Factory Overhead—Rs. 4,000; (*iv*) Administrative Overhead—Rs. 5,754 and (*v*) Selling and Distribution Overhead—Rs. 1,500.
   The products are sold at a price of Rs. 400 per unit.
   The above expenditure are classified into fixed and variable as follows :

Expenditure	*Fixed*	*Variable*
(*i*) Materials	Nil	100%
(*ii*) Labour	50%	50%
(*iii*) Factory Overhead	25%	78.5%
(*iv*) Administrative Overhead	100%	Nil
(*v*) Selling & Distribution Overhead	60%	40%

[Ans. Total variable Cost Rs. 43,600 and Fixed Cost Rs. 17,654, (b) Contribution in Total Rs. 36,400 and per unit Rs. 182. (c) P/V Ratio 45·5%, (d) B.E.P. Sales Rs. 38,800, in units—97.]

4. X Ltd. sells 8,000 units of its products at a loss of Rs. 16,000.
   Variable cost per unit is Rs. 12 and total fixed cost is Rs. 48,000.
   Calculate : (*i*) Profit-Volume Ratio, (*ii*) The number of units to be sold to earn a profit of Rs. 10,000 (*iii*) The amount of profit from a sale of 20,000 units. *[C.U. B.Com. 1999]*

   [Ans. (*i*) 25% (*ii*) 14,500 units (*iii*) Rs. 32,000.]

5. The projected output of a plant, when sold, would earn Rs. 70,000 as sales income to Mixers Ltd. The variable costs for this production volume would be Rs. 30,000. The fixed costs are Rs. 20,000. Determine the following :
   (*i*) The break-even point of the company.
   (*ii*) The Profit or Loss to the company on sales of Rs. 49,000 and Rs. 28,000.
   (*iii*) The amount of sales that will enable the company to earn a net profit of Rs. 28,000. *[Delhi Univ. B.Com. (H) 1990]*

   [Ans. (*i*) Rs. 35,000, (*ii*) Profit when sales are Rs. 49,000 : Rs. 8,000, Loss when sales are Rs. 28,000 : Rs. 4,000, (*iii*) Rs. 84,000]

6. From the following data, calculate :
   (*a*) Break-even point expressed in terms of units sold and sales value.
   (*b*) Number of units to be sold for earning a profit of Rs. 70,000 per year.
   (*c*) How many units are to be sold to earn a net profit of 15% on sales ?

	Rs.
Selling price per unit	20
Variable manufacturing cost per unit	11
Variable selling cost per unit	2
Fixed factory overhead	1,04,000
Fixed selling expenses	15,000

[Ans. (*a*) Rs. 17,000; Sales value Rs. 3,40,000]

(*b*) 27,000 units. (*c*) 29,750 units.

Hints : No. of units to be sold is x.

$$x = \frac{\text{Fixed cost + Desired Profit}}{\text{Contribution per unit}}$$

$$\therefore \quad x = \frac{1,19,000 + \frac{15}{100}(x \times \text{Rs. } 20)}{7}$$

or $7x = 1,19,000 + 3x$ or $x = 29,750$ units.

7. Rainbow Ltd sold goods for Rs. 30,00,000 in a year. In that year the variable costs were Rs. 6,00,000 and fixed costs were Rs. 8,00,000.

Find out :

(*i*) P/V ratio.

(*ii*) Break-even Sales.

(*iii*) Break-even sales if selling price was reduced by 10% and fixed costs were increased by Rs. 1,00,000. ***[C.U. B.Com. (H) 2000]***

[Ans. (*i*) P/V ratio = 80%; (*ii*) Break-even sales : Rs. 10,00,000; (*iii*) Rs. 11,57,143]

8. The following figures are available from the records of Venus Enterprise as at 31st March:

	1988	*1989*
	Rs. Lakhs	*Rs. Lakhs*
Sales	150	200
Profit	30	50

Calculate (*a*) The P/V ratio and total fixed expenses (*b*) The break-even level of sales ; (*c*) Sales required to earn a profit of Rs. 90 Lakhs (*d*) Profit or Loss that would arise if the sales were Rs. 280 Lakhs. ***[C.A. Inter., May 1989]***

[Ans. (*a*) 40%, fixed expenses Rs. 3,00,000 ; (*b*) Rs. 75,00,000 ; (*c*) Rs. 3,00,000 ; (*d*) Rs. 82,00,000]

9. On the basis of the following information, you are required to ascertain:

(*a*) Sales to break-even.

(*b*) Sales to earn a profit of Rs. 60,000 if selling price is reduced by Re. 1.

Sales (10,000 units)	Rs. 1,60,000
Variable cost	Rs. 96,000
Fixed cost	Rs. 48,000

[C.U., B.Com. (H) 2001]

[Ans. (*a*) Sales to break even Rs. 1,20,000; (*b*) Rs. 3,00,000]

10. From the following information, calculate profit :

Sales	Rs. 8,00,000
Variable cost	Rs. 6,00,000
Break-even sales	Rs. 6,00,000

[C.U., B.Com. (H) 2002]

[Ans. Rs. 50,000]

11. The price structure of a cycle made by Cycle Co. Ltd. is as follows :

	Rs.	*Rs.*
Material	60	
Labour	20	
Variable overhead	20	100
Fixed O/H		50
Profit		50
Selling Price		200

This is based on the manufacturing of one lakh cycles per annum. The company expects that due to competition, they will have to reduce selling prices, but they want to keep the total profits intact. What level of production will have to be reached, i.e. how many cycles will have to be made to get the same amount of profits if :

(*a*) The selling price is reduced by 10% (*b*) the selling price is reduced by 20%.

[I.C.W.A. Inter]

[Ans. (*a*) Rs. 1,25,000; (*b*) Rs. 1,66,667]

12. The operating results of a company for the last 2 years are as follows :

Year	Sales (Rs.)	Profit (Rs.)
2003	2,70,000	6,000
2004	3,00,000	15,000

Assuming that the cost structure and selling prices remain the same in both the years, find out
(*i*) P/V ratio
(*ii*) Fixed cost
(*iii*) Break-even point
(*iv*) Margin of safety at a profit of Rs. 24,000. *[C.U. B.Com. (H) 2003]*

[Ans. (*a*) P.V. ratio : 30% (*b*) Rs. 75,000 (*c*) Rs. 2,50,000 (*d*) Rs. 80,000]

13. Micado Ltd. furnishes you the following information relating to the half year ending 30th June 2000 :

	Rs.
Fixed Expenses	50,000
Sales value	2,00,000
Profit	50,000

During the second half of the same year the company has projected a loss of Rs. 10,000. Calculate
(*a*) The profit volume ratio, break-even point and margin of safety for six months ending 30th June 2000.
(*b*) Expected sales volume for second half of the year assuming that selling price and fixed expenses remain unchanged in the second half of the year also.
(*c*) The break-even point and margin of safety for the whole year 2000. *[I.C.W.A. Inter]*

[Ans. (*a*) 50%; Rs. 1,00,000 (*b*) Rs. 80,000 (*c*) Rs. 2,00,000; Rs. 80,000]

14. Alpha Ltd. furnished the following information :

Selling price	Rs. 10 per unit
Variable cost	Rs. 6 per unit

It is expected that variable cost will increase by 20%. What will be the selling price per unit if the company wishes to maintain the same P/V ratio ? *[C.U. B.Com. (H) 2004]*

[Ans. Selling price per unit : Rs. 12]

15. Merry manufactures Ltd. has supplied you the following information in respect of one of its products :

	Rs.
Total fixed costs	18,000
Total variable costs	30,000
Total Sales	60,000
Units sold	20,000

Find out (*a*) contribution per unit (*b*) break-even point (*c*) Margin of safety (*d*) profit and (*e*) volume of sales to earn a profit of Rs. 24,000. *[C.S. Final]*

[Ans. (*a*) Rs. 150; (*b*) 12,000 units (*c*) 8,000 units (*d*) Rs. 12,000; (*e*) 28,000 units.]

16. (*a*) A company has fixed expenses of Rs. 90,000 with sales at Rs. 3,00,000 and a profit of Rs. 60,000. Calculate the profit volume ratio. If in the next period, the company suffered a loss of Rs. 30,000. Calculate the sales volume.
(*b*) What is the margin of safety for a profit of Rs. 60,000 in (a) above ?

[I.C.M.A. Inter]

[Ans. (*a*) 50%; Rs. 1,20,000 (*b*) Rs. 1,80,000]

17. A company budgets for a production of 1,50,000 units. The variable cost per unit is Rs. 14 and fixed cost is Rs. 2 per unit. The company fixes its selling price to fetch a profit of Rs. 15% on cost.

(*a*) What is break-even point ?
(*b*) What is profit volume ratio ?
(*c*) If it reduces its selling price by 5% how does the revised selling price affect the break even point and the profit-volume ratio ?
(*d*) If a profit increase of 10% is desired more than the budget what should be the sales at the reduced prices ?

[Ans. (*a*) 68,182; (*b*) 23.91% (*c*) 19.91% (*d*) 2,00,000 units]

18.

	Sales	Profit
Period 1	10,000	2,000
Period 2	15,000	4,000

You are required to calculate :
(*i*) P.V. ratio; (*ii*) Fixed cost; (*iii*) Break even sales volume; (*iv*) Sales to earn a profit of Rs. 8,000. *[C.S. Inter]*

[Ans. (*i*) P. V. ratio = 40%; (*ii*) Fixed cost = Rs. 2,000; (*iii*) B.E.P. = Rs. 50,000; (*iv*) Rs. 12,500; Additional sale Rs. 2,500; (*v*) Profit Rs. 1,200]

19. Following information is given :

Fixed Cost	Rs. 18,000
Sales	5,000 units
Break-even point	3,000 units
Selling price per unit	Rs. 20

Calculate :
(*a*) Profit/volume Ratio; (*b*) Margin of safety; (*c*) Profit if sales are Rs. 1,30,000; (*d*) Additional units to be sold increasing the present profit by Rs. 5,400. *[M.Com. Kanpur]*

[Ans. (*a*) 30%; (*b*) Rs. 40,000 (*c*) Rs. 21,000; (*d*) 900 units.]

20. The sales of a company in the first half of 2004, amounted to Rs. 2,70,000 and profit earned was Rs. 7,200. The sales in the 2nd half registered an increase and amounted to Rs. 3,42,000. The profit earned was Rs. 20,700 in that half year. Assuming no change in fixed costs, calculate :
(*i*) P.V. ratio.
(*ii*) The amount of profit when sales are Rs. 2,16,000.
(*iii*) The amount of sales required to earn a profit of Rs. 36,000. *[B.Com. Delhi]*

[Ans. (*i*) 18.75%; (*ii*) Loss : Rs. 2,925; (*iii*) 4,23,600.]

21. A company budgets for a production of 1,50,000 units. The variable cost per unit is Rs. 14 and fixed cost is Rs. 2 per unit. The company fixes its selling price to fetch a profit of 15% of cost.
(*a*) What is break-even point ?
(*b*) What is profit-volume ratio ?
(*c*) If it reduces its selling price by 5%, how does the revised selling price affect the break even point and P/V ratio ?
(*d*) If a profit increase of 10% is desired more than the budget, what should be the sale at the reduced price ? *[C.A. Inter]*

[Ans. (*a*) B.E.P. : 68,182 units; (*b*) P/V ratio : 23·91%; (*c*) B.E.P. : 86,207 units, P/V ratio : 19·9%; (*d*) Sales 2,00,000 units, Rs. 34,96,000]

22. From the following information, calculate the break even point and turnover required to earn a profit of Rs. 36,000 :

	Rs.
Fixed Overheads	Rs. 1,80,000
Variable cost per unit	Rs. 2
Selling price	Rs. 20

If the company is earning a profit of Rs. 36,000, then express the margin of safety available to it. *[C.A. Inter]*

[Ans. (*a*) B.E.P : 10,000 units, Rs. 2,00,000; (*b*) Rs. 2,40,000 (*c*) Margin of safety Rs. 40,000]

23. Expansion Ltd. manufactures automobile accessories and parts. The following are the total costs of processing 1,00,000 units :

	Rs. (Lakhs)
Direct Material cost	5
Direct Labour cost	8
Variable factory overhead	6
Fixed factory overhead	5

The purchase price of the component is Rs. 22. The fixed overhead would continue to be incurred even when the component is bought from outside, although there would have been reduction to the extent of Rs. 2,00,000.

Required :

(*a*) Should the part be made or bought considering that the present facility when released following a buying decision would remain idle ?

(*b*) In case the released capacity can be rented out to another manufacturer for Rs. 1,50,000 having good demand, what should be the decision ? *[C.S. (Inter), June 1990]*

[Ans. (*a*) Total cost : Make : Rs. 24 Buy : Rs. 25; Decision. The part should be made.; (*b*) Cost : Make : Rs. 24, Buy, Rs. 23·50; Decision : The part should be bought.]

24. The following data has been obtained from the records of a factory :

Sales 4,000 units @ Rs. 25 each		Rs. 1,00,000
	Rs.	
Material consumed	40,000	
Variable overheads	10,000	
Labour Charges	20,000	
Fixed overheads	18,000	Rs. 88,000
Net Profit		Rs. 12,000

Calculate :

(*i*) The number of units by selling which the company will neither lose nor gain anything.

(*ii*) The sales needed to earn a profit of 20% on sales.

(*iii*) The extra units which should be sold to obtain the present profit if it is proposed to reduce the selling price by 20% and 25%, and

(*iv*) The selling price to be fixed to bring down its break even point to 500 units under present conditions.

[Ans. (*i*) 2,400 units; (*ii*) Rs. 1,80,000; (*iii*) 8,000 units and 20,000 units; (*iv*) Rs. 53.50 per unit.]

25. Polestar Electronics decides to effect a 10% reduction in the price of its product because it is felt that such a step may lead to a greater volume of sales.

It is anticipated that there are no prospects of a change in total fixed costs and variable cost per unit. The directors wish to maintain the net profits at the present level.

The following information has been obtained from its books :

Sales : 10,000 units	Rs. 2,00,000
Variable costs	Rs. 15 per unit
Fixed costs	Rs. 40,000

How would management proceed to implement this decision ? *[B.Com. (H) Delhi]*

[Ans. Profit Rs. 10,000; units to be sold 16,667. Management should reduce selling price only when it is sure of increasing sales by 6,667 units.]

26. The trading result of Oxfam Ltd. for the first year of business which ended on 31st Dec. 1991 are :

		Rs.	*Rs.*
Sales (at Rs. 40 per unit)			32,00,000
Less :	Material	12,00,000	
	Labour	4,80,000	
	Variable overhead	2,40,000	
	Fixed overhead	5,00,000	24,20,000
	Profit		7,80,000

During 1991 the factory has been working at 50% capacity and the marketing manager has estimated that the quantity sold could be doubled in 1992 if the selling price was reduced to Rs. 35 per unit. No change is anticipated in unit variable cost, but certain administration change to cope with the additional volume of work would increase fixed overhead by Rs. 40,000.

You are required to :

(*a*) Evaluate the marketing manager's proposal; and

(*b*) Assuming the selling price was reduced, as proposed, unit variable cost remaining as in 1991 and fixed overhead increased by Rs. 40,000, calculate what quantity would need to be sold in 1992, in order to yield a profit of Rs. 10,00,000. *[C.A. Final]*

[Ans. (*a*) The proposal should be accepted since this will increase profit by—Rs. 4,40,000; (*b*) 1,40,000 units.]

27. A company is at present working at 90% capacity and producing 13,500 units per annum. It operates a flexible budgetary control system.

The following figures (excluding material and labour cost) are obtained from its budget :

	90% Rs.	100% Rs.
(*a*) Sales	15,00,000	16,00,000
(*b*) Fixed Expenses	3,00,500	3,00,500
(*c*) Semi Fixed Expenses	97,500	1,00,500
(*d*) Variable Expenses	1,42,000	1,49,500

Material and labour cost per unit are constant under present conditions, profit margin is 10% at 90% capacity.

(*a*) You are required to determine the cost of production of additional 1,500 units.

(*b*) What would you recommend for an export price for these 1,500 units taking into account that overseas prices are much lower than indigenous prices ? ***[I.C.W.A. Inter June 1990]***

[Ans. (*a*) Rs. 1,00,500 (*b*) Indigenous price = 111·11 per unit. Total cost $\frac{13,50,000}{13,500}$ = 100 per unit. Cost per unit of additional units = Rs. 67

Recommendation : Though the overseas prices are much lower than indigenous prices, these 1,500 units can be exported even at Rs. 70 per unit, Balance 10% capacity can be utilised and foreign exchange of Rs. 1,05,000 can be earned. There will be a profit of Rs. 4,500 also.]

28. (a) Product pricing is an important area for management decision making. State very briefly the broad objectives of the pricing policy. Mention specifically situations where prices are fixed below the variable cost.

(b) Two plants manufacturing the same product decide to merge. Particulars of operation of the two plants before the merger were as follows :

	Plant A	*Plant B*
Capacity utilised	80%	60%
Sales	Rs. 4.80 crores	Rs. 2.40 crores
Variable cost	3.52 crores	1.80 crores
Fixed cost	0.80 crores	0.40 crores

Your are required to work out :

(*i*) Break even capacity of the merged plant.

(*ii*) Profit earned at 75% capacity of the merged plant.

(*iii*) Sales required to earn a profit or Rs. one crore. ***[I.C.W.A. Inter, Dec. 2004]***

[Ans. (*i*) B.E.S. : Rs. 4,61,54,000. P.V. ratio : (Merged) : 26% : Capacity utilisation : 46·15%; (*ii*) Rs. 75,00,000; (*iii*) Rs. 8,46,15,000]

29. The Pupils' Book Co. has two book selling outlets : Kalidas Book House and Tulsidas Book House. Each store has a manager who has great deal of decision authority over the individual stores. A central office, however, handles advertising, marketing research, acquisition of books, legal services, and other staff functions. The Pupils' Book Co.'s current accounting system allocates all costs to the stores. Results for 2002-03 were :

Amount in Rs.

Item	*Total Company*	*Kalidas Book House*	*Tulsidas Book House*
Sales Revenue	7,00,000	3,50,000	3,50,000
Cost of merchandise sold	4,50,000	2,25,000	2,25,000
Gross Margin	2,500	1,25,000	1,25,000
Operating Expenses :			
Salaries and Wages	63,000	30,000	33,000
Supplies	45,000	22,500	22,500
Rent and Utilities	60,000	40,000	20,000
Depreciation	15,000	7,000	8,000
Allocated staff cost	60,000	30,000	30,000
Total operating expenses	2,43,000	1,29,500	1,13,500
Operating income (Loss)	7,000	(4,500)	11,500

Each bookstore manager makes decisions that affect salaries and wages, supplies and depreciation. In contrast, rent and utilities are beyond the managers' control because the managers did not choose the location or size of the store.

Supplies are variable costs. Variable salaries and wages are equal to 8% of the cost of merchandise sold ; the remainder of salaries and wages is a fixed cost. Rent. utilities, and depreciation are also fixed costs. Allocated staff costs are unaffected by any events at the bookstores, but they are allocated as a proportion of sales revenue.

Required :

(*i*) Using the contribution approach, prepare a Performance report that distinguishes the performance of each bookstore from that of the bookstore manager.

(*ii*) Evaluate the performanace of each bookstore.

(*iii*) Evaluate the performance of each manager. *[I.C.W.A. Inter Dec. 2004]*

30. A toy manufacturer earns an average net profit of Rs. 3 per price in a selling price of Rs. 15 by producing and selling 60,000 pieces at 60% of the potential capacity. Composition of his cost of sales is :

Direct Material	Rs. 4
Direct wages	Re. 1
Works overhead	Rs. 6 (50% fixed)
Sales overhead	Rs. 1 (25% varying)

During the current year, he intends to produce the same number but anticipates that :

(*a*) his fixed charges will go up by 10%.

(*b*) rates of direct labour will increase by 20%

(*c*) rates of direct material will increase by 5%

(*d*) selling price cannot be increased.

Under these circumstances, he obtains an order for a further 20% of his capacity. What minimum price will you recommend for accepting the order to ensure the manufacturer an overall profit of Rs. 1,80,500 ? *[M.Com. Rajasthan]*

[Ans. Rs. 11 per unit. Marginal Cost per unit Rs. 8·65, extra profit of Rs. 47,000 is to be earned on 20,000 units.]

31. A paint manufacturing company manufactures 2,00,000 per annum medium sized tims of "Spray Lac Paints" when working at normal capacity. It incurs the following costs of manufacturing per unit :

	Rs.
Direct Material	7·80
Direct Labour	2·10
Variable overhead	2·50
Fixed overhead	4·00
Product cost (per unit)	16·40

Each unit (tin) of the product is sold for Rs. 21 with variable selling and administration expenses of 60 paise per tin.

During the next quarter only 10,000 units can be produced and sold. Management plans to shut down the plant estimating that the fixed manufacturing cost can be reduced to Rs. 74,000 for the quarter.

When the plant is operating, the overheads are incurred at a uniform rate throughout the year. Additional costs of plant shut-down for the quarater are estimated at Rs. 14,000.

You are required :

(*a*) to express your opinion, along with the calculations as to whether the plant should be shut down during the quarter, and

(*b*) to calculate the shutdown point for quarter in units of products (i.e. in terms of number of tins). *[C.A. Final, May 1991]*

[Ans. (*a*) Loss when plant is operated Rs. 1,20,000, Loss when plant is shut down Rs. 80,000. The management should shut down the plant

(b) Shut down point at output of 14,000 units of products (i.e. Rs. 1,12,000 ÷ 8)]

32. A company has furnished the following cost data :

	Rs. Per unit
Direct material	11·20
Direct wages	3·00
Variable overhead	0·80
Fixed Factory overhead	6,60,000 p.a.
Fixed selling and administration overhead	3,60,000 p.a.
Capital employed in fixed Assets	9,00,000
Annual Sales	4,00,000 units

Capital employed in current assets in 50% of sales. Determine the selling price per unit to yield 20% return on capital employed. *[I.C.W.A. Final, Dec. 1989]*

[Ans. Selling price per unit Rs. 20]

33. A small scale manufacturer produces an article at the operated capacity of 10,000 units while the normal capacity of his plant is 14,000. Working at a profit margin at 20% on sales realisation, he has formulated his budget as under :

Units	10,000	14,000
Sales Realisation	Rs. 2,00,000	Rs. 2,80,000
Variable overhead	Rs. 50,000	Rs. 70,000
Semi-variable overheads	Rs. 20,000	Rs. 22,000
Fixed overhead	Rs. 40,000	Rs. 40,000

He gets an order for a quantity equivalent to 20% of the operated capacity and even on this additional production profit margin is desired at the same percentage sales realisation are for production to operated capacity.

Assuming prime cost is constant per unit of production, what would be the minimum price to realise this objective ? *[C.A. Final, May 1988]*

[Ans. Differential cost Rs. 10·50 per unit; Minimum selling price Rs. 10·50 + 2·625 = Rs. 13·125 per unit.]

34. A factory produces 1,000 articles for home consumption at the following costs :

	Rs.	*Rs.*
Materials		40,000
Wages		36,000
Factory overheads :		
Fixed	12,000	
Variable	20,000	32,000
Administration overheads—fixed		18,000
Selling overheads :		
Fixed	10,000	
Variable	16,000	26,000
		1,52,000

The home market can consume only 1,000 articles at a selling price of Rs. 155 per article; it can consume no more articles. The foreign market for this product can, however, consume additional 4,000 articles if the price is reduced to Rs. 125.

Is the foreign market worth trying ? *[M.Com., Kolkata]*

[Ans. Contribution Rs. 13 per unit and total contribution Rs. 52,000. The foreign market is worth trying.]

35. A company manufactures a machine which has a variable cost structure as follows :

	Rs.
Material	40
Labour	10
Overhead	4
Selling price	90

Sales during the current year are expected to be Rs. 13,50,000 and fixed overhead Rs. 1,40,000. Under a wage agreement, an increase of 10% is payable to all direct workers from the beginning for the forthcoming year, while material costs are expected to increase by 7·5%, variable overhead costs by 5% and fixed overhead costs 3%.

You are required to calculate :

(*a*) The new selling price if the current profit/volume ratio is to be maintained; and

(*b*) The quantity to be sold during the forthcoming year to yield the same amount of profit as the current year assuming the selling price to remain at Rs. 90. *[C.A. Inter]*

[Ans. (*a*) P/V ratio : 40%, New selling price Rs. 97·00

(*b*) Contribution required : Rs. 5,44,200; No. of machines : 17,113]

36. Sterling Industries Ltd. manufactures a product 'Z' by making and assembling three components A, B and C. The components are made in a machine shop using three identical machines each of which can make any of the three components. However, the total capacity of the three machines is only 12,000 machine-hours per month and is just sufficient to meet the current demand. Labour for assembling is available according to requirements. Further details are given below :

Components.	*Machine-Hours required per unit*	*Variable cost per unit* Rs.	*Market price at which component can be bought* Rs.
A	4	48	64
B	5	60	75
C	6	80	110
Assembling	—	30 (z)	—

Fixed cost per month amount to Rs. 50,000. Product Z is sold at Rs. 300 per unit. From next month onwards the company expects the demand for Z to rise by 25%. As the machine capacity is limited, the company wants to meet the increase in demand by buying such numbers of A, B or C which is most profitable.

You are asked to find out the following :

(*a*) Current demand and profit made by the company.

(*b*) Which component and how many units of the same should be bought from the market to meet the increase in demand ?

(*c*) Profit made by the company if suggession in (b) is accepted. *[I.C.W.A. Inter, Dec 1998]*

[Ans. (*a*) Maximum production in units : 800, Net profit : 15,600;

(*b*) 600 units of component B should be purchased

(*c*) Net profit : 23,000]

13 Standard Costing

Authors' Comments and suggestions :

1. ***This chapter is most important for students of degree courses, I.C.W.A., C.A. and C.S. students, as well as for different professional examinations.***
2. ***Any problem on standard cost for working out different variances like Material cost variances, Labour cost variances, Overhead variances, Sales variances, Sales Margin variances can be workedout by using a standard format applicable to all variance analysis.***
3. ***Most of the students are afraid of this important chapter only because of different formulae for different analysis. But the standard format introduced in this chapter tries to eliminate such difficulties.***
4. ***The calculation of Mix variance is necessary only when there are more than one type of component for producing an article.***
5. ***Standard cost means the standard cost for the actual production.***
6. ***Sometimes variances are given and actual cost or standard cost/rate are to find out.***

Introduction; Standard, Standard Cost and Standard Costing; Types of standards—Current Standard, Basic Standard, Ideal Standard, Attainable Standard; Terminology on Standards; Problems in setting Standard Cost; Standard Costing and Budgetary Control; Standard Cost and Estimated Cost; Advantages of Standard Costing; Limitation of Standard Costing; Analysis of Variances; Illustration; Workedout Problems.

Introduction

It is very difficult to compare and find out the reasons of cost fluctuation through Historical Costing, as it ascertains costs after they have been incurred. The reasons for cost fluctuation apart from variations in output (or units produced) may be detected through introductions of standard costing. Its utility are increasing day by day in advanced countries, like U.S.A., Great Britain etc.

Standard, Standard-cost and Standard costing

The term ***standard*** is a predetermined measurable quantity set in defined conditions against which actual performance can be compared. In a word, we can say the term ***standard*** refers to predetermined rate against which performance is judged.

Standard-cost is defined by CIMA in the following way :—A predetermined calculation of how much cost should be used under specified working conditions. It is built up from an assessment of the value of cost elements and correlates technical specification and qualification of material, labour and other costs to the prices and/or usage rates expected to apply during the period in which the standard cost is intended to be used. Its main purpose is to provide basis for control through variance accounting for the valuation of stock and work-in-progress and in some cases for setting prices.

The technique by which standard costs are used is known as—***Standard costing.*** It involves the setting of predetermined cost estimates in order to provide a basis for comparison with actual. Standard cost is universally accepted as an effective tool for cost control in industries.

Objective of Standard Costing

The objectives of standard costing are :

(*a*) To provide an accepted basis for assessing performance and efficiency.

(*b*) To control cost by introducing standards and analysis of variances.

(*c*) To assist in setting budgets.

(*d*) To motivate staff and management.

(*e*) To help in assigning responsibility for non-standard performance in order to correct deficiencies or to capitalise the benefits.

(*f*) To provide basis for estimating.

(*g*) To provide guidance on possible ways for improving performance.

Type of standards

(A) Current Standard

(B) Basic Standard

(C) Ideal Standard

(D) Attainable Standard.

Current Standard

It is a standard established for use over a short period of time related to current conditions. The main shortcoming is that it does not try to improve on current levels of efficiency.

Basic Standard

It is a standard which is established for use over a long period from which a current standard can be developed. The main disadvantage of this standard is that as it has remained unaltered over a long period of time, it may be out of date. The main advantage is in showing the changes in trend of price and efficiency from year to year.

Ideal Standard

Ideal standard is a standard which can be attained under the favorable conditions. This standard is not widely used in practice beacause it may influence employee motivation adversely.

Attainable Standard

It is a standard which can be performed if a standard unit of work is carried out efficiently and properly. It has the greatest motivational impact on the employees. It represents the objectives which are reasonably attainable.

Terminology on standards

Generally, the following terminologies are widely used in standard costing :

(*a*) Standard hour;

(*b*) Standard time;

(*c*) Standard unit of work;

(*d*) Standard material cost;

(*e*) Standard material usage;

(*f*) Standard direct labour;

(*g*) Standard overhead cost;

(*h*) Standard production cost;

(*i*) Standard price;

(*j*) Standard profit.

Problems in setting Standard costs

The problems involved in setting standard costs are :

(*a*) Deciding how to deal inflation into planned unit costs;

(b) Deciding on the quality of materials to be used;

(*c*) Estimating material prices where seasonal price variations or bulk purchase discount may be significant.

(*d*) Deciding on the appropriate mixture where some change in the mix is possible.

(*e*) The cost of setting up and maintaining a system for establishing standards.

Standard costing and Budgetary control :

Both standard costing and Budgetary control are used for controlling the business operations by establishing predetermined standard and comparing the standard with actual. Budgetary control is usually operated without standard costing but it is difficult to implement the standard costing without budgetary control. A system of budgetary control in conjunction with standard costing is more helpful. Thus, although both are helpful to management in controlling costs, they differ in respect of scope and technique as follows :

Standard Costing	Budgetary Control
1. Standards are based on technical assessments.	1. Budgets are based on past actual with necessary adjustments.
2. Standard costing is mainly related to manufacturing departments.	2. Budgetary control deals with the departments or business as a whole.
3. Standards are the minimum targets, which are to be attained.	3. Budgets are the maximum limits of expenses about which expenditure should not be incurred.
4. Standards are usually for expenditure only.	4. Budgets include both income and expenditure.
5. Analysis of variances are necessary whether they are favorable or adverse.	5. In case of costs within the budget, no further analysis is necessary.
6. Standards are expressed per unit of production.	6. Budgets are expressed in total and not per unit.
7. Standards costs are planned under specific assumed, conditions of production performance.	7. Budgets are expected cost used for forecasting profit.

Standard cost and Estimated cost :

While both the standard costs and estimated costs are predetermined costs, their objectives are different. Following are the main points of differences :

Standard Cost	Estimated Cost
1. Standard costs aim at what the cost should be.	1. Estimated costs aim at what cost will be.
2. Standard costs are planned cost determined on scientific basis and are based on certain assumed conditions of production.	2. Estimated costs are based on average of past actual figure adjusted for future.
3. It serves as an effective tool for cost control.	3. It is used for price quotations.
4. Here variances are accounted for in the books.	4. Here variance analysis is only a statistical data.

Advantage of Standard costing :

A standard costing has many advantages, some of them are :

(*a*) Standard costing provides the guidance which helps the management in performing their managerial functions such as in formulating policies, in determining prices etc.

(*b*) Standard costing highlights areas on strengths and weaknesses.

(*c*) It acts as yardsticks against which actual costs are compared. Thus it facilitates effective cost control and provides necessary information for cost reduction.

(*d*) It acts as a form of feed forward control that allows an organisation to plan the manufacturing inputs required for different levels of output.

(e) It will help prompt preparation of profit and loss account for short period.

(f) It stimulates cost conciousness of all executives because in the variance analysis the responsibility for favorable or adverse performances is identified.

(g) It helps to trace or allocate manufacturing costs to each individual unit produced.

Limitation of Standard costing :

The following limitations are levelled against Standard costing :

1. Standard costing is generally used in such organisation whose processess or jobs are repetitive i.e. it cannot be used in all organizations.
2. A lot of input data is required which is expensive.
3. If standards are not revised it will be harmful instead of helpful.
4. Revision of standards is costly.
5. Standard costing may be unsuitable to the non-standard jobs which are manufactured according to customers' specifications.
6. It is very difficult to distinguish between controllable and uncontrollable variances.
7. Some variances cannot be explained properly.
8. It may require high degree of technical skill as standard is based on technical assessments.

Computation of Standard cost and Actual cost and Analysis of Variances :

First we are to work out the standard cost elementwise for the actual output or production, say standard cost of material for the actual units produced or the standard cost of labour for the output, or the standard overhead cost for the actual production. Thereafter each standard cost figure is to be deducted from the actual cost of inputs of materials or cost of labour or cost of overheads respectively, and the result is called cost variances. If the standard cost is higher than the actual cost then this variance is to be considered as favorable to an organisation. But if the actual cost is higher than the standard cost then the result is to be considered as adverse.

Now these elementwise cost variances are analysed critically to find out the exact causes or circumstances leading to it, so that the management can exercise proper control. A suitable analysis will reveal that some of the variances are controllable while others are not so. For example if materials are mixed at the time of production deviating from the standard ratio as fixed by the experts or engineers and due to that cost is more than the standard fixed, the result is adverse to the organisation and then the responsibility can be fixed on the production supervisor and this cost is controllable. But if the adverse cost is due to increase of extraneous causes such as general increase in wage rates, devaluation of currency, fall in demand due to change in tastes among the customers, no responsibility can be assigned to any individual. Such variances would, therefore, be non-controllable. A detailed probe into the variances, particularly the controllable variances, helps the management to ascertain (i) the amount of the variances, (ii) the causes of its occurences, (iii) the factors responsible for it, (iv) the responsibility to be laid on executives/departments, and (v) corrective actions which should be taken to eliminate or reduce the variance.

Variances under each element of cost are analysed below :

Material cost variances :

Material cost variance is the difference between the actual direct material cost incurred and the standard direct material cost specified for the production achieved. Material cost variances are analysed under two heads, viz. material price variance and material usage variance.

(a) Material price variance : This is that portion of cost variance which is due to difference in rate of material between standard and actual per unit of material applied to the actual quantity of material purchased or used.

(b) Material usage variance : This is that portion of material cost variance which is due to the difference between the actual quantity used and the amount which should have been used, valued at standard price as was fixed beforehand. Material usage variances can be further analysed under two heads (*i*) Material mix variance, (*ii*) Material yield variance.

(*i*) Material mix variance :

One of the reasons for material usage variance is the change in the composition of the material mix. The mix variance is the difference between actual composition of mix and standard composition of mixing of the total quantity of input of production used.

(*ii*) Material yield variances :

It is the difference between the standard cost of production achieved and the actual total quantity of materials used at standard ratio/composition at standard price. A low actual output or yield will give adverse result which indicates that the consumption of material was more than the standard. A high actual yield indicates efficiency, but a consistent high yield is a pointer for the revision of the standard.

Material Cost Variance and its subdivisions are presented in the chart below :

MATERIAL COST VARIANCE
(MCV)
↓

MATERIAL PRICE VARIANCE (MPV) | MATERIAL USAGE VARIANCE (MUV)

↓ (MUV)

Material Mix Variance (MMV) | **Material Yield Variance** (MYV)

For finding out the material cost variances the format below can be used. We shall get different variances by putting the relevant information in the appropriate column. Same format can be used in case of labour cost variances, overhead variances and also sales, sales margin variances.

MATERIAL COST VARIANCE ANALYSIS

STANDARD COST	STANDARD COST OF ACTUAL INPUT		ACTUAL COST
	at standard mix	at actual mix	
St. Cost per unit × Output	A.Q. in standard ratio × S.R.	A.Q. × S.R.	Actual Quantity × AC. Rate
M_4	M_3	M_2	M_1

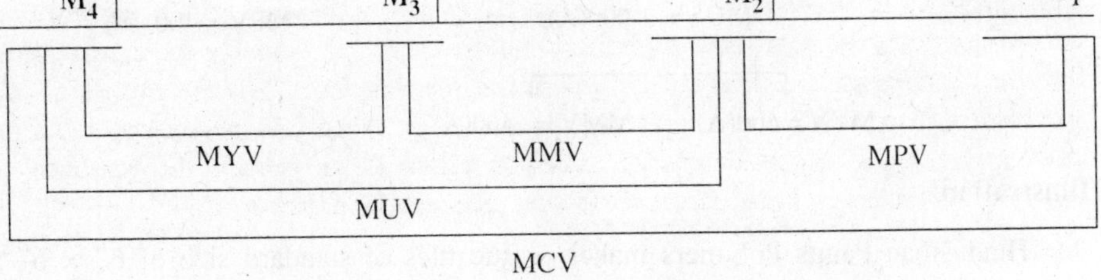

*Deduct from left to right. If positive then (F); if negative then (A)

Illustration

The following standard and actual data relate to a manufacturing concern :

Standards :

Material X : 40 Kgs. @ 6 = Rs. 240
Material Y : 60 Kgs. @ 4 = Rs. 240
Rs. 480

Standard output is 80% of input.

Actuals :

Material X : 600 Kgs. @ 5·00
Material Y : 400 Kgs. @ 4·50

Actual output is 70% of input, i.e. 700 Kgs.

You are required to calculate Material Variances.

Solution

MATERIAL COST VARIANCE ANALYSIS

STANDARD COST	STANDARD COST OF ACTUAL INPUT		ACTUAL COST
	at standard mix	at actual mix	
*S.C. × Output 6·00 × 700 Kg	St. mix × S.R. X : 400 Kgs. @ 6·00 = 2,400 Y : 600 Kgs. @ 4·00 = 2,400 1,000 St. mix ratio : 2 :3	Ac. mix × S.R. X : 600 Kgs. × Rs. 6·00 = 3,600 Y : 400 Kgs. × Rs. 4·00 = 1,600 1,000	AC. Qnt. × A.R. X : 600 Kgs. × Rs. 5 = 3,000 Y : 400 Kgs. × Rs. 4·50 = 1,800
4,200	4,800	5,200	4,800
M_4	M_3	M_2	M_1

MYV = 600 (A) MMV = 400 (A) MPV = 400 (F)

MUV= 1,000 (A)

MCV = 600 (A)

* S.C. *i.e.* Standard Cost of Unit of Output.

$$\frac{\text{Standard Mat. Cost}}{\text{Standard Output}} = \frac{\text{Rs. } 480}{80 \text{ Kgs.}} = 6{\cdot}00 \text{ per Kg}$$

Reconciliation

MCV 600(A)
↓
MUV = 1,000(A) MPV = 400 (F)
↓
MYV = 600(A) MMV = 400(A)

Illustration

Hindusthan Paints Polymers makes plastic tiles of standard size of 6″ × 6″ × $\frac{1}{2}$″. From the following information, you are required to calculate all the direct material cost variances :

A standard mix of the compound required to produce an output of 20,000 sq. ft. of tiles, $\frac{1}{2}$″ thick is :

Direct Materials	*Qnt. Kgs.*	*Price Per Kg.* *Rs.*
A	600	0·90
B	400	0·65
C	500	0·40

During a month eight mixes were processed and actual materials consumed were :

Direct Materials	*Qnt. Kgs.*	*Price Per Kg.* Rs.
A.	5,000	0·85
B.	2,900	0·60
C.	4,400	0·45

Actual production for the month was 6,20,000 tiles.

Solution

MATERIAL COST OF VARIANCE ANALYSIS

STANDARD COST	STANDARD COST OF ACTUAL INPUT at standard mix		at actual mix	ACTUAL COST
*S.C. × Output	St. mix × S.R.		Ac. mix × S.R.	AC. Qnt. × A.R.
Re. 0·0125 × 6,20,000			Kgs.	Kgs.
= 7,750	A : 4,920 @ 0·90 =	4,428	A : 5,000 @ 0·90 = 4,500	A : 5,000 @ 0·85 = 4,250
	B : 3,280 @ 0·65 =	2,132	B : 2,900 @ 0·65 = 1,885	B 2,900 @ 0·60 = 1,740
	C = 4,100 @ 0·40 =	1,640	C : 4,400 @ 0·40 = 1,760	C : 4,400 @ 0·45 = 1,980
	12,300			
	St. mix ratio : 6 : 4 :5		12,300	
7,750		8,200	8,145	7,970
M_4		M_3	M_2	M_1

MYV = 450 (A) MMV = 55 (F) M.P.V. = 175 (F)

MUV= 395 (A)

MCV = 220 (A)

* S.C. *i.e.* Standard cost of one unit of output :

Standard cost of one mix :

600 Kgs. × 0·90 + 400 Kgs. × 0·65 + 500 Kgs × 0·40 = Rs. 1,000

$$\text{Standard output from one mix} = \frac{20{,}000\ \text{Sq. ft} \times \frac{1}{2}''\ \text{thick}}{6'' \times 6'' \times \frac{1}{2}''\ \text{thick}} \text{ or, } \frac{20{,}000\ \text{Sq.ft} \times \frac{1}{2}''\ \text{thick}}{0\cdot5\ \text{ft} \times 0\cdot5\ \text{ft} \times \frac{1}{2}''}$$

= 80,000 tiles

$$\text{S.C. of one tile} = \frac{\text{Rs. } 1{,}000}{80{,}000\ \text{tiles}} = 0\cdot0125$$

RECONCILIATION

MCV = Rs. 220 (A)

↓

MUV = 395 (A) MPV = Rs. 175 (F)

↓

MYV = 450(A) MMV = 55(F)

Direct Labour Cost Variance :

Direct Labour Cost variance is the difference between the actual direct wages paid and the standard direct wages specified for the activity achieved.

As in the case of material cost variances, labour cost variance is analysed into two separate variances, viz. Labour rate variance and Labour efficiency variance.

(*a*) **Labour rate variance** (Wages rate variance) **:** This is due to difference between the actual and standard wage rate per hour applied to the total hours worked. Labour rate variance is comparable with material price variance and is calculated in the similar manner.

(*b*) **Labour efficiency variance :** This is due to the difference between the standard cost of labour for the actual output or the cost of standard hours which should have been worked for the output and the hour actually paid, valued at standard wage rate. This is similar to the material usage variance. The labour efficiency variances are sub-divided in three parts :

(*i*) Labour mix or Gang. variance, (ii) Labour idle time variance, (iii) Labour yield variance.

(*i*) **Labour mix variance :** It is that portion of labour efficiency variance which is due to difference between actual composition of gang at standard rate and the actual hour or days in standard ratio of composition specified for a gang.

(*ii*) **Idle time variance :** This variance—which forms a portion of labour efficiency variance—is represented by the standard cost of the actual hours for which the workers remain idle due to abnormal circumstances. It is the standard cost of difference between the actual hours paid and the actual hours worked.

(*iii*) **Labour yield variance :** It is that part of the labour efficiency variance which is due to difference between actual output at standard rate for each unit of finished product and the standard cost of the actual hours worked at standard composition.

LABOUR COST VARIANCES

↓

LABOUR RATE VARIANCE — LABOUR EFFICIENCY VARIANCE

LABOUR EFFICIENCY VARIANCE ↓

Labour Yield variance — **Labour Idle time variance** — **Labour Mix variance**

Any problem can be worked out by putting the information in the following format. When there is no mix or idle time only three columns to be drawn; extra column to be drawn for mix and idle time.

LABOUR COST VARIANCE ANALYSIS

STANDARD COST	STANDARD COST OF ACTUAL HOURS			ACTUAL COST
	Worked at St. mix	Paid at St. mix	Paid at actual mix	
S.C × Output	St. mix × SR	St. mix of Ac. hour × S.R.	Ac. Hrs. × S.R.	Ac. Hrs. × Ac. rate
L_5	L_4	L_3	L_2	L_1

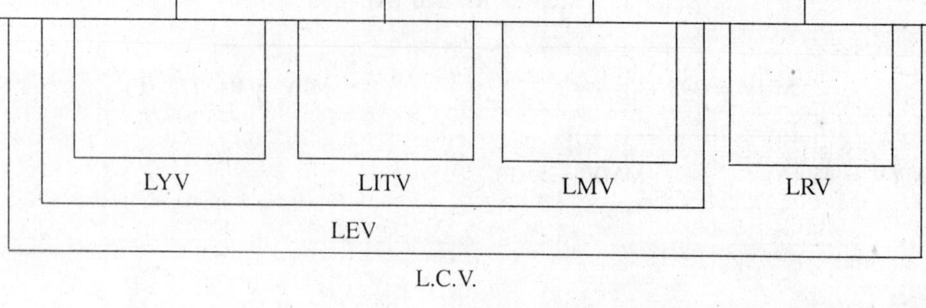

Always deduct the right hand figure from the left hand figure and, if result is positive, it is (F) *i.e.* favourable, and, if it is negative, then result is (A) *i.e.* adverse.

Illustration

From the following information of Orient Manufacturing Co. Ltd., determine the Labour cost variance, Labour Efficiency variance and Labour Rate variance :

(*i*) Standard Labour cost per unit of production is Rs. 15.
(*ii*) Time allotted per unit is 30 hours.
(*iii*) During the month of March 2004, 3,000 units are produced in 75,000 hours.
(*iv*) Actual payment of wages for the month is Rs. 45,000.

[*C.U. B.Com. (H) 1996*]

Solution

STANDARD COST FOR ACTUAL PRODUCTION Rs.	STANDARD COST OF ACTUAL LABOUR HOUR Rs.	ACTUAL COST Rs.
S.C. per unit × output. Rs. 15 × 3,000 units = 45,000	Actual Labour Hours × S.R. per hour. 75,000 Hrs. × *0·50 Per Hour = 37,500 $* S.R. = \frac{\text{Rs. 15 P.V.}}{\text{30 Hrs. P.V.}} = 0{\cdot}50$ Per Hrs	45,000
45,000	37,500	45,000
L_3	L_2	L_1

LEV = 7,500 (F) LRV = 7,500 (A)

LCV = NIL

Alternatively

LRV = $L_2 - L_1$ = 7,500 (A)
LEV = $L_3 - L_2$ = 7,500 (F)
LCV = $L_3 - L_1$ = NIL

Note. The abvoe format is same as is followed in case of analysis of Material variances. When there is no mix then draw three columns and when there is mix then draw four columns like material variances.

An extra column is to be drawn for actual hours worked when there is any information regarding idle time.

Illustration

The following details are available from the records of ABC Ltd engaged in manufacturing Article 'A' for a week.

The standard labour hours and rates of payment per article 'A' were as follows :

	Hrs.	*Rate/Hr.*	*Total*
Skilled Labour	10	Rs. 3·00	Rs. 30
Semi-skilled Labour	8	Rs. 1·50	Rs. 12
Unskilled Labour	16	Rs. 1·00	Rs. 16
			Rs. 58

The actual production was 1,000 units of article 'A' for which the actual hours worked and rates are given below :

	Hrs.	*Rate/Hr.* *Rs.*	*Total* *Rs.*
Skilled Labour	9,000	4	36,000
Semi Skilled Labour	8,400	1·50	12,600
Unskilled Labour	20,000	0·90	18,000
			66,600

From the above set of data you are asked to calculate :

(*a*) Labour Cost variance.
(*b*) Labour Rate variance.
(*c*) Labour Efficiency variance.
(*d*) Labour Mix variance.

[*I.C.W.A. Inter, Dec. 1987*]

Solution

STANDARD COST	STANDARD COST OF ACTUAL HOURS at St. mix	STANDARD COST OF ACTUAL HOURS at Ac. mix	ACTUAL COST
S.C × Output. S.C. of one Unit has been given Rs. 58 × 1,000 Units	St. mix × S.R. *Hrs.* Sk. 11,000 × 3·00 = 33,000 S.Sk. 8,800 × 1·50 = 13,200 U.Sk. 17,600 × 1·00 = 17,600 37,400 St. ratio : 10:8:16	Ac. Hours × S.R. *Hrs.* *Rs.* Sk. 9,000 × 3·00 = 27,000 S.Sk. 8,400 × 1·50 = 12,600 U.Sk. 20,000 × 1·00 = 20,000 37,400	Ac. Hrs. × Ac. Rate *Rs.* SK. 36,000 S.Sk. 12,600 U.Sk. 18,000
58,000	63,800	59,600	66,600
L_4	L_3	L_2	L_1

LYV = 5,800 (A) LMV = 4,200 (F) LRV = 7,000 (A)

LEV = 1,600 (A)

LCV = 8,600 (A)

Overhead Cost variance :

Overhead Cost variance or overall overhead variance is the difference between the actual overhead incurred and the overhead charged or applied into the Job or process at the standard overhead rate. Overhead cost variance and its component variance may be computed and analysed separately for fixed and variable overheads and for each cost centre.

Variable overhead variance :

Variable overhead per unit does not change with the change in units. Total variable cost increases or decreases with change in unit like direct material cost or direct labour cost. Variable overhead costs are sub-divided in two divisions (i) V/OH Expenditure variance (ii) V/O.H. Efficiency variance.

VARIABLE OVERHEAD VARIANCE

↓

V/OH. EXPENDITURE VARIANCE ↓ V/OH EFFICIENCY VARIANCE ↓

Variable Overhead variance :

It represents the difference between actual overhead incurred and the standard overhead for actual production.

(*i*) Variable Overhead Expenditure Variance :

This is the difference between the actual variable overhead and standard variable overhead for the actual hours worked.

(*ii*) Variable Overhead efficiency variance : This represents the difference between standard variable overhead for actual production and the cost of Actual hours worked at standard rate. Following format can be used in working out any variable overhead analysis :

VARIABLE OVERHEAD VARIANCE ANALYSIS

STANDARD COST	STANDARD COST OF ACTUAL HOURS WORKED	ACTUAL COST
S.C × Output. S.C. = St. V/O. for one Unit of output.	Actual Hours Worked × Standard V/O H. rate per Hour (S.R.)	
V_3	V_2	V_1

V. Efficiency Variance (V_3 – V_2) V. Exp. variance (V_2 – V_1)

Variable O/H. variance

Illustration

Following information is relating to X. Ltd. :

(*i*) Budgeted production	300 units
(*ii*) Budgeted variable overhead	Rs. 7,200
(*iii*) Standard time for one unit	25 hours
(*iv*) Actual production for the period	400 units
(*v*) Actual variable overhead	Rs. 7,000
(*vi*) Actual hours worked	9,000

Calculate the following variance :

(*a*) Variable overhead Expenditure variance.

(*b*) Variable overhead efficiency variance.

(*c*) Variable overhead variance.

Solution

VARIABLE OVERHEAD VARIANCE

STANDARD COST	STANDARD COST OF ACTUAL HOURS WORKED	ACTUAL COST
S.C × Output. $S.C. = \frac{7,200}{300 \text{ units}} = \text{Rs. } 24$ ∴ 24 × 400	Actual Hours × S.R. $S.R = \frac{\text{Budgeted O/H.}}{\text{St. Hrs. for Ac. Prod.}}$ $\frac{\text{Rs. } 7,200}{25 \text{ Hrs.} \times 400 \text{ units}} = 0{\cdot}72$ 9,000 Hrs × 0·72 6,480	Rs. 7,000
9,600	6,480	Rs. 7,000
V_3	V_2	V_1

V/Efficiency Variance 3120 (F) V/Exp. variance 520(A)

V.O.H. Variance = 2,600 (F)

Fixed Overhead Variance

Fixed overhead variance may be classified as follows :

FIXED O/H COST VARIANCE
(FOCV)

- F/O.H. EXPENDITURE VARIANCE (F.O. Exp. V)
- FIXED O/H. VOLUME VARAINCE (FOVV)
  - **Idle time variance/Calendar** (FO IT. V)
  - **Capacity variance** (FOCV)
  - **Efficiency variance** (FOEFV)

Fixed Overhead variance :

It represents the difference between actual fixed overhead incurred and standard cost of fixed overhead for production.

(*i*) **Fixed overhead expenditure variance :**

It is the difference between actual fixed overhead incurred and the amount of fixed overhead which should be spent according to budget or standard during the period.

(*ii*) **Fixed overhead volume variance :**

It is the difference between budgeted fixed overhead for the period and the standard fixed overhead for actual production.

(*a*) **Calendar variance/Idle time variance :**

The difference between budgeted fixed overhead and fixed overhead for days available during the period at standard rate.

(*b*) **Capacity variance :**

It is the difference between capacity utilised and planned capacity. The difference between bugeted fixed overhead for the hours available at standard rate and the fixed overhead for actual hours worked at standard rate. Capacity varaince arises when the budgeted capacity differs from capacity available.

(*c*) **Efficiency variance :**

Fixed overhead efficiency variance is that portion of volume variance which reflects output arising from efficiency being above or below standard. It is due to the difference between budgeted or standard efficiency and actual efficiency in utilisation of fixed common facilities.

The following format will help you to find out the fixed overhead variances :

FIXED OVERHEAD VARIANCE ANALYSIS

STANDARD COST	STANDARD FIXED O/H FOR ACTUAL		BUDGETED COST	ACTUAL COST
	hours worked	days available		
FO_5	**FO_4**	**FO_3**	**FO_2**	**FO_1**

FO (Eff.) V. (FO_5 – FO_4) FO (Cap) V. (FO_4 – FO_3) F.O. (Cal) V (FO_3 – FO_2) FO (Exp.) V (FO_2 – FO_1)

FO (Volume) V (FO_5 – FO_2)

FOV (FO_5 – FO_1)

Illustration

From the following cost data, calculate the Fixed overehad variance.

	Budget	**Actual**
No. of working days.	22	25
Man-hours per day	6,500	7,500
Output per man-hour in units.	1·00	1·20
Overheads (Fixed)	1,50,000	1,72,000

Solution

STANDARD COST	STANDARD FIXED O/H FOR ACTUAL hours worked	STANDARD FIXED O/H FOR ACTUAL days available	BUDGETED FIXED O/H	ACTUAL COST
*S.C × Output 1·04895 × 2,25,000	S.R. per hour × Actual Hours worked $S.R = \frac{1,50,000}{22 \times 6,500} = 1{\cdot}0489$ AC. Hours = 25 days × 7,500 = 1,87,500 ∴ 1·0489 × 1,87,500	St. O/H per day × AC. days $\frac{\text{Rs. } 1,50,000}{22 \text{ days}} \times 25 \text{ days}$ = 1,70,455	(Given) Rs. 1,50,000	(Given) Rs. 1,72,000
2,36,014	1,96,678	1,70,455	1,50,000	1,72,000
FO_5	FO_4	FO_3	FO_2	FO_1

F.O. Eff. V = 39,336 (F) (FO_5 – FO_4)

F.O. Cap. V = 26,223 (F) (FO_4 – FO_3)

F.O. Cal. V = 20,455 (F) (FO_3 – FO_2)

F.O. Exp. V. = 22,000 (A) (FO_2 – FO_1)

F.O. Vol. V = 86,014 (F) (FO_5 – FO_2)

FOV = 64,014 (F) (FO_5 – FO_1)

*S.C. *i.e.* Standard cost of one Unit of Output :

$$i.e. \quad \frac{\text{Budgeted Cost}}{\text{Budgeted Unit}}$$

$$i.e. \quad \frac{1,50,000}{22 \text{ days} \times 6,500 \text{ hours per day} \times 1 \text{ unit}}$$

$$= \frac{1,50,000}{1,43,000 \text{ Unit}} = 1{\cdot}04895$$

Output = 25 days × 7,500 units × 1·20 units = 2,25,000 units.

Readers may compare the variable or Fixed Expenditure variance with Labour rate variance or Material price variance. The nature of differences are same. Similarly, Volume variance is like M.U.V. and LEV. Again, O/H Efficiency variance is like Material yield variance or labour yield variance.

Sales variances :

Sales variance is the difference between the actual value of sales achieved in a given period and budgeted value of sales. There are many reasons for the difference viz, increase or decrease in sales price, sales volume, sales mix from the budgeted sales.

Sales variances are analysed by using two methods :

(*i*) Sales variances based on turnover.

(*ii*) Sales variances based on margin.

(i) Sales variance based on turnover :

SALES VALUE VARIANCE (S.V.V.)

↓

SALES PRICE VARIANCE (SPV) | SALES VOLUME VARIANCE (SVV)

SALES VOLUME VARIANCE (SVV) ↓

Sales Mix variance (SMV) | **Sales Quantity Variance** (SQV)

Illustration

From the following information about sales, calculate :

(a) Total Sales variance.
(b) Sales Price variance.
(c) Sales volume variance.
(d) Sales mix variance.
(e) Sales Quantity variance.

	Budgeted Units	*S.R.*	*Rs.*	*Actual Units*	*A.R.*	*Rs.*
A	5,000	5	25,000	6,000	6	36,000
B	4,000	6	24,000	5,000	5	25,000
C	3,000	7	21,000	4,000	8	32,000
	12,000		70,000	15,000		93,000

[*I.C.W.A. Inter 1984*]

Solution

BUDGETED/ STANDARD SALES	STANDARD SALES VALUE OF ACTUAL QUANTITY at standard mix	STANDARD SALES VALUE OF ACTUAL QUANTITY at actual mix	ACTUAL SALES
(Given) Rs. 70,000	A 6,250 × 5 = 31,250 B 5,000 × 6 = 30,000 C 3,750 × 7 = 26,250 15,000 S/Ratio : 5:4:3	AC. Qnt. × S.R. A 6,000 × 5 = 30,000 B 5,000 × 6 = 30,000 C 4,000 × 7 = 28,000 15,000	(Given) Rs. 93,000
70,000	87,500	88,000	93,000
SV_4	SV_3	SV_2	SV_1

SQV = 17,500 (F) | S.M.V = 500 (F) | S.P.V = 5,000 (F)

S.V.V. = 18,000 (F)

Sales Value variance = 23,000 (F)

Reconciliation

SALES VALUE VARIANCE (SVV)
Rs. 23,000 (F)
↓

SALES VOLUME VARIANCE (SVV) Rs. 18,000 (F) | SALES PRICE VARIANCE (SPV) Rs. 5,000 (F)

↓

Sales Mix variance (SMV) Rs. 500 (F) | **Sales Quantity variance** (SQV) Rs. 17,500 (F)

Note : The Sales variance analysis is like Material Cost variance analysis, the only difference is that when actual sale is higher than standard or budgeted sales then result is (F), but in case of cost variance analysis, when actual cost is higher, result is (A).

(ii) Sales variances based on Margin :

This approach shows the difference in actual profit and budgeted profit. The following sales variances are calculated :

TOTAL SALES MARGIN VARIANCE
(SMV)
↓

SALES MARGIN VOLUME VARIANCE (SMVV) | SALES MARGIN PRICE-VARIANCE (SMPV)

↓

Sales Margin Mix variance (SMMV) | **Sales Margin Quantity Variance** (SMQV)

To work out any problem on Sales margin variance analysis we are to follow the same format as is used in case of Sales value variance analysis. Instead of Sales value we shall put the profit element.

Illustration

Compute the variances from the data given below :

(*i*) Total Sales margin variance.
(*ii*) Sales margin price variance.
(*iii*) Sales margin volume variance.
(*iv*) Sales margin mix variance.
(*v*) Sales margin quantity variance.

	Standard Cost	*Budgeted Quantity*	*Actual Qnt.*	*Budgeted Sales price*	*Actual Sales Price*
X	Rs. 30 P.U.	240 Units	400 Units	Rs. 50 P.U.	Rs. 45 P.U
Y	Rs. 15 P.U.	160 Unis	200 Unis	Rs. 25 P.U.	Rs. 20 P.U.

[C.A. *Inter, May 1992*]

SALES MARGIN VARIANCE ANALYSIS

BUDGETED PROFIT	BUDGETED PRICE FOR ACTUAL QUANTITY		ACTUAL PROFIT
	for St. mix	for Ac. mix	
Budgeted Qnt. × (BSP – S.C.) X : 240 (50 – 30) = 4,800 Y : 160 (25 – 15) = 1,600	AC. Qnt. at St. ratio × Budgeted margin. X : 360 (50 – 30) = 7,200 Y : 240 (25 – 15) = 2,400 600 unit 3 : 2 9,600	AC. Qnt. × Budgeted margin X : 400 × (50 – 30) = 8,000 Y : 200 (25 – 15) = 2,000 600 unit.	Ac. Qnt. Sold × (A.S.P – S.C) X = 400 (45 – 30) = 6,000 Y= 200 (20 – 15) = 1,000
6,400	9,600	10,000	7,000
SM_4	**SM_3**	**SM_2**	**SM_1**

SMQV = 3,200 (F)   SMMV = 400 (F)   SMPV = 3,000 (A)

SMVV = 3,600 (F)

SMV = 600 (F)

Reconciliation

SMV = 600 (F)

- SMVV Rs. 3,600 (F)
  - SMQV = 3,200 (F)
  - SMMV = 400 (F)
- SMPV Rs. 3,000 (A)

WORKEDOUT PROBLEMS ON MATERIAL COST VARIANCES

Problem 1

The standard raw materials costs of producing 300 units of product A were as follows :

600 Units of Raw material @ Rs. 50 per unit : Rs. 30,000

But actual Raw material costs of producing 300 units of product A were as follows : 1,000 units of raw material @ Rs. 40 per unit : Rs. 40,000.

Determine Material cost variance, Material Price variance and Material Usage Variance.

[*C.U. B.Com. (H), 1998*]

Solution

STANDARD COST *S.C. × Output	STANDARD COST OF ACTUAL INPUT	ACTUAL COST (Actual input × Actual rate)
Rs. Rs. 100 × 300 Units 30,000	*Rs.* 1,000 units × Rs. 50 (Ac. input × S.R.) 50,000	*Rs.* 1000 Units × Rs. 40 : 40,000
30,000	50,000	40,000
M_3	M_2	M_1

MUV = 20,000 (A)   MPV = 10,000 (F)

MCV = 10,000 (A)

*S.C. *i.e.* Standard cost of one Unit of output : $\frac{\text{Rs. } 30{,}000}{300 \text{ Units}}$ = 100 P.U.

From above :

Material Price variance (MPV) = $M_2 - M$ = 10,000 (F)

Material Usage variance (MUV) = $M_3 - M_2$ = 20,000 (A)

Material Cost variance (MCV) = $M_3 - M_1$= 10,000 (A).

Problem 2

The standard material cost of producing each unit of product K is :

4·8 Kg of material @ Rs. 5 per Kg.

The actual material cost of producing 200 units of product K is :

1,200 Kg. of material costing Rs, 4,800.

Compute :

(*i*) Material Cost variance (*ii*) Material Price variance (*iii*) Material usage variance.

[*C.U. B.Com. (H), 2004*]

Solution

STANDARD COST		STANDARD COST OF ACTUAL INPUT		ACTUAL COST	
	Rs.		*Rs.*		*Rs.*
*S.C. × Output (Rs. 24 × 200 Units.)	4,800	Actual input × St. Rate (1,200 Kg × Rs.5)	6,000	(1,200 Kg. @ Rs.4)	4,800
	4,800		6,000		4,800
	M_3		**M_2**		**M_1**

M.U.V = 1,200 (A) M.P.V. = 1,200 (F)

MCV = NIL

*S.C. *i.e.* Standard cost of one unit of output :

4·8 Kg × Rs. 5 = Rs. 24

From above :

1. Material Price variance (MPV) : $M_2 - M_1$ = 1,200 (F)
2. Material Usage variance (MUV) : $M_3 - M_2$ = 1,200 (A)
3. Material Cost variance (MCV) : $M_3 - M_1$ = Nil.

Problem 3

Compute material cost variances from the following data :

Production for the period is 192 units.

	Mat. X	*Mat. Y*
	Rs.	*Rs.*
Standard price per ton	24·00	22·00
Actual Price per ton	22·75	30·80
Actual Weights	16 tons	13 tons

The standard production for the period is 400 units for which standard quantities of materials are 30 tons of X and 25 tons of Y.

Solution

STANDARD COST	STANDARD COST OF ACTUAL INPUT		ACTUAL COST
	at standard mix	at actual mix	
*S.C. × Output 3·175 × 192	Standard mix × St. rate. X = 15·818 × Rs. 24 = 379·64 Y = 13·181 × Rs. 22 = 290·00 29 tons in the ratio 30:25	AC. mix × St. rate. X = 16 tons × 24 = 384 Y = 13 tons × 22 = 286 29 tons.	AC. Qnt. × Ac. Rate X=16 Tons × 22·75 Y=13 Tons × 30·80
609·60	669·64	670	764·40
M_4	M_3	M_2	M_1

MYV = 60·04 (A) M.M.V = 0·36 (A) MPV = 94·40 (A)

MUV = 60·40 (A)

MCV = 154·80 (A)

*S.C. *i.e.* Standard cost for one unit of output :

S.Q. × SR = SC

X = 30 tons × 24 = 720

Y = 25 tons × 22 = 550

1,270

$$\text{S.C. of one unit} = \frac{\text{Rs. } 1{,}270}{400 \text{ units}} = 3{\cdot}175$$

From above :

1. Material Price variance (MPV) = $M_2 - M_1$ = 94·40 (A)
2. Material Mix variance (MMV) = $M_3 - M_2$ = 0·36 (A)
3. Material Yield variance (MYV) = $M_4 - M_3$ = 60·04 (A)
4. Material Usage variance (MUV) = $M_4 - M_2$ = 60·40 (A)
5. Material Cost variance (MCV) = $M_4 - M_1$ = 154·80 (A)

An analysis of the above format :

1. Draw the format as above (in three segments when there is no mix and in four segments when there is mix).
2. Put the figures of the problem in your format.
3. The results to be drawn and marked from right hand side as M_1 M_2 M_3 M_4.
4. Simply deduct from left to right as per format and if it is positive then answer is (F) i.e. Favorable, and if it is negative then answer is (A) i.e. Adverse.

* The same format can also be applied in the variance analysis of Labour, Overhead, Sales based on turnover or based on margin with a little variation.

Problem 4

80 Kg of material A at a standard price of Rs.2 per Kg and 40 kg of material B at a standard price of Rs. 5 per Kg. were to be used to manufacture 100 Kg of a chemical.

During a month, 70 Kg of material A priced at Rs. 2·10 per kg and 50 Kg of material B priced at Rs. 4·50 per Kg were actually used and the output of the chemical was 102 Kg.

Find out the material variances.

[*I.C.W.A. Inter, June 1991*]

Solution

STANDARD COST	STANDARD COST OF ACTUAL INPUT		ACTUAL COST
	at standard mix	at actual mix	
*S.C. × Output Rs. 3·60 × 102 Kg.	Kg. SR Rs. A : 80 × 2·00 = 160 B : 40 × 5·00 = 200 120 Kg. St. ratio : 80 : 40 .	Kg. SR Rs. A : 70 × 2·00 = 140 B : 50 × 5·00 = 250 120 Kg.	Ac Qnt. × Ac. Rate Kg. Rate Rs. A : 70 × 2·10 = 147 B : 50 × 4·50 = 225
367·20	360	390	372

M_4 M_3 M_2 M_1

MYV = 7·20 (F) M.M.V = 30 (A) MPV = 18 (F)

MUV = 22·80 (A)

MCV = 4·80 (A)

*S.C. *i.e.* standard cost of one unit of output :

A = 80 Kg × Rs. 2 = 160
B = 40 Kg × Rs. 5 = 200
360

$$\text{S.C. per Kg. of output} = \frac{\text{Rs. } 360}{100 \text{ Kg}} = 3{\cdot}60$$

Problem 5

The standard cost of a chemical mixture is :

16 tons of material A at Rs. 40 per ton
12 tons of material B at Rs. 60 per ton

Standard yield is 90% of output :

Actual cost for the month of June 2000 is as under :

20 tons of material A at Rs. 30 per ton
40 tons of material B at Rs. 68 per ton

Actual yield is 53 tons. Compute all material variances.

Solution

STANDARD COST	STANDARD COST OF ACTUAL INPUT		ACTUAL COST
	at standard mix	at actual mix	
*S.C. × Output Rs. 53·968 × 53 tons.	St. mix SR Rs. A : 34·28 × 40 = 1,371·15 B : 25·71 × 60 = 1,542·85 60 tons St. ratio : 16 : 12	Ac. mix SR Rs. A : 20 × 40 = 800 B : 40 × 60 = 2,400 60 tons.	Ac Qnt. × Ac. Rate Tons. Rs. Rs. A : 20 × 30 = 600 B : 40 × 68 = 2,720
2,860	2,914	3,200	3,320

M_4 M_3 M_2 M_1

MYV = 54 (A) MMV = 286 (A) MPV = 120 (A)

MUV = 340 (A)

MCV = 460 (A)

*S.C. *i.e.* standard cost for one unit of output :

	S.Q.	S.R.		Rs.
A :	16 tons.	× Rs. 40	=	640
B :	12 tons.	× Rs. 60	=	720
	28 tons.			1,360
Less, Normal Loss				
10%	2.80 tons			×
	25·20 tons			1360

S.C. of one ton of output $\frac{1,360}{25 \cdot 20}$ = Rs. 53·968

Problem 6

S.V. Ltd. manufactures BXE by mixing three raw materials. For every batch of 100 Kgs. of BXE, 125 Kgs. of Raw materials are used. In April 1999, 60 batches were prepared to produce an output of 5,600 Kgs of BXE. The standard and actual particulars for April 1999 are as follows :

Raw Material	*Standard*		*Actual*		*Raw Material*
	Mix %	*Per Kg.* *Rs.*	*Mix %*	*Per Kg.* *Rs.*	*Purchased* *Kg.*
A	50	20	60	21	5,000
B	30	10	20	8	2,000
C	20	5	20	6	1,200

Calculate all variances.

[*C.A. Inter*]

Solution

STANDARD COST	STANDARD COST OF ACTUAL INPUT at standard mix	STANDARD COST OF ACTUAL INPUT at actual mix	ACTUAL COST
Note 2 S.C. × Output Rs. 17·50 × 5,600 Kg.	**St. mix × S.R.** *Kg.* *Rs.* *Rs.* A : 3,750 × 20 = 75,000 B : 2,250 × 10 = 22,500 C : 1,500 × 5 = 7,500 7,500 Kg. in St. ratio.	**Ac. mix × S.R.** *Kg.* *Rs.* *Rs.* A : 4,500 × 20 = 90,000 B : 1,500 × 10 = 15,000 C : 1,500 × 5 = 7,500 7,500 Kg.	**Note 1** Kg. Rs. Rs. A : 4,500 × 21 = 94,500 B : 1,500 × 8 = 12,000 C : 1,500 × 6 = 9,000
98,000	1,05,000	1,12,500	1,15,500
M_4	M_3	M_2	M_1

MYV = 7,000 (A) MMV = 7,500 (A) MPV = 3000 (A)

MUV = 14,500 (A)

MCV = 17,500 (A)

Note 1

60 batches were prepared. For every batch 125 Kgs. of input are required. Actual input = 60 × 125 = 7,500 Kg.

Actual mix ratio : A = 7,500 × 60% = 4,500 Kg.
B = 7,500 × 20% = 1,500 Kg.
C = 7,500 × 20% = 1,500 Kg.

Note 2

S.C. *i.e.* standard cost for one Kg. of output. Standard Cost of one batch :

	Rs.
A : 125 × 50% = 62·50 Kg × 20 =	1,250
B : 125 × 30% = 37·50 Kg × 10 =	375
C : 125 × 20% = 25·00 Kg × 5 =	125
	1,750

$$\text{Standard cost of output} = \frac{\text{Total Cost}}{\text{Actual Output}}$$

$$\frac{\text{Rs. } 1,750}{100 \text{ Kg.}} = 17\cdot50 \text{ Per Kg. of Output.}$$

Problem 7

A company produces a finished product by using three basic raw materials. The following standards have been set up for raw materials :

Material	*Standard Mix*	*Standard Price*
A	25%	Rs. 4 per Kg
B	35%	Rs. 3 per Kg.
C	40%	Rs. 2 per Kg.

The standard loss in process is 20% of input. During a particular month, the company produced 2,400 Kgs. of finished product. The details of stock and purchases for the month are as under :

Material	*Opening Stock*	*Closing Stock*	*Purchase Qnt.*	*During the month Cost*
A	200 Kgs.	350 Kgs.	800 Kgs.	Rs. 3,600
B	150 Kgs.	200 Kgs.	1,000 Kgs.	Rs, 3,500
C	300 Kgs.	200 Kgs.	1,100 Kgs.	Rs. 1,980

The opening stock is valued at standard cost. Compute the variances taking the issue to material on L.I.F.O basis.

[C.A. Inter, Nov., 2000]

Solution

STANDARD COST	STANDARD COST OF ACTUAL INPUT at standard mix	STANDARD COST OF ACTUAL INPUT at actual mix	ACTUAL COST
*S.C. × Output	St. mix × S.R.	Ac. mix × S.R.	Note 1 Ac. Qnt. × Ac. Rate
Rs. 3·5625 × 2,400 Kg.	*Kgs.* *Rs.*	*Kgs.* *SR.* *Rs.*	*Rs.* *Rs.* *Rs.*
	A : 700 × 4·00 = 2,800	A : 650 × 4·00 = 2,600	A : 650 × 4·50 = 2,925
	B : 980 × 3·00 = 2,940	B : 950 × 3·00 = 2,850	B : 950 × 3·50 = 3,325
	C : 1,120 × 2·00 = 2,240	C : 1,200 × 2·00 = 2,400	C : 1,100 × 1·80 = 1,980
	2,800	2,800	100 × 2·00 = 200
	St. mix ratio : 25 : 35 : 40.		
8,550	7,980	7,850	8,430
M_4	M_3	M_2	M_1

MYV = 570 (F)
MMV = 130 (F)
MPV = 580 (A)
MUV = 700 (F)
MCV = 120 (F)

Note

Material issued to Production Dept. = Op. Stock + Purchase – Closing Stock.

	Kgs.	*Kgs.*	*Kgs.*	*Kgs.*
A =	200 +	800 –	350 =	650
B =	150 +	1,000 –	200 =	950
C =	300 +	1,100 –	200 =	1,200
			Total	2,800

Under LIFO basis, materials from current purchases are issued first, thereafter from opening stock at old rate.

* S.C. *i.e.* standard cost for one unit of output.

Let 100 Kg. is our input.

∴ A : 25 Kg. × Rs. 4 = Rs. 100
B : 35 Kg × Rs. 3 = Rs. 105
C : 40 Kg. × Rs. 2 = Rs. 80
100 Kg. Rs. 285

$$\text{S.C. per kg.} = \frac{\text{Rs. } 285}{100\text{ Kg} - 20\text{ Kg}} = \frac{\text{Rs. } 285}{80\text{ Kg}} = 3{\cdot}5625$$

Problem 8

ABC Ltd. produces an article by blending two basic raw materials. It operates a standard costing system and the following standards have been set for raw materials :

Material	*Standard Mix*	*Standard Price per Kg.*
A	40%	Rs. 4
B	60%	Rs. 3

The standard loss in processing is 15%. During April 1990 the company produced 1,700 Kgs. of finished output.

The position of stock and purchases for the month of April 1990 are as under :

Material	*Stock on 1.4.90*	*Stock on 30.4.1990*	*Purchased in April 1990*	
	Kgs.	*Kgs.*	*Kgs.*	*Rs.*
A	35	5	800	3,400
B	40	50	1,200	3,000

Opening Stock are valued at standard price *i.e.* under FIFO basis.

Calculate the following variances :

(*i*) Material price variance.
(*ii*) Material usage variance.
(*iii*) Material yield varaince.
(*iv*) Material mix variance.
(*v*) Material cost variance.

[C.S. Inter, Dec. 1991]
[C.A. Inter, Nov. 1991]

Solution

S.C. *i.e.* Standard cost for one Kg. of output :
Let 100 Kgs. were the input.

		Rs.
A : 40 Kg @ Rs. 4	=	160
B : 60 Kg. @ Rs. 3	=	180
100 Kg.	=	340
Less : 15% Normal Loss 15 Kg		
85 Kg.	=	340

$$\text{S.C.} = \frac{340}{85} = \text{Rs. 4 per Kg.}$$

STANDARD COST	STANDARD COST OF ACTUAL INPUT at standard mix	STANDARD COST OF ACTUAL INPUT at actual mix	ACTUAL COST
S.C. × Output 4 × 1,700	St. mix × S.R. *Kg. Rate Rs.* A : 808 × 4 = 3,232 B : 1,212 × 3 = 3,636 2,020 St. ratio : 2,020 in 40 : 60.	Ac. mix × St. Rate *Kgs. Rate Rs.* A : 830 × 4 = 3,320 B : 1,190 × 3 = 3,570 2,020	A.Q. × Ac. Rate *Kg. Rate Rs.* A : 35 4·00 140 795 4·25 3,378 B : 40 3·00 120 1,150 2·50 2,875
6,800	6,868	6,890	6,513·75
M_4	M_3	M_2	M_1

MYV = 68 (A)　　MMV = 22 (A)　　MPV = 376·25 (F)

MUV = 90 (A)

MCV = 286·25 (F)

∴ Material Price variance = $M_2 - M_1$ = 376·25
Material Mix variance = $M_3 - M_2$ = 22(A)
Material Yield variance = $M_4 - M_3$ = 68(A)
Material Usage variance = $M_4 - M_1$ = 286·25 (F)

Reconciliation

MCV : Rs. 286·25 (F)

↓

MPV : Rs. 376·25 (F)　　MUV : Rs. 90 (A)

↓

MMV : Rs. 22(A)　　MYV Rs. 68 (A)

Problem 9

Gemini Chemical Industries provide the following information from their records :

For making 10 Kgs. of GEMCO, the standard material requirement is :

Material	*Quantity*	*Rate per Kg.*
A	8 Kgs.	Rs. 6·00
B	4 Kgs.	Rs. 4·00

During April 2004, 1000 Kgs. of GEMCO were produced. The actual consumption of material is as under :

Material	*Quantity*	*Rate per Kg.*
A	750 Kgs.	Rs. 7·00
B	500 Kgs.	Rs. 5·00

Calculate :

(*a*) Material Cost variance.

(*b*) Material Price variance.

(*c*) Material Usage variance.

[*C.A. Inter*]

Solution

STANDARD COST	STANDARD COST OF ACTUAL INPUT		ACTUAL COST
	at standard mix	at actual mix	
*S.C. × Actual Output 6·40 × 1,000 Kg.	St. mix × S.R. *Kgs.* × *S.R.* *Rs.* A : 833·33 × 6·00 = 5,000 B : 416·67 × 4·00 = 1,667 1,250 St. ratio : 8 : 4	Ac. Qnt. × S.R. *Kgs.* *SR.* *Rs.* A : 750 × 6·00 = 4,500 B : 500 × 4·00 = 2,000 1,250	Ac. Qnt. × Ac. Rate Kgs. AR Rs. A : 750 × 7·00 = 5,250 B : 500 × 5·00 = 2,500
6,400	6,667	6,500	7,750
M_4	M_3	M_2	M_1

MYV = 267 (A) MMV = 167 (F) MPV = 1,250 (A)

MUV = 100 (A)

MCV = 1,350 (A)

* S.C. *i.e.* Standard cost of one Kg. of output :

A = 8 Kg × Rs. 6·00 = 48·00

B = 4 Kg × Rs. 4·00 = 16·00

Total Cost Rs. 64·00 to produce 10 Kg. Output.

∴ S.C. of Kg. = Rs. 64 ÷ 10 Kg. = 6·40 Per Kg.

Problem 10

The standard material inputs required for 1,000 Kgs. of a finished product are given below :

Material	*Quantity* Kg.	*Standard rate Per Kg.* Rs.
P	450	20
Q	400	40
R	250	60
	1,100	
Less : Standard Loss	100	
Standard Output	1,000	

Actual production in a period was 20,000 Kgs. of the finished product for which the actual quantities of material used and the prices paid thereof, are as under :

Material	***Quantity used***	***Price Per Kg.***
P	10,000 Kgs.	Rs. 19
Q	8,500 Kgs.	Rs. 42
R	4,500 Kgs.	Rs. 65

Calculate the :

(*i*) Material cost variance; (*ii*) Material Price variance, (*iii*) Material usage variance, (*iv*) Material Mix variance, (*v*) Material yield variance.

[*I.C.W.A. Inter June 1996*]

Solution

STANDARD COST	STANDARD COST OF ACTUAL INPUT		ACTUAL COST
	at standard mix	at actual mix	
* S.C. × Actual Output Rs. 40 × 20,000 Kg.	St. mix × S.R. *Kg. × Rs.* *Rs.* P : 9,409 × 20 = 1,88,182 Q : 8,363·63 × 40 = 3,34545 R : 5,227·27 × 60 = 3,13,636 23,000 St. ratio : 9:8:5	AQ × S.R *Kgs. × Rs.* *Rs.* P : 10,000 × 20 = 2,00,000 Q : 8,500 × 40 = 3,40,000 R : 4,500 × 60 = 2,70,000 23,000	A.Q. × A.R *Kg. Rate Rs.* P : 10,000 × 19 = 1,90,000 Q : 8,500×42 = 3,57,000 R : 4,500 × 65 = 2,92,500
8,00,000	8,36,363	8,10,000	8,39,500
M_4	M_3	M_2	M_1

MYV = 36,363 (A) MMV = 26,363 (F) MPV = 29,500 (A)

MUV = 10,000 (A)

MCV = 39,500 (A)

*S.C. *i.e.* standard cost of one Kg. of output.

Let the input is of 1,100 Kg. in total.

P	450 Kg.	× Rs. 20 =	9,000
Q	400 Kg.	× Rs. 40 =	16,000
R	250 Kg.	× Rs. 60 =	15,000
	1,100 Kg.		Rs. 40,000
Less : Normal Loss	100 Kg.		×
Cost of	1,000 Kg.	=	Rs. 40,000

$\therefore$ Standard cost of 1 Kg. $= \frac{40,000}{1,000} =$ Rs. 40

Note If we are to know the variance itemwise then the following analysis is to be done in addition to the above format :

1. Material Price variance (itemwise)

	M_2	–	M_1	=	
P	2,00,000	–	1,90,000	=	10,000 (F)
Q	3,40,000	–	3,57,000	=	17,000 (A)
R	2,70,000	–	2,92,500	=	22,500 (A)
	8,10,000		8,39,500		29,500 (A)

2. Material mix variance (itemwise).

	M_3	–	M_2		
P :	1,88,182	–	2,00,000	=	11,818 (A)
Q :	3,34,545	–	3,40,000	=	5,455 (A)
R :	3,13,636	–	2,70,000	=	43,636 (F)
					26,363 (F)

3. Material usage variance (Itemwise)

M_4 = 8,00,000. This cost of Material is to be apportioned in the standard input Cost ratio *i.e.* 9,000 : 16,000 : 15,000.

i.e. 9:16:15

		M_4	–	M_2		
P : $8{,}00{,}000 \times \frac{9}{40}$	=	1,80,000	–	2,00,000	=	20,000 (A)
Q : $8{,}00{,}000 \times \frac{16}{40}$	=	3,20,000	–	3,40,000	=	20,000 (A)
R : $8{,}00{,}000 \times \frac{15}{60}$	=	3,00,000	–	2,70,000	=	30,000 (F)
						10,000 (A)

4. Material Cost variance and Material yield variance are based on output and variances on the basis of items or inputs are not workedout.

WORKEDOUT PROBLEMS ON LABOUR COST VARIANCES

Problem 11

A gang of workers normally consists of 30 men, 15 women and 10 boys. They are paid at standard hourly rates as under :

Men	Re. 0·80
Women	Re. 0·60
Boys	Re. 0·40

In a normal working week of 40 hours, the gang is expected to produce 2,000 units of output.

During the week ending 31st Dec. 1987 the gang consisted of 40 men, 10 women and 5 boys. The actual wages paid were @ Re. 0·70, Re. 0·65 and Re. 0·30, respectively; four hours were lost due to abnormal idle time and 1,600 units were produced.

Calculate : (*i*) Labour cost variance, (*ii*) Labour rate variance, (*iii*) Labour efficiency variance, (*iv*) Labour Mix variance, (*v*) Labour idle time variance.

[*B.Com.(Hons.), Delhi, 1993*]

Solution

STANDARD COST	STANDARD COST OF ACTUAL HOURS: Worked at St. mix	STANDARD COST OF ACTUAL HOURS: Paid at St. mix	STANDARD COST OF ACTUAL HOURS: Paid at Ac. mix	ACTUAL COST
**S.C. × Output	St. mix × S.R.	*St. mix × S.R.	A.C. Hrs. × S.R	A.C. Hrs. × A.C. Rate
Re. 0·74 × 1,600	M : 1,080 × 0·80 = 864	M :1,200 × 0·80 = 960	M :1,600 × 0·80 =1,280	M :1600 × 0·70 =1,120
	W : 540 × 0·60 = 324	W : 600 × 0·60 = 360	W : 400 × 0·60 = 240	W : 400 × 0·65 = 260
	B : 360 × 0·40 = 144	B : 400 × 0·40 = 160	B : 200 × 0·40 = 80	B : 200 × 0·30 = 60
	1,980	2,200 Hrs.	2,200 Hrs.	
	St. ratio : 6:3:2	6 : 3 : 2 (St. Mix)		
1,184	1,332	1,480	1,600	1,440
L_5	L_4	L_3	L_2	L_1

LYV = 148 (A) LITV = 148 (A) LMV = 120 (A) LRV = 160 (F)

LEV = 416 (A)

LCV = 256 (A)

Note 1

*Standard mix = Actual hours paid at standard ratio.
Standard ratio = Men : Women : Boys.
30 : 15 : 10
i.e. 6 : 3 : 2

Note 2

Actual Hours paid = 40 men + 10 women + 5 boys
= 55 workers × 40 Hrs.
= 2,200 Hours

Note 3

Actual hours worked = 55 Workers × 36 Hrs.
= 1,980 Hrs.

Note 4

**S.C. of one Unit :

$$\frac{40 \text{ Hrs. } (30 \text{ Men} \times \cdot 80 + 15 \text{ women} \times \cdot 60 + 10 \text{ boys} \times \cdot 40)}{2{,}000 \text{ Units}}$$

$$= \frac{1{,}480}{2{,}000 \text{ Units}} = \cdot 74 \text{ per unit.}$$

Problem 12

The following was the composition of a gang of workers in a factory during a particular month, in one of the production departments. The standard coposition of workers and wage rate per hour were as below :

Skilled : 2 workers @ Rs. 20 per hour each.
Semi-skilled : 4 workers @ Rs. 12 per hour each.
Unskilled : 4 workers @ Rs. 8 per hour each.

The standard output of the gang was four units per hour, of the product.

During the month in question, however, the actual composition of the gang and hourly rates paid were as under :

	No. of Workers	
Skilled	2	Rs. 20 per hour per worker
Semi-skilled	3	Rs. 14 " " "
Unskilled	5	Rs. 10 " " "

The gang was engaged for 200 hours during the month, which included 12 hours when no production was possible, due to machine break down, 810 units of the product were recorded as output of the gang during the month.

Calculate the Labour variances.

[*I.C.W.A. Inter, Dec. 1996*]

Solution

STANDARD COST	STANDARD COST OF ACTUAL HOURS			ACTUAL COST
	Worked at St. mix	Paid at Ac. mix	Paid at Ac. mix	
* S.C. × Output. Rs. 30 × 810 Units	St. mix × S.R. Sk. : 376 × 20 = 7,520 S.Sk. : 752× 12 = 9,024 U.Sk. 752 × 8 = 6,016 1,880 St. ratio : 2:4:4	St. mix × S.R. Sk. : 400 × 20 = 8,000 S. Sk. 800×12 = 9,600 U.Sk. 800× 8 = 6,400 2,000 Hrs. St. ratio 2:4:4	AC. Hours. × S.R Sk. 400 × 20 = 8,000 S. Sk. 600 × 12 = 7,200 U.Sk. 1,000 × 8 = 8,000 2,000 Hrs.	A.C. Hrs. × A.C. Rate Sk : 400×20 = 8,000 S.Sk. : 600×14 = 8,400 U.Sk : 1,000×10 = 10,000
24,300	22,560	24,000	23,200	26,400
L_5	L_4	L_3	L_2	L_1

LYV = 1,740 (F) LITV = 1,440 (A) LMV = 800 (F) LRV = 3,200 (A)

LEV = 1,100 (F)

LCV = 2,100 (A)

Note 1

1. Actual hours in a month = No. of workers × 200 Hrs.
2. Standard ratio means actual hours in standard ratio.
3. Actual Hours worked = No. of workers × 188 Hours.
   = 10 workers × 188 Hrs. = 1,880 Hours.

* S.C. *i.e.* Standard Labour Cost of one unit. The standard cost of 4 units has been given.

$$\frac{2 \times 20 + 4 \times 12 + 4 \times 8}{4 \text{ Units}} = \frac{\text{Rs. } 120}{4} = 30 \text{ per unit.}$$

Labour variances and its sub-divisions are summarised in a flow chart.

LCV = 2,100 (A)

↓

LRV = 3,200 (A) LEV = 1,100 (F)

↓

LMV = 800 (F) LITV = 1,440 (A) LYV = 1,740 (F)

Problem 13

Direct Labour strength of a section of a factory is 100 workers, paid at the rate of 6·00 per day of 8 hours each. The normal production level is 1,000 pieces per week of 48 hours. During a particular week an order for 1,500 pieces was completed working in all 7,650 hours, out of which 6,300 hours at normal wages and the balance 1,350 hours at overtime wages at double the normal rate. Total wages came to Rs. 6,300.

Calculate the average Labour cost per piece during the week and also analyse the various Labour cost variances for the week.

[*I.C.W.A. Inter*]

Solution

Average Labour cost per piece = $\frac{\text{Rs. } 6{,}300}{1{,}500 \text{ Units}}$ = Rs. 4·20

STANDARD COST	STANDARD COST OF AC. HOURS at S.R.	ACTUAL COST
*S.C. × Actual Output 3·60 × 1,500 Units	Ac. Hours × S.R. 7,650 Hrs. × 0·75 (S.R. = $\frac{6.00}{8 \text{ Hrs.}}$)	**Given** Ac. Hrs. × Ac. Rate 6,300 × 0·70 = 4,410 1,350 × 1·40 = 1,890
5,400	5,737·50	6,300
L_3	L_2	L_1

LEV = 337·50 (A) LRV = 562·50 (A)

LCV = 900 (A)

*S.C. *i.e.* Standard cost of one Unit :

$$\frac{100 \text{ workers} \times 48 \text{ Hours} \times \text{Re. } 0.75 \text{ Per Hour}}{1{,}000 \text{ pcs.}} = \frac{3{,}600}{1{,}000} = 3.60 \text{ Per unit}$$

Note 1

Actual rate per Hour :

6,300 Hours at Normal rate

1,300 Hours at Double rate

Equivalent normal hour

= 6,300 Hours + 1,300 Hours × 2 = 9,000 normal Hours.

Rate for normal hours

= $\frac{\text{Rs. } 6{,}300}{9{,}000 \text{ Hours}}$ = 0·70 P.H.

Rate for overtime period

= Re. 0·70 × 2 = Rs. 1·40 P.H.

Note 2

LRV (Labour rate variance) include an extra rate in the shape of overtime premium. And due to that the L.R.V. has become adverse, although the actual normal rate is less than the standard rate by 0·05 paise per hour. If overtime premium is separately shown *i.e.* 1,350 Hours × ·70 = 945 (A); then the L.R.V. will be = Actual hours × fall in rate than the S.R.

L.R.V. = 7,650 Hours × 0·05 = 382·50 (F). But the L.R.V. (in combined form will be as shown in format) *i.e.* 945A + 382·50 = 562·50 (A).

Problem 14

The standard Labour component and the actual Labour component engaged in a week for a job are as under.

	Skilled	*Semi-skilled*	*Unskilled*
(*a*) Standard number of workers in the gang	32	12	6
(*b*) Standard rate per Hour (Rs.)	3	2	1
(*c*) Actual No. of workers.	28	18	4
(*d*) Actual wage rate per Hour (Rs.)	4	3	2

During the 40 hours working week the gang produced 1,800 standard labour-hours of work.

Calculate : (*i*) Labour efficiency variance.

(*ii*) Labour Mix variance.

(*iii*) Labour rate variance.

(*iv*) Labour Cost variance.

[*B.Com. (Hons.), Delhi*]

Solution

STANDARD COST	STANDARD COST OF ACTUAL HOURS at standard mix.	STANDARD COST OF ACTUAL HOURS at Actual mix.	ACTUAL COST 1 week = 40 Hrs.
*S.C. × Output. 2·52 × 1,800 Hrs.	St. mix × S.R. Sk. : 1,280 × 3 = 3,840 S.Sk. : 480 × 2 = 960 U.Sk. 240 × 1 = 240 2,000 Hrs. St. ratio : 32:12:6	Ac. Hours × S.R. Sk. : 1,120 × 3 = 3,360 S. Sk. 720 × 2 = 1,440 U.Sk. 160 × 1 = 160 2,000 Hrs.	AC. Hours. × A.R Sk. 1,120 × 4 = 4,480 S. Sk. 720 × 3 = 2,160 U.Sk. 160 × 2 = 320
4,536	5,040	4,960	6,960
L_4	L_3	L_2	L_1

LYV = 504 (A) LMV = 80 (F) L.R.V = 2,000 (A)

LEV = 424 (A)

LCV = 2,424 (A)

*S.C. *i.e.* standard cost of one hour :

$$\frac{(32 \times 3 + 12 \times 2 + 6 \times 1)}{50 \text{ Hours.}} = \frac{126}{50} = \text{Rs. } 2{\cdot}52$$

Problem 15

100 skilled workmen, 40 semi-skilled workmen and 60 unskilled workmen were to work for 30 weeks to get a contract Job completed. The standard weekly wages were Rs. 60, Rs. 36 and Rs. 24, respectively. The Job was actually completed in 32 weeks by 80 skilled, 50 semi-skilled and 70 unskillled workmen who were paid Rs. 65, Rs. 40 and Rs. 20, respectively, as weekly wages.

Find out the Labour cost variance, Labour rate variance, Labour mix variance and Labour efficiency variance.

[*I.C.W.A. Inter, June 1992*]

Solution

STANDARD COST	STANDARD COST OF ACTUAL WEEKS at standard mix.	STANDARD COST OF ACTUAL WEEKS at Actual mix.	ACTUAL COST
*S.C. × Output. 2,66,400 × 1 Job.	Ac. weeks in St. ratio × S.R. Sk. : 3,200 × 60 =1,92,000 S.Sk. : 1,280 × 36 = 46,080 U.Sk. 1,920 × 24 = 46,080 6,400 Weeks. St. ratio : 100:40:60	Ac. Weeks × S.R. Sk. : 2,560× 60= 1,53,600 S. Sk. 1,600× 36 = 57,600 U.Sk. 2,240× 24 = 53,760 6,400 Weeks.	AC. Week × A.R Sk. 2,560× 65 = 1,66,400 S. Sk. 1,600× 40 = 64,000 U.Sk. 2,240× 20 = 44,800
2,66,400	2,84,160	2,64,960	2,75,200
L_4	L_3	L_2	L_1

LYV = 17,760 (A) LMV = 19,200 (F) LRV = 10,240 (A)

LEV = 1,440 (F)

LCV = 8,800 (A)

1. Ac Week = Man Power × 32 Weeks. Viz : Sk = 80 × 32 = 2,560 weeks.

2. * S.C. *i.e.* standard cost of one Unit of output. Here the output is the contract itself of which the standard cost has been given. S.C. = (100 × 60 + 40 × 36 + 60 × 24) 30 Weeks = 2,66,400.

WORKEDOUT PROBLEMS ON COMBINED MATERIAL AND LABOUR COST VARIANCES

Problem 16

The following details relating to the product 'x' during the month of March 1989 are available. You are required to compute the material and Labour Cost variances and also to reconcile the standard and the actual cost with the help of such variances.

Standard cost per Unit :

Material 50 Kg. @ Rs. 40 per Kg.

Labour 400 hours @ Rs. 1·00 per hour.

Actual cost for the month—

Material 4,900 Kgs. @ Rs. 42 per kg.

Labour 39,600 hours @ Rs. 1·10 per hour.

Actual production—100 Units.

[*I.C.W.A. Inter, June 1989*]

Solution

Material Variances

STANDARD COST	STANDARD COST OF AC. INPUT	ACTUAL COST
S.C. × Output S.C. of one Unit = 50 Kg. × 40 = 2,000 Rs. 2,000 × 100 Units.	4,900 Kgs. @ Rs. 40	4,900 Kgs. × 42
2,00,000	1,96,000	2,05,800
M_3	M_2	M_1

MUV = 4,000 (F) MPV = 9,800 (A)

MCV = 5,800 (A)

Labour Variances

STANDARD COST	STANDARD COST OF AC. HOURS	ACTUAL COST
Rs. 400 × 100 Units	39,600 Hours. @ Rs. 1·00	39,600 Hours × Rs. 1·10
40,000	39,600	43,560
L_3	L_2	L_1

LEV = 400 (F) LRV = 3,960 (A)

LCV = 3,560 (A)

Problem 17

The following standards have been set to manufacture a product :

Direct Material :

	Rs.
2 Units of A @ Rs. 4 per Unit	8·00
3 Units of B @ Rs. 3 per Unit	9·00
15 Units of C @ Rs. 1 per Unit	15·00
	32·00
Direct Labour : 3 hrs. @ 8 per hour	24·00
Total standard prime cost	56·00

The company manufactured and sold 6,000 units of the product during the year. Direct material costs were as follows :

12,500 Units of A at Rs. 4·40 per Unit
18,000 Units of B at Rs. 2·80 per Unit
88,500 Units of C at Rs. 1·20 per Unit

The company worked 17,500 direct Labour hours during the year. For 2,500 of these hours, the company paid at Rs. 12 per hour while for the ramaining, the wages were paid at standard rate.

Calculate material price variance and Usage variance and Labour rate and efficiency variances.

[*C.A. Inter*]

Solution

Material Variance Analysis

STANDARD COST	STANDARD COST OF ACTUAL INPUT		ACTUAL COST
S.C. × Output	A 12,500 @ 4·00 =	50,000	*Units* *Rs.* *Rs.*
Rs. 32 × 6,000 Units	B 18,000 @ 3·00 =	54,000	A 12,500 @ 4·40 = 55,000
	C 88,500 @ 1·00 =	88,500	B 18,000 @ 2·80 = 50,400
			C 88,500 @ 1·20 = 1,06,200
1,92,000		1,92,500	2,11,600
M_3		M_2	M_1

MUV = 500 (A)   MRV = 19,100 (A)

Labour Variance Analysis

STANDARD COST	STANDARD COST OF ACTUAL HOURS		ACTUAL COST
S.C. × Output	17,500 hours @ 8 =	1,40,000	2,500 Hrs. × 12 = 30,000
Rs. 24 × 6,000 Units			15,000 Hrs. × 8 = 1,20,000
1,44,000		1,40,000	1,50,000
L_3		L_2	L_1

LEV = 4,000 (F)   LRV = 10,000 (A)

Problem 18

Calculate the variances from the following information according to originating causes :

Standard direct cost per unit :

Material Cost : 5 Kg. Rs. 50

Labour Cost : 20 Hours Rs. 10

For production of 500 Units, material consumption amounted to Rs. 25,650 against 2·7 M.T.

Wages payment was Rs. 6,050 for 11,000 hours including 20 hours idle time due to machine break-down.

[*C.U. M.Com.*]

Solution

Material Variance Analysis

STANDARD COST	STANDARD COST OF ACTUAL INPUT	ACTUAL COST
S.C. × Output Rs. 50 × 500 Units	Ac. Qnt × S.R. 2,700 Kg. @ 10 = 27,000	Rs. 25,650
25,000	27,000	25,650
M_3	M_2	M_1

MUV = 2,000 (A) MPV = 1,350 (F)

MCV = 650 (A)

Labour Variance Analysis

STANDARD COST	STANDARD COST OF ACTUAL		ACTUAL COST (Given)
	Hours worked	Hours paid	
S.C. for Actual Output Rs. 10 × 500 Units	10,980 Hrs. @ 0·50	11,000 Hrs. @ 0·50	Rs. 6,050
5,000	5,490	5,500	6,050
L_4	L_3	L_2	L_1

LYV = 490 (A) LITV = 10 (A) LRV = 550 (A)

LEV = 500 (A)

LCV = 1,050 (A)

Problem 19

From the following particulars given below, compute : Material Price variance, Material Usage variance, Labour Rate variance, Idle time variance and Labour Efficiency variance.

One tonne of material input yields a standard of 1,00,000 Units. The standard price of material is Rs. 20 per Kg. Number of employees engaged is 200. The standard wage rate per employee per day is Rs. 6. The standard daily ouput per employee is 100 Units. The actual quantity of material used is 10 tonnes and the actual price paid is Rs. 21 per Kg. Actual output obtained is 9,00,000 units. Actual number of days worked is 50 and actual rate of wages paid is Rs. 6·50 per day. Idle time paid for and included in above time is $\frac{1}{2}$ day.

[*C.A. Inter, May 96*]

Solution

Material Variance Analysis

STANDARD COST	STANDARD COST OF ACTUAL INPUT	ACTUAL COST
S.C. × Output * Re. ·20 × 9,00,000 * $\left(\frac{1{,}000 \text{ Kg.} \times 20}{1{,}00{,}000 \text{ Units}} = 0{\cdot}20\right)$	10,000 Kg. @ 20 (1 Ton = 1,000 Kg)	10,000 Kg. @ 21
1,80,000	2,00,000	2,10,000

M_3 — M_2 — M_1

MUV = 20,000 (A) M.P.V = 10,000 (A)

MCV = 30,000 (A)

Labour Variance Analysis

STANDARD COST	STANDARD COST OF ACTUAL DAYS		ACTUAL COST
	Worked	Paid	
* S.C. = $\frac{\text{Rs. } 6}{100 \text{ Unit}}$ = ·06 * S.C. × Output * ·06 × 9,00,000	200 × 49·5 days × 6·00	200 × 50 × 6·00	200 employees × 50 days @ 6·50 per day
54,000	59,400	60,000	65,000

L_4 — L_3 — L_2 — L_1

LYV = 5,400 (A) LITV = 600 (A) LRV = 5,000 (A)

LEV = 6,000 (A)

LCV = 11,000 (A)

WORKEDOUT PROBLEMS ON VARIABLE AND FIXED OVERHEAD VARIANCES

Problem 20

A.B. Company Limited is having standard costing system in operation for quite some time. The following data relating to the month of April '05 is available from cost records :

	Budgeted	*Actual*
Output (in Units)	30,000	32,500
Operating hours	30,000	33,000
Fixed Overheads (Rs.)	45,000	50,000
Variable overheads (Rs.)	60,000	68,000
Working days	25	26

You are required to work out the relevant variances.

[*I.C.W.A. (Inter), June 1994*]

Solution

Variable Overhead Variance Analysis

STANDARD COST	STANDARD COST OF ACTUAL Hours worked	ACTUAL COST
*S.C. per unit × Output Rs. 2 × 32,500	Actual hours × S.R. $S.R. = \frac{\text{Budgeted O/H}}{\text{Budgeted Hours}} = \frac{\text{Rs. } 60,000}{30,000} = \text{Rs.} 2$ ∴ 33,000 Hours × Rs. 2 = 66,000	Given Rs. 68,000
65,000	66,000	68,000

V_3 — V_2 — V_1

V. Eff. V = 1,000 (A) V. Exp. V. = 2,000 (A)

V.O.V = 3,000 (A)

$$*\text{S.C. per Unit} = \frac{\text{Budgeted O/H}}{\text{Budgeted Unit}} : \frac{\text{Rs. } 60,000}{30,000 \text{ Units}} = \text{Rs. 2 per Unit}$$

Fixed Overhead Variance Analysis

STANDARD COST	STANDARD FIXED O/H FOR ACTUAL hours worked	STANDARD FIXED O/H FOR ACTUAL days available	BUDGETED F. O/H	ACTUAL COST
S.C. per Unit × Output $S.C. = \frac{\text{Rs. } 45,000}{30,000 \text{ Units}} = 1{\cdot}5$ P.V. 1·5 P.V. × 32,500 Units	A.C. Hour × S.R. $S.R. = \frac{\text{Rs. } 45,000}{30,000 \text{ Hrs.}}$ = 1·5 per hrs. 33,000 Hrs. × Rs. 1·5 = Rs. 49,500	$\text{Rs. } 45,000 \times \frac{26 \text{ days}}{25 \text{ days}}$ = Rs. 46,800	Given Rs. 45,000	Given Rs. 50,000
48,750	49,500	46,800	45,000	50,000

F_5 — F_4 — F_3 — F_2 — F_1

F.O. Eff. V = 750 (A) F.O. Cap. V = 2,700 (F) F.O. Cal. V = 1,800 (F) F.O. Exp. V = 5,000 (A)

F.O. Vol. V = 3,750 (F)

F.O.V = 1,250 (A).

Problem 21

S.V. Ltd. has furnished the following data :

	Budget	*Actual (In July 1999)*
No of working days	25	27
Production in units	20,000	22,000
Fixed overhead	30,000	31,000

Budgeted fixed overhead rate is Re. 1·00 per hour. In July 1999, the actual hours worked were 31,500.

Calculate :

(*i*) Efficiency variance.
(*ii*) Capacity variance.
(*iii*) Calendar variance.

(*iv*) Volume variance.

(*v*) Expenditure variance.

(*vi*) Total overhead variance.

[C.S. Inter, June 1999]

STANDARD COST	STANDARD FIXED O/H FOR ACTUAL hours worked	STANDARD FIXED O/H FOR ACTUAL days available	BUDGETED F. O/H	ACTUAL COST
S.C. × Output $S.C. = \frac{Rs.\ 30{,}000}{20{,}000\ Units} = 1{\cdot}5$ P.U. Rs. 1·50 × 22,000 Units	A.C. Hours × S.R. 31,500 × 1·00 P.H.	$Rs.\ 30{,}000 \times \frac{27\ days}{25\ days}$ = Rs. 32,400	Given Rs. 30,000	Given Rs. 31,000
33,000	31,500	32,400	30,000	31,000

FO_5 FO_4 FO_3 FO_2 FO_1

F.O. Eff. V = 1,500 (A) | F.O. Cap. V = 900 (A) | F.O. Cal. V = 2,400 (F) | F.O. Exp. V = 1,000 (A)

F.O. Volume V. = 3,000 (F)

F.O.V = 2,000 (F).

Reconciliation

F.O. VARIANCE

2,000 (F)

F.O. Expenditure variance 1,000 (A) — F.O. volume variance 3,000 (F)

F.O. volume variance 3,000 (F) → F.O. Eff. variance 1,500 (F) — F.O. Capacity variance 900 (A) — F.O. calender Variance 2,400 (F)

Problem 22

A Cost Accountant of a company was given the following information regarding the overheads for February 2005 :

(*a*) Overhead Cost variance Rs. 1,400 (A).

(*b*) Overhead volume variance Rs. 1,000 (A).

(*c*) Budgeted hours for February 2005 1,200 hours.

(*d*) Budgeted overheads for February 2005 Rs. 6,000.

(*e*) Actual rate of recovery of overheads Rs. 8 per hour.

You are required to assist him in computing the following for Feb. 2005 :

1. Overhead expenditure variance.
2. Actual overheads incurred.
3. Actual hours for actual production.
4. Overhead capacity variance.
5. Overhead efficiency variance.
6. Standard hours for actual production.

[C.A. Inter (Adopted)]

Solution

STANDARD COST	STANDARD F.O.H. FOR ACTUAL Hours Worked		BUDGETED OVERHEAD	ACTUAL COST
	Actual Hour Worked × S.R. S.R. $= \frac{\text{B.O.H.}}{\text{B. Hours}}$ $= \frac{6{,}000}{1{,}200} =$ Rs.5 ∴ 800 Hrs. × 5 =	4,000	Given Rs. 6,000	Ac. Hours × A.R. A.C. Hrs. × Rs. 8 800 Hrs. × 8
5,000		4,000	6,000	6,400
FO_4		FO_3	FO_2	FO_1

F.O. Eff. V = 1,000 (F)

F.O. Cap. V = 2,000 (A)

F.O. Exp. V. = 400 (A)

F.O. Volume V Rs. 1,000 (A)

F.O. Cost Variance = 1,400 (A)

Note. If we put the available information in the format, the required information will come out one after another automatically as balancing figure :

1. Overhead Expenditure variance = Rs. 400 (A)
2. Actual overhead incurred : Rs. 6,400
3. Actual hours for production = 800 Hours.
4. Overhead capacity variance = 2,000 (A)
5. Overhead Efficiency variance = 1,000 (F)
6. Standard hours for Actual production :

   Standard cost = Rs. 5,000

   S.R. per hour = Rs. 5

   $\therefore$ Standard hour $= \frac{5{,}000}{5} = 1{,}000$ Hours.

Problem 23

The following information was obtained from the records of a manufacturing unit using standard costing system :

	Standard	Actual
	4,000 Units	3,800 Units
Working days	20	21
Fixed overhead	Rs. 40,000	Rs. 39,000
Variable overhead	Rs. 12,000	Rs. 12,000

You are required to calculate the following overhead variance :

(*a*) Variable overhead variance.

(*b*) Fixed overhead variance

(*i*) Expenditure variance.

(*ii*) Volume variance.

(*iii*) Efficiency variance.

(*iv*) Calendar variance.

(*c*) Also prepare a Reconciliation statement for the standard fixed expenses workedout at standard fixed overhead rate and the actual overhead.

[*I.C.W.A. Inter, Dec. 1991*]

Solution

Variable Overhead Variance Analysis

STANDARD COST		ACTUAL COST
* S.C. of one Unit × Output 3·00 × 3,800 = 11,400		Given 12,000
11,400		12,000

$* \text{ S.C.} = \dfrac{\text{Rs. } 12{,}000}{4{,}000 \text{ Units}}$

= Rs. 3·00 Per Unit

V_2 ——— V_1

VOV = 600 (A)

Fixed Overhead Variance Analysis

STANDARD COST	STANDARD FIXED O/H for Actual days	BUDGETED FIXED OVERHEAD	ACTUAL COST
Standard Cost for Actual production S.C. × Output 10 × 3,800	$40{,}000 \times \dfrac{21 \text{ days}}{20 \text{ days}} = 42{,}000$	Given Rs. 40,000	Given Rs. 39,000
38,000	42,000	40,000	39,000
FO_4	FO_3	FO_2	FO_1

F.O. Eff. V = 4,000 (A) F.O.Cal.V. - 2,000 (F) F.O.Exp. V. = 1,000 (F)

F.O. Volume V = 2,000 (A)

FOV = 1,000 (A)

Note. Readers will follow that we are to drop one or two columns as per requirement of problem. Keeping that portion aside you are to follow same procedure as per format for the rest portion.

Problem 24

The following information is available from the records of a factory :

	Budget	*Actual*
Fixed overhead for June 2004	10,000	12,000
Production for June 2004 (Units)	2,000	2,100
Standard time per Unit (Hours)	10	—
Actual hours worked in June 2004	—	22,000

Compute— (*i*) Fixed overhead cost variance.
(*ii*) Expenditure variance.
(*iii*) Volume variance.
(*iv*) Capacity variance.
(*v*) Efficiency variance.

[*C.A. Inter (Adopted)*]

Solution

Note. Calendar variance need not be worked out. When there is no information on days or actual days are same as budgeted days, then there will be no calendar variance. Now we are to draw four columns instead of five.

Fixed Overhead Variance Analysis

STANDARD COST		STANDARD F.O. FOR ACTUAL Hours worked		BUDGETED COST	ACTUAL COST
St. Cost × Output. S.C. = ·50 × 10 Hours = 5·00 P.V. 5·00 × 2,100 =	10,500	Actual Hours × S.R. S.R. = $\frac{\text{Budgeted Amount}}{\text{Budgeted hours}}$ = $\frac{\text{Rs. } 10{,}000}{2{,}000 \text{ Units} \times 10 \text{ Hrs.}}$ = 0·50 P.H. 22,000 Hrs. × ·50 =	Rs. 11,000	Given Rs. 10,000	Given Rs. 12,000
	10,500		11,000	10,000	12,000
FO_4			FO_3	FO_2	FO_1

F.O.H. Eff. Variane = 500 (A)

F.O.H. Cap. Variance = 1,000 (F)

F.O.H. Exp. V. = 2,000 (A)

F.O.H. Volume Variance = 500 (F)

F.O.H. Variance = 1,500 (A)

Problem 25

A company has a normal capacity of 120 machines, working 8 hours per day of 25 days in a month. The fixed overheads are budgeted at Rs. 1,44,000 per month. The standard time required to manufacture one unit of product is 4 hours.

In April 1998, the company worked 24 days of 840 machine hours per day and produced 5,305 units of output. The actual fixed overhead were Rs. 1,42,000.

Compute :

(*i*) Efficiency variance, (*ii*) Capacity variance, (*iii*) Calendar variance, (*iv*) Expenditure variance, (*v*) Volume variance, (*vi*) Total Fixed overhead variance. **[*C.A. Inter, May 1998*]**

Solution

FIXED OVERHEAD VARIANCE ANALYSIS

STANDARD COST	STANDARD FIXED O/H FOR ACTUAL hours worked	STANDARD FIXED O/H FOR ACTUAL days available	BUDGETED F.O.	ACTUAL COST
*S.C. × Output. Rs. 24 × 5,305 = 1,27,320	Actual Hours × S.R. S.R. = $\frac{\text{Bud. F.O.}}{\text{Bud. Hours.}}$ = $\frac{1{,}44{,}000}{120 \times 8 \times 25 \text{ days}}$ = 6 P.H. Ac. Hours = 24 × 840 = 20,160 ∴ 20,160 × 6 = 1,20,960	$\frac{\text{Bud. F.O.}}{\text{Bud. day}} \times \text{Ac days.}$ ∴ $\frac{1{,}44{,}000}{25 \text{ days}} \times 24 \text{ days}$ = 1,38,240	Given Rs. 1,44,000	Given Rs. 1,42,000
1,27,320	1,20,960	1,38,240	1,44,000	1,42,000
FO_5	FO_4	FO_3	FO_2	FO_1

F.O. Eff. V = 6,360 (F)

F.O. Cap. V. = 17,280 (A)

F.O. Cal. V. = 5,760 (A)

F.O. Exp.. V. = 2,000 (F)

F.O. Volume Variance = Rs. 16,680 (A)

F.O. Variance 14,680(A)

*S.C. = Rs. 1,44,000 ÷ 6,000 Units = 24 p.u. $\frac{120 \text{ Machines} \times 8 \text{ Hrs} \times 24 \text{ days}}{4 \text{ Hrs. per Unit}}$ = 6,000 Units

Problem 26

The following data have been obtained from the records of a machine shop for an average month :

Budget :

No. of working days	25
Working hours per day	8
Number of direct workers	16
Efficiency : One standard hour per clock hour	
Down time : 20%	
Fixed overhead	Rs. 15,360
Variable overhead	Rs. 20,480

The actual data for the month of September 2004 are as under :

Fixed Overhead	Rs. 16,500
Variable Overhead	Rs. 14,500
Net operator hours worked	1,920
Standard hours produced	2,112

There was a special holiday in September 2004.

You are required to present reports to Departmental Manager

(*i*) Showing the cost ratios you have chosen.

(*ii*) Setting out the analysis of variances.

[*C.A. Final, (Adopted*]

Solution

(*i*) Report to Dept. Manager : Cost ratios

Budgeted Hours = 25 days × 8 Hours × 16 Workers = 3,200

Less, 20% down-time 640

2,560 Hours

Maximum possible hours = 3,200 Hours

1. Efficiency ratio $= \dfrac{\text{Standard hours produced}}{\text{Actual Hours worked}} \times 100$

$= \dfrac{2{,}112}{1{,}920} \times 100 = 110\%$

2. Activity ratio : $\dfrac{\text{Standard Hour Produced}}{\text{Budgeted Hours}} \times 100$

$= \dfrac{2{,}112}{2{,}560} \times 100 = 82{\cdot}5\%$

3. Standard capacity usage Ratio $= \dfrac{\text{Budgeted Hours}}{\text{Max. Possible Hours}} \times 100$

$= \dfrac{2{,}560}{3{,}200} \times 100 = 80\%$

4. Actual capacity Utilisation Ratio : $\dfrac{\text{Actual Hours Worked}}{\text{Budgeted Hours}} \times 100$

$= \dfrac{1{,}920}{2{,}560} \times 100 = 75\%$

5. Calendar Ratio : $\dfrac{\text{Actual days worked}}{\text{Budgeted Days}} \times 100 = \dfrac{24}{25} \times 100 = 96\%$

(ii)

STANDARD COST	STANDARD COST FOR ACTUAL hours worked	STANDARD COST FOR ACTUAL days available	BUDGETED F.O.H.	ACTUAL COST
S.C. × Output S.C. = $\frac{15,360}{2,560}$ = Rs. 6·00 Rs. 6·00 × 2,112	Ac. Hours. × S.R. 1,920 × 6	B.F.O. × $\frac{\text{Ac. days}}{\text{Bud. days}}$ 15,360 × $\frac{24}{25}$	Given Rs. 15,360	Given Rs. 16,500
12,672	11,520	14,745·60	15,360	16,500
FO_5	FO_4	FO_3	FO_2	FO_1

F.O. Eff. Variance = Rs. 1,152 (F)
F.O. Cap. V = Rs. 3,225·60 (A)
F.O. Cal. V. = 614·40 (A)
F.O. Exp. V. = 2,688 (A)
F.O. Volume Variance = 2,688 (A)
F.O. Variance = Rs. 3,828 (A)

WORKEDOUT PROBLEMS ON ALL COST VARIANCES

Problem 27

A Ltd. operates a system of standard costs.

Following information is available :

Actuals :

	Rs.
Materials consumed (3,600 Units at Rs. 52·50 per Unit)	1,89,000
Direct Wages	22,100
Fixed Expenses	1,88,000
Variable Expenses	62,000
	4,61,000

Output during the period was 3,500 Units of finished product.

For the above period, the standard production capacity was 4,800 Units and the break-up of standard cost per unit was as under :

	Rs.
Materials (One Unit @ 50 per Unit)	50·00
Direct Wages	6·00
Fixed Expenses	40·00
Variable Expenses	20·00
Total standard cost per Unit	116·00

Total standard wages per Unit is based on 9,600 hours for the above period at a rate of Rs. 3·00 per hour. 6,400 hours were actually worked during the above period and in addition, wages for 400 hours were paid to compensate for idle time due to break-down of a machine, and overall wage rate was Rs. 3·25 per hour.

You are required to calculate the following variances :

(*a*) Material cost variance (*b*) Material Price variance (*c*) Material Usage variance (*d*) Labour cost variance (*e*) Wages rate variance (*f*) Labour efficiency variance (*g*) Idle time variance (*h*) Variable expenses variance (*i*) Fixed Expenses Expenditure variances (*j*) Fixed expenses volume variance (*k*) Fixed Expenses capacity variance (*l*) Fixed Expenses Efficiency variance (*m*) Total cost variance.

[*C.A. Inter, Nov. 1993*]

Solution

Material Cost Variance Analysis

STANDARD COST	STANDARD COST OF ACTUAL INPUT		ACTUAL COST
		at actual quantity/mix	
Standard Cost. 3,500 × 50	As mix variance and yield variance are not required this column is to be dropped.	(3,600 Units × 50)	Given Rs. 1,89,000
1,75,000		1,80,000	1,89,000
M_3		M_2	M_1

Mat. Usage variance = 5,000 (A) MPV = 9,000 (A)

Material Cost variance = 14,000 (A)

Labour Cost Variance Analysis

STANDARD COST	STANDARD COST OF ACTUAL HOURS			ACTUAL COST
	Worked		Paid (Ac. mix)	
3,500 @ 6 Rs. 21,000	6,400 @ 3	No. mix variance	6,800 hours @ 3	Given Rs. 22,100
21,000	19,200		20,400	22,100
L_4	L_3		L_2	L_1

LYV = 1,800 (F) LITV = 1,200 (A) LRV = 1,700 (A)

LEV = 600 (F)

L.C.V 1,100 (A)

Variable Overhead Variance Analysis

STANDARD COST		ACTUAL COST
3,500 unit × 20		Rs. 62,000
70,000		62,000
Vo_2		Vo_1

Variable O/H Variance = 8,000 (F)

Fixed Overhead Variance Analysis.

STANDARD COST	STANDARD FIXED OVERHEAD for Actual hours worked at S.R.		BUDGETED F.O.	ACTUAL COST
3,500 Units × 40	Ac. Hours. × S.R. $S.R. = \frac{\text{Budgeted F.O.}}{\text{Budgeted Hours}}$ *i.e.* $\frac{1,92,000}{9,600} = 20$ ∴ 6,800 × 20 = 1,36,000	No Calendar Variance	4,800 Units @ 40	Rs. 1,88,000
1,40,000	1,36,000		1,92,000	1,88,000
FO_4	**FO_3**		**FO_2**	**FO_1**

F.O. Eff. V. = 4,000 (F) F.O. Cap. V. = 56,000 (A) F.O. Exp. V. = 4,000 (F)

F.O. Volume Variance = 52,000 (A)

F.O. Variance = 48,000 (A)

Total Cost variance :

Standard Cost (Sc × Output)	–	Actual Cost.
3,500 × 116	–	4,61,000

55,100 (A)

Alternatively : Total Cost Variance = MCV + LCV + VOV + FOV *i.e.* 14,000 (A) + 1,100 (A) + 8,000 (F) + 48,000 (A) = 55,100.

WORKEDOUT PROBLEMS ON SALES VARIANCES

Problem 28

Budgeted and actual sales for the month of December 2004 of two products A & B of XY Ltd. were :

Product	*Budgeted Units*	*Budgeted Price*	*Actual Units*	*Actual Price*
A :	6,000	5·00 P.U.	5,000	5·00 P.U.
			1,500	4·75 P.U.
B :	10,000	2·00 P.U.	7,500	2·00 P.U.
			1,750	1·90 P.U.

Budgeted costs for products A and B were Rs. 4·00 and Rs. 1·50 per Units' respectively. Workout from the above data the following variances.

(*i*) Sales value variance (*ii*) Sales volume variance (*iii*) Sales Price variance (*iv*) Sales Mixture variance (*v*) Sales Quantity variance.

[*I.C.W.A. Inter, Adopted*]

Solution

BUDGETED SALES	STANDARD SALES VALUE OF ACTUAL QUANTITY at standard mix	STANDARD SALES VALUE OF ACTUAL QUANTITY at actual mix	ACTUAL SALES
A : 6,000 @ 5 = 30,000 B : 10,000 @ 2 = 20,000	A : 5,906·25 @5·00=29,531·25 B : 9,843·75 @2·00=19,687·50 15,750 49,218·75 St. ratio : (3:5)	Ac. Qnt × S.R. A : 6,500 @ 5 = 32,500 9,250 @ 2 = 18,500 15,750 51,000	A : 5,000 @ 5·00 =25,000 1,500 @ 4·75 = 7,125 B : 7,500 @ 2·00 =15,000 1,750 @ 1·90 = 3,325 15,750 50,450
50,000	49,218·75	51,000	50,450
SV_4	SV_3	SV_2	SV_1

SQV = 781·25(A) SMV = 1781·25(F) S. Price Variance = 550(A)

S.Volume variance 1,000(F)

Sales Value variance = 450(F)

Problem 29

X Ltd. operates a budgetary control and standard costing system. From the following data calculate :

(*i*) Sales variance (*ii*) Sales volume variance (*iii*) Sales price variance.

Product	*Budgeted Units*	*Sales Value Rs.*	*Actual. Units Sold*	*Sales Value Rs.*
A	100	1,200	100	1,100
B	50	600	50	600
C	100	900	200	1,700
D	75	450	50	300
	325	3,150	400	3,700

[*C.S. Final*]

Solution

SALES VARIANCE ANALYSIS

BUDGETED SALES	STANDARD SALES VALUE OF ACTUAL UNITS SOLD AC. MIX.	ACTUAL SALES
Given. Rs. 3,150	A : 100 @ 12 P.U. = 1,200 B : 50 @ 12 P.U. = 600 C : 200 @ 9 P.U. = 1,800 D : 50 @ 6 P.U. = 300 400	Given. Rs. 3,700
3,150	3,900	3,700
SV_3	SV_2	SV_1

Sales Volume Variance = Rs. 750(F) Sales Price Variance = Rs. 200(A)

Sales Value Variance = Rs. 550(F)

Note. You have not been asked to work out mix variance or quantity variance. So you are not to find out standard Sales Value of standard mix. Keeping this portion aside rest to be done on usual process.

EXERCISES

OBJECTIVE TYPE QUESTIONS

1. *Which of the suggested answers is correct ?*

(*a*) Standard costing implies :

(*i*) The use of predetermined levels of price and performance as the standard.
(*ii*) The use of the previous year's actual figures as the standard.
(*iii*) The use of fixed budgeting.
(*iv*) The use of ideal costs which are useful control aids.

[Ans. (*i*)]

(*b*) The labour cost variance may be expressed as :

(*i*) (Standard wage rate – Actual wages rate) × Actual Hours.
(*ii*) Budgeted Labour Cost – Actual Labour Cost.
(*iii*) St. Wage rate × Output achieved – Actual wage cost.
(*iv*) (Standard hours produced – actual hours) × Standard Wage rate.

[Ans. (*iii*)]

(*c*) Fixed overhead volume variance may be subdivided into :

(*i*) Expenditure variance + Capacity Variance.
(*ii*) Productivity variance + Expenditure variance.
(*iii*) Productivity variance + Capacity variance.
(*iv*) None of the above.

[Ans. (*iii*)]

(*d*) Excess direct wages will be disclosed in :

(*i*) Yield variance.
(*ii*) Quantity variance.
(*iii*) Labour efficiency variance.
(*iv*) Labour rate variance.

[Ans. (*iii*)]

(*e*) When standard costs are used, the amount of detailed record-keeping will :

(*i*) Reduce.
(*ii*) Increase.
(*iii*) Stay the same.
(*iv*) Be more time-consuming.

[Ans. (*i*)]

THEORETICAL QUESTIONS

1. What do you mean by standard costing ? How does it differ from Budgetary Control ?
[*C.U. B.Com. 1994; 2000*]

2. Define Standard costing. What are its obejcts ? **[*C.U. B.Com. 1995*]**

3. What is standard costing ? What are its advantages ? **[*C.U. B.Com. 1996*]**

4. Write short notes on :

(*a*) Material usage variance.
(*b*) Calendar variance.

[*C.S. Inter, June 1994*]

5. Explain the possible causes of material price variances and material usage varainces in standard costing. What are the remedial measures ?

[*I.C.W.A. Inter, June 1990*]

6. What do you understand by the term standard Labour hour, labour efficiency ratio and labour activity ratio ?

[*I.C.W.A. Inter, Dec. 1983*]

7. Write short notes on (*i*) Variance Analysis (*ii*) Standard costing.

[*C.S. Inter., Dec. 1991*]

8. Distinguish between 'estimated cost and standard cost'. **[*C.S. Inter, June 1990*]**

PROBLEMS

1. A manufacturing concern which has adopted standard costing furnishes the following information :

1. Standard for 70 Kgs. finished product 100 Kgs. raw material are required.
2. Standard price per Kg. of raw material Re. 1·00.
3. Actual output 2,10,000 Kg.
4. Material Used : 2,80,000 Kg.
5. Cost of Material : Rs. 2,52,000.

Calculate :

(*a*) Material Usage variance,
(*b*) Material Price variance,
(*c*) Material Cost variance.

[Ans. (*a*) Rs. 20,000(F); (*b*) Rs. 28,000(F) (*c*) Total cost variance : 48,000 (F)]

2. From the following particulars in respect of an output produced in a factory for the quarter ended on 31st Dec. 2003, compute material cost variance :

Quantity of Material purchased	3,000 Units
Value of Material Purchased	Rs. 9,000
Standard quantity of Material required per ton of output	30 Units
Standard rate of material per unit	Rs. 2·50
Opening stock of material	Nil
Closing stock of material	500 Units
Output during the period	8 Units

[Ans. MCV : 1,500 (A); M.P.V. : 1,250(A); 250 (A).]
[B.Com (H) Delhi]

3. From the following particulars compute material cost variances :

Standard quantity of Material per ton of Output.	50 Units
Standard rate of materials per unit	Rs. 4·50
Quantity of materials purchased	2,900 Units
Cost of materials purchased	Rs. 12,180.
Opening stock of materials	50 Units (Cost Rs. 220)
Closing stock of materials	550 Units
Actual output during the quarter	40 tons

Compute the material cost variances (Assume FIFO Method).

[Ans. MCV : 1,090(A); MPV : 710(F); MUV : 1,800 (A).]

4. A company manufacturing 'distemper' operates a costing system. The standard cost for one of the products of the company shows the following material standards :

Material	*Quantity*	*St. Rate Per Kg.*	*Total*
A	40 Kg.	Rs. 75	Rs. 3,000
B	10 Kg.	Rs, 50	Rs. 500
C	50 Kg.	Rs. 20	Rs. 1,000
			Rs. 4,500

Material cost per Unit (Total)
The standard input mix is 100 Kg. and the standard output of the finished product is 90 Kg.
The actual results for a period are :
Material Used :

A = 2,40,000 Kg. at Rs. 80 per Kg.
B = 40,000 Kg. at Rs. 52 per Kg.
C = 2,20,000 Kg. at Rs. 21 per Kg.

Actual output of the finished product = 4,20,000 Kg.
You are required to calculate the material price, mix and yield variances.

[I.C.W.A. Inter, Dec. 1989]

[Ans. (*i*) MPV : Rs. 15,00,000(A) (*ii*) M.M.V. : 19,00,000(A) (*iii*) MYV : 15,00,000(A) (*iv*) MCV : 49,00,000(A)]

5. The standard mix of product A is :

Kgs.	*Material*	*Price Per Kg.* *Rs.*
45	X	6·00
25	Y	4·50
30	Z	9·50

The standard loss in production is 10% of input. There is no scrap value. Actual production for a month was 7,425 Kgs. of A from 80 mixes.

Actual purchases and consumption of material during the month were :

Kgs.	*Material*	*Price Per Kg.* *Rs.*
4,200	X	6·50
1,700	Y	4·25
2,600	Z	9·75

You are required to calculate the following variances for presentation to the management :

(*i*) Material cost variance.
(*ii*) Material price variance.
(*iii*) Material mix variance.
(*iv*) Material yield variances.

[*C.S. Inter*]

[Ans. MCV : Rs. 4,806(A); M.P.V. : Rs. 2,325(A); MMV : Rs. 812·50 (A); MYV : Rs. 1,668·50(A)]

6. One Kilogram of product 'K' requires two chemicals A and B. The following were the details of product 'K' for the month of June 1987 :

(*a*) Standard mix chemical 'A' 50% and Chemical 'B' 50%.
(*b*) Standard price per Kilogram of 'A' Rs. 12 and chemical 'B' Rs. 15.
(*c*) Actual input of chemical 'B' 70 Kilograms.
(*d*) Actual price per Kilogram of chemical 'A' Rs. 15.
(*e*) Standard normal loss 10% of total input.
(*f*) Material cost variance total Rs. 650 adverse.
(*g*) Material yield variance total Rs. 135 adverse.

You are required to calculate :

(1) Material mix variances (2) Material usage variance (3) Material Price variance (4) Actual Loss of input (5) Actual input of chemcial 'A' (6) Actual price per-kilogram of chemcial 'B'.

[*C.A. Inter*]

[Ans. (1) MMV: Rs. 45(A); (2) MUV : Rs. 180(A); (3) MPV : 470(A); (4) Actual Loss = 20 Kg; (5) Actual input of A : 40 Kg; (6) Ac. Price : Rs. 20 per Kg]

7. XYZ Company manufactures a product ABC by mixing three raw materials. For every 100 Kg. of ABC, 125 Kg of raw materials are used. In April 1999, there was an output of 5,600 Kg of ABC. The standard and actual particulars of April 1999 are :

Raw Materials	**Standard**		**Actual**	
	Mix	Price per Kg.	Mix	Price per Kg.
Raw Material I	50%	40	60%	42
Raw Material II	30%	20	20%	16
Raw Material III	20%	10	20%	12

Calculate all variances :

[*I.C.W.A. Inter, June 1990*]

Ans. **(*a*) Material Cost variances : 19,600 (A).**
(*b*) Material Price variances : 5,600 (A).
(*c*) Material Mix variance : 14,000(A)
(*d*) Material Yield variance : NIL

8. S.V. Ltd. manufactures a simple product, the standard mix of which is :

Material A : 60% at Rs. 20 per Kg.
Material B : 40% at Rs. 10 per Kg.

Normal loss in production is 20% of input. Due to shortage of material A, the standard mix was changed. Actual result for March 1989, were :

Material A :	105 Kg.	at Rs. 20 per kg.
Material B :	95 Kg.	at Rs. 9 per Kg.
	200 Kg.	
Loss	35 Kg.	
Output	165 Kg.	

(*i*) Material Price variances, (*ii*) Material Usage variance, (*iii*) Material Mix variances, (*iv*) Material yield variances.

[*I.C.W.A. Inter, Dec. 1984, Dec. 2000*]

[Ans. MPV : 95(F); MMV : 150(F); MYV : 100(F); MUV : 250(F).]

9. The standard cost of a certain chemical mixture is :

35% Material A : at Rs. 25 per Kg.
65% Material B : at Rs. 36 per Kg.

A standard Loss of 5% is expected in production.
During a period the actual uses are :

125 Kg. of Material A : at Rs. 27 per Kg.
275 Kg. of Material B : at Rs. 34 per Kg.

The actual output was 365 Kg.
Calculate :

(*a*) Material Cost variance.
(*b*) Material Price variance.
(*c*) Material Mix variance.
(*d*) Material Yield variance.

[*B.Com. (Hons.), Delhi, 1985*]

[Ans. MCV : 373(A); MPV : 300(F); M.M.V : 165(A); MYV : 508(A).]

10. The standard material cost to produce a tonne of chemical X is :

300 Kg. of material A @ Rs. 10 per Kg.
400 Kg. of material B @ Rs. 5 per Kg.
500 Kg. of material C @ Rs. 6 per Kg.

During a period, 100 tonnes of mixtures X was produced from the usage of :

35 tonnes of material A at a cost of Rs. 9,000 per tonne.
42 tonnes of material B at a cost of Rs. 6,000 per tonne.
53 tonnes of material C at a cost of Rs. 7,000 per tonne.

Calculate the price, usage and mix variances.

[*B.Com. (Hons.), Delhi*]

[Ans. MCV : Rs. 1,38,000 (A); MPV : 60,000(A); MUV : Rs. 78,000 (A); MMV : 11,333(A)]

11. The standard material cost for 100 Kgs. of chemical 'D' is made up of :

Chemical A : 30 Kgs. @ Rs. 4·00 per Kg.
" B : 40 Kgs. @ Rs. 5·00 per Kg.
" C : 80 Kgs. @ Rs. 6·00 per Kg.

In a batch, 500 Kgs. of Chemical 'D' were produced from a mix of

Chemical A : 140 Kgs. at a cost of Rs. 588
" B : 220 Kgs. at a cost of Rs. 1,056
" C : 440 Kgs. at a cost of Rs 2,860.

How do the yield, mix, and the price factors contribute to the variance in the actual cost per 100 Kg. of chemical 'D' over the standard cost ?

[*I.C.W.A. Final*]

[Ans. MCV : Rs. 100·80(A); M.P.V. : Rs. 40·80(A); MMV : Rs. 6·67(A); MYV : 53·33(A); MUV : Rs. 60·00(A)]

12. In a manufacturing process, the following standards apply :

Standard price : Raw material A : Rs. 1 Per Kg.
Raw material B : Rs. 5 Per Kg.

Standard mix : 75% A; 25% B (by weight)

Standard yield (weight of product as % of weight of raw materials) : 90%

In a period, the actual costs, usages and output were as follows :

Used : 4,400 Kgs. A, Costing Rs. 4,650
1,600 Kgs. B, Costing Rs. 7,850

Output : 5,670 Kgs. of products.

The budgeted output for the period was 7,200 Kgs.

Prepare an operating statement, showing how the material cost variance is built up.

[*I.C.M.A. Adopted*]

[Ans. MCV : Rs. 100(F); MPV : 100(A); MMV : 400(A); MYV : 600(F); MUV = 200(F)]

13. A gang of workers usually consists of 10 men, 5 women and 5 boys in a factory. They are paid at standard hourly rates of Rs. 1·25, Re. 0·80 and Re. 0·70, respectively. In a normal working week of 40 hours the gang is expected to produce 1,000 units of output.

In a certain week, the gang consisted of 13 men, 4 women and 3 boys. Actual wages were paid at the rates of Rs. 1·20, Re 0·85 and Re. 0·65, respectively. Two hours were lost due to abnormal idle time and 960 Units of output were produced.

Calculate various labour variances.

[*C.S. Inter, June 93*]

[Ans. Labour cost variance : Rs. 70(A)
Labour rate variance : Rs. 19·10(A)
Labour mix variance : Rs. 58·90(A)
Labour yield variance : Rs. 8(F)]

14. Using the following information, calculate Labour Cost variance, Labour rate variance, Labour efficiency and idle time variance :

Standard hours :	5,000 Hours
Standard wage rate :	Rs. 4 per hour
Actual hours :	Rs. 6,000 hours
Actual wage rate :	3·50 per hour

Time lost on account of machinery breakdown ....300 hours.

[*B.Com. Calicut*]

[Ans. LCV : Rs. 1,000(A); LRV : 3,000(F); LEV : 4,000(A); LITV : Rs. 1,200(A)]

15. The standard production of X Ltd. for January 2004 was : 20,000 big containers and 40,000 small containers.

A standard hour represents 5 big containers or 4 small containers. The standard rate of wages is @ 0·25 per hour. During January payment was made for 15,000 hours @ Re. 0·30 per hour. Out of 15,000 hours, 700 hours were lost due to unbudgeted holidays. Also there was a loss of production of 500 big containers due to machine break down. Actual production for January was 24,000 big containers and 38,000 small containers.

Calculate Labour variances.

[*M.Com. Kolkata*]

[Ans. LCV : 925(A); LRV : 750(A); LEV : 25(F); LITV : 200(A)]

16. From the following figures, calculate (a) Labour cost variance, (b) Wages rate-variance and (c) Labour efficiency variance :

Actual hours worked	5,600 Hrs.
Actual wages paid	Rs. 7,840
Standard rate per hour	Rs. 2
Standard hours	4,000 Hours.

[Ans. (*a*) Labour Cost variance : 160(F); (*b*) Labour rate variance : Rs. 3,360(F); (*c*) LEV : Rs. 3,200 (A)]

17. A factory specialises in the production of a product. From the following information calculate material cost variance and Labour cost variance :

	Rs.
Material used : 2,000 Units @ 5·20	10,400
Labour : 2,000 hours @ Rs. 3	6,000
	16,400

The output at the close of the month was 1,800 Units completed and 200 Units for which materials were drawn fully, but only 50% completed with reference to labour.
The standard cost for 2 Units of the product was Rs. 16 consisting of :

	Rs.
Material (2 Units)	10
Labour (2 hours @ Rs. 3 per hour)	6
	16

[Ans. Effective output in respect of material = 1,800 + 200 Units = 2,000 Units, but effective output in respect of Labour = 1,800 Units + 50% of 200 = 1,900 Units.]
M.C.V. : Rs. 400(A); L.C.V. = Rs. 30(A).

18. The particulars of standard cost card for a product are given below :

	Per Unit
Material cost : 2 Kg. @ 2·50 each	5·00
Wages : 2 hours @ 0·50 each	1·00

The actuals which have emerged from business operation are :
Production : 8,000 Units.
Material consumed : 16,500 Kg. @ Rs. 2·40 each = Rs. 39,600.
Wages paid : 18,000 hours @ 40 paise each. = Rs. 7,200.
Calculate appropriate material and labour cost variances.

[B.Com. (H) Delhi]

[Ans. MCV : Rs. 400(F); MPV = 1,650 (F); MUV =1,250(A)
LCV = 800(F); LRV=1,800(F); LEV : 1,000(A)]

19. From the following particulars, calculate the variable overhead variances :

Actual variable overhead Expenses	Rs. 28,500
Budgeted variable overhead Expenses	Rs. 34,000
Actual level of production	8,000 Hours
Normal capacity	10,000 Hours

[C.U. B.Com. 2003]
Ans. Rs. 1,300(A).

20. S.V. Ltd. has furnished you with the following data :

	Budget	Actual
No. of Working days	25	27
Production in Units	20,000	22,000
Fixed Overheads	Rs. 30,000	Rs. 31,000

Budgeted fixed overhead rate is Re. 1·00 per hour. In July 2004, the actual hours worked were 31,500.
Calculate the following variances :
(i) Total overhead variance
(ii) Expenditure variance
(iii) Volume variance
(iv) Efficiency variance
(v) Capacity variance
(vi) Calendar variance

[C.A. Inter. (Adopted)]

[Ans. *(i)* Total O.H. variance : Rs. 2,000(F)
***(ii)* O.H. Exp. variance : Rs. 1,000(A)**
***(iii)* Volume variance : Rs. 3,000(F)**
***(iv)* Efficiency variance : Rs. 1,500(F)**
***(v)* Capacity variance : Rs. 900(A)**
***(vi)* Calendar variance : Rs. 2,400(F).]**

21. Vinak Ltd. has furnished you the following information for the month of August 2004 :

	Budget	*Actual*
Output (units)	30,000	32,500
Hours	30,000	33,000
Fixed Overhead	Rs. 45,000	Rs. 50,000
Variable overhead	Rs. 60,000	Rs. 68,000
Working days	25	26

Calculate the variance.

[I.C.W.A. Inter, Adopted]

[Ans. (*i*) Total O.H. Cost variance Rs. 4,250(A).
(*ii*) Variable O.H. Cost variance Rs. 3,000(A)
(*iii*) F.O. cost variance Rs. 1,250(A)
(*iv*) Expenditure variance Rs. 1,250(A)
(*v*) Volume variance Rs. 3,750(F)
(*vi*) Efficiency variance Rs. 750(A)
(*vii*) Capacity variance Rs. 4,500(F)
(*viii*) Calendar variance Rs. 1,800(F).]

22. S. Ltd. has furnished you the following information for the month of August 2004 :

	Budget	*Actual*
Output (Units)	33,000	35,500
Hours	36,000	43,000
Fixed Overhead	Rs. 50,000	Rs. 55,000
Variable overhead	Rs. 60,000	Rs. 65,000
Working days	24	26

Calculate the variances.

[Ans. (*i*) Variable O/H Expenditure Variance Rs. 455(A)
(*ii*) F/O.H. Cost variance Rs. 1,212(A)
(*iii*) F/O.H. Expenditure variance Rs. 5,000(A)
(*iv*) F/O.H. Volume variance Rs. 3,788(F).]

23. As the senior Cost Analyst you have been asked to prepare a Profit and Loss Statement on Standard costing basis for week ended 31st December from the following available information :

Sales for week Rs. 50,000
Direct Material— Price variance(A) Rs. 400
Usage variance(A) Rs. 300

Standard price of direct Material used Rs. 600 per M.T.
Standard labour rate per hour Rs. 4·00
Actual Material issued 20 M.T. @ Rs. 620 per M.T.
Actual Payment to workmen :
4 employees @ 4·20 per hour
6 employees @ 3·80 per hour
Others were paid at standard rate.
Budgeted Fixed overheads for December (4 weeks) Rs. 76,800.
Actual overhead incurred Rs. 18,000.
Each M.T. of material is expected to produce 2,400 Units.
The company operates a forty hour week and there are 60 direct employees. The standard performance is that each employee should produce one unit of product in three minutes.

[I.C.W.A. Final, June 1990]

[Ans. Labour rate variance Rs. 16(F)
Labour Efficiency variance Rs. 240(A)
Overhead Expenditure variance Rs. 1,200(F)
Overhead Volume variance Rs. 480(A)
Actual Profit as per P/L statement Rs. 10,016.]

24. Bronte Ltd. manufactures a single product, a laminated Kitchen Unit which has a standard cost of Rs. 80 made up as :

		Rs.
Direct materials	15 Square metre @ Rs. 3 per Square metre	45
Direct Labour	5 hours @ Rs. 4 per hour	20
Variable Overheads	5 hours @ Rs. 2 per hour	10
Fixed overheads	5 hours @ Re. 1 per hour	5
		80

The standard selling price of the Kitchen unit is Rs. 100.
The monthly budget project production and sales of Rs. 1,000.
Actual figures for the month of April are :

Sales 1,200 Units @ Rs. 102.
Production 1,400 Units.
Direct materials 22,000 Square meter @ Rs. 4 per Square meter.
Direct wages 6,800 hours @ Rs. 5.
Variable overheads Rs. 11,000
Fixed overheads Rs. 5,000.

You are required to prepare :

(a) A Trading Account reconciling actual and budgeted profit and showing all the appropriate varainces.
[*I.C.A.E.W. UK. May 1981 (Adopted)*]

[**Ans. Reconciliation of Budgeted profit and Actual profit :**

			Rs.
Budgeted profit			**20,000**
	Adverese	***Favourable***	
Sales Margin price variance	**—**	**24,000**	
Sales Margin volume variance	**—**	**4,000**	
Material price variance	**22,000**		
Material usage variance	**3,000**		
Labour Rate variance	**6,800**		
Labour efficiency variance	**—**	**800**	
Fixed overhead efficiency variance	**1,000**	**—**	
Fixed overhead efficiency variance	**—**	**200**	
Fixed overhead capacity variance	**—**	**1,800**	
Variable overhead expenditure variance	**—**	**2,600**	
Variable overhead efficiency variance	**—**	**400**	
	32,800	**12,200**	**20,600**
Actual Profit (Loss)			**(600)**]

25. The records of Conwest Engineering Corporation indicated the following for the month of April 2005 :

Standards		***Rs.*** ***Per Unit***
Direct materials	4 gallons @ Rs. 1·20	4·80
Direct Labour	3 hours @ Rs. 1·80	5·40
Factory Overhead	Re. 0·60 per Lab. hour	1·80
	Total manufacturing Cost	12·00

Actual :

(*i*) Production during the month of April 2005 has been 6,500 Units with no beginning or ending work-in-progress inventories.

(*ii*) Materials :
Purchased 32,000 gallons @ Rs. 1·18 per gallon. Used in production 25,600 gallons.

(*iii*) Labour :
Hours worked 20,000
Average hourly wage rate Rs. 1·75.

(*iv*) Factory Overheads :
Total overhead cost incurred Rs. 12,500.
Calculate material variances, Labour variances and total variance for factory overhead.

[*B.Com. (Hons.), Delhi, 1982*]

[**Ans. Material price variance**	**Rs.**	**512 (F)**
Material usage variance	**Rs.**	**418 (F)**
Material Cost variance	**Rs.**	**992 (F)**
Labour rate variance	**Rs.**	**1,000 (F)**]

Labour time variance	Rs. 900 (A)
Labour cost variance	Rs. 100 (F)
Total overhead variance	Rs. 800 (A)

26. The following data are obtained from Pritam Ltd. manufacturing a single product A :

(*a*) **Standard Cost.**

	Per Unit *Rs.*
Material Cost : 2 Kg. at Rs. 2·50.	5·00
Wages : 2 hours at Re. 0·50 per hour.	1·00
Direct Expenses—royalty (to be revised at Re. 0·15 per unit)	0·10
Variable overhead : 2 hours at Re. 0·45	0·90
Fixed overhead : 2 hours at Re. 1 per hour	2·00
Standard Cost	9·00
Standard Margin	1·00
Standard Price	10·00

(*b*) Budgeted production and sales 10,000 Units
Budgeted Fixed overhead Rs. 20,000
Budgeted working hours 20,000 Hours
Budgeted Profit Rs. 10,000

(*c*) Actuals : Sales at cash 8,000 Units @ Rs. 10·20 per Unit
Production : 8,000 Units
Materials purchased and consumed :

	Rs.
16,500 Kg. @ Rs. 2·40	39,600
Wages : 18,000 hours @ Re. 0·40	7,200
Direct Expenses	1,200
Variable overheads	7,500
Fixed overhead	19,000

You are required to :

(a) Compute the cost, revision and sales variances;

(b) Present the information to show clearly the profit variances.

(c) A reconciliation statement of Cost and Profit variances.

[Ans. Material Price variance : 1650 (F); Material usage variance : 1,250 (A); Material cost variance Rs. 400 (F). Labour rate variance : Rs. 1,800 (F) ; Labour efficiency variance : 1,000 (A); Labour Cost variance : 800 (F); Direct Expenses variance : 400 (A); Variable O.H. Expenditure variance : 600(F); Variable overhead efficiency variance : 900 (A) ; Variable overhead variance : 300 (A); Fixed overhead variance : Expenditure variance : 1,000 (F); Capacity variance : 2,000 (A); Volume variance 2,000 (A); Total Fixed overhead variance : 3,000 (A). Sales Margin price variance : 1,600 (F); Sales Margin Volume variance : 2,000 (A); Sales Margin variance : 400 (A).]

Note : Actual sales are Rs. 81,600 and actual total costs are Rs. 74,500. Actual Profit : 81,600 – 74,500 = 7,100. This can be reconciled with budgeted profit and presented to management as follows :

	Favourable	*Adverse*	*Rs.*
Budgeted profit @ Re. 1 per Unit :			10,000
Sales Margin variance			
Price	1,600	—	
Volume		2,000	
Sales Margin variance (Total)			(400)
			9,600
Cost Variance			
Material variances :			
Price	1,650	—	
Usage	—	1,250	

Wages variances :	1,800	—	
Rate	—	1,000	
Efficiency	—	400	
Direct Expenses Variance			
Variable overhead :			
Expenditure	600	—	
Efficiency	—	900	
Fixed overhead :			
Expenditure	1,000	—	
Efficiency	—	2,000	
Capacity	—	2,000	(2,500)
Actual Net Profit			7,100

27. From the following data for a particular period compute the Sales margin variances :

Budgeted Sales : A. 600 Units at Rs. 10 (Standard Cost Rs. 6)
B. 400 Units at Rs. 5 (Standard cost Rs. 3)

Actual Sales : A. 1,000 Units at Rs. 9 each
B. 500 Units at Rs. 4 each

[Ans. Sales Margin Price variance : 1,500 (A); Mix variance : Rs. 200 (F) ; Quantity variance : 1,600 (F); Volume variance : 1,800 (F); Sales margin variance : 300 (F).]

28. Compute the missing data indicated by the Question marks from the following :

	Product R	*Product S*
Sales Quantity		
Standard (Units)	?	400
Actual (Units)	500	?
Price (Unit)		
Standard	Rs. 12	Rs. 15
Actual	Rs. 15	Rs. 20
Sales Price variance	?	?
Sales Volume variance	Rs. 1,200 (F)	?
Sales Value variance	?	?

Sales mix variance for both the products together was Rs. 450 (F). "F" denotes Favourable.

[CA Inter, November 88]

[Ans. Product R
Sales Price variance = Rs. 1,500 (F)
Standard (Budgeted) Units sold = 400
Sales Value variance = Rs. 2,700 (F)
Product S
Actual Sales Quantity = 800 Units
Sales Price variance = 4,000 (F)
Sales Volume variance = 6,000 (F)
Sales Value variance = 10,000 (F).]

29. A product is manufactured by mixing and processing three raw materials X, Y and Z as per standard data given below :

Raw material	*Percentage of input*	*Cost per kg.*
X	40%	Rs. 40
Y	40%	Rs. 60
Z	20%	Rs, 85

Note : Loss during processing is 5% of input and this has no realisable value.